Microeconomic Theory

CONCEPTS AND APPLICATIONS

Thomas M. Carroll

Memphis State University

Microeconomic Theory

CONCEPTS AND APPLICATIONS

St. Martin's Press • New York

For Regina and Michael

Library of Congress Catalog Card Number: 82-60454

Manufactured in the United States of America.
76543
fedcba

For information, write St. Martin's Press, Inc.,
175 Fifth Avenue, New York, N.Y. 10010

cover design: Judith Getman
book design: Leon Bolognese

ISBN: 0-312-53178-8

Thomas M. Carroll

Memphis State University

Microeconomic Theory

CONCEPTS AND APPLICATIONS

St. Martin's Press • New York

For Regina and Michael

Library of Congress Catalog Card Number: 82-60454

Copyright © 1983 by St. Martin's Press, Inc.
All Rights Reserved.

Manufactured in the United States of America.
76543
fedcba

For information, write St. Martin's Press, Inc.,
175 Fifth Avenue, New York, N.Y. 10010

cover design: Judith Getman
book design: Leon Bolognese

ISBN: 0–312–53178–8

Contents

v

PART THREE: PRODUCTION AND COST   179

Chapter 5: Production   181

Chapter 6: Input Selection and Production Costs   230

PART FIVE: INCOME DISTRIBUTION AND ECONOMIC WELFARE 517

Preface

I enjoy economics, especially microeconomic theory, and I have written this book in the hope that students will share my enthusiasm. Astonishingly, considering the number of microeconomics texts available, I have been unable to find even one text that provides the particular combination I want for my own classes—that of lively writing, abundant and relevant applications, and objective analysis. The problem, I suspect, is that it is so very difficult for those of us who teach the courses and write the textbooks to remember what it was like *not* to know the material. We either overestimate what students understand or underrate what they are capable of understanding. If, as I hope, this book succeeds in avoiding both pitfalls, much of the credit is due to the many students who have read parts of the manuscript and been generous with both their criticism and praise. I am able to thank a few of these students by name at the end of this preface, but I wish to thank all my students here at the beginning: the book is, initially, for you.

Teaching Premises and Objectives

First, and most important, I believe that microeconomics is something to be understood, not just memorized. For this reason, I have developed the various topics in this book so that students will not merely learn a lot of models and theories, but will understand why a model or theory is important and useful, what assumptions underlie it, and how it has developed over time. The text carefully maintains the distinction between models, which are abstract logical constructs, and theories, which use models to predict and explain reality.

Second, I believe that students should not have to "psych out" the instructor's political philosophy in order to pass a microeconomic theory (or any other) course. Too many books present as positive economics what in fact stems from a particular ideological perspective: the market always works, or government intervention is required to make the market work, and so on. I have tried instead to present microeconomic theory as an array of objective, highly useful analytical tools with which economists can improve things for themselves, their clients, and perhaps society at large. Rather than treating controversial issues as clear-cut cases of the "correct" and "incorrect" application of economic reasoning,

I have tried—by presenting balanced analyses of property rights, markets, antitrust laws, advertising, and labor unions, to mention just a few topics—to show how individuals or groups with different interests can use the same theories or variations of the same theories to advocate different social and business policies.

I have also attempted to present as broad a spectrum of ideas in microeconomics as possible. Instructors will recognize the recent work of such people as Becker, Stigler, Coase, Lancaster, and Leibenstein, as well as that of older economists like Robinson, Chamberlin, Sweezy, and Galbraith.

Third, I believe that humor need not be banished from any course and is especially welcome in microeconomics, which has an undeserved reputation for being dry. Textbooks do little good if they are so boring that they are read grudgingly or not at all. I have allowed a bit of humor, even a little irreverence to breathe through these pages.

Features and Organization

This book, like several other microeconomics texts, contains many real-world applications and examples. Here, however, they are carefully integrated with the presentation of economic analysis and relate not only to social and economic policy but also to the operation of business firms. I have made a special effort to use comparisons and contrasts with material from various business fields to clarify economic concepts. For example, in chapter six the different definitions of costs and of profit used in economics and accounting are shown to reflect the differing goals of those professions. In chapters nine and ten the traditional approach to profit maximization is compared with the break-even analysis often encountered in management courses. In chapter eleven the economics of product differentiation is developed using Lancaster's "goods and characteristics" approach, which is similar to product-cycle analysis, an approach used in marketing. Also in chapter eleven, the equivalence of markup pricing with the marginal-revenue—equals—marginal-cost approach to pricing shows that economics complements rather than contradicts the other business disciplines.

In addition to the applications and examples in the text proper, there are numerous boxed "illustrations." These unique sections—which appear in every chapter after the first—are of two kinds, policy and business, and enrich the discussion in the text proper. Chapter four, for example, contains a policy illustration on price elasticity and drug-related crime and a business illustration on practical difficulties in estimating elasticity.

The book is organized flexibly. Basic concepts are introduced in seven core chapters, giving the instructor maximum flexibility in selecting among the remaining eight optional chapters and three end-of-chapter appendices. The core chapters deal with the fundamental microeconomic theory topics: consumer choice (chapter two), demand (four), production (five), costs (six), competitive and monopolistic product markets (nine and ten), and ideal input markets (thirteen). The eight optional chapters cover methodology (chapter one), extensions of household choice theory (three), linear programming and simple technology (seven), property rights and market structure (eight), monopolistic competition (eleven), oligopoly (twelve), unions and discrimination (fourteen), and general equilibrium and welfare economics (fifteen). These optional chapters are both important and relevant; indeed, I have often found that the topics in them are the ones that interest students most. However, I have often found it necessary to slow the pace of my course when students seemed to have difficulty grasping the material, and I realize it helps to know what topics can be sacrificed with the least detriment to subsequent learning.

Further enhancing the book's flexibility is its optional employment of calculus. I have discovered in my teaching that investing one or two class periods in the concepts of calculus increases students' understanding of change and marginal analysis. But because many students' attitude toward calculus lies somewhere between dread and terror, I have limited the calculus in the book to certain footnotes; the text itself makes use only of geometry and some basic algebra, and none of the calculation exercises requires more mathematics than high school algebra. Since most undergraduate and many graduate students have not taken a course in calculus, appendix A provides sufficient information to enable them to follow the calculus used in the quantitative footnotes. In fact, students may discover that knowledge of economics actually facilitates their understanding of calculus.

Learning Aids

Each chapter opens with an outline of its content and concludes with numbered highlights and a glossary. Suggestions for additional reading are also provided. Students may test their progress with the exercises which follow each chapter. The exercises are of three kinds: evaluation, calculation, and contemplation or essay. Few of them are of the easy, regurgitory type; hence they are well-suited for homework and even take-home exams. Answers to the calculation exercises are provided in appendix B; answers to all the exercises, along with additional, easier exercises and their answers, may be found in the separate *Instructor's Manual*. A *Study Guide* that offers chapter summaries and concept reviews, as well as a wealth of exercises, is also available.

Use in the Classroom

Every class of students is unique, varying in ability, interest, and preparation. Microeconomic theory is frequently the course undergraduates take to determine whether to major in economics; their experience with microeconomic theory may well determine their attitudes toward economics.

I have used the manuscript for this book in three different classes. In my undergraduate intermediate microeconomic theory course, I assigned chapters one and eight as readings, then covered chapters two through six and eight through fourteen in lectures. In an equivalent course for MBA students, which emphasized microeconomics but also touched on macroeconomic topics, I covered the appendices to chapters two and nine in addition to the chapters studied in the undergraduate course. Finally, my course for master's students began with appendix A, covered all chapters and end-of-chapter appendices, and utilized various outside readings. The approaches I have used are merely suggestions; each instructor will of course tailor the course to the needs and interests of the class.

Acknowledgments

I would like to express grateful appreciation to the many reviewers of the text, whose criticisms were consistently constructive:

Frederick W. Bell of Florida State University
Robert B. Carson of State University College, Oneonta, New York
James Elliott of Georgetown University
William Forgang of Mercer College
Errol Glustoff of the University of Tennessee, Knoxville
Thomas Koplin of the University of Oregon
William P. Rogerson of Stanford University
Frederick E. Tank of the University of Toledo

Many other people suggested improvements in the manuscript as this book was taking shape. Carol Abbt Parsons and Barbara Wilson-Relyea, who wrote the *Study Guide*, were also helpful in bettering the text. Many undergraduate and graduate students read portions of the book; in particular, I thank Teresa McLendon, Barbara Gasquet, Michael Davidson, Jimmy Smithson, Mark Caruso, Christine Munson, Tim Butler, and Bernadette Pian. Several colleagues—David Ciscel, Roger Chisholm, Robert Bean, and Barbara Vatter—and I jointly developed ideas that have been incorporated in the book. All, however, are innocent of any misinterpretations I may have made. I also thank my colleagues Tom Depperschmidt, Cyril Chang, Dale Bails, Kurt Flexner, K. K. Fung, and Howard Tuckman for helpful comments on the manuscript. Special thanks are extended to the heroic staff of St. Martin's Press: Michael Weber, Patricia Mansfield, and Carolyn Eggleston.

My deepest appreciation I extend to my wife, Regina, and our son, Michael. Regina read various drafts of the manuscript and was responsible for many improvements. She also provided encouragement and sympathy in copious quantities. Michael, although only three, kept us both entertained through many trying times and reminded me of how important it is to leave our children with a better world than the one we found when we got here.

THOMAS M. CARROLL

PART ONE
Introduction

1 *The Nature and Purpose of Microeconomics*

Part one is about economic methods: what economists do and how they do it. Many economists look upon methodology as artists regard criticism; that is, if one is to find fault with another's work, it is first necessary to understand the work being criticized. For this reason, part one is optional. Some students prefer to find things out for themselves and thus may wish to start with part two. However, reading part one now will prepare the reader for some of the surprises, paradoxes, and controversies in the field of economics that come later.

The first four sections of chapter one place the social science of economics in its historical, intellectual, and scientific contexts. The central role of scarcity in creating an economic perspective is explored, particularly as it paralleled the development of the scientific method. Scarcity is also seen as the intersection of human and physical phenomena, which gives economics its character as a bridge between the social and natural sciences.

The second half of chapter one is devoted to the nature of economic theory. How scarcity gives rise to the efficient use of abstract logic—that is, models—is contrasted with the use of those models to explain and predict the real world. Controversies in economics are shown to involve the scope of alternative models (e.g., competition and monopoly) rather than the logical content of the models per se.

Chapter 1

The Nature and Purpose of Microeconomics

The great economist Frank Knight stated:

> [I]t ought to be the highest objective in the study of economics to hasten the day when the study and the practice of economy will recede into the background of men's thoughts, when food and shelter, and all provision for physical needs, can be taken for granted without serious thought, when "production" and "consumption" and "distribution" shall cease from troubling and pass below the threshold of consciousness and the effort and planning of the mass of mankind may be mainly devoted to problems of beauty, truth, right human relations and cultural growth.[1]

These sentiments might have been uttered by a member of any profession about its ultimate goal. Physicians, for example, wish to eradicate all disease, and police officers dream of an end to crime. Psychiatrists labor for a future in which all are sane. Lawyers yearn for a judicial system so fair and logical that anyone can negotiate a contract without legal assistance. Insurance actuaries strive for a world with no hazards, moral or otherwise. And just as every general works for a lasting peace and clergy foster universal salvation, each accountant looks forward to the day of glorious tax reform that will make complex accounting rules unnecessary.

Cynics may scoff, "If a person's livelihood is derived from helping people cope with persistent problems, aren't that person's interests fer-

---

[1] Frank H. Knight, "Social Economic Organization" in *The Economic Organization* (New York: Harper & Row, 1951); reprinted in William Breit and Harold Hochman, eds., *Readings in Microeconomics*, 2nd ed. (New York: Holt, Rinehart and Winston, 1971), p. 5.

2

vently vested in perpetuating those problems? Why should economists behave any more nobly than other professionals?" The answer lies in the nature of what economists do, not in some superior moral character they possess. Why it is necessary for people to earn their living is one of the central concerns of economic inquiry. If the world no longer concerned itself with motivating people to work rather than "play," there would be no need for economists.

Although economists can be magnanimous in their desire for a solution to economic problems, realism dictates that they not promise something they cannot provide. The most that can be expected from economists is advice on how to make the available resources, including human time and energy, stretch as far as possible in desirable directions. As long as human beings want more than can be produced with available resources, economic problems will exist. Furthermore, economists' solutions to these problems compete with those of other social scientists and business specialists. Like these other professionals, economists must provide practical solutions to real problems. As an example of how economists accomplish this, which in turn provides an insight into what economics is, consider the following debate about what priorities should govern the use of natural resources.

APPLICATION
Ecology versus Industry

Ecologists believe that every species of animal and plant is valuable and that all endangered species should be preserved, even at the expense of industrial activity. Most industrialists, on the other hand, wonder why untapped resources are lying idle rather than being developed. The debate between ecologists and industrialists involves three related issues:

1. Who should have the authority to determine whether nonrenewable resources are used now or preserved in their original state?
2. Who should bear the cost of despoiling beauty or reducing society's material output?
3. How should resources be allocated between preserving beauty and producing commodities?

As will be seen, economists tend to focus on the third question. However, they cannot overlook how the answers to the first two questions influence an answer to the third. And it is fairly clear that no consensus can be established on the third question because of disagreements among economists about the answers to the first two questions.

Into the fray steps an attorney, who points out legal principles and precedents that support each side and then sells his services to the highest bidder. Others join in. A sociologist argues convincingly that social cohesion depends upon the reinforcement of increasing standards of living and upon leaving unspoiled resources to posterity. A philosopher cites categorical imperatives to husband resources and to preserve beauty. Quoting opinion polls, a political scientist relates that 78 percent of the population believe that a clean environment should be pursued at any cost, while 82 percent oppose all regulations which inhibit production or threaten jobs. Above the din, an economist shouts, "Hold on! Everybody is missing the central issue."

Imagine that the lawyer, sociologist, philosopher, and political scientist stop their bickering as the economist continues to speak.

"Let us begin with a couple of observations—call them *assumptions*, if you will," says the economist. The others wait expectantly. "First, both natural beauty and material production are good things to have." The others nod in agreement. "Second, the conflict between ecologists and industrialists arises because they have two different goals and resources are inadequate to achieve them both. Therefore, does it not follow that the first task is to maximize the rate of material production which is compatible with each state of environmental quality? In other words, shouldn't resources be allocated to maximize the environmental quality for the chosen material standard of living?"

"Of course!" cry the specialists. "How could we have been so blind! Tell us, oh wise and practical economist, how can the best combination of environmental purity and material plenty be achieved?"

"I'm glad you asked," replies the economist, as appreciative of a leading question as Socrates in his *Dialogues*. "Although sacrifice is inevitable in the face of inadequate resources to satisfy competing goals, sacrifice can be minimized by using resources efficiently. Generally speaking, efficient outcomes result from selfish actions which are transformed into social benefits under the guidance of market competition. You know, to really understand the impact of scarce resources on human behavior and social institutions, you ought to study microeconomic theory."

"I knew there would be a catch," says the lawyer.

"With economics there is always a catch," adds the sociologist.

"A pragmatic approach to knowledge is not without drawbacks," murmurs the philosopher.

"Watch, now we'll be told why economists are better than we are," complains the political scientist.

"Well, allow me to say that the economic perspective on social problems is different and, properly used, will complement other approaches," soothes the economist. "The important point is that the goals of each of your disciplines will be enhanced when the resources needed to achieve those goals are allocated efficiently. Economics does not indicate whether ecological purity or material largess should be given higher priority. Economics shows that when resource users are unable to enjoy the benefits they produce, or are able to escape the costs they cause, society will suffer unnecessary sacrifices of both comfort and beauty. At the same time, an objective economic analysis does not invalidate the prescriptions of your disciplines.''

"Then economists do not think they know everything!" exclaim the assembled specialists. "Economics allows room for disagreement just like our specialties do! Please, dear friend, join our discussions. The economic perspective on the ecologist-industrialist debate should prove most interesting," says the philosopher.

"Thank you," replies the economist. "Do you mind if I bring a few of my colleagues? I'd hate to give the impression that all economists think alike."

A Whirlwind History of Economic Ideas

The word *economics* is of both humble and practical origins: it is derived from the ancient Greek word *oikonomia*, which means "household management." Technically, "home economics" is redundant. Greek philosophers, such as Plato and Aristotle, believed that issues such as the care and feeding of slaves, the importance of keeping an estate's expenses below its revenue, and whether to plant grapes or figs were too mundane to occupy a philosopher's attention. After all, there were more important issues to be considered: beauty, truth, proper human relations, and cultural growth. Yet, with all its disease and starvation, not to mention the enslavement of most of humanity, that ancient era can hardly be characterized as a golden age. Today, those in power have many more economists on retainer than philosophers. What caused the change in focus?

If human wants exceed the means available for satisfying them, two solutions can be tried. One is to harness the desire for more in order to motivate socially desirable behavior. Societies have universally rewarded their leaders and heroes with control over resources (i.e., wealth) and command over people (i.e., power). The other approach is to condemn human cravings for more. It is no accident that most Eastern and Western religions have their roots in Stoic philosophies which require willing acceptance of one's lot in life. In societies which yearn for stability and whose technology barely allows for survival, **scarcity** is approached as a condition requiring that desires be limited to what is available.[2]

The Stoic approach to scarcity stunted the development of an eco-

---

[2] Words included in the end-of-chapter glossary are designated in **boldface** the first time they appear.

nomic perspective until relatively recent times. Throughout ancient and medieval history, what we now call economics was the province of religion and ethics. And the moral perspective was by no means unique to economic issues. The scientific revolution and the age of enlightenment were responsible for purging the natural sciences of their mysticism. The intellectual revolutions of the seventeenth and eighteenth centuries, which freed scientific inquiry from the shackles of superstition, changed the focus of scarcity from the management of wants to the management of resources. How fitting that the universally proclaimed father of modern economics was a moral philosopher named Adam, whose revolutionary treatise on economic ideas was published in 1776.

Adam Smith's *An Inquiry into the Nature and Causes of the Wealth of Nations*, a work of brilliant scholarship, provided practical advice to merchants and radical proposals to governments. Monarchs, whose political authority was no longer bolstered by a universal belief in the divine right of kings, found that power and "purse" were closely linked. The crown treasury, whose gold was needed to hire mercenary soldiers, depended upon trade with other nations. Both international trade and domestic economic activity seemed too important to trust to chance; hence, monarchs bestowed monopoly grants on lackeys who were better known for their court manners than their business acumen. Smith's condemnation of government meddling in economic affairs was both blistering and ironic:

> As every individual . . . endeavors as much as he can both to employ his capital in the support of domestic industry, and so to direct that industry that its produce may be of the greatest value; every individual necessarily labours to render the annual revenue of the society as great as he can. He generally, indeed, neither intends to promote the public interest nor knows how much he is promoting it. By preferring the support of domestic to that of foreign industry, he intends only his own security; and by directing that industry in such a manner as its produce may be of the greatest value, he intends only his own gain, and he is in this, as in many other cases, led by an invisible hand to promote an end which was no part of his intention. Nor is it always the worse for society that it was no part of it. By pursuing his own self interest he frequently promotes that of the society more effectually than when he really intends to promote it. I have never known much good done by those who affected to trade for the public good. It is an affectation, indeed, not very common among merchants, and very few words need be employed in dissuading them from it.[3]

Smith's message smacked more of an underground newspaper than of the *Wall Street Journal*. This cynical praise of self-interest was his

---

[3] Adam Smith, *An Inquiry into the Nature and Causes of the Wealth of Nations* (Chicago: University of Chicago Press, 1976), pp. 477–478.

way of depersonalizing economic activity. Economic events follow their own laws if allowed to operate free from interference. Smith's prescription for economic harmony was **laissez-faire**, literally, "let it be." To Smith, merchants and entrepreneurs were not heroes but pawns; their pursuit of selfish ends led to the betterment of society because of the impersonal forces of the market (i.e., "the invisible hand").

For two hundred years economists have elaborated upon and refined the ideas in *The Wealth of Nations*, but the ideal of market competition remains largely unchanged. The new science was initially dubbed "political economy," thereby transcending the "household management" limitation of the original Greek word. The infamous population theory of the English economist Thomas Robert Malthus had its origins in a debate about the liberalization of British poor laws to ease the miserable lot of early nineteenth-century workers. Malthus believed that income redistribution through government intervention or private charity would cause population growth to outpace food production, leading to increased misery. The iron law of wages—that wages would tend toward subsistence levels—earned economics the label of "the dismal science."

Another debate pitted Malthus against a great economist of the nineteenth century, David Ricardo, who, like Malthus, believed in the iron law of wages. Malthus suggested the possibility that a market economy might produce more than it consumed, leading to a glut of commodities, falling wages and prices, and, ultimately, depression and widespread unemployment. Only landlords, whose income from rents financed aristocratic living, would continue to spend during economic downturns, while profit-minded capitalists postponed investments until economic conditions improved. To support rental incomes, Malthus favored a continuation of the Corn Laws, which restricted grain imports. Ricardo countered with two refinements in economic logic. First, the principle of comparative advantage indicated that a society's well-being was determined by the *relative* cost of production at home and abroad; Britain could produce bread more cheaply by exporting manufactured goods and importing grain. Second, Ricardo refuted the possibility of prolonged depression by citing a principle enunciated by a contemporary French economist, Jean Baptiste Say. According to Say's law, producing a commodity always generates enough income to purchase it. Hence, supply creates its own demand; relative prices may change, but full employment will persist.

Throughout the first century of its existence, economics continued as "political economy." In the last quarter of the nineteenth century, economic concern gradually shifted from the wealth of nations to the behavior of individual markets. "Political economy" as a discipline became known simply as *economics*. Sixty years later, when worldwide depression challenged the simplicity of Say's law, attention was again focused on the causes of economic prosperity. At this juncture, economics cleaved into two perspectives: macroeconomics and microeconomics.

Defining Economics

Up to this point we have sidestepped formal definitions of economics. When one defines something, one seeks to place it in an appropriate class which distinguishes it from other things. A definition is both inclusive and exclusive. As we will see throughout this book, there remain many unresolved controversies and differences of opinion which embarrass some economists. A delightful tolerance motivated economist Jacob Viner's definition: "Economics is what economists do." Since there is no crown, uniform, or physical attribute which distinguishes economists from other mortals, the only way to determine whether someone is an economist is to ask.[4] There is no licensing exam for economists; no one can be arrested for practicing economics without a license. Thus, we are led to conclude that economists are individuals who "do economics." Such circular logic may prevent economists from building walls around their profession, but it is hardly satisfying to students with important things like exams to consider.

In this book, we will try to define economics in a way that reveals "what economists do," while allowing that different economists practice economics in different ways. **Economics** is the *science of how scarcity influences behavior and shapes social interactions.* Something is scarce when there is not enough to go around. Scarcity implies choice. If a man does not have enough time to do everything he wants to do, he must choose to do some things and consciously give up other things; otherwise, he will end up doing nothing well. If there are not enough resources to produce all the commodities which we and future generations might desire, then the cost of using nonrenewable resources today will be a lower standard of living for posterity.

Not only do economists study problems associated with scarcity, their attitudes about scarcity influence the methods they use. Human wants are taken as assumptions; economists claim no special expertise in explaining why most people want more than they can have or why different people want different things. The goal of economic analysis is to advise people how to use resources efficiently. Economists do not have special insight into why people buy more recordings of rock music than of classical music. Nor do economists explain why some fashions catch on and others flop. However, they do attempt to explain and predict how people, acting as consumers or producers, react and adapt to changes in their economic incentives.

Figure 1-1 communicates the essence of economic inquiry as the interaction of the physical and social sciences. The circle on the left, physical science topics, depicts the domain of the physical, natural, or

---

[4] Walk down any street in the United States and ask passersby, "What happened in 1776?" Anyone who answers "the publication of *The Wealth of Nations*" is probably an economist.

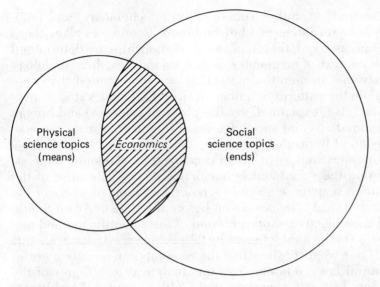

Figure 1-1
The Subject Matter of Economics

"hard" sciences (e.g., physics, chemistry, biology, engineering). The physical sciences employ similar methods to uncover and explain natural forces which rule or influence those aspects of reality not subject to human initiative. The essence of the scientific method employed in the hard sciences is to depersonalize nature, that is, to show how natural events occur without human or supernatural intervention. The controversy between creationists and evolutionists demonstrates that the impersonal approach to natural phenomena is not universally popular. Scientists themselves acknowledge that the appearance of nonhuman events is often biased by the human observer. Nevertheless, the goal of the physical sciences involves discovering objective reality, in contrast to painting reality to conform to mythical notions.

The right-hand circle, social science topics, encompasses the concerns of the social sciences (e.g., psychology, anthropology, history, sociology, political science). Social scientists analyze questions involving human interactions, the creation and behavior of social groupings, the process of rule formation and the enforcement of those rules, the struggle between animal instincts and civilizing aspirations, and so on. The social sciences involve the study of humans by humans.

The subject matter of economics—the impact of scarcity on human and social behavior—stands at the intersection of physical science topics (resources, the "means") and social science topics (desires, the "ends"). To emphasize the limitation of resources relative to human desires, the right-hand circle is larger than the left. Note that economists do not lay claim to the entirety of either sphere. Physics, chemistry, and engineering study how resources can be combined. Economics takes these physical relations as given; that is, physical relationships are determined outside of the context of economics. Social sciences such as sociology and psychology, not to mention marketing, are more suited than economics to explain the patterns of human desires. Economics studies how resource limitations ("explained" by the physical sciences) and human desires ("explained" by the social sciences) interact to create the economic dimension of human experience.

Since economics studies behavior organized by economic motives, it belongs among the social and behavioral sciences.[5] Because of the focus on resource scarcity, economic science has adopted many of the features of the physical sciences. Even before the time of Adam Smith, admiration of the objectivity and precision of the scientific method motivated emulation of the hard sciences by those concerned with economic phenomena. If one wants to show that the economy can operate by rules much like natural laws, one employs the analytical techniques of the natural sciences. Just as Copernicus and Galileo struggled to liberate astronomy from the moral authority of the Church, Smith sought to emancipate economic affairs from the heavy hand of political patronage. A clockwork market system, whose pendulum is steadied by the invisible hand discerned by Smith, has much in common with the clockwork universe of Isaac Newton.

The prominence of physical phenomena within economics allows economists to measure their subject matter with more precision than is possible in the other social sciences. This precision enhances the logical rigor of economic theory. Although economic theory may resemble the theories of physics in its logic, structure, and complexity, it is the nature of scarcity which explains the economist's concern (some might say *preoccupation*) with theory.

The set of economic phenomena, like any slice of human experience, is incredibly complex; unlike atomic particles or chemical compounds, each human being is unique. Yet the intellectual energies of humankind are scarce; attention given to one aspect of experience must be limited in order to understand other facets of that experience. A theory allows an investigator to develop a general explanation of many phenomena by abstracting the details that make every event unique.

Used prudently, a theory enhances the productivity of intellectual effort. A model, which reflects the common, vital elements of a class of

---

[5] "Economics deals with the social organization of economic activity. In practice its scope is much narrower still; there are many ways in which economic activity may be socially organized, but the predominant method of modern nations is the price system, or free enterprise. Consequently it is the structure and working of the system of free enterprise which constitutes the principle topic of discussion in a treatise on economics" (Knight, "Social Economic Organization," p. 5).

phenomena, saves the investigator the trouble of "starting from scratch" with each new problem encountered. The art of using abstract logic is to account for enough detail of a particular situation to make the theory relevant while excluding irrelevant details which would only make the model unwieldy. The choice of a level of generality is not a costless decision.

The first cost is the intellectual effort required to learn to reason abstractly. There is no denying that students preparing for a career in economics load a great deal of intellectual effort at the front end of their careers. The payoff is that mastering the logic of economic theory qualifies one as an expert, one who can perform tasks that many others do not understand. This expertise gives business and government economists more autonomy than generalists enjoy. For example, economists are often assigned tasks their supervisors do not understand. And a task that would take a noneconomist several weeks, an economist can often complete in a day or two. Many professional economists find that the extra work as a student is handsomely rewarded in both financial and intellectual terms in their careers. But the cost of doing one's own thing later is doing something hard now.

The second cost of abstraction is that cutting away detail reveals sharp differences of opinion. If different scholars use different terms and employ different models, then differences in conclusions could be attributed to different points of view. With most economists using the same set of abstract models (or slight variations on standard models), however, the amount of disagreement among economists seems almost nonprofessional.

Tools of Economic Analysis

A craftsman's pride in his work shows in his care of his tools. Good workers protect their tools, even when they do not own them. As mental constructs, economists' tools are communal. A noble sentiment: thoughts are free. But what is free can be taken, carelessly used, and even abused. A wood carver whose chisel is ruined by a thoughtless apprentice has only himself to blame; he should never have loaned the tool. Economic theories are the public domain of an unlicensed profession. Proud economists must stand helpless as their prized theories are mangled by dilettantes and charlatans.

Economic theories have more than one use. As scientists, economists seek truth, which they may not always recognize if it is not what they expect. As practical men and women, economists apply their theories in business, government, and nonprofit institutions; the advice they give must be understood. As advocates of divergent political and economic philosophies, economists use their theories to persuade doubters, entertain believers, and vanquish opponents. A theory which is well suited for one task may not work well for another. One way of postponing controversies in order to get down to the business of learning economics is to distinguish *hypothesis, model,* and *theory* from one another.[6]

In searching for truth, economists begin with a simple **hypothesis**, that is, a testable assertion of a cause-and-effect or if-then relationship. For example: Consumers buy less of a commodity after its price rises. This statement is objective since there is unambiguous evidence which, if presented, would render the statement false. If sales of a certain commodity rise following an increase in its price, the hypothesis is diversified; that is, it does not apply to at least one real event.

The lessons learned from testing simple hypotheses guide the construction of economic models. A **model** is an abstract pattern which captures the essential structure of a set of phenomena while stripping away unnecessary detail. Since influences other than price also affect the amount of a commodity consumers wish to buy, the economic model of consumer behavior states that when other factors are held constant, consumption of a good varies inversely with its price. The observation that purchases of a commodity increased after its price increased does not disprove the model of consumer demand. The evidence would indicate that some other influence on consumer behavior (e.g., consumer tastes) set off the increase in price when consumers wished to purchase more than producers were willing to supply at the prevailing price. As the price rose, producers offered more for sale (the model of supply). The price stopped increasing when consumers were no longer trying to buy more than the amount available at that price. Because of their abstract structure, models of economic behavior are less vulnerable to contradiction by evidence than are simple hypotheses. A model is not so much true or false as it is relevant or irrelevant.

According to Andreas Papandreou, a theory emerges when an abstract model is applied to real-world phenomena.[7] A **theory** is a systematically organized statement, applicable to a wide variety of circumstances, composed of a set of assumptions, accepted principles, and rules of procedure designed to analyze, predict, or otherwise explain a specified set of phenomena. The **applicability assumption** of a theory specifies the scope of the theory; most disagreements within economics involve controversies about the scope of economic theories.

Virtually every economist is willing to apply the model of a competitive market to show the impact of natural forces on price and quantity

---

[6] Much of this section is inspired by Martin Bronfenbrenner, "A 'Middlebrow' Introduction to Economic Methodology," in Sherman Roy Krupp, ed., *The Structure of Economic Science* (Englewood Cliffs, N.J.: Prentice-Hall, 1966), pp. 9–10.

[7] Andreas G. Papandreou, *Economics As a Science* (Philadelphia: Lippincott, 1958).

in a market with many producers and many consumers. A hailstorm in Florida which wipes out a portion of the orange crop would increase the price of oranges and reduce consumption. The model of supply and demand works; hence, it becomes the theory of competitive markets.

Most economists would be content to treat changes in consumer tastes as unexplained, since those changes would only manifest themselves through the willingness of consumers to buy a larger quantity of a commodity at the prevailing price. The theory of competitive markets predicts that price would increase in the wake of a consumer-induced shortage, until, at some higher price, the quantity offered for sale increased while the quantity demanded by consumers was less than the (unobserved) quantity demanded at the lower price. According to liberal economist John Kenneth Galbraith, changes in consumer tastes are frequently the result of manipulation by powerful sellers who wish to increase price without reducing quantity. The prediction—price and quantity rise together when consumer tastes change—is the same, but the "feeling" is quite different in the Galbraith version.

Consensus erodes still further when the model of competition is applied to an industry some suspect of behaving noncompetitively. According to competitive theory, artificially low prices create unnecessary shortages; the solution to shortages is to remove arbitrary restrictions on market adjustment. The model of monopoly explains events differently. The way a monopoly raises prices is by creating an artificial shortage; decontrol of prices set by monopolists allows price gougers to extract their tribute from helpless consumers.

The distinction between models and theories may seem subtle, but it has important implications for students of economics. Since almost all economists accept the relevance of the competitive model to *some* real events, this model will be presented first, in chapter nine. The monopoly model, which nearly all economists accept as a reasonable predictor of events in *some* markets, will follow in chapter ten. Disagreement occurs when more than two models are required; many economists dispute the scope of models of imperfect competition. Nevertheless, these models, which are presented in chapters eleven and twelve, can be studied without taking sides as to whether or not they should be called theories. Even though some analysts use the word *model* in a somewhat pejorative sense (regarding a model as an abstract construct with no relevance), this book will avoid debate about the relevance of alternative models until the logic of those models has been developed. Hence, since all theories are models, use of the word *model* is not meant to belittle a theory. On the other hand, those who doubt the relevance of a model should nevertheless devote some time to learning its logic.

We will see in chapter eleven that conservative economist Milton Friedman dismisses the model of monopolistic (or differentiated) competition because it provides no "theory" of the industry. Yet, for those advising dress manufacturers on how to price their fall fashions, this model provides a link between the characteristics of commodities and consumer desires for variety. How well a tool works depends on what it is used for. As a tool, the theory of competitive markets is something like a hammer; we can do many things with that tool, albeit imprecisely. An automatic screw machine does fewer things than a hammer, but it does one thing with speed and precision. Then, by analogy, the fact that models of imperfect competition have less scope than the model of perfect competition may be counterbalanced by the greater depth of analysis that models of imperfect markets allow.

The Role of Assumptions in Economic Theory

One attitude toward the role of assumptions in economic theory is clearly articulated by Milton Friedman, professor of economics at the University of Chicago, Nobel Prize winner, and one of the leading spokesmen for conservative economic philosophies:

> Truly important and significant hypotheses will be found to have "assumptions" that are wildly inaccurate descriptive representations of reality, and in general, the more significant the theory, the more unrealistic the assumptions. . . . The reason is simple. A hypothesis is important if it "explains" much by little, that is, if it abstracts the common and crucial elements from the mass of complex and detailed circumstances surrounding the phenomena to be explained and permits valid predictions on the basis of them alone. To be important, therefore, a hypothesis must be descriptively false in its assumptions; it takes account of, and accounts for, none of the many other attendant circumstances, since its very success shows them to be irrelevant for the phenomena to be explained.[8]

According to Friedman and his followers, the model of ideal economic organization—the modern version of Adam Smith's invisible hand—is adequate to predict real-world events with little or no modification in its structure. This "idealist" position is sharply contrasted by the "realist" position espoused by John Kenneth Galbraith, who takes issue with the notion that false assumptions can lead to relevant predictions. According to Galbraith, conventional economic theory holds

> that the best society is the one that best serves the economic needs of the individual. Wants are original with the individual; the more of these wants that are supplied the greater the general good. Generally speaking the wants to be supplied are effectively translated

---

[8] Milton Friedman, "The Methodology of Positive Economics," in William Breit and Harold Hochman, eds., *Readings in Microeconomics*, 2nd ed. (New York: Holt, Rinehart and Winston, 1971), p. 30.

by the market to firms maximizing profits therein. If firms maximize profits they respond to the sovereign choices of the consumer. Such is the frame and given its acceptance a myriad of scholarly activities can be designed and fitted together in the knowledge that they are appropriate to—that they fit in—the larger structure. There can be differences of opinion as to what best serves the purposes of the larger structure. Mathematical theorists and model builders can squabble with those who insist on empirical measurement. But this is a quarrel between friends.

Should it happen, however, that the individual ceases to be sovereign—should he become, however subtly, the instrument or vessel of those who supply him, the frame no longer serves. Even to accommodate the possibility that humans are better served by collective than by individual consumption requires the framework to be badly warped. Should the society no longer accord priority to economic goals—should it accord priority to aesthetic accomplishment or mere idleness—it would no longer serve. And no one quite knows the effect of such a change. One can only be certain that, for a long time, economics, like the lesser social sciences, will be struggling with new scaffolding. And the work of economists will be far less precise, far less elegant, seemingly far less scientific than those who are fitting pieces into a structure the nature of which is known and approved and accepted.[9]

More than a difference of opinion about the appropriate level of abstraction in economic theory separates Galbraith and Friedman. They also have different perspectives on economic issues. Friedman's claim that a theory's ability to predict should be the sole basis for judging its merit presumes the existence of objective tests of the accuracy of those predictions. Economists can show that specific events (e.g., a change in the quantity purchased in reaction to a price change, a change in the number of suppliers in response to a change in profits) usually conform to the predictions of the theory of perfect competition. Exceptions can be accounted for and incorporated in variations of this theory.

The issues raised by Galbraith go deeper, since economists draw untestable inferences from observable events. For instance, the theory of perfect competition (presented in chapter nine) predicts that an increase in consumer demand for a product will increase the product's price in the short run, but ultimately will cause an increase in the number of sellers in the market, which will in turn lower the price. Merely showing that a product's price rises in the wake of increased demand for a product is not sufficient, by itself, to prove that the industry in question is free of monopolistic distortions of the product price (see chapter ten).

---

[9] John Kenneth Galbraith, "The New Industrial State: A Review of a Review," *Public Interest* (fall 1967), p. 117.

To take another example, economists simplify the model of consumer choice by assuming that buyers are accurately informed about the characteristics of products before they purchase them. The theory of consumer demand (presented in chapter four) is then built on this model. According to the theory of demand, an increase in a product's price will reduce the quantity consumers purchase, other influences on consumer demand remaining constant. If some consumers mistakenly infer that products with higher prices have better quality—a violation of the simplifying assumption of accurate knowledge by consumers—the adjustment of consumers' purchases will take a longer time. Eventually, experience teaches buyers that quality is not as good as they expected, and their consumption declines. In this context, the predictions of the model are not sensitive to the simplifying assumption of accurate information. However, we cannot logically infer that the assumption of accurate consumer information makes no difference in another context, such as whether producers should be legally required to display the ingredients of products on their containers, when some consumers may be allergic, for example, to certain food preservatives.

Robert Solow, an economist at the Massachusetts Institute of Technology and a member of the Council of Economic Advisors in the Kennedy administration, expressed an eclectic attitude toward economic assumptions which synthesizes the major points made by Friedman and Galbraith:

> All theory depends on assumptions which are not quite true. That is what makes it theory. The art of successful theorizing is to make the inevitable simplifying assumptions in such a way that the final results are not very sensitive. A "crucial" assumption is one on which the conclusions do depend sensitively, and it is important that crucial assumptions be reasonably realistic. When the results of a theory seem to flow from a special crucial assumption, then if the assumption is dubious, the results are suspect.[10]

In regard to simplifying assumptions, requiring accuracy of economic models would require that economic theories cease being theories, since a different model would be needed each time any assumption of a model became technically inaccurate. Economics would become, as Galbraith admits, less precise and less scientific. There is a fundamental difference between a simplifying assumption and a crucial assumption. We can change an assumption and see whether the predictions of a model are materially affected by the change. If they are not, the model is robust with respect to that assumption; the accuracy of the assumption is not germane in that context. If changing an assumption changes a model's prediction, that assumption is crucial in some contexts.

---

[10] Robert Solow, "A Contribution to the Theory of Economic Growth," *Quarterly Journal of Economics* (February 1956), p. 65.

When the accuracy of a prediction rests on one or more crucial, but dubious, assumptions, it may be reasonable to question the applicability of that model to real problems.

Normative Statements and Positive Economics

When we inquire whether a hypothesis predicts actual events, we are concerned with a **positive statement**, a statement whose accuracy can be determined, at least ideally, by an examination of experimental or statistical evidence. For instance, if an economist asserts that labor unions raise wages of union members only when they lower the number of jobs in an industry, another economist can check that claim against actual wage data. If it can be shown that the number of jobs increased *because* of a union-won wage hike, the universal validity of the assertion will have been disproved. Economists will continue their research until it becomes clear under what circumstances unions raise wages by reducing jobs, and under what circumstances unions raise wages without reducing jobs (see chapter fourteen).

When we state an opinion about what *ought* to be, we are making a **normative statement**, a statement that cannot be proven true or false. Employers do not like unions, and they may attempt to attract public sympathy for antiunion legislation (e.g., a right-to-work law) by arguing that unions are bad because they raise wages and reduce the number of jobs. Showing that unions can sometimes raise wages without decreasing employment would not necessarily change an employer's opinion about labor unions, because employers do not like to pay higher wages. However, as Milton Friedman explains, positive economics can still contribute to the advancement of truth by testing the validity of assertions made by those with a stake in economic policy:

> I venture the judgement . . . that currently in the Western world, and especially in the United States, differences about economic policy among disinterested citizens derived predominantly from different predictions about the economic consequences of taking action—differences that in principle can be eliminated by the progress of positive economics—rather than from fundamental differences in basic values, differences about which men can ultimately only fight.[11]

Two qualifications, or elaborations, can be appended to Friedman's noble sentiments. First, while disinterested citizens may be persuaded to change their opinion about the desirability of actions by use of objective arguments and evidence, it is usually "interested parties" (e.g.,

---

[11] Friedman, "The Methodology of Positive Economics," p. 30.

labor unions or employers' associations) who hire economists to make an "objective case" for their cause. A labor-union president will probably not be dissuaded from seeking pro-union legislation by evidence that union wages are increased at the expense of the wages received by nonunion workers. Nor will employers cease resenting unions, even if it can be shown that unions raise wages from artificially low (subcompetitive) levels. As long as evidence is inconclusive or subject to various interpretations, economists will continue to use positive economics in the support of opinionated special interests.

Second, it is a fundamental precept of human nature that opinions with which we disagree are easier to spot than the subjectivity of opinions with which we agree. Few politicians complain about press reports that are biased in their favor;[12] few business representatives condemn regulations that give their companies a competitive edge. It is a rare scholar who seeks to disprove his or her favorite theory with the same vigor used to attack the theories espoused by rival ideologies. If the problem of "fundamental differences" is that "men can ultimately only fight" about them, conflict can be avoided by associating only with people who share one's own prejudices. The danger is that different schools of thought will calcify around unquestioned beliefs, demanding ideological conformity as a condition for admission into the brotherhood of positive economics. Such a perversion of logic was eloquently condemned by Frank Knight:

> [The] emotional pronouncement of value judgements condemning emotion and value judgements seems to [be] a symptom of a defective sense of humor. The attempt to build a social science on these foundations suggests that the human race, and especially its "best minds," having at long last (a very long last) found out that the objects of nature are not like human beings—are not actuated by love and hate and caprice and contrariness, and subject to persuasion, cajolery and threats—have logically inferred that human beings must be like natural objects, and so viewed by the seeker of knowledge about them.[13]

The distinction between positive economics and normative statements reflects an ethical commitment to perfection in an admittedly imperfect world. Because economics is relevant, it is not easy to distinguish between disprovable facts and unprovable opinions. Economic policy

---

[12] In a delightful display of candor, the difference between opinions and objective evidence was demonstrated by a presidential spokesman. When an unforeseen economic slowdown led the Carter administration to seek a tax cut and spending increases, a member of the White House press corps queried how it would affect the administration's "dream" of a balanced budget. "Not at all," was the reply.

[13] Frank H. Knight, "Review of T. W. Hutchinson's *The Significance of Basic Postulates of Economic Theory*" in *On the History and Method of Economics* (Chicago: University of Chicago Press, 1963), p. 151.

does affect different groups in desirable and undesirable ways, and there will always be a demand for economic arguments that a policy which is most advantageous to one's clients is the only one that works. But the economics of the 1980s is not limited to purely political issues. There are more economists employed in business and government whose jobs entail objective evaluation of business and government practices than there are economists employed as polemicists. Perhaps the most important feature of positive economics is, quite simply, the fact that it sells.

Microeconomics and Macroeconomics

The fundamental unit of analysis in **microeconomic** theory is the market for particular outputs or inputs. We begin with models of how a "typical" consumer and a "typical" producer cope with scarcity through the process of constrained maximization (of utility and profit, respectively). The models of buyer and seller behavior are integrated into a theory of supply and demand. In a competitive market, autonomous buyers and autonomous sellers are predicted to react independently to changes in the market price, which adjusts itself to a shortage or surplus of the commodity being traded until market equilibrium is achieved or restored.

The fundamental unit of analysis in **macroeconomic** theory is the aggregate sector: the household sector, representing all consumers; the business sector, representing all purchases of plant and equipment; the government sector, representing all federal, state, and local government purchases of goods and services; and the foreign sector, representing imports and exports. But more than mere size separates microeconomic theory and macroeconomic theory. The split between these two "levels" of theory represents a breakdown in the one-time consensus about the scope of microeconomic models. The classical economists' belief in Say's law (i.e., supply creates its own demand) led them to the notion that economy-wide aggregates would behave like individual markets. Just as lower wage rates within an industry would increase employment within an industry, so falling wages during depressions would eventually cure economy-wide unemployment crises.

During the Great Depression, British economist John Maynard Keynes (and many of his contemporaries) challenged Say's law as a bridge between isolated (i.e., single-market) adjustments and the behavior of an economic system to major traumas such as economy-wide unemployment and inflation. Unemployment in one industry might be resolved by reducing real wage rates, because workers in one industry generally make up a small fraction of consumers in that industry; any decline in demand due to lower wage income in that industry could be ignored. However, a general decline in wages would correspond to a general decline in consumer income; reduced consumer spending would cause prices to fall, negating the impact of wage cuts on employment.

Macroeconomic theory arises because many economists no longer believe that economy-wide issues like unemployment, inflation, and economic growth can be adequately handled by microeconomic theory. Modern disciples of Keynes believe that unemployment stems from a shortfall in the amount that firms, consumers, and the government are willing to spend, and that inflation occurs when these groups try to buy more than a fully employed economy can produce. Keynesians recommend that the government budget (i.e., fiscal policy) be used to stimulate or dampen aggregate spending. Monetarists see economic downturns as resulting from dysfunctions in monetary institutions. If the money supply is inadequate to sustain a full-employment rate of spending, prices and wages fall until adequate cash reserves are established. With too much money, inflation results when people try to reduce unwanted cash balances. The moral is thus: assure that the money supply grows at a constant known rate. Aggregate economic stability *should* result.

In their simplest form, neither the Keynesian nor the monetarist model accounts adequately for simultaneous inflation and unemployment; yet these phenomena have been occurring together with such regularity that their joint occurrence can hardly be considered an anomaly. Modifications in macroeconomic theories have again immersed macroeconomic policies in microeconomic controversies.

The liberal modification of Keynesian theory, associated with John Kenneth Galbraith and other liberals, charges that real markets are so dominated by the economic power of big business used to administer prices and to control demand that traditional stimulation policies no longer work. What is needed, they argue, is a policy of wage and price controls to stifle inflation so that policies designed to expand employment do not run afoul of stable price goals. The major problem with this theory is that wage-price controls were tried in the early 1970s, with undesirable microeconomic consequences (e.g., the 1973–74 gasoline shortage).

A new conservative approach—"supply-side economics"—to macroeconomic problems is associated with Arthur Laffer of the University of Southern California and the economic policies of the Reagan administration. Supply-side economists argue that government spending, taxation, and income redistribution all weaken microeconomic incentives, so that workers produce less, businesses invest less, and households save less. By cutting tax rates, they argue, government could stimulate output while actually increasing tax collections (see policy illustration, p. 98). If inflation is caused by too much money chasing too few goods (as both monetarists and Keynesians admit), then supply-side inspired tax cuts would fight inflation on two fronts: tax revenue increases would reduce the money in circulation, while output increases would sop up the rest of the (formerly) excess purchasing power. Their problem is similar to that of the post-Keynesians: supply-side tax cuts initiated in 1981 resulted in increasing unemployment (less output) and larger deficits (declining tax revenue). Ironically, tight monetary policy, and the resulting high interest rates, did seem to be making a dent in the rate of inflation.

The separation of topics into macroeconomics and microeconomics, which has facilitated teaching, is becoming strained. A simplifying assumption of distinct microeconomic and macroeconomic phenomena appears to be a crucial assumption after all. More and more, macroeconomic problems seem to stem, at least in part, from microeconomic causes. Thus, certain topics, in the past reserved exclusively for macroeconomic theory and policy courses, must now be analyzed with tools developed in a microeconomic theory course. For this reason, this book is sprinkled with macroeconomic applications of microeconomic principles. (Because some instructors and students like their microeconomics "straight up," these examples have been placed in appendices and in optional sections.)

The disagreement about the scope of ideal and imperfect market models has led to sharp divisions over economic policies. This implies, perhaps paradoxically, that a textbook in microeconomic theory should not be identifiable with any one viewpoint. Therefore, this book presents models of ideal and imperfect markets that allow students to decide the merits of the conservative and liberal points of view for themselves. If some students have already taken sides, it behooves them to understand the logic of their opponents; if others see merit in both sides, so much the better. The author believes that scholarship flourishes in the middle of the road.

The Study of Microeconomics

Your first exposure to thinking like an economist will be a practical one: How should economics be studied? Your time is scarce. There are many other activities you might have pursued instead of enrolling in a microeconomic theory course. You could have taken a job or worked extra hours at the one you have. You could be enjoying recreation. You could be sleeping. Or you could be contemplating the meaning of life and your role in the scheme of things. By committing valuable time to the study of microeconomics, you have implied that the benefits you expect exceed the cost that this commitment imposes on you.

Perhaps you chose this course because you are interested in the ideas and skills it will help you develop. You may have enrolled in microeconomic theory to establish a foundation for applied courses in economics, business, or the social sciences. Perhaps this is a course which you must pass in order to graduate (i.e., your demand for microeconomic theory is derived from your desire for a college degree). Whatever your motivation, approaching microeconomic theory as an exercise in efficient resource use will maximize your understanding in relation to the time and effort you allocate.

Economics in general and microeconomic theory in particular are not subjects that lend themselves to memorization. The road to knowledge (or a passing grade) is paved with abstract concepts and strewn with complicated diagrams. Each theory has its own set of assumptions leading to different conclusions, and you may be required to apply theories which you dislike or whose relevance you question. How are you supposed to commit all this to memory? The answer is simple: you are not expected to memorize microeconomic theory; you are expected to understand it.

Memorization is not an efficient way to learn economics. In the amount of time it takes to memorize a set of definitions, a complex theory, or how to reproduce a complicated diagram, you could be mastering the logic of microeconomics. By understanding and using a few basic concepts, you will retain the essence of microeconomic reasoning long after you have finished the course. You will also have developed the mental discipline needed to derive the details for yourself. Instead of spending time trying to memorize what may seem to be meaningless formulas, you should concentrate on understanding basic concepts, which will enable you to remember particular formulas or derive them as needed.

Another aspect of microeconomics which makes it unsuited for rote learning is the cumulative process of theory development. Virtually every new concept you explore will be based on ideas covered previously. If you study economics efficiently, you will learn gradually and you will retain what you learn. You can work hard early and learn enough economics that you begin to enjoy it, or you can relax early and bequeath yourself endless drudgery later.

The study of microeconomics is an investment. Just as more consumer goods can ultimately be produced if resources are first diverted to produce tools, time spent studying economic theory will pay off in enhanced understanding of the real world. Our basic goal is learning to do what successful economists do: *they think clearly.*

Plan of Study

The remaining fourteen chapters in this book are divided into four parts. Part two (chapters two through four) deals with the reaction of households to income and price changes, and the relationship between household demand and market demand for commodities. Part three (chapters five through seven) concerns the producer's choice of inputs and how efficient production translates input scarcity into production costs. Part four (chapters eight through twelve) is devoted to the various models of the firm under ideal competition, pure monopoly, and imperfect competition. Part five (chapters thirteen through fifteen) presents theories of income determination in ideal and imperfect factor markets, and takes an updated look at how well the market mechanism facilitates the attainment of economic well-being.

HIGHLIGHTS

1. Modern economics traces its beginning from Adam Smith's *The Wealth of Nations*, which discussed political economy and the resolution of political issues. Smith's doctrine was that the market would allocate resources more efficiently than the government, an idea at odds with the then prevailing philosophy of mercantilism.

2. Modern economics emerged during the eighteenth century after the scientific method was adopted as an ideal for the physical sciences. The question of scarcity was recast as a problem of resource allocation, rather than the moral concern of restricting the expression of desires.

3. The methodology of economics can be understood as a combination of (a) the mathematical and scientific methods by which physical phenomena are investigated and (b) the restrictions on experimentation and the temptations of subjectivity posed by the social phenomena at the heart of economic issues.

4. Theories in economics and other systems of deductive logic emerge from a three-step process. First, a hypothesis is expressed as a testable, conditional relationship: whenever *A* happens, *B* will follow. Second, what is learned from testing (and generally disproving) hypotheses leads to the formation of abstract models, which are generally immune from disproof. Third, an applicability assumption specifies the range of phenomena to which the model is meant to apply, thereby elevating the model into a theory.

5. Assumptions can either be simplifying (i.e., pedagogical) or crucial. A simplifying assumption can be relaxed without significant change in a theory's prediction; a crucial assumption is one upon which the results depend sensitively. Many of the controversies among economists concern how realistic economic assumptions should be. The Friedman position holds that assumptions need never be true, as long as a theory predicts accurately; the Galbraithian position implies that when assumptions are untrue, the theory is irrelevant. The eclectic position of Robert Solow holds that simplifying assumptions need not be true, while crucial assumptions must be reasonably accurate.

6. The distinction between positive and normative economics ideally rests with whether or not a statement can be tested. A positive statement can be proven false (under some circumstances); a normative statement (or value judgment) is not subject to the conventions of truth or falsehood.

7. The distinction between microeconomics and macroeconomics rests in whether or not the precepts of how parts of the economy behave (e.g., markets, firms, and households) can be applied to the behavior of the economy as a whole (e.g., the interaction of the household sector, the investment sector, the financial sector, and the government sector of the economy in the determination of total output, employment, and price level).

GLOSSARY

Applicability assumption Statement, either explicit or implied, that an economic model is meant to apply to a particular set of real-world events.

Economics From the Greek *oikonomia* ("household management"), now used to refer to the social science concerned with how scarce resources are allocated among competing ends.

Hypothesis Testable assertion of a cause-and-effect or if-then relationship; the first step in the development of an economic theory.

Laissez-faire French phrase meaning "let it be"; the economic and social philosophy that individuals, pursuing their own ends, will serve the social good if a market is free to operate on its own.

Macroeconomics Branch of economic theory concerned with the behavior of economic aggregates: the price level; the unemployment and economic growth rates; and the interaction of household, government, and business sectors of the economy.

Microeconomics Branch of economic theory concerned with the behavior and interaction of individuals (households and firms) through markets, thus determining relative prices and income distribution.

Model Abstract logical construct emphasizing only the essential detail that characterizes a set of economic phenomena. Since it is basically designed to be immune from empirical disproof, a model is better characterized as relevant or irrelevant, rather than true or false.

Normative statement A statement which reflects an opinion or emotional sentiment. As such, one agrees or disagrees with normative statements; they are not designed to be true or false.

Positive statement A statement which can be proven false, or at least can be considered as false if specified evidence is produced.

Scarcity A condition in which the available means are inadequate for the attainment of all desirable ends. Scarcity implies choice and sacrifice.

Theory The result of proposing the relevance of an abstract model to a broad class of phenomena. Hence, the theory of perfect competition rests on the assertion that the predictions of the perfectly competitive model of the firm (or the market) adequately approximate real-world events.

SUGGESTED READINGS

Blaug, Mark. *The Methodology of Economics.* Cambridge: Cambridge University Press, 1980.

Boulding, Kenneth E. *Economics as a Science.* New York: McGraw-Hill, 1970.

Elliott, John E., and John Cownie, eds. *Competing Philosophies in American Political Economics: Selected Readings with Essays and Editorial Commentaries.* Pacific Palisades, Calif.: Goodyear Publishing Company, 1975.

Friedman, Milton. "The Methodology of Positive Economics." In *Essays in Positive Economics.* Chicago: University of Chicago Press, 1966.

Knight, Frank H. "Social Economic Organization." In *The Economic Organization.* New York: Harper & Row, 1951. Reprinted in William Breit and Harold Hochman, eds. *Readings in Microeconomics.* 2nd ed. New York:

Holt, Rinehart and Winston, 1971, pp. 3–19.

Krupp, Sherman Roy, ed. *The Structure of Economic Science.* Englewood Cliffs, N.J.: Prentice-Hall, 1966.

Machlup, Fritz. *Methodology of Economics and Other Social Sciences.* New York: Academic Press, 1978.

Morgenstern, Oskar. "Thirteen Critical Points in Contemporary Economy Theory: An Interpretation." *Journal of Economic Literature* (December 1972), 1163–1189.

Smith, Adam. *An Inquiry into the Nature and Causes of the Wealth of Nations.* Chicago: University of Chicago Press, 1976.

Ward, Benjamin. *What's Wrong with Economics?* New York: Basic Books, 1972.

EXERCISES

Evaluate

Indicate whether each of the following statements is true (agrees with economic theory), false (is contradicted by economic theory), or uncertain (could be true or false, given additional information). Briefly explain your answer.

1. Scarcity ceases to be a problem when resources are allocated efficiently.
2. The objectives of positive economics would be better served if fledgling economists were required to pass a licensing exam, so that those not dedicated to the principles of free enterprise could be kept from damaging the reputations of competent economists.
3. If a model is "bad in practice," it is also "bad in theory."
4. Economics is what people think economists do.
5. When real-world evidence contradicts the predictions of an economic model, the model must be discarded.
6. Economic theory, which assumes that individuals pursue their own self-interest, cannot be applied to altruists, who consider the welfare of others in making decisions.
7. A good theory should be true in all circumstances.
8. A relevant theory is a contradiction in terms.
9. To Milton Friedman, no assumption is crucial; to John Kenneth Galbraith, all assumptions are crucial.
10. A thorough understanding of economics makes the other social sciences irrelevant to solving human problems.

Contemplate

Answer each of the following questions in a brief but complete essay.

11. According to Milton Friedman: "[C]urrently in the Western world and especially in the United States, differences about economic policy among disinterested citizens derive predominantly from different predictions about the economic consequences of taking action—differences that in principle can be eliminated by the progress of positive economics—rather than from fundamental differences in basic values—differences about which men can ultimately only fight."
    a. Who is more likely to pay an economist's salary: a disinterested citizen in search of the truth or a client interested in furthering some special interest?
    b. For those economists who serve the "special interests" in business and government, what is the value of objective analysis?
    c. Is widespread disagreement among economists about economic policy a reflection of a *positive* economics atmosphere or a *normative* economics atmosphere?

12. "It is not as important for a theory to explain why something is; rather, a theory is meant to predict how something is likely to change." Do you agree or disagree? Explain your answer.

13. "As in most professions, a good economist is a successful economist, and a successful economist must have influence. But the only way to have influence is to tailor one's advice to fit one's audience. Positive economics may be a noble goal, but it is not a realistic goal." Do you agree? Explain your answer.

14. Indicate whether each of the following statements is a positive statement (capable of disproof in the light of objective evidence), a normative statement (with which one can agree or disagree, but not prove to be true or false), or a tautology (a statement which is true by definition).
    a. The costs of unemployment are not as great, in the long run, as the costs of labor market inefficiency generated by unemployment compensation.
    b. In order to raise wage rates, a union must reduce employment.
    c. A producer who wastes inputs cannot be efficient.
    d. Only good theories stand the test of time.
    e. Honest economists make lower salaries than dishonest economists.
    f. Economics is the highest paying profession in which no occupational license is required.
    g. This question is too hard.

15. The law of demand states, "If one good's price rises relative to another good's price, people will tend to consume less of the good whose price has increased, other factors constant." Which of the following statements, if accurate reflections of the facts, constitute valid refutations of the law of demand? Explain your answer.

   a. When a good's price increases, people fear greater price increases in the future, so they stock up.

   b. Some people believe that they increase their status by consuming high priced goods.

   c. People do not reduce their consumption of individual commodities during inflationary periods.

   d. People believe that higher priced goods have better quality.

PART TWO
Household Choice and Consumer Demand

Economic theory, like charity, begins at home. In part two we consider the nature and consequences of consumer management of the household budget. Chapter two presents a model of constrained utility maximization, whereby consumers attempt to obtain as much satisfaction as possible from their limited income. This model serves as a basis for predicting reactions to changes in the household budget. An increase in purchasing power (i.e., real income) normally leads to increased consumption of commodities, although some commodities, *inferior goods*, may be consumed in smaller amounts as income rises. Of particular relevance to the rest of the book is the analysis of the substitution effect of price changes on the commodities included in the household budget. The appendix to chapter two explains the analytical difficulties of measuring real income accurately during periods of inflation, when price indexes are incapable of picking up the substitution effect of relative price changes on the quantities of goods consumed.

Chapter three elaborates the material in chapter two. The resilience of the theory of consumer choice—when the three simplifying assumptions made in chapter two are relaxed—is demonstrated. The economic theory of choice is extended to take into account the opportunity cost of time when the hours of work are varied by changing the hours of leisure, the allocation of consumption over time, and the impact of risk and attitudes about risk on the allocation of the household budget. Chapter three is highlighted by a running example of the economic aspects of the education decision. The applications presented in chapter three provide in-depth illustrations of the process of constrained utility maximization to social and business issues.

Chapter four develops the household demand and market demand curve. The household demand curve represents the schedule of desired purchases of consumer goods that correspond to alternative prices. The household demand curve results from constrained utility maximization and is derived by allowing the price of one good to vary while other commodity prices, money income, and tastes are held constant. The demand curves of many households are added together to form the market demand curve, which shows the quantity demanded for market-wide commodity prices. The law of demand, reflected in the negative slope of the market demand curve, explains that once other influences on consumer behavior are accounted for, the consumption of a commodity tends to be inversely related to its price. The concept of elasticity of demand explains how a price change affects expenditures on a commodity. The chapter concludes by comparing the usual *ceteris paribus* demand curve, which assumes that quantity responds only to a price change, with the *mutatis mutandis* demand curve, which takes into account changes in tastes, real income, or expectations (which occur because of a change in price or the quantity response to that price change).

Chapter 2

Consumption and the Household Budget

For a society, scarcity means that resources are inadequate to satisfy all human desires. Scarcity makes choices inevitable. It forces people to compete for resources, but also leads them to cooperate through exchange, production, and shared consumption. The basic units of analysis in microeconomics are the household and the firm. Sometimes one person consumes alone, just as one person sometimes works alone. But most of the time, an individual acts as a member of a multiple-person household—first as a dependent, later as a provider. Single-person households can be analyzed by assuming that the person is an *egoist*, that his or her decisions are motivated by what will make him or her better off. The decisions made by providers in multiple-person households are often altruistically motivated; nevertheless, the household can be analyzed as an egoistic entity. Parents who want the best for their children place their family's interests first.

    The inevitability of scarcity is communicated to the household through the insufficiency of its income for purchasing all that might be desired. In a market economy, money represents a *claim* on goods and services. Once that claim has been exercised, purchasing power has been transferred to another. The cost of consuming one thing is the sacrifice of something else. The boy with a quarter in his pocket, his nose pressed against the window of a candy store, is rich to the limits of his imagination. What wonderful things he can buy! But before the chocolate has been wiped from his face, the memory of the candy bar he purchased begins to fade, along with the dreams of everything else he might have bought. The quarter is gone. But the real price of the candy bar was the other goodies he had to give up.

Since income and wealth are limited, consumers will try to get as much pleasure—or relieve as much pain—*as possible*. Efficient households establish priorities. Ultimately, preferences must be expressed in the amount of one commodity that a person would sacrifice to obtain more of another, even though having more of both would be nicer. When limited income is taken to the market, the amount of one good that must be given up to obtain another good is bluntly apparent in the *relative* prices of commodities. If a pair of shoes costs $40 and a shirt costs $20, the *real* cost of a pair of shoes is two shirts.

The Household Budget Constraint

In its most familiar form, the household budget presents a relation among monetary equivalents of commodities: money income must equal or exceed the sum of expenditures on all commodities. Letting Y represent monthly income, p represent price, and q represent the quantity of various commodities consumed each month, the **budget constraint** for the Smith family may be written as:

$$Y = p_1 q_1 + p_2 q_2 + \cdots + p_n q_n$$

The subscripts on p and q indicate different commodities (housing, subscriptions to magazines or cable television, college tuition, food, and so on). The message of the budget constraint is simple: household providers must mind their ps and qs. If Mr. Smith brings home $700 per month and Mrs. Smith earns a net income of $800, the Smith family can average up to $1,500 per month for consumer expenditures.

To simplify the analysis of household consumption, we will pretend (that is, assume) that all income must be spent on two commodities. Since we wish to relate how changes in income or price affect the consumption of one commodity at a time, it will simplify matters if we lump all other goods purchased into one composite commodity.[1] In the next chapter we will extend the principles of choice to allow the household to change its income by varying the allocation of time between work and leisure activities. We will also allow saving and borrowing as a means

---

[1] Scarcity of space limits our discussion (and diagrams) to two goods. The use of calculus, briefly summarized in appendix A, frees us from the artificial constraint of a two-commodity world. Those familiar with calculus can follow the extension of two-commodity examples to multiple-good examples through the footnotes.

of relaxing the rigid assumption that money income in each period must equal expenditures in that period. But for now, we will limit our analysis to the basics.

This is an important step. Pause and read carefully. As we have expressed it, the budget constraint appears to involve money quantities:

$$Y = p_1 q_1 + p_2 q_2$$

When we divide the entire budget equation by the price of one of the commodities, say p_2, and isolate that commodity on the left side of the resulting equation, our money relationship becomes a *real* relationship between the quantity of good 1 and the quantity of good 2:

$$q_2 = \frac{Y}{p_2} - \frac{p_1}{p_2} \cdot q_1$$

This menu of alternative combinations of two commodities can now be depicted by a diagram which further underscores the *real* dimensions of the budget constraint. In Figure 2-1, we have plotted quantities of

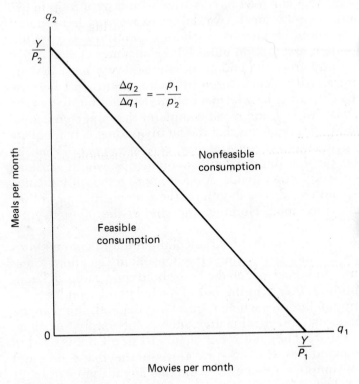

Figure 2-1
The Household Budget Constraint

good 2 (meals) on the vertical axis, which may be familiar to you as the Y-axis in algebra. If all income were spent on meals, the maximum consumption of this good would equal money income divided by its price. If each meal costs $5, the Smith family's $1,500 monthly income would support 300 meals per month. A family with ten meals per day would never go hungry, but then they wouldn't go anywhere else either. In the figure, points above the intercept Y/p_2 are not feasible. Even if only meals were purchased, income is inadequate to purchase more than 300 per month, given $1,500 monthly income and the $5 price per meal. In Figure 2-1, consumption of less than Y/p_2 meals per month leaves purchasing power which can be spent on the other commodity. Since a typical household faces constant prices—that is, its choice of which commodities to consume does not change the prices of those commodities— each unit of good 1 consumed requires the sacrifice of p_1/p_2 units of good 2. If movies cost $4, each movie seen by a member of the family costs 4/5 of a meal.

The intercept of the *budget line* on the horizontal axis (or X-axis) depicts the maximum number of movies this family could see per month: a $1,500 monthly income and a $4 movie price would permit up to 375 movies each month. As with meals, we do not expect any household's entire budget to be spent on movies. Such an expenditure is *possible*, however. An important assumption underlying consumer choice is that household preferences are independent of commodity prices. (Exceptions to this premise will be considered in chapter four.) Just because we do not expect a consumer to select an option does not imply that the option does not exist. In fact, the usual complaint that a person cannot "afford" a commodity rarely means that the family budget is inadequate to purchase that commodity *if nothing else were consumed*. What the person really means is that purchasing that commodity would cause an unacceptable sacrifice of other goods. A family with a monthly income of $1,500 could spend two days a month on the French Riviera, if they were willing to sacrifice food, clothing, and shelter the other twenty-eight days.

Note that the budget line divides the combination of commodities depicted in Figure 2-1 into those which the household can afford ("feasible consumption") and those which the household cannot afford ("non-feasible consumption"). Points to the left of, or below, the budget line represent consumption bundles which require less expenditure than the household's income. As a practical matter, such points imply that some income is saved or that money not spent.on good 1 or good 2 is used to purchase other commodities. However, we are assuming that good 1 and good 2 exhaust consumption possibilities and that any income not spent is simply wasted or lost. When all income is spent on meals, each movie "costs" eight-tenths of a meal; the slope of the budget line, $\Delta q_2/\Delta q_1$, is equal to the negative ratio of the price of movies to the price of meals.

Principles of Consumer Preference

The economic theory of consumer choice is based on some basic **assumptions of consumer behavior**. As we shall see, these assumptions are more analytical conveniences than testable assertions about the way consumers actually behave. The first premise merely asserts that consumers are capable of ordering alternative consumption prospects:

> **Completeness:** Between any two collections of consumer goods, an individual either prefers one combination to another or is indifferent between them.

The completeness principle assumes that consumer choice is a costless process. If you are offered a choice between an apple and an orange and you prefer the apple, you choose the apple. If you have no preference, you do not care which fruit you are given, since either would leave you equally satisfied.

The concept of *indifference* presented considerable difficulty for the fourteenth-century philosopher Jean Buridan, who related the following fable. After a long day's work, a thoughtless master returned his hungry and thirsty donkey to its stall in such a way that its head was midway between feed bags containing equal quantities of oats and between buckets containing equal quantities of water. The animal had no reason to choose the meal on the right instead of the one on the left; nor was there any reason to choose the meal on the left instead of the meal on the right. Alas, lacking a basis for choice, the donkey starved to death.

Of course, we know that such behavior is not typical of hungry animals, let alone people; the completeness principle assumes away such atypical behavior. Furthermore, the completeness principle indicates that people contemplate outcomes of options they face and pick those actions they think will lead to the most agreeable outcomes. The significance of the completeness principle for this chapter lies in our assumption that individuals have accurate information about the consequences of their choices prior to making a decision. It is assumed that choice is based on known outcomes of the options. This is a simplifying assumption which postpones the complications of risk (to be considered in chapter three) until the theory of choice is better understood. The completeness assumption implies that the decision process itself is effortless.

The second assumption about consumer preferences is equally noncontroversial:

> **Dominance:** If two consumption prospects are identical, a consumer is indifferent between them. If one prospect contains more of at least one commodity and no less of any other commodity, it will be preferred and is said to *dominate* the alternative prospect.

The dominance principle assumes that *more* is preferred to *less*. When this principle does not hold, a person is said to be *sated* with the commodity in question. There are, in fact, many commodities for which more *is not* preferred to less. Few of us desire more headaches, more smog, more germs, more homework, or more exams. But few of us consciously spend our hard earned income to acquire more smog, germs, or homework; these **bads** are not relevant to the theory of consumer choice. The dominance principle merely focuses the theory of consumer choice on the relevant choice among desirable combinations of **goods**.

The third principle of consumer behavior is that preferences are transitive. Suppose that you are given a choice between steak and chicken and you choose steak. However, you learn that there has been a mistake and your options are chicken and liver. You now pick chicken. If your preferences are transitive, you would pick steak if offered a choice between steak and liver. Stating this assumption formally:

Transitivity: If a person prefers alternative *A* to alternative *B* and prefers alternative *B* to alternative *C*, then that person prefers alternative *A* to alternative *C*. Similarly, if a person is indifferent between alternatives *A* and *B* and between alternatives *B* and *C*, then that person is also indifferent between alternative *A* and alternative *C*.

The principle of transitive preferences, or transitivity, means that the consumer is able to rank all available consumption prospects in a logically consistent fashion. This allows an observer to deduce the individual's preferences from choices actually made. Transitivity means that consumption preferences follow a pattern similar to the real number system, which we use to measure temperature, age, weight, height, and exam scores. Knowing that Frank is taller (or older or heavier) than Mary and knowing that Mary is taller (or older or heavier) than Lee allows us to infer that Frank is also taller (or older or heavier) than Lee. Income, prices, and rates of consumption can all be measured using real numbers, although the units of measurement (e.g., dollars per month, dollars per pound, pounds per month) may be arbitrarily chosen. The three principles of consumer behavior—completeness, dominance, and transitivity—allow economists to discuss preferences *as if* some standard unit for measuring them existed. This measure is called *utility*.

Utility

Economists have long been concerned with explaining the value of commodities. In fact, microeconomic theory (which some economists prefer to call price theory) was once referred to as value theory. Even in ancient times, philosophers realized that a commodity is valuable only if it is useful. If an object, such as a weed or a parasite, has no useful or beneficial function, people are not willing to sacrifice anything to obtain it. It is not the best things in life that are free; the worst things in life are free!

Adam Smith argued in *The Wealth of Nations* that an object's value, relative to other objects, should be proportionate to its usefulness. Goods would exchange, he speculated, according to their **utility**. However, this obviously was not the case then, or now:

> The word *value*, it is to be observed, has two different meanings, and sometimes expresses the utility of some particular object and sometimes the power of purchasing other goods which the possession of that object conveys. The one may be called "value in use"; the other "value in exchange." The things which have the greatest value in use frequently have little or no value in exchange; and, on the contrary, those which have the greatest value in exchange have frequently little or no value in use. Nothing is more useful than water; but it will purchase scarce any thing; scarce any thing can be had in exchange for it. A diamond, on the contrary, has scarce any value in use; but a very great quantity of other goods may frequently be had in exchange for it.[2]

While the "value in exchange" of diamonds is normally greater than that of water, there are circumstances, familiar to connoisseurs of desert adventure movies, when the need for water takes precedence over the desire for gold or diamonds. If water were so scarce that people faced death from thirst, most of them would willingly trade a diamond for a drink of water.

Scarcity, of course, provides the key to this diamond-water paradox. Although utility is a precondition for value (a positive exchange price), the exchange values of commodities reflect their relative scarcity. Smith provided the following illustration. If it took two hours to trap a beaver and one hour to bring down a deer, hunters would exchange two deer for one beaver. If the price of a beaver was more than twice the price of a deer, it would take a person less time to trap a beaver than to shoot the deer needed to exchange for a beaver. No one would hunt deer, so no deer would be available to exchange for beaver. But if deer were useful, people would be encouraged to hunt them by being offered more beaver in exchange. The price of deer would rise relative to the price of beaver until their exchange values reflected their relative scarcity and the relative time (labor) required to obtain them.

This reasoning led to the **labor theory of value**, which predicted that two commodities would exchange for prices roughly proportional to labor required to produce them. The theory was objective since the

[2] Adam Smith, *An Inquiry into the Nature and Causes of the Wealth of Nations* (Chicago: University of Chicago Press, 1976), pp. 32–33.

labor required to obtain (or produce) an item could be measured independently of the item's price. This avoided the circular reasoning encountered if scarcity was used as an explanation for price and then price was used as an explanation for scarcity; for example:

Q: Why are diamonds so expensive?
A: Because they are scarce, of course.
Q: And why are diamonds so scarce?
A: That's obvious! They are so expensive that very few people can afford them!

This is not very informative reasoning. Contrast it with the following:

Q: Why are diamonds so expensive?
A: Because diamonds are hard to find, people must be offered an adequate incentive to search for them. If people who find diamonds can exchange them for a large amount of other commodities which are easier to produce, enough people will look for diamonds and some will be found.

Unfortunately, the labor theory of value posed several problems, which ultimately led to its abandonment by most economists. Except for the simplest of handicraft economies, the exchange values of goods would *not* reflect their "embodied labor." The problem of accounting for the contribution of machinery to output was handled by reducing the contribution of capital to the "indirect labor" it provides (first labor is "stored" in capital, then released in production). For instance, suppose that two identical amounts of labor produce two identical vats of crushed grapes, and the juice is then bottled. Some bottles are immediately sold as grape juice. The remaining bottles are stored for several years and later sold as wine. Even with the identical amount of labor, wine exchanges for more than grape juice. The labor theory of value did not explain the "reward for waiting," namely, interest. (The influence of interest rates on consumption decisions over time is discussed in chapter three.)

Labor is a heterogeneous factor of production; one worker may be more or less productive than another at the same task, and there are many different kinds of tasks to be performed. Karl Marx attempted to deal with heterogeneous labor by defining "socially necessary labor time." However, since labor time is also a commodity, whose "price" reflects the labor time necessary to produce wage goods, the problem remained. (The modern problem of defining capital is discussed in chapter five.) The labor theory of value ultimately foundered on the inability to provide a unique "unit" of labor.

Around 1870, three economists, apparently unaware of one another's work, developed another explanation of the diamond-water paradox. William Stanley Jevons (England), Carl Menger (Germany), and Leon Walras (Austria) argued that the exchange value of a commodity is not determined by its total utility, but by its **marginal utility**, that is, by the *additional* satisfaction obtained from the last unit consumed (per period). The diamond-water paradox is easily explained. Since no water at all means death, the first gallon of water consumed (say during a week) provides an incredibly high degree of utility, since such consumption means the difference between life and death. But as more and more water is drunk per week, the person's thirst is quenched; additional water is then relegated to meeting less urgent needs, such as bathing. As still more water becomes available, clothes are washed, plants are watered, and so on. Since diamonds are less plentiful than water, their marginal utility is higher; hence, people will not usually sacrifice diamonds for more water.

During recent years, cities on the east and west coasts of the United States have been hit with droughts and water shortages, so that less water was available than people had been accustomed to at prevailing prices. Residents were urged to adopt voluntary conservation methods designed to forestall mandatory rationing, either by increases in water rates or by nonprice means. Watering lawns and filling swimming pools were discouraged. It was suggested that people shower instead of bathe, take shorter showers, or shower together. Dishwater could be used to flush toilets; rubber gloves replaced automatic dishwashers. At no time was anyone found in a dehydrated condition on his well-watered lawn.

The concept of diminishing utility explains the mutual benefit of voluntary exchange. For example, Joe has a lot of candy bars and very few cigarettes; for him, the marginal utility of eating a candy bar is low relative to the marginal utility of smoking an additional cigarette. Since Mary has several cartons of cigarettes but no candy bars, she finds the marginal utility of smoking low relative to the marginal utility of eating candy. Thus, Mary is willing to trade cigarettes for candy, while Joe is willing to trade candy for cigarettes. Mary and Joe both expect to be better off, *in their own estimation*, after the exchange. If not, the exchange would not occur.

While the idea of **diminishing marginal utility** provides a logical solution to the diamond-water paradox, we cannot characterize this principle as "scientific" in the same sense that the labor theory of value can be so characterized. Unless marginal utility can be measured independently of the prices of goods or the terms at which commodities are traded, we eventually encounter circular logic:

Q: Why are diamonds more valuable than water?
A: Because the additional utility gained from the last gallon of water is less than the utility gained from the last carat.
Q: How do you know that?
A: It's simple. People are willing to give up many gallons of water for an extra one-carat diamond.
Q: And why is that?
A: Because diamonds have more value than water.

And so it goes.

Policy Illustration
Social Choice and Individual Values

The principles of completeness, dominance, and transitivity allow an observer to infer what people believe makes them better off from the choices they actually make. Since utility maximization is presumed to spring from individual preference functions, which differ from one individual to another, most economists place the burden of proof on policies which interfere with voluntary choice. It seems the height of arrogance to coerce individuals into changing their behavior when our only reliable measure of what is "good" for people is what they decide for themselves.

There are many instances in which group choice is unavoidable. For instance, if only one candidate can win an election, some mechanism must be found to determine *whose* preferences (e.g., those of Republicans or those of Democrats) will be decisive. In his classic work *Social Choice and Individual Values*, economist Kenneth Arrow attempted to determine a set of principles of social choice which would parallel the principles of individual choice upon which consumer behavior theory is founded.* His results were startling. If a researcher sets down criteria which embody the notions of political democracy (e.g., one person—one vote and majority rule), it is possible that the social-choice mechanism will cause either arbitrary or intransitive results.

Let us consider two social-choice processes. First, take the process of plurality choice, wherein the policy or candidate receiving the most votes (but not necessarily a majority) wins the contest. Imagine an election in which there are three candidates. Each party ranks its own candidate first but the remaining two candidates differently.

Party A (40%)	Party B (35%)	Party C (25%)
Smith	Jones	Marx
Marx	Marx	Jones
Jones	Smith	Smith

If all three candidates are placed on the ballot, and members of each party vote for their candidate, Smith wins with 40 percent of the vote, even though a majority (members of party B and party C) prefer either Jones or Marx to Smith. Had Marx withdrawn from the race, Jones would have won; had Jones withdrawn, Marx would have won. Plurality voting yields arbitrary results since the social choice depends (arbitrarily) upon whether losing candidates remain in the race. Had a majority been required, Smith and Jones (the first two finishers) would have entered a run-off election, and, with Marx's votes transferred to Jones, Jones would have won with 60 percent of the vote.

---

* Kenneth J. Arrow, *Social Choice and Individual Values*, 2nd ed. (New Haven, Conn.: Yale University Press, 1970).

The problem with simple majority voting is that the social-choice mechanism could be intransitive. Consider a slightly different set of preferences, in this case for a high, medium, or low school budget, with corresponding property tax rates. Suppose three income groups have the following preferences:

> *High Income*
> High budget
> Low budget
> Medium budget
>
> *Middle Income*
> Medium budget
> High budget
> Low budget
>
> *Low Income*
> Low budget
> Medium budget
> High budget

If households desire to consume more (or higher quality) education as their incomes rise, the preferences of the middle- and low-income groups appear consistent, while the high-income group decides that if the high budget is not passed, its children will go to private schools, so the low budget is fine for other people's children. If no single group constitutes a majority, intransitive preferences will result. Regardless of which budget is adopted, a majority will prefer an alternative. If the high budget is adopted, a majority will prefer the medium budget. If the medium budget is adopted, a majority will prefer the low budget. But if the low budget is adopted, a majority will prefer the high budget.

There are several accommodations that can be made to minimize the impact of intransitive social preferences. The first is frequent elections, so that temporary majorities are continually monitored. The second is a "bill of rights" which allows individual preferences to take precedence over majority preferences—if a majority of citizens want to sleep on their backs, I am still free to sleep on my stomach. The third is to allow decisions to be made, where practical, at the local level, thereby establishing voting blocs with consistent preferences. But since local communities are often segregated by income (e.g., inner city versus suburbs), local elections make the distribution of public services more a function of "ability to pay" than of need, thus favoring the rich over the poor. Nevertheless, the apparent preference of most economists for individual-choice economic institutions (i.e., markets, households, private enterprise) over social-choice institutions (i.e., governments) probably reflects, at least in part, their confidence in the consistency of individual preferences. Yet, as we shall see, it is only through a social choice to enforce private property rights that private exchange relations can exist.

Early developers of utility theory, such as Jeremy Bentham (founder of the London School of Economics, who died in 1832, before the principle of diminishing marginal utility had been well articulated), believed that utility was measurable, at least in principle. By fostering policies which produced more pleasure in some than discomfort in others, governments could hope to obtain the greatest good for the greatest number.[3] Suppose that Democrats were determined to be better "pleasure producers and pain avoiders" than Republicans. Would there be any justification in redistributing wealth from Republicans to Democrats to achieve a higher "total utility" for society? (Before answering, imagine that the direction of redistribution were reversed.)

The answer, of course, is no. Even if utility could be measured, there is no objective reason for using such a measure as a basis for social policies.[4] Furthermore, there would be no basis for making interpersonal comparisons of utility even if measures of individual utility were possible. The assumption that individual preferences are transitive cannot be extended to the preferences of a group of people. A simple example will illustrate. The Smith family decides to watch television. Pat Smith prefers a cooking show to football and prefers football to *Sesame Street.* Lee Smith prefers the football game to *Sesame Street* and likes *Sesame Street* more than the cooking show. Their son Johnny likes *Sesame Street* better than the cooking program, but considers cooking preferable to football. There is only one television set; watching any program requires sacrificing the other two. Pat Smith calls for a vote and agrees to vote only to break a tie.

First, Pat calls for a vote between the football game and *Sesame Street.* Johnny votes for *Sesame Street,* Lee votes for football; Pat breaks the tie by voting for football. Next, Johnny votes for the cooking show, while Lee votes for football. This time Pat votes for the cooking show. The cooking show wins. As Pat settles down to watch the program, Lee and Johnny are suspicious. How did Pat's favorite show win when both of them preferred *Sesame Street* over the cooking show?

An examination of the family's preference ranking in Table 2-1 shows that no matter which program is watched, the majority will prefer another program. If Lee gets to watch football, Pat and Johnny would prefer to watch cooking. If Johnny watches *Sesame Street,* his parents would prefer football. So even though there are transitive preferences

---

[3] "The balance, if it be on the side of pleasure, will give the good tendency of the act upon the whole; if in the side of pain, the bad tendency of it upon the whole" (W. Stark, ed., *Jeremy Bentham's Economic Writings* [London: George Allen & Unwin, Ltd., 1954], pp. 436–37).

[4] Lionel Robbins's *An Essay on the Nature and Significance of Economic Science,* 2nd ed. (New York: Darby Books, 1981), is generally credited as being the most influential in dissuading economists from the goal of making interpersonal comparisons of utility by arguing that such a process had no grounding in scientific objectivity.

TABLE 2-1

	Cooking	Football	*Sesame Street*
Pat	First	Second	Third
Lee	Third	First	Second
Johnny	Second	Third	First

for all three individuals, there is no guarantee that "aggregated preferences" will be transitive.

Transitivity implies that *individual* preferences are subject to ranking as if a good's utility for an individual could be measured using real numbers. However, unless marginal utility is measurable independently of the relative prices of commodities, there is no way to test the marginal utility solution to the diamond-water paradox in a scientific fashion. "Utility" is, at best, a metaphor: a shorthand method of relating a person's willingness to trade (or substitute) one commodity for another to the rate at which those commodities are already being consumed. Ironically, the original use of marginal utility to "explain" commodity substitution has been replaced by the use of an individual's willingness to substitute commodities to represent their relative marginal utility.

Indifference Curves

Once economists gave up what seemed to be a futile search for an objective measure of utility, they discovered that measurable utility was unnecessary for the economic theory of choice. If the principles of completeness, dominance, and transitivity hold, the diminishing marginal utility can be replaced by the observation that individuals appear less willing to sacrifice one commodity to obtain more of another. Nonobservable utility can be inferred from observable choices. Figure 2-2 depicts combinations of movies (q_1) and meals (q_2). The dominance principle implies that point B (q_1^B movies, q_2^B meals) would be preferred to point A (q_1^A, q_2^A) by any person or household that was not sated with meals, since combination B has the same number of movies as combination A plus more meals (i.e., $q_1^B = q_1^A$ and $q_2^B > q_2^A$). By similar logic, point C is preferred to point B, since combination C has more movies than combination B but the same number of meals per month. Finally, by either the transitivity principle or the dominance principle, we can deduce that point C is also preferred to point A.

Neither the dominance nor the transitivity principle can be used to compare points B and D, since point B has more meals than point D, while point D has more movies than point B. The completeness principle indicates that either point D is preferred to point B, point B is preferred

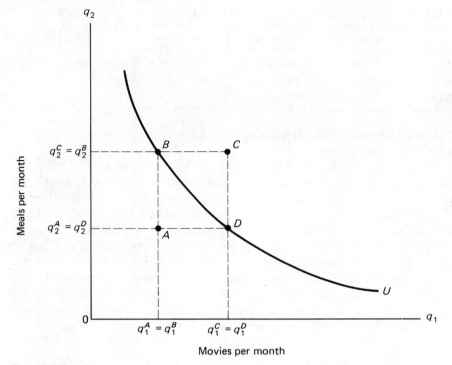

Figure 2-2
Indifference Curve of Two Commodities. The dominance principle implies that point C is preferred to point B and also to point D. Dominance indicates that both B and D are preferred to point A also. However, when one combination has more of one commodity and less of the other commodity relative to another combination, as with B and D, it is possible that neither is preferred.

to point D, or a person will be indifferent between the two. However, because different people have different tastes, any of these three contingencies is possible. If a consumer were indifferent between points B and D, an observer might discern a willingness on that person's part to trade up to $(q^B - q^D)$ meals per month for $(q^D - q^B)$ movies per month, or vice versa. Seeing more movies or having to give up fewer meals would, of course, be preferred; only when the individual is indifferent would the choice be reversible.

An **indifference curve** represents all combinations of q_1 and q_2 which yield the same satisfaction for a consumer. As long as the dominance principle holds, combinations with more of one commodity and no less of the other commodity (or both commodities) will be preferred to combinations with less. Two points can lie on the same indifference curve only if one has more of one commodity and the other has more of the other commodity. Otherwise, points on indifference curves farther from the origin (indicating zero amounts of both commodities) are preferred to points closer to the origin.

The most relevant characteristic of an indifference curve for our purposes is its *slope*, which measures the maximum amount of one good a consumer would sacrifice to obtain one more unit of the other good (or vice versa). In Figure 2-3, we imagine a consumer rearranging consumption from point B to point D, that is, substituting movies for meals, in a two-step process. First, the consumer is given extra movie tickets, depicted as a movement of consumption from point B to point C. The increase in movies, by itself, causes satisfaction to increase, here represented by a movement to a higher indifference curve. This change in utility can be represented as $(\Delta U/\Delta q_1)(\Delta q_1)$, where the symbol Δ (the Greek letter *delta*) means "change in." The change in satisfaction due

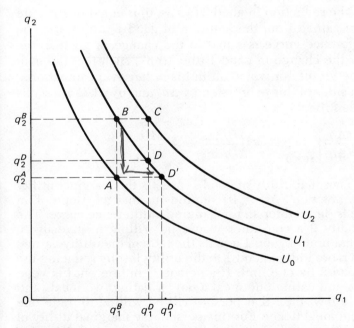

Figure 2-3
Marginal Rate of Substitution (MRS). Increase in good 1 from q_1^B to q_1^D increases satisfaction from U_1 to U_2 (which only the consumer can measure); reduction in good 2 from q_2^B to q_2^D brings utility back to original level (U_1). The willingness of the consumer to substitute $(q_1^D - q_1^B)$ for $(q_2^B - q_2^D)$ reveals the relative marginal utility (MU) of those two commodities: $MRS_{2,1} = \Delta q_2/\Delta q_1 = -(MU_1/MU_2)$. A similar pattern results from moving to point D' from point B via point A.

to the change in the consumption of movies equals the extra satisfaction per movie times the number of movie tickets received.[5]

Suppose the person receiving the extra movie tickets has a binding contract which forces him or her to yield a promised amount of good 2. The second step of the substitution of movies for meals returns the consumer to the original indifference curve and moves consumption from point C to point D. The change in utility due to this reduction in good 2 can be represented as $(\Delta U/\Delta q_2)(\Delta q_2)$. By construction, the overall change in utility after the move from point B to point D is zero:

$$\Delta U = \frac{\Delta U}{\Delta q_2}\cdot\Delta q_2 + \frac{\Delta U}{\Delta q_1}\cdot\Delta q_1 = 0$$

or

$$\frac{\Delta U}{\Delta q_1}\cdot\Delta q_1 = -\frac{\Delta U}{\Delta q_2}\cdot\Delta q_2$$

The utility lost by the reduction in good 2 ($\Delta q_2 < 0$) is equal in absolute value to the utility gained from the addition of good 1 ($\Delta q_1 > 0$). The slope of the indifference curve is equal to the change in good 2 (the "rise") divided by the change in good 1 (the "run") such that the consumer is neither better off nor worse off in his or her own estimation.

Dividing both sides of this expression by Δq_1 and by $\Delta U/\Delta q_2$ results in an intriguing identity:

$$\left.\frac{\Delta q_2}{\Delta q_1}\right|_{\Delta U=0} = -\frac{\Delta U/\Delta q_1}{\Delta U/\Delta q_2} = -\frac{MU_1}{MU_2}$$

where MU_1 is the marginal utility of good 1. MU_2 is the marginal utility of good 2, and the notation "$\Delta U = 0$" reminds us that the slope of an indifference curve is defined for an unchanging indifference curve. The amount of commodity 2 a consumer would be willing to give up to receive an additional unit of good 1 equals the ratio of the utility gained by consuming one more unit of good 1 to the utility lost by reducing the consumption of good 2 by one unit. If a person is indifferent between seeing two movies and eating one meal a day or eating two meals and seeing one movie a day, then that person will be willing to trade one movie ticket for one meal ticket. For this person, the marginal utility of a movie must equal the marginal utility of a meal. We know the relative marginal utility of commodities from observed behavior, even though we do not know how utility is measured.

---

[5] Because of the principle of diminishing marginal utility, this is not precisely true, unless the change in q_1 is very small. Those familiar with calculus know that this means:

$$dU = \frac{\partial U}{\partial q_1}\cdot dq_1 = \lim_{\Delta q_1 \to 0} \frac{\Delta U}{\Delta q_1}\cdot\Delta q_1$$

The slope of an indifference curve is called the **marginal rate of substitution (MRS)**. The dominance principle requires that the marginal rate of substitution is negative. As long as receiving more of one commodity would increase utility—the consumption of other commodities being held constant—then marginal utility of that commodity is positive. Assuming that the marginal utility of good 1 is positive ($MU_1 > 0$) and that the marginal utility of good 2 is positive ($MU_2 > 0$), then the ratio of MU_1 to MU_2 must also be positive. Since the marginal rate of substitution equals the ratio of MU_1 to MU_2 preceded by a negative sign, the marginal rate of substitution is negative.

Transitive preferences rule out intersecting indifference curves. In Figure 2-4, indifference curves U_0 and U_1 intersect at point A. Since points A and B are both on U_0, the consumer is indifferent between them. Point C, on indifference curve U_1, has more of both goods than point B. Therefore, point C is preferred to point B, and by transitivity, point C should also be preferred to point A. However, since point A also lies on indifference curve U', the consumer is indifferent between A and C. This is a contradiction. Indifference curves cannot intersect when preferences are transitive.

Diminishing marginal utility implies that interesting indifference

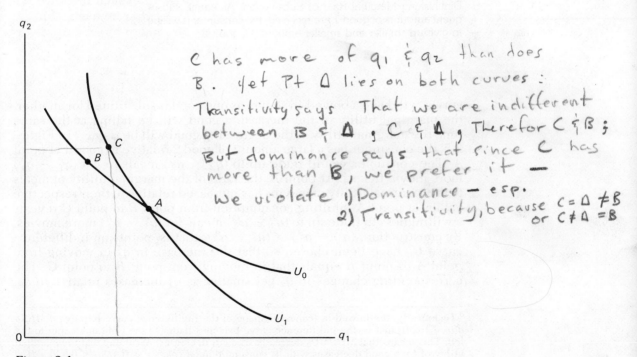

C has more of q_1 & q_2 than does B. Yet Pt A lies on both curves: Transitivity says That we are indifferent between B & A , C & A , Therefor C & B; But dominance says that since C has more than B, we prefer it — We violate 1) Dominance — esp.
2) Transitivity, because $C = A \ne B$ or $C \ne A = B$

Figure 2-4
Intersecting Indifference Curves Violate the Assumption of Transitive Preferences.

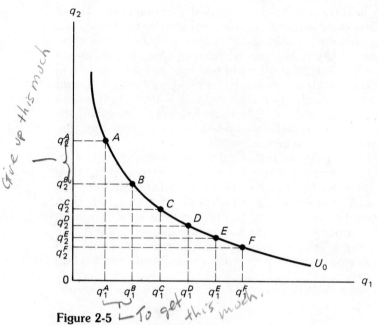

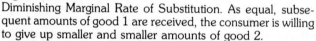

Figure 2-5
Diminishing Marginal Rate of Substitution. As equal, subsequent amounts of good 1 are received, the consumer is willing to give up smaller and smaller amounts of good 2.

curves will have a bowed-in shape; as one good is substituted for another, the marginal utility of the increasing good will be falling at the same time the marginal utility of the decreasing good will be rising.[6] In Figure 2-5, the consumer has a large amount of good 2 relative to good 1 at point A. The consumer would trade up to $(q_2^A - q_2^B)$ meals to get $(q_1^B - q_1^A)$ more movie tickets. At point B, the ratio of the marginal utility of meals to the marginal utility of movies has increased relative to their respective values at point A. Shifting consumption from point B to point C reveals a willingness to trade up to $(q_2^B - q_2^C)$ meals for $(q_1^C - q_1^B)$ more movies. By construction, $(q_1^C - q_1^B) = (q_1^B - q_1^A)$; that is, points on indifference curve U_0 have been chosen so that the increase in q_1 in moving from point A to point B equals that in moving from point B to point C. The corresponding changes in q_2 get smaller as q_1 increases relative to q_2:

---

[6] Technically, the bowed-in (concave) shape of the indifference curve requires $d(MRS)/d(q_2/q_1) < 0$; that is, the indifference curve becomes flatter to the right or steeper to the left. This means that MU_1/MU_2 decreases as q_2/q_1 decreases. Assuming that the marginal utility of each good decreases with its consumption ($\partial U^2/\partial q^2 = \partial MU_1/\partial q_1 < 0$ and $\partial MU_2/\partial q_2 < 0$), indifference curves will be bowed-in toward the origin if the marginal utility of one commodity does not decrease as the consumption of the other commodity increases: $\partial MU_1/\partial q_2 \geqq 0$ and $\partial MU_2/\partial q_1 \geqq 0$.

$(q_2^B - q_2^A) > (q_1^C - q_1^B)$. As more movies are seen, fewer meals are willingly sacrificed to see yet more movies.

The bowed-in shape of the indifference curve reflects what is formally known as the principle of diminishing marginal rate of substitution:

> **Diminishing marginal rate of substitution:** As commodity substitution occurs in such a way that consumption prospects remain on the same indifference curve, an individual willingly sacrifices smaller and smaller amounts of one commodity to receive a constant increase in the other commodity. Equivalently, it will take larger and larger increases in one commodity to compensate an individual for a constant reduction in the other commodity. The indifference curve becomes flatter (i.e., its slope approaches zero) as consumption prospects move to the right.

The typical consumer prefers variety in consumption. Diminishing marginal rates of substitution mean that the amount of q_2 one will sacrifice to get more q_1 is directly related to the amount of q_1 one has and inversely related to the amount of q_2 one has.

Utility Maximization with a Budget Constraint

The completeness principle means that any imaginable combination of commodities must lie on some indifference curve. The transitivity principle requires that each consumption prospect lie on only one indifference curve. The consumer is able to rank the consumption opportunities indicated by the budget line. By juxtaposing the diagram of consumer preferences (i.e., the indifference map) in Figure 2-2 with the diagram of consumer options (the budget line) in Figure 2-1, we can simulate the process of consumer choice.[7] A consumer maximizes utility by purchasing that combination of goods on the budget line which is also on the highest (attainable) indifference curve.

In Figure 2-6, we imagine that the Smith family has been spending all its income on meals; the maximum amount of meals, given by Y/p_2, lies on indifference curve U_0. According to the slope of indifference curve U_0, they would be willing to reduce their consumption of meals to q_2' to obtain q_1^0 movie tickets. However, the budget line indicates that the consumption of meals would only have to be reduced to q_2^0 in order

---

[7] Actually, for multiple-person households, the adults who do the shopping are maximizing their own utility by looking after family members' health and (expressions of) happiness. The role of empathy in allocating a household budget has been investigated by Gary S. Becker in "A Theory of Social Interactions," *Journal of Political Economy* (November/December 1974), 1163–91. However, to avoid complex mathematics, we will continue to discuss allocating a "household budget" and allocating a "consumer's budget" interchangeably.

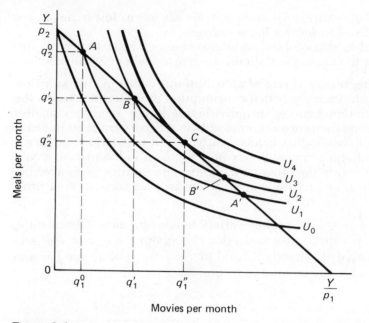

Movies per month

Figure 2-6
Utility Maximization with a Budget Constraint. As long as consumption occurs at a point of intersection between the budget line and an indifference curve, satisfaction can be increased by substituting purchases along the budget line until the point of tangency is reached. At utility maximum (point C), the marginal rate of substitution equals the slope of the budget line.

to attend q_1^0 movies per month. The market gives the Smiths a bargain; by moving along the budget line, trading meals for movies at the rate of $(\Delta q_2/\Delta q_1) = -(p_1/p_2)$, the family is able to move to a higher indifference curve.

At point A, the Smiths would sacrifice up to $(q_2^0 - q_2'')$ meals to obtain $(q_1' - q_1^0)$ additional movie tickets, indicated along indifference curve U_1. The market provides a better deal than what is necessary to keep the Smith family indifferent. By yielding only $(q_2^0 - q_2')$ meals per month, the household moves to indifference curve U_2 by spending the money saved on meals for $(q_1' - q_1^0)$ movie tickets per month. Once more, by purchasing $(q_1'' - q_1')$ movie tickets per month instead of $(q_2' - q_2'')$ meals, the satisfaction level moves from U_2 (point B) to U_3 (point C).

At point C the household has reached the limits of its budget constraint. Indifference curve U_4 would be preferred to indifference curve U_3, but "U-foria" is not attainable. The household must settle for what is feasible. Points to the left of point C (e.g., A, B), and points to the right of point C (e.g., A', B') involve intersections of the budget line and the relevant indifference curve. Reallocating expenditures along the budget line raises consumers to higher indifference curves because their marginal rate of substitution (the slope of their indifference curve) indicates they are willing to give up more of one commodity to obtain the other commodity than the market requires (as indicated by the slope of the budget line). Point C is a *tangency* point between the budget line and the highest attainable indifference curve. The budget line and indifference curve U_3 are moving together as point C is approached. At point C, the two lines touch briefly. At one instant, that indifference curve and the budget line are moving in harmony. But beyond point C, the indifference curve once again goes its own way.

Intersection of an indifference curve with the budget line at point A or point B indicates:[8]

$$-\frac{MU_1}{MU_2} < -\frac{p_1}{p_2} \quad \text{or} \quad \frac{MU_1}{p_1} > \frac{MU_2}{p_2}$$

indicating that the last dollar spent on movies (good 1) yields greater satisfaction than the last dollar spent on meals (good 2). Reducing expenditure on meals and using the money saved to buy movie tickets increases total satisfaction. At point C, the last dollar spent on movie tickets yields the same satisfaction as the last dollar spent on meals:

$$-\frac{MU_1}{MU_2} = -\frac{p_1}{p_2} \quad \text{or} \quad \frac{MU_1}{p_1} = \frac{MU_2}{p_2}$$

It makes no difference (to satisfaction) how the last dollar of the consumer budget is spent, since the marginal utility of each commodity is proportional to its price. Since utility cannot be increased by reallocating purchases, it follows that the household has reached the highest possible utility level (indifference curve) given its income.

Consumers use their limited budget most effectively by allocating purchasing power so that the marginal utility of each commodity purchased is proportional to its price. Although Figure 2-6 is limited to only two commodities, the rule which states that consumers should equate the marginal utility of the last dollar spent on every commodity is true for any number of goods purchased. Allowing n to stand for the number of goods purchased, this rule is:

$$\frac{MU_1}{p_1} = \frac{MU_2}{p_2} = \cdots = \frac{MU_n}{p_n}$$

Utility maximization does not imply buying the "best" (i.e., highest marginal utility) or the "cheapest" (i.e., lowest price) commodities; the

---

[8] Points A' and B' (indeed, all points to the right of point C) are characterized by $-(MU_1/MU_2) > -(p_1/p_2)$, so that $(MU_1/p_1) < (MU_2/p_2)$; satisfaction is increased by substituting meals for movie tickets.

most economical purchases provide the highest marginal utility per dollar spent.

APPLICATION
Changes in the Budget Constraint: Income

So far, our discussion of consumer behavior has merely set the stage for the theory of consumer behavior. Because of the critical role played by consumer tastes in reaching the indifference-curve/budget-line tangency solution, economic theory does not explain which commodities different households actually purchase.[9] What economic theory does seek to predict is how consumers respond to changes in observable influences on consumption, namely, prices and/or income.

Figure 2-7a depicts a household spending its Y_0 income on a combination of meals and movies given by point A. An increase in money income from Y_0 to Y_1 which leaves the relative prices of the two goods the same would cause a parallel displacement of the budget line. An equal percentage decrease in both p_1 and p_2 which left relative prices unchanged, with constant money income, would have the same effect. Either way, the effect of a change in purchasing power (relative prices constant) is shown as a parallel shift in the budget line.

The increase in purchasing power places point A below the new budget line in Figure 2-7a. The combination of commodities which maximized utility at a lower level of income is no longer the best combination attainable. By spending the extra income, $\Delta Y = Y_1 - Y_0 = Y_1 - (p_1q_1^0 + p_2q_2^0)$, on meals and movie tickets, the Smith household is able to attain a degree of happiness previously beyond their purchasing power.

In Figure 2-7a, the increase in money income, the prices of the two goods (and tastes) being constant, results in a relocation of the optimal consumption point from point A to point C. Note that the amount of each good consumed increases in response to the income increase. In such a case, both good 1 and good 2 are called normal goods. A **normal good** is a commodity whose consumption changes in the same direction as the change in real income (other factors being constant). Note that were money income to decrease from Y_1 to Y_0, the optimal combination of movies and meals would decrease from q_1' to q_1^0 and from q_2' to q_2^0, respectively. A decrease in income causes the consumption of a normal good to decrease, *ceteris paribus*. **Ceteris paribus** is a Latin phrase meaning "other things remaining equal."

---

[9] Some economists, most notably Gary S. Becker, have extended the principles of consumer behavior to explain alleged differences in tastes in terms of differences in the opportunity cost of time. See "A Theory of the Allocation of Time," in *The Economic Approach to Human Behavior* (Chicago: University of Chicago Press, 1976), pp. 89–114.

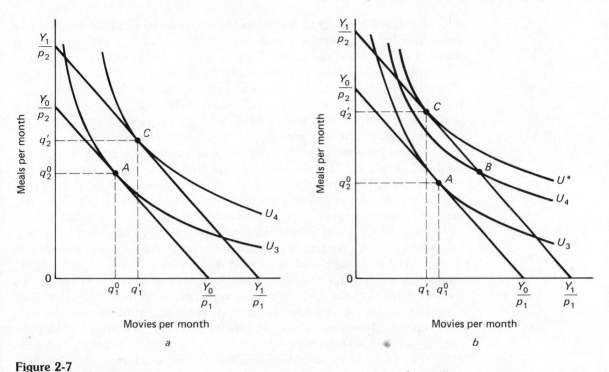

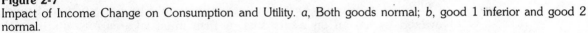

Figure 2-7
Impact of Income Change on Consumption and Utility. *a*, Both goods normal; *b*, good 1 inferior and good 2 normal.

Figure 2-7*b* shows what happens when one of the commodities is an **inferior good**, a commodity whose consumption varies in the opposite direction as income varies, *ceteris paribus*. In Figure 2-7*b*, the increase in money income means that the previous utility-maximizing consumption point, *A*, is no longer best. The household begins to spend its extra income on meals and movies, but discovers at point *B* that utility can be further enhanced by substituting meals for movies until, at point *C*, as much satisfaction as possible has been derived from the higher purchasing power. The new consumption optimum shows more meals being consumed: the consumption of good 2 indicates that meals are normal goods. However, the reduced consumption of movies indicates that they are inferior goods.

At this juncture, our simplifying assumption of two commodities—meals and movies—begins to strain credibility, so a verbal explanation is in order. The typical household consumes literally hundreds of different kinds of commodities, most of which fit into broad budget categories (e.g., food, shelter, clothing, entertainment, transportation). Each of these categories can contain basic necessities (bland food, drab clothing, a used car) or luxurious substitutes for the "basics" (rich pastries and expensive wines, designer clothes, a finely engineered sports car).

For example, both peanut butter and chicken necks provide protein, but steak and lobster are often preferred by households which can afford them. A secondhand sedan may be an adequate source of transportation, but a new Mercedes also confers status. As income rises, the consumption of some narrowly defined commodities may fall. If income falls (e.g., from Y_1 to Y_0 in Figure 2-7*b*), consumers will find the impact on their standard of living is minimized by substituting basic (inferior) goods for more desirable (normal) goods.

Income increases are more likely to cause the substitution of "high quality" goods for "low quality" goods than an actual increase in the rate of consumption of narrowly defined commodities. The dividing line between normal and inferior goods depends upon the broadness of the consumption categories. All major budget items for a household seem to behave like normal goods: expenditure on food, clothing, housing, education, transportation, medical care, entertainment, and even children.[10] Within these broad categories, however, individual components may behave like inferior goods. For example, generic beer gives way to imported ale; off-the-rack suits are replaced by tailor-made clothing; camping trips are eliminated in favor of vacations at plush resorts.

Many businesses attempt to identify potential customers by income range, perhaps to target an advertising campaign. A luxury good purchased by swinging young professionals would be advertised in *Playboy* or *Playgirl*, while low-priced necessities would be more efficiently advertised by a sign on a city bus. A firm must take care to distinguish between income differences, identifying which groups at a particular time are likely to buy its product, and income changes, which predict whether its sales would be helped or hurt by a recession. Time series data, collected from the same households over time, are likely to show the effects of fads and temporary business downturns as well as the trend in consumption. Cross-sectional data, collected for many households at the same time, may attribute differences in tastes coincidental with differences in income (e.g., due to education or the number of workers) to differences in income per se. The relationship between changes in consumption and changes in income is a *ceteris paribus* relationship; that is, the change in consumption due to the change in income is that change in consumption which remains with other influences held constant (or accounted for separately).

To analyze the consumption of a commodity over a broad range of income, economists attempt to relate the consumption that would occur at various levels of income, other factors being constant. By connecting the points of tangency between indifference curves and their associated budget lines, we generate the **income-consumption path** in Figure 2-8. Then by plotting the quantity of each good (e.g., meals, movie tickets)

---

[10] Gary S. Becker, "On the Interaction Between the Quantity and Quality of Children," *Journal of Political Economy* (March/April 1973), S279–S288.

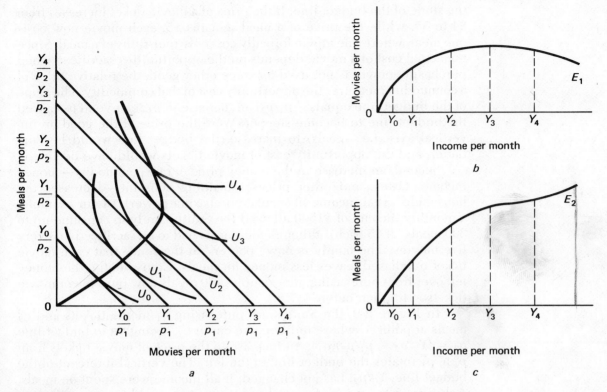

Figure 2-8
Income-Consumption Path (*a*) and Associated Engel Curves for One Inferior Good (*b*) and One Normal Good (*c*)

on the vertical (dependent variable) axis against the associated income (on the horizontal axis), we generate an **Engel curve** (named for the German statistician Ernst Engel).

Hypothetical Engel curves for movies and meals are displayed in Figure 2-8*b* and *c*, respectively. As in Figure 2-7*b*, movies become an inferior good above income level Y_3. When this household's income exceeds Y_3, the income-consumption curve in Figure 2-8*a* bends backward, indicating that as q_2 increases, q_1 decreases. The corresponding Engel curve for meals, assumed to be a normal good, is positively sloped for all levels of income (Y).

APPLICATION

Changes in the Budget Constraint: Money Prices

A change in the money price of one commodity—money income, tastes, and other prices remaining constant—has two effects on the household's budget line. First, a change in the relative price of commodities changes the slope of the budget line. If the price of a movie ticket increases from $4 to $5, while the price of a meal remains $5, each movie now costs one meal, where one movie formally cost only four-fifths of a meal. Since the actual cost of a movie depends on the opportunities sacrificed when purchasing power is not used for some other good, the relative price of a commodity measures the **opportunity cost** of that commodity. The slope of the budget line equals $-p_1/p_2$; an increase in p_1 relative to p_2 caused the budget line to become steeper. Were the price of the good on the vertical axis (i.e., meals) to increase, the budget line would become flatter, and the opportunity cost of movie tickets would have declined.

Second, an increase in the money price of one commodity—money income, tastes, and other prices remaining constant—decreases the household's **real income** (its actual purchasing power). In our example, a monthly income of $1500 allowed the Smith family to consume up to 300 meals (at $5 each), although four meals had to be sacrificed for every five movies. The family is now "poorer" in the sense that each movie ticket purchased leaves less money for meals. Equivalently, the money left over from purchasing, for example, 160 meals now buys fewer movie tickets (140) than before (175).

In Figure 2-9, the Smiths are purchasing q_1^0 movie tickets and q_2^0 meals at point A, where indifference curve U_0 is tangent to budget line $q_2 = (Y_0/p_2 - p_1^0/p_2)(q_1)$. An increase in the price of movie tickets from p_1^0 to p_1' rotates the budget line to the left. The vertical intercept of the budget line, Y_0/p_2, has not changed; if all income were spent on meals, a change in the price of a good not purchased would have no effect on the amount of the other good(s) consumed. The increase in the price of movie tickets moves the horizontal intercept toward the origin, from Y_0/p_1^0 to Y_0/p_1'. The original utility maximum is no longer feasible. As with a decrease in money income, the impact of a price increase is minimized by reducing consumption of the two goods until the point of tangency on the new budget line is achieved at point C on indifference curve U'.

As usual, the optimal consumption point on budget line $(Y_0/p_2; Y_0/p_1')$ is characterized by the equality of the consumer's marginal rate of substitution and the (negative) price ratio:

$$MRS = \frac{\Delta q_2}{\Delta q_1} = -\frac{MU_1}{MU_2} = -\frac{p_1'}{p_2}$$

so that:

$$\frac{MU_1}{p_1'} = \frac{MU_2}{p_2}$$

The Smiths have reduced their consumption of movies relative to meals in such a way that the higher relative price of movies is now associated with a higher relative marginal utility.

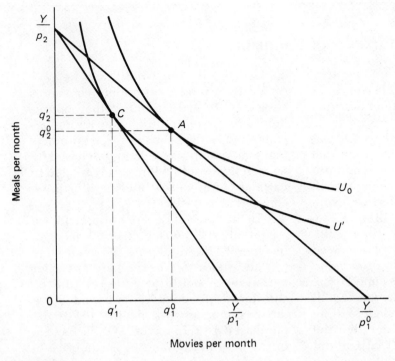

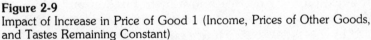

Figure 2-9
Impact of Increase in Price of Good 1 (Income, Prices of Other Goods,
and Tastes Remaining Constant)

The impact of a money price change for one good (other prices,
utility, and money income remaining constant) can be separated into a
substitution effect and an **income effect**. The substitution effect of a price
change is always the same: the quantity of a good purchased will vary
inversely with changes in its relative price, other factors (including *real
income*) remaining constant. Since (as the appendix to this chapter
shows) real income usually changes for individual households in the
wake of a price change, demonstrating a pure substitution effect of a
money price change requires the use of imagination. To isolate the impact of a relative price change on the consumption of our two goods, we
will pretend that money income changes by exactly enough to hold
utility constant before and after an increase in the price of movie tickets.

Figure 2-10 reprises the events in Figure 2-9: an increase in the
money price of movie tickets switches the optimal consumption point
from A to C. However, we pause in the middle of the adjustment process
to identify the point on indifference curve U_0 where the marginal rate
of substitution is equal to the new relative price ratio, $\Delta q_2/\Delta q_1 = -(p_1'/p_2) < -(p_1^0/p_2)$. By locating the dashed line $(Y'/p_2, Y'/p_1')$ parallel
to the new budget line and tangent to indifference curve U_0 at point B,

Business Illustration
Economic Theory and Irrational Behavior

As we shall see in subsequent chapters, the theory of individual choice serves as a basis of the theory of consumer demand, which predicts market-wide responses to changes in economic incentives. Of particular relevance is the proposition that income-compensated demand schedules will always have a negative slope; that is, a price increase will always have a dampening impact on consumer willingness to buy a particular good, once other influences on consumer behavior have been taken into account. This *law of demand* (defined in chapter four) is assumed to act as a constraint on seller behavior. If sellers offer more than consumers are willing to buy at the prevailing price, either the price of the commodity must fall, output must be cut, or some other influence on consumer behavior (e.g., advertising, tastes) must change. Whether they believe the law of demand or not, sellers are not happy with it; they prefer the law of supply, which says that buyers must offer sellers more for a commodity if buyers offer to pay higher prices.

Most economists have been unconcerned about the literal truth of the model of constrained utility maximization. However, a few economists and many non-economists criticize the notion that consumers attempt to maximize well-defined utility functions (represented by indifference curves) and use this criticism to reject the prediction that an increase in the relative price of a good will reduce its consumption, real income remaining constant. Economist Gary S. Becker argues that the market behavior of consumers, inferred from the theory of consumer

choice (see p. 33), would also be predicted by a model of random consumer choice.[*] Merely assuming that households are prevented from consuming beyond their budget constraints, he predicts that total quantity of a good purchased by households would be inversely related to its relative price, real income remaining constant.

In the spirit of Becker's argument, we assume that 10 households each have an income of $60 to allocate between wine (q_1) and steak (q_2). In the base or earlier period, each bottle of wine sells for $5 and steak is priced at $4 per pound. Since the maximum amount of wine that can be purchased is Y_0/p_1, where Y_0 is income in the base period and p_1 is the price of wine, we allow q_1 to take on any value between 0 and 12 with a probability of 0.0825, using a random-number generator program from a pocket calculator. Once the value of q_1 is determined, we solve for the amount of steak as: $q_2 Y_0 - p_1 q_1/p_2$, where p_2 is the price of steak.

Next, we determine the impact of a price increase for wine, with the price of steak remaining constant. Holding money income constant (see Table 1) means that only 10 bottles of wine can be purchased; the calculator is programmed so that q_1 takes on any value from 0 to 10 with an equal probability of 10 percent. Since the price of steak has not changed, the residual amount of steak is determined in the same manner. Note that while three

---

[*] Gary S. Becker, "Irrational Behavior and Economic Theory," *Journal of Political Economy* (February 1962), 1–13.

TABLE 1
Simulated Market Demand from Random Household Behavior, Money Income Being Constant ($Y_0 = 60$, $Y_1 = 60$)

Household	$p_1 = 5$	$p_2 = 4$	$p_1 = 6$	$p_2 = 4$		
	q_1	q_2	q_1	q_2	Δq_1	Δq_2
1	10	2.5	7	4.5	−3	+2
2	12	0	7	4.5	−5	+4.5
3	4	10	7	4.5	+3	−5.5
4	2	12.5	5	7.5	+3	−5
5	6	7.5	6	6	0	−1.5
6	1	13.5	0	15	−1	+1.5
7	8	5	8	3	0	−2
8	11	1.25	7	4.5	−4	+3.25
9	7	6.25	1	13.5	−6	+7.25
10	3	11.25	9	1.5	+6	−9.75
Total	64	69.75	57	64.5	−7	−5.25

households actually consumed more wine, and two households consumed the same amount of wine, five households consumed less wine at the $6 price than at the $5 price, with money income remaining constant, even though the data were randomly generated. That is, with an increase in the price of wine, the probability of consuming 11 or 12 bottles went to zero, while the probability of consuming each quantity from 0 to 10 increased from 8.25 to 10 percent. Note also that the total quantity of steak decreased although its relative price decreased: the income effect due to the increase in the price of wine offset the substitution effect of a lower relative price of steak.

Table 2 shows the results of "random" consumption patterns when real income is held constant in the wake of an increase in the price of wine. Had a household spent one-half of its budget on wine and one-half on steak in the base period, it would have purchased 6 bottles of wine and 7.5 pounds of steak: $q_1 = \frac{1}{2}(60/5) = 6$, $q_2 = [60 − (5 \times 6)]/4 = 7.5$. An increase in the price of wine to $6 per bottle would raise the cost of 6 bottles of wine and 7.5 pounds of steak to $66. Assuming that each household has a money income of $66 allows the average household to purchase the same combination of wine and steak in the current period as in the base period.† Hence, the probability for each rate of wine consumption between 0 and 11 is $1/11 \simeq 0.091$, and the

---

† Obviously, if we deny the existence of indifference curves, we cannot use the Hicks approach to real income measurement to neutralize the income effect of a money price change. Hence, we have employed the Slutsky approach, which defines real income as the ability to purchase the same bundle of commodities in two periods. This approach is discussed further in the appendix to chapter two and in chapter three.

TABLE 2
Simulated Market Demand from Random Household Behavior, Real Income Being Constant ($Y_0 = 60$, $Y_1 = 66$)

	$p_1 = 5$	$p_2 = 4$	$p_1 = 6$	$p_2 = 4$		
Household	q_1	q_2	q_1	q_2	Δq_1	Δq_2
1	6	7.5	6	7.5	0	0
2	1	13.75	1	15	0	+ 1.25
3	2	12.5	2	13.5	0	+ 1
4	1	13.75	1	15	0	+ 1.25
5	7	6.25	4	10.5	− 3	+ 4.25
6	9	3.75	1	15	− 8	+ 11.25
7	9	3.75	6	7.5	− 3	+ 3.75
8	10	2.5	8	4.5	− 2	+ 2
9	6	7.5	8	4.5	+ 2	− 3
10	4	10	9	3	+ 5	− 7
Total	55	81.25	46	96	−9	+ 14.75

value of q_2 is determined as $q_2 = (66 - 6q_1)/4$.

As in the case of constant money income, the randomly determined pattern of household expenditures resulted in a net reduction of wine. Furthermore, higher real income resulted in an increase in the consumption of steak. While luck necessarily had to play a part in the pattern of consumption observed, this simple experiment has supported Becker's argument: in order to observe an inverse relationship between the quantity of a good households consume in the aggregate and the relative price of that good, it is only necessary to hold real income constant. The model of constrained utility maximization, which provides an insight into how changes in economic incentives change consumption decisions, might indeed be untrue. Nevertheless, there is evidence that the predictions of this model would still hold, even if households are asssumed to behave in a completely irrational fashion.

we have isolated the pure substitution effect. By construction, point B indicates the amount of movie tickets (q_1^B) and the number of meals (q_2^B) that would be consumed were the Smith family given just enough additional income, $\Delta Y = Y' - Y_0$, to keep them as happy as they were at point A. Since real income remains constant (by definition), the change in the consumption of movie tickets and meals from point A to point B reflects the impact of the higher relative price of movie tickets.

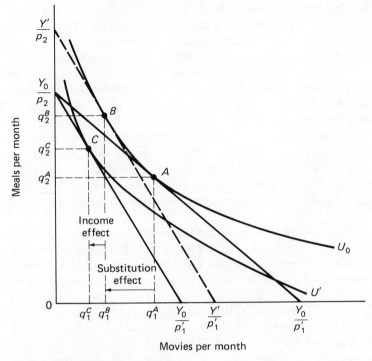

Figure 2-10
Income and Substitution Effects of Price Increase. Increase in the relative price of good 1 reduces its consumption from q_1^A to q_1^B; lower real income further reduces consumption of this normal good from q_1^B to q_1^C.

Having traced the substitution effect, the income effect is easy to see. It was all a fake! There was no compensation for the Smith family to offset the increase in the price of movie tickets. The loss of that income supplement (which they never had) reduces consumption of both goods, from the combination indicated by point B to the combination indicated by point C. In this case, movies and meals are both normal goods; the loss of real income, due to an increase in the price of one good, money income and other prices constant, led to a reduction in the consumption of both goods relative to what they would have been had real income not fallen. For normal goods, the income effect of a money price change reinforces the substitution effect of that price change. That is, the change in consumption due to the change in real income (the change in real income is in the opposite direction from the change in the money price) will be in the same direction as the substitution effect (which is in the opposite direction from the change in the relative price of the good). Let's trace through a numerical example involving meals and movies.

Suppose that the Smith family spends $800 per month on meals ($q_2$ = 160 meals at $5 each) and $700 on movies ($q_1$ = 175 when movie tickets cost $4 each). This unfortunate family, already plagued by a pathetic lack of imagination, is devastated when the price of a movie ticket increases from $4 to $5. But, by coincidence (and poetic license), Pat Smith receives a one-time bonus of $150. For one month, the family has $1650 to spend. They decide to reduce their consumption of movies to 160 while raising their consumption of meals to 170 for that month. At the end of month, the members of the Smith household agree that, although they substituted ten meals for fifteen movies, they felt just as happy as they did before. Although their lifestyle is dull, the Smiths are very sensitive to changes in their relative happiness. The substitution effect led to a reduction in movie consumption relative to meal consumption.

The next month, without the one-time income supplement, the full impact of the price increase for movie tickets is felt. The Smiths' money income of $1500 allows them to consume only 155 meals and 145 movies. The loss of compensating income caused the Smiths' consumption of movies to fall even further: the income effect reinforced the substitution effect. Overall, movie attendance fell by approximately 17 percent, half due to the substitution effect and half due to the income effect. While the income effect caused the consumption of meals to fall also (by about 3 percent), the magnitude of the change in meal consumption was much smaller.

Now suppose, as in Figure 2-8, movie tickets are inferior goods for the Smith family. Then, as shown in Figure 2-11, the income effect of a price change in movie tickets would operate in the opposite direction from the substitution effect. Again we imagine a household maximizing utility at point A, where indifference curve U_0 is tangent to budget line (Y_0/p_2, Y_0/p_1^0). This time, we imagine a decrease in the price of movie tickets from p_1^0 to p_1'. The total impact of the decline in ticket prices results in an increase in the number of movies from q_1^A to q_1^C. This may "look normal," but good 1 is not a normal good, as the dashed line tangent to indifference curve U_0 at point B attests. If money income were somehow reduced just enough to constrain the choice to the original indifference curve, the substitution effect implies a consumption of movie tickets of $q_1^B > q_1^C$. For an inferior good (in this case, movie tickets) the income effect reduces the change in consumption of a good relative to what its consumption would have been because of the substitution effect alone. Nevertheless, as in Figure 2-11, the substitution effect is usually strong enough to dominate the change in consumption.

Restriction of our examples to two commodities means that only one commodity can be an inferior good. If an increase in real income reduces consumption of one commodity, all the increase in real income, plus the money saved by reducing consumption of the inferior good, must be

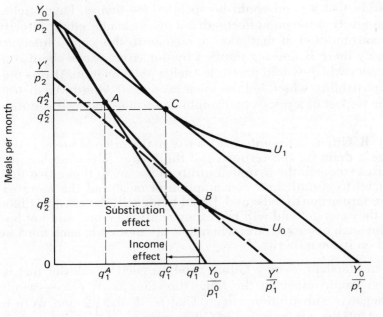

Figure 2-11
Income and Substitution Effects of Price Decrease for an Inferior Good.
The relative price decline of movie tickets results in a substitution effect
from point A to point B; gain in real income reduces consumption of
tickets from q_1^B to q_1^C. However, the substitution effect is still dominant
and the number of movie tickets purchased increases.

spent on the other (normal) good. In real life, of course, there are many
commodities in the household budget, so more than one commodity
could be an inferior good. However, by the same reasoning, not all
commodities could be inferior goods, since there must exist at least one
commodity whose consumption increases as real income increases and
whose consumption decreases as real income decreases. After all, a
household's real income can be defined only by its consumption, since
neither utility nor indifference curves can be directly observed.

The Strange Paradox of Sir R. Giffen

Most economists are perplexed by the popular resistance to the notion
that consumption of a commodity falls as its relative price rises, once
coincidental changes in tastes, income, or other prices are taken into
account. Nevertheless, the resistance is there, and by no means is it a
recent phenomenon. One way of expressing this skepticism is to ask: Is

it not possible that a good could be so inferior—that is, have such a strong counteracting income effect—that a price change might directly cause the consumption of that good to change in the same direction? Yes. In theory there is nothing implied by the assumptions about consumer behavior which would preclude such a phenomenon. It was precisely this possibility which led the great economist Alfred Marshall to separate the impact of a price change into an income and a substitution effect:

> [A]s Sir R. Giffen has pointed out, a rise in the price of bread makes so large a drain on the resources of the poorer labouring families and raises so much the marginal utility of money to them, that they are forced to curtail their consumption of meat and the more expensive farinaceous foods: and, bread being still the cheapest food which they can get and will take, they consume more, and not less of it. But such cases are rare; when they are met with, each must be treated on its own merits.[11]

According to Marshall, even a **Giffen good**—a good so inferior that its consumption would move in the same direction as its price—would exhibit a negative substitution effect. That is, if real income were to remain constant, the consumption of Giffen goods would vary inversely with their relative prices. If money income, rather than real income, were held constant, then the situation suggested by Giffen would be hypothetically possible.

Even our movie addicts, the Smith family, may exhibit the consumption behavior suggested by Giffen and cited by Marshall. Hence we imagine that the commodity on the horizontal axis (q_1) is bread and that the commodity on the vertical axis (q_2) is "other goods." Since only the price of bread is allowed to rise, we will assume that the price of "other goods" is one, so that the vertical intercept is Y_0, that is, money income.

In Figure 2-12, a low-income household, the Bob Cratchit family, spends most of its income on bread, using what little remains to buy turkeys and other foods. An increase in the relative price of bread from p_1^0 to p_1' would cause the substitution of turkey for bread if Mr. Scrooge would give Cratchit a raise to Y' per month, just enough to maintain consumption along U_1. Like everyone else, Bob Cratchit has indifference curves characterized by diminishing marginal rates of substitution. If real income remained constant, optimal consumption would shift from point A to point B, since the higher relative price of bread would require a higher marginal utility of bread for utility to be maximized.

Alas, Scrooge thinks income and substitution effects are all humbug; he is even less enthusiastic about providing compensating income in-

---

[11] Alfred Marshall, *Principles of Political Economy*, 8th ed. (New York: Macmillan, 1947), p. 132.

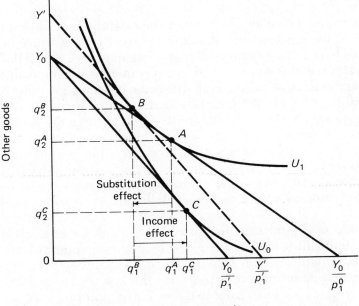

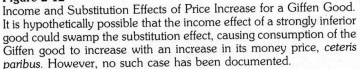

Bread per month

Figure 2-12
Income and Substitution Effects of Price Increase for a Giffen Good.
It is hypothetically possible that the income effect of a strongly inferior
good could swamp the substitution effect, causing consumption of the
Giffen good to increase with an increase in its money price, *ceteris
paribus*. However, no such case has been documented.

creases out of his own pocket. Since money income remains Y_0, the
Cratchits discover that they cannot purchase enough turkeys and other
food in sufficient quantities to prevent malnutrition. Their only alternative to starvation is to substitute bread for more expensive types of
food. By substituting carbohydrates for protein, the Cratchit household
ends up consuming more bread (point C on U_0).

Although a Giffen good is theoretically possible, there has never
been an empirically verified instance of a Giffen good as a market-wide
phenomenon. In our example, the Cratchits decide to dress up like ghosts
and extort a raise and free turkeys from Scrooge. In other cases, logic
dictates asking where extra bread would come from, since a shortage of
bread was likely to have caused its price to increase in the first place.
That is, if less bread caused prices to rise, how could the price increase
lead to the consumption of more bread? It is more likely that a change
in income or a change in tastes caused the consumption of bread to
increase, while the price increase was necessary to encourage bakers to
produce more bread (see the appendix to chapter nine).

Consumer Surplus

Analysis of consumer behavior leads to an important, albeit abstract, implication about the performance of an ideal market system which allows households to purchase commodities at constant prices. Recall that the diamond-water paradox was resolved by the principle of diminishing marginal utility: the price of a commodity (its value in exchange) reflects its marginal utility, whereas the total satisfaction that commodity provides (its value in use) reflects its total utility. By allocating the household budget so that the marginal rate of substitution (negative ratio of marginal utilities) equals the market allowed rate of substitution (negative ratio of prices), the household "breaks even" on the last dollar spent on each good. The last dollar spent on movies gives the same addition to satisfaction as would one more dollar spent on meals (and vice versa).

The principle of diminishing marginal utility (and the equivalent concept of the diminishing marginal rate of substitution) implies that the next-to-last dollar spent on each commodity in the household budget provides a greater amount of satisfaction than the last dollar spent. In fact, the *inframarginal* (all units prior to the last) expenditure on a commodity returns more satisfaction than expenditure on the last unit. When each unit of a commodity can be purchased at the price paid for the last unit, a household receives a surplus on those inframarginal units. This excess of the "value in use" (total utility) over "value in exchange" (total expenditure) is called, appropriately, the **consumer surplus**.

The indifference curve interpretation of consumer surplus is presented in Figure 2-13. On the horizontal axis we have plotted the monthly bread consumption of the Cratchit family, measured as q_1 and whose price is given as p_1. Plotted on the vertical axis is the composite commodity y. Often called *Hicks-Marshall money* (after the economists who introduced the technique, Sir John Hicks and Alfred Marshall), this composite commodity is defined as the purchasing power available for purchases of all commodities other than bread: $y = Y - p_1q_1$, where Y is money income. Again, the "price" of this composite good is taken as 1, so that if no bread is purchased, consumption of the composite good equals total income, $y = Y$, which is the vertical intercept of the budget line.

As in Figure 2-12, the Cratchit family maximizes its utility at point A, consuming q_1^* loaves of bread per month and leaving $y^* = Y_0 - p_1q_1^*$ for other goods. For drama, imagine that Ebenezer Scrooge cornered the bread market and forced Bob Cratchit to pay tribute for the right to buy bread at price p_1. Note that indifference curve U_0 emanates from point Y_0; if Bob Cratchit were unable to buy bread at any price, utility would fall from U^* to U_0. Now, note that U_0 also passes through point (q^*, y_0), meaning that Bob Cratchit is indifferent between doing

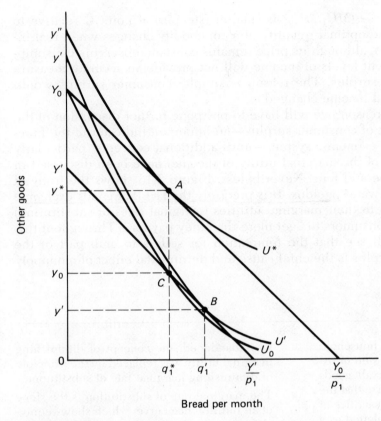

Other goods

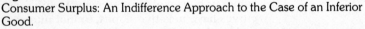

Bread per month

Figure 2-13
Consumer Surplus: An Indifference Approach to the Case of an Inferior
Good.

without bread and spending his income on other goods and having q_1^*
loaves of bread per month and y_0 worth of other goods. In other words,
the maximum amount the Cratchit family would spend for q_1^* loaves of
bread would appear to be $Y_0 - y_0 = y^* - y_0 + p_1 q_1^*$.

Unless Jacob Marley is communicating the Cratchit household's
indifference curves to Mr. Scrooge, the maximum tribute which can be
extracted must be estimated from Cratchit's behavior. Figure 2-13 shows
some of the measurement errors which are likely when researchers attempt to estimate consumer surplus from actual expenditures. If bread
is an inferior good, reducing money income by $\Delta Y = Y_0 - Y' = y^* -
y_0$ would cause the consumption of bread to increase to q', since indif-
ference curve $U' (>U_0)$ is tangent to the budget line $y = Y' - p_1 q_1$ at
point B, while money left for other goods, y', would be less than y_0. As
the quote by Marshall indicated, loss of real income by consumers of an
inferior good would imply a reduction in the marginal utility of income,

since $MRS = -(MU_1/MU_y)$ is smaller (steeper) at point C relative to point A. If the optimal quantity of a commodity changes when real income changes, although its price remains constant, observing consumption at different levels of income will not provide an accurate measure of consumer surplus. The reason is simple: consumer surplus would change as real income changed.

For this reason, we will have to postpone further discussion of the measurement of consumer surplus—an important indicator of the functioning of an economic system—until additional concepts (particularly the meaning of the marginal utility of income) have been discussed in chapters three and four. Nevertheless, Figure 2-13 shows the irony of the diamond-water paradox. It is precisely the fact that goods exchange in proportion to their marginal utilities (marginal rates of substitution) that allows consumers to "get more than they pay for." Throughout this book, we will see that the temptation for sellers to grab part of the consumer surplus is the chief cause and detrimental effect of monopoly power.

HIGHLIGHTS

1. Scarcity is communicated to a household through its budget constraint: the sum of expenditures (price × quantity) for all goods cannot exceed income. To emphasize that the cost of consuming one good is the sacrifice of another, the budget constraint is plotted as a relation between quantities of goods: $q_2 = Y/p_2 - (p_1/p_2) \times q_1$.

2. There are four principles of consumer preference:
    a. Completeness: all consumption prospects can be ranked.
    b. Dominance: more is preferred to less.
    c. Transitivity: prospects with more of one good are preferred to prospects with less of that good and no more of any other good.
    d. Diminishing marginal rate of substitution): as consumption of one good increases relative to other goods, the consumer is less and less willing to give up other commodities to consume more of that commodity.

3. The idea of diminishing marginal utility was proposed in the 1870s as an explanation of the diamond-water paradox: why the exchange values of commodities deviated from their use values. After the search for measurable utility

was abandoned, the concept of diminishing marginal utility was replaced by the principle of diminishing marginal rate of substitution.

4. The marginal rate of substitution is the slope of an indifference curve, which shows equivalent consumption prospects according to consumer or household preferences. Indifference curves have negative slopes, cannot intersect, and are bowed-in toward the origin.

5. A consumer maximizes utility under a budget constraint by purchasing commodities in order of the marginal utility they generate per dollar spent.
    a. When the budget is exhausted, the ratio of the marginal utility to the price of each good will be identical for all goods purchased.
    b. The utility maximizing consumption prospect is identified by the tangency of the highest attainable indifference curve to the consumer's budget line.

6. Real income can increase (decrease) either because money income rises (falls), money prices being constant, or because the money prices of all goods fall (rise) by the same proportion, money income being constant: an in-

come change (other factors being constant) changes the consumer's ability to consume, without changing the opportunity cost of one commodity in terms of another.

a. Consumption of a normal good changes in the same direction as the change in real income, *ceteris paribus*.

b. Consumption of an inferior good changes in the opposite direction from the change in real income, *ceteris paribus*. This follows from the tendency of consumers to substitute higher quality goods for commodities they consider to be of lower quality as their standard of living rises.

7. A change in the price of one good, other prices and money income being constant, changes both the position and the slope of the budget line.

a. The substitution effect of a price change is always negative. For a given set of tastes, a consumer will substitute commodities whose relative prices have decreased for a commodity whose relative price has increased; consumption of a good and its price change in opposite directions (real income, tastes, and the prices of other goods being constant).

b. The income effect for a normal good reinforces the substitution effect. The loss of

real income due to a price increase will reduce the consumption of a good below the level given by the substitution effect; an increase in real income due to the fall in the price of a good will increase its consumption beyond the level determined by the substitution effect.

c. The income effect of an inferior good reduces the impact of the substitution effect. The fall in real income due to a price increase tends to increase the consumption of a good relative to its level after the substitution effect; the increase in real income due to a price decrease tends to reduce the consumption of an inferior good below its level after the substitution effect.

d. A Giffen good is a theoretical possibility whereby the income effect of a price change for an inferior good is stronger than the substitution effect. So far, there has been no reliable evidence of the occurrence of a Giffen good.

8. Consumer surplus refers to the extra value a consumer receives when able to purchase a commodity at a constant price. The price paid for each unit reflects the marginal utility of the last unit; that is, the total value of the commodity to the consumer exceeds the opportunity cost of the money spent.

GLOSSARY

Assumptions of consumer behavior The principles upon which the model of consumer choice is based. The three basic assumptions are:

a. **Completeness.** For any two consumption prospects, an individual either prefers one prospect to the other or is indifferent between them.

b. **Dominance.** More is preferred to less; rules out satiation and bads.

c. **Transitivity.** Consumption prospects are uniquely ordered: if prospect A is preferred to prospect B and prospect B is preferred to prospect C, then prospect A is also preferred to prospect C.

Bad Opposite of a good; a commodity with negative marginal utility.

Budget constraint The equation $Y = p_1q_1 + p_2q_2$, which gives combinations of commodities which are within the household's purchasing power. Solving the equation for one of the commodities $[q_2 = (Y/p_2) - (p_1/p_2)\,q_1]$ describes the budget line: the amount of one good consumed equals the maximum the household can afford (Y/p_2) minus the opportunity cost of the other commodity $[(p_1/p_2)\,q_1]$.

Ceteris paribus Latin phrase meaning "other things remaining equal."

Completeness See **Assumptions of consumer behavior**.

Consumer surplus The difference between the value of a consumer good (its total utility) and the value of the expenditure on that good (marginal utility of last dollar times number of dollars spent).

Diminishing marginal rate of substitution The principle of consumer behavior that the amount of one good that will be sacrificed to attain an extra unit of another good is directly related to the amount of the former being consumed and inversely related to the amount of the latter.

Diminishing marginal utility The assumption that as the rate of consumption for one commodity increases—tastes and the consumption of other commodities being held constant—the satisfaction from the last unit will get progressively smaller.

Dominance See **Assumptions of consumer behavior**.

Engel curve A diagram depicting the consumption of a commodity at alternative income levels, other factors (i.e., prices and tastes) being constant.

Giffen good A hypothetical case whereby an inferior good has such a strong income effect that the substitution effect of a price change causes consumption of the commodity to change in the same direction as the change in price.

Good Opposite of a bad; a commodity whose consumption generates positive marginal utility.

Income effect The change in consumption of a commodity resulting from the change in real income due to a money price change. An inferior good has an income effect which mitigates the substitution effect since real income falls when the price of a good rises. The income effect of a normal good reinforces the substitution effect.

Income-consumption path The locus of indifference curve–budget line tangencies for alternative income levels, prices and tastes remaining constant

Indifference curve A diagram of consumption prospects which provide the same level of utility. Points on higher indifference curves are preferred to points on lower indifference curves, but a consumer (household) does not care at which point on a given indifference curve consumption actually occurs. The principles of consumer preference imply that indifference curves are negatively sloped, nonintersecting, and bowed in toward the origin.

Inferior goods Commodities whose consumption tends to decrease as income increases (and vice versa), other factors being constant. Inferior goods reflect the tendency of consumers to substitute higher quality goods for commodities they consider to be of lower quality as income increases.

Labor theory of value The notion in classical economic theory that the relative scarcity of commodities could be measured by the labor required to produce them (and the machinery used up in that production). The labor theory of value was eventually replaced by the marginal utility explanation of the deviation between exchange values and use values.

Marginal rate of substitution (MRS) The slope of an indifference curve, measuring the maximum amount of one good a consumer would give up in order to consume one more unit of another good, in such a way that total utility remained constant. Observation of the marginal rate of substitution reveals the relative marginal utilities for two commodities, since $MRS = \Delta q_2/\Delta q_1 = -(MU_1/MU_2)$. The assumption of diminishing marginal utility gives rise to the bowed-in shape of indifference curves, known as the diminishing marginal rate of substitution.

Marginal utility The additional satisfaction gained from the last unit of a commodity consumed. The idea of diminishing marginal utility holds that as more of one commodity is consumed per unit of time, the consumption of other commodities and tastes being constant, additions to satisfaction become progressively smaller.

Normal goods Commodities whose consumption tends to increase as income increases (and vice versa), other factors being constant. The income effect of a price change for a normal good reinforces the substitution effect.

Opportunity cost The economic cost of one activity, measured by the sacrifice of the next-highest-valued use of resources or purchasing power.

Real income The ability to purchase goods and

services; purchasing power adjusted for price changes.

Substitution effect   The change in the combination of goods consumed due to a change in their relative prices, real income being held constant. If consumption is constrained to the same indifference curve, the consumer reacts to an increase in the relative price of a commodity by consuming less of it, substituting a commodity whose relative price has decreased.

Transitivity   See **Assumptions of consumer behavior**.

Utility   The abstract consequence of consumption.

SUGGESTED READINGS

Becker, Gary S. "Irrational Behavior and Economic Theory." In *The Economic Approach to Human Behavior*. Chicago: University of Chicago Press, 1975, pp. 153–168.

Galbraith, John Kenneth. *The Affluent Society*. New York: Houghton Mifflin, 1958, pp. 139–160.

Kauder, Emil. "The Retarded Acceptance of the Marginal Utility Theory." *Quarterly Journal of Economics* (November 1953), 564–575.

Marshall, Alfred. *Principles of Economics*. 9th ed. London: Macmillan, 1960, pp. 83–137.

Samuelson, Paul, A. *Economics*. 11th ed. New York: McGraw-Hill, 1980, pp. 405–425.

Smith, Adam. *An Inquiry into the Nature and Causes of the Wealth of Nations*. Chicago: University of Chicago Press, 1976, pp. 34–71.

Stigler, George J. "The Development of Utility Theory." *Journal of Political Economy* (August–October, 1950).

Von Hayek, F. A. "The Non Sequitur of the Dependence Effect." *Southern Economic Journal* (April 1961).

EXERCISES

Evaluate

Indicate whether each of the following statements is true (agrees with economic theory), false (is contradicted by economic theory), or uncertain (could be true or false, given additional information). Briefly explain your answer.

1. Since knowledge of the prices of any pair of commodities purchased by consumers indicates their marginal rate of substitution for those commodities, consumer preferences must be caused by relative prices.
2. All that is necessary for a consumer's indifference curve for two commodities to have a negative slope is that both commodities be goods (provide positive marginal utility) or that both commodities be bads (provide negative marginal utility).
3. The bowed-in shape of a consumer indifference curve is consistent with the saying "variety is the spice of life."
4. If a consumer purchased an equal quantity of apples and oranges, the marginal rate of substitution of those commodities must have been equal to −1.
5. All Giffen goods are (would be) inferior goods, but not all inferior goods are Giffen goods.
6. The consumer receives no surplus on the last unit of a good consumed if utility is maximized under a budget constraint.
7. A diminishing marginal rate of substitution is responsible for the conclusion "the substitution effect of a relative price change is always negative."
8. That consumers seem to maintain their spending habits during inflationary periods, even though prices are rising, invalidates the theory of consumer behavior.
9. If the marginal rate of substitution is −1, two commodities are perfect substitutes.
10. If a consumer refuses to purchase a commod-

ity, the marginal utility of the first dollar spent on that commodity would have provided less satisfaction than the marginal utility of the last dollar spent on commodities actually purchased.

Calculate

Determine the numerical value (or range) of the marginal rate of substitution for each pair of commodities mentioned in the following statements. Be careful about the sign of MRS, and indicate whether an equality or inequality is implied. For example: "I don't care whether I have one more orange or two more apples" implies $MRS_{a/o} = -2$ or $MRS_{o/a} = -0.5$; "I'll give you two apples for one orange" implies $MRS_{a/o} \leq -2$ (I may be willing to give up more than two apples).

11. A bird in the hand is worth two in the bush.
12. I like ice cream better than cake.
13. Anita went shopping and found a sale on hats and gloves. Hats were \$15 each, and gloves were \$10 a pair. She bought four hats and two pairs of gloves.
14. A horse! A horse! My kingdom for a horse!
15. I would give anything for a cigarette!
16. Five dollars for this piece of junk? You must be joking!
17. 'Tis better to have loved and lost than never to have loved at all.
18. *Q:* Your money or your life? *A:* Don't shoot!

Contemplate

The following questions, which are designed to test your reasoning ability, require you to think beyond the material in chapter two. Note that the

right answer may not always be obvious; many of these issues are still being debated by professional economists.

19. Is it accurate to say that the economic model of constrained utility maximization "explains" consumer tastes? What does it mean when one says that the economic analysis of consumer behavior really does not begin until after the maximization process has been described?

20. Which, if any, of our assumptions about consumer behavior are violated by these hypothetical events?
    a. An advertising blitz causes a consumer to try a placebo cold remedy.
    b. A guest at a party remarks, "Gee, I shouldn't have eaten that green stuff."
    c. People pay extra for sweaters with little reptiles embroidered on them.
    d. Coffee prices rise sharply and unexpectedly. People rush out to buy more coffee.
    e. Some people like to buy expensive goods in order to distinguish themselves from the common folk.
    f. Sellers sometimes sell more of a product after its price goes up.

21. Using the concept of consumer surplus, explain why sellers of illegal commodities, such as drugs, often oppose making these goods legal.

22. Using an indifference diagram for food and shelter, explain why welfare recipients would probably be better off, in their own estimation, if they got cash instead of the equivalent value of food stamps. Also show the consequences of allowing individuals to sell their food stamps.

APPENDIX TO CHAPTER 2

Microeconomic Foundations of Macroeconomic Policy: Measuring Inflation and Real Income

Inflation, which is the result of price level changes, is a topic usually reserved for courses in macroeconomic theory. This may explain why many students of economics confuse the impact of *relative price changes*—the subject matter of microeconomics—with the effect of *price level changes*. In this appendix we will apply the distinctions between income and substitution effects of price changes to illuminate why price indexes, which are designed to adjust nominal income for the changing purchasing power of money due to inflation or deflation, may give distorted measures of the actual impact of inflation.

The Index Number Problem

When the price level is changing through time, the change in a household's money income will not accurately reflect changes in the household's standard of living. Various types of price indexes or deflators are employed to translate changes in money income into estimated changes in real income. The index number problem is the inability to measure changes in both prices and quantities, because a price index requires that quantities remain the same and a quantity index requires that prices remain the same. As explained in chapter two, when relative prices change, consumers substitute relatively less expensive goods for those which become more expensive. We will now explore why a price index cannot make use of the price system.

If inflation occurred in a world of constant relative prices, there would be no index number problem. If all prices (including the prices of input services) changed by the same percentage, then the household's money income could be adjusted for inflation by dividing this year's income by this year's price level: one plus the annual rate of change in prices. If a household's money income increased by 10 percent, but all prices increased by 5 percent over last year's level, money income this year would represent slightly less than 105 percent of last year's purchasing power. Since this year's expenditure will be 110 percent of last year's expenditure in nominal terms, but $1.05 is required to buy what $1.00 would have bought last year, then this year's real income is 104.8 percent (110/105) of last year's real income. Note that in the absence of relative price changes, the same measure of real income is found, regardless of whether constant real income is measured by the income required to buy last year's consumer goods, or the income last year that would have been necessary to buy this year's consumer goods.

Relative prices are constantly changing in response to changes in consumer tastes, commodity availability, technological knowledge, and even the weather; that is what prices in a market system are designed to do. At the same time, increases in the money supply in excess of increases in output may be changing the purchasing power of the monetary unit—e.g., the dollar.[1] A price index is supposed to measure the size of average price changes for all commodities, but that average depends on which commodities are purchased.

Although energy prices more than doubled during the 1970s, the price of

---

[1] Suggesting that inflation occurs by "too much money chasing too few goods" does not imply a taste for monetarist theories over Keynesian theories; such money could have been created when firms took out investment loans at full employment.

pocket calculators fell by more than 50 percent. Did the two price changes cancel each other out? Obviously, the "typical" household spends a considerably greater proportion of its budget on energy than on pocket calculators. Determination of the average price level means that each commodity in the household's budget must be given a *weight* which reflects its relative importance. Since total expenditure on all goods must equal the household's income, it follows that quantity purchased is the logical choice for a quantity weight. However, the question remains: from which period—the base period or the current period—should the quantities of various goods be selected? Picking the base period quantities means prices are given their weights before the price change; picking current period quantities means weights are assigned after commodity substitution has occurred.

The Slutsky Approach to Real Income

In chapter two, constant real income was simulated by constraining a consumer's choices of commodities to the same indifference curve, so that any welfare changes resulting from price changes could be depicted (after the substitution effect) by changes in indifference curves. The advantage of the Hicks approach to the income and substitution effects of a price change is that the consumer's own preferences form the basis of real income.[2] The disadvantage is that indifference curves are introspective; that is, one can only determine changes in one's own well-being, and the economic incentives for revealing such changes to others are, at best, dubious, as a simple example can illustrate.

Suppose that last year Mrs. Smith, a New England senior citizen, bought q_{10} gallons of heating oil and q_{20} sweaters to keep warm (Figure 2A-1). This year, the combination of higher heating oil prices and a fixed income have reduced Mrs. Smith's consumption of both commodities. She therefore experiences a decline in utility from U_1 to U_0; an observer would only be able to determine that consumption had gone from point A (q_{10}, q_{20}) to point C (q_{11}, q_{21}).

Suppose that the government, sensitive to the plight and voting habits of senior citizens, institutes a program to neutralize the impact of higher energy prices on retired persons. A cash transfer of $(Y' - Y_0)$ would allow Mrs. Smith to consume at point B, where indifference curve U_1 is tangent to budget line $(Y'/p_{11}, Y'/p_{20})$, which reflects the higher relative price of heating oil. The precise location of point B can be determined only by Mrs. Smith, for she alone knows her marginal rate of substitution of sweaters for heating oil. It would be naive of the agency distributing the grants to depend upon those receiving cash to say when they have had enough. By the principle that more is preferred to less, Mrs. Smith—and almost everyone else in her circumstances—would prefer to understate the transfer necessary to restore lost welfare. This does not imply that

---

[2] As explained in chapter two, the Hicks approach is named for Sir John Hicks, a British Nobel laureate in economics and early pioneer of indifference curve analysis. Ironically, it was Hicks who rediscovered the work of Eugene Slutsky, whose formula for income and substitution effects is the basis of the Slutsky approach.

transfer recipients would be dishonest. However, as will be argued in several contexts (chapters three, eight, and fifteen), a program which has no other check on dishonesty or selfishness than the recipient's conscience creates an incentive system whereby antisocial behavior is rewarded and altruistic behavior may look foolish.

Is there no limit to government largess? The answer is contained in the Slutsky approach to real income measurement. In Figure 2A-1, the income compensated budget line $(Y''/p_{11}, Y''/p_{20})$ passes through point A but has a slope reflecting the higher relative price of heating oil; that is, $Y'' = p_{11}q_{10} + p_{20}q_{20}$. When she receives $(Y'' - Y_0)$, Mrs. Smith would have enough income to purchase the same bundle of commodities she purchased last year. Ruling out taste changes, Mrs. Smith would be no worse off after the price change than before, because she could be consuming the same combinations of goods. When money income is sufficient in the current period to purchase the combination of commodities consumed in the base period, the consumer is no worse off in this period than in the last period, *ceteris paribus*.

In addition, if the transfer equal to $(Y'' - Y_0)$ were made, Mrs. Smith's behavior would reveal an improvement in her economic well-being. (Unless, of course, purchasing patterns formed the basis of the transfer policy, whereby any consumption change implying an improvement of well-being causes a reduction in the transfer.) Like the Hicks approach, the Slutsky approach to real income measurement implies that a change in relative prices, real income held constant,

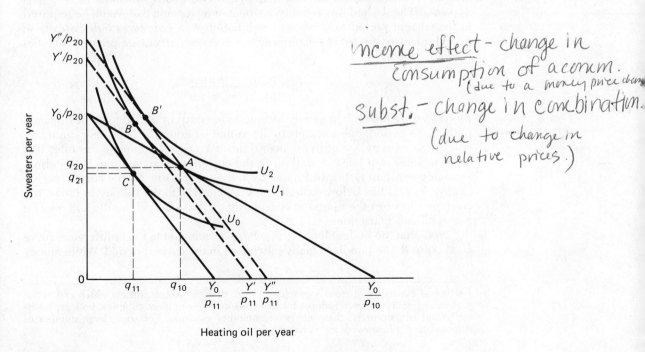

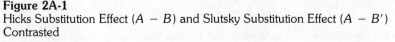

Figure 2A-1
Hicks Substitution Effect $(A - B)$ and Slutsky Substitution Effect $(A - B')$ Contrasted

will result in a substitution of commodities with lower relative prices for commodities whose relative prices have increased, *ceteris paribus*. Note that point B' is identified by the tangency of budget line $(Y''/p_{11}, Y''/p_{20})$ and indifference curve U_2. The Slutsky approach to holding real income constant, while having the advantage of being empirically observable, has the disadvantage that the substitution effect (here, from point A to point B') involves an increase of the consumer's satisfaction.

Base Period and Current Period Quantity Weights

The index number problem is an unavoidable consequence of the Slutsky approach to real income measurement. Because the income-compensated budget line of the Slutsky approach implies a utility increase for a relative price change, the Slutsky income effect overstates the income necessary to maintain constant real income when base period quantity weights are used. When current consumption provides the reference for the real income change, the Slutsky approach will understate the real income change due to inflation.

Figure 2A-2 depicts a consumer purchasing at point A in the base period, when prices are p_{10} and p_{20} and income is Y_0. Maintaining our assumption that income is exhausted on the consumption of two goods, we have $Y_0 = p_{10}q_{10} + p_{20}q_{20}$. The dashed line L indicates the money income that would be required in the current period to purchase combination A; a *Laspeyres index* uses base period quantity weights to determine the average percentage price change between periods:[3]

$$L = \frac{p_{11}q_{10} + p_{21}q_{20}}{p_{10}q_{10} + p_{20}q_{20}}$$

By comparing the ratio of money income in the current period to money income in the base period, one attempts to determine whether the consumer can maintain the same standard of living over time. If $Y_1/Y_0 > L$, then we can infer that the consumer is at least as well off in the current period as in the base period, assuming constant tastes. In Figure 2A-2, the budget line for the current period $(Y_1/p_{11}, Y_1/p_{21})$ lies below dashed line L. According to the Laspeyres index, the consumer has lost the option of consuming the base period bundle and *may* be worse off as a consequence.

Note that the budget line $(Y_1/p_{11}, Y_1/p_{21})$ is tangent to the indifference curve U_0 at point B, the bundle actually purchased in the current period. While money

---

[3] A typical consumer obviously purchases more than two commodities, which makes the problem of devising price indexes for real consumers even more complex, both arithmetically and conceptually, than our two-commodity example. For some large number of commodities, a Laspeyres index has the form:

$$L = \sum_{i=1}^{n} \frac{p_{i1}q_{i0}}{p_{i0}q_{i0}}$$

where 0 refers to base prices and quantities, and 1 refers to current period prices.

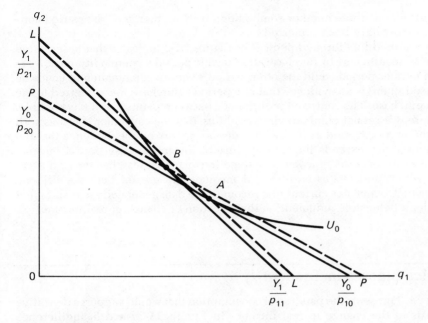

Figure 2A-2
Insufficient Data to Determine Change in Real Income

income has not increased enough to purchase point *A*, as indicated by the Laspeyres index, money income has increased just enough to maintain the same standard of income, according to the Hicks approach. By ignoring commodity substitution, with which consumers minimize the utility lost (or maximize the utility gained) due to a change in relative prices, the Slutsky approach biases the measure of real income. The use of base period quantity weights, as in Laspeyres indexes like the consumer price index (CPI) and the producer price index (PPI), usually overstates the change in real income necessary to maintain a constant real income during inflation.[4]

The Slutsky approach can never give an accurate rendering of the Hicks measure of real income, which is nonobservable. However, the use of inferences made on the basis of a Laspeyres index, which tends to understate real income in the current period, can be tempered by the use of a *Paasche index*, which is biased in the opposite direction. A Paasche price index is computed as the ratio of current expenditures to the expenditure that would have been required in the base period to purchase the current combination of commodities:

$$P = \frac{p_{11}q_{11} + p_{21}q_{21}}{p_{10}q_{11} + p_{20}q_{21}}$$

If the consumer could have purchased the current consumption bundle in the

---

[4] Measuring the extent of this bias requires simulating the marginal rate of substitution for a typical consumer. See S. D. Braithwait, "The Substitution Bias of the Laspeyres Price Index," *American Economic Review* (March 1980), 355–371.

base period, but chose another combination instead, then the base period combination must have been preferred.

The dashed line through point B in Figure 2A-2 indicates that base period income is insufficient to purchase the current period's commodity mix: $Y_1/Y_0 > P$. In neither period could the other period's chosen combination of goods be purchased; there is no evidence that one period's purchase was preferred to the other's purchase. The contrived indifference between points A and B is possible. Therefore, we cannot eliminate the possibility that the consumer is just as well off in the current period as in the base period, purely on the evidence that the Laspeyres index exceeds the ratio of current income to base period income. When the ratio of current income to base period income is less than the Laspeyres index (which understates current real income) and greater than the Paasche index (which overstates current real income), the data generated are insufficient to render a defensible judgment on the direction of change in real income.

Revealed Preference: Price Indexes in Tandem

Figure 2A-3 presents the patterns of consumption that would support a definitive diagnosis of the change in real income. In Figure 2A-3a and b, indifference curves have been suppressed to conform to the type of evidence available to objective observers of other people's consumption. In Figure 2A-3a—as in Figure 2A-2—point A, the base period consumption combination, lies outside the

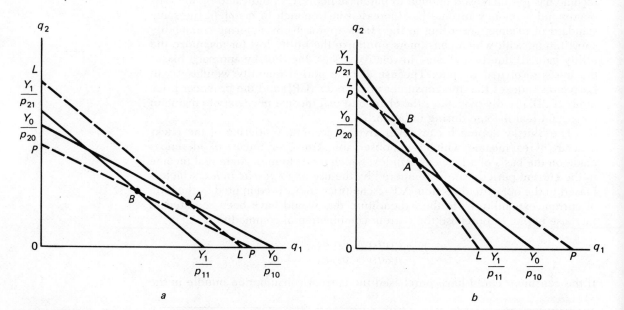

Figure 2A-3
Data Permit Inferences about Real Income Changes When Both Laspeyres and Paasche Price Indexes Agree: (a) $Y_1/Y_0 < L$ and $Y_1/Y_0 < P$ (real income has fallen); (b) $Y_1/Y_0 > L$ and $Y_1/Y_0 > P$ (real income has increased).

current period's budget line: $L > Y_1/Y_0$. The consumer could not have chosen point A in the current period, even if it had been preferred; the choice of point B in the current period does *not* imply that point B is preferred to point A. The current period's bundle was within the budget constraint in the base period: $Y_0 > p_{10}q_{11} + p_{20}q_{21}$. Since point A was picked instead of point B, the consumer revealed a preference for point A in the base period. When the ratio of current income to base period income is *less* than both the Laspeyres *and* the Paasche indexes, real income in the present is *less* than real income was in the base period, *tastes constant*.

Figure 2A-3*b* shows the opposite pattern. In the current period, the consumer can afford point A, but point B is chosen instead. The availability of bundle A in the current period implies $Y_1 > p_{11}q_{10} + p_{21}q_{20}$. Dividing both sides of the inequality by the equation $Y_0 = p_{10}q_{10} + p_{20}q_{20}$ yields:

$$\frac{Y_1}{Y_0} > \frac{p_{11}q_{10} + p_{21}q_{20}}{p_{10}q_{10} + p_{20}q_{20}} > L$$

The ratio of current income to base period income exceeds the Laspeyres index; that is, the chosen combination of goods in the present is the preferred combination of goods. This result is reinforced by the consumer's inability to consume combination B in the base year: $p_{10}q_{11} + p_{20}q_{21} > Y_0$. Dividing both sides of this inequality of $p_{11}q_{11} + p_{21}q_{21} = Y_1$, we have:

$$\frac{p_{10}q_{11} + p_{20}q_{21}}{p_{11}q_{11} + p_{21}q_{21}} > \frac{Y_0}{Y_1}$$

Inverting the two ratios changes the direction of the inequality, revealing $Y_1/Y_0 > P$. When the ratio of current income to base period income is *greater* than both the Laspeyres index *and* the Paasche index, real income is *higher* in the current period than in the base period, *tastes constant*.

We have established that when the ratio of income in the current period to income in the base period exceeds *both* the price index using base quantity weights and the price index using current quantity weights, real income has increased. We have also established that when the ratio of income in the present to income in the base period is smaller than *both* types of price indexes, then real income has decreased. Since constant tastes imply a substitution of commodities with lower relative prices for commodities with higher relative prices, a Laspeyres index will usually exceed a Paasche index, because the former index uses quantity weights before output substitution and the latter uses quantity weights after. It is therefore possible that the ratio of present to base period income could fall between the Laspeyres and the Paasche price index for a typical household. Remember, when $L > Y_1/Y_0 > P$, insufficient evidence exists to determine whether real income has increased, decreased, or remained the same.

One final conceivable pattern for the change in income and the relative size of the two price indexes remains, namely, $P > Y_1/Y_0 > L$. Although this pattern is unlikely (for reasons which will be elaborated), the implications of the Paasche index exceeding the Laspeyres index, with the ratio of incomes falling in between, can be derived from Figure 2A-4. According to this pattern, point A was picked in the base period although point B was available. Thus, the consumer

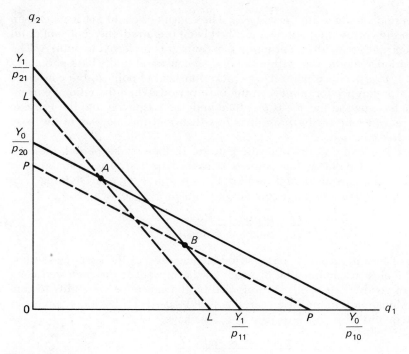

Figure 2A-4
Changing Tastes Lead to Contradictory Diagnosis When $P > Y_1/Y_0 > L$.

revealed a preference for point A to point B during the base period. This implies that $p_{10}q_{10} + p_{20}q_{20} > p_{10}q_{11} + p_{20}q_{21}$; hence,

$$\frac{p_{10}q_{10} + p_{20}q_{20}}{p_{11}q_{11} + p_{21}q_{21}} > \frac{p_{10}q_{11} + p_{20}q_{21}}{p_{11}q_{11} + p_{21}q_{21}}$$

That is, $Y_0/Y_1 > 1/P$, or $P > Y_1/Y_0$. As we have seen, when the Paasche index exceeds the ratio of current income to past (base period) income, the consumer had a choice of both combinations of goods in the base period; the choice of the base period bundle indicated a preference for that combination over the combination consumed in the present.

Figure 2A-4 also indicates that the choice in the present is the preferred alternative. Point A, which lies on budget line $(Y_0/p_{20}, Y_0/p_{10})$, lies *below* the budget constraint for the current period. Thus, the base period bundle could be purchased at prevailing prices: $p_{11}q_{11} + p_{21}q_{21} > p_{11}q_{10} + p_{21}q_{20}$. Dividing through by $(Y_0 = p_{10}q_{10} + p_{20}q_{20})$,

$$\frac{p_{11}q_{11} + p_{21}q_{21}}{p_{10}q_{10} + p_{20}q_{20}} > \frac{p_{11}q_{10} + p_{21}q_{20}}{p_{10}q_{10} + p_{20}q_{20}}$$

That is, $Y_1/Y_0 > L$. When the ratio of present income to base period income exceeds the Laspeyres index, the consumer's income has kept up with the cost of the base period bundle; then, the current period combination is preferred to the commodity mix of the base period.

Figure 2A-4 indicates that point A is the preferred combination in the base period and point B is the preferred combination in the current period. However, point B would not have exhausted income in the base period, and point A would not have exhausted income in the current period. The only explanation is that tastes have changed in the opposite direction to the change in relative prices. Although point A was preferred over point B in the base period, the consumer would have been better off, in his or her own estimation, had the income and relative prices of the current period prevailed. Similarly, although point B is chosen over point A in the present, the consumer would be better off, *given current tastes*, if the income and relative prices of the base period prevailed in the present.

The concept of revealed preference, which forms the theoretical basis of the use of price indexes in diagnosing changes in real income, is based upon the assumption of constant tastes. Evidence that tastes have changed thus invalidates any inferences otherwise drawn from comparing the percentage change in money income and the percentage change in either (or, ideally, both) of the two price indexes.

Table 2A-1 summarizes the possible patterns of income ratios and price indexes which one might observe for a particular household. As we have shown, whenever *both* the Paasche index and the Laspeyres index yield the same diagnosis, one can be reasonably confident about the change in real income. If income has increased by a greater percentage than either price index, evidence indicates that the consumption choice of the present period is the preferred combination, and no evidence exists of taste changes. The household is apparently better off, in its own estimation, during the present period. If the percentage change in income falls short of both price indexes, then the base period bundle was the preferred bundle when it was chosen, but the unavailability of the base bundle in the present means the household settles for less. Real income has apparently fallen.

When the Laspeyres index, which usually understates real income in the present, exceeds the ratio of the two incomes, the diagnosis of declining real

TABLE 2A-1
Appropriate Inferences from Price Index Patterns

Result	Diagnosis
$\dfrac{Y_1}{Y_0} > L,P$	By either price index, money income has increased more than the cost of living; real income is higher in the present.
$L,P > \dfrac{Y_1}{Y_0}$	By either price index, money income has not kept pace with the cost of living; real income is lower in the current period.
$L > \dfrac{Y_1}{Y_0} > P$	The change in income falls within the predictable biases of the two indexes; data are insufficient to determine the direction of change in real income.
$P > \dfrac{Y_1}{Y_0} > L$	The change in consumption is in the opposite direction to the expected substitution of relatively less expensive commodities for more expensive ones. Evidence of taste changes invalidates any diagnosis about real income change.

income can be erroneous. This prognosis is even more likely when reinforced by a contradictory indication from the Paasche index, which tends to understate base period real income. Hence, if $L > Y_1/Y_0 > P$, insufficient evidence exists to support any diagnosis about the change in real income.

Finally, no inference can be supported if the Laspeyres index exceeds the ratio of current income to base year income. First, each index implies a real income change which contradicts the implication of the other index. The Laspeyres index indicates that real income is higher in the present; the Paasche index implies higher real income in the base period. Second, taken together, the relative size of the Paasche and Laspeyres indexes indicate a change in tastes, since commodity substitution occurred in the opposite direction to the change in relative prices.

Consumer Price Index

Few households have either the data or the inclination for calculating their own price indexes. Most of us rely on price indexes published by the government. Probably the best known of these is the consumer price index (CPI), reported monthly by the Bureau of Labor Statistics. The consumer price index is based on the prices of food, clothing, shelter, fuel, drugs, transportation fares, doctor's and dentist's fees, and other goods and services a "typical" household buys. Through 1982, the consumer price index was based on 1967 quantity weights, with price and rent data collected from 18,000 tenants, 24,000 retail establishments, and 18,000 housing units in eighty-five urban areas across the United States.

Originally designed to measure the cost of living for urban wage earners and clerical workers, the Bureau of Labor Statistics began calculating a second, broader based index in 1978 for all urban consumers. In addition to wage earners and clerical workers, this index was extended to cover professional, managerial, and technical workers, in addition to short-term workers, the self-employed, the unemployed, and others not in the labor force. There is an obvious trade-off between the scope of the consumer price index and how closely its quantity weights will approximate the base year consumption habits of an actual household. The traditional price index for wage earners and clerical workers now covers only about 40 percent of the labor force, but that group tends to be more homogeneous than the group from which data for the all-urban consumer price index are collected, namely, 80 percent of all households. In addition to the distortions of using base year quantity weights, the consumer price index has the extra disadvantage of using quantity weights which may be more or less arbitrary for actual households. As every statistician knows, the most typical thing about an American household is that it is likely to be atypical.

We have already established that the use of base year quantity weights tends to overstate the amount of money income necessary for a household to sustain a constant real income. In attempting to hold the price level constant, statisticians are forced to ignore the operation of the price system. Few households were consuming as many gallons of gasoline per dollar of (real) income in 1982 as they did in 1967, but most households had more electronic gadgets than they did a decade and a half ago. By giving too much weight to gasoline and too little weight to electronic devices, the typical household appears to have less real income than it *probably* has (we say "probably" because taste changes in the opposite direction to the change in relative prices would confound any inferences). This inflationary bias of the CPI has led to a number of fundamental misconceptions about the causes and cures of inflation.

First, the use of fixed, base year quantity weights tends to give the erroneous impression that inflation is caused by changes in the relative prices of particular commodities. We are all familiar with the monthly ritual whereby television and newspaper commentators break down the overall rate of change in the consumer price index to determine how much inflation was due to changes in gasoline prices, how much was due to changes in food prices, how much was due to changes in housing costs, and so on.

Attributing inflation to individual components of the household budget leads to a second misconception: the belief that if the price index can be kept from changing, inflation will be cured—or at least people will think that inflation is cured, which might be just as good. If traders write inflationary expectations into contracts, then inflation will be that much harder to cure, since a reduction in the money supply (or aggregate demand) would cause default on contracts whose nominal terms suddenly become real terms. Rather than experience massive economic disruption, the government continues to foster inflation. Hence, if we get inflation out of contracts, it will melt away.

Wage-price controls, like those imposed by President Nixon in August 1971 at the urging of Congress, are intended to stop upward price movements by freezing prices in their tracks. Freezing prices to make inflation go away is like freezing a thermostat to make a room cooler. There are two problems in using wage-price controls to fight inflation. First, they do not work when relative prices are changing. If prices are frozen or legally controlled, the price system cannot encourage commodity substitution when shortages occur. This leads to short-term nonprice rationing (e.g., the gasoline rationing of the early 1970s) and selective permits that allow some sellers to raise their prices. Being able to raise prices when all others have their prices frozen implies a real price increase; suddenly sellers, especially sellers of products with inelastic demand (see chapter four), have an incentive to create artificial shortages. On the other hand, sellers facing temporary surpluses will be reluctant to reduce their prices, lest those price cuts become frozen. But as more and more exceptions are granted, the public will perceive a failure of price controls, and inflationary expectations will strengthen, rather than weaken. Second, even if relative prices were not changing, wage-price controls would not work because they would do nothing about the underlying causes of inflation: excess monetary growth or excess aggregate demand.

The third distortion created by widespread reliance on the consumer price index as a measure of the cost of living involves the indexing of welfare payments, pensions, and wage rates. If the measured rate of inflation (according to the rate of change in the consumer price index) is 11 percent, but the "real" rate of inflation is only 7.5 percent (although there is no means of measuring the "real" rate of inflation[5]), then social security recipients and government pensioners who receive an 11 percent cost-of-living adjustment actually receive a 3.5 percent real income increase after substituting commodities. But if the economy is not growing by 3.5 percent or more in real terms, higher real income for retired people means lower real income for others. Either the government must raise taxes, borrow funds from the private sector (crowding out private investment and driving up interest rates), or print money to cover the resulting deficit. If the last method is chosen, the ironic result is that the use of an inflation-biased index to adjust transfers may end up creating inflation.

The Implicit Price Deflator

We have seen that one way to avoid the pitfalls of a Laspeyres price index is to double-check results with the use of a comparable Paasche index. However, the construction of a reliable Paasche index for consumer prices is considerably more difficult than the construction of a Laspeyres index. Constructing a Paasche index requires considerably more data than that required for a comparable Laspeyres index. Once the base year weights are constructed, calculating the most recent month's consumer price index is a relatively simple process of collecting new price data and using the fixed quantity weights. But a Paasche index uses new quantity weights each year; as a result, all prices must be kept on record for the base year, so that the revised weights can recompute the base year cost of this year's consumption bundle.

Another problem with the Paasche index is one of interpretation. Since quantity weights change from year to year, the only valid comparison is between the current year's prices and the base year's prices. If the base year is 1972, then the Paasche price index for that year will be 100.0; a price index of 105.5 for 1973 indicates that the combination of commodities chosen for a representative consumer in 1973 cost 5.5 percent more than that combination would have cost in 1972. An index of 116.9 for 1974 shows that the combination of commodities for a representative consumer in 1974 cost 16.9 percent more than it would have cost in 1972. However, it cannot be logically inferred that a 10.8 percent rate of inflation occurred between 1973 and 1974, even though $(116.9/105.5) \times 100 = 1.108$, because the 1974 index is based on different quantity weights than the 1973 index. However, some economists believe that comparing Paasche price indexes for nonbase years is a more accurate measure of the change in real income than a comparable Laspeyres indexes for those two years, since changes in quantity weights of the former can be taken as the price substitution effect of relative price changes.

One Paasche index has been receiving more attention from government and academic economists as a tempering influence on the distorted inferences re-

---

[5] One suggested method of measuring the "real" rate of inflation is to compare the nominal prime rate of interest with the "real prime (or riskless) rate," calling the difference the rate of inflation. Of course, one reason price indexes are used is to adjust the nominal rate to determine what the prime rate is.

sulting from sole reliance on the consumer price index as the measure of inflation. When the U.S. Department of Commerce collects statistics for the gross national product (GNP), it calculates the *GNP implicit price deflator*, which is used to translate nominal GNP into real GNP. The GNP implicit price deflator is based on the actual output of a calendar year; the problem of defining a "typical" consumer is avoided, since quantity weights are based upon observed production. Furthermore, using current period weights gives a measure of price changes which is biased in the opposite direction to the consumer price index.

Table 2A-2 compares the annual consumer price index and the GNP implicit price deflators for the period 1960 through 1979. Although the base year for the consumer price index is 1967, the series can be translated into a 1972 base by merely dividing each year's consumer price index by 1.253, the ratio of the consumer price index in 1972 to the consumer price index in 1967. The implicit price deflator cannot be directly translated into another base year because of the changing quantity weights from year to year. In addition, the implicit price deflator for all goods and services includes commodities not consumed by the typical household. Therefore, the implicit price deflator for the consumer goods sector of the gross national product accounts is actually a more appropriate Paasche index to contrast with the consumer price index.

TABLE 2A-2
Comparison of Consumer Price (Laspeyres) Index and GNP Implicit (Paasche) Price Deflator

Year	Consumer Price Index		Implicit Price Deflator		$\dfrac{\text{CPI}}{\text{IPD}} \times 100$
	1967 Base	*1972 Base*	*Total GNP*	*Consumer Goods*	
1960	88.7	70.8	68.7	71.7	98.7
1961	89.6	71.5	69.3	72.5	98.6
1962	90.6	72.3	70.6	73.6	98.2
1963	91.7	73.2	71.6	74.7	98.0
1964	92.9	74.1	72.7	75.7	97.9
1965	94.5	75.4	74.3	77.1	97.8
1966	97.2	77.6	76.8	79.3	97.9
1967	100.0	79.8	79.0	81.3	98.2
1968	104.2	83.2	82.6	84.6	98.3
1969	109.8	87.4	86.7	88.5	98.8
1970	116.3	92.8	91.5	92.5	100.3
1971	121.3	96.8	96.0	96.6	100.2
1972	125.3	100.0	100.0	100.0	100.0
1973	133.1	106.2	105.8	105.5	100.7
1974	147.7	117.9	116.6	116.9	100.9
1975	161.2	128.7	127.2	126.5	101.7
1976	170.5	136.1	133.9	131.6	103.4
1977	181.5	144.9	139.8	139.5	103.9
1978	195.4	155.9	152.1	149.1	104.6
1979	214.1	173.7	162.8	162.3	107.0

Source: *Statistical Abstract of the United States, 1981.* Washington, D.C.: U.S. Government Printing Office, 1981

For the years prior to 1967, the consumer price index is actually a Paasche index, since the base year (1967) occurs after the year in question. By similar logic, the implicit price deflator is actually a Laspeyres index prior to 1972, since the "current" year, whose output is the basis of quantity weights, occurred before the base year (1972). Although the base year for the consumer price index is transformed to 1972, the ratio of the transformed consumer price index to the implicit price deflator is less than 100 for the years 1960 to 1966—a predictable consequence of taking the ratio of a Paasche index to a Laspeyres index. Between 1967 and 1972, both indexes are Laspeyres indexes, and so there is no predictable pattern for the ratio of consumer price index to implicit price deflator, except that their ratio must equal 100 in 1972.

The real meaning of Table 2A-2 is reflected in the relative size of the consumer price index and the implicit price deflator (for consumer goods) from 1973 to 1979. Since the last column measures the ratio of a Laspeyres index to a Paasche index, the ratio is consistently greater than 100 percent and the disparity becomes progressively greater.[6] By 1979 there is a 7 percent discrepancy in the two measures of inflation. The consumer price index implies that household income in 1979 must have been 73.7 percent greater in 1979 if nominal income were to have kept pace with inflation. According to the implicit price deflator, the commodities consumed in 1979 required an expenditure of 162.3 percent of their cost in 1972. As indicated previously, we could confidently conclude that real income had increased between 1972 and 1979 only if nominal income had increased by 73.9 percent or more over that period. We would be justified in concluding that real income had fallen only if nominal income increased by 62.3 percent or less. If tastes had changed—not implausible when the average age of a household increased by seven years—any inferences about real income changes would be even more suspect.

Conclusion

By now, it should be apparent that the overestimation of inflation which results from the reliance on and misinterpretation of the consumer price index is the consequence neither of an evil conspiracy nor of inexcusable incompetence. Too many phenomena—the price level, relative prices, money income, and relative quantities—are changing simultaneously for a single number to measure any of these things accurately.

As a practical matter, the use of past quantity weights requires much less data and allows one's measure of the cost of living to be anchored by the same combination of commodities from year to year. The consumer price index also has the advantage of allowing year-to-year comparisons of the rate of change in prices, whereas the implicit price deflator and other Paasche indexes allow comparisons only between the base year and the current year. Year-to-year com-

---

[6] A simple trend analysis indicated that the ratio could be predicted by (CPI/IPD) × 100 = $(99.2)e^{0.0098t}$, where t is time and $t = 1$ in 1973 and $t = 7$ in 1979; this equation appears to "explain" 94 percent of the variation in that ratio.

parisons are arithmetically suspect. However, year-to-year comparisons of the implicit price deflator may be preferable on theoretical grounds.

Nevertheless, there is a political reason for preferring to use a Paasche index to measure inflation rather than a Laspeyres index. Compared to the political incentives for fighting recessions (e.g., cutting taxes or raising spending for Keynesians, increasing the rate of growth of the money supply for applied monetarists), fighting inflation is not politically popular.[7] If administrations and governments are politically vulnerable when they cut popular spending programs, raise taxes, or foster tight monetary policy, one would think politicians would favor a measure which understated the rate of inflation rather than overestimated it, given the absence of a statistically reliable measure. If one has to be biased, why not be biased in one's own favor? If one is likely to be run from office for creating recessions as a side effect of fighting inflation, one should not create larger recessions than necessary.

During the closing months of the 1980 presidential campaign, inflation, as measured by the consumer price index, was running at an annual rate of 18 percent. Yet the prime interest rate hovered around 15 to 17 percent. Unless one believes that the banks did not anticipate inflation in 1980, it should be obvious that the real rate of interest of -3 to -1 percent was downwardly biased. If the actual rate of inflation was, say, 12 percent (implying a real prime rate of 3 to 5 percent), then fully one-third of the measured inflation problem was a statistical illusion. Had the Carter administration announced that the official measure of inflation had been changed to the implicit price deflator, the official rate of inflation could have been cut by 50 percent, from 18 to 9 percent, with the stroke of a pen. If a guess of 12 percent inflation were correct, changing the official measure of inflation to the implicit price deflator would have replaced a measure which overestimated inflation by $33\frac{1}{3}$ percent with one that underestimated inflation by 25 percent. Instead, the administration followed a more modest course. In October 1980 the Bureau of Labor Statistics took end-of-the-model-year price cuts for automobiles into account when calculating that month's consumer price index. This reduced the reported rate of inflation by 1 percent. The press howled.

In December 1980, Professor Murray Weidenbaum, then the designated chairman of the Council of Economic Advisors for the incoming administration, gave a speech which the author attended. During the question session, the author asked the speaker if the Reagan administration would consider using the implicit price deflator as the measure of inflation, thereby relieving the pressure to follow excessively contractionary policies.

Weidenbaum replied that the public would never stand for it. Until a significant proportion of the press and public understood the index number problem, dropping the consumer price index in favor of the implicit price deflator would be politically suicidal.

---

[7] The possible exception, of course, is the "supply-side" argument that inflation can be attacked from both sides at once by cutting tax rates: once by increasing output and also by increasing tax collections from the extra economic activity (see chapter three). Experiences by Margaret Thatcher's government in Great Britain and Ronald Reagan's administration through 1982 seemed to indicate that the incentives offered to politicians by "supply-side" anti-inflation policies may not be matched by economic performance.

To paraphrase Abraham Lincoln, one can fool some of the people some of the time, but that tends to make all of the people suspicious all of the time. Unlike many of the controversies surrounding macroeconomic policy, the appropriate way to report inflation should not in itself be controversial. That it is controversial indicates an education priority so important that it is worth putting macroeconomic theory appendices into microeconomic theory texts.

Chapter 3

Applications and Extensions of Economics of Choice

In developing the model of consumer choice in chapter two, we made the following simplifying assumptions:

1. Consumer options are limited to two commodities.
2. Households neither save nor borrow.
3. Consumers are never sated.
4. Money income is fixed.
5. All prices and consumption outcomes are known in advance.

With an understanding of the process of constrained utility maximization, some of those assumptions can now be relaxed. If you are still having difficulty with the material in chapter two, please reread it. Much of the material in microeconomics is cumulative; the efficient approach to learning economics is to seek assistance as soon as you realize you are having difficulty. Otherwise, you will be missing a solid foundation in the techniques of analysis.

The topics of this chapter include the allocation of time between work and leisure activities, the consumption decision when saving and borrowing are possible, and the influence of risk on decisions. As we explore these topics, you will obtain additional practice in using the techniques and ideas of chapter two. You will also see that the theory of consumer choice is robust; many of the assumptions used to simplify the analysis can be safely relaxed. In addition, you will discover the broad range of issues which can be better understood with economic insights.

The Choice between Income and Leisure

Up until now, we have assumed that household income is fixed and beyond the control of members of the household. We now allow income to change according to how time is allocated between work (i.e., income-generating activities) and leisure (i.e., utility-producing activities). We will also assume that work is not pursued for its own sake, but rather to generate income to purchase commodities.[1] The consumer derives satisfaction from real income, y, and leisure time, t_L. Real income is the sum of nonlabor earnings (e.g., rents, dividends, transfer payments) and wage income. Since wage income is the product of the wage rate, w, and the number of hours worked, we have

$$y = y_0 + wt_h = y_0 + w(\bar{t} - t_L)$$

where y_0 is nonlabor income, t_h is the amount of time worked, and $\bar{t}$ is the total time available.

The consumer-worker's budget line for income and leisure has been reproduced in Figure 3-1. Each individual has a fixed amount of time, $\bar{t}$, which must be allocated between work and leisure. Maximum possible income, $y_0 + w\bar{t}$, is the intercept of the budget line for income and leisure on the vertical (income) axis. The opportunity cost of leisure is the wage rate; for each additional hour of leisure consumed, the individual sacrifices 1 hour's worth of money income: $\Delta y/\Delta t_L = -w$.

The budget constraint for the income-leisure choice in Figure 3-1 differs in two fundamental ways from the figures encountered in chapter two. First, the intercept on the leisure (horizontal) axis is anchored at $\bar{t}$. The number of hours per day (or week) cannot be changed. Second, since most households have some source of nonlabor income, the budget line becomes vertical at leisure time $\underline{t}$; if all time were devoted to leisure, the consumer would still have y_0 income.

The expression "all work and no play makes Jack a dull boy" implies

---

[1] Gary S. Becker distinguishes between market production, which generates money income to purchase inputs for consumption, and household production, which transforms those raw materials into utility (see *The Economic Approach to Human Behavior* [Chicago: University of Chicago Press, 1975], pp. 89–115). The possibility that work activities may produce utility directly will be considered in chapter thirteen.

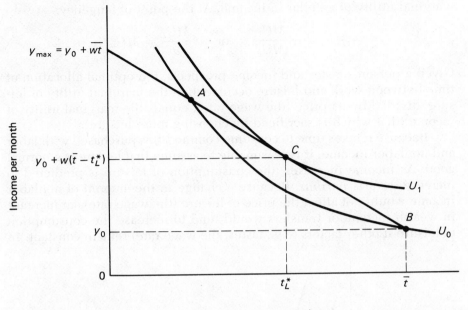

Figure 3-1
Utility Maximum for Allocation of Time between Income-Generating Activities and Leisure Activities

a diminishing marginal rate of substitution of income for leisure. The longer one works, the higher one's money income, but the less one's time for consumption. A typical worker requires greater and greater amounts of money to compensate for subsequent reductions in leisure, *ceteris paribus*. A typical indifference curve for income and leisure has a negative slope, since both income and leisure provide positive marginal utility, and it will be bowed in toward the origin due to a diminishing marginal rate of substitution.

According to the preferences simulated in Figure 3-1, the person would be indifferent between point A (large income and little leisure) and point B (only nonlabor income since all time is devoted to leisure). Since indifference curve U_0 lies below the budget line between points A and B, satisfaction improves by substituting leisure for income (from point A to C) or by substituting income for leisure (from point B to C) until, at point C, indifference curve U_1 is tangent to the budget line.

The marginal rate of substitution of income for leisure is:

$$MRS = \frac{\Delta y}{\Delta t_L} = -\frac{MU_L}{MU_y}$$

where MU_L is the marginal utility of an hour of leisure and MU_y is the marginal utility of a dollar in income. At the point of tangency:

$$-w = -\frac{MU_L}{MU_y} \quad \text{or} \quad \frac{MU_L}{w} = MU_y$$

Given a person's tastes and income prospects, the optimal allocation of time between work and leisure occurs when the marginal utility of leisure, divided by its price (the wage rate), equals the marginal utility of income (that which is sacrificed by choosing more leisure).

Because it takes time to consume commodities purchased with labor and nonlabor income, it is reasonable to assume that leisure is a normal good. As income increases, the consumption of leisure is predicted to increase, *ceteris paribus*. Because a change in the amount of nonlabor income would not affect the price of leisure (the wage rate), an increase in wealth income or transfers would tend to increase the consumption of leisure if other factors (e.g., tastes, the wage rate) remain constant. In

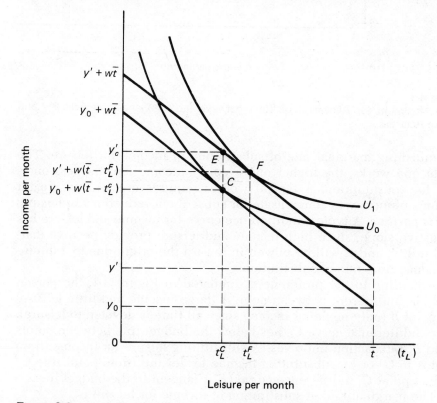

Figure 3-2
Effect of Increase in Nonlabor Income on the Allocation of Time to Work and Leisure. An increase in nonlabor income from y_0 to y' enhances the marginal utility of leisure, encouraging reduced work effort to enjoy more leisure (leisure as a normal good).

Figure 3-2, an increase in nonlabor income from y_0 to y' causes an upward, parallel shift in the budget line. If the household continued to allocate t_L^C hours to leisure, income would be $y_C' > y_0 + w(\bar{t} - t_L^C)$; however, utility would increase if part of these higher earnings were spent on leisure. At the new tangency point F, both income (the consumption of goods) and leisure (time spent consuming) would have increased relative to the previous optimum point C.

APPLICATION
The Economics of Education: The Cost of Time

Figures 3-1 and 3-2 suggest that the opportunity cost of time allocated to education would be the same whether a student reduced working time or sacrificed leisure activities. This may seem paradoxical. Recall the principle of transitivity from chapter two. If Barbara is indifferent between an hour of leisure and an hour's worth of income, then the value of her last hour of leisure is proportional to her wage rate. When Barbara sacrifices labor income to attend college, the cost of time spent in class and time spent studying is the sacrifice of wage income for that time. If Barbara decides to schedule all her classes on weekday mornings so she can work during afternoons, evenings, and weekends, her time spent in class would also be valued at her wage rate. But how can this be? Barbara is already working afternoons, evenings, and weekends; she would not also work mornings if she were not attending school. Precisely. The opportunity cost of time spent in class and studying is the value of leisure time that must be sacrificed. What is the value of leisure? The opportunity cost of an hour of leisure is the marginal utility of goods which could have been purchased with an hour's earnings.

Consider how the income-leisure choice can clarify another apparent anomaly. As we will see throughout this chapter (and in chapter thirteen), a major motive for pursuing a higher education is the prospect of enhanced earning ability. Since there are also nonpecuniary motives for attending school (e.g., friendship, parental approval, love of learning), we expect (and evidence indicates) that education is a normal good. Yet during recessions and periods of high unemployment, a greater proportion of recent high school graduates and older adults enroll in college than during periods of low unemployment, *ceteris paribus*. Although income is usually lower—thus encouraging a student to substitute lower-cost state colleges for high-tuition private universities—the opportunity cost of time is considerably lower when a student has no attractive employment opportunities. Although short-term job prospects for college graduates may not be good, the prospects for those with less than a college education are probably bleaker. Hence, while people are unavoidably unemployed, their wage is effectively zero, thus encouraging them to allocate their time to education and other time-intensive activities.

APPLICATION

Work Incentives and Overtime Pay

Unlike the predictable influence of a change in nonlabor income on leisure time, the impact of a wage rate change on the allocation of time between work and leisure is ambiguous. The wage rate is both the price of leisure and a major determinant of total income. The income and substitution effects of a wage change operate in opposite directions. This opposition of income and substitution effects may seem confusing. In chapter two we saw that real income changed in the opposite direction to a change in the price of a good a household was consuming, *ceteris paribus*. But an increase in the price of leisure (i.e., the wage rate) increases real income, *ceteris paribus*. Since the substitution effect is always in the opposite direction to a price change, the income effect, when positive, works against the substitution effect. The decline in real income caused by a nominal price increase in an inferior good leads to a counteracting income effect. Since an increase in the price of leisure (which equals an increase in the wage rate) increases real income, the income effect is positive if leisure is a normal good.[2]

An increase in the wage rate, w, increases the opportunity cost of leisure, so that the substitution effect tends to reduce the amount of time spent in leisure. In Figure 3-3, we imagine that Ed Collins experiences a coincidental wage rate increase, from w_0 to w_1, and reduction in nonlabor income, from y_0 to y_1. Notice that total income would remain at y_A if Ed continued to allot t_L^A to leisure activities. Since (by grace of poetic license) the steeper (dashed) budget line intersects indifference curve U_0 at point A, utility could be increased by substituting income for leisure. By reducing leisure to t_L^B, Ed raises satisfaction to U_1 at point B, where the income-compensated budget line, $y = y_1 + w_1(t - t_L)$, is tangent to that indifference curve.

Figure 3-3 shows the **Slutsky approach** to holding real income constant (discussed in detail in the appendix to chapter two). Instead of constraining choice to the original indifference curve, U_0, as in the **Hicks approach**, the Slutsky approach defines constant real income as the ability to consume the same combination of goods before and after a price change. Both Figures 3-3a and b are drawn in such a way that constant real income allows Ed Collins to achieve a higher rate of utility by

Hicks – constrains to same U curve.

---

[2] Using calculus, the chain rule gives the income effect of a change in the price of an inferior good as the product of two negative partial derivatives: $(\partial q_i/\partial y)(\partial y/\partial p_i) > 0$ when $\partial q_i/\partial y < 0$ and $\partial y/\partial p_i < 0$. The income effect of a wage change is the product of two positive partial derivatives: $(\partial t_L/\partial y)(\partial y/\partial w) > 0$ when $\partial t_L/\partial y > 0$ and $\partial y/\partial w > 0$.

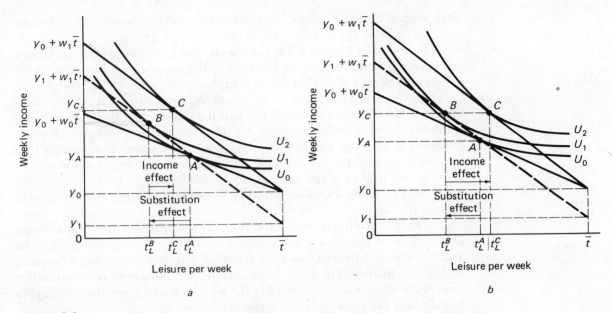

Figure 3-3
Income and Substitution Effects of Wage Increase on Leisure and Income. *a*, Substitution effect dominant; *b*, income effect dominant.

substituting income for leisure. The substitution effect is identified by the movement of the (imagined) utility maximum from point A to point B. The income effect is shown by restoring nonlabor income to y_0, thus allowing Ed to achieve indifference curve U_2 at point C.

In Figure 3-3*a*, the income effect, which dampens the reduction in leisure time, is not as strong as the substitution effect; the overall impact of the wage increase from w_0 to w_1 is to reduce leisure time from t_L^A to t_L^C. In Figure 3-3*b*, the income effect is so strong that the substitution effect of a wage increase on leisure is completely overcome. Although the substitution effect would reduce leisure from t_L^A to t_L^B, the overriding income effect increases leisure from t_L^B to t_L^C, resulting in less work effort at the higher wage rate than was the case with artificially depressed nonlabor income.

The opposing income and substitution effects of a wage increase have a highly practical business application. Suppose that Ed's boss, Mr. Crank, wished to increase output for a short period of time, a period too short to hire and train additional workers. If Mr. Crank offered Ed a higher wage rate for all time worked, the best Crank could hope for is the situation depicted in Figure 3-3*a*: a small increase in Ed's work effort $(t_L^A - t_L^C)$ resulting from a fairly substantial increase in wage payments (equal to $y_C - y_A$, since nonwage income remains constant). The outcome depicted in Figure 3-3*b* is even worse from Crank's perspective; Ed, however, would be delighted. Mr. Crank ends up paying higher total wages to Ed Collins, but actually receives fewer labor hours: $(\bar{t} - t_L^C) - (\bar{t} - t_L^A) = (t_L^A - t_L^C) < 0$.

The moral of Figure 3-3 is that across-the-board wage rate increases are relatively ineffective in increasing the number of hours worked. Figure 3-4 shows that by setting a higher wage rate for overtime (i.e., for work in excess of $\bar{t} - t_L^A$), Mr. Crank can maximize Ed's work effort for a specified wage payment. Ed Collins is assumed to be in equilibrium, maximizing utility at point A with wage rate w_0, receiving a wage payment of $y_A - y_0$ and allocating t_L^A hours to leisure. The budget line for overtime pay passes through point A, with a steeper slope representing the higher wage rate w_1 for work in excess of $\bar{t} - t_L^A$; if Ed continued to work the same number of hours, his wage income would remain the same.

Note that paying a wage rate one-and-a-half times the normal wage for overtime is equivalent to counting overtime as "time-and-a-half." In a plant where different workers are paid different wage rates because they perform different jobs, have different experience, or even suffer from wage discrimination, paying time-and-a-half allows the employers to maintain the same relative wage structure.

Figure 3-4 illustrates why employers prefer overtime pay to across-the-board wage increases. Since indifference curve U_0 intersects the budget line offering a wage of w_1 for work in excess of $\bar{t} - t_L^A$, Ed

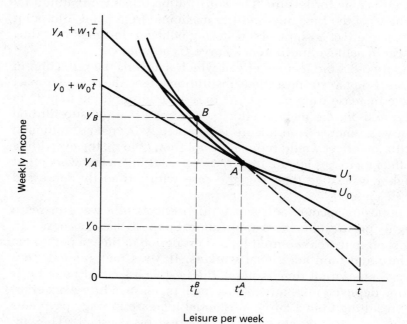

Figure 3-4
Overtime Pay and Work Effort

increases his utility to U_1 by reducing his leisure to t_L^B. If Ed is free to turn down the offer of overtime work at a higher rate of pay, Mr. Crank would not expect him to complain. Crank ends up paying higher wages only for the extra hours worked.

APPLICATION
Welfare Reform and Work Incentives

Another application of the theory of choice between income and leisure explains the frustrating contradictions of government antipoverty programs designed to increase the income of the working poor. Programs meant (1) to provide a minimum income to those in need and (2) to limit payments to "the deserving poor" have an unintended side effect: leisure is treated as a free good.

In Figure 3-5 we depict the plight of Alice Smith, whose earnings,

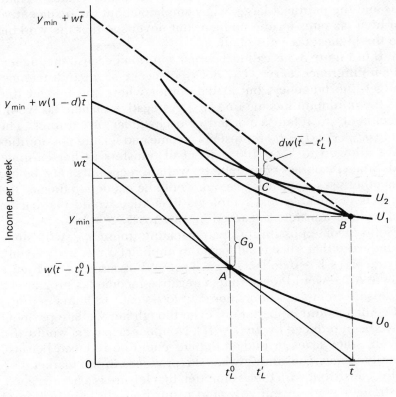

Figure 3-5
Transfer Programs and Work Incentives

$w(\bar{t} - t_L^0)$, are so meager that she and her children consume below the officially designated poverty level, y_{min}. She applies for Aid to Families with Dependent Children (AFDC) payments, and a social worker determines her grant by applying a **means test**. Her transfer benefits (e.g., food stamps, public housing, medicaid payments, and AFDC payments) are initially set at G_0, which is the difference between what her social worker determines the family "needs" and earned income, which represents their "means."

As long as leisure, which includes such activities as taking care of her own children, is a good, Alice can increase her family's well-being by reducing her labor income to zero and receiving the maximum grant of y_{min}. Perhaps the most insidious feature of the plight of the welfare mother is the popular attitude that the poor should feel remorse for their choice of maximum transfers in the wake of what is, effectively, a 100 percent tax on earned income, since \$1 of benefits are taken back for each \$1 of reported earnings. Making "leisure" (i.e., child-care) a "bad" does shame some of the poor into working, but it also alienates welfare recipients and the public at large, who complain about the disincentive effects of high tax rates for the nonpoor but never see that the working poor face the highest tax rates of all.

Point B in Figure 3-5 is called a *corner solution* because the highest attainable indifference curve, U_1, does not occur at an indifference-curve/budget-line tangency, but at the corner where the budget line intersects the minimum income line y_{min}. A **negative income tax** would permit recipients to retain a portion of each dollar of earnings. The dashed line $y_{min} + w(\bar{t} - t_L)$ represents income and leisure possibilities were Alice allowed to keep 100 percent of transfers as her earnings increased. Since resources consumed by welfare recipients must be bid away from other uses, some tax program would be needed to finance the transfers; it is reasonable that recipients like Alice would pay back a portion of welfare transfers as earned income rose.

The solid income possibility line emanating from $\bar{t}, y_{min}$ with slope $w(1 - d)$ indicates that Alice is subject to an implicit tax rate of d percent: her family receives $1 - d$ dollars for each extra \$1 of earnings. As Figure 3-5 is drawn, Alice would respond to a negative income tax program by reducing leisure from $\bar{t}$ (24 hours per day) to t_L' (e.g., 18 hours per day) at point C. Alice would be better off, even though her welfare payment would have been reduced by $dw(\bar{t} - t_L')$. Nonpoor taxpayers would also be better off, since taxes or budget deficits could be reduced because Alice's family is now consuming what she produces in the market.

Finally, consistent with the assumption that leisure is a normal good, an even stronger work incentive would result from the elimination of transfer programs entirely. Given the choice of earning sub–poverty-level income or seeing her family starve, Alice would choose point A. There

TABLE 3-1
Feasible Welfare Programs

Program	Criteria		
	Income Floor	*No Leakage*	*Work Incentive*
None	No	Yes	Yes
AFDC	Yes	Yes, by design; no, in practice.	No
Negative income tax	Yes	No	Yes

are only two ways of adding work incentives to transfer programs: (1) set the benefit level substantially below the poverty level (as with no transfers at all), so that no one receives benefits above the poverty level, or (2) allow total income from earnings and transfers to exceed the poverty level so that benefits may be reduced gradually as income rises.

This observation led A. Dale Tussing of Syracuse University to develop an "impossibility theorem" for welfare reform.[3] According to Tussing, if the "perfect" welfare program is defined as having a minimum floor on income at the poverty level, no "leakage" of payments to households with incomes above the poverty level, and a work incentive, then the results of real welfare reform will be disappointing. As we have seen, a program which sets a floor on income at the poverty level but takes away $1 of transfers for each $1 of earnings offers the prospect that increasing labor time will not increase income until the poverty level is exceeded. Table 3-1 also demonstrates that any two of these criteria can be achieved, at least in theory.[4]

If programs to redistribute income were dropped entirely, the poor who could not work (e.g., young children) would starve, steal, or survive by private charity. But a strong work incentive would exist for those able to work; and with no payments to anyone, there would be no fear of payments going to "cheaters." The current system, which tries to assure that only the "deserving poor" receive transfer payments, minimizes the work incentive because benefits are reduced by $1 for every $1 of reported income. Only by cheating—by keeping earnings secret—do welfare recipients have an incentive to work. Finally, a negative income tax

---

[3] A. Dale Tussing, *Poverty and the Dual Economy* (New York: St. Martin's Press, 1975).

[4] The results of a negative income tax experiment, reported in Joseph Pechman and P. Michael Timpane, eds., *Work Incentives and Income Guarantees: The New Jersey Negative Income Tax Experiment* (Washington, D.C.: Brookings Institution, 1975), seemed to indicate that a work incentive may not exist when a negative income tax replaces the traditional means test approach. However, since part of the control group included the working poor receiving no transfers, the results of the experiment are consistent with the prediction that eliminating transfers would have a stronger work incentive than a negative income tax program.

Policy Illustration
The Microeconomic Legacy of Supply-Side Macroeconomics

The work disincentive of high marginal tax rates has been generalized as the microeconomic basis for supply-side macroeconomic policy, particularly the Reagan administration's 1981 tax cuts. The extreme arguments used by advocates of cutting tax rates to stimulate output and fight inflation are simple. Suppose a 100 percent tax rate were imposed on all earnings, the proceeds to be distributed equally among households. With income divorced from work effort, output would quickly shrink toward zero and society's standard of living would fall. The zero price of leisure would encourage a reduction in work effort, while promised transfers would neutralize any income effect of lower labor earnings. Conversely, so the argument runs, reducing the tax rate below 100 percent would encourage work effort and raise tax collections.

But we do not live in a society where tax rates (except for the working poor) are nearly so high, or transfer programs (including the imputed value of tax-financed government services) are quite so generous. Whether cutting tax *rates* would increase work effort (dominant substitution effect) or encourage additional leisure (dominant income effect) depends upon two factors: (1) whether or not budgets are cut in such a way that workers perceive a lower real income as a result, and (2) the trade-off between the substitution effects of higher after-tax wage rates and the income effects of higher after-tax nonlabor income. Ironically, the attitude of the Reagan administration that social spending was "wasteful" and that tax cuts should be concentrated in upper income brackets (where nonlabor income is prevalent) tended to encourage, rather than discourage, the income effect of tax cuts on the leisure-income choice. The accompanying figure demonstrates why.

Assume that John Q. Publique earns a wage income of $w(1 - \delta_0)t_h^0$ where $t_h^0 = \bar{t} - t_L^0$, and δ_0 is the tax rate on labor earnings (including social security taxes), and y_0 is his net nonlabor income, which includes the value John places on services provided by the government (e.g., the present value of expected social security payments, unemployment compensation, college loans for his children, national defense, etc.). The gap between the budget line, $(y_0 + w[1 - \delta_0]\bar{t}, \bar{t})$, tangent to U_0 at point A and $y_0 + w(\bar{t} - t_L^0)$ is the tax paid on labor income: $T_0 = \delta_0 w(\bar{t} - t_L^0)$.

To isolate the substitution effect of a tax cut on the hours of leisure, we assume simultaneous cuts of the tax rate to δ_1, and a decrease in the value of government services, which causes nonlabor income to fall to y'. The budget line reflecting the lower tax rate, $y = y_1 + w(1 - \delta_1)t_h$, intersects indifference curve U_0 at point A; real income has been held constant by the Slutsky approach. The higher price of leisure, $w(1 - \delta_1) > w(1 - \delta_0)$, encourages John Q. to reduce leisure to t_L', thereby increasing hours of work and increasing tax payments relative to $\delta_1 w(\bar{t} - t_L^0) = \delta_1 w t_h^0$. Hence, if the tax rate cut and the government spending cuts had been geared to balance the budget if work effort remained constant, the substitution of earnings for leisure would have resulted in a budget surplus. If inflation occurs because of "too much money chas-

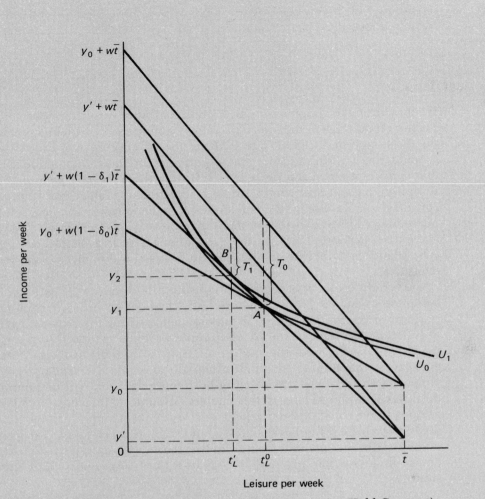

Impact of a Tax Cut on Work Effort (Real Income Being Held Constant)

ing too few goods," the results depicted in the accompanying figure would have fought inflation on two fronts: (1) by increasing output and (2) by reducing the rate of money balances of households.

By the spring of 1982, there was some indication that the rate of inflation was beginning to ebb, although many critics of the tax cut attributed this to the continued tight money policy of the Federal Reserve. The budget deficit grew after the tax cut, in large part because of the recession which occurred. What happened? The figure indicates that the tax cut idea might have been "good in theory." What happened in practice was a violation of the assumption that the substitution effect of higher after-tax income would not be offset by an adverse income effect. Paradoxically, the spending cuts did not hurt enough for the whole impact of higher after-tax income to be felt through increased work effort.

encourages some work effort, although only by setting minimum payments well below the poverty level or by setting the cut-off level of income above the poverty level.

Consumption over Time

We now drop the simplifying assumption that current consumption must exactly equal present income. This allows saving and borrowing to enter the consumption decision. The analysis of consumption over time is not fundamentally different from single-period utility maximization, except that consumption in the present is substituted for the prospect of consumption in the future wholly through adjustments in the rate of current consumption. *Saving* means consuming less than present income, while *borrowing* implies consuming more than present income allows. Utility maximization today involves the consequences of irrevocable past decisions and the anticipation of uncertain future consequences of present decisions.

We define our two goods as "consumption today" (C_t) and "consumption tomorrow" (C_{t+1}), where individual commodities in each period are measured in "constant dollars" adjusted for the expected rate of inflation. (In light of the index number problem explored in the appendix to chapter two, the rate of inflation is difficult to measure accurately, so that future consumption actually amounts to a *risky* prospect. However, this feature of the saving-borrowing decision will be ignored until risk is explored later in this chapter. In limiting the analysis to two periods (where each period equals one year), we assume that a similar decision will be made between C_{t+1} and C_{t+2} next year, based, in part, upon wealth or debts inherited from this period. Given the existence of banks, financial markets, and loan sharks, the two-period budget constraint is:

$$C_{t+1} = Y_{t+1} + (1 + r)(Y_t - C_t)$$

where r is the **real rate of interest** (the nominal rate of interest minus the rate of change in prices, i.e., adjusted for inflation), and Y_t and Y_{t-1} equal actual real income in the present and anticipated real income in the future, respectively. Planned consumption next year equals next year's expected income, plus the principle and interest for the portion of this year's income saved, or minus this year's debt and the interest on that debt. If current consumption exceeds current income, next year's consumption must be reduced by the principal of the loan (the difference between Y_t and C_t), plus the interest which must be paid on that loan. If current consumption is less than current income, the difference ($Y_t - C_t$) plus the interest these savings earn are added to next year's income before determining expected consumption.

Whether it reduces the amount saved or increases debt, each extra dollar of consumption this year reduces planned consumption next period by $(1 + r)$ dollars:

$$\frac{\Delta C_{t+1}}{\Delta C_t} = -(1 + r)$$

Figure 3-6 shows that the budget line (or consumption possibility line) must pass through the balanced budget point (Y_t, Y_{t+1}). Regardless of the (real) rate of interest, if consumption this year exactly equals current income, planned consumption next year will exactly equal expected income next year. The horizontal-axis intercept of this budget line equals present income plus the *present value* of expected future income:

$$C_t^{max} = Y_t + \frac{Y_{t+1}}{1 + r}$$

If the market rate of interest is 10 percent, $1.00 of consumption next year must be sacrificed for $0.91 of consumption this year. However, if the rate of inflation is expected to equal 5 percent, that dollar next year would buy only slightly more than $0.95 worth of goods at current prices.
    The vertical intercept indicates the maximum amount of planned

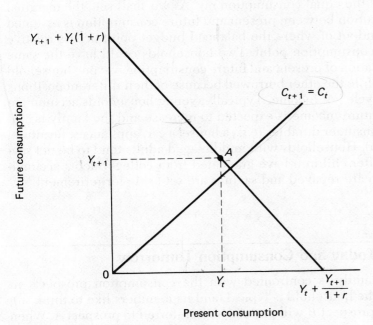

Figure 3-6
Present and (Prospective) Future Consumption Possibilities

future consumption if all income this year were saved:

$$C_{t+1}^{\max} = Y_{t+1} + Y_t(1 + r)$$

Consumption would not likely occur at either extreme of the budget line in Figure 3-6, but this is because of preferences rather than possibilities. Consuming nothing this year means starvation; few people have so much altruism that they save all their income to enhance the future consumption of their heirs. Nor is it likely that one could find a lender who would be willing to mortgage all of next year's income without substantial collateral (e.g., unbroken knees); such profligate spenders tend to have high default rates on loan repayments. Nevertheless, simple diagrams such as Figure 3-6 can be used if irrelevant complications are ignored. The intercepts would become bothersome only if a corner solution to utility maximization were indicated.

A particularly important point on every multiperiod budget line is identified by the intersection of the budget line and the ray labeled $C_{t+1} = C_t$, which indicates equal consumption in the two periods. In Figure 3-6, real future income is expected to be greater than current income; equalizing planned consumption in the two periods implies consuming more than current income and thus using some of next year's income to repay this year's debt. If future income were expected to be less than present income, the balanced budget point A ($C_t = Y_t$) would be located to the right of the equal consumption ray. As we shall see, the marginal rate of substitution between present and future consumption is assumed to be independent of where the balanced budget point occurs relative to the equal consumption point. Two households could have the same relative evaluation of present and future consumption, yet one household would save while the other borrowed because of their different positions on the "life cycle" of income. Typically, young households accumulate debts since future income is expected to increase and the family is "investing" in consumer durables (e.g., a house, a car, appliances, furniture, even children). Households with middle-aged adults tend to be net savers, at least after children have graduated from college: debts accumulated in youth are repaid and savings are set aside for retirement.

Preferences for Consumption Today and Consumption Tomorrow

The Carroll family is confronted with the consumption prospects in Table 3-2. If the household is typical (and its members like to think so), consumption prospect B will probably be preferred to prospect A. When the publisher's representative asks, "Would you prefer an advance against royalties of $3,000?" Tom Carroll says yes. The future involves

TABLE 3-2
Alternative Consumption Prospects

Prospect	Consumption	
	1982	*1983*
A	$25,000	$31,000
B	28,000	28,000
C	47,000	9,000

much uncertainty, including the prospect of death. Most people seem to prefer $1 today instead of $1 tomorrow when consumption prospects are approximately equal. Nevertheless, most people tend to feel insecure when presented with the prospect of a destitute future. If the publisher told Carroll that he could have a $22,000 loan against royalties, but only on the condition that he consume that amount, the uncertain author would likely balk. When the prospect of future consumption enters into the present consumption decision, a diminishing marginal rate of substitution of present consumption for expected future consumption is likely. It would not be surprising if the Carrolls, who prefer prospect B to prospect A, also prefer prospect B (or even prospect A) to prospect C.

The assumption that present consumption is preferred to future consumption implies that the marginal rate of substitution of present consumption for future consumption, $\Delta C_{t+1}/\Delta C_t = -MU_t/MU_{t+1}$, is less than -1 when consumption prospects are equal (along $C_{t+1} = C_t$). This implies that prospect A is on a lower indifference curve than prospect B. The assumption of a diminishing marginal rate of substitution means that households would be willing to sacrifice smaller and smaller amounts of future consumption for an extra dollar's worth of present consumption. Hence, prospect C would be on a lower indifference curve than prospect B, and possibly prospect A would also be preferred to prospect C.

An indifference curve relating present and expected future consumption, like those in Figure 3-7, would feature a bowed-in shape typical of indifference curves reflecting a diminishing marginal rate of substitution. As C_t increases at the expense of C_{t+1}, so that total utility remains on indifference curve U_0, the marginal utility of present consumption would fall relative to the marginal utility of the prospect of future consumption. Note that MU_{t+1} does *not* refer to the marginal utility that will actually be experienced next year; consumers are not assumed to be clairvoyant. Rather, MU_{t+1} implies satisfaction *today* due to contemplating consumption in the future.

Impatience suggests that where indifference curve U_0 intersects the equal consumption ray, $C_{t+1} = C_t$, $MU_t/MU_{t+1} > 1$, so that $\Delta C_{t+1}/\Delta C_t < -1$. To the right of the equal consumption ray, indifference curves

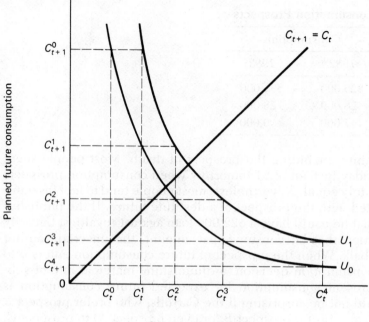

Figure 3-7
Diminishing Marginal Rate of Substitution of Present Consumption for Planned Future Consumption. By construction, the consumer is indifferent between (C_t^0, C_{t+1}^0), (C_t^1, C_{t+1}^1), (C_t^2, C_{t+1}^2), (C_t^3, C_{t+1}^3), and (C_t^4, C_{t+1}^4).

are assumed to flatten as present consumption increases at the expense of the prospect of future consumption. To the left of the equal consumption line, U_0 becomes steeper as C_{t+1} increases at the expense of C_t.

Utility Maximization with a Multiperiod Income Constraint

The assumption that consumption must exactly equal present income simplified the analysis of consumer choice but at the cost of ignoring the important role of saving and borrowing in the household budget. Now, by making household consumption more general, we also complicate the process of consumer choice when utility depends on both current consumption and implied future consumption. The maximization of utility with a two-period income constraint is presented in Figure 3-8, in which two households are assumed to choose the same combi-

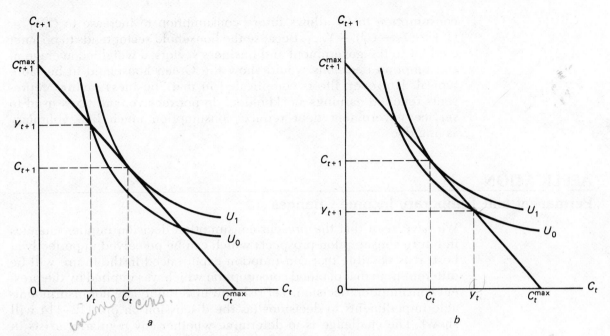

Figure 3-8
Utility Maximum under Multiperiod Income Constraint for (*a*) a Borrower and (*b*) a Saver

nation of present consumption, C_t^0, and future consumption, C_{t+1}^0. The two families differ only in the location of this chosen consumption point relative to their balanced budget point. The Browns, depicted in Figure 3-8*a*, spend more than their income in the current period and become debtors. The Greens, depicted in Figure 3-8*b*, consume less than their present income today and are savers. In both cases, satisfaction is maximized by adjusting current consumption so that:

$$MRS = \frac{\Delta C_{t+1}}{\Delta C_t} = -\frac{MU_t}{MU_{t+1}} = -(1 + r) \quad \text{or} \quad \frac{MU_t}{1 + r} = MU_{t+1}$$

where r is the natural rate of interest; that is, $-(1 + r)$ is the slope of the multiperiod budget line. Current consumption increases until the satisfaction gained from the last dollar spent today equals the satisfaction of the prospect of spending $1 + r$ dollars tomorrow.

The Browns (Figure 3-8*a*) would have a meager current standard of living if it were not possible for them to borrow against expected future income. Since loans must be secured, it is easy to imagine that the Browns purchase consumer durables (e.g., a car, a house, a new television) which serve as collateral and supply a stream of consumer services. If the Greens (Figure 3-8*b*) consumed all their income in the present, their future consumption prospects would be bleak. Reducing consumption to C_t^0 allows future consumption to increase to $C_{t+1}^0 = (1 + r)(Y_t - C_t^0) + Y_{t+1}$. Because the household sector tends to be a net creditor to the government and business sectors, a weighted average of consumption decisions would show the Green household to be more typical. However, life is complicated in that "business saving" represents retained earnings stockholders do not receive, and taxes used to service government debt reduce consumption much like voluntary saving does.

APPLICATION
Permanent and Temporary Income Changes

We have seen that the present consumption decision implies changes in future consumption prospects which can be perceived imperfectly at best. It is possible that consumption experienced in the future will be different from that planned consumption which was implied by the present consumption decision. Yet risk and uncertainty are not insurmountable impediments to decisions (as the discussion on pp. 112–114 will show). The challenge is to determine whether any regularity exists in the consumption behavior of many households. Two well-known approaches will be explored: the Keynesian consumption function and Milton Friedman's permanent consumption hypothesis. How the *perception* of an income change affects consumption behavior is a common theme which makes these two opposing models of consumer behavior complement each other.

In trying to explain the causes of the Great Depression and its unprecedented duration, John Maynard Keynes invoked what some modern economists have called (often disparagingly) "disequilibrium" economics. Households were surprised by the sudden decrease of their incomes and wealth, and they cut back on consumption to salvage some resources for the future. Yet, if the downturn in income was believed to be temporary, consumption would decline by a smaller proportion than current income. The attempts by households to sustain their former lifestyles through borrowing would arrest the general decline of income.

Figure 3-9a shows a decline in present income from Y_t^0 to Y_t', while expected future income remains at $\overline{Y}_{t+1}$. Note that the two-period budget line shifts toward the origin, parallel to the former budget line. If the real interest rate remains the same, the slope of the new budget line must be the same as the slope of the old one. Present consumption possibilities decline for the obvious reason that present income has declined. Future consumption possibilities decline proportionately because, with fewer dollars to save today, there will be fewer opportunities at the maximum end of the consumption spectrum tomorrow. For convenience, Figure 3-9a has been drawn so that the tangency of indiffer-

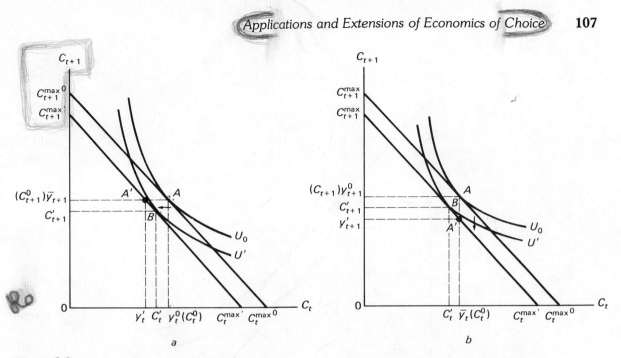

Figure 3-9
Microeconomic Roots of Keynesian Consumption Function. *a*, Transitory decrease in present income; *b*, anticipated decrease in future income.

ence curve U_0 to the higher budget line occurs at the balanced budget point A (Y_t^0, $\bar{Y}_{t+1}$). The decline in present income (with constant expected future income) shifts the balanced budget point to the left to point A' (Y_t', Y_{t+1}). Since both present consumption and planned future consumption are assumed to be normal goods, indifference curve U' is tangent to the lower budget line at point B, which is to the right of its balanced budget point. A decrease in present income which is not expected to become permanent will reduce both present and future consumption, hence reducing planned future consumption relative to expected future income. This household goes from a balanced budget to a position of borrower. Figure 3-9*b* illustrates the Keynesian explanation for the epidemic character of severe recessions. If learning that others have lost their jobs caused a consumer to expect future income to decline from Y_{t+1}^0 to Y_{t+1}', both planned future consumption and actual present consumption would decrease, even if present income remained at $\bar{y}^t$. Because both present and planned future consumption are assumed to be normal goods, an anticipated decline of future income would reduce present consumption immediately. In Figure 3-9*b*, the decline in expected future income creates a vertical downward shift in the balanced budget point from point A to point A', while the budget line for present and future consumption, which shifts toward the origin, retains its original slope, assuming that the real rate of interest does not change. The

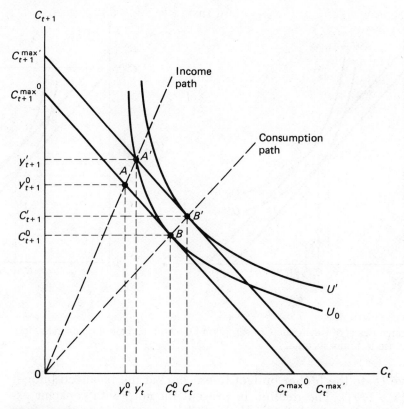

Figure 3-10
Permanent Income and Consumption. An increase in present income
from y_t to y_t' and a proportionate increase in expected future income
from y_{t+1} to y_{t+1}' will tend to increase both present and planned future
consumption, *ceteris paribus.*

tangency point shifts from point *A* to point *B*. Once we realize, as Keynes
did, that a decline in current consumption reduces sales of consumer
goods (particularly durable goods), we see the paradox of thrift: if business investment changes in the same direction as national income, an
increase in household saving (e.g., in anticipation of future income declines) can actually create a recession, which in turn reduces total saving.

Since Keynes published *The General Theory of Employment, Interest and Money,*[5] many of the economic factors which encouraged
panic saving by households have been blunted. Unemployment insurance and seniority systems reduce the multiplier effect of recessions;
those with jobs are less apt to reduce consumption in anticipation of

---

[5] John Maynard Keynes (New York: Macmillan, 1936).

their own unemployment. Government insurance of bank deposits, social security, and other transfer programs also mitigate the recessionary consequences of temporary unemployment.

With social insurance against **transitory income** losses, variations in **permanent income** have an enhanced influence on household saving and consumption behavior. Milton Friedman has argued that a change in income that is considered permanent will have a greater influence on consumption than a change in income that is expected to be transitory.[6] The impact of a change in permanent income on present and planned future consumption is presented in Figure 3-10.

In Figure 3-10, present income and expected future income increase by the same proportion, moving the balanced budget point from A to A'. Since present consumption and the prospect of future consumption are both assumed to be normal goods and since increased consumption in each period can be financed out of that period's income, we cannot predict, a priori, how an increase in income which is perceived to be permanent will affect the proportion of income consumed. If planned future consumption increases relative to present consumption, borrowing will decrease (saving will increase). However, present consumption might increase relative to planned future consumption if the household reduced its precautionary saving. Figure 3-10 shows the same proportion of income consumed at the new tangency point B', as at the old tangency point B.

Present Value

The indifference-curve/budget-line tangency for the allocation of consumption over time gives a straightforward meaning to the concept of **present value**. The consumer maximizes utility by allocating present consumption such that the marginal rate of substitution of present consumption for planned future consumption equals the market rate of substitution, $-(1 + r)$. At the margin, the consumer is indifferent between either having an extra dollar's worth of consumption today or saving that dollar and receiving $(1 + r)$ dollars of real purchasing power next year. This is equivalent to saying that the prospect of one dollar's worth of consumption next year has a present value of $1/(1 + r)$.

Generalizing to n time periods, the present value of the prospect of $1 in n years is equal to $1/[(1 + r)^n]$ today if the rate of interest is assumed to remain constant and interest is compounded annually. Throwing simplicity to the wind, the present value (PV) of the prospect of a multiperiod

---

[6] Milton Friedman, *A Theory of the Consumption Function* (Princeton, N.J.: Princeton University Press, 1957).

consumption flow worth C_i in period $t + i$ (in constant dollars), with a real interest rate of r_i in that period, and with interest compounded m times per period, is:

$$PV = C_0 + \frac{C_1}{\left(1 + \frac{r_1}{m}\right)^m} + \frac{C_2}{\left(1 + \frac{r_2}{m}\right)^{2m}} + \cdots$$
$$+ \frac{C_i}{\left(1 + \frac{r_i}{m}\right)^{im}} + \cdots + \frac{C_n}{\left(1 + \frac{r_n}{m}\right)^{nm}}$$

where n is the number of periods the payment is expected or promised. Using summation notation, the present value of the consumption stream depicted above is:

$$PV = \sum_{i=1}^{n} \frac{C_i}{\left(1 + \frac{r_i}{m}\right)^{im}}$$

Table 3-3 displays the present values for annuities paying $1,000 per year. Note that present value varies with the number of years the payment is expected, n; with the expected rate of interest, r; and with the frequency of compounding, m. If a household had reached the optimal rate of present consumption (implying a plan for consumption in future years), the present value of the annuity would equal the subjective evaluation of the payment stream to the household.

The greater the number of years a payment is expected, the greater will be the present value of the annuity, given tastes and values of r and m. But even if payments were expected to last forever, there is a maximum amount that a utility-maximizing (financial) investor would pay to acquire the income stream; the present value of a perpetuity is the annual payment divided by the expected rate of interest.

The higher the prevailing or expected rate of interest, the lower will be the present value of a given expected payment stream, *ceteris paribus*. There are two mutually reinforcing explanations for this. One, the higher the market rate of interest, the greater is the opportunity cost of funds committed to the purchase of any particular financial asset. Two, assuming a person's consumption plans have resulted in indifference-curve/budget-line tangency, the higher the rate of interest, the greater is the marginal rate of substitution between present and future consumption implied by that tangency.

Understanding the process of consumer utility maximization brings us to an ironic, but important, insight. Economists have no expertise for explaining tastes; ultimately, why two individuals of similar age, income, and future prospects differ in their allocation of consumption between the present and the future does not have a uniquely economic expla-

TABLE 3-3
Selected Present Values for Annuities Paying $1,000 per Year[a]

n	m	i = 5%	i = 10%	i = 20%
1	1	$ 952.38	$ 909.09	$ 833.32
	2	951.81	907.03	826.44
	4	951.52	905.97	822.70
	12	951.33	905.21	819.41
	∞	951.23	904.84	818.73
	(continuous)			
2	1	1,859.41	1,735.54	1,527.78
	2	1,857.77	1,729.73	1,509.44
	4	1,856.92	1,726.70	1,499.54
	12	1,856.35	1,724.62	1,492.62
	∞	1,856.07	1,723.57	1,489.05
5	1	4,329.48	3,790.79	2,990.61
	2	4,322.01	3,766.70	2,925.98
	4	4,318.19	3,754.15	2,891.38
	12	4,315.61	3,745.48	2,867.37
	∞	4,314.31	3,741.24	2,855.07
10	1	7,721.73	6,144.57	4,192.47
	2	7,698.36	6,079.12	4,054.08
	4	7,686.41	6,045.20	3,981.11
	12	7,678.35	6,022.10	3,930.95
	∞	7,674.29	6,010.41	3,905.39
20	1	12,462.21	8,513.57	4,869.69
	2	12,396.44	8,370.28	4,656.69
	5	12,362.98	8,296.62	4,596.77
	12	12,340.34	8,246.71	4,546.61
	∞	12,328.98	8,221.50	4,433.93
∞	1	20,000.00	10,000.00	5,000.00
	2	19,753.09	9,756.10	4,761.90
	4	19,628.88	9,638.72	4,640.24
	12	19,545.80	9,549.91	4,558.07
	∞	19,504.17	9,508.33	4,516.66

[a] An annuity is a guaranteed series of payments in the future, purchased in the present, either for a lump sum (e.g., for a gift) or by contributions (e.g., a pension). An annuity can begin immediately upon purchase or may be deferred. In this table, payments are assumed to commence 1 year from the purchase date.

nation. Yet, when economists analyze investment decisions or other activities which involve current costs and the prospect of future revenue, they compare the present value of that revenue with the current costs. Are they not guilty of imposing their value judgments on the rest of society?

If you have been following the logic of the last two chapters, you may anticipate the economists' defense of calculating present value as an *objective* means of evaluation. Decisions are continually being made—indeed must be made—about how to allocate consumption between the present and the future. Hence, in the absence of contrary evidence, we may *assume* that the household has allocated its current budget in such a way that the relative marginal utility of a consumption (income) prospect is proportional to its present value.

APPLICATION

The Economics of Education: Discounting Educational Benefits

With our understanding of how anticipation of future events influences current decisions, we can return to the investment of time (valued at the present wage) in regard to educational activities. According to the theory of human capital (presented in detail in chapter thirteen), the optimal amount of education occurs when the present value of future benefits attributed to the last year of schooling equals the present cost of an extra year of education. Assuming that Δy_{t+i} is the payoff for one more year of schooling i periods in the future, w_0 is the present wage, t_e is time devoted to education, and c includes other costs (tuition and books, but not room and board), a student would invest an additional year in school if:

$$w_0 t_e + c \leq \sum_{i=1}^{n} \frac{\Delta y_{t+i}}{(1 + r_i)^i}$$

where r_i is the real rate of interest in period i.

There are, of course, a number of complications. First, education does not increase income at a smooth rate; the payoff of a degree means that the fourth year of college usually has a much greater "value added" than any of the three preceding years. Second, the opportunity cost of an hour spent in class is the wage rate, regardless of whether the student actually sacrificed leisure or earned income. However, to the extent that part of the payoff of an education is enhanced enjoyment of leisure, looking only at the financial payoff will understate the present value of an education. Third, the payoff of an education depends upon what happens after graduation. Will earnings be high or low in the graduate's chosen profession? Will he or she be admitted to professional school? Will the graduate be at the right place when opportunity knocks? It is time to turn our attention to risk.

Decisions under Risk

Every choice we make requires predicting the future consequences of alternative courses of action before action is taken. So far, it has been convenient to assume that the individual knows the consequence of each option, at least in terms of a preference ordering, at the time of decision making. In the last sections of this chapter, we will consider how imperfect control over the outcomes of decisions influences the way in which they are made.

Economics involves the allocation of scarce means to achieve alternative ends; people try to simplify the connection between actions (purchasing different commodities, taking one job instead of another) and outcomes (utility, income). The *assumption* of **certainty** really involves two related, but distinguishable, characteristics about the decision environment.[7] First, for each option, there is only one outcome which will occur if that alternative is chosen. This one-to-one correspondence between options and outcomes gives individuals complete control; they cause their preferred outcome merely by selecting the appropriate action. Second, individuals know in advance what the outcome of each known alternative will be; this complete knowledge of the relation between alternatives and outcomes means that no surprises occur after decisions have been taken. Usually individuals have, at best, only incomplete control over the outcomes of their decisions; a chosen course of action may result in any one of a number of mutually exclusive events.

Suppose you go to Hollywood to become a movie star. Whether you end up making hamburgers or making films depends on whether you are discovered by a movie producer or a fast-food entrepreneur. A student's exam grade depends in part upon material studied, but also upon which questions are asked. Whether your clothes stay dry depends partly on whether you carry an umbrella, but also upon whether it rains.

The conditions of risk and uncertainty create complications in the analysis of how decisions are made. A condition of **risk** exists when there are multiple possible, but mutually exclusive, outcomes to one or more options that a person has. However, that individual has the most complete information possible under such circumstances, that is, has knowledge of the relative likelihood or probability of those outcomes if the alternative is chosen. A state of **uncertainty** exists when the individual not only lacks perfect control over the outcome of a decision, but also has incomplete or inaccurate knowledge about the probability of outcomes.

Decision making under risk is similar to the allocation of consumption over time. In the latter case, a person consuming in the present must anticipate the cost of not consuming later. The marginal rate of substitution of present consumption for future consumption equals the ratio of the marginal utility of present consumption to the marginal utility of the prospect of future consumption. Under risk, a decision maker must

---

[7] This characterization of certainty is taken from Robert J. Wolfson and Thomas M. Carroll, "Ignorance, Error and Information in the Classic Theory of Decision," *Behavioral Science* (March 1976), pp. 107–115.

choose a course of action by comparing the marginal utility of prospective outcomes. Over time, individuals compare the present value of prospective future consumption possibilities. Under risk, individuals are assumed to compare the **expected value** of alternative (risky) prospects, only one of which will actually come to pass.

APPLICATION

The Economics of Crime

Building upon the pioneering work of economists Gary Becker, George Stigler, and Isaac Ehrlich,[8] many economists have analyzed criminal activity as a predictable reaction to economic incentives. The act of breaking into someone's house and stealing a television set can have successful or unsuccessful outcomes: the thief may be caught and punished, caught and let go, inadvertently shoot the victim (and face punishment for a more serious offense), or escape with the loot. Suppose that reliable statistics indicate that 10 percent of burglaries result in arrest and conviction. To keep the analysis simple, suppose that every successful burglar gets $100 from a "fence" for each stolen television set, and those convicted of burglary are fined $2,000 and must return the set. We calculate the expected value (*EV*) of burglary by adding the products of the value of each outcome times its probability:

$$EV = (1 - \rho)\$100 + \rho(-\$2000) = 0.9(\$100) + 0.1(-\$2000)$$
$$= \$90 - \$200 = -\$110$$

where ρ (the Greek letter "rho") is the probability of punishment. According to this calculation, a person can expect to lose $110 every time he or she attempts to steal a television set.

The assumption that decision makers have accurate information about the likelihood of outcomes—knowledge which separates risk from uncertainty—becomes a *crucial assumption* when the model of decision making under risk is used to diagnose behavior. (An assumption becomes crucial when changing that assumption modifies the predictions of a theory in a nontrivial way. See chapter one.)

Suppose Mugsy Mitty is apprehended leaving the apartment of Albert Nerd with Albert's television set. Having calculated that the act had an expected value of $-\$110$, we might conclude not only that Mugsy

---

[8] Gary S. Becker, "Crime and Punishment: An Economic Approach," *Journal of Political Economy* (March/April 1968), pp. 169–217; George Stigler, "The Optimal Enforcement of Laws," *Journal of Political Economy* (May/June 1970), pp. 526–536; Isaac Ehrlich, "Participation in Illegitimate Activities: A Theoretical and Empirical Investigation," *Journal of Political Economy* (May/June 1973), pp. 521–564, and "The Deterrent Effect of Capital Punishment: A Case of Life and Death," *American Economic Review* (June 1975), pp. 397–417.

was unlucky (he was the one burglar in ten to get caught), but that the thrill of breaking the law must have been worth $110 to him. A **risk lover** is someone who behaves as if risk itself provided satisfaction, over and above the expected (monetary) payoff of the action. That someone gets a "charge" out of danger is occasionally offered by noneconomists as a criticism of the economic approach to crime. Before we explore this criticism further, let us consider an alternative explanation for risky behavior.

Suppose Mugsy believed that his chances of being caught and punished were only one in fifty, perhaps because he considered himself particularly skilled at avoiding detection. Given a subjective probability of $\rho = 0.02$, Mugsy's expected payoff from burglary would be:

$$EV = 0.98(\$100) + 0.02(-\$2000) = \$98 - \$40 = \$58$$

This optimistic but misguided soul considered $58 an acceptable rate of pay for a job that allows him to keep his own hours, be his own boss, and occasionally meet interesting, if not altogether pleasant, people.

Because the decision maker under risk is *assumed* to have accurate information about the relative frequency of outcomes, the researcher uses his or her own estimate of the probability of outcomes to calculate the expected value of each option.[9] This attitude can lead to complications. If a person chooses an action other than the one thought to have the highest expected value, that person appears to reveal a taste for risk. However, if the decision maker (or the observer) has erroneously calculated the probability of outcomes, what appears to be a preference for risky prospects is actually a disagreement between observer and observed about the estimated probability of outcomes.

When information is insufficient to calculate the probability of outcomes, a state of uncertainty exists. Decisions can still be observed, but the observer has no prior knowledge of the probability estimates used by the subject to calculate the expected values of options. Furthermore, decisions may be postponed while information is collected, which leads to the "satisficing" behavior attributed to many corporate executive (to be discussed in chapter twelve). Uncertainty makes it difficult, if not impossible, to assess risk preferences accurately. If we believe that "crime does not pay," we may err in attributing a taste for risk to criminals who are more optimistic than we are about their chances for success.

---

[9] Distinguishing between "objective" and "subjective" probability is a classical attitude which assumes that probability numbers exist independently of human measures of it. In contrast, Bayesian probability theory, named for the eighteenth-century mathematician Thomas Bayes, treats all probability measures as subjective in nature and assumes that experience causes people to modify their beliefs about the relative likelihood of events. The use of Bayesian probability theory in an economic context is given in Thomas M. Carroll and Robert D. Dean, "A Bayesian Approach to Plant Location," *Decision Sciences* (January 1980), pp. 81–89.

Do some people enter risky occupations which offer low average incomes and a very few high incomes (e.g., boxing, acting, textbook writing) because they enjoy the prospect of beating the odds? Perhaps they consider their chances better than average.

Risk Preferences

The decision to commit a crime seems to reflect the conventional notion of risk as exposure to danger: to make a "good" outcome possible, criminals take the chance of something bad happening to them. Yet the essence of risk involves imperfect control over outcomes, because whether an outcome constitutes a gain or a loss is often a matter of perspective. Consider the alternative games of chance presented in Table 3-4. A coin is flipped: if it shows heads, players receive payoff A; if the coin shows tails, the players receive payoff B. Prospect 1 appears to guarantee that the players are better off than when they started; but the relevant cost of picking prospect 1 is what they sacrificed, namely, prospect 2 or prospect 3.

The prospects in Table 3-4 would not be risky prospects if the players could specify the payoff combination *after* the coin was tossed. If heads, they would pick prospect 2; if tails, prospect 1 would be best. If they picked prospect 1, knowing that heads was going to appear, they would lose $98.50; they might be $1.50 better off than before the coin was flipped, but they would be $98.50 poorer than they could have been. In selecting a payoff combination *before* the outcome of a gamble is determined, two types of information are available: the expected value of outcomes, explained in the previous section, and the variation in outcomes, which can be measured as the average deviation between possible outcomes and the expected value of a prospect.

TABLE 3-4
Alternative Risky Prospects

Prospect	Payoff A (Heads)	Payoff B (Tails)	Expected Value $(EV)^a$	Standard Deviation $(SD)^b$
1	$ 1.50	$ 1.00	$1.25	$ 0.25
2	100.00	−97.50	1.25	98.75
3	11.00	−8.00	1.50	9.50

$$\rho_A = \tfrac{1}{2}; \quad \rho_B = (1 - \rho_A) = \tfrac{1}{2}$$

$^a EV = \rho_A(A) + \rho_B(B) = \tfrac{1}{2}(A) + \tfrac{1}{2}(B)$

$^b SD = \{\rho_A[\rho_A(A) - EV]^2 + \rho_B[\rho_B(B) - EV]^2\}^{1/2}$
$\quad = \{\tfrac{1}{2}[\tfrac{1}{2}(A) - EV]^2 + \tfrac{1}{2}[\tfrac{1}{2}(B) - EV]^2\}^{1/2}$

What makes prospect 2 more risky than prospect 1 is the greater variability of outcomes associated with prospect 2 relative to prospect 1. Ranking these two prospects by their "riskiness" is simplified by the fact that both prospects have an expected value of $1.25:

$$EV(1) = \tfrac{1}{2}(\$1.50) + \tfrac{1}{2}(\$1.00) = \$0.75 + \$0.50 = \$1.25$$
$$EV(2) = \tfrac{1}{2}(\$100) + \tfrac{1}{2}(-\$97.50) = \$50.00 - \$48.75 = \$1.25$$

Among prospects with equal expected values, a risk averter would prefer prospects in reverse order of their standard deviation (i.e., a **risk averter** would prefer prospect 1 to prospect 2); a **risk lover** would rank prospects with equal expected values in the order of their standard deviations (a risk lover would prefer prospect 2 to prospect 1).

Note that prospect 3 has a higher expected value than either prospect 1 or prospect 2, although the standard deviation of outcomes for prospect 3 is greater than the standard deviation of prospect 1 but smaller than the standard deviation of prospect 2. A **risk neutral** decision maker ranks prospects strictly in terms of their expected values; a risk neutral individual would select prospect 3 instead of prospect 1 or 2. Like a risk neutral individual, risk averse and risk-loving persons are also assumed to prefer prospects with higher expected values, *ceteris paribus*. However, because the prospects in Table 3-4 differ in their standard deviations, it is possible that a risk averter would pick a prospect with a smaller expected value in order to reduce the variability of outcomes. Similarly, a risk lover might select a prospect with a lower expected value in order to increase the variability of outcomes.

Although we cannot predict how a risk lover or a risk averter would pick among prospects 2 and 3 or 1 and 3, respectively, failure of a subject to pick the prospect with the highest expected value does reveal his or her risk preferences. Hence, if we observed a person select prospect 3, we would be unable to determine whether that person was risk neutral, who picked prospect 3 because its expected value was $0.25 higher than the other two, a risk averter who considered the $0.25 difference between the expected values of prospect 2 and prospect 1 too much to give up to reduce his or her risk, or a risk lover who was unwilling to pay the $0.25 difference in the expected values of prospect 3 and prospect 2 to obtain the higher variation in outcomes. However, a person who picked prospect 1 would reveal risk averse preferences; the $0.25 difference in the expected values of prospect 3 and prospect 1 is the **risk premium** that person pays to avoid risk. Finally, a person picking prospect 2 would reveal risk-loving preferences; the $0.25 difference between the expected values of prospect 3 and prospect 2 is the risk premium this person pays to increase risk.

To summarize, in ranking risky prospects, all individuals are assumed to prefer prospects with higher expected values to those with lower expected values, among prospects with equal average variations in outcomes. Risk neutral preferences involve ordering risky prospects as if utility were proportional to the expected value of prospects; the variation in outcomes neither adds to nor subtracts from the expected utility of risky prospects. Risk aversion implies that greater variation in outcomes reduces the expected utility from risky prospects. Finally, risk-loving preferences imply that increasing the variation in outcomes enhances the utility derived from the expected value of prospects.

Risk Aversion and Insurance

Imagine that Rebecca Sunnybrook inherits a farm with a market value of $10,000. Bull Dozer, a contractor, offers her $50,000 for the land if it can be zoned for commercial development, thus allowing Bull to build a shopping center. Rebecca and Dozer agree that there is a 75 percent likelihood that the zoning commission will approve a petition for a change in the land's use. Figure 3-11 depicts two alternative futures. If the property is not rezoned (future A), Rebecca's wealth will remain $10,000; if the property is rezoned (future B), her wealth will increase to $50,000. The pair of prospective futures are represented as point P.

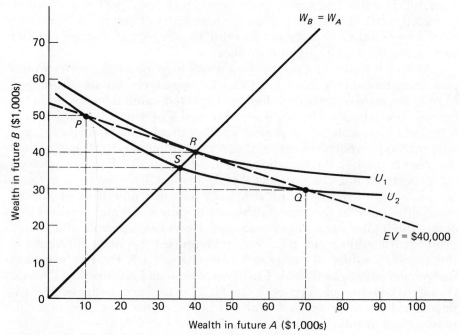

Figure 3-11
Indifference Curves for a Risk Averter

By multiplying the value of her land in each possible future by the probability of that outcome, then summing, we can calculate the expected value of Rebecca's land as:

$$EV(P) = (1 - \rho_B)(\$10,000) + \rho_B(\$50,000) = 0.25(\$10,000)$$
$$+ \ 0.75(\$50,000) = \$2,500 + \$37,500 = \$40,000$$

where ρ_B is the probability that the land will be rezoned. By imagining other payoffs in future A and future B, while maintaining the assumption that $\rho_B = 0.75$, we can plot other risky prospects and compare them to point P. For instance, suppose that there was a 25 percent chance that members of the Society for the Preservation of Curious Anachronisms would pay \$70,000 to develop the Sunnybrook Museum if rezoning were denied, but that it would take a bribe of \$20,000 to prevent them from suing to stop construction of the shopping center if rezoning were approved. Since that \$20,000 would come at Rebecca's expense, point Q identifies a risky prospect which has a payoff of \$70,000 in future A and \$30,000 in future B. Not only does point Q have the same expected value as P:

$$EV(Q) = 0.25(\$70,000) + 0.75(\$30,000) = \$40,000$$

but both have the same standard deviation in outcomes. The average, or standard, deviation in outcomes is determined by subtracting the value of each outcome from the expected value of that prospect, squaring the result and multiplying by the probability of that outcome, summing, and then taking the square root:

$$SD_P = [0.25(\$40,000 - \$10,000)^2 + 0.75(\$40,000 - \$50,000)^2]^{1/2}$$
$$= \$17,320.51$$
$$SD_Q = [0.25(\$40,000 - \$70,000)^2 + 0.75(\$40,000 - \$30,000)^2]^{1/2}$$
$$= \$17,320.51$$

Regardless of her tastes for risk, we would expect Rebecca to be indifferent between prospects P and Q in Figure 3-11.

A person's attitude toward risk is reflected in the marginal rate of substitution among outcomes in different possible futures, just as a person's time preference is revealed through his or her willingness to substitute present consumption for planned future consumption. Assuming that the probability of outcomes cannot be changed, a person is depicted as maximizing **expected utility** (EU) where the utility from each prospective outcome is weighted by the probability of that outcome:

$$EU = \rho_A U(W_A) + \rho_B U(W_B) = (1 - \rho_B)U(W_A) + \rho_B U(W_B)$$

Since the expected utility would change if either wealth prospect changed, an indifference curve for risky prospects would consist of higher wealth in one future and lower wealth in the alternative future, the probability of outcomes being constant:

$$\Delta EU = (1 - \rho_B)\frac{\Delta U}{\Delta W_A}\Delta W_A + \rho_B\frac{\Delta U}{\Delta W_B}\Delta W_B$$

Setting the change in expected utility equal to zero, the marginal rate of substitution between W_B and W_A is determined by solving for $\Delta W_B/\Delta W_A$:[10]

$$\Delta EU = 0 \text{ implies } (1 - \rho_B)\frac{\Delta U}{\Delta W_A}\Delta W_A = -\rho_B\frac{\Delta U}{\Delta W_B}\Delta W_B$$

or

$$MRS_{W_B \text{ for } W_A} = \frac{\Delta W_B}{\Delta W_A} = -\frac{1 - \rho_B}{\rho_B}\frac{MU_A}{MU_B}$$

The indifference map in Figure 3-11 shows point R, depicting equal wealth of \$40,000 in each state, residing on a higher indifference curve (U_1), relative to points P and Q (i.e., U_0). For a risk averter, smaller variations in outcomes are preferred to larger variations among risk prospects with equal expected values. With equal wealth in the two states, identified by the certainty ray, $W_B = W_A$, it follows that $MU_A = MU_B$. Regardless of risk preferences, when wealth is equal, the marginal rate of substitution of wealth between future states equals the ratio of the probability of each state: $MU_A = MU_B$ implies that MRS $= -(1 - \rho_B)/\rho_B$.

For a risk neutral individual, satisfaction results only from the expected value of a prospect; hence, the marginal rate of substitution among risky prospects equals the negative ratio of the likelihood of the two states. In Figure 3-11, the dashed line through points P, R, and Q represents an indifference curve for a risk neutral decision maker. In this example, Bull Dozer might be indifferent between purchasing the property for \$40,000 before the zoning decision, or agreeing to pay \$50,000 if it were zoned for commercial use and \$10,000 if it remained zoned only for agricultural use. However, risk averse Rebecca Sunny-

---

[10] Using calculus, the marginal rate of substitution is obtained by taking the total derivative of expected utility:

$$EU = (1 - \rho_B)U(W_A) + \rho_B U(W_B)$$

with respect to W_A and W_B, setting the result equal to 0:

$$dEU = (1 - \rho_B)\frac{\partial U}{\partial W_A}dW_A + \rho_B\frac{\partial U}{\partial W_B}dW_B = 0$$

and solving for dW_B/dW_A:

$$\frac{dW_B}{dW_A} = -\frac{1 - \rho_B}{\rho_B}\frac{MU_A}{MU_B}$$

brook would clearly prefer to receive $40,000 *before* the zoning board's decision; her utility would be increased if the risk of the zoning decision could be transferred to Dozer.

Although the risk averters clearly prefer to receive the certainty equivalent of a risky prospect, one can rarely escape risk without paying a fee for that service. Figure 3-11 shows an indifference curve passing through point S on the certainty line, representing approximately $36,000 in each possible future. So although the certainty equivalent of point P (i.e., point R) is clearly preferred, Rebecca would sacrifice up to $4,000 in expected wealth to escape the risk associated with point P or point Q. The preferences of risk averse households establish a market for insurance.

In Figure 3-12, the dashed line through points P and R represent the budget line for *actuarily fair* insurance policies which allow individuals to transfer wealth from the "good" state (state B) to the "bad" state (state A) at the rate of $\Delta W_B / \Delta W_A = -(1 - \rho_B)/\rho_B$. Suppose 1,000 individuals each face the same prospects as the individual in Figure 3-12. Some event, with a probability of 75 percent, would result in $50,000 wealth; if that event did not occur (probability $= 1 - 0.75 = 25$ percent),

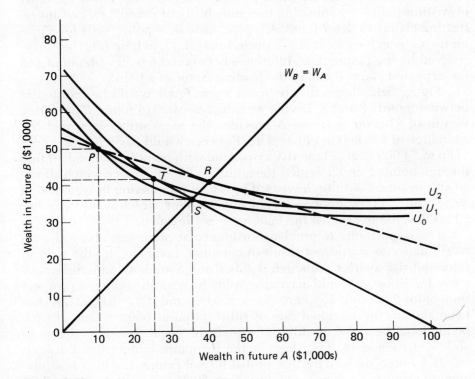

Figure 3-12
Reduction of Risk through Market Insurance

wealth would be only $10,000. By buying insurance policies for $10,000 which pay $40,000 if event A occurs, each person could be assured of $40,000 in either state. If event B occurs, each person would "lose" the premium of $10,000 and keep the $40,000 which remained. If event A occurs, the loss of the $10,000 premium would be compensated by a gain of $40,000. In this case, each $1 reduction in wealth in state B would result in a $3 increase in wealth in state A. Approximately 25 percent of insured households would have claims; therefore, the $1 million collected from all households would roughly equal payments. Not even insurance companies can escape the risk of policy claims deviating from their expected value, even if the probability of the insured calamity had been accurately predicted. Nevertheless, the standard deviation of outcomes does decline dramatically when many independent risk prospects are pooled. In this case, the probability is better than 95 percent that total claims would range from $986,000 ($14,000 profit) to $1,014,000 ($14,000 loss).

To remain in business, private enterprise insurance companies must sell policies for premiums which generate revenue in excess of expected claims (i.e., actuarially fair rates). If a company's revenue from premiums were exhausted by the payment of claims, it could not cover the costs of writing policies, estimating the probability of calamities, and investigating claims to deter fraud. A typical insurance policy sells for a premium, G, which exceeds the expected payoff, ρL, where L is the "loss" covered by the policy. The difference between the policy premium and the expected claim is called the **loading factor** of a policy.

Figure 3-12 shows that Rebecca Sunnybrook would be indifferent between points P and S; having wealth of $50,000 in future B or having wealth of $10,000 in future A provides the same utility as would the guarantee of $36,000 in either state. Rebecca would pay a risk premium of up to $4,000 to avoid the risk associated with point P. The budget line through points P and S depicts the ability to buy insurance which allows wealth in future A to be increased by $1 for a reduction in wealth B of $0.54; for $14,000, Rebecca could buy a policy which would pay her $26,000 in the event that the land were not rezoned.

The opportunity to purchase insurance at premiums above the actuarially fair rate would not result in complete insurance for the typical, informed risk averter. Although points P and S are both on indifference curve U_0, Rebecca would maximize utility by relocating the risk prospect from point P to point T, where $W_A = \$25,000$ and $W_B = \$41,923$. As has been shown, the marginal rate of substitution at point S (and at each point along the equal wealth line) equals the negative ratio of the probability of each state. The slope of the insurance-budget line between points P and S understates the probability of future A, which is equivalent to requiring a sacrifice of more than $0.25 in wealth in future B for an increase of $0.75 in wealth in future A. Instead of remaining on indifference curve U_0 by switching from risk prospect P to risk prospect S, Rebecca would maximize utility by choosing that risk prospect, T, identified by the tangency of the insurance-budget line to indifference curve U_0.

In light of this result, the student may better understand the trend in recent years for insurance companies to urge policyholders to buy enough fire insurance so that their homes could be completely restored in the event of fire. One does not advertise a product which people would buy anyway; our analysis indicates that the informed policyholder would be underinsured if premiums represented greater than actuarily fair rates. On the other hand, government programs designed to encourage urban renewal by subsidizing fire insurance premiums not only encourage excessive amounts of insurance in deteriorating neighborhoods, but often make buildings worth more after they have been gutted by fire. Ironically, and tragically, programs intended to encourage urban renewal create incentives for arson. The term **moral hazard** refers to the perverse incentives created by subsidized insurance; if persons are no worse off, or even better off, if avoidable catastrophes occur, those persons will not take steps needed to avoid accidents, and may even try to cause otherwise harmful events.

Gamblers and Risk Takers

In a classic article, Milton Friedman and L. J. Savage sought to explain behavior which appears to contradict the model of decisions under risk.[11] Why do many people purchase insurance policies to protect themselves against large losses, while at the same time wagering small amounts of money in gambles which might result in large winnings (with a small probability), even though these gambles have negative expected values? Friedman and Savage suggested that individual risk preferences may reflect risk aversion when great losses are contemplated, but that individuals may be risk takers when potential losses are small.

Variable risk preferences would cause "wavy" indifference curves like those in Figure 3-13. As in Figure 3-12, imagine that Rebecca Sunnybrook confronts risk prospect P, which promises \$10,000 in future A (with probability 0.25) and \$50,000 in future B (with probability 0.75). Note that indifference curve U_0 passes through point P, with expected value of \$40,000, and through point S on the certainty ray, identified by \$36,000 in either state. Rebecca's willingness to sacrifice up to \$4,000 (the risk premium) to equalize wealth prospects in the two futures re-

---

[11] Milton Friedman and L. J. Savage, "The Utility Analysis of Choices Involving Risk," *Journal of Political Economy* (August 1948), pp. 279–304.

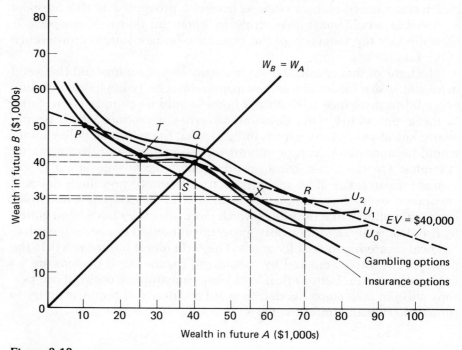

Figure 3-13
Gambling and Mixed Risk Preferences

flects risk aversion. As in Figure 3-12, Rebecca would purchase enough insurance to shift future prospects to point T. By reducing the variability of wealth prospects from \$10,000 and \$50,000 to \$25,000 and \$41,923, she also reduces her expected wealth to \$37,692. Moving from point P to point T involves paying a risk premium of \$2,307.70.

The striking difference between Figures 3-12 and 3-13 is the bowed-out shape of the indifference map along the certainty ray in Figure 3-13. Suppose that Rebecca were able to transfer all risk associated with point P to Bull Dozer. The option of moving from point P to point Q, which has the same expected wealth but zero variability of outcomes, would bring Rebecca to a *lower* indifference curve than incomplete insurance at actuarily unfair rates. Dare we let such a person run around loose?

To pose the question is to answer it; if behavior contradicts the assumption of risk aversion, it is the assumption, rather than the behavior that is deemed "wrong" by positive economics. Suppose Rebecca were initially endowed at point Q on the certainty line. Figure 3-13 is constructed so that indifference curve U_0 has the same slope as the budget line for actuarial insurance: $MRS = -(1 - \rho_B)/\rho_B$, since $MU_A = MU_B$

when $W_A = W_B$. (The assumption that $MU_A = MU_B$ when $W_A = W_B$ is equivalent to assuming that the probability mechanism which determines which outcome occurs provides neither utility nor disutility. For gambling this assumption need not be true; one may prefer playing poker and breaking even to not playing poker at all because the game itself is fun.) However, that indifference curve is bowed out at point Q; the marginal rate of substitution of W_B for W_A is increasing in the neighborhood of point Q. At point Q, Rebecca would be willing to trade increasing amounts of wealth in one state to increase wealth prospects in the future associated with the other state.

If Rebecca could get a gamble at "fair" odds—that is, so that the expected loss equals the expected gain (also called a zero sum game)—utility would be maximized at risk prospect R, where $W_A = \$70,000$ and $W_B = \$30,000$. For example, instead of buying \$40,000 worth of safe government bonds with the proceeds from the farm, Rebecca might invest \$10,000 in a wildcat oil-drilling venture with a 75 percent chance of failure (resulting in the loss of \$10,000) and a 25 percent chance of success (returning \$30,000). Stockbrokers and bookies must cover their costs just as insurance companies do; one rarely is presented with a "fair" gamble. In Figure 3-13, imagine that Rebecca receives the same terms as those for the insurance options line. Just as "unfair" insurance results in less insurance than "actuarily fair" insurance would for a risk averter,[12] a person with variable risk preferences will gamble less at

Business Illustration
Risk and the Professional Economist

How well might an economics major fare in the job market? The data in the accompanying tables present evidence from the 1980 salary survey reported by the National Association of Business Economists. Table 1 presents the distribution of earnings for all those reporting, uncorrected for such factors as type of job held, years of experience, or level of education. Table 2 reports the median and modal base salaries for different types of

jobs business economists do. Again, the data are uncorrected for other relevant factors.

Like the data for alternative careers in Table 3-5 (in the next section), these data reveal the role of risk (or luck) in the determination of earnings for economists. Table 2 contrasts the expected salaries for typical entry-level jobs (roughly the bottom five categories) and the types of jobs attained with experience. If nothing else,

---

[12] See Isaac Ehrlich and Gary S. Becker, "Market Insurance, Self-Insurance and Self Protection," *Journal of Political Economy* (July/August 1972), pp. 623–648.

TABLE 1
Percentage Distribution of Base Salary of Business Economists by Income Class

Base Salary	Respondents (%)
Under $25,000	12.2
$25,000–29,999	11.4
30,000–34,999	16.6
35,000–39,999	13.4
40,000–44,999	11.7
45,000–49,999	8.3
50,000–54,999	8.1
55,000–59,999	4.3
60,000–64,999	3.4
65,000–69,999	2.1
70,000–74,999	1.7
75,000–79,999	2.0
80,000–84,999	a
85,000–89,999	1.3
90,000 and over	2.8
Median	$38,000
Mode	$30,000
Interquartile range	$25,421–$51,111

a Distribution withheld.
Source: National Association of Business Economists, "Salary Characteristics, 1980."

these tables hint at the need to separate random influences (what economists usually mean by risk) from factors that can be controlled (e.g., hours worked, educational attainment, and years of experience).

Given adequate data, there are techniques for sorting the causes of predictable variation in economic phenomena; these techniques can be learned in courses in statistics, particularly in that branch of economics devoted to statistical analysis, econometrics. Economists who engage in empirical research are participating in a special type of risky decision making. Because of unavoidable errors of observation, measurement, data reporting, and interpretation of results, they can never be 100 percent certain that empirical data accurately depict real events. The best they can hope for is to minimize the cost of unavoidable error by following the rules of statistical inference.

TABLE 2
Compensation by Area of Responsibility

Title	No. Reporting	Median Base Salary	Modal Base Salary
General administration economist	153	$47,000	$50,000
Economic adviser	192	46,000	50,000
Research administration	96	43,250	30,000
Financial administration	67	42,000	25,000
General administration	63	40,000	30,000
Corporate planning	182	40,000	40,000
Economic analyst	275	33,000	50,000
Financial analyst	58	32,750	25,000
Marketing research	89	32,600	30,000
Teaching	93	30,000	30,000
Econometrician	30	29,400	30,000

Source: National Association of Business Economists, "Salary Characteristics, 1980."

An economist working for a large corporation, a large government agency, or some other powerful organization occasionally uncovers evidence that a prevailing practice is inefficient or counterproductive. Given the reluctance of those in authority to admit mistakes, it behooves the economist to behave in a risk averse manner, double-checking results before announcing or publishing them. This practice is formalized in the specification of a null hypothesis that the economist would accept if evidence in support of his or her own beliefs is unsubstantial. As a practical matter, a professional only contradicts the boss or client when the chance of being proved wrong (and getting a bad report) is less than, say, 5 percent.

Specifying a viable null hypothesis is also a type of "code of ethics" for the academic economist. When attacking an accepted theory, it is traditional to specify the "conventional wisdom" as the null hypothesis. Most journals publish "heresy" only if there is a good chance that it will later become accepted theory; no editor wants a reputation for accepting shoddy heresy. Thus, it is not really surprising that most empirical work published in professional journals supports the conventional wisdom; the risk of having an article rejected by a journal is smaller when the writer disproves someone else's heresy than when he or she attacks the sacred truths of colleagues.

It is often said that economics is not an exact science. Error and bias will influence any researcher; those who refuse to question accepted ideas practice dogmatism, not science. What is remarkable about research in economics is that recognition of the risk of being wrong stands at the very heart of the methods used. Following the rules of evidence laid down in econometric theory allows researchers to minimize their risk of being wrong. It also provides a basis for deciding when contrary or unpopular evidence is worth presenting.

unfair odds than at fair odds, *ceteris paribus*. In Figure 3-13, when presented with a gamble with a negative expected value, Rebecca wagers $8,077 hoping to win $15,000 if event A transpires.

To summarize, risk averse behavior implies a willingness to pay a risk premium to reduce the variability of prospective futures; this is equivalent to assuming that the marginal utility of wealth decreases as wealth increases. A person who will have $50,000 with a 75 percent probability and $10,000 with a probability of 25 percent, but who has wealth prospects of $41,923 and $25,000, respectively, is indicating that the marginal utility of an extra dollar in future B is less than that of an extra dollar in state A. However, a person who prefers variable outcomes to a "sure thing" is behaving as if the marginal utility of wealth increases as wealth increases. Figure 3-13 shows that the same person may exhibit both types of behavior; the ability of microeconomic theory to account for both risk aversion and risk taking is important, of course, because both types of behavior are, indeed, observed.

APPLICATION

The Economics of Education: Choosing a Career

In the previous sections, we have shown how the model of individual choice can be extended to account for behavior under risk: when the decision maker knows there are multiple possible outcomes to alternative courses of action and when the probabilities of outcomes are known, alternatives can be weighted according to their expected utility. A major complication is encountered when, as is usually the case, risk enters into the computation of expected utility; only for risk neutral individuals can the expected utility of alternatives be taken as proportional to the expected value (e.g., in terms of money) of risk prospects.

Consider Table 3-5, which gives the average present value and the standard deviation of the present value for alternative career choices in 1970. Note that occupations which have high present values tend also to have high standard deviations in present value.[13] This indicates a mild tendency toward risk aversion in occupational choice. However,

TABLE 3-5
Rankings of Eleven Occupations by Level and Variability of Earnings (1 = most preferred, 11 = least preferred)

	Present Value of Lifetime Earnings	
Census Occupational Title	*Mean (Rank)*	*Standard Deviation (Rank)*
Insurance agents	$136,516 (1)	$55,089 (11)
Engineers, mechanical	124,447 (2)	18,056 (1)
Bank, financial managers	123,641 (3)	29,776 (7)
Sales representatives, wholesale	121,264 (4)	48,093 (9)
Engineers, electrical	121,244 (5)	25,009 (5)
Accountants	112,788 (6)	23,530 (3)
Foremen	112,677 (7)	24,245 (4)
Sales representatives, manufacturing	110,656 (8)	49,073 (10)
Personnel, labor relations	95,757 (9)	38,482 (8)
Secondary-school teachers	80,491 (10)	25,630 (6)
Elementary-school teachers	72,801 (11)	20,935 (2)

Source: Richard Evans and Robert Weinstein, "Ranking Occupations as Risky Income Prospects," *Industrial and Labor Relations Review* (January 1982), pp. 252–259.

---

[13] The correlation between mean present value and standard deviation is +0.17, which is significant at the 0.16 level; that is, the chance that there is no relation is only 16 percent (Evans and Weinstein, "Ranking Occupations," p. 253).

because other factors are not taken into account in Table 3-5, such evidence must be considered with some skepticism.

While the data in Table 3-5 are adjusted for age differences for workers in 1970 (the purpose of calculating present value), there were a number of factors which could not be easily controlled. For instance, it is entirely likely that individual income differences will reflect personal preferences for income or leisure; an insurance salesperson who works 50 hours per week will tend to have higher income than one who works 40 hours. Moreover, engineers and accountants with master's degrees will usually earn higher salaries than those with only a bachelor's degree, but they will also have sacrificed income or leisure to achieve their higher education. Table 3-5 adjusts for income differences, but does not pick up the impact of education "financed" out of leisure. Nevertheless, the table does indicate that to pick a career on the basis of average or expected earnings alone is to overlook the importance of risk in determining the variability of earnings.

HIGHLIGHTS

1. The theory of consumer choice developed in chapter two is expanded by relaxing the following assumptions:
   a. Money income is fixed.
   b. All current income is spent.
   c. Consumers have perfect information about the consequences of their decisions.

2. The household maximizes utility with respect to income and leisure, $U = U(y, t_L)$. Utility is maximized when the marginal utility of leisure divided by the wage rate equals the marginal utility of income: $MU_L/w = MU_y$.

3. Assuming that leisure is a normal good, an increase in nonlabor income reduces the hours of work, *ceteris paribus*.

4. Because either income or leisure must be sacrificed to allocate time to education, the opportunity cost of educational time is the wage rate that could be earned. This explains why college enrollments tend to increase when the unemployment rate increases.

5. A change in the wage rate has an ambiguous effect on the consumption of leisure time. The substitution effect, due to a change in the price of leisure, tends to cause hours of leisure to decline as the wage rate increases. However, since wages are a major source of income, the income effect of a wage change tends to work in the opposite direction from the substitution effect.

6. The lack of work by welfare recipients is traceable to the high implicit tax rate of welfare programs, rather than to the tastes or characteristics of the recipients. To provide a work incentive, either welfare payments must be reduced substantially for those not working or benefits must be reduced by less than a dollar for each additional dollar of earnings.

7. Whether a cut in income tax rates increases hours worked and hence increases total taxes paid depends on the relative influence of income and substitution effects. Ironically, the more valuable government services are to workers, the less would be the offsetting income effect of a simultaneous tax-rate–expenditure cut.

8. The decision to consume more in the present reduces future planned consumption according to the following formula: $\Delta C_{t+1}/\Delta C_t = -(1 + r)$, where all terms are measured in

constant dollars. Utility is maximized when the marginal rate of substitution between present consumption and the prospect of future consumption equals the slope of the budget line, $-(1 + r)$, where r is the real rate of interest.

9. Whether a household saves or borrows depends in part on the relative size of present income and expected future income, as well as on the marginal rate of substitution between C_{t+1} and C_t.

10. Consumption will change by a larger percentage when income changes are permanent than when they are expected to be transitory, *ceteris paribus.*

11. The tangency between indifference curves for present and future consumption and the budget line for consumption over time establishes an objective basis for discounting future income prospects to their present value.

12. The optimal investment in education can be defined as that amount for which the present cost of education equals the present value of future benefits (both monetary and nonmonetary) attributed to that extra education.

13. The model of decision making under certainty really amounts to assuming:
    a. Each alternative action only has one outcome.
    b. The decision maker has accurate information about which actions lead to which outcomes.

14. Risk is a state of affairs when there are multiple possible outcomes to alternative actions and the individual knows the probability of each outcome before the decision is made. By contrast, uncertainty exists when the probability of outcomes is not known. The practical distinction between these two situations is that the researcher assumes that the decision maker is using the same probability numbers as the researcher to evaluate the expected utility of risk prospects. This allows the observer to infer the risk preferences of the observed. Under uncertainty, the observer may think an option has one expected

value while the decision maker has calculated another.

15. The expected value of a risky prospect is determined by multiplying each outcome by its probability, then summing.

16. Economists have gained insights into criminal behavior by assuming that criminal acts are predictable responses to incentives.

17. Risk preferences are revealed by how and which risky prospects are chosen, assuming accurate information about the expected value and standard deviation associated with risky prospects:
    a. A risk neutral person ranks prospects only by their expected values.
    b. A risk averter ranks prospects with equal expected values in reverse order of their standard deviations.
    c. A risk lover ranks prospects with equal expected values in order of their standard deviations.

18. Households of risk averse members increase utility by transferring wealth from the "good" state to the "bad" state until the rate at which wealth can be transferred is equal to the weighted marginal utility for wealth in the two states, where the weights equal the probability of each state.

19. When risk averters purchase insurance at rates exceeding actuarily fair values (due to the loading factor), wealth will not be equalized in the "good" and the "bad" future.

20. Risk averters behave as if the marginal utility of wealth were a decreasing function of wealth; risk lovers behave as if the marginal utility of wealth increased as wealth increased. That some people insure against major calamities but wager small amounts of money at unfair odds is explained by "wavy" (mixed bowed-out and bowed-in) indifference curves.

21. Individuals tend to choose careers on the basis of expected earnings and the standard deviation of earnings. Some tendency toward risk aversion is indicated by the positive relationship between the expected earnings of careers and the standard deviation of earnings.

GLOSSARY

Certainty A decision environment in which each option has only one possible outcome (complete control) and the relationship between alternatives and outcomes is accurately understood (complete information).

Expected utility In a risky environment, the sum of the utility from the prospect of each outcome times the probability of that outcome. A risk neutral person's expected utility from a risky alternative is proportional to the expected value of that alternative.

Expected value The weighted average value—usually in money terms—of outcomes for a risky prospect, where weights are the objective (i.e., actuarial) probabilities of those outcomes. Also called the certainty equivalent.

Hicks approach An approach, named for British economist Sir John Hicks, that holds real income constant by restricting consumer choice to the same indifference curve before and after a relative price change. Contrast **Slutsky approach**.

Loading factor The difference between the expected payoff and the premium paid for an insurance policy. The loading factor covers the insurance company's costs over and above paying claims, and represents the risk premium paid by a knowledgeable risk averter in order to avoid risk.

Means test A feature of many transfer programs for the poor, which requires that the transfer recipient prove need. Because evidence of increased earnings would reduce the recipient's need, programs with a means test tend to lack a work incentive.

Moral hazard The problem which develops when, fully insured against undesirable events, people become indifferent to whether those events occur and lose their incentive to take precautions.

Negative income tax A proposed welfare reform in which transfer recipients are allowed to keep a portion of their transfers as they earn income. To encourage welfare recipients to work, either (1) benefits must be placed considerably below the poverty level so that cutting off benefits at the poverty level does not constitute a high marginal tax rate or (2) families must continue to receive benefits after their total income (earnings plus transfers) exceeds the poverty level.

Permanent income Income, expressed in annual or monthly terms, which is expected to continue indefinitely.

Present value The amount of money in the present which would provide the same utility as the prospect of income or wealth in the future. When utility is maximized by allocating consumption over time, the present value of \$1, n years in the future, is $1/(1 + r)^n$, where r is the rate of interest.

Real rate of interest The nominal rate of interest minus the rate of change in prices.

Risk A decision environment in which some alternatives have multiple possible, but mutually exclusive, outcomes (i.e, the individual has incomplete control) and the individual has complete information, that is, accurate knowledge of the probabilities of outcomes prior to the decision.

Risk averter A decision maker for whom expected utility increases with the expected value of a risky prospect, but decreases with the variance, or expected deviation, of outcomes. A risk averter is willing to pay a risk premium to reduce the variability of possible outcomes.

Risk lover A decision maker for whom the expected utility of a risky prospect increases with the expected value and with the expected deviation. A risk lover, or risk taker, is willing to pay a risk premium for the opportunity to assume risk (and possibly obtain a higher reward).

Risk neutral A preference by which risky prospects are ranked strictly according to their expected values, without regard to the variability of outcomes.

Risk premium The difference between the expected value of a risky prospect and what a person pays for that prospect. Risk averters pay risk premiums to reduce the variability of outcomes; risk lovers pay risk premiums to increase the variability of outcomes.

Slutsky approach An approach, named for Russian economist Eugene Slutsky, that defines constant real income as the ability to purchase the same bundle of commodities before and after a relative price change.

Transitory income The opposite of permanent income; a temporary gain or loss of income which has a smaller impact on household consumption than an equal change in permanent income.

Uncertainty A decision environment in which some alternatives have multiple possible outcomes (i.e., incomplete control) and the decision maker is either ignorant of the probability distribution or has inaccurate information about probability (i.e., incomplete information).

SUGGESTED READINGS

Becker, Gary S. *The Economic Approach to Human Behavior.* Chicago: University of Chicago Press, 1975, readings 1, 4, 5, 6.

Ehrlich, Isaac. "Participation in Illegal Activities: A Theoretical and Empirical Investigation." *Journal of Political Economy* (July/August, 1972). pp. 521–564.

——— and Gary S. Becker. "Market Insurance, Self-Insurance and Self-Protection." *Journal of Political Economy* (June 1975).

Evans, Richard, and Robert Weinstein. "Ranking Occupations as Risky Income Prospects." *Industrial and Labor Relations Review* (January 1982), pp. 252–259.

Friedman, Milton. *A Theory of the Consumption Function.* Princeton, N.J.: Princeton University Press, 1957.

——— and L. J. Savage. "The Utility Analysis of Choices Involving Risk." *Journal of Political Economy* (August 1948).

Hellman, Daryl A. *The Economics of Crime.* New York: St. Martin's Press, 1980.

Pechman, Joseph and P. Michael Timpane (eds.). *Work Incentives and Income Guarantees: The New Jersey Negative Income Tax Experiment.* Washington, D.C.: Brookings Institution, 1975.

Tussing, A. Dale. *Poverty and the Dual Economy.* New York: St. Martin's Press, 1975.

Wolfson, Robert J. and Thomas M. Carroll. "Ignorance, Error and Information in the Classic Theory of Decision." *Behavioral Science* (March 1976), pp. 107–115.

EXERCISES

Evaluate

Indicate whether each statement is true (agrees with economic theory), false (is contradicted by theory), or uncertain (could be true or false, given additional information). Briefly explain your answer.

1. Employers who pay higher wages for overtime work than for the first 40 hours of work per week are trying to encourage the income effect of a higher wage rate over the substitution effect.

2. A rise in one spouse's earnings will tend to reduce the amount of time the other spouse works outside the home, *ceteris paribus.*

3. Compared to wage earners, welfare recipients reveal a pronounced preference for leisure instead of income.

4. High interest rates during periods of inflation do not seem to discourage present consumption very much. Therefore, inflation must change consumer tastes for present, as opposed to future, consumption.

5. As long as people prefer present consumption to future consumption, no one would save at a zero real rate of interest.

6. An increase in the interest rate will increase the planned future consumption for a saver, but may not increase the proportion of current income saved.

7. A risk lover always prefers a gamble to a sure thing.

8. When people buy accident insurance, they are betting the insurance carrier that they will have an accident. Hence, buying insurance indicates a taste for risk.

9. That exconvicts are prone to commit more crimes after getting out of prison contradicts the economic theory of choice under risk.

10. If crimes were punished by fines instead of imprisonment, the average legal incomes of law breakers would increase.

Calculate

Answer each of the following, showing all your work.

11. An individual who owns a $60,000 house calculates that there is a 1 percent chance that the house will be destroyed by fire within a year.
    a. What would be the maximum insurance premium a risk neutral person would pay for a policy which paid $60,000 in the event the house was destroyed? Assume claims are limited to one per year.
    b. What is the minimum premium payment a risk averse person would be willing to pay?
    c. What would you infer if the homeowner paid $750 for the policy?
    d. Suppose that the government allows fire insurance premiums to be deducted from taxable income. How do your answers to parts (a) and (b) of this question change if the homeowner is in a 25 percent tax bracket? if the homeowner is in a 40 percent tax bracket?

12. For each of the following combinations of current income (Y_0), expected future income (Y_1), and interest rate (r), draw a budget line for present and future consumption possibilities. On each diagram, identify the balanced budget point $(Y_t = C_t)$ and the equal consumption point $(C_{t+1} = C_t)$.
    a. $Y_0 = \$20,000$, $Y_1 = \$20,000$, $r = 10$ percent
    b. $Y_0 = \$15,000$, $Y_1 = \$25,000$, $r = 10$ percent
    c. $Y_0 = \$40,000$, $Y_1 = 0$, $r = 10$ percent
    d. $Y_0 = 0$, $Y_1 = \$40,000$, $r = 10$ percent
    e. $Y_0 = \$10,000$, $Y_1 = \$30,000$, r_s (for saving) $= 8$ percent, r_b (for borrowing) $= 16$ percent.

Contemplate

Answer each of the following questions in a brief but complete essay.

13. On the eve of election day, candidate X promises a welfare reform program designed to: (a) guarantee that each family receives a total income (earnings plus transfers) equal to or greater than the officially designated poverty level; (b) guarantee that only the deserving poor receive benefits; and (c) assure that every able-bodied adult will get off welfare and work. Imagine that you are a speechwriter for this politician's opponent, candidate Y. Write a brief statement for the press explaining why candidate X is unfit for office. Make sure you explain in terms easily understood by noneconomists.

14. Explain how the labor-leisure choice can cause individuals to offer fewer hours of work at high wage rates rather than at lower ones. Is such a phenomenon likely to create greater supply problems in a licensed profession such as medicine or in an unlicensed profession such as economics? Explain.

15. If the government wanted to increase the number of hours worked by the typical blue-collar worker, would it be more effective to cut income tax rates or to cut the payroll tax for social security (assuming an equal percent reduction)? Would it be more effective to increase, decrease, or maintain promised social security payments for future retirees? Explain.

Chapter 4

Household Demand and Market Demand

Chapter four is the culmination of our discussion of consumer behavior. We begin by showing how market demand is generated by the independent behavior of many price-taking households. The household demand curve is developed from the price-consumption curve, showing budget-line/indifference-curve tangencies for a given set of tastes, money income, and prices of other goods. The distinction between a change in quantity demanded, which occurs when the price of a good changes, and a change in **demand**, which results from a change in income, tastes, or the prices of other goods, is carefully investigated.

The process of deriving market demand from the summation of quantities demanded for all households at each possible market price is shown to depend upon the exclusivity of consumption and the homogeneity of the product. How the law of large numbers allows economics to avoid irrelevant complications of the aggregation process is also discussed.

The nature of price elasticity of demand is explored at length. Confusion between the law of demand and the impact of a change in price on expenditure (revenue) is avoided by measuring elasticity—the percentage change in quantity due to a 1 percent increase in price, *ceteris paribus*. The two methods of measuring the sensitivity of quantity demanded to price—point elasticity and arc elasticity—are also discussed.

The chapter concludes by contrasting *ceteris paribus* demand curves, which allow price to influence quantity without other variables changing, with *mutatis mutandis* demand curves, which result when a price change causes other variables to change. *Mutatis mutandis* demand curves occur because of predictable income effects; the use of price as a quality proxy; bandwagon, snob, and Veblen effects; and speculative effects of changes in expectations.

From Utility Maximization to Household Demand

While economic theory builds its analysis of consumer behavior on the model of utility maximization, the more relevant concern of the business operation is consumer demand. Sellers want to determine how much of an item households will actually purchase at different prices, or, what amounts to the same thing, what the market clearing price is for various rates of sales. *Consumer demand* relates the quantity of a commodity which consumers would attempt to purchase to each conceivable market price, other factors (prices of substitute and complementary goods, income, and tastes) being held constant. The *demand curve* is a two-dimensional diagram which relates quantity demanded to price, other factors being constant.

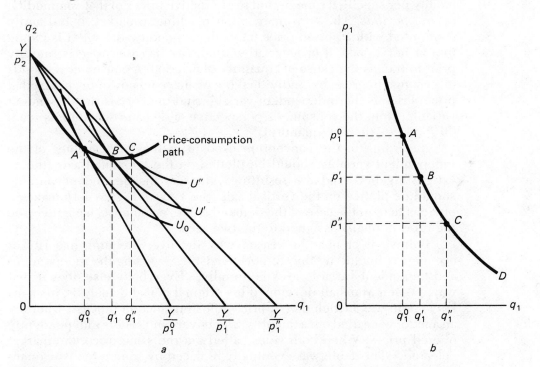

Figure 4-1
Data from the Price Consumption Path (*a*) Are Used to Plot the Household Demand Curve (*b*).

In Figure 4-1*a*, we see the various combinations of good 1 and good 2 which would maximize utility for various budgets, each budget line identified by a different price for good 1, with the price of good 2, the level of money income (Y), and the indifference map (representing consumer tastes) remaining unchanged. The locus of equilibrium points traced in Figure 4-1*a* is appropriately dubbed the **price-consumption path**. Except in the incredibly unlikely case of a Giffen good, a price-consumption path will associate higher levels of q_1 with lower values of p_1. As the budget lines fan out along the q_1 axis (depicting declining values of p_1), q_1 increases.

We saw in chapter two that plotting optimal consumption levels against the associated money income levels given by an income-consumption path gave rise to an Engel curve. We can also visualize an important relationship by plotting optimal consumption levels obtained from a price-consumption path against the associated values of the commodity's price. If we followed the precedent of the Engel curve and named such a diagram for its originator, Figure 4-1*b* would be called a Marshall curve, in honor of Alfred Marshall. However, it is known by a more familiar name—the **demand curve**.

A demand curve is a diagram relating intended purchases of a commodity per specified time period to alternative prices of that commodity, *ceteris paribus*. The consumer, upon reaching a market, is ordinarily confronted with a posted price for each commodity; the seller is giving him or her a "take it or leave it" option. In this case, price is causally prior to (i.e., is the cause of) quantity demanded. A consumer responds to a change in price, but individual buyers have no power to change that price. Price is the independent variable and quantity is the dependent variable; from the consumer's perspective, a demand schedule is read: "if P (price), then Q (quantity)."

According to the convention used in mathematics, values of the independent variable should be plotted on the horizontal axis (the X-axis in algebra), and the resulting values of the dependent variable should be plotted on the vertical axis (the Y-axis). Figure 4-1*b* makes it obvious that, in the case of the demand curve, economists have reversed the roles normally assigned to the two axes.

Believe it or not, the reason why the overwhelming majority of economists (including this author) persist in reversing the independent and dependent variable axes is literally, "Everybody else does it that way." When Marshall developed his original demand analysis, his market system was modeled on a price-adjusting auction process, whereby an auctioneer called out a quantity, and buyers and sellers independently offered prices. When both sides called out the same price, the market "cleared." This fable was eventually replaced by a more realistic quantity adjustment model (to be discussed in chapter nine). Nevertheless, the Marshallian demand curve, with price on the vertical axis, became a fixture of textbooks. After Marshall's *Principles* had served more than a generation of economists, no one dared produce a microeconomics text with mathematically correct demand curve diagrams, lest students and especially professors be confused by their unconventional appearance.

After the fact, we can justify, or rationalize, the conventional demand curve model since, when dealing with imperfectly competitive firms, it will be convenient to think of the firm's output as "finding its own (market clearing price) level." In that case, it will be correct to consider quantity as the determinant of average revenue (i.e., price).

Because of the transposition of the axes, the consumer demand curve is read by finding the prevailing price on the vertical axis, following the horizontal line at that price to the demand curve, then dropping a perpendicular line to the horizontal axis to find the resulting quantity. The rectangle formed when reading a demand curve (e.g., $p_1^0 A q_1^0 0$, $p_1' B q_1' 0$, $P_1'' C q_1'' 0$ in Figure 4-1b) will form the basis of another important analytical technique discussed later in this chapter.

The slope of the demand curve, $\Delta q_1 / \Delta p_1$ = change in quantity/change in price, is the ratio of the "run" to the "rise," that is, the reciprocal of the conventional measure of slope. Luckily, the most important characteristic of the demand curve, namely, the inverse relationship between quantity and price, is displayed by a *negatively sloped* demand curve regardless of how the variables are situated on the two axes. The **law of demand** states that *price and quantity demanded always change in opposite directions*, other factors being constant.

Changes in Other Variables

The law of demand does not say that price is the only influence on consumer willingness to purchase a particular commodity. We have already seen in chapter two that changes in income, prices of other goods, and even tastes can also influence the amount of a commodity a household is willing to purchase. What the law of demand does require is that changes in other variables do not change the inverse relationship between the price of a commodity and the quantity consumers are willing to purchase.[1]

---

[1] A multivariable demand function is expressed in mathematical form as: $q_1^D = f(p_1, p_2, \ldots, p_n, M, \alpha)$, where q_1^D is the amount of good 1 consumers wish to buy (per unit of time), p_1 is the price of good 1, P_2 through P_n are the prices of other goods, M is money income (for the same time period), and α is some proxy for tastes or other influences, such as expectations. The total change in q_1^D is:

$$dq_1^D = \frac{\partial q_1}{\partial p_1}(dp_1) + \frac{\partial q_1}{\partial p_2}(dP_2) + \ldots + \frac{\partial q_1}{\partial p_n}(dP_n) + \frac{\partial q_1}{\partial M}(dM) + \frac{\partial q_1}{\partial \alpha}(d\alpha)$$

The law of demand requires that whatever happens to the values of P_2 through p_n, M, or α, $\partial q_1 / \partial p_1$ always remains negative, even if the observed change in q_1 happens to be in the same direction as the observed change in p_1 because the net effect of other variables masked the relationship between price and quantity demanded.

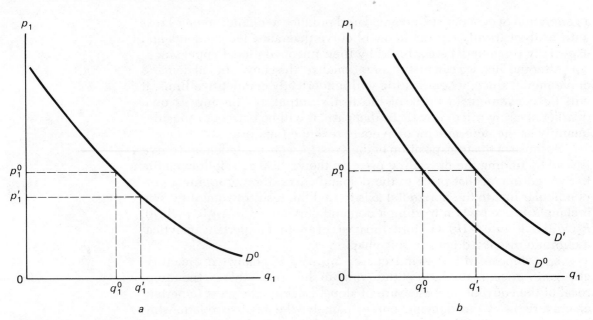

Figure 4-2
Change in Quantity Demanded (*a*) and Change in Demand (*b*)

The convention in economics is to distinguish between a **change in quantity demanded** and a **change in demand**. Since a demand curve reflects an entire set of different quantities a household would attempt to purchase at different prices, a change in price alone would merely relocate the relevant point along a demand curve. The change in price (the cause) selects a different quantity (the effect) without changing the relationship between them. This change in quantity demanded is depicted in Figure 4-2*a*.

A change in demand is shown in Figure 4-2*b*. Although the price remains at p_1^0, the amount of good 1 demanded increases from q_1^0 to q_1'. Obviously, a price change was not responsible for this change in consumer behavior; something else must have altered the relationship between p_1 and q_1. Rather than a violation of the law of demand, an observed increase in the quantity of good 1 purchased in the absence of an observed decrease in its price would indicate a violation of the **ceteris paribus** assumptions.

Any number of events could have changed the demand for good 1, which is shown in Figure 4-2*b* as a displacement of D° to D'. The price of a substitute good may have increased; for example, an observed increase in chicken purchases might stem from an increase in the price of beef.[2] The price of a complementary good may have decreased; since people usually consume hamburgers and buns together, a decrease in the price of ground beef would not only increase the consumption of ground beef itself, but would also increase the number of hamburger buns purchased. An increase in income will increase demand for a normal good; for inferior goods, demand will increase if income decreases. Finally, a change in a measurable proxy for tastes (e.g., education, average local temperature, age, or number of children) might correspond to an increase in the demand for a product.

A decrease in demand (an inward or downward shift of the demand curve) would result from changes in other variables in the opposite direction to those cited above: a decrease in the price of a substitute, an increase in the price of a complement, an income decrease for normal goods or an income increase for inferior goods, or a change in proxy for taste, indicating decreased demand. But regardless of whether a demand curve shifts outward or inward, once a change in demand has taken place, a consumer will respond to price increases by reducing consumption along the new demand curve; or when the price falls, consumption will increase along the new demand curve.

Market Demand

Just as sellers are more interested in household demand than in the process of utility maximization per se, they are generally more concerned with the total amount of their product they can sell at various market prices than with the amount sold to a particular household. The **market demand** for a commodity relates the total amount of a product all consumers are willing and able to buy at various prices (per time period), *ceteris paribus*. The simplest method for deriving market demand is by the *horizontal summation* of household demand curves, that is, adding up the amount each household wishes to purchase at each price. However, for the horizontal summation of household demand curves to be realistic, certain simplifying (pedagogical) assumptions should be made explicit.

First, we assume that the commodity in question is a **pure private good**, meaning that all benefits and costs associated with consumption are experienced solely by the household which makes the purchase.

---

[2] Good j is a *substitute* for commodity i if the consumption of good i varies in the same direction as the price of good j; that is, $\partial q_i/\partial p_j > 0$. On the other hand, if $\partial q_i/\partial p_j < 0$, good j is a *complement* of good i. The chain rule will provide a logical insight that should make this distinction easier to understand: $\partial q_i/\partial p_j = (\partial q_i/\partial q_j)(\partial q_j/\partial p_j)$. The law of demand assures us that $\partial q_j/\partial p_j < 0$, for all commodities. Hence, if people tend to consume good i *instead* of good j, $\partial q_i/\partial q_j < 0$, so $\partial q_i/\partial P_j > 0$. If goods i and j are consumed together, $\partial q_i/\partial q_j > 0$, so that $\partial q_i/\partial p_j < 0$.

Only when a commodity is a pure private good can we be assured that a household reveals its true preferences regarding that item. If a family is able to enjoy benefits from someone else's purchases, the household demand curve may understate that family's true preferences. But, for pure private goods, the purchase of a commodity by one household reduces the amount of that commodity available to other households. The problems of measuring demand for public goods are discussed in chapter fifteen.

Second, we assume that the product is homogeneous in the minds of consumers, so that they distinguish among sellers solely on the basis of the price charged. This assumption of perfect price competition, which also depends on the next assumption, assures us that only one market price will prevail at any particular time.

Third, we assume that consumers have accurate knowledge of product quality and price. This allows us to avoid for the present the complications of consumer search and also to postpone consideration of changes in consumer attitudes about product quality in the wake of a price change.

Figure 4-3 shows the process of demand aggregation. The subscript on q now identifies the household consuming the commodity, rather than the commodity itself. In the market demand diagram, Q refers to *total quantity demanded*[3] at each price, and *ut* means "per unit of time," to emphasize that market demand, like household demand and consumption activity, is a *flow* concept. (A *flow* concept can only be understood in the context of a stated or implied period of time. To learn that a person consumed fifty hot dogs does not mean much until we are told whether those hot dogs were consumed during one meal, one month, one year, or one lifetime.) To obtain the market demand curve, we add the quantity demanded by each household at each price. If the market price is p^0, the quantity demanded is registered as: $Q^0 = q_1^0 + q_2^0 + \ldots + q_n^0$; when the market price is p', $Q' = q_1' + q_2' + \ldots + q_n'$. Obviously, if all households (or even most) have negatively sloped demand curves, the market demand curve will also be negatively sloped.[4]

Once we have aggregated household demand curves to obtain the market demand curve, we must carefully distinguish between events which cause the market demand curve to *shift* (a change in demand) and changes in market price, which move the relevant point from one location

---

[3] That is, $Q = \sum_{i=1}^{i=n} q_i$.

[4] In his classic article "Irrational Behavior and Economic Theory" (*The Economic Approach to Human Behavior* [Chicago: University of Chicago Press, 1975]), Gary S. Becker shows that negatively sloped demand curves do not necessarily imply that each consumer is a utility maximizer, and in fact might still result if all households were irrational! An example of how random consumer behavior leads to an inverse relationship between total quantity demanded and price was explored in the business illustration in chapter two.

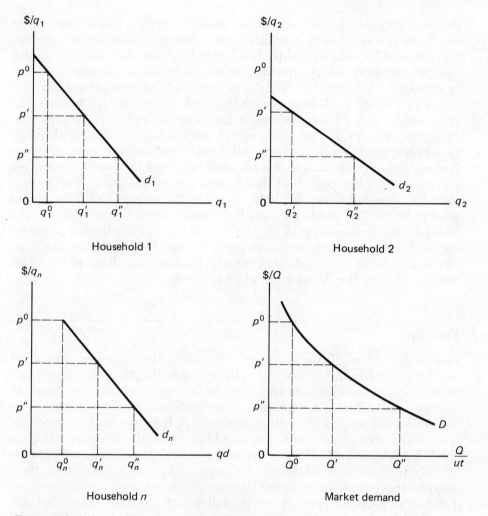

Figure 4-3
The Aggregation of Household Demand into Market Demand

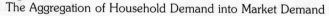

to another along a stationary demand curve. Since market demand is generated by the aggregation of household demand, it follows that a shift in the market demand curve would occur only if household demand curves shifted or if there was a change in the *number* of household demand curves (e.g., population growth or the introduction of a product into a new area). Furthermore, only those events which cause a significant number of households to change their behavior in the same manner are likely to have a noticeable impact on the position of the market demand curve. For instance, an individual household's demand curve may shift because an illness reduces that family's income and hence its demand for normal goods. However, another family's chief wage-earner may have just recovered from an illness, increasing that family's income and demand for normal goods. The law of large numbers assures us that random variations which affect individual elements of a population (often in different ways) tend to cancel out through the aggregation process.

Thus, when analyzing market demand, we generally concern ourselves only with changes in important variables and with average consumption patterns. For instance, most households that consume alcoholic beverages would consider beer and wine as *substitutes*, even though a few nonconformists may thrive on wine followed by a beer chaser. We can be reasonably confident that a decrease in the price of wine will shift the demand curve for beer closer to the origin. Similarly, steaks tend to be normal goods for most households, even though a few of the conspicuously affluent may be in the process of substituting pheasant for beef, or sparrow tongue for pheasant. We may be reasonably confident that a growth in per capita income will increase the demand for steak, while reducing the demand for chicken necks.

Price Elasticity of Demand

One of the causes of confusion and skepticism about the law of demand on the part of both buyers and sellers is that they tend to mistakenly infer that a *change in quantity demanded* is equivalent to a change in money expenditure. Expenditures or receipts provide convenient media for record keeping, both written and mental, because market prices are a natural common denominator for adding up and comparing all commodities bought and sold in a market economy. Household budgets are usually records of expenditures for major categories such as rent, food, and transportation, rather than elaborate enumerations of square feet per person, pounds of hamburger, or gallons of gasoline consumed per month. A business income statement contains a simple line item for total revenue; exhaustive inventories of the rate of turnover of individual items can rarely be remembered except by the computer.

But the law of demand does not imply a universal relationship between a change in the price of a commodity and expenditure on that item. Total expenditure (TE = \$/period of time) for a commodity is equal to the product of price (p = \$/unit) and quantity bought (Q = units/period of time); that is, $TE = p \cdot Q$. An increase in price causes a decrease in quantity; a decrease in price causes an increase in quantity, *ceteris paribus*. The net effect of a change in price on total consumer expenditure (which is definitionally equivalent to total seller revenue) depends upon the strength of the quantity response to the price change.

The law of demand guarantees that, along a given demand curve, the percentage change in expenditure can never be as great as the percentage change in price when price and expenditure change in the same direction. It is natural to expect an increase in price to increase expenditure, since consumers spend more on each unit they continue to purchase. However, consumers purchase fewer units of a commodity when its price rises. Therefore, whether price and expenditure change in the same direction depends upon the strength of the quantity response to a price change. We say that demand is *price elastic* if the quantity response to a price change is so strong that *total expenditure* moves in the *same direction* as the change in *quantity* or (equivalently) in the *opposite direction* from the change in *price*. A seller who raises the price of his merchandise 10 percent will receive 10 percent more revenue for each item he continues to sell. However, if he sells 20 percent *less* because of the 10 percent price increase, his total revenue actually falls by 10 percent. The quantity response was so strong that the quantity change turned the expenditure change around.

Demand is *price inelastic* if the quantity response to a price change is too weak to overturn the tendency of expenditure to move in the same direction as price. If a seller raises the price of an item by 10 percent and the quantity sold falls by only 5 percent, total revenue will increase by 5 percent. In the case of inelastic demand, the quantity response can only reduce the magnitude of an expenditure change; *total expenditure* will change in the *same direction* as *price*.

Suppose that the quantity response was of exactly the same magnitude as the price change (although, obviously, the two variables would change in opposite directions)—for every 1 percent increase in price, quantity would fall by 1 percent; for every 1 percent decrease in price, quantity would rise by 1 percent. The counteracting influences on total expenditure would be exactly balanced; thus total expenditure would not change. Because these offsetting effects occur when the *percentage change in quantity equals the percentage change in price*, we call this intermediate, or dividing, case *unitary elastic* demand.

It is difficult to overemphasize the importance of price elasticity in applying economic theory to real-world events. A seller who uses a 10 percent markup is acting *as if* there were more consumer resistance to price increases than a seller who uses a 100 percent markup. By calculating price elasticity for the two sellers, an economist could advise them on whether their markup formulas were appropriate for their markets. When an airline charges business people higher ticket prices than it charges students, it is charging higher prices to buyers whose expense accounts make their demand relatively price inelastic, and lower prices to those buyers most sensitive to high airline fares. The frustration voiced by farmers whose prices tend to fall drastically in years with bumper crops is understandable, but falling farm prices can be explained by the inelastic demand for agricultural products. The Organization of Petroleum Exporting Countries (OPEC) learned in the early 1970s that revenues could be increased dramatically by raising the price of petroleum exports: world demand for oil was price inelastic. The early 1980s confronted OPEC with an oil glut and price cutting by individual members of the cartel. Although the world demand for oil may still be relatively inelastic (but not as price inelastic as in the early 1970s), the demand for the oil produced by one country is highly price elastic if price is cut below the official OPEC price.

Given the critical importance of elasticity, it is worthwhile spending additional time learning the concept thoroughly now, lessening the chance that confusion will occur later. In Figure 4-4, a price of p_0 results in quantity demanded of Q_0; total expenditure is given by the rectangle $p_0 A Q_0 0$. (Remember from geometry that the area of a rectangle [a right-angled quadrilateral] is given by the length [here, height on the price axis] times the width [quantity].) A decrease in price from p_0 to p_1 increases quantity demanded to Q_1, so that total expenditure changes to $p_1 B Q_1 0$. Unlike the inverse relationship between price and quantity, the relationship between the price and the total expenditure rectangle it generates is not obvious. Some way must be found to determine which rectangle has the larger area.

Notice that the two rectangles have a large area in common; $p_1 C Q_0 0$ represents the invariant revenue for the seller. When the price falls, consumers who purchased Q_0 units at the higher price continue to buy *at least* that much, only now the first Q_0 units can be purchased for p_1 instead of p_0. The net effect of the price decrease on revenue now merely requires comparing the relative sizes of the two "slivers" outside the larger (common) rectangle. The rectangle $Q_1 B C Q_0 = p_1(Q_1 - Q_0) = p_1(\Delta Q)$ represents the gross increase in revenue since additional units are sold at the lower price. The rectangle $P_1 P_0 A C = Q_0(p_0 - p_1) = Q_0(-\Delta p)$ reflects the decline in revenue for the first Q_0 units sold.[5] That is, algebraically:

$$\Delta TE = p_1(\Delta Q) - Q_0(-\Delta p) = p_1(\Delta Q) + Q_0(\Delta p)$$

We wish to find the ratio of the change in total expenditure to the change in price. A positive ratio means total expenditure moves in the same direction as price; a negative ratio means the two change in opposite directions. Dividing ΔTE by ΔP, we obtain:

$$\frac{\Delta TE}{\Delta p} = p_1\left(\frac{\Delta Q}{\Delta p}\right) + Q_0 = Q_0 + p_1\left(\frac{\Delta Q}{\Delta p}\right)$$

By factoring out the Q_0 term, we discover:

$$\frac{\Delta TE}{\Delta p} = Q_0\left[1 + \left(\frac{p_1}{Q_0}\right)\left(\frac{\Delta Q}{\Delta p}\right)\right] = Q_0\left(1 + \frac{\Delta Q/Q_0}{\Delta p/p_1}\right)$$

---

[5] Note that the price change is from p_0 to p_1, which is negative. Since conventional geometry does not easily handle "negative area," the minus sign in front of ΔP allows us to define the area of rectangle $p_1 p_0 A C$ as a positive number.

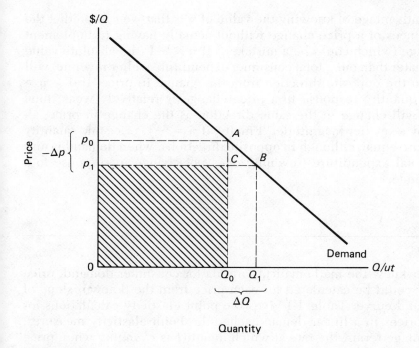

Figure 4-4
Graphical Interpretation of Price and Expenditure Relationship

If we ignore the subscripts on price and quantity, the last term inside the parentheses is the *percentage change in quantity divided by the percentage change in price.* This formula for the **price elasticity of demand** is algebraically equivalent to the inverse slope of the demand curve ($\Delta Q/\Delta p$) times the ratio of price to quantity (p/Q):

$$\eta = \frac{\Delta Q/Q}{\Delta p/p} = \left(\frac{\Delta Q}{\Delta p}\right)\left(\frac{p}{Q}\right)$$

The Greek letter "eta" (η) is used to designate the *point elasticity formula,* which economists use when the demand equation is known. From the law of demand, we know that $\Delta Q/\Delta p < 0$ (*ceteris paribus*). Since $p/Q > 0$, it follows that η will always be a negative number.[6]

---

[6] Instructors of microeconomics are divided about whether elasticity should be defined as a negative number (as is done here) or as a positive number (the approach used in most principles of economics texts). There is an initial pedagogical advantage in the latter method, since students seem to remember "elastic demand is bigger than one" more easily than "demand is elastic when $\eta < -1$." The author feels that the modest benefit of easier memorization is more than offset by the contradiction of the law of demand implicit in defining elasticity of demand as a positive number. Once the point formula is *understood,* the student will have a much easier time coping with empirical estimates, in which demand elasticities are negative and supply elasticities are positive.

The advantage of knowing the value of η is that we can predict the consequences of a price change without actually having to implement that change (which could be a mistake).[7] If $\eta < -1$ (the absolute value of η is greater than one), total consumer expenditure (seller revenue) will change in the opposite direction from the change in price. If $0 > \eta > -1$, the quantity response to a price change is relatively weak; total revenue will change in the same direction as the change in price, although by a smaller magnitude.[8] Finally, if $\eta = -1$, price and quantity changes are equal, although in opposite directions; when demand is unit elastic, total expenditure (revenue) does not change in response to a price change.

APPLICATION
Measuring Point Elasticity

If a seller knew the mathematical formula for consumer demand, price elasticity could be calculated for each price from the (known) slope of the demand curve. Table 4-1 gives the point elasticity calculations for various prices in a linear demand schedule. **Point elasticity** measures, in percentage terms, the rate at which quantity is *changing* when price changes by 1 percent, other factors remaining constant. We can think of point elasticity as performing a function similar to that of an automobile speedometer; although a car's speed is calculated in miles per hour, a person does not have to drive at a constant speed for an entire hour to measure its velocity. Similarly, while price elasticity is calibrated as the ratio of the percentage change in quantity to the percentage change in price, we do not have to change price to measure what the quantity response would be.

The data in Table 4-1 were generated by using the formula $Q_D = 1100 - (100)p$. Although this formula is an expository invention designed

---

[7] Taking the derivative of pQ with respect to p:

$$\frac{d(PQ)}{dP} = Q + p\left(\frac{dQ}{dQ}\right) = Q\left[1 + \left(\frac{p}{Q}\right)\left(\frac{dQ}{dp}\right)\right] = Q(1 + \eta)$$

$$\frac{d(pQ)}{dp} \gtreqless 0 \text{ as } \eta \gtreqless -1$$

[8] The responsiveness of revenue to price is:

$$\frac{d(pQ)/pQ}{dp/p} = \frac{d(pQ)}{dQ} \times \frac{p}{pQ} = \frac{1}{Q}[Q(1 + \eta)] = 1 + \eta$$

The percentage change in revenue due to a 1 percent increase in price is simply one plus the elasticity of demand.

TABLE 4-1
Point Elasticity Measures for Demand Equation: $Q_D = 1100 - 100(p)$

Price (p)	Quantity Demanded (Q_D)	$\Delta Q_D/\Delta P$	Point Elasticity (η)	Total Revenue (Expenditure)
$11.00	0	−100	∞	0
10.00	100	−100	−10.00	$1,000
9.00	200	−100	−4.50	1,800
8.00	300	−100	−2.67	2,400
7.00	400	−100	−1.75	2,800
6.00	500	−100	−1.20	3,000
5.50	550	−100	−1.00	3,025
5.00	600	−100	−0.83	3,000
4.00	700	−100	−0.57	2,800
3.00	800	−100	−0.38	2,400
2.00	900	−100	−0.22	1,800
1.00	1,000	−100	−0.10	1,000
0	1,100	−100	0	0

(handwritten note: "← optima price" pointing to the 5.50 row)

to keep the analysis simple,[9] we can assume that these data represent consumer demand for movie tickets, per showing, at a theater which seats 1,000 persons. Note that the slope of the demand curve (column 3) is always − 100; regardless of what the price is, a $1 change in price is always associated with a change of 100 in the number of tickets demanded (in the opposite direction). To calculate the point elasticity for a constant-slope demand equation, we merely divide price by quantity, then multiply by the (constant) slope value.

By knowing the point elasticity value associated with each possible ticket price, the theater operator would be able to set the price at the revenue maximizing level, rather than experimenting with various prices and earning less than the maximum possible revenue until the appropriate price was found. Table 4-1 shows that when price exceeds $5.50, demand is elastic, and revenue would rise if the price were cut. At prices below $5.50, demand is inelastic, and revenue could be increased by raising the price. It follows that revenue will be maximized when a price

---

[9] In the appendix to chapter nine, the process of estimating economic formulas from empirical data is discussed in detail. Mistakes are unavoidable when one tries to estimate a *ceteris paribus* relation, since many variables will be changing at the same time in actual markets. Econometric methods designed to sort the influence of a price change from the impact of coincidental changes in other prices, incomes, or tastes, not to mention influences on seller behavior, are imperfect, at best. While demand theory may be fairly simple, once it is mastered, implementing that logic with the use of actual market information can be quite tricky. Real-world demand equations tend to be much more complex, and much less precise, than the pedagogical example presented in Table 4-1.

change in either direction would cause revenue to decline. If she can calculate the price at which demand is unit elastic before any tickets are sold, the theater operator will be able to maximize revenue for every performance. (In chapter ten we will see that revenue maximization is consistent with profit maximization—the motive usually attributed to sellers—only when it costs nothing to sell one more unit. Once a movie is being shown, it costs virtually nothing to seat one more patron in a theater with empty seats.)

The relationship between price and total expenditure is depicted in Figure 4-5. A linear demand curve has two prices associated with each possible level of revenue, except for the revenue maximizing price, which occurs at the precise midpoint of a linear demand curve. Figure 4-5a shows the linear demand curve for the equation used in Table 4-1. The quantity intercept is the number of tickets people would take if tickets were free; we imagine that 1,100 tickets could be given away at a zero price. Since sitting through a movie will still have a high opportunity cost in terms of time, only a finite number of "free" tickets will be demanded. Since each $1 price increase reduces quantity demanded by 100, the price intercept equals $11. Were the price of a ticket $11 or more, quantity demanded would equal zero. We have already seen that the point of unit elasticity occurs when $p = \$5.50$ and $Q_D = 550$, which is exactly one-half the value of the price and quantity intercepts, respectively.

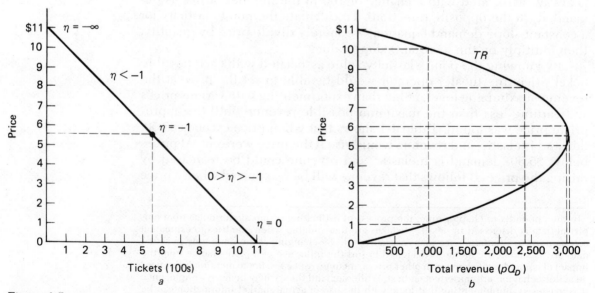

Figure 4-5
Linear Demand (a) and Resulting Total Revenue (b)

Figure 4-5*b* shows the total revenue (*TR*) associated with each price; total revenue is plotted on the horizontal axis to preserve continuity with Figure 4-5*a*. Note the symmetry in Figure 4-5*b*. Zero revenue occurs at the two intercepts, since $pQ = 0$ when either p or Q equals zero. $pQ = \$1,000$ when $p = \$10$ ($Q_D = 100$) and when $p = \$1$ ($Q_D = 1,000$), and total revenue is \$2,400 when $p = \$3$ and when $p = \$8$. If the theater owner did not know the demand equation for movie tickets, she would have to estimate elasticity of demand by comparing the percentage change in quantity and the percentage change in price over two discrete points in Figure 4-5*a*.

Suppose that the theater operator is unaware of the precise formula for the demand for tickets. Let the price of tickets be \$8 each; the movie house is selling 300 tickets per show, leaving 300 seats empty. Playing a hunch, the operator lowers her price to \$4 and her ticket sales rise to 700 per performance. Her revenue has risen from \$2,400 (\$8 times 300 tickets) to \$2,800 (\$4 times 700 tickets) per show. If she estimates elasticity on the basis of the \$8 price, it will appear that a 50 percent decrease in price resulted in a 133 percent increase in quantity demanded. Clearly, over the price range from \$8 to \$4, demand was price elastic; revenue did increase in the wake of the price cut. But can the operator infer anything about the elasticity of demand at a \$4 price from the experience of lowering the \$8 price? Unfortunately, in this case, the answer is: very little.

Table 4-1 gives the point elasticity for $p = \$8$ as -2.67; this is consistent with the experience of the theater operator because she based her interpretation on an \$8 price. She still has 300 empty seats. If she assumes that elasticity is still -2.67, she will conclude that a 16 percent price cut is sufficient to increase quantity demanded by 43 percent (i.e., $0.16 = 0.43/2.67$). So the price is cut to \$3.35 to sell 1,000 tickets. Expected revenue is \$3,350. In fact, quantity demanded only increases to 765 tickets, and revenue falls to \$2,562.75. What went wrong?

What went wrong, of course, was that the theater operator was ignorant of the fact that a linear demand curve has a different point elasticity at each price. Applying the elasticity measure calculated for a price of \$8 to predict the consequences of a price change from \$4 led to an erroneous prediction of the impact of a price change on revenue. Returning to Table 4-1, we see that $\eta = -0.571$ when $p = \$4$. When price is in the neighborhood of \$4, a 1 percent price change will change quantity demanded by slightly more than 0.5 percent (i.e., by one-half of one percent). If a seller is ignorant of the formula which describes consumer demand, it is safer to rely on the average elasticity, or **arc elasticity**, of demand, a measure of elasticity which equals the average percent change in quantity divided by the average percent change in price between two points on an unseen demand curve.

APPLICATION

Measuring Arc Elasticity

In our movie theater example, we saw how a relatively large (50 percent) price reduction led to a revenue increase. By reducing price from $8 to $4 per ticket, the theater operator missed the opportunity to charge the revenue maximizing price. Had price been reduced by only 31.25 percent (from $8 to $5.50), revenue would have increased from $2,400 to $3,025; a smaller percentage price reduction would have led to a greater revenue increase. Quantity is more responsive to price over the range $8 to $5.50 than over the range $8 to $4. Obviously, calculating the point elasticity at $8 would not indicate that the sensitivity of quantity demanded to price changes at lower prices.

If we can calculate point elasticity at every price (because we have accurate knowledge of the demand formula), we can see that the absolute value of η declines as price falls. If we are ignorant of the formula for quantity demanded as a function of price, the more appropriate measure is arc elasticity. Arc elasticity measures the *average* percentage change in quantity divided by the average percentage change in price, for the price and quantity combinations actually observed.

The formula for arc elasticity (E) is:

$$E = \frac{\dfrac{Q_1 - Q_2}{1/2(Q_1 + Q_2)}}{\dfrac{p_1 - p_2}{1/2(p_1 + p_2)}} = \frac{\Delta Q / \overline{Q}}{\Delta p / \overline{p}}$$

If we let $p_1 = \$8$ (so that $Q_1 = 300$) and $p_2 = \$4$ (so that $Q_2 = 700$), the arc elasticity for that price range is:

$$E = \frac{\dfrac{300 - 700}{1/2(300 + 700)}}{\dfrac{8 - 4}{1/2(8 + 4)}} = \frac{\dfrac{-400}{1/2(1000)}}{\dfrac{4}{1/2(12)}} = \frac{-400/500}{4/6} = -1.2$$

Note that the arc elasticity for a price change from $8 to $4 is the same as the point elasticity at the average price of $6. If the price had been reduced from $8 to $5.50, the arc elasticity would have been measured as:

$$E = \frac{\dfrac{300 - 550}{1/2(300 + 550)}}{\dfrac{8 - 5.50}{1/2(8 + 5.50)}} = \frac{-250/425}{250/6.75} = -1.59$$

Arc elasticity measures the average elasticity between the two observed points. *If* the underlying demand equation which generated the observed prices and quantities is a linear equation, the arc elasticity of demand will equal the point elasticity for the average price and quantity between the two observations. However, this is usually not the case if the underlying demand formula is not linear.

Generally speaking, economists use two general formulas or functional forms when estimating demand equations from market data: linear equations, with the form $Q_D = a - bp$, and power (or log-linear) equations, with the form $Q_D = ap^{-b}$. A linear demand function will always have the same slope, $\Delta Q_D/\Delta p = -b$, while the other constant, a, indicates the price at which quantity demanded falls to zero. The power function has a differing slope but a constant elasticity: $\eta = -b$, while a is merely a constant to translate price units into quantity units. Except when $\eta = -1$, calculating arc elasticity will not yield an accurate measure of the constant elasticity of a power function demand equation.

The real advantage of using arc elasticity is in locating the point of maximum revenue from limited market data. In our example, the seller who calculates an arc elasticity of -1.2 for the price range $p_1 = \$8$ and $p_2 = \$4$ will know that demand is elastic over that range; however, considering the closeness of -1.2 to -1, the possibility exists that demand is actually inelastic when $p = \$4$. Assuming that the demand equation is linear (as a first approximation), she estimates that $\eta = -1.2$ at $p = \$6$, and that the price where point elasticity is unitary is probably between $p = \$6$ and $p = \$4$. Therefore, she sets the price at $5, and revenue rises from \$2,800 to \$3,000. Clearly, demand is inelastic between $p = \$4$ and $p = \$5$; in fact $E = -0.75$. Splitting the difference again, she sets the price at \$5.50. Revenue rises to \$3,025, and $E = -0.913$, which is very close to -1.

Let us try one more example. Consider each of the following price-quantity pairs. What do all three have in common?

$p_1 = \$10, Q_1 = 100$	$p_1 = \$8, Q_1 = 300$	$p_1 = \$6, Q_1 = 500$
$p_2 = \$1, Q_2 = 1000$	$p_2 = \$3, Q_2 = 800$	$p_2 = \$5, Q_2 = 600$

In each case, a price reduction from p_1 to p_2 (or a price increase from p_2 to p_1) would leave revenue unchanged. In each case, arc elasticity is $E = -1$. When a discrete price reduction (or increase) leaves total revenue unchanged, calculating arc elasticity will suggest that the point of maximum revenue has been bypassed and that the price decrease (or increase) was too great.

To summarize, since the estimation of point elasticity assumes knowledge of the demand equation, arc elasticity should be used when knowledge of the underlying demand conditions is limited to the two prices and quantity pairs actually observed. When we calculate the average elasticity (i.e., arc elasticity) over the range of observed prices, we are less likely to make erroneous inferences about elasticity outside the

Policy Illustration
Price Elasticity and Drug-Related Crime

One of the more controversial applications of price elasticity of demand is explaining the lack of success of sumptuary taxes and other laws designed to reduce the consumption of commodities deemed to be harmful to the consumer. For instance, most states levy high excise taxes on tobacco and liquor. Often, these taxes are defended as a means of discouraging the consumption of harmful commodities. Ironically, sumptuary taxes are major sources of revenues for state and local governments. Addiction to tobacco or reliance on alcohol tends to make the demand for these "bads" price inelastic, because the increase in price due to the excise tax causes only a slight decrease in consumption. After the tax is imposed, consumer expenditure (which includes most of the tax) is greater than before the tax was imposed. With inelastic demand, sellers can shift most of the tax to buyers, reducing the antitax lobbying efforts of sellers.

Even more extreme, and certainly more tragic, consequences follow attempts to prohibit the sale or purchase of forbidden commodities. When a state outlaws the activities of bookies, prostitutes, or purveyors of pornography, it defines these sellers of bets, illicit sex, or pornographic material as criminals. When consumers are willing to pay a price high enough to cover the seller's risk premium (see chapter three), unsavory characters provide the "bads" that buyers consider "goods." Since laws are already being broken, sale of these illegal commodities is often associated with potentially more

serious crimes, such as loansharking, shakedowns, bribery, mugging, rape, and child abuse. Advocates of the illegality of what some people consider "victimless" crimes point to the associated crimes (i.e., those with victims) to justify their viewpoint. Nevertheless, in Nevada, where gambling and prostitution are legal but heavily regulated (and taxed!), there is a lower incidence of associated secondary crimes than in states where gambling and prostitution are illegal.

Perhaps the most compelling link between the illegality of a consumption commodity and other criminal activity involves prohibitions against the sale and use of narcotics, particularly heroin.* By definition, an addictive drug such as heroin has few acceptable substitutes in the mind of its addicts. Hence, the demand for the substance is likely to be very price-inelastic. Consider the accompanying figure. Although obvious problems exist in obtaining a reliable estimate of the demand curve for an illegal commodity, we assume that at a price that roughly reflects the production price of a drug—say, $1 per ounce—200,000 ounces per day would be consumed (price times quantity [rectangle p_0Aq_00] = $200,000 per day). A higher price, charged by a monopoly seller of an illegal drug, would reduce consumption; that is what the law of de-

---

* See Simon Rottenberg, "The Clandestine Distribution of Heroin, Its Discovery and Suppression," *Journal of Political Economy* 76 (January–February 1968), 78–90; also see Daryl A. Hellman, *The Economics of Crime* (New York: St. Martin's Press, 1980), pp. 143–166.

Hypothetical Demand Curve for Addictive Drug. An increase of price from p_0 = \$1 to p_1 = \$100 reduces quantity demanded from q_0 = 200,000 ounces per day to 190,000 ounces per day; total expenditure rises from \$200,000 per day to \$19 million per day.

mand says. However, if a price of \$100 per ounce reduces consumption to 190,000 ounces per day, total expenditure would *increase* to \$19 million per day. In this example, the arc elasticity of demand is:

$$E = \frac{q_0 - q_1/q_0 + q_1}{p_0 - p_1/p_0 + p_1}$$

$$= \frac{200,000 - 190,000/(200,000 + 190,000)}{1 - 100/1 + 100}$$

$$= \frac{10,000/390,000}{-99/101} = -0.026$$

The ultimate paradox stems from the means by which many, if not most, addicts support their addiction. According to some antidrug crusaders, injecting heroin into one's body generates an uncontrollable urge to steal television sets; hence the logic that increasing the penalities for heroin sales will reduce the quantity of heroin available, thus reducing the incidence of theft. Economic analysis suggests that the incidence of theft is dependent on the expenditure on heroin; increasing penalties reduces consumption but increases expenditure on a commodity with very inelastic demand.

The accompanying figure suggests a dilemma, a choice between two undesirable options: (1) when society interferes with the use of harmful drugs by employing criminal penalties, the cost is a high incidence of theft by drug addicts; and (2) minimizing crimes by drug addicts implies legalizing dangerous drugs. Here, inelastic demand works in the opposite direction: a decrease in the street price of heroin by as much as 99 percent might not increase its use by more than 5 percent.

Economic analysis in no way implies that people should be allowed to buy harmful commodities; nor does it imply they should be prohibited from purchasing them. Those are normative issues that cannot be subjected to clear tests for truth or falsehood. However, economic theory does predict that theft and other crimes would be lower if heroin were sold at a much lower price. Hence, the cost of making heroin illegal is the high degree of drug-related crime. Only society as a whole can decide if the benefits of anti-drug laws are worth the cost.

range of observed prices than if we were to calculate point elasticity by assuming a demand equation from only two observations of price and quantity.

Income Elasticity

Any variable which can cause the demand curve for a commodity to shift can also be evaluated in **elasticity** terms. We know that the consumption of normal goods changes in the same direction as real income, *ceteris paribus*. Just as the magnitude of slope of the demand curve is sensitive to the units measuring quantity, price, or the period of time, the change in quantity demanded due to a change in income is also sensitive to the way in which income is measured. Suppose that a manufacturer of calculators discovers that sales increase by 1,000 units per year for each $1 increase in per capita income in the United States, while sales increase by 1,800 units per year for each £1 increase in per capita income in Great Britain. In which market is the demand for the company's calculators more sensitive to changes in income? What is the relative size of the company's markets in the two countries? These questions can be answered by calculating the good's income inelasticity.

By defining the **income elasticity** of demand, we can measure the responsiveness of demand for a commodity to a change in income, other things being equal, in terms of a pure (i.e., a number independent of how time, money, or quantity is measured). Income elasticity is defined as the percentage change in quantity demanded divided by the percentage change in income, *ceteris paribus*:

$$\eta_{iY} = \frac{\Delta q_i / q_i}{\Delta Y / Y} = \left(\frac{\Delta q_i}{\Delta Y}\right)\left(\frac{Y}{q_i}\right)$$

We know that the sign of the coefficient for income elasticity will depend upon how a good's consumption changes with income: $\eta_{iY} > 0$ for a normal good, and $\eta_{iY} < 0$ for an inferior good. Unlike price elasticity of demand, knowledge of income elasticity is not necessary to determine how expenditure on a commodity changes as income changes. We know that as income rises, people spend more of their income on normal goods and less of their income on inferior goods. The concept of income elasticity of demand clarifies how the proportions of a household's budget spent on various commodities change as income changes.

If $\eta_{iY} > 1$, we say that the demand for commodity i is *income elastic*. If the percentage change in quantity is greater than the percentage change in income, it follows that income-elastic commodities will absorb a large share of a family's budget as income rises.[10] Commodities such as travel, entertainment, and many services are income elastic. Income-elastic commodities are often called *luxuries* or *superior goods*, reflecting the tendency of a household to substitute high quality goods for more basic goods as real income rises. Since income elasticity is a *ceteris paribus* concept, relative prices are assumed constant as real income increases. Goods can be counted as income elastic even if "quantity" in the narrow sense does not increase. If Ivy League college tuition takes a larger share of household budgets than state college tuition, despite the fact that families who send their sons and daughters to Ivy League colleges tend to have higher incomes than families who send their children to state colleges, then an Ivy League education can be considered a superior good.

If $1 > \eta_{iY} > 0$, the commodity is a normal good which is income *inelastic*; as income rises, consumption of that good (or expenditure on it) rises, but the proportion of the household budget allocated to that commodity falls. Food and clothing appear to be the most obvious income-inelastic commodities. Income-inelastic commodities are often called necessities, and they represent a larger share of the budgets of lower-income households. Between income-elastic and income-inelastic commodities, the case of unitary income elasticity simply indicates a

---

[10] Given a budget constraint for many commodities, $Y = \sum_{i=1}^{n} p_i q_i$, the change in income will be accounted for in the change in the quantity of all goods consumed if prices remain constant (we can now allow saving, borrowing, and leisure—see chapter three): $\Delta Y = \sum_{i=1}^{n} p_1(\Delta q_i)$. Dividing both sides by ΔY, multiplying by $\dfrac{Y/Y}{q_i/q_i} = 1$, and regrouping terms:

$$\frac{\Delta Y}{\Delta Y} = \frac{\Delta q_i}{\Delta Y} \cdot \frac{Y}{q_i} \cdot \frac{p_i q_i}{Y} = \eta_{iY}\theta_i$$

where θ_i is the *share* of the budget allocated to good i. The weighted sum of income elasticities must equal one. If one commodity is income elastic, there must be another which is income inelastic. If one good is inferior, another good must exist which is not only normal but income elastic. However, not all goods can be income inelastic.

commodity whose consumption tends to change in the same proportion and direction as income. There is some evidence that, given time for adjustment, housing tends to be a unitary income-elastic commodity. Finally, of course, inferior goods are really a special case of income-inelastic commodities; $\eta_{iY} < 0$ means $\eta_{iY} < 1$.

Knowing the income elasticity of demand for one's product can be almost as important to a seller as knowing the price elasticity of demand. If a firm produces a commodity with income-elastic demand, it may find it profitable to offer a diversified product line, reflecting higher quality at a higher price. It is no accident that the major automobile manufacturers offer low, medium, and high price models, hoping to attract some consumers in each bracket as they work their way up the income ladder.

Income elasticity may also tell a manufacturer how to target an advertising campaign. Income-inelastic commodities are presented as "good buys," or as economical or practical; income-elastic commodities are "stylish" or "luxurious." When did you last see an inferior good advertised?

When state and local governments impose sales or excise taxes, the *progressivity* of the tax system depends upon how heavily income-elastic and income-inelastic commodities are taxed. Many states exempt food and medicines from sales taxes; this practice tends to increase the progressivity of sales taxes. Few, if any, states impose a sales tax on personal services such as tax advice, haircuts, or visits to the dentist. If these services are income elastic, then sales taxes tend to be less progressive. Taxes on hotel rooms and entertainment tend to take a larger share of high-income budgets than of low-income ones, *ceteris paribus*, but taxes on cigarettes and alcohol tend to take a larger bite out of the low-income budget.

Cross Elasticity

The **cross elasticity of demand** between good i and the price of good j is defined as the percentage change in the demand for good i due to a 1 percent change in the price of good j, other factors being constant:

$$\eta_{ij} = \frac{\Delta q_i / q_i}{\Delta p_j / p_j} = \left(\frac{\Delta q_i}{\Delta p_j}\right)\left(\frac{p_j}{q_i}\right)$$

The sign of η_{ij} is determined by the sign of $\Delta q_i / \Delta p_j$. (Given this notation, η_{ii} is the elasticity of q_i with respect to P_i; a commodity's *own* price elasticity is simply a special case of cross elasticity.) A simple algebraic transformation may make the concept of cross elasticity easier to remember. First, we have already established the law of demand: the consumption of a good will change in the opposite direction to a change in its price, *ceteris paribus*. An increase in the price of good *j* will cause the consumption of good *j* to fall, *ceteris paribus*. A reduction in the consumption of good *j* (due to a rise in its price) will cause the consumption of good *i* to rise if *i* and *j* are substitutes. Indeed, if *i* and *j* are substitutes, the relative price of good *i* will fall (and hence the relative consumption of good *i* will rise) either because P_i falls or P_j increases.

By writing $\Delta q_i/\Delta p_j = (\Delta q_i/\Delta q_j)(\Delta q_j/\Delta p_j)$, we discover that the sign of η_{ij} is determined by the relative change in q_i and q_j. Since $\Delta q_j/\Delta p_j$ is always negative, if $\Delta q_i/\Delta q_j$ is also negative, η_{ij} will be positive. If the cross elasticity between good *i* and the price of good *j* is positive, the two goods are substitutes.[11] If the consumption of good *i* and the consumption of good *j* move together, the two goods are complements, and the cross elasticity between q_1 and p_j will be negative. Consumers of good *i* will react to increases of p_j in much the same way as they would react to an increase in good *i*'s own price.

The most important uses of cross elasticity—in forecasting demand and in identifying potential rivals—tend to be empirical. If every time seller A lowers his price by 1 percent, my sales fall by 5 percent, it would behoove me to monitor seller A's pricing behavior closely. If a 1 percent decrease in the price of product A reduces my firm's sales by 0.005 percent, I will ignore the other firm's price changes. In chapter twelve, we will see that *rivalry* tends to characterize a market in which sellers are few and substitutes are imperfect. If I find that my firm's product has a strong negative cross elasticity with another commodity, I may wish to buy out the producer of that commodity or sell a similar product of my own. Thus, a perfume manufacturer typically offers additional fragrance products—soaps, bath oils, powders, and so on—since men and women like to coordinate their olfactory adornments.

Combining the elasticity concepts we have considered allows us to derive some general principles about price elasticity:

1. A good's price elasticity of demand tends to be greater, the greater its income elasticity of demand. This is because income-elastic commodities will have income effects which greatly magnify the substitution effect of a change in the price of that good.

---

[11] Using the chain rule from calculus, η_{ij} can be written as:

$$\eta_{ij} = \left(\frac{\partial q_i}{\partial p_i}\right)\left(\frac{p_i}{q_i}\right) = \left(\frac{\partial q_i}{\partial q_j}\right)\left(\frac{\partial q_j}{\partial p_j}\right)\left(\frac{p_j}{q_i}\right)\left(\frac{q_j}{q_j}\right) = \left(\frac{\partial q_i}{\partial q_j}\right)\left(\frac{q_j}{q_j}\right)\left(\frac{\partial q_j}{\partial p_j}\right)\left(\frac{p_j}{q_j}\right) = \eta_{ij}\left(\frac{\partial q_i/q_i}{\partial q_j/q_j}\right)$$

The cross elasticity of demand between good *i* and the price of good *j* is equal to the elasticity of demand for good *j* with respect to its own price times the elasticity of q_i with respect to q_j. If good *i* and good *j* must be used in constant proportions, so that a 1 percent increase in the consumption of good *j* automatically increases the consumption of good *i* by 1 percent, then the cross elasticity of good *i* with respect to the price of good *j* will equal the price elasticity of good *j*. If *i* and *j* were perfect substitutes, consumers would purchase the less expensive "brand." If prices were equal, cross elasticity would approach ∞; if one good's price rose relative to the other, its consumption would fall to zero.

2.   The larger the percentage of a household's budget a commodity absorbs, the more price elastic the demand for that commodity will tend to be.
3.   The greater the number of substitutes a good has, and the greater the (positive) cross elasticity between it and any substitute(s), the more price elastic the demand for that good will be.
4.   The greater the number of complements a good has, and the greater the cross elasticity (in absolute value) between it and any complement(s), the less elastic will be the demand for that good in response to a change in its own price.
5.   Since households develop consumption habits, demand tends to become more price elastic the longer the period of time over which consumers are observed to adjust to a price change.

APPLICATION

Ceteris Paribus and *Mutatis Mutandis* Demand Curves

So far we have accounted for many independent changes in the demand for a good, and we have distinguished between a shift of a demand curve (*ceteris paribus* conditions violated) and a movement along a stable demand curve (*ceteris paribus* conditions in force). *Ceteris paribus* is a useful logical technique which allows us to isolate the impact of each independent variable change on the change in the intended consumption of a particular good. But this logic is not limited to events in which only one variable changes, since economic logic allows us to add the effects of independent variables to obtain a total change in quantity demanded.

Suppose that a change in the price of a variable causes a change in other variables in the demand equation. For instance, suppose we are

Business Illustration
Practical Difficulties in Estimating Elasticity

Somewhat paradoxically, estimates of market-wide price and income elasticities are complicated by the operation of the market itself. In an ideal market, all households pay the same price for identical commodities. Were markets ideal, the differences in consumption among households could not be attributed to differences in price. In reality, of course,

markets are not perfect, and it is possible that different households pay different prices for the same commodity due to their location, the time they spend hunting for bargains, and perhaps whom they know. However, it is highly likely that markets are imperfect because consumers consider different brands, or even commodities available at different locations, as imperfect substitutes. That one person buys one six-pack of generic beer for $2 while another buys twelve cans of a "premium" brew at $4 a six-pack does *not* imply a violation of the law of demand; income and tastes are likely to differ across households.

Estimating price elasticity of demand usually requires time series data. Through time, the relative price of a commodity can move up or down in response to changes in supply and/or changes in demand. As discussed in the appendix to chapter nine, separating supply-induced price changes (which allow points along a stable demand curve to be observed) from demand-induced price changes can be difficult, and sometimes impossible. Furthermore, to isolate the impact of price on the percentage change in quantity demanded, it is also necessary to account for changes in income, the prices of substitutes and complements, and even tastes. One common approach is to relate the change in a price index for one commodity group (e.g., food, health care, transportation) to changes in *real income* and changes in the overall price index. Holding real income, rather than nominal income, constant means that most empirical demand equations describe constant real income (*mutatis mutandis*) demand curves.

A further complication of using time series data to estimate price elasticities is that demand tends to be more elastic the longer the time period allowed for adjustment. Hence, the percentage change in price and quantity from, say, one month to the next may underestimate the true responsiveness of quantity demanded to price. Even worse, only part of the adjustment this month may be due to the price change last month, while part may be due to a price change two or more months before. If the relative price of a commodity changes frequently in both directions, short-run demand elasticities may be poor estimates of consumer behavior. This problem is often remedied by using *lagged* prices: quantity demanded this month is related to prices over the past several months, with empirical weights used to accord importance to various time periods.

Ultimately, the complexity of empirical estimation of elasticity requires a clear understanding of theory in analyzing empirical results. For instance, if we estimated that the price elasticity of demand for gasoline was $+0.2$, it is more likely that we inadvertently measured elasticity of supply, or failed to account for the change in some exogenous variable, than that the law of demand was violated. In fact, it is the problem of empirical estimation which represents the final nail in the coffin of the Giffen good. Economists have learned by bitter experience that when consumption changes in the same direction as price, it is virtually certain that the demand curve has shifted, so that elasticity of demand cannot be estimated by the techniques used. Whenever a positive price elasticity of demand is found, empirical results are rejected. Who knows how many times Giffen good demand curves have been mistaken for supply curves and rejected. Ask yourself: What would happen if a supply curve were mistaken for a Giffen good demand curve? Which prospect would you stake your career as a professional economist on?

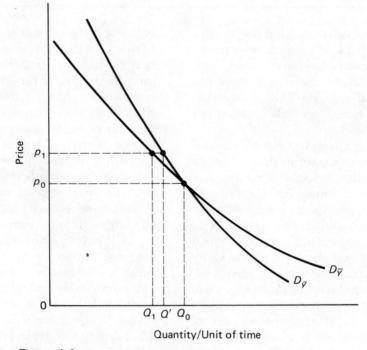

Figure 4-6
Constant Money Income (*Ceteris Paribus*) Demand and Constant
Real Income (*Mutatis Mutandis*) Demand

dealing with the effect of a relative increase in the price of an important
commodity (say, medical care) in the context of a fully employed economy without international trade.[12] The price increase, which reduces
consumption of nonessential medical services by those whose medical
costs are not covered by insurance, changes the real incomes of buyers
and sellers in opposite directions. If demand for medical care is price
elastic, expenditure on other goods increases; if demand is inelastic,
expenditure on medical care increases. The income effects of the price
change may cancel out by the time the changes in expenditure on various
goods have become changes in money income. In Figure 4-6, $D_{\bar{y}}$ is the
usual type of *ceteris paribus* demand curve, constructed under the assumption of constant money income. An increase in price from p_0 to p_1
reduces quantity demanded to Q_1 if *money* income is held constant.
However, if the income effect is cancelled by changes in money income
induced by the price change, the demand curve will display the char-

[12] This discussion is loosely based on Milton Friedman's "The Marshallian Demand
Curve," *Journal of Political Economy* (December 1949); reprinted in William Breit and
Harold Hochman, eds., *Readings in Microeconomics*, 2nd ed. (New York: Holt, Rinehart
and Winston, 1971), pp. 92–102.

acteristic of constant real income. Demand curve $D_{\bar{y}}$ is an **income-compensated demand curve**, whereby real income, as opposed to money income, is held constant.[13] When price rises from p_0 to p_1, quantity demanded decreases along $D_{\bar{y}}$ only to Q'. For normal goods, the income-compensated demand curve has a lower price elasticity of demand than the constant money income demand curve. For inferior goods, the income-compensated demand curve is more price elastic than the constant money income demand curve.

When a change in the price of a commodity also causes one of the *ceteris paribus* conditions to change, it is necessary to take the resulting "shift" in the demand curve into account before proceeding with the analysis of the price change. For this reason, we define **mutatis mutandis** demand curves using the Latin phrase meaning "all necessary changes having been made." Another interesting application of the *mutatis mutandis* demand curve is the salesman's dream of the consumer who uses the price of a commodity as a proxy for its quality. According to one marketing fable, a department store priced a new brand of lipstick at 50¢ a tube, but sold little of the item. The store manager decided to *raise* the price of the lipstick to $1 per tube (thinking what was lost in volume could be regained from a larger mark-up). And, miracle of miracles, the number of lipstick tubes sold per week actually increased after the price hike.

The story ends there, supposedly with everyone (especially the store manager) living happily ever after. But the economist demands an epilogue. After all, if customers are so easily fleeced, why not raise the price still further, to $2, $4, or even $100 a tube? The answer, of course, is that the change in consumer tastes (or information) may have shifted the demand curve outward, but subsequent consumer experience must confirm the inference from the quality proxy, or the demand curve will shift back to its original position (or even further inward).

In Figure 4-7, the initial state of consumer impressions of the product generates demand curve D_0. The increase in price from p_0 to p_1, which also changes consumer opinion about the good, causes D_0 to shift to D_1. Note that quantity demanded rises from Q_0 to Q_1, but this is hardly a refutation of the law of demand. Had advertising or dispensing free samples been used to persuade consumers of the product's higher quality and price remained at p_0, quantity demanded would have increased to Q_0'. Since $Q_1 < Q_0'$, the new demand curve also has a negative slope. But if consumers discover (after trying the product) that its quality really is as poor as they originally believed, D_1 will return to D_0, where the good is now priced out of the market at p_1.

Three additional ways in which price changes might induce pre-

---

[13] Since most empirical demand equations attempt to hold real income constant, most empirically estimated demand curves are *income-compensated* demand curves.

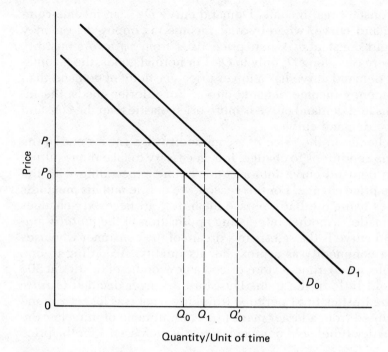

Figure 4-7
Price as a Proxy for Quality. If a price increase causes consumers to believe a product's quality is better, the increase in price from p_0 to p_1 will shift the demand curve from D_0 to D_1, causing quantity to increase to Q_1. If consumers' expectations are reinforced by experience, a reduction in price to P_0 will raise quantity demanded to Q_0'.

dictable changes in demand have been explored by Harvey Liebenstein.[14] **A bandwagon effect** occurs when some consumers' demand for a product increases as the popularity of the good increases. In Figure 4-8*a*, a group of consumers are purchasing Q_0 units of a good (say, an Adam Smith T-shirt) at price p_0. Demand curve D_0 reflects the usual *ceteris paribus* conditions: income, prices of substitutes and complements, and tastes are held constant. However, in this case, tastes are a function of the observed consumption of Adam Smith T-shirts, here Q_0.

If p_0 decreases to p_1, consumption initially rises to Q' along demand curve D_0. However, consumers discover that total consumption has increased, and demand increases until a stable point, Q_1, is reached on demand curve D_1, where actual and anticipated market consumption

---

[14] "Bandwagon, Snob and Veblen Effects in the Theory of Consumer Demand," *Quarterly Journal of Economics* (May 1950), pp. 183–207; reprinted in William Breit and Harold Hochman, eds., *Readings in Microeconomics*, 2nd ed. (New York: Holt, Rinehart and Winston, 1971), pp. 111–127.

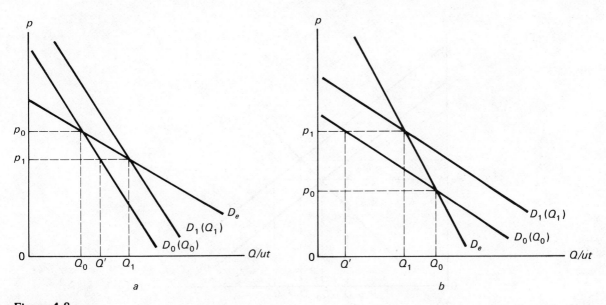

Figure 4-8
Mutatis Mutandis Demand Curves When Tastes Depend on Total Quantity Consumed. *a*, Bandwagon effect; *b*, snob effect.

once again coincide. The *mutatis mutandis* demand curve, D_e, is more elastic than any of the *ceteris paribus* demand curves which assume an expectation of constant total consumption.

Figure 4-8*b* illustrates a **snob effect**, whereby tastes are inversely related to Q_d (which, of course, is inversely related to p). People who value "exclusivity" wish to consume more of a commodity (at a given price) when they believe other people are consuming less. At a price of p_0, consumption is at Q_0 along demand curve D_0, for which the *expected* market consumption corresponds to the observed Q_0. If p_0 increases to p_1, consumption will initially fall to Q', since for a given expected level of consumption, quantity demanded is inversely related to price. However, the reduced market consumption will cause demand to increase, shifting the demand curve out from D_0 to D_1, but the increased consumption dampens the snob effect. When consumption reaches Q_1, which conforms to the expected consumption for D_1, the "snob reaction" to the price increase has been played out.

It should be clear that the *mutatis mutandis* demand curve, D_e, must be negatively sloped. If a decrease in consumption due to a price increase to p_1 shifted the demand curve so much that consumption returned to its former level at p_0, the *expectation* of reduced consumption would not be confirmed by experience. The demand curve would shift again, this time back toward D_0. A snob effect makes the *mutatis mutandis* demand curve less elastic than the *ceteris paribus* demand curve,

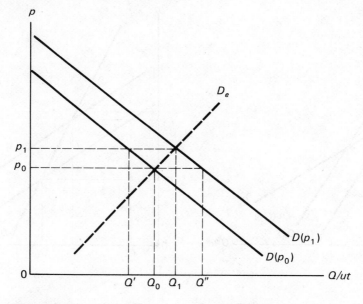

Figure 4-9
Mutatis Mutandis Demand with Veblen Effect. Quantity demanded is a function of perceived price.

but it does not completely overturn the inverse relationship between price and quantity demanded.

A **Veblen effect**, or *conspicuous consumption*, could hypothetically generate a positive relationship between price and quantity demanded.[15] But a market-wide observation of conspicuous consumption is unlikely. Imagine an expensive automobile which provides two services: transportation and prestige. The amount of transportation demanded is inversely related to price; an increase in the price of a car causes most people to turn to other means of transportation. But when few people are purchasing that car, the prestige of owning it may increase, thereby shifting the demand curve to the right, as shown in Figure 4-9.

An increase in price from p_0 to p_1 would decrease purchases to Q' if no prestige were associated with the higher price. However, if the prestige of the commodity increased, the demand curve might shift outward. In the case depicted in Figure 4-9, consumption would rise above Q', perhaps even above the original consumption level of Q_0 (say, to Q_1). Thus, there is a hypothetical basis for the possibility of a positively sloped *mutatis mutandis* demand curve like D_e in the figure. However, a strong motive would exist for sellers and conspicuous consumers to

---

[15] According to Liebenstein ("Bandwagon, Snob and Veblen Effects"), the concept of conspicuous consumption did not originate with the American economist Thorstein Veblen, but with John Rae's *The Sociological Theory of Capital* nearly a half-century earlier.

falsify the true price of the commodity. If the actual price were p_0 but believed to be p_1 (because sellers had been encouraged to overstate the price), consumption would be greater than if the consumer had to pay p_1 (perhaps Q'' as in Figure 4-9). And, in fact, the condescending retort "If you have to ask the price you can't afford it" might actually reflect the embarrassment of a lying seller. Finally, as demonstrated by the disdain in which "old money" holds "the new rich," an increase in consumption due to an increase in price would eventually cease to be impressive.

Our final example really belongs later in the book, since a situation in which expectations react perversely to a price change have more to do with market adjustment than with the slope of a demand curve per se. (See the appendix to chapter nine.) Nevertheless, the phenomenon which is often (mis)labeled "inflationary expectations" is sometimes used as a last defense by those who stubbornly support the case of the positively sloped demand curve. In the case of simple monetary inflation, whereby all prices are changing by the same percentage, the *ceteris paribus* conditions are violated.[16] Since the prices of substitutes and money income also increase, inflation causes demand curves to shift upward, and observed consumption need not change.

Suppose, however, an unexpected *relative* price increase occurs. Consumers have been purchasing a particular commodity (say, beef) at a steady rate, having experienced stable relative prices for some time. Yesterday consumers were "storing" their future purchases of beef in the producer's inventory (on the hoof), rather than going to the expense of freezing their own beef. Suddenly the price increases, contradicting the presumption of stable prices. "If only I had bought more when I had the chance," moans the consumer, to no avail. Yesterday's price is but a memory.

"But today's price is lower than tomorrow's will be," harried consumers think. So they try to purchase more before prices increase further, thereby transferring inventories from producers to themselves. The anticipation of higher prices in the future, by temporarily increasing the rate of purchases, creates a self-fulfilling prophecy. Consumers cause the price increases they were trying to avoid.

This process must eventually come to an end; an increase in the relative price of a commodity will not cause a permanent increase in the

---

[16] In the absence of a money illusion, a demand equation is assumed to be homogeneous of degree zero, meaning that if all variables were increased by the same percentage, quantity demanded would remain constant. Formally, if $Q_{10} = D(p_{10}, p_{20}, \ldots, p_{n0}, Y_0)$, where p_1 is the price of good 1, Q_1 is the total quantity demanded, p_2 through p_n are all prices of related goods, and Y is money income, with the subscript "0" identifying specific values, then multiplying all variables by the same positive number, λ, would cause quantity demanded to remain the same:

$$Q_{10} = D(\lambda p_{10}, \lambda p_{20}, \ldots, \lambda p_{n0}, \lambda Y_0) = D(p_{10}, p_{20}, \ldots, p_{n0}, Y_0)$$

rate of consumption. The transfer of inventories from sellers to buyers compresses purchases into a shorter time period; the rate of consumption will fall as higher beef prices increase the replacement cost of the commodity. When prices stop increasing, the rate of purchases will decline below the rate of consumption as inventories are consumed and not entirely replaced. And should the relative price of the commodity fall, inventories would be transferred back to sellers. However, the market might "crash" before inventories of consumers had been adjusted downward and the rate of purchases had increased.

Ceteris paribus demand curves, which ordinarily assist economists in sorting out the independent influences on consumer behavior, often generate unjustified abuse by skeptical noneconomists. We have seen that *ceteris paribus* analysis does not require that exogenous forces literally remain constant, since shifts in market demand curves can usually be analyzed independently of changes in a good's price or the quantity of that good demanded. Only when normally outside influences are predictably dependent on either price or quantity demanded will *ceteris paribus* logic lead to erroneous predictions about the responsiveness of quantity demanded to a change in price. For that purpose, we have introduced the *mutatis mutandis* demand curve. In this chapter, *mutatis mutandis* logic has been limited to exceptions to the usually reliable concept of a *ceteris paribus* demand curve. In later chapters, *mutatis mutandis* logic would help smooth out complications in real market situations.

HIGHLIGHTS

1. The household demand for a commodity can be derived from the price-consumption curve, which is constructed from the indifference-curve/budget-line tangencies for constant money income and a constant price for one commodity, with different budget lines identified by different prices for the commodity in question. Because the demand curve depicts a set of contingencies for the same point in time, the household is assumed to have constant tastes.

2. The law of demand states that price and quantity always change in opposite directions, other factors being constant. The law of demand implies that all demand curves have a negative slope.

3. Economists distinguish between a change in quantity demanded, which refers to a change in the amount of a good a household wishes to purchase when only the price of the good changes (movement along a stable demand curve), and a change in demand, which results in a shift of the entire demand curve. A change in demand can occur because of a change in consumer income, in the prices of other goods, or in consumer tastes.

4. Market demand for a commodity relates the total amount of a good consumers are willing and able to buy at various prices, *ceteris paribus*. The market demand is obtained by adding up the quantities demanded by all consumers at each hypothetical market price.

5. The price elasticity of demand measures the percentage change in quantity demanded divided by the percentage change in price, other factors remaining constant. Elastic demand means that quantity is so responsive to a change in price that consumer expenditure

changes in the opposite direction to the change in price. Inelastic demand means that the percentage change in quantity is smaller (in absolute value) than the percentage change in price, so that consumer expenditure changes in the same direction as, but by a smaller percentage than, price. When demand is unit elastic, the percentage change in quantity exactly offsets the percentage change in price (in the opposite direction), and consumer expenditure does not change when price changes.

6. There are two methods of measuring price elasticity: (1) point elasticity uses the known value of the change in quantity resulting from a change in price (the inverse slope of the demand curve); and (2) arc elasticity uses the average values of observed quantities and prices when the precise formula for the demand curve is not known.

7. Income elasticity measures the percentage change in quantity demanded due to a 1 percent change in income, other factors remaining constant. Income elasticity of demand is positive for normal goods and negative for inferior goods. Income-elastic demand means that a commodity absorbs a larger share of a household's budget as income rises; income-inelastic demand means that a commodity's share of a household's budget falls as income rises.

8. Cross elasticity relates the percentage change in the quantity demanded of one good to the percentage change in the price of some other good. The cross elasticity of demand is positive for substitute goods and negative for complementary goods. When the cross elasticity of demand is zero, the two goods are said to be unrelated.

9. When the demand curve shifts because a variable normally held constant changes when either price or quantity changes, the *ceteris paribus* demand curve must be replaced by a *mutatis mutandis* demand curve. *Mutatis mutandis* is a Latin phrase meaning "necessary changes having been made."

10. When producers of a commodity also make up a substantial share of consumers, a price change may redistribute income in such a way that real income, as opposed to money income, remains constant. The *mutatis mutandis* (constant real income) demand curve tends to be less elastic than the *ceteris paribus* (constant money income) demand curve for normal goods, whereas the reverse is true for inferior goods.

11. Bandwagon, snob, and Veblen effects all result in *mutatis mutandis* demand curves, whereby tastes, which influence consumption, are a function of quantity consumed (bandwagon and snob effects) or of perceived price (Veblen effect). Bandwagon effects make demand more price elastic, and snob effects make demand less price elastic, compared with *ceteris paribus* (constant taste) demand curves. While it is theoretically possible that an increase in price may increase demand enough to offset reduced quantity demanded along the *ceteris paribus* demand curve when Veblen effects are present, there is reason to doubt the real-world relevance of such a phenomenon for market demand curves.

12. Commodity speculation, resulting from an unexpected change in price, tends to delay, rather than overturn, the normal consumer reaction to a price change.

GLOSSARY

Arc elasticity of demand The average percentage change in quantity divided by the average percentage change in price, for two observations of price and quantity; used for calculating price elasticity when the precise formula for the demand curve is not known.

Bandwagon effect A *mutatis mutandis* demand function in which consumer tastes are a positive function of total quantity consumed. A reduction in price, which increases consumption along the *ceteris paribus* demand curve, also causes demand to increase. Bandwagon effects make market demand more price elastic than any *ceteris paribus* demand curve would indicate.

Ceteris paribus   Latin phrase meaning "other things remaining the same"; used for a demand function when quantity demanded is the only variable which changes when price changes.

Change in demand   The horizontal (or equivalent vertical) displacement of the demand curve due to a change in an exogenous variable (e.g., consumer tastes, number of consumers, consumer income, consumer expectations, prices of complementary or substitute commodities).

Change in quantity demanded   The change in the quantity of a commodity consumers are willing and able to buy when its price changes, other factors remaining constant. A change in quantity demanded involves a movement from one point to another on a stable demand curve.

Cross elasticity of demand   The percentage change in quantity demanded of one good due to a 1 percent change in the price of another good, other factors being constant. The cross elasticity between a good and the price of a substitute(s) is positive; the cross elasticity between a good and the price of a complement(s) is negative. If cross elasticity is zero, the two goods are unrelated.

Demand   The relationship between the quantity of a commodity consumers are willing and able to buy during a specified time period and the price of that commodity, other factors (e.g., income, tastes, prices of substitutes and complements) being constant.

Demand curve   The diagram relating the quantity of a good which consumers wish to purchase each period to each hypothetical market price, assuming that relevant prices of other goods, money income, and consumer tastes remain constant.

Elasticity   A relationship between variables measured by the percentage change in the dependent variable divided by the percentage change in the independent variable.

Income-compensated demand curve   A *mutatis mutandis* demand curve adjusted to account for the fact that a relative price change will redistribute purchasing power, but often not change the aggregate level of real income; contrast with the constant money income (*ceteris paribus*) demand curve derived from price-consumption path.

Income elasticity   The percentage change in quantity demanded divided by the percentage change in income, other factors remaining constant. The income elasticity of an inferior good is negative; the income elasticity of a normal good is positive. Income-elastic demand means that expenditure on a commodity takes a larger percentage of a household's budget as income rises; income-inelastic demand means that expenditure on a commodity takes a smaller percentage of a household's budget as income rises.

Law of demand   The quantity of a good demanded varies inversely with its price, *ceteris paribus*. As a result, a demand curve has a negative slope.

Market demand   Total amount of a commodity all consumers are willing to purchase at different market-determined prices, *ceteris paribus*. Market demand is the result of the horizontal summation of household demand curves at each price.

Mutatis mutandis   Latin phrase meaning "all necessary changes having been made." *Mutatis mutandis* logic replaces *ceteris paribus* logic when variables formerly treated as exogenous or independent actually respond predictably to changes in the endogenous variables.

Point elasticity   The formula used for calculating price elasticity when the equation for the demand curve is known. For instance, if market demand has been estimated as $Q_d = a - bp$ (where $\Delta Q/\Delta p = -b$), elasticity equals $\eta = -b(p/Q) = -bp/(a - bp)$.

Price elasticity of demand   The percentage change in quantity demanded due to a 1 percent change in price, other factors being constant: $\eta = \dfrac{\Delta Q/Q}{\Delta p/p}$. If demand is price elastic ($\eta < -1$; $|\eta| > 1$), consumer expenditure on a good is inversely related to price; if demand is price inelastic ($0 > \eta > -1$; $1 > |\eta| > 0$), consumer expenditure changes in the opposite direction to a change in price. When demand is unit elastic ($\eta = -1; |\eta| = 1$), a price change leaves expenditure on that commodity unchanged.

Price-consumption path The locus of points of maximum consumer utility for a given set of tastes and income, a range of prices for the commodity in question, and a constant money price for the other commodity.

Pure private good A commodity whose benefits and costs are associated solely with the purchaser.

Snob effect A *mutatis mutandis* demand function in which a reduction in consumption by some increases the attractiveness of a commodity to others. A price increase, which reduces quantity demanded along the *ceteris paribus* demand curve, will be partly offset by an increase in demand. A snob effect makes market demand less price elastic than the underlying *ceteris paribus* demand curve would indicate.

Veblen effect The consequence when conspicuous consumers obtain status by purchasing goods thought to have high prices. Hence, a price increase would cause the demand curve to shift to the right. Since quantity demanded increases as actual price falls (perceived price held constant), a Veblen good may be susceptible to fraudulent price announcements.

SUGGESTED READINGS

Bailey, Martin J. "The Marshallian Demand Curve." *Journal of Political Economy* (June 1954). Reprinted in William Breit and Harold Hochman, eds. *Readings in Microeconomics*. 2nd ed. New York: Holt, Rinehart and Winston, 1971, pp. 103–110.

Baumol, William. "The Empirical Determination of Demand Relationships." Chapter 10 in *Economic Theory and Operations Analysis*. 4th ed. Englewood Cliffs, N.J.: Prentice-Hall, 1977, pp. 227–266.

Becker, Gary S. "Irrational Behavior and Economic Theory." In *The Economic Approach to Human Behavior*. Chicago: University of Chicago Press, 1975, pp. 153–168.

Ferber, R. "Consumer Economics: A Survey." *Journal of Economic Literature* (December 1973).

Friedman, Milton. "The Marshallian Demand Curve." *Journal of Political Economy* (December 1949). Reprinted in William Breit and Harold Hochman, eds. *Readings in Microeconomics*. 2nd ed. New York: Holt, Rinehart and Winston, 1971, pp. 92–102.

Houthakker, Hendrik S., and Lester D. Taylor. *Consumer Demand in the United States: Analysis and Projections*. Cambridge, Mass.: Harvard University Press, 1970.

Liebenstein, Harvey. "Bandwagon, Snob and Veblen Effects in the Theory of Consumer Behavior." *Quarterly Journal of Economics* (May 1950), pp. 183–287. Reprinted in William Breit, and Harold Hochman, eds. *Readings in Microeconomics*. 2nd ed. New York: Holt, Rinehart and Winston, 1971, pp. 111–127.

Machlup, Fritz. "Professor Hicks' Revision of Demand Theory." *American Economic Review* (March 1957). Reprinted in William Breit and Harold Hochman, eds. *Readings in Economics*. 2nd ed. New York: Holt, Rinehart and Winston, 1971, pp. 77–91.

Marshall, Alfred. *Principles of Economics*. 9th ed. London: Macmillan, 1960, book 3.

Scitovsky, Tibor. *The Joyless Economy*. London: Oxford University Press, 1976.

Usher, Dan. "The Derivation of Demand Curves from Indifferent Curves." *Oxford Economic Papers* (March 1963). Reprinted in Richard E. Neel, ed. *Readings in Price Theory*. Cincinnati: Southwestern Publishing, 1973, pp. 165–188.

Veblen, Thorstein B. *The Theory of the Leisure Class*. New York: Macmillan, 1899.

Willig, R. "Consumer Surplus without Apology." *American Economic Review* (September 1976), 589–597.

EXERCISES

Evaluate

Indicate whether each statement is true (agrees with economic theory), false (is contradicted by theory), or uncertain (could be true or false, given additional information). Briefly explain your answer.

1. Inelastic demand means that a change in the price of a commodity has no effect upon quantity demanded.

2. A change in price will never shift a *ceteris paribus* demand curve.

3. Both arc elasticity and point elasticity calculations use all the information which is available to the observer.

4. A constant-elasticity demand curve (i.e., a demand curve with the same value of point elasticity at every price) would *not* have a common slope.

5. If the demand for a commodity is price elastic, that commodity must have at least one substitute.

6. An excise tax on a price-elastic commodity would raise more revenue than an excise tax on a price-inelastic commodity, *ceteris paribus*.

7. Consumer surplus can be measured as the area under the income-compensated demand curve, up to the quantity purchased, minus the rectangle representing consumer expenditure.

8. Demand for a particular brand of gasoline will tend to be more price elastic than the demand for gasoline in general, *ceteris paribus*.

9. For each 1 percent increase in their real income, consumers increase the proportion of income spent on education by 0.5 percent; hence, the income elasticity of education is 1.5 percent.

10. Brazil produces one-third of the world's coffee crop. If the price elasticity of demand for coffee is -0.6, then the price elasticity of demand for Brazilian coffee must be -0.2.

Calculate

Answer each of the following, showing all your work.

11. For the linear demand equation $Q_d = 800 - 50p$, answer the following questions:
    a. What is the slope of the demand equation?
    b. What is the quantity demanded when price is zero?
    c. At what price would the good be priced out of the market?
    d. At what price would point elasticity equal -1?

12. Calculate the arc elasticity of demand for each pair of prices and quantities below:
    a. $p_1 = 100$ $p_2 = 75$
       $Q_1 = 50$ $Q_2 = 60$
    b. $p_1 = 10$ $p_2 = 0$
       $Q_1 = 0$ $Q_2 = 100$
    c. $p_1 = 125$ $p_2 = 200$
       $Q_1 = 75$ $Q_2 = 50$

Contemplate

Answer each of the following questions in a brief but complete essay. These questions require creative thinking or anticipate topics which will be covered later in the text.

13. Suppose that your firm were accused of illegally conspiring with other sellers in the industry to charge an artificially high monopoly price. In looking around for an expert witness, you discover one economist who has calculated the elasticity of demand in your industry as -1.05, while another has calculated a price elasticity of demand of -0.86. Which economist would you hire to testify on behalf of your firm? Explain your answer.

14. In response to increasing thefts and muggings by heroin users, the legislature of your state passes a bill increasing both the penalty and the probability of punishment for heroin

sellers. What would you predict would happen to the rate of property crime committed by heroin addicts if the price elasticity of demand for heroin is $\eta = -0.01$? Explain your answer.

15. Producers sometimes discover that when they raise their price, they end up selling more of their product than they sold at a lower price. As concisely and diplomatically as possible, write a memo to your boss explaining why increasing price is not a good strategy for increasing sales revenue.

APPENDIX TO CHAPTER 4

Geometric Measures of Elasticity and Consumer Surplus

The purpose of this appendix is to show how price elasticity and consumer surplus can be measured by the use of simple geometry. We will first relate the value of point elasticity to a linear (constant-slope) demand curve, then show how this technique can be extended to measure the elasticity of a nonlinear (variable-slope) demand curve. We will then show how the price elasticity of demand for a commodity can be inferred from the change in expenditure for other goods in the household budget line–indifference curve tangency. Finally, we will show how these expenditures on other goods allow a monetary approximation of consumer surplus.

Measuring Point Elasticity on the Demand Curve

If the known or estimated demand function is linear (which most empirical demand functions are), it will have an equation of the form $Q_D = Q_{max} - \overline{b}p$, where Q_{max} is the quantity demanded at a zero price, and $-\overline{b} = \Delta Q/\Delta p$, which is constant for a linear demand curve. Setting $Q_D = 0$, we find that the price intercept is $p_{max} = Q_{max}/\overline{b}$: at this price, the commodity is priced out of the market. When $p = 0$ or when $Q = 0$, total expenditure equals zero. At prices between $p = 0$ and $p = p_{max}$, expenditure is positive. At the price intercept, $p = p_{max}$ and $Q = 0$: $\eta = -\infty$, since a finite reduction in price would cause an infinite percentage increase in quantity demanded. Note that the fact that price and quantity change in opposite directions still makes elasticity a negative number. At the quantity intercept, $p = 0$ and $Q = Q_{max}$; hence, $\eta = -b(0/Q_{max}) = 0$. Geometrically, the elasticity of demand at a point on a linear demand curve can be measured as the ratio of the distance from that point to the quantity intercept (a positive distance) to the distance from that point to the price intercept (a negative distance).

In Figure 4A-1, point A is associated with price p_a and quantity Q_a, so that the ratio of price to quantity equals the distance from the origin to p_a along the

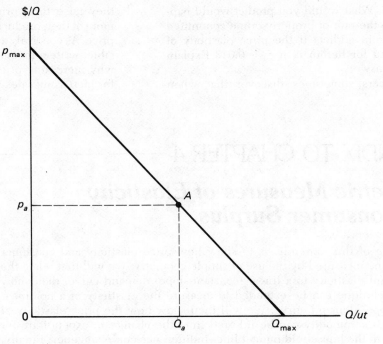

Figure 4A-1
Geometric Calculation of Point Elasticity for a Linear Demand
Curve: $\eta = Op_a/p_{max}p_a = Q_{max}Q_a/OQ_a = Q_{max}A/p_{max}A$.

price axis divided by the distance from the origin to Q_a along the quantity axis: $p/Q = Op_a/OQ_a$. The slope is everywhere the same along a linear demand curve, so that we can measure $\dfrac{\Delta Q}{\Delta p}$ as $\dfrac{OQ_a}{p_{max}p_a}$, since quantity demanded goes from zero to Q_a as price falls from p_{max} to p_a, where $p_{max} = \dfrac{Q_{max}}{b}$. Thus:

$$\eta = \frac{\Delta Q}{\Delta p} \times \frac{p}{Q} = \frac{Op_a}{OQ_a} \times \frac{OQ_a}{p_{max}p_a} = \frac{Op_a}{p_{max}p_a}$$

Also, the inverse slope of the demand curve can be measured as $\Delta Q/\Delta p = Q_{max}Q_a/Op_a$: quantity demanded falls from Q_a to zero when price rises from zero to p_a. By this measure:

$$\eta = \frac{Op_a}{OQ_a} \times \frac{Q_{max}Q_a}{Op_a} = \frac{Q_{max}Q_a}{OQ_a}$$

Given these equivalent measures of elasticity,

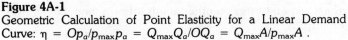

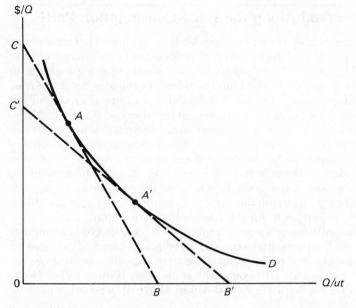

Figure 4A-2
Geometric Calculation of Point Elasticity for a Nonlinear Demand
Curve. At point A, $\eta = AB/AC$; at point A', $\eta = A'B'/A'C'$.

we see that triangle $p_{\max}p_aA$ is geometrically similar to triangle $AQ_aQ_{\max}$, since both are right triangles and we have shown that two sides of each triangle are proportional. And since similar triangles have three proportional sides, it follows that: $\eta = Q_{\max}A/p_{\max}A$, which is the result we wished to prove.

If point A were at the midpoint of the demand curve in Figure 4A-1, then $Q_{\max}A = -p_{\max}A$, so that $\eta = -1$. As point A moves toward $p_{\max}$, demand becomes more price elastic (η approaches negative infinity). As point A moves toward $Q_{\max}$, $Q_aQ_{\max}$ approaches zero, and demand becomes less price elastic (η approaches zero). The geometric approach to the measurement of point elasticity indicates that each point on a linear demand curve has a different price elasticity, from infinitely elastic at the price intercept to zero elastic at the quantity intercept.

Figure 4A-2 depicts a nonlinear demand curve: each point is associated with a different change in quantity relative to the change in price. However, the slope of the curve itself at a particular point is the same as the slope of the line tangent to the curve at that point. At point A, both the slope and the values of p and Q are the same on demand curve D and the tangent line CB. Using the techniques developed for linear demand curves, $\eta = AB/AC$. At point A', the demand curve has the same slope and the same values for p and Q as those of tangent line $C'B'$ at point A'. By similar logic, we know $\eta = A'B'/A'C'$ at point A'. To determine the geometric measure of point elasticity for a nonlinear demand curve, we merely apply the procedures for calculating the elasticity for a point on a linear demand curve to the tangent line at that point.

Determining Price Elasticity of Demand Along the Price-Consumption Path

Instead of going to the trouble of first plotting the demand curve from information obtained from the price-consumption path of a household's indifference curve map, we could calculate whether demand is price elastic or price inelastic by calculating how much money in the household budget remains for other commodities at alternative prices. If evidence indicates that a price decrease for one commodity leads to a decrease in the money spent for other goods, then it follows that the money spent on the good in question must have risen, since tastes (the indifference map), prices of other goods, and money income are held constant along a price consumption path. Hence, changes in the consumption of other goods can only be due to changes in money left over after the household has changed its consumption of the good in question. By monitoring changes in expenditures for other goods along the price consumption curve, we are able to infer the changes in expenditure for the commodity in question.

Figure 4A-3 presents the price-consumption path for a specific commodity, cheese, measured on the horizontal axis, and a composite commodity, x, which is defined as real purchasing power remaining after a specific amount of commodity 1 has been purchased. This composite commodity is often called *Hicks-Marshall money*, after Sir John Hicks and Alfred Marshall, who originated the

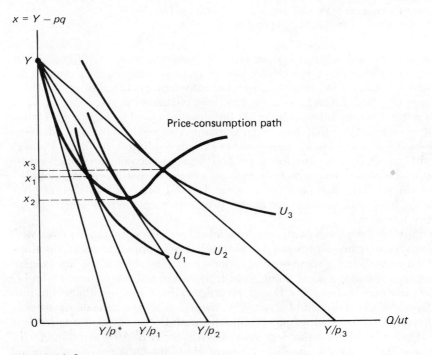

Figure 4A-3
Measuring Price Elasticity of Demand for a Good (q) Using Hicks-Marshall Money (x)

composite commodity approach. It is measured as $x = Y - pq$, where Y is money income per period, p is the relative price of cheese, and q is the quantity of cheese purchased. Note that the price-consumption path emanates from the vertical intercept of budget line Y, Y/p^*: p^* is the price at which cheese is priced out of this household's budget (given income, tastes, and other prices). For prices equal to p^* and above, expenditure on good 1 is zero, and $x = Y$.

As budget lines fan out away from budget line Y, Y/p^*, the price consumption path is associated with increasing consumption of cheese implying, at least initially, increasing expenditure on this good. As seen in the case of a linear demand curve, demand is price elastic in the neighborhood of the price intercept of a demand curve. Figure 4A-3 shows that price elastic demand is associated with a negatively sloped price-consumption path: if, as the price of a good decreases, less is spent on other commodities, *ceteris paribus*, demand for the good in question is price elastic.

In Figure 4A-3, the price consumption path reaches its lowest price (relative to the vertical axis) at the tangency of indifference curve U_2 to budget line Y, Y/p_2. Since x_2 is the lowest expenditure on "other goods," it follows that $p_2q_2 = Y - x_2$ is the maximum expenditure on cheese, given money income tastes and the relative prices of other goods. Prices greater than p_2 are associated with less expenditure on cheese, implying elastic demand for cheese in the price range $p^* > p > p_2$. Prices less than p_2 are also associated with expenditure less than p_2q_2, meaning that a price increase (to p_2) would increase expenditure. Demand is price inelastic for prices in the range $p_2 > p > 0$. An unbroken price consumption path, like the one in Figure 4A-3, implies that demand is unit elastic when the slope of the price consumption path is zero. Finally, a positively sloped price-consumption path means expenditure on other goods increases as the price of cheese decreases; demand for the good plotted on the horizontal axis must be inelastic.

Geometric Measurement of Consumer Surplus

In chapter two we saw how the opportunity to purchase any amount of a commodity at a constant price allows the household to get more utility than it gives up (in the utility sacrificed by not purchasing other commodities instead of the one in question). As we will see throughout this text, one of economists' major claims for the system of private enterprise is that a competitive market tends to allocate resources in a way which maximizes consumer surplus, given the distribution of purchasing power and prevailing consumer tastes. We will conclude this appendix by showing the conditions under which consumer surplus can be approximated from household and market demand curves.

Figure 4A-4 shows a household purchasing q_0 pounds of cheese, at a constant price of p_0 per pound. The negative slope of the demand curve indicates that this implies that this household would have been willing to pay higher prices for the inframarginal $(q_0 - 1)$ pounds of cheese purchased that income period. In fact, the distance from the horizontal axis to the demand curve may, under some conditions, be interpreted as the maximum price that would be paid for

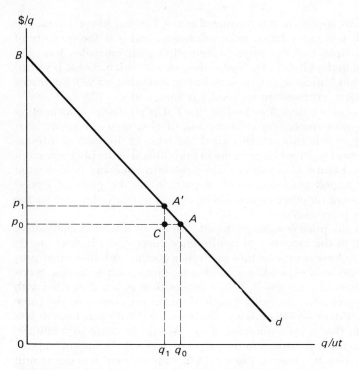

Figure 4A-4
Measuring Consumer Surplus from Demand Curve

each unit. Following this logic, the area beneath the demand curve from the origin to q_0 is the money equivalent of total utility gained from consuming q_0 pounds of cheese. Subtract expenditure $p_0 q_0$, equal to the area of rectangle $p_0 A q_0 0$, and consumer surplus equals the area of triangle $p_0 A B$.

Knowledge of demand curves presumes, of course, that data exist (in the form of observed prices and quantities), which allows the area of triangle $p_0 A B$ to be estimated. Even if a researcher could control for changes in tastes, income, and other prices, would an empirical demand curve allow the researcher to draw reliable conclusions about the size of consumer surplus? In light of the distinction between *ceteris paribus* and *mutatis mutandis* demand curves in chapter four, we can answer in the affirmative.

Consider an increase in the price of cheese from p_0 to p_1 in Figure 4A-4; consumption would fall to q_1 pounds of cheese per month and consumer surplus would decline by $q_1(p_1 - p_0)$, the increased expenditure on units purchased, plus the area of triangle $AA'C$, which is the lost consumer surplus on the last $(q_1 - q_0)$ units no longer purchased at the higher price.

As explained in chapter two, a typical money price increase will reduce consumption by the combined impact of the income and the substitution effects. If the demand curve in Figure 4A-4 were a constant money income demand curve, price p_1 would be associated with a lower real income than price p_0. And, if the marginal utility of purchasing power changed in response to a change in real income, the money measure of consumer surplus would give an inaccurate picture of true consumer surplus. However, as mentioned previously, empirical demand curves tend to be constant *real* income, or income-compensated demand curves, since empirical data are time series data, requiring adjustments for the change in the purchasing power of money. Ironically, when measuring consumer surplus along income-compensated demand curves, the assumption of constant marginal utility of income is less crucial than were one to use constant money income demand curves derived directly from a household's price-consumption path.

Economists are often required to warn their clients that an empirical estimation of an economic relationship is, at best, only a rough approximation of the ideal concept being discussed. How ironic, and fortunate, that an important concept like consumer surplus can, at least in principle, be more adequately measured by empirical techniques which imply income-adjusted demand curves, than from household price-consumption paths, which assume constant money income.

PART THREE
Production and Cost

Part three complements the theory of household choice by exploring how producers choose combinations of scarce resources with which to produce commodities. Despite the similarity of diagrams and analytical techniques, the economics of input choice involves the study of a means (economic efficiency) to achieving a more remote end (economic profit, analyzed in part four). While consumer choice is taken as a revelation of underlying, nonobservable preferences, producer choice involves a relation between measurable input services and measurable rates of output.

Chapter five concentrates on the physical aspects of production: without knowing the opportunity costs of inputs, analysis of efficiency is limited to whether or not input services are being wasted. Production cannot be technically efficient if the rate of output can be increased without the services of one or more inputs being increased. The chapter begins by considering how the rate of output varies when the amount of one input is varied while other input services are held constant. Next, the services of two or more inputs are varied, first with output remaining constant (factor substitution) and then with output changing as inputs are increased or decreased proportionately (changes in scale).

Chapter six builds on the material in chapter five, extending the analysis to the economic costs of production. Producers confront scarcity through the opportunity cost of inputs; the valuation of inputs ultimately reflects society's preferences for the alternative commodities inputs could produce. The chosen combination of inputs for any rate of output is said to be economically efficient only if it is impossible to reduce production costs without also reducing the rate of output. Equivalently, a combination of inputs is economically efficient when it is impossible to increase the rate of outputs unless the cost of input services also increases. Once the minimum cost of producing each rate of output has been identified, the firm is able to define a cost function, which relates the economic cost of producing each rate of output. The chapter concludes by showing how production planning is related to the day-to-day production costs the firm actually experiences once long-range plans have been implemented.

Chapter seven extends the concepts developed in chapters five and six by presenting a nontechnical overview of the simple production technologies often encountered in industry. Since input substitution often entails changing the technology of production, we explore how treating different techniques as discrete processes leads to isoquants with linear segments. The chapter deals with input selection when a given output can be produced with alternative production processes. It concludes with a description of cost curves which result from technology characterized by fixed input proportions.

Chapter 5
Production

Much like the choice of consumer goods, the selection of inputs juxtaposes technical possibilities and human priorities. Factor prices (or opportunity costs) communicate to the user of scarce resources the value of alternatives foregone. The production isoquant, whose characteristics are similar to consumer indifference curves, embody technical possibilities for input substitution.

In this chapter we concentrate on the physical aspects of production, laying the groundwork for the investigation of production costs in chapter six. We see how producers winnow technically efficient production methods, discarding techniques which waste resources. Chapter six will then show how the producer selects the least costly process from among the technically efficient ones by considering relative factor prices.

We begin by emphasizing the behavioral context of efficiency, showing how human values influence the way we define and measure productive inputs. The physical aspects of production are first manifest through the analysis of the marginal product and the average product of a single factor of production. After exploring the relation between change in one input and the resulting change in output, we turn our attention to the definition of technical efficiency when several factors are variable. An *isoquant* is developed as the production analogue of the indifference curve.

The most relevant characteristic of the isoquant is the marginal rate of technical substitution, which relates the producer's ability to substitute inputs to the marginal productivity of those factors. We also consider returns to scale, which relates different rates of output (i.e., different isoquants) to proportional changes in all inputs. For empirical research, economists often specify homogeneous production functions, whereby output change can be predicted by the proportional change in the scale of input use. After considering the characteristics of homogeneous production functions, the chapter ends by relating technical efficiency to the preconditions for economically efficient input use.

Efficiency and the Definition of Inputs

The complex set of influences that motivate consumer choice is neatly packaged in the concept of utility. Individuals are presumed to be the best judge of their own welfare. The choices consumers make are taken as revelations of their preferences. In turning our attention to production, emphasis shifts from utility to efficiency. **Production** is a process whereby resources are transformed into more useful—hence more valuable—forms. Production is *efficient* when no additional output can be produced unless additional input services are obtained by increasing cost or sacrificing some other commodity. In a world of scarcity, potential human welfare cannot be maximized if some resources are squandered. Efficient resource use will not vanquish scarcity, but efficient use of inputs does lessen the sting of scarcity.

Efficiency is a term widely used in the physical and engineering sciences. This leads some to treat efficiency as a physical phenomenon. But all human goals, including efficiency, must be expressed in human terms. As Frank Knight stated some five decades ago:

> There is the common misconception that it is possible to measure or discuss efficiency in purely physical terms. The first principle of physics or engineering science teaches us that this is not true, that the term efficiency involves the idea of value, and some measure of value as well. It is perhaps the most important principle of physical science that neither matter nor energy can be created or destroyed, that whatever goes into any process must come out in some form, and hence as a mere matter of physical quantity, the efficiency of all operations would equal one hundred percent. The correct definition of efficiency is the ratio, not between "output" and "input," but between *useful* output and total output or input. Hence efficiency, even in the simplest energy transformation, is meaningless without a measure of usefulness or value.[1]

---

[1] Frank H. Knight, "Social Economic Organization," *The Economic Organization* (New York: Harper & Row, 1933, 1951), reprinted in William Breit and Harold Hochman, eds., *Readings in Microeconomics*, 2nd ed. (New York: Holt, Rinehart and Winston, 1971), p. 7.

Knight's words are still true. The study of production must provide a role for human values in separating desirable production techniques from undesirable or wasteful ones. Production which uses scarce resources to create desirable commodities is efficient when an output is created with the minimum opportunity cost. **Opportunity cost** is the sacrifice of one commodity when resources are allocated to the production of another. Scarce resources used to produce one commodity cannot be used to produce another commodity; human preferences for different commodities ultimately determine whether the benefits from the commodities actually produced justify the cost of other commodities sacrificed. Human values even color the definition and measurement of inputs themselves.

Classical economists used the **labor theory of value** to explain input prices and to measure factors of production. We saw in chapter two that measuring relative scarcity of two commodities (e.g., grape juice and wine) wholly in terms of embodied labor failed to account for interest payments. To Karl Marx, all nonlabor income was a result of the exploitation of workers; if labor produced all value, workers should receive the full value of what they produced. Profit, interest, and rent all sprang from the surplus value that went to privileged classes.

The demise of the labor theory of value resulted from more than disagreement with Marx's denunciation of nonlabor income. Ultimately, the labor theory of value foundered on its inability to measure labor itself. While capital could be measured in terms of the labor embodied in its production, which was released as machinery was used to produce other goods, labor was measured in terms of the necessities workers purchased with their subsistence wages. Yet, since some workers were more productive than others, a "standard" measure of labor was necessary. Marx defined socially necessary labor time as the minimum (i.e., efficient) amount of unskilled labor used to produce basic necessities. But using "wage goods" to measure labor and using labor to measure the price of "wage goods" caused the labor theory of value to get bogged down in a morass of tautology.

After diminishing marginal utility had displaced embodied labor as the explanation for exchange values, Alfred Marshall reintroduced the role of production costs into price determination as half of his supply-demand framework.[2] John Bates Clark, one of the first American economists of international repute, extended the principle of marginalism to the supply side of price determination.[3] Under ideal competitive conditions, each input would gravitate to its highest valued use, and the owner of each factor of production would be paid the market value of

[2] *Principles of Political Economy* (London: Macmillan, 1890).
[3] *The Distribution of Wealth* (London: Macmillan, 1899).

that factor's **marginal product**, defined as the change in output due to the use of one more unit of that input, *ceteris paribus*. The wage earned by each worker was equal to the change in output attributed to the last labor hour hired. The rent of land corresponded to the output obtained from the marginal acre. The return to capital was not labor exploitation; owners of capital received the value of output which would have been lost if one unit of capital were withdrawn from production, other inputs remaining constant.

Marginal productivity theory was anticipated in David Ricardo's explanation of rental income.[4] Ricardo had shown that the rent paid on a parcel of land would equal the difference between output produced on that land and the output produced on the least fertile land under cultivation (other factors being constant). Marginal productivity theory extended the meaning of rent to include the payment to the owners of any nonreplicable input. Labor and capital could also earn rent. Further, the price of transferable inputs equals the present value of its expected yield. A plot of land, expected to earn $3,000 per year in perpetuity, would be worth exactly $30,000 if the market rate of interest were expected to remain at 10 percent per year.

Marginal productivity theory links each factor's reward to its influence on output. Differences in labor productivity due to inherited traits would, like land, receive economic rent. Productivity differences resulting from education, on-the-job training, and other resource-using activities would ultimately be explained as returns to the investment in **human capital**.[5]

And what of capital itself? The value of a machine to a producer would equal the present value of the machine's marginal product. A machine expected to produce $250 worth of output in excess of its operating costs for its 10-year life would be worth $2,026.96 if the market rate of interest were 5 percent, $1,689.96 if the interest rate were 10 percent, and only $1,257.74 at a 20 percent rate of interest.

Today capitalized value provides the common denominator for all factors of production. The selling price of land is its capitalized value, or the present value of expected rental receipts (see chapters three and thirteen). Workers, as we have seen, can be crudely characterized as globs of human capital. Microeconomic theory has come full circle; a century after the labor theory of value was abandoned, neoclassical economics now stands on a **capital theory of value**.

Is a capital theory of value any more objective, or less circular in its logic, than the labor theory of value it replaced? After an extended debate between economists at Cambridge University in England (led by Joan

---

[4] *Principles of Political Economy and Taxation* (1817).

[5] See George F. Kneller, *Education and Economic Thought* (New York: Wiley, 1968).

Robinson) and those in Cambridge, Massachusetts (e.g., Paul Samuelson and Robert Solow of M.I.T.),[6] there is some agreement that, ultimately, the capital theory of value founders on its inability to define exactly what a unit of capital is. The payment to the owners of capital goods depends upon the value of commodities which capital produces, but to compare the change in output to the change in the amount of capital used, capital must be measured. The services of one machine can be measured by the length of time that machine is used, but some common denominator must be found if several different types of machines (e.g., lathes, punch presses, fork lifts) are used in the production process.

Different types of machines cannot be compared as "embodied labor," since different types of workers are defined as having different quantities (and perhaps qualities) of human capital. Different types of machines can be weighted by their relative market prices, but we have already seen that the market will cause the price of a machine to equal the present value of the machine marginal product. The circle is complete. We cannot determine capital's marginal product without knowing its price, but the price of a capital good cannot be determined without knowledge of its marginal product.

The implications of the circularity of the definition of capital mean that economics, like any science, must accept some terms as undefined. In geometry, a line can be defined as the shortest distance between two points, or a point can be defined by the intersection of two lines. One of the two terms—point or line—must remain undefined so that the other can be defined. In economics, we can define capital as embodied labor, or we can define labor as embodied capital. If we accept the first definition of capital, we cannot define labor. If we use the human capital approach to measure labor differences, we sacrifice a clear meaning of capital.

As a practical matter, the working economist rarely needs to be concerned with the problems of defining inputs. If we are concerned with one firm, or even one industry, the relative prices of capital goods can be taken as given. Answers to questions of productive efficiency and minimizing cost or maximizing profit are not materially affected by the circularity in the definition of capital.

The deeper implication of the capital controversy brings us back to Frank Knight's warning against thinking of efficiency, upon which distribution theory is based, as a purely objective concept. Marx's concept of socially necessary labor time was based on the operation of an efficient firm, but defining labor as embodied capital did not avoid the fact that what labor "ought to receive" is a subjective question. In neoclassical economics, the relative prices of capital goods are based on the as-

---

[6] See James Tobin, "Cambridge (UK) vs. Cambridge (Mass.)," *The Public Interest* (spring 1972).

sumption that competitive capital markets are in equilibrium, but characterizing labor differences as differences in human capital does not justify unequal income distribution. (Because of the awarding of patents for inventions, the assumption that capital goods sell for competitive prices may be violated in most industries. This issue is explored in depth in chapter twelve.)

Distribution of income and output is a social process, the result of human decisions rather than unchanging natural laws. The definitions and measurement of factors of production reflect the prevailing attitudes and institutions which make up the environment in which economic theory is shaped. As long as we remember that definitions themselves are factors of production, we can judge the usefulness of those definitions in terms of the goals we wish our theories to help us achieve.

The Production Function

Production, as mentioned, involves the transformation of scarce resources into something people value. *Manufacturing* is a productive activity; both human and machine energy shape raw materials into usable finished goods. A *service* is also a productive activity in which the commodity is consumed at the same instant it is produced. Other forms of production include transportation, storaging, and packaging. Even so-called leisure can entail *household production*: the time (labor) of different members of the household is spent using appliances (capital) to transform food items (raw materials) into the finished product (a meal).[7]

Production is a process; like consumption, production can be measured only if a time dimension is specified. It makes no sense to talk about producing "half a car" except as a time-based expression: producing one car every two hours is equivalent to producing at the *rate* of one-half car per hour. Because production is measured as output per unit of time, inputs are measured in terms of services per unit of time: four worker-hours and four machine-hours may mean four workers each using one machine for one hour, or one worker using one machine for four hours. Either way, the capital-to-labor ratio is one.

Mindful of Frank Knight's warning that efficiency reflects human values, we may distinguish between technical efficiency, which requires that scarce inputs not be wasted, and economic efficiency, which requires that each commodity be produced with minimum opportunity cost. Technical efficiency is analogous to the dominance assumption of consumer preferences, as long as more output is preferred to less output,

[7] Gary S. Becker, *The Economic Approach to Human Behavior* (Chicago: University of Chicago Press, 1975), readings 1, 5, 6, and 7.

the use of inputs being constant. A production process is technically efficient only when it is impossible to produce more output without increasing input services. When more inputs are used, but no more output results, those additional inputs are being wasted—society has sacrificed whatever commodities those inputs might have produced and has nothing to show for it.

Regardless of relative factor prices, a technically inefficient production process can never be the economically efficient (least-cost) process. By identifying and discarding technically inefficient combinations of inputs, we reduce the number of processes that must be screened to determine which is the minimum cost process. Economic efficiency depends upon society's relative evaluation of inputs, which is communicated through factor markets in a private enterprise economy. A process which is economically efficient at one time or in one place may not be the least-cost process at other times or in different places. Consider how three different societies choose to grow rice. Japan produces the most rice per acre of land; the United States produces the most rice per labor-hour; Thailand produces the most rice per unit of capital. (We have some confidence that using tractors and combines is more capital intensive than using oxen to cultivate rice. However, it can be perplexing to explain how many oxen are equivalent to one tractor, especially if the relative prices of oxen and tractors differ in different countries.) Since there is no unique agricultural process which simultaneously maximizes rice output for each input, there can be more than one technically efficient process, and which process is economically efficient depends upon local conditions. Without knowledge of relative factor prices (the relative evaluation of input services), it is impossible to determine which, if any, of the three countries is producing rice inefficiently.

Since factor and output prices vary across time and space, a process which minimizes cost today may be supplanted by a different process if relative input prices change. Producers in oil consuming countries have learned that changing modes of production can soften the blow of increasing energy costs. In this chapter we will concentrate on identifying the technically efficient production methods, which form a menu from which the least-cost process will be selected. The set of all technically efficient production processes for a commodity is called the **production function** for that commodity.

The production function relates the maximum rate of output to each technically efficient combination of input services. In our rice growing example, the production function has the form $q = f(L,K,T)$, which is read: The quantity of rice produced (per unit of time) is a function of the amount of labor services (L), capital services (K), and land services (T for "terra") employed in rice production. In more general form, if we allow q to stand for output(s) and v to stand for inputs, a single-commodity production function has the general form $q = f(v_1,$

$v_2, \ldots, v_m$), where each v denotes a different type of labor, machine, raw material, land, or energy input.

As often as not, a firm produces several outputs at the same time, either because different commodities require the same machinery or labor skills, or because two or more outputs are linked together as *joint products*. Joint products can involve the simultaneous production of two goods: wool and mutton, chickens and eggs, gasoline and diesel fuel. Combinations of "goods" and "bads" can also occur: steel and dirty air, chemicals and polluted water, nuclear energy and radioactive waste. When multiple inputs and outputs are interrelated through joint production, increasing the rate of output of a finished good requires either increasing one or more inputs or reducing one or more outputs. As we will see in chapter fifteen, producing more of one good by producing less of some other good can be viewed as transforming the latter good into the former. When joint products are involved, production is depicted as a relationship between a production function for inputs and a transformation function for outputs:

$$f(v_1, v_2, \ldots, v_m) = g\,(q_1, q_2, \ldots, q_n)$$

With joint production, technical efficiency requires that all inputs in the production function, f, are accounted for among the outputs in the transformation function, g. Efficiency means that it is impossible to increase any of the outputs unless either (1) one or more input services are increased, or (2) one or more outputs are decreased. If any of the outputs (for example, q_i), is a "bad" (e.g., pollution, worker injuries), it is represented as a negative output. Any time that pollution were avoidable, production would be inefficient: it would be possible to increase q_i (the absolute value of q_i could be reduced) without increasing the use of inputs or sacrificing any other (good) output.

Before we venture further into the economics of production, it is wise to get a fix on our direction. Economists use production functions to show how producers select input combinations in response to relative prices of input services. Assuming that producers attempt to minimize the cost of producing the chosen rate of output is equivalent to assuming that only technically efficient input combinations are candidates for selection. But there is more to production than hiring workers and operating machines. Plant supervisors and production managers are paid to encourage, cajole, and even threaten workers to perform at their peak efficiency. Sometimes managers push too hard: workers quit or go on strike. Sometimes managers give dumb orders, and output falls below its potential.

Although economic production theory bypasses the important considerations such as personnel administration, machine maintenance, and quality control, this does not mean that economists consider these issues unimportant or irrelevant. However, economists in general claim no special expertise in how inputs are actually turned into outputs. Yet, economic insights into input selection are useful for improving mismanaged firms as well as for describing well-managed ones. Economic theory provides a description of how efficient input combinations are achieved, so that inefficient combinations can be recognized and modified. The fact that all firms do not behave in accordance with the assumptions of production theory means that business economists, in cooperation with other business and engineering experts, can improve upon the methods used in industry, thereby earning a fee for their advice.

Marginal and Average Productivity of Input Services

There are two methods by which a firm can hire the services of inputs (which we will consider in detail in chapter six). If an input is readily available in a consistent quality at a known price (e.g., electricity can be obtained by flipping a switch), the producer will take the chance that the input will be available on demand and hire that input on a pay-as-you-go basis. By buying factor services only as needed, the firm avoids having to pay for those which cannot be used efficiently. Inputs whose cost varies with their use (resulting in variable costs) are termed **variable inputs**.

When a machine must be custom-made, when a worker must be specially trained, or when raw materials are in uncertain supply, firms often incur fixed costs to assure that needed input services will be available when needed. Computer time may be leased from a computer firm or business that owns its own computer; but concern for the safety of sensitive files and the need for instant access often causes a firm to purchase its own computer. Entertainers, athletes, university professors, and other people with scarce, hard-to-replace talents are hired under contracts which often require that they be paid even if their services are not used. Workers whose training is extensive and expensive are often retained on a company's payroll even when there is no useful work for them to do. The employer who tries to save a few dollars by firing workers who are not needed runs the risk of incurring much greater costs if new workers must be trained at the company's expense. The specter of a labor stoppage or other supply interruption causes firms to build up raw material inventories to assure the continuation of production, even if the current price is greater than that which might prevail later.

The disadvantage of hiring inputs by contracts, or buying equipment outright that could be leased, is that factor costs become fixed, that is, unrelated to the firm's rate of production. A **fixed input** is an input whose costs do not vary with its use. The opportunity cost of a machine's purchase price will be incurred, regardless of whether the machine is used or remains idle. An injured football player cannot help his team win games, but his contract assures that his paychecks continue. The price of using raw materials purchased at premium prices is their replacement cost; outrageous prices paid in the past cannot be recovered.

Not all inputs whose cost is fixed must be used to capacity. A farmer may have signed a lease requiring him to pay rent on 1,000 acres of land; but if he chooses, he can plant only 500 acres. There is an upper limit on factor availability, but no lower limit. On the other hand, the purchase of a multi-ton earth mover implies using all of the machine or none of it. So much horsepower is required to move the machine, that it may be almost as costly to move a little dirt as it is to move a lot of dirt. Bulky capital goods, in particular, tend to have fixed costs and to be fixed inputs as well.

The periods of production correspond to the length of contracts which require factor payments. The **long run** is really the firm's planning horizon—a period long enough that all contracts will expire so that all inputs can be varied. Obviously, a person who has not yet entered an industry has signed no contracts; he or she is paying for no factor services and is receiving no revenue since no output can be produced.

Once a person quits his or her job to start a business, signs a lease for land or a building, borrows from a bank to buy machinery, invests in an inventory of raw materials, or hires accountants, attorneys, or other specialists under contract, some costs will become fixed. But production can take place only after input services have been acquired; hence, a firm operates under the dual constraints of minimum payments for some inputs and maximum availability of those inputs to the quantity contracted for or owned outright.

The **short run** is a period of time—determined by the duration of contracts or by the replacement cycle for fixed inputs—during which some factor services will have a maximum availability and some costs cannot be reduced below predetermined levels. When the cost of a factor is fixed, the cost of using an input involves the sacrifice of alternative uses; the contract cost is not a cost of using the input, since that cost must be paid even if the input were not used. If I leased 500 acres of farmland, but planted only 100 acres, I must still pay the rent for the 400 acres which lie idle. If I decide to plant the remaining 400 acres, I will incur only labor, seed, and machinery cost; if the land has no alternative use, the cost of using it is zero.

Even though a producer is required to pay for a factor of production, that input will be used only if variable costs are lower as a result. To take a silly example, a secretarial pool in a large office might contain 25 typewriters; but if the firm employed only one typist, the typist's time would be more productive if he or she used only one typewriter, instead of typing one line on each machine.

We define the **short-run production function** as the formula which gives the maximum rate of output for each employment level of a variable input, other input services being fixed. For expository purposes, we will assume that a commodity's output depends upon the amount of land, $\overline{T}$, and capital, $\overline{K}$, which are both fixed, and the amount of labor services, L, which are assumed to be variable. To concentrate on how the productivity of labor changes as the ratio of labor services to other inputs increases, we will assume that labor is *homogeneous*. This means that individual workers are perfect substitutes: they can be hired in any order without changing the output or the cost associated with each quantity of labor services employed. (The complications introduced by dropping the assumption of homogeneous labor will be discussed in chapter fourteen.)

In the short-run production function, $q = f(L, \overline{K}, \overline{T})$, capital and land operate as *parameters*, potential variables which are treated as constants. The **short-run total product of labor**, TP_L, is illustrated in the upper diagrams in Figure 5-1*a* and *b*. Short-run total product of labor is defined as the maximum rate of output associated with each rate of employment of labor, other input services held constant. In Figure 5-1*a*, the output of labor first rises rapidly as employment increases from $L = 0$ to $L = L_0$; then output rises more gradually when employment increases from L_0 to L_2, until the maximum possible output of q_{max} is reached when $L = L_2$. In Figure 5-1*b*, total output increases at a constant rate until reaching its maximum at L^*. Beyond L_2, output is shown to decline in Figure 5-1*a*; if more than L^* units of labor are used in Figure 5-1*b*, output is assumed to remain constant at q_{max}. Figure 5-1*a* represents the case in which the marginal product of a variable input varies with the amount employed because the variable and fixed inputs are *used* in differing proportions. In Figure 5-1*b*, labor and capital (and land) are used in fixed proportions; when less than L^* units of labor are used, some machinery and land are idle. A production function which requires fixed input proportions for each unit of output results in a linear total product, which rises with the use of labor, until all fixed inputs are used, at q_{max}.

The bottom diagrams in Figure 5-1*a* and *b* depict the marginal product of labor under different assumptions about how output changes as the use of labor changes. The *marginal product of labor* curve, MP_L, shows the slope, or rate of change, of the *total product* of labor curve in the top diagram. Marginal product measures the change in output due to the change in the use of the variable input, other factor services remaining constant.[8] When many tasks are necessary to produce a com-

---

[8] Using calculus, the marginal product of each input is the partial derivative of output with respect to that input. Given $q = f(L, K, T)$, $MP_L = \delta q/\delta L$, $MP_K = \delta q/\delta K$, and $MP_T = \delta q/\delta T$. For a discussion of partial derivatives, see appendix A.

modity and machinery is specialized (e.g., the sequence of machines on an assembly line), all jobs must be performed by the same person when only one worker is available. Hiring a second worker allows both workers to specialize: each worker can devote more time to work because less time is wasted switching tools and moving from one place to another. Figure 5-1*a* shows the marginal product of labor initially increasing as each additional worker enhances the effectiveness of workers already employed. The range of *increasing* marginal productivity is from $L = 0$ to $L = L_0$.

As the amount of variable input use increases, given a maximum availability of other inputs, there must come a point where the marginal product of the variable input will begin to decline. In Figure 5-1*a*, *diminishing marginal productivity* commences at $L = L_0$. As more and more workers are used, the increases in the rate of output become smaller and

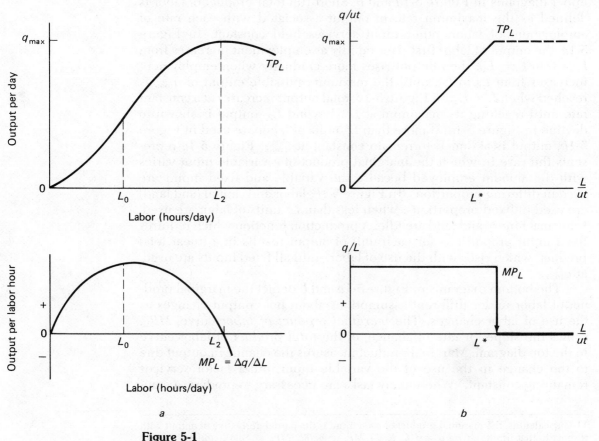

Figure 5-1
Total and Marginal Product of Labor: *a*, Variable Proportions; *b*, Fixed Input Proportions.

smaller until, at L_2, total output per unit of time is maximum. When inputs can be used in variable proportions, diminishing marginal productivity reflects the fact that labor services are, at best, only imperfect substitutes for limited capital and land services. As more workers are added to a fixed amount of capital and land, the effect of crowding will eventually outweigh further gains from labor specialization. Workers will be idled when needed tools are being used by others; obviously, idle workers will not increase output. Too many workers in a limited space would increase breakage and lower morale, further snarling the production process. If more than L_2 workers were employed in Figure 5-1a, the marginal product of labor would actually become negative: output would decline as employment increased. For obvious reasons, profit-conscious firms would not knowingly hire so many workers that the last worker hired caused output to fall.

Figure 5-1b shows a different pattern. Some types of machinery (e.g., typewriters, computer terminals, sewing machines) can only be used in fixed proportions to labor. One typist cannot work effectively with more than one typewriter at a time, nor can more than one typist work with a single typewriter at the same time. Once a number of machines have been installed, total output will rise at a constant rate (due to our assumption of homogeneous labor), and the marginal product of labor will remain constant as long as idle machines are available. Once machinery has been used to capacity, additional workers could add nothing to output; and, since technology would not allow additional workers to operate machines used by the appropriate number of workers, they would not decrease output either. In Figure 5-1b, diminishing marginal productivity is represented by the positive horizontal line from $L = 0$ to $L = L^*$, then plunges to the labor axis, where $MP_L = 0$, for $L > L^*$.

Allowing for either gradual (Figure 5-1a) or discrete (Figure 5-1b) drops in labor productivity, we can state the **law of diminishing marginal productivity** (sometimes called the **law of diminishing returns**) as follows: beyond some rate of variable input use (L_0 in Figure 5-1a and L^* in Figure 5-1b), the marginal product of that input will decline as more of the input is used. A common mistake is to confuse diminishing marginal productivity with negative marginal productivity. Once the marginal product of labor has peaked, each additional unit of labor service causes the rate of output to increase, but by smaller and smaller amounts, until as much output as possible has been produced. At L_2 in Figure 5-1a, the last unit of labor hired neither adds nor detracts from output: total product is maximized.[9] Only if employment were to expand beyond

---

[9] Given the short-run production function, $q = f(L, \overline{K}, \overline{T})$, q is maximized for specified value of K and T by hiring labor such that $\partial q/\partial L = 0$ and $\partial^2 q/\partial L^2 < 0$. Since $\partial^2 q/\partial L^2 = \partial MP_L/\partial L$, the total product of labor is maximized when marginal product of labor equals zero and is declining (that is, would be negative if more labor were hired). See appendix A.

its output maximizing rate would diminishing returns cause output to fall. Thus, negative marginal productivity is an extreme consequence of diminishing marginal productivity: the fact that marginal product is getting smaller does not imply that output is actually declining as use of that output increases.

A moment's reflection should convince the reader that negative marginal productivity for a variable input is seldom encountered among healthy businesses because it represents such a blatant violation of technical efficiency. A firm which hired so many workers that output began to decline would in effect be hiring extra workers to destroy the output of other workers. A less expensive way of producing the resulting net output would be to stop hiring workers while the marginal product of labor was still positive.

For more subtle reasons, a firm which stopped hiring labor before diminishing marginal productivity commenced would also violate technical efficiency. An increasing marginal product of the variable input implies a negative marginal product for the fixed factor(s). Too little labor for optimal specialization could also be interpreted as too much capital, or too much land for the labor services hired, or both. For example, a farmer with 1,000 acres who has only his own labor available might grow and harvest more food by tilling 100 acres, and by leaving other land and capital idle, than by trying to work his entire spread single-handedly.

Sometimes, capital goods come in discrete units (e.g., earth movers), which have a narrow range on their rate of operation; this is called a case of *lumpy* inputs. Figure 5-2 shows a production function for lumpy capital. When fewer than L' workers are employed, the total product curve for K_1 units of capital lies below the total product curve for K_0 units of capital, even though $K_1 > K_0$. The marginal product of capital, MP_K, is negative when fewer than L' units of labor are used, that is, when $L < L'$, $MP_K < 0$. When $L = L'$, output is the same whether K_0 or K_1 units of capital are used; the marginal product of capital must be zero: $MP_K = 0$ when $L = L'$. If use of capital could be varied only by discrete units (e.g., the number of earth movers used must be one or two), the firm would operate efficiently by using only K_0 units of capital until L' workers were hired, then using K_1 units of capital only when more than L' workers were hired.

If use of a fixed factor could not be varied, the firm which had installed K_2 units of capital would not produce efficiently if it hired fewer than L' units of capital. Blast furnaces come in different sizes and capacities, but once one has been installed in a steel plant, efficient use requires a minimum number of workers. The only plausible example of a firm purposefully using too little labor for available production capacity would be a monopoly seller contriving an artificial shortage to raise price. As we will see in chapter ten, it is because monopoly sellers often

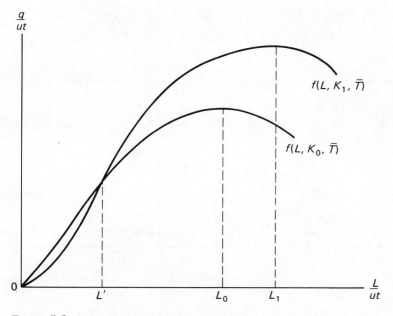

Figure 5-2
Total Product of Labor Curves for Two Levels of Capital. If capital use could be varied only discretely, the firm would use K_0 units until L' workers had been hired, then use K_1 units of capital. Even when cost is fixed, the firm will try to avoid using inputs at levels which cause the factor's marginal product to become negative.

behave inefficiently relative to their technical potential that many economists are critical of monopoly market structure.

Somewhat more familiar than the concept of marginal productivity is the **average product** of an input, which is defined as the ratio of the rate of output to the rate of employment of an input. Geometrically, the average product of labor is measured by the slope of a ray drawn from the origin to the relevant point on the total product of labor curve. The "rise" of the line from the origin to point A in Figure 5-3a is output q_A, and the "run" is the quantity of labor, L_A. Hence, $AP_L = q_A/L_A =$ rise/run from the origin ($L = 0$, $q = 0$) to the point in question ($L = L_A$, $q = q_A$).

Note that the line used to measure the average product of labor at point A can also be used to measure the average product of labor at point C, since both points on the total product of labor curve lie on the same ray. As Figure 5-3a is constructed, marginal product of labor is maximum at $L = L_A$. The average product of labor falls back to $q_A/L_A = q_c/L_c$ at point C; thus, AP_L must still be increasing at point A. At $L = L_B$, $AP_L = q_B/L_B$ is at its maximum. The ray from the origin is tangent to the total product curve at point B: all other points on $TP_L = f(L, \overline{K}, \overline{T})$ lie below

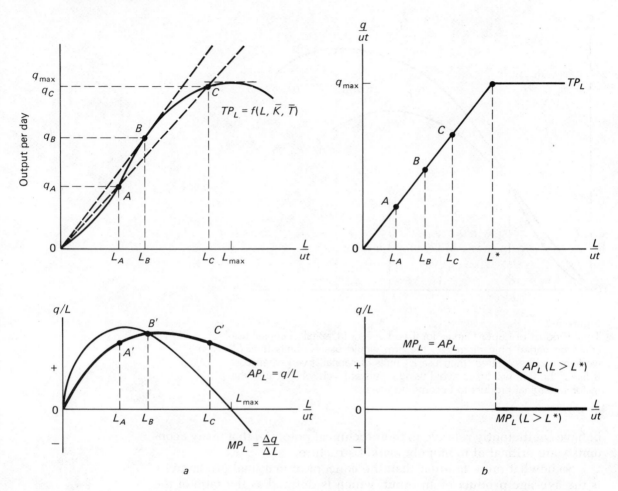

Figure 5-3
Relationship Between Total Product, Marginal Product, and Average Product of Labor. a, Variable input proportions; b, fixed input proportions.

this tangent line. Since *tangency* means that the curve and its tangent line have the same slope at their point of contact, average product (the slope of ray *OB*) must be equal to marginal product (the slope of the total product of labor curve) at point *B*.[10]

---

[10] The change in AP_L with respect to L, other factors remaining constant, is:

$$\frac{\delta AP_L}{\delta L} = \frac{\delta\left(\dfrac{q}{L}\right)}{\delta L} = \frac{L\left(\dfrac{\delta q}{\delta L}\right) - q\left(\dfrac{\delta L}{\delta L}\right)}{L^2} = \frac{1}{L}\left(\frac{\delta q}{\delta L} - \frac{q}{L}\right) = \frac{1}{L}(MP_L - AP_L)$$

If $MP_L > AP_L$, then AP_L is increasing; if $MP_L < AP_L$, then AP_L is decreasing. Since AP_L is maximum when its slope is zero, setting $\delta AP_L/\delta L = 0$ implies that AP_L is maximum when $AP_L = MP_L$.

APPLICATION
Changing Productivity of a Student's Time

An example will illustrate the relationship between the marginal and average products of labor more meaningfully. Imagine that State University requires that students complete 120 semester hours for a bachelor's degree and have a minimum grade point average of 2.0 on a 4.0 scale. Suppose that Annie Anxiety takes 15 hours per semester and passes all her courses with a grade of "C" (2.0) or better. Her transcript, after eight semesters, is reproduced as Table 5-1.

During her first three semesters, Annie develops improved study habits and finds a major which suits her interests and ability; this period of increased specialization corresponds to her increasing marginal productivity period. As her semester grades improve (marginal product), her grade point average (average product) also improves. Midway through her second year, her grade point average is 3.00; then sophomore slump sets in. Her grades begin to slide downward. Yet, even though Annie's fourth-semester grades (3.0) are lower than her third-semester grades (3.2), her grade point average remains at 3.00. Her semester grades and her grade point average are identical at the end of the fourth semester: 3.00; her grade point average is neither increased nor decreased by the fourth-semester performance. From the fifth through the eighth semesters, her semester grades dip below her grade point average, causing it to fall. However, her grade point average never falls as much as her semester grades, since her outstanding performance the first two years adds buoyancy to her average. Thus, by the time Annie Anxiety graduates her semester grade average is 2.2, but her grade point average is 2.75.

TABLE 5-1
Marginal and Average Products Reflected in a Hypothetical College Transcript

Semester	Semester Grades (MP_L)	Grade Point Average (AP_L)
1	2.8	2.80
2	3.0	2.90
3	3.2	3.00
4	3.0	3.00
5	2.8	2.96
6	2.6	2.90
7	2.4	2.83
8	2.2	2.75

APPLICATION

The Short-Run Stages of Production

Figure 5-4 illustrates the ranges of the total product curve which economists call the **stages of production**. Stage I occurs when the average product of the variable input increases as use of the input increases. Stage I includes the range of increasing marginal productivity ($\Delta MP_L / \Delta L > 0$): as the marginal product rises, the average product increases also. After diminishing marginal productivity of the variable input commences (at L_0), the average product continues to rise until (at L_1) it equals the marginal product. Whether AP_L increases or decreases depends upon whether MP_L is greater or less than AP_L. Hence AP_L is maximum after MP_L has begun to decrease, since AP_L rises more slowly than MP_L.

Stage II of production occurs when the average product exceeds marginal product and marginal product exceeds zero. (i.e., $AP_L > MP_L > 0$). In Stage II, both average product and marginal product are increasing as the use of labor increases. Stage II is the operating range for the efficient firm when some inputs are fixed. A firm would not stop hiring the variable input until its average product had reached its maximum, since each unit hired enhances the productivity of input services already employed. We will see in chapter nine that a firm operating in a competitive market would never maximize profit by limiting employment of a variable input so that production occurred in stage I.[11]

Stage III occurs after the marginal product becomes negative, meaning total output declines as more of the variable input is employed. Even if a firm were coerced into signing a "featherbedding" contract, which required paying a minimum number of workers, a producer would never *use* so much labor that the marginal product of labor became negative. It would be better to honor the contract and pay for those workers, but allow some of them to remain idle. Clearly, if the cost of labor could be reduced by cutting employment (the case of a variable input), then producing in stage III would amount to throwing money away.

Table 5-2 should clear up another source of confusion about production with one variable input. The first worker is assumed to produce 10 units of output in a plant with ten machines that must be operated in sequence. Since output would be zero if no workers were employed, the total, average, and marginal product of the first worker equals 10

---

[11] The competitive firm maximizes profit by producing that rate of output for which marginal cost equals the market determined price. If this rate of output occurs in stage I of the short-run production function, either marginal cost is decreasing (implying a profit minimizing or loss maximizing rate of output) or marginal cost is below the minimum point on the average variable cost curve (implying that losses could be reduced by shutting down the plant and producing nothing).

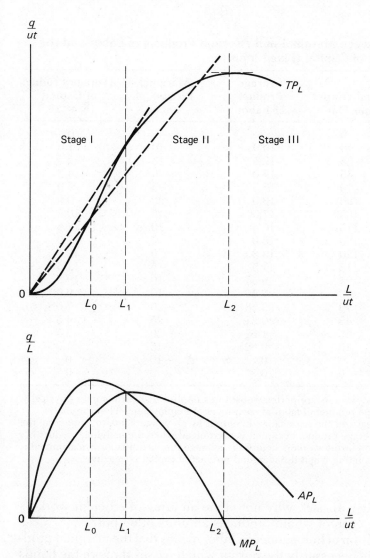

Figure 5-4
The Stages of Production. The efficient firm will produce somewhere within stage II between L_1 and L_2. Production in stage II
means that marginal product of the variable input is positive but
falling, while average product is also falling with use of that input
($AP_L > MP_L > 0$).

units per day. Hiring the second worker allows output to increase to 25
units; the marginal product of the second worker is 15. The third worker's
employment increases output from 25 to 45 units; that worker's marginal
product is 20. Hiring the fourth worker increases output from 45 to 70
units; her marginal product is 25. It seems inefficient not to hire the

TABLE 5-2
Relationship between Marginal and Average Products of Labor and the Average Product of Capital (Fixed Input)

No. Workers	Total Output per Day	Average Product of Labor	Marginal Product of Labor	Average Product of Capital $(\overline{K} = 10)$
0	0	–	–	0
1	10	10.0	10	1.0
2	25	12.5	15	2.5
3	45	15.0	20	4.5
4	70	17.5	25	7.0
5	90	18.0	20	9.0
6	105	17.5	15	10.5
7	115	16.4	10	11.5
8	120	15.0	5	12.0
9	120	13.3	0	12.0
10	115	11.5	– 5	11.5
11	105	9.54	– 10	10.5
12	90	7.50	– 15	9.0
13	70	5.38	– 20	7.0
14	45	3.21	– 25	4.5
15	25	1.67	– 20	2.5
16	10	0.625	– 15	1.0
17	0	0	– 10	0
18	0	0	0	0

Note: Assuming that workers are perfect substitutes implies that each worker physically produces the average product of labor at each level of employment. The marginal product of labor measures the net change in output by all workers due to employing the last worker. The average product of capital is maximized when the marginal product of labor is zero. To stop hiring workers before the average product of labor is maximized (stage I) implies operating when the marginal product of capital is negative.

fourth worker first. In fact, why not clone an army of efficient workers from the fourth, each of whom produces 25 units of output?

Our assumption of homogeneous labor means that the marginal product of labor is not necessarily the output which passes through the hands of the last worker hired. The first worker, no matter who he or she is, must perform all jobs necessary for the production of the commodity (operating ten machines). Time is diverted from production every time that worker moves from one machine to another, or puts down one tool to pick up another. Hiring the second worker permits some specialization. The first worker can produce 12.5 units of output when each of two workers uses five machines. Hiring the third worker permits the first two workers to produce 15 units of output. *Five units of the third worker's marginal product pass through the hands of the first two workers.* Because we have assumed that individuals are perfect substitutes as workers, the average product of labor reflects the output which passes through each worker's hands. (If workers were imperfect substitutes because some were more productive than others, the employer would attempt to hire the most able workers, relative to their wage costs, first. Gains from specialization would be diluted by the declining quality of labor as employment expanded. Average product would overstate the output actually produced by the last worker hired. Nevertheless, a pattern like the one in Table 5-2 would tend to emerge. The assumption that workers have identical skills and temperaments simplifies the analysis of diminishing marginal productivity of a variable input; the implications of heterogeneous labor will be discussed in greater detail in chapter fourteen.)

The fourth worker's marginal product is 25 and her average product is 17.5. Our assumption of homogeneous labor means that each worker

Policy Illustration
Sexual Equality and Household Production

Sometimes, when economic insights are most valuable, they are likely to be least popular. One such time is when economic logic shows that the "ideal" solution to a controversial problem—a solution which would satisfy both sides of the controversy—is impossible. Chapter three showed how the trade-offs between setting a minimum guaranteed income, limiting antipoverty transfers to the poor, and encouraging the poor to work made achieving those three goals infeasible. We now tackle the matter of assuring economic rights for women and the fear that equal rights will undermine the stability of the family. Ideally, one would like to show how economic equality can enhance marital stability. By enhancing a woman's self-respect and by encouraging communication among husband, wife, and children, equal rights might indeed strengthen marital and parental relationships. However, economic logic suggests that lessening the economic inequality between men and women might reduce the strictly economic incentive for marriage.

According to economist Gary S. Becker, a family can be analyzed as an economic entity formed to facilitate joint consumption between spouses and with children.[*] The consumption per family member depends upon the extent to which consumption activities are shared, either directly, through joint use of consumer goods and family outings, or vicariously, through altruistic concern for the well-being of others. Empathy—the abstract sharing of another's joy or sorrow—depends upon love, which is generally considered to be a noneconomic phenomenon: unlike most goods, love increases when it is given to another.[†] And,

[*] Gary S. Becker, "A Theory of Marriage: The Economics of the Family," *The Economic Approach to Human Behavior* (Chicago: University of Chicago Press, 1976), pp. 205–250.

[†] For an exception to this rule, see K. K. Fung, "On Romantic Love—An Analysis of Open System Economic Behavior," *Policy Sciences* 11 (1979), 179–186.

romantic factors held constant, the more activities a husband and wife enjoy together, the more satisfaction each can receive from a family's limited income. If two cannot live as cheaply as one, they can live less expensively by sharing consumption activities than by consuming dissimilar commodities.

On the other hand, household production, like market production, tends to be enhanced by specialization. The amount of utility derived from household consumption depends upon the amount of commodities purchased with market income and on the productivity of labor used to transform raw materials (food, fabric, grass seed) into enjoyable entities (meals, clothing, a well-kept lawn). The opportunity cost of time used in household production is the goods which could have been purchased with income earned if the same amount of time were allocated to market production (i.e., a job). The greater the inequality of the market wage earned by a husband and a wife relative to their respective talents at household activities, the less will be the income sacrificed for a given amount of household production.

Here is the rub. A person's market wage tends to be positively related to education, *ceteris paribus*, although men usually earn more than women with the same amount of education. Yet education has a strong influence on life-style, as do religion, ethnic background, and family wealth. Such characteristics tend to be positively assortive traits: in seeking mates with consumption tastes similar to their own, people tend to marry those who have a similar education and a similar background. However, because specialization in household production or in market production enhances household consumption, wage rates operate as negatively assortive traits: material advantages from marriage are maximized when a high-wage earner marries a low-wage earner, so that the former specializes in market activities while the latter specializes in turning "income" into "utility."

Note that one way—albeit unjust—of resolving the conflict between the advantages of similar education and the gains from unequal wages is for society to discriminate so that women earn less than men with the same education. Of course, a pattern of lower wages for men than for women with the same education would represent an equivalent compromise. However, those who benefit from the current arrangement defend the status quo by claiming a "natural order" to economic inequality. This is a non sequitur: economics teaches us that problems have multiple solutions and that the obvious solution is not always the only solution. But economics also teaches us to be realists. Proponents of equal opportunity for women must deal with the real concerns of the defenders of inequality.

The economic approach to marriage is a limited, although useful, perspective on the issues of redressing the imbalances in the typical family. It is entirely possible that noneconomic issues such as justice, self-image, and child psychology transcend the trade-off between similar consumption tastes and dissimilar production activities. But the economic issues will remain, and ignoring them will postpone any workable compromise of conflicting interests, which, in a democratic society, is the only form lasting solutions can take.

produces 17.5, implying that 7.5 units of the fourth worker's marginal product measures the increase in the average product of the other three workers. Diminishing returns commence with the fifth worker, even though the average product of labor continues to rise. The fifth worker "contributes" only 2 units to increasing the average product of the other four workers, which is 5 units less than the fourth worker's "contribution" to the average product. After the fifth worker has been hired, gains from specialization have been exhausted. Average product begins to decline with the employment of the sixth worker.

This firm would never hire more than eight workers, since the marginal product of the ninth worker is zero. Although the ninth worker appears to produce 13.3 units (see Table 5-2), employing this worker would reduce the total output of the other eight workers by the same 13.3 units. When workers are idled because of too little capital or too little space, average product falls as employment increases. When marginal product reaches zero, the firm has reached the maximum output that can be produced with its fixed inputs.

The average product of capital, one of the fixed inputs, is at a maximum when the marginal product of the variable input is zero. To use more than 9 units of labor would cause the average product of capital to fall. Were labor fixed (say, at ten workers) and capital the variable input, the marginal product of capital would increase if the number of machines were increased (since new machines would absorb redundant labor). Output could also be increased by using fewer than the ten workers available. As long as *use* of the fixed input can be varied, a firm can avoid producing in stage I by reducing the amount of the fixed input used until its marginal product is no longer negative.

Production Isoquants: Two Variable Inputs

There is an obvious geometric difficulty in trying to analyze the simultaneous influence of more than one variable input on the rate of production. Diagrams of more than two dimensions are difficult to depict on two-dimensional pages; pages of more than two dimensions make books difficult to close. Economists depict production with two variable inputs by using an **isoquant map**, which is analogous to the indifference curve map encountered in the study of consumer choice. An **isoquant** is the set of combinations of the services of two variable inputs which produce the same rate of output.[12] For expository simplicity, we will

[12] One of the many benefits of calculus in microeconomics is that it frees us of the geometric constraint of considering only two variables at a time. Given a production function of the form $q = f(v_1, v_2, \ldots, v_m)$, the total change in output is:

$$dq = \frac{\partial q}{\partial v_1}(dv_1) + \frac{\partial q}{\partial v_2}(dv_2) + \ldots + \frac{\partial q}{\partial v_m}(dv_m)$$

temporarily assume that the commodity in question is produced with only labor and capital: $q = f(L, K)$. We will shortly return to our original three input production function, $q = f(L, K, F)$, where F indicates that land is fixed, so that only labor and capital services vary.

Figure 5-5 depicts the isoquant for output q_0. The figure looks suspiciously like an indifference curve. In a sense, an isoquant is an indifference curve for a profit-maximizing producer: without knowledge of input prices, a producer is assumed to be indifferent among technically efficient combinations of inputs. As we shall see in chapter six, the "best" point on an isoquant is identified by relative factor prices. (In chapter ten, we will identify the inefficient operation of regulated utilities in managers' preferences for higher capital expenditure than would be justified by profit maximization; in chapter fourteen, discrimination will be shown to be an employment practice incompatible with profit maximization.)

While the characteristics of indifference curves were deduced from assumptions about consumer preferences, the characteristics of isoquants are inferred from the requirements for technical efficiency. The major characteristics which concern us are that isoquants (1) have negative slopes, (2) are smooth and continuous, (3) do not intersect, and (4) are bowed-in toward the origin.

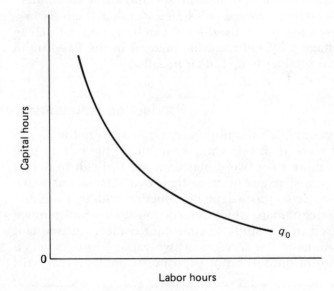

Figure 5-5
Production Isoquant. An *isoquant*, or iso-product curve, depicts all combinations of two variable inputs which produce a specified labor output efficiency (without wasting inputs).

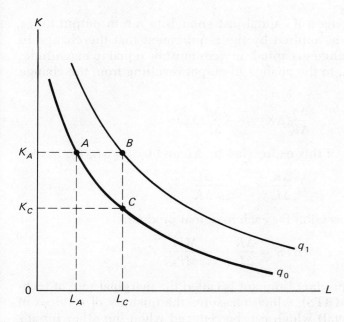

Figure 5-6
Derivation of the Marginal Rate of Technical Substitution. The firm is able to substitute $(L_C - L_A)$ units of labor for $(K_A - K_C)$ units of capital, keeping output constant at q_0. The ratio of the change in capital to the change in labor, $\Delta K/\Delta L = (K_A - K_C)/(L_A - L_C)$, equals the negative ratio of the marginal product of labor to the marginal product of capital: $MRTS = -MP_L/MP_K$.

Figure 5-6 develops the reasoning of the negative slope of an isoquant. Both points A and C lie on isoquant q_0: input combinations (L_A, K_A) and (L_C, K_C) both produce a maximum output of q_0. Moving from point A to point C along isoquant q_0 is equivalent to substituting labor for capital. If we break the substitution process into two steps, we can relate the slope of the isoquant to the marginal products of labor and capital.

An increase in labor services from L_A to L_C would increase output from q_0 to q_1 if capital services remained at K_A. Since q_0 and q_1 are physical measures of output, say so many tons per day, there is no ambiguity in the labeling of isoquants. For convenience, we can represent the output resulting from an increase in labor as:

$$\Delta q = (q_1 - q_0) = \frac{\Delta q}{\Delta L}(\Delta L)$$

Input substitution means changing factor proportions while holding output constant. In Figure 5-6, substituting labor for capital is completed by reducing the services of capital just enough to return output to q_0. Reducing K_A to K_C is implied by the requirement that the change in output due to the change in capital services must be equal in magnitude, but opposite in sign, to the change in output resulting from the change in labor:

$$\frac{\Delta q}{\Delta K}(\Delta K) = -\frac{\Delta q}{\Delta L}(\Delta L)$$

Dividing both sides of this expression by ΔL and by $\Delta q/\Delta L$, we have:

$$\frac{\Delta K}{\Delta L} = -\frac{\Delta q/\Delta L}{\Delta q/\Delta K}$$

Substituting the expression for each marginal product:

$$MRTS = \frac{\Delta K}{\Delta L} = -\frac{MP_L}{MP_K}$$

The slope of a product isoquant is called the **marginal rate of technical substitution (MRTS)**, which measures the quantity of services of one input (e.g., capital) which can be reduced when the other input's services (e.g., labor) are increased by one unit, so that output remains constant.[13] The slope of the isoquant is equal to the (negative) ratio of the marginal products of the two inputs. An input combination is technically efficient only if output would fall if either input were decreased, the other input remaining constant. This condition is satisfied if both inputs have positive marginal products: $MP_L > 0$ *and* $MP_K > 0$. Since the ratio of two positive numbers is also a positive number, multiplying the ratio of MP_L to MP_K by -1 yields a negative number when production is technically efficient.

The second characteristic of isoquants—that isoquants are smooth and continuous—is analogous to the assumption that there are an infinite number of technically efficient ways of producing a rate of output. Since capital and labor services are both measured as amounts of time, it is conceivable that labor and capital are infinitely divisible. However, since changing the proportions of labor and capital usually involves changing the manner by which a commodity is produced, some economists balk at the assumption of smooth isoquants. Chapter seven shows that the major consequence of dropping the assumption of smooth isoquants is that cost curves become "jagged" rather than "smooth." And since it is more convenient to talk about the slope of a smooth curve than

---

[13] Using calculus: $dq = \partial q/\partial L(dL) + \partial q/\partial dK(dK)$. By definition of an isoquant, $dq = 0$, so that $-\partial q/\partial K(dK) = \partial q/\partial L(dL)$, or:

$$MRTS = \frac{dK}{dL}\bigg|_{dq=0} = -\frac{\partial q/\delta L}{\partial q/\delta K} = -\frac{MP_L}{MP_K}$$

of the changing slopes of line segments of jagged isoquants, we will maintain the assumption of smooth isoquants until chapter seven.

The third characteristic of isoquants—that two isoquants cannot intersect (or become mutually tangent)—can be demonstrated by **reductio ad absurdum**: intersecting isoquants would violate the conditions of technical efficiency. Suppose that isoquants q_0 and q_1 did intersect, say, at point A in Figure 5-7. Since isoquants represent measurable rates of output, it follows that $q_1 > q_0$, or $q_0 > q_1$, or $q_0 = q_1$. If q_1 is larger, points on isoquant q_0 to the left of (and including) point A imply inefficient input combinations: point like C' would not belong on an isoquant. If q_0 is larger, points on isoquant q_1 to the right of (and including) point A cannot be technically efficient. For instance, point C contains more capital services and more labor services than point B; if $q_0 > q_1$, then point C would be a technically inefficient method of producing this commodity. Finally, if $q_1 = q_0$, all points to the right of point A on isoquant q_1 (e.g., point C) and all points to the left of point A on isoquant q_0 (e.g., point C') must be rejected as inefficient input combinations. In all cases, only one isoquant remains after inefficient points are deleted from Figure 5-7.

The fourth characteristic of isoquants—that isoquants bow in toward the origin—results from the assumption that the two input services in question are imperfect substitutes. As labor services are increased relative to capital services, the marginal product of labor tends to fall and

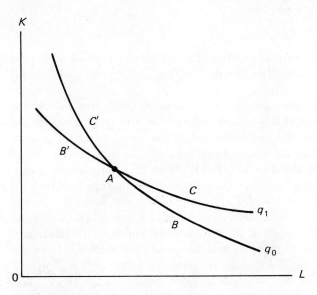

Figure 5-7
Intersecting isoquants violate the requirement that input combinations be technically efficient.

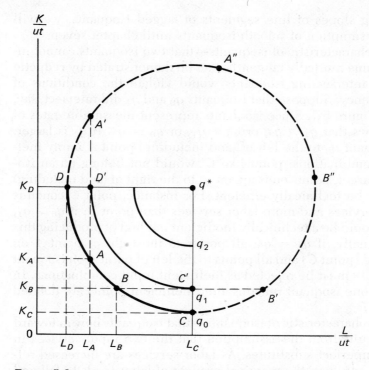

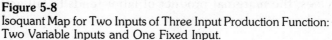

Figure 5-8
Isoquant Map for Two Inputs of Three Input Production Function:
Two Variable Inputs and One Fixed Input.

the marginal product of capital to rise. The marginal rate of technical substitution approaches zero (its absolute value decreases) as labor increases at the expense of capital.

The shape of isoquants may be easier to appreciate if we drop our unrealistic assumption that labor and capital are the only two inputs. When more than two inputs are involved in the production of a commodity, it is possible that some combinations of two inputs (e.g., labor and capital services) are not technically efficient, given maximum availability of other inputs (e.g., land). Consider our production function for an agricultural commodity, $q = f(L, K, \overline{T})$. The annual harvest of some crop, q, depends upon the combination of labor (L), capital (K), and land (T) *used*. In Figure 5-8, we treat land as a fixed input, with labor and capital services variable. Output q_0 can be produced with L_A hours of labor *and* K_A hours of capital goods, or with L_B labor and K_B capital. Hence, ($L_B - L_A$) hours of labor could be substituted for ($K_A - K_B$) hours of capital, output remaining constant. The negative slope of isoquant q_0 between points A and B in Figure 5-8 implies that the marginal product of labor and the marginal product of capital are both positive—

or that both marginal products are negative. We have seen that the existence of positive marginal products for both variable inputs implies a negative marginal rate of technical substitution. Close inspection of Figure 5-8 shows that the converse of that proposition is not necessarily true: the negative slope of an isoquant does not necessarily imply that both marginal products are positive (i.e., that input combinations represented by the points on the isoquant are technically efficient).

Suppose that farmer N. D. Dale substituted farmworkers for tractors along isoquant q_0 in Figure 5-8 until point C was reached. To the right of point C, using more labor would cause output to fall, unless either land or tractors were increased to compensate for the negative marginal product of labor. Since we are assuming that land is fixed, Dale must increase capital services, whose marginal product is positive, to counteract the destructive influence of too much labor. When one input has a negative marginal product while the other has a positive marginal product, the slope of the isoquant is positive.

Commonsense notions of input substitution are violated when we refer to the positive slope of an isoquant as the marginal rate of technical substitution. One does not "substitute" one input for another by increasing the use of both of them. An efficient producer would not purposefully operate at a point on the positively sloped portion of an isoquant. This is obvious when we consider what happens to the rate of output as labor is increased along the line segment BB' in Figure 5-8 (where capital is held constant at $K = K_B$). When labor is increased from L_B to L_C, with capital services held constant, output increases from q_0 to q_1 (at point C'). Were labor to be increased past L_C, output would fall. At point B', the rate of production would once again equal q_0. Since point B' has the same amount of capital and more labor than point B, while both combinations produce the same output, point B' must be technically inefficient.

Figure 5-8 is constructed so that the marginal product of capital becomes negative when $K > K_D$ (i.e., above point D). With labor held to L_A, increasing capital from K_A to K_D would increase output from q_0 to q_1. Increasing capital still further would cause output to decline if labor were not also increased. At point A', output would have returned to q_0—the same output associated with point A. Point A' cannot be technically efficient, since the same output (q_0) could be produced with less of both inputs (at point D, for instance).

Finally, compare points A'' and B'' with A and B, respectively. By construction, points A and A'' have the same ratio of capital to labor. Although point A'' represents more of both inputs than point A, output is the same at both points. At point A'', the marginal product of labor is negative ($L > L_C$) and the marginal product of capital is negative ($K > K_D$). At point B'', the ratio of capital to labor is the same as at point B. Although point B'' represents more of both inputs, only q_0 output is obtained each harvest. At point B'', as at point A'', the marginal product of labor and the marginal product of capital are both negative.

Point B'' has more labor and less capital than point A''. Moving from A'' to B'' appears to result from substituting labor for capital. But "factor substitution" from A'' to B'' is perverse. At point A'', Dale is using so much labor and so much capital that crops are being trampled by workers and ground under the wheels of tractors. Increasing labor relative to point A'' would threaten to destroy the few crops available for harvest, unless those extra workers merely destroyed the output which would otherwise have been ruined by capital. To increase one input with a negative marginal product, use of the other input with a negative marginal product must be reduced.

With our minds reeling from contemplating combinations of (marginally) destructive inputs, it should be obvious that production theory loses none of its relevance, and is considerably simplified, if we restrict the relevant range of isoquants to combinations of inputs which both have nonnegative marginal products. The perpendicular lines at K_D and L_C in Figure 5-8 are the **ridge lines** marking the boundary on the isoquant

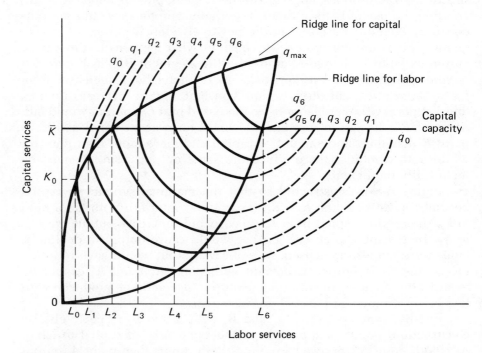

Figure 5-9
Production in the Short Run and Factor Proportions. If *use* of fixed (limited) input can be reduced below capacity, more output can be produced at low employment rates of the variable input by using the "fixed" input where its marginal product is zero, along the capital ridge line.

map, separating inefficient input combinations from technically efficient input combinations. Note that in Figure 5-8, the two ridge lines meet at a point labeled q^*, which represents L_C units of labor and K_D units of capital. When the marginal products of all variable inputs are zero, the absolute limit of output possibilities for the fixed input has been reached. No more than q^* units of output can be produced on the land available, no matter how much labor and capital are employed. As we said earlier, land, labor, and capital are, at best, only imperfect substitutes for one another.

The relevant range of the isoquant lies between the capital and labor ridge lines and is characterized by a bowed-in shape, formerly called a **diminishing marginal rate of technical substitution**. This characteristic, sometimes referred to as the **law of variable proportions**, implies that as one input is substituted for another, the marginal product of the former increases relative to the marginal product of the latter. Figure 5-8 is constructed so that $(K_D - K_A) > (K_A - K_B)$, although $(L_B - L_A) = (L_A - L_D)$: as labor increases at the expense of capital, less capital is released for equal subsequent additions of labor. Similarly, we see that $(L_C - L_B) > (L_B - L_A)$, although $(K_B - K_C) = (K_A - K_B)$: when capital is substituted for labor, the falling marginal product of capital means that less labor can be replaced with each "dose" of capital.[14]

Production with one variable input can be illustrated by setting an upper limit on the availability of one input (here, capital services) and tracing how changes in the other input (labor time) changes the rate of output. In Figure 5-9, we assume that Whatsit Widgets has contracted for $\overline{K}$ machine-hours per day; acquiring additional capital services would require at least a month until new contracts could be negotiated and the extra machines delivered. In Figure 5-9, the $\overline{K}$ machine-hours represent a minimum purchase requirement and a maximum availability production constraint.

In Figure 5-9, the *capital capacity line* (the horizontal line at $\overline{K}$) intersects the ridge line for capital at point $(L_2, \overline{K})$. Unlike Figure 5-8, in which the marginal product of each input was independent of the amount of the other input, Figure 5-9 is drawn so that the marginal product of capital increases as the amount of labor increases. For less than L_2 hours of labor per day, the marginal product of capital would be

---

[14] The change in *MRTS* as K/L decreases is:

$$\frac{d(MRTS)}{dL} = \frac{d(-MP_L/MP_K)}{dL} = -\frac{MP_K(dMP_L/dL) - MP_L(dMP_K/dL)}{(MP_K)^2}$$

As long as capital and labor services are complements in the sense that the marginal product of one input increases when services of the other input increase, the numerator of this expression is positive: the absolute value of *MRTS* approaches zero as labor increases and as capital is decreased in order to maintain the rate of output.

negative if all $\overline{K}$ machine-hours were used. If widget production requires that each machine on an assembly line be in continuous operation, producing q_0 widgets per day would require L_1 labor hours daily. If widget production involves replication of a simple process which allows using less than $\overline{K}$ machine-hours per day (e.g., machine-shop technology), q_0 widgets could be produced with L_0 labor hours and K_0 capital hours. When the fixed input cannot be used below capacity, the extra labor required does not produce extra output: $(L_1 - L_0)$ labor is required to compensate for the negative marginal productivity of $(\overline{K} - K_0)$ machine-hours.

In Figure 5-9, the cost of the variable input would be minimized by using L_1 labor hours and K_1 capital hours to produce q_1 widgets per day and L_2 labor hours and K_2 machine-hours to produce q_2 widgets each day. The firm could avoid stage I production, characterized by negative marginal productivity of the fixed input, by using the fixed input below capacity to produce less than q_2 widgets per day, or by using at least L_2 labor hours per day, never producing less than q_2 widgets per day.

When producing q_2 or more widgets per day, available capital services can be used to capacity without any detrimental effect on the amount of labor services required. By following the capital capacity line as it intersects the relevant isoquants, the firm uses L_3 hours of labor to produce q_3 widgets per day, L_4 hours to produce q_4 per day, and L_5 hours of labor to produce q_5 widgets each day. The capital capacity line intersects the labor ridge line at point $(L_6, \overline{K})$ on isoquant q_6. Using more than L_6 labor hours would cause the marginal product of labor to become negative, and total output to fall below q_6 widgets per day. Insufficient capital services are available in the short run to produce more than q_6 widgets per day, regardless of the amount of labor employed. The isoquant associated with the intersection of the capital capacity line and the labor ridge line determines the firm's maximum possible rate of output as long as the capital availability constraint holds.

APPLICATION
Output Elasticities of Productive Inputs

So far we have ignored the measurement problems encountered by most producers who produce many commodities, using a variety of labor with different skills, machines with different designs, in plants at different locations. At best, records on the production function for individual commodities will be kept in terms of hours of labor or total wages paid, with machinery measured as the book value of assets, and so forth. Hence, it may be much easier for managers or accountants to measure the percentage change of input services than to provide an accurate picture of the physical flow of either input or output. Accordingly, business economists make use of the **output elasticity** (which is represented by the Greek letter *epsilon*, ϵ_i) for any input v_i, which is defined as the *percentage change* in output due to a 1 percent increase in that input's services, other input services remaining constant:

$$\epsilon_i = \frac{\Delta q/q}{\Delta v_i/v_i} = \left(\frac{\Delta q}{\Delta v_i}\right)\left(\frac{v_i}{q}\right) = \frac{MP_i}{AP_i}$$

The output elasticity of labor is the marginal product of labor divided by the average product of labor. In stage I, a factor's marginal product exceeds its average product, causing the average product to increase as use of the input increases: $\epsilon_L > 1$ implies that some input other than labor (e.g., land, capital, management) has a negative marginal product. In stage II, average product exceeds marginal product, and marginal product is positive: $1 > \epsilon_L > 0$. In stage III, $AP_L > 0 > MP_L$, so that $\epsilon_L < 0$.

The output elasticity of labor for the numerical example encountered in Table 5-2 is presented in Table 5-3. From $L = 1$ to $L = 4$, where the marginal product of labor is increasing, labor's output elasticity not only exceeds 1, but ϵ_L increases as more labor is hired. When diminishing returns commence ($L = 4$), ϵ_L begins to decrease with labor increases, although remaining greater than 1 until stage II begins (between $L = 5$ and $L = 6$). Because the marginal product of labor falls faster than the

TABLE 5-3
Output Elasticity of Variable Labor

No. Workers	Total Output	Average Product of Labor	Marginal Product of Labor	Output Elasticity of Labor	Stage
0	0	–	–	–	–
1	10	10.0	10	1.00	I
2	25	12.5	15	1.20	I
3	45	15.0	20	1.33	I
4	70	17.5	25	1.43	I
5	90	18.0	20	1.11	I
6	105	17.5	15	0.857	II
7	115	16.4	10	0.608	II
8	120	15.0	5	0.333	II
9	120	13.33	0	0	II
10	115	11.50	−5	−0.435	III
11	105	9.54	−10	−1.05	III
12	90	7.50	−15	−2.00	III
13	70	5.38	−20	−3.71	III
14	45	3.21	−25	−7.71	III
15	25	1.67	−20	−12.0	III
16	10	0.625	−15	−24.0	III
17	0	0	−10	−∞	III

average product of labor in stage II, ϵ_L approaches zero as employment expands in this range. Output elasticity becomes negative in stage III, since marginal product is negative while average product is positive.

Returns to Scale and Production Planning

At least once during the life of a firm—at its birth—all input services and all production costs will be variable. Before the owners have signed any contracts or produced any output, all costs and all input services will be zero. But the old adage in business is relevant to economic theory: one must spend money (i.e., commit resources) to make money (i.e., produce output to earn revenue). Once contracts have been signed and inputs purchased, the firm must operate under the minimum purchase requirements of those contracts and the maximum availability constraints on fixed input services. Through time, contracts will expire and inputs will depreciate, and the firm will select new input services based on the technology and relative input prices prevailing at that time, as chapter six will show. Nevertheless, managers attempt to anticipate the best combinations of inputs through long-range planning; when the time comes for replacing capital goods or renewing building leases, fortune often favors firms which can act swiftly and decisively.

Business planning necessarily involves incomplete information about conditions which will prevail when those plans are implemented. Frequently, planning involves the extrapolation of current trends and practices. For instance, what would happen to the firm's rate of output if all inputs were increased or decreased by a common percentage—for example, the firm duplicated one of its production facilities at a new location, or let an existing plant close? Of course, actual events would depend upon information which became available as the firm approached the implementation date, but practical planning involves concepts which do not require detailed information the firm is unlikely to have.

One concept which requires only knowledge of the physical aspects of production is the **returns to scale** of a production function, defined as the percentage change in output which would result from a 1 percent change in all inputs. Diminishing marginal productivity results when one input's services are increased while all other inputs remain constant; eventually, increasing one input will cause changes in output to get progressively smaller. However, when all inputs increase together, output might increase by a greater proportion (increasing returns to scale), by the same proportion (constant returns to scale), or by a smaller proportion (decreasing returns to scale) than the common percentage change in all input services.

The total change in output can be represented as the sum of the impacts of individual input increases. In our three input agricultural production function, $q = f(L, K, T)$, the total change in output per growing season will equal the sum of the influences of the changes in labor, capital, and land services:

$$\Delta q = \left(\frac{\Delta q}{\Delta L} \times \Delta L \right) + \left(\frac{\Delta q}{\Delta K} \times \Delta K \right) + \left(\frac{\Delta q}{\Delta T} \times \Delta T \right)$$

Dividing both sides of this expression by the rate of output, q, we obtain an expression for the percentage change in the rate of output:

$$\frac{\Delta q}{q} = \left(\frac{\Delta q}{\Delta L} \times \frac{\Delta L}{q} \right) + \left(\frac{\Delta q}{\Delta K} \times \frac{\Delta K}{q} \right) + \left(\frac{\Delta q}{\Delta T} \times \frac{\Delta T}{q} \right)$$

As such, this expression appears to relate relevant relationships (the marginal product of each input) to a meaningless ratio of the change in that input's services to the rate of output. However, through the simple step of multiplying each term by the ratio of each input to itself (e.g., L/L, K/K), and rearranging, a more appealing pattern results:

$$\frac{\Delta q}{q} = \left(\frac{\Delta q}{\Delta L} \times \frac{L}{q} \times \frac{\Delta L}{L} \right) + \left(\frac{\Delta q}{\Delta K} \times \frac{K}{q} \times \frac{\Delta K}{K} \right) + \left(\frac{\Delta q}{\Delta T} \times \frac{T}{q} \times \frac{\Delta T}{T} \right)$$

The percentage change in output is the sum of the output elasticity of each input times the change in that output:[15]

$$\frac{\Delta q}{q} = \left(\epsilon_L \times \frac{\Delta L}{L} \right) + \left(\epsilon_K \times \frac{\Delta K}{K} \right) + \left(\epsilon_T \times \frac{\Delta T}{T} \right)$$

As we will see in chapter six, the change in inputs over time will reflect the combined influence of changing input prices (either because demand and/or supply conditions change through time, or because factor prices change as the firm hires more or less of a particular input.) In the absence of information about future prices (and since we have yet to discuss the influence of relative input price on input choice), it is prudent to standardize the percentage change in input services. Changing the *scale* of production has been defined as the change in output which results when all inputs are increased by 1 percent. In more general

---

[15] Given the production function, $q = f(v_1, v_2, \ldots, v_m)$, the total derivative of q relates the change in output to the change in each input:

$$dq = \left(\frac{\partial q}{\partial v_1} \times dv_1 \right) + \left(\frac{\partial q}{\partial v_2} \times dv_2 \right) + \cdots + \left(\frac{\partial q}{\partial v_m} \times dv_m \right)$$

Dividing both sides by q, then multiplying each term by the relevant ratio of that input divided by itself, the equation is preserved since $v_i/v_i = 1$:

$$\frac{dq}{q} = \left(\frac{\partial q}{\partial v_1} \times \frac{v_1}{q} \times \frac{dv_1}{v_1} \right) + \left(\frac{\partial q}{\partial v_2} \times \frac{v_2}{q} \times \frac{dv_2}{v_2} \right) + \cdots + \left(\frac{\partial q}{\partial v_m} \times \frac{v_m}{q} \times \frac{dv_m}{v_m} \right) = \sum_{i=1}^{m} \epsilon_i \times \frac{dv_i}{v_i}$$

terms, we can set the common percentage change in all inputs equal to the same number, which we will represent by the Greek letter *lambda*, λ:

$$\lambda = \frac{\Delta L}{L} = \frac{\Delta K}{K} = \frac{\Delta T}{T}$$

Then, by substitution, we discover:

$$\frac{\Delta q}{q} = \epsilon_L(\lambda) + \epsilon_K(\lambda) + \epsilon_K(\lambda) = (\epsilon_L + \epsilon_K + \epsilon_T)\lambda$$

$$\therefore \epsilon = \frac{\Delta q/q}{\lambda} = \epsilon_L + \epsilon_K + \epsilon_T$$

Epsilon (ϵ) without a subscript equals the returns to scale of the production function, $q = f(L, K, T)$. We have now discovered that returns to scale of a production function can be obtained by adding together the output elasticities for all inputs. This relationship underscores the fact that changing all input services by the same proportion is an assumption made in the ignorance of future relative input prices. The earlier steps in deriving this relationship allow planners to predict the consequences of changing input services by unequal percentages.

Returning to our running example, suppose that N. D. Dale hires an econometrician to estimate the output elasticities of labor, capital, and land. After consulting Dale's own records and those of government reports on farms similar to Dale's, the economist determines that $\epsilon_L \simeq$ 0.6, $\epsilon_K \simeq 0.25$, and $\epsilon_T \simeq 0.15$, where the symbol "$\simeq$" means "approximately equals," since statistical estimations always involve possible error. From this information, Dale concludes that the farm is characterized by *constant returns to scale*, meaning that if all inputs were increased by the same percentage, output would also increase by that percentage. This result follows, since $\epsilon = \epsilon_L + \epsilon_K + \epsilon_T \simeq 0.6 + 0.25 + 0.15 = 1.0$. However, if the econometrician had underestimated those elasticities, the production function would actually be characterized by *increasing returns to scale*: if all inputs were increased by the same proportion, output would increase by a larger proportion. Finally, if all output elasticities had been underestimated, *decreasing returns to scale* would prevail: an increase in all inputs by the same proportion would cause output to increase, but by a smaller percentage.

Suppose that Dale wishes to double the farm's annual harvest. According to the estimated returns to scale, doubling all inputs would have the desired effect. But suppose that land can be increased by only 50 percent, since only one adjoining farm can be purchased at a price Dale deems economical. According to the equations used to derive our returns to scale formula, the percentage change in output can be generalized to equal the sum of each input elasticity times the percentage change in each input. If land is increased by only 50 percent, while labor and capital were increased by 100 percent each, total change in output would approximately equal:

$$0.6(100\%) + 0.25(100\%) + 0.15(50\%) = 60\% + 25\% + 7.5\% = 92.5\%$$

A long-run constraint on the availability of land implies that labor and capital inputs would have to be increased by more than 100 percent to compensate for the limited amount of land.

Hypothetically, the shortfall in land could be made up by increasing labor by 112.5 percent (since 7.5%/0.6 = 12.5%) or by increasing capital by 130 percent (since 7.5%/0.25 = 30%). However, the law of variable proportions tells us that increasing one factor while holding other factors constant will eventually result in declining marginal products for variable inputs. By holding factor proportions constant, the returns to scale avoid the complications introduced by diminishing marginal productivity of one or more inputs, which would tend to cause output elasticities to change. Whether this assumption of constant input proportions is a simplifying or crucial assumption depends upon the context in which that assumption is used. In this context, Dale learns that a planned output increase of 50 percent could be accomplished by increasing outlay for inputs by 50 percent, *if factor prices remain constant.* However, if Dale plans to increase output by more than 50 percent, the inability to increase land by more than 50 percent means that other inputs will have to increase by more than 50 percent. Diminishing returns to nonland inputs imply that increasing output by 50 percent will increase costs by more than 50 percent.

In chapter seven we will discuss in detail the most typical example of constant returns to scale, which occur when a simple process can be replicated over a wide range of output. A small office may employ one typist, working at one typewriter. A typing pool of twenty typists working at twenty typewriters would produce approximately twenty times the number of typed pages per day as the small office, assuming that all twenty-one typists typed the same number of hours and at the same rate. A machine shop is another example of how side-by-side replication of a small-scale operation can result in output changes roughly proportionate to the percentage change in all inputs.

Increasing returns to "scale" usually result when inputs become more specialized as output increases. Technology may allow typewriters to be replaced by word processors and high-speed printers, so that ten operators can do the work of twenty typists. Ten computer operators are only half as many employees as twenty typists, but their wages are likely to exceed half the wages paid to twenty typists. Similarly, using the cost of capital as a common denominator, those word processors and high-speed printers are likely to represent more than twenty "units" of capital. Ironically, while designed to avoid requiring knowledge of input prices, returns to scale often use input prices to calculate the percentage changes in heterogeneous inputs. Furthermore, when increasing returns are encountered, it is likely that planned input proportions must change as the planned rate of output changes: this complication is compounded by systematic or coincidental changes in input prices as the amounts of input services change.

The reason usually cited for decreasing returns to scale is the exhaustion of gains from specialization of labor, and particularly capital, along with the organizational problems encountered as an enterprise expands. A simple plant might operate with one foreperson-manager and ten specialized workers. As output expands through building a larger facility, specialization of labor and capital will require specialization of

---

Business Illustration
Returns to Scale and the "Natural" Laws of Production

The "natural law of competition" was displaced by the notion of "natural monopoly" among owners and managers in the United States iron and steel industry at the turn of the century, reflecting the structural changes that had occurred as many small firms began to give way to a few large ones. Andrew Carnegie, the telegrapher turned steel producer, participated in the industry from its competitive beginnings to the creation of U.S. Steel Corporation in 1901, when his firm was merged with the holdings of J. P. Morgan and the W. H. Moore Company.

In 1867 many small producers delivered 1,600 tons of steel to the United States market; in 1897 an oligopoly core and competitive fringe firms produced 7.2 million tons for that market. In the early 1870s, efforts to control pig iron production by a system of withholding output from the market in relatively low demand years failed. In "The Bugaboo of Trusts" (*Iron Age*, February 1889), Carnegie called the reader's attention to all the trusts that had failed and emphasized

that the process of competition is a law of nature by which new firms spring up to replace incompetent firms and to undermine trusts: "Such is the law, such has been the law, and such promises to be the law."

Within a few months, Carnegie was to modify his views in keeping with his consolidation of his holdings into the Carnegie Steel Corporation. In April 1889 Carnegie informed his *Iron Age* readers of the effects of economies of scale, which accommodated so well the state of technology of the iron and steel industry at that time:

Economic laws force the manufacture of all articles of general consumption into the hands of a few enormous concerns, that their costs to the consumer may be less. The manufacture of such articles cannot be conducted on a small scale: works costing millions are required, as the amount per ton or per yard of "fixed charges" is so great in the total cost that whether a concern management, which in turn will require more managers to manage the managers. Furthermore, larger plants mean greater spaces, causing transportation and communication problems. Decreasing returns to scale explain why large manufacturing firms operate multiple plants, roughly characterized by constant returns to scale, rather than one huge plant, which would have been plagued by decreasing returns to scale.

As in the case of increasing returns to scale, decreasing returns to scale are likely to involve changing input proportions as the planned level of output changes. But this problem is overshadowed by an even more obvious empirical problem: in a competitive business environment, firms which have experienced decreasing returns to scale are not likely to survive long. Hence, decreasing returns to scale are difficult to

can run or not in many cases depends upon whether it divides these fixed charges—which are practically the same in a large establishment as in a small—whether we can divide them by 1000 tons per day or by 500 tons per day of product . . . (*Iron Age*, April 4, 1889).

As economies of scale in steel production continued through the 1890s, highlighted by Carnegie's absorption of several firms into the Carnegie Steel Corporation, steel manufacturers began to encompass multiple stages of a process called vertical integration. As charcoal was replaced by coke, wood gave way to coal in steel smelting encouraging steel firms to mine their own coal. In 1896, Carnegie obtained a lease on the great Mesabi iron range in Minnesota by steel firms. Steel producers also began to develop new uses for steel, thereby increasing demands for semifinished steel products. In the steel industry, attitudes about natural law turned away from "survival

of the fittest" to seek biblical precedents for rule by the mighty. Charles M. Schwab, president of the U.S. Steel Corporation in 1901, made the following statement to the Banker's Club of Chicago on December 21 of that year:

> The consolidation of [steel firms] today is proper policy. It has been borne out in everything, even in Genesis, and so on down. The rivers combine to make the great sea; trees combine to make the forests. Combinations have gone on in nature forever, and they will go on in politics and business.
> You might just as well try to dam the Mississippi . . . as to stop natural consolidation of business interests . . . .
> King Cotton is now dethroned and King Steel has taken his place . . . (quoted in *Iron Age*, December 26, 1901, p. 26).

Based on an untitled paper by Barbara Vatter, Department of Economics, Memphis State University.

observe except in protected markets. Indeed, much of the "inefficiency" attributed to government activities probably results from the fact that by necessity or design, governments produce commodities with facilities plagued with decreasing returns to scale. Those services private enterprises do perform are, for the most part, less wasteful because of the process of selection the market performs.

APPLICATION

Homogeneous Production Functions

A special type of production function economists use extensively in empirical research is the **homogeneous production function**.[16] A production function is called homogeneous of degree b if, for any technically efficient combination of inputs, say (L_0, K_0), such that $q_0 = f(L_0, K_0)$, $f(\lambda L_0, \lambda K_0) = \lambda^b f(L_0, K_0)$, where λ is any positive constant. If $b = 1$, that is, if $f(\lambda L, \lambda K) = \lambda f(L, K)$, the production function is said to be homogeneous of degree one, or *linearly homogeneous*. A linearly homogeneous production function exhibits constant returns to scale for all technically efficient input combinations. If $b > 1$, changing all inputs by the same proportion causes output to change by a greater proportion. If all inputs are doubled, output more than doubles; if all inputs are cut by 50 percent, output falls by more than 50 percent. When a production function is homogeneous to a degree greater than one, it exhibits increasing returns to scale for all technically efficient input combinations. A production function will exhibit decreasing returns to scale over all relevant input combinations if $b < 1$. Note that since output must be defined as a nonnegative number, λ is restricted to real numbers greater than or equal to zero. Further, since increasing all inputs must increase output for production to be technically efficient, b can never be less than zero.

One convenient characteristic of homogeneous production functions is the fact that isoquants are parallel: along any ray through the origin (representing a constant input ratio), each isoquant will have the same marginal rate of technical substitution.[17] This implies that ridge lines

[16] Almost always, the homogeneity of empirically estimated production functions results from the assumptions used by the estimators of those functions, rather than representing a feature of reality discovered by the use of statistical techniques which might have allowed estimated production functions to have mathematical formulas which are not homogeneous.

[17] A homothetic production function is a production function which has parallel isoquants; a homogeneous production function is a special case of a homothetic production function, which need not represent the same returns to scale for all input combinations.

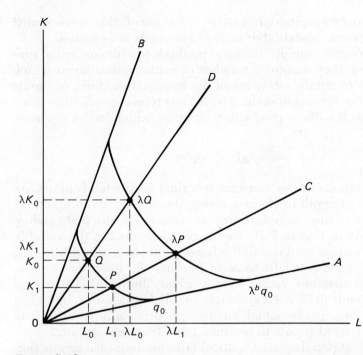

Figure 5-10
Isoquant Map for a Homogeneous Production Function. For any
ray, indicating a constant ratio of capital to labor, the marginal rate
of technical substitution must be the same on every isoquant that
the ray crosses.

are themselves rays. In Figure 5-10, ray *OB* represents those combinations of inputs when $MP_K = 0$ and $MP_L > 0$, so that $MRTS = -\infty$. Ray
OA represents the ridge line for which $MP_L = 0$ and $MP_K > 0$, so $MRTS
= 0$. All points along ray *OC* have a capital-labor ratio equal to K_0/L_0.
Moving from point P (L_0, K_0) to point λP $(\lambda L_0, \lambda K_0)$ increases output
from q_0 to $\lambda^b q_0$. If $b > 1$, isoquants bunch closer together as production
moves along ray *OC* away from the origin (i.e., as labor and capital are
increased proportionately). If $b < 1$, isoquants move farther apart at
higher outputs. Point Q (L_1, K_1) is also on isoquant q_0. Therefore, point
λQ $(\lambda L_1, \lambda K_1)$ must be on isoquant $\lambda^b q_0$. Moving from point Q to point
P means substituting $(L_1 - L_0)$ units of labor for $(K_0 - K_1)$ units of
capital. Moving from λQ to λP along isoquant $\lambda^b q_0$ means substituting
$(\lambda L_1 - \lambda L_0) = \lambda(L_1 - L_0)$ units of labor for $(\lambda K_0 - \lambda K_1) = \lambda(K_0 - K_1)$
units of capital. Along both isoquants, the ratio of the change in capital
to the change in labor is the same. Since this must be true for any two

isoquants and any two capital-labor ratios, the slope of all isoquants must be the same for each capital-labor ratio.[18] Isoquants are parallel.

When economists employ statistical methods to estimate actual production functions, they employ a number of mathematical forms which they can specify to obtain estimates of the marginal products of inputs and to measure the returns to scale. The easiest type of production function to estimate is the linear production function, which has an equation of the form:

$$q = aL + bK$$

where a and b represent the constant marginal products of inputs. As will be explored in depth in chapter seven, linear production functions arise *between* ridge lines which represent technically efficient production processes. As in Figure 5-1*b*, the marginal product of the variable input remains constant until use of the fixed input has reached capacity, then the marginal product falls to zero. Because the linear production function exhibits discrete, rather than gradual, diminishing marginal productivity, it tends to be used sparingly in scholarly studies, but it has limited applications inside actual businesses, especially when a firm uses one or more fixed inputs to produce more than one output.

By far the most popular mathematical form for empirical production function estimates is named for C. W. Cobb and P. H. Douglas,[19] who produced the first estimates of empirical production functions with the mathematical form:

$$q = AL^\alpha K^\beta$$

Unlike the linear production function, the Cobb-Douglas production function is characterized by marginal products of labor and capital which vary as the proportion of labor to capital varies. An additional advantage of the Cobb-Douglas function is that the two parameters, α and β, represent output elasticities. Hence, the returns to scale for a Cobb-Douglas production function simply equal the sum of the two estimated

---

[18] Given $f(\lambda L, \lambda K) = \lambda^b f(L, K)$ for all points (L, K) such that $MP_L > 0$ and $MP_K > 0$, it follows that:

$$\frac{\partial q}{\partial \lambda L}(d\lambda L) + \frac{\partial q}{\partial \lambda K}(d\lambda K) = \lambda^b \left[\frac{\partial q}{\partial L}(dL) + \frac{\partial q}{\partial K}(dK) \right] = dq$$

Since $dq = 0$ along an isoquant, it follows that:

$$\frac{d\lambda K}{d\lambda L} = -\frac{\partial q/\partial \lambda L}{\partial q/\partial \lambda K} = \frac{dK}{dL} = -\frac{\partial q/\partial L}{\partial q/\partial K}$$

[19] Paul H. Douglas, *The Theory of Wages* (New York: Crowell Collier & Macmillan, 1934).

parameters:[20]

$$\epsilon = \epsilon_L + \epsilon_K = \alpha + \beta$$

Using simple algebra, we can substitute λL and λK for L and K, respectively, and obtain:

$$q = A(\lambda L)^\alpha (\lambda K)^\beta = \lambda^{\alpha + \beta}(AL^\alpha K^\beta)$$

The Cobb-Douglas production function is homogeneous of degree α + β. Thus, if $\alpha = 0.75$ and $\beta = 0.25$, the Cobb-Douglas function would exhibit constant returns to scale. If $\alpha + \beta > 1$, increasing returns to scale are indicated, and if $\alpha + \beta < 1$, the estimated production function has decreasing returns to scale.

From Technical to Economic Efficiency

In this chapter we have developed general relationships between inputs and output. Of all possible combinations of inputs, we narrowed our attention to those which are technically efficient. In the short run, characterized by minimum payment requirements and maximum availability constraints for one or more inputs, the law of diminishing marginal productivity limits the ability of the producer to squeeze output from variable input increases. Technical efficiency requires that the firm use variable inputs so that both the marginal product and the average product of each variable input are positive and declining with increases in that input. This defines stage II of production, the operating range of the efficient firm. The precise amount of a variable input that is used cannot be determined without knowledge of the relative costs of inputs. Technical efficiency is a necessary, but not a sufficient, condition for economic efficiency.

The possibility of input substitution increases options for the firm. The isoquant represents a menu of technically efficient input combinations; but, once again, which input combination is economically efficient depends upon the relative values society places on various input services. As we shall see, the relative evaluation of inputs ultimately reflects society's evaluation of commodities those inputs can produce.

It is important to emphasize that inferences about production costs cannot begin until the technical aspects of production are understood.

---

[20] As a power function, the Cobb-Douglas function is actually estimated by linear regression technique, since $q = AL^\alpha K^\beta$ can be transformed into $\ln q = \ln A + \alpha(\ln L) + \beta(\ln K)$. By first transforming measures of capital (usually measured in dollar value of machines or assets) and labor (measured in workers or man-hours) into natural logarithms, the Cobb-Douglas function can be measured with relatively simple statistical techniques.

But knowledge of how changes in input services change the rate of output, and how inputs can be substituted efficiently, is only the first step to an understanding of the nature of economic costs. How relative factor prices or opportunity costs influence the firm's choice of inputs is the subject of chapter six. How the business economist uses simple technology assumptions to plan a firm's production is the topic of chapter seven. And how the market for outputs and the market for inputs reward owners of factors of production and influence consumer welfare will sustain our attention through the rest of the book.

HIGHLIGHTS

1. Despite the technical ring to the word *efficiency*, evaluating the relative merits of different production methods involves subjective evaluation. For simplicity, we have divided the concept of efficiency into technical efficiency, which requires that input services not be wasted, and economic efficiency, which requires that each level of output be produced at minimum opportunity cost.

2. Both the labor theory of value and the capital theory of value are plagued by the ambiguity of the input used to define other inputs. Capital can be defined as embodied labor or labor can be defined as embodied capital, but one term must be accepted as an undefined primitive. The moral of this controversy about input definitions is that various theories of distribution (Marxian and marginal productivity, for instance) are based partly on subjective as well as objective (i.e., testable) premises.

3. A production function relates efficient combinations of inputs to the highest possible rate of output that those inputs can produce. Like consumption, production is a flow concept. Broadly defined, production involves the transformation of scarce resources into more valuable commodities.

4. When only one or more input services are subject to a maximum availability constraint, the additional output obtained from an increase in the services of that input must eventually become smaller and smaller. This is known as the law of diminishing marginal productivity (or the law of diminishing returns).

5. It is important to distinguish between inputs whose costs are fixed (usually the result of a minimum purchase contract) and inputs whose services are fixed. If a contractually hired input can be used below capacity, fewer variable inputs may be required to produce small rates of output.

6. The average product of a variable factor increases when the marginal product of that factor is greater than its average product, and decreases when marginal product is less than average product. Technical efficiency requires that variable inputs be employed so that the average product of each exceeds its marginal product and that the marginal product is positive.

7. The characteristics of isoquants—negatively sloped, nonintersecting curves, which are bowed-in toward the origin—come from the requirements of technical efficiency when there are two or more variable inputs. The positively sloped and bowed-out regions of isoquants are eliminated by the definition of ridge lines, where the marginal product of one of the factors is zero. In addition, assumption of smooth isoquants is usually made to simplify analysis of the firm's input choice.

8. Output elasticity is defined as the percentage change in output due to a 1 percent change in one input, other factors held constant. The

percentage change in output can be predicted by multiplying each input's output elasticity times the percentage change in that input and summing the results for all inputs.

9. Economists define returns to scale as the change in output caused by a 1 percent increase in all inputs. Increasing returns to scale reflect increasing specialization: if a particular rate of output is required to keep a specialized machine or worker employed continuously, doubling the rate of output may not require doubling all inputs. By contrast, decreasing returns to scale reflect the problems of coordinating inputs or deteriorating input quality as output expands. The returns to scale of a production function can be determined as the sum of the output elasticities of all inputs.

10. When simple production processes can be replicated side-by-side (e.g., typing pools or machine shops), constant returns to scale may result. This case comes closest to the idea that all inputs are changed by the same proportion, resulting in a consistent proportional response of output.

11. For empirical research, economists make considerable use of homogeneous production functions, which are designed to show the same returns to scale at all rates of output. The analytical advantage of homogeneous production functions is that they exhibit parallel isoquant maps.

GLOSSARY

Average product The rate of output divided by the quantity of services of one input.

Capital theory of value A way of characterizing modern theories of production and distribution which measure all inputs as embodied capital.

Diminishing marginal rate of substitution See **law of variable proportions.**

Diminishing marginal rate of technical substitution The technical name for the bowed-in shape of isoquants: as labor is substituted for capital, the slope of the isoquant becomes flatter.

Efficiency The production of commodities at minimum opportunity cost. (1) Economic efficiency exists when it is impossible to reduce the cost of inputs without reducing the rate of output. (2) Technical efficiency exists when it is impossible to increase the rate of output unless services of at least one input are increased.

Fixed input An input whose costs do not vary with its use.

Homogeneous production function A production function is said to be homogeneous to degree b when changing all inputs by a factor of λ changes output by a factor of λ^b. If $b = 1$, the production function is said to be linearly homogeneous and exhibits constant returns to scale. If $b > 1$, the production function exhibits increasing returns to scale, and if $b < 1$, the production function displays decreasing returns to scale.

Human capital The present value of a worker's expected earnings attributed to an investment-like expenditure of scarce resources on formal education, other training, and similar activities.

Isoquant A set of combinations of the services of two variable inputs which produce the same rate of output.

Isoquant map The set of isoquants for representative rates of output of a specific commodity.

Labor theory of value The classical economic theory that used embodied labor to measure all inputs and hypothesized that all goods would exchange in proportion to the amount of labor and other inputs, also measured in labor units, used to produce them.

Law of diminishing marginal productivity If production occurs with one variable input, it will eventually take larger and larger increases in that input to obtain equal subsequent increases in the rate of output, other factor services being fixed. Also known as the **law of diminishing returns.**

Law of diminishing returns   See **law of diminishing marginal productivity.**

Law of variable proportions   As inputs are substituted along an isoquant, it will take progressively greater quantities of the increasing input to compensate for equal subsequent reductions of the other input. Also known as **diminishing marginal rate of technical substitution.**

Long run   A period of time long enough for all inputs to vary. It usually corresponds to the duration of minimum purchase contracts and/ or maximum availability constraints of fixed inputs.

Marginal product   The change in output due to the use of one more unit of a given input, other factor services being constant.

Marginal rate of technical substitution (MRTS)   The slope of an isoquant, relating the amount by which one input can be reduced when another input's services are increased in such a way that the rate of output remains constant. The marginal rate of technical substitution equals the negative ratio of the marginal product of the increasing factor to the marginal product of the decreasing factor:

$$MRTS = \frac{\Delta K}{\Delta L}\bigg|_{\Delta q = 0} = -\frac{MP_L}{MP_K}$$

Opportunity cost   The sacrifice of benefits of goods not produced when scarce input services are used to produce a given commodity.

Output elasticity   The percentage change in output due to a 1 percent increase in one input's services, other input services remaining constant. Output elasticity can be calculated as the ratio of a factor's average product to its marginal product:

$$\epsilon_i = \frac{\Delta q/q}{\Delta v_i/v_i} = \frac{\Delta q}{\Delta v_i} \times \frac{v_i}{q} = \frac{MP_i}{AP_i}$$

Production   Any process which transforms scarce

resource services into a form considered more valuable.

Production function   A mathematical expression relating the maximum possible rate of output to each technically efficient combination of input services.

Reductio ad absurdum   Latin phrase meaning "reduction to an absurdity." An analytical method or debating tactic by which an assumption or argument is shown to be false by demonstrating that its truth would result in a logical contradiction.

Returns to scale   The percentage change in output resulting from a common percentage change in all inputs. Increasing returns to scale mean output changes by a greater proportion than the common percentage change in all inputs; constant returns to scale result when the percentage change in output equals the common percentage change in all inputs; and decreasing returns to scale occur when output changes by a smaller percentage than the common percentage changes in all inputs. The returns to scale can be calculated by adding up the output elasticities for all inputs.

Ridge lines   Limits to the relevant range of an isoquant map, obtained by connecting all points where the marginal product of a variable input is zero.

Short run   A period of time during which (1) the costs of one or more inputs are fixed and/or (2) one or more inputs are subject to a maximum availability constraint.

Short-run production function   The formula which gives the maximum possible output for each employment level of a variable input, other input services being limited to their fixed amounts.

Short-run total product of labor   The maximum rate of output associated with each rate of employment of labor, other input services held constant.

Stages of production   The possible relations between the average product and marginal product of one variable input and the employment rate for that input.

1. *Stage I* $MP_i > AP_i > 0$. The average product of the factor is increasing with its use, indicating that the marginal product of a

fixed input is negative. Stage I can be avoided either by increasing the use of the variable input, or reducing the use of the affected fixed input below its capacity.

2. *Stage II* $AP_i > MP_i > 0$. Since both the marginal product and the average product of the variable input are decreasing as more of that input is used, the firm will find it efficient to stop hiring that input somewhere in stage II.

3. *Stage III* $AP_i > 0 > MP_i$. This implies that too much of the variable input is being used, since output could be increased by using less of that factor. Once the marginal product of the variable input has reached zero (at the boundary between stage II and stage III), output can be increased only by increasing the services of one or more fixed inputs.

Variable input A factor of production available in adequate amounts without a minimum purchase contract. A factor whose costs change with its use.

SUGGESTED READINGS

Cassels, John M. "On the Law of Variable Proportions." In *Explorations in Economics*. New York: McGraw-Hill, 1936.

Douglas, Paul H. "Are There Laws of Production?" *American Economic Review* (March 1948), pp. 1–41.

Georgescu-Roegen, Nicholas. "The Economics of Production." *American Economic Review* (May 1970), pp. 1–9.

Knight, Frank H. "Social Economic Organization." *The Economic Organization*. New York: Harper & Row, 1933, 1951. Reprinted in William Breit and Harold Hochman. eds. *Readings in Microeconomics*. 2nd ed. New York: Holt, Rinehart and Winston, 1971, pp. 3–19.

Leibenstein, Harvey. "The Proportionality Controversy and the Theory of Production." *Quarterly Journal of Economics* (November 1955), pp. 619–625.

Moore, Frederick T. "Economies of Scale: Some Statistical Evidence." *Quarterly Journal of Economics* (May 1959), pp. 232–245.

Samuelson, Paul. *Economics*. 11th ed. New York: McGraw-Hill, 1980, pp. 513–522.

Smith, Adam. *An Inquiry into the Nature and Causes of the Wealth of Nations*. Chicago: University of Chicago Press, 1976, book I, chapters I–III.

Stigler, George. "The Division of Labor Is Limited by the Extent of the Market." *Journal of Political Economy* (June 1951), pp. 185–193. Reprinted in William Breit and Harold Hochman. eds. *Readings in Microeconomics*. 2nd ed. New York: Holt, Rinehart and Winston, 1971, pp. 140–148.

Tobin, James. "Cambridge (UK) vs. Cambridge (Mass.)" *The Public Interest* (spring 1972).

EXERCISES

Evaluate

Indicate whether each statement is true (agrees with economic theory), false (is contradicted by theory), or uncertain (could be true or false, given additional information). Explain your answer.

1. If the average product of a fixed factor is increasing, the marginal product of the variable factor must be negative.

2. As long as the firm has to pay for an input, it would be wasteful not to use all input services purchased.

3. Increasing returns to scale mean that the output elasticity of at least one input must be greater than one.

4. If two inputs are variable and a third input is fixed, the maximum output consistent with the fixed input is identified by the isoquant-

point where both variable inputs have a zero marginal product.

5. An input combination must be technically efficient if it is economically efficient, but not all technically efficient combinations have to be economically efficient.

6. When a factor's marginal product is less than its average product, too much of the input is being used.

7. Isoquants have negative slopes because of diminishing marginal productivity of both inputs.

8. As long as all factor services are variable, a firm need never experience negative marginal productivity.

9. If all inputs were perfect substitutes, diminishing marginal productivity would not occur.

10. An input's average product can never be negative.

Calculate

Answer each of the following questions, showing all your calculations.

11. The Peacock Cab Company has signed a contract with the Municipal Airport Authority to supply 20 cabs each day to service arriving passengers. Since taxis will be in constant use, they will break down occasionally. The chief mechanic has devised the following plans for assuring a minimum of 20 cabs in operating condition at all times:

Plan	Taxis	Mechanics
A	40	2
B	35	3
C	31	4
D	28	5
E	30	6

a. Which, if any, of the plans are technically inefficient? Explain.

b. What is the marginal rate of technical substitution for each technically efficient pair of processes?

12. A producer has contracted for 100 units of capital per day, deciding it is better to pay a fixed cost than risk the prospect of no capital goods, since only 100 units are available.

After a month's experience working with all the capital and different amounts of labor, the following schedule is drawn up:

Labor	Output	Capital/Worker
1	5	100
5	40	20
10	100	10
20	180	5
30	240	$3\frac{1}{3}$
40	280	$2\frac{1}{2}$
50	300	2
60	280	$1\frac{2}{3}$

a. Calculate the average and marginal products of labor for each employment rate.

b. If capital services could be varied, and production were characterized by constant returns to scale, what would be the maximum output which could be produced with 1 unit of labor services? What is the maximum output that could be produced with 5 units of labor?

c. Calculate the marginal product of capital for each employment level of labor.

Contemplate

Answer each of the following in a brief but complete essay.

13. Economists define capital as commodities which produce other commodities, while most noneconomists define it as an amount of money. What sorts of confusions result from these two definitions of the same term? What do you suppose the impact is of using the price of machines as their common denominator in aggregating and comparing capital? Do you think these problems are avoidable?

14. Evaluate the following: "Increasing returns to scale is a misnomer, since gains from increasing the output capacity of a production facility involve changes in factor proportions. However, without knowledge of relative input prices, one cannot explain why or how factor proportions change. Therefore, returns to scale is a reasonable starting point."

15. Many nonprofit organizations (e.g., universities, hospitals, museums) receive bequests and gifts in the form of buildings, equipment,

or exhibits, requiring that these institutions expand employment to maintain and operate that paraphernalia, which increases operating costs. Does this practice contradict the economic approach to production, which emphasizes input substitution? If so, what do you think accounts for this contradiction? If not, what sorts of returns to "scale" result when all inputs are increased in the wake of a gift of capital goods?

Chapter 6

Input Selection and Production Costs

Having defined technical efficiency in chapter five, we now consider how the firm selects that input combination which minimizes opportunity cost. The economically efficient process is determined by comparing the marginal rate of technical substitution (the slope of the isoquant) with the relative prices of inputs (the slope of the isocost line for a price taker in the input market). After developing the firm's output-expansion path, we explore the ways in which input prices influence the firm's long-range planning.

Once a firm has begun production, it is likely that some inputs can be increased only after considerable delay. The operating firm must contend with problems of decreasing marginal productivity of variable inputs when other inputs have limited availability. Also, because many payments result from binding contracts, the firm will discover that total costs do not fall as rapidly as output can contract in the short run. Considerable attention is devoted to the behavior of production costs in the short run.

Finally, the relation between total costs, average costs, and marginal cost in the long run (the planning horizon) and the short run (operating experience) is developed. The chapter concludes by showing how the long-run average cost curve represents an "envelope curve" for the set of short-run (fixed plant) average total cost curves.

Opportunity Cost

In economics, *cost* reflects what must be given up to achieve something. To an economist, who is concerned about the scarcity of inputs, the *cost of producing one commodity is the sacrifice of alternative goods and services which could have been produced instead.* To an accountant, who is concerned about the tax liability of his or her client, a cost is what the government allows to be deducted from revenue in calculating taxable income. In general, accounting costs are outlays, whereas economic costs are **opportunity costs.** If the price paid for the service of a factor of production equals the payment the owner of that factor could receive from an alternative source, the outlay for input services equals the opportunity cost of those services—economic costs and accounting costs are equivalent. The two concepts diverge when producers use their own labor, land, or capital. What is left over after outlays have been deducted from revenue will constitute the producer's taxable income. The economist, in determining economic profit, would deduct the foregone income which could have been earned if that labor, land, or capital had been used by another producer in exchange for money income.

Since the accountant's job is to determine tax liability, accounting costs are naturally sensitive to who owns a resource. An entrepreneur who hires another to manage his or her business will deduct the manager's salary when calculating the firm's taxable income. An entrepreneur who manages his or her own business must pay taxes on income attributable to managerial effort; it matters not whether the entrepreneur could have earned a higher income managing someone else's business. However, economic costs are independent of the identity of owners of scarce resources. Suppose Sonny Day quits a $50,000-a-year job, invests $200,000 of his own money to build a factory on land that was earning $10,000 a year in rent, and "clears" $75,000 at the end of the first year after all out-of-pocket expenses (plus allowable depreciation) have been deducted from revenue. Day's taxable income is $75,000. However, the economist, who is interested in how well resources are doing in this industry, would point out that $50,000 must be deducted for the opportunity cost of Day's foregone salary, $10,000 for foregone rent, and $20,000 foregone interest (assuming an interest rate of 10 percent). With total implicit costs of $80,000, that $75,000 taxable income is also a $5,000 economic loss.

As a barometer of efficient resource use, economic costs reflect current alternatives, not past decisions. Suppose Mr. Hooper has purchased a shipment of coffee at $2 per pound. Adding 25 percent to cover overhead and profit he sets the retail price at $2.50 (an economic analysis of markup price will be presented in chapter eleven). While Hooper still has 75 percent of the coffee in stock, the wholesale price jumps to $4 per pound. Should Hooper first deplete his inventory of "cheap" coffee and raise the price only after paying the higher wholesale price on the next shipment? Or should he be a "price gouger," extorting tribute from customers by marking up the $2 coffee to, say, $5 and making windfall gains of $3 per pound?

For all its nefarious overtones, the second action would correspond to economic logic. The cost of selling a commodity is what must be paid to replace it, not what was originally paid for it. The "windfall gain" may determine Hooper's tax liability, but economic logic indicates that this is not real income. A large difference between the wholesale and retail price of coffee may enrage consumers, who always prefer lower prices to higher ones. But tax liability and shoppers' preferences have little to do with the way economists measure costs.

Before you conclude that economists favor price gouging, let's reverse this example. Suppose that just after paying $4,000 for 1,000 pounds of coffee, Mr. Hooper learns that the wholesale price has fallen to $2 per pound. Should he hold the price above $4 per pound until he recovers his investment in inventory? If so, he will eventually learn the retail price of *stale* coffee. Economic logic is consistent: the cost of selling goods out of inventory is their replacement cost, not their original cost. The grocer who sells coffee at $2.50 per pound when all others sell at prices above $4 will find his stock depleted in short order. His customers may be delighted; but later, if he tries to unload $4 coffee when others charge about $2.50, he will find consumer gratitude is fleeting.

APPLICATION
Accounting Costs and Economic Costs

Another example illustrates how the economist's definition of cost is tailored to the things economists do. Suppose that the management of Sparky Electronics Inc., impressed by the growing popularity of videogames, is considering a venture into this expanding market. I. U. Snumbers, the firm's accountant, determines that Sparky Electronics can produce a million videogames, at an average cost of $10.91 each for parts, labor, and overhead. Adding 10 percent for profit, Snumbers suggests that the game sell for $12 to provide Sparky's investors with an acceptable dividend. Note that the accountant's advice is based entirely on the estimated cost of variable inputs, arbitrarily assigned overhead, and a desired rate of profit. The information used does not indicate whether consumers would be willing to buy 1 million videogames at the suggested price of $12 each.

Sparky Electronics hires an economic consultant, I. C. Clearly, to estimate the demand for the new product. Using data on the prices of competing games, the past trends in sales, and a couple of educated hunches, Clearly estimates that only 600,000 videogames could be sold annually at the $12 price. To sell a million games, he calculates that the price should be set at $10 per game. Since this falls short of the accountant's recommended price of $12, should Sparky Electronics venture into the videogame market? Ever daring, I. C. Clearly makes his recommendation. "It depends," he tells the Sparky executives.

"How so?" queries J. P. Mortimer, the president.

"Well, what would be the consequences of not introducing the new product?" asks Clearly.

"We'd have lower costs, that's what," replies an irritated Mortimer.

"Ah, but how much lower? If your plant is operating at capacity, producing videogames means installing new machinery or diverting machinery from other products. Either way, machinery costs of producing videogames would be a variable cost, and they should be considered as a cost of producing the new commodity. On the other hand, if your plant has idle capacity, which could be used to make the games, the only relevant costs are the cost of materials, labor, and energy—costs which would occur only if the commodity is actually produced."

"Well," replies Mortimer, "We are currently operating at approximately 50 percent of our plant capacity. If we continue at this rate we stand to lose almost five million dollars this year. But I don't see what this loss has to do with the price of videogames."

"Precisely!" shouts I. C. Clearly, triumphantly. "The price of videogames depends upon what consumers are willing to pay, the quantity they are willing to purchase at that price, and the extent of competition in the market. And, unfortunately, we will not be ready to talk about the last topic until later in the book."

"What book?" asks Mortimer, incredulously.

"Never mind," replies Clearly. "The point is that since you will be losing money without producing the new commodity, your decision about whether to produce the videogame should depend upon whether the new product would reduce your losses. My interpretation of Boring's data indicates that each game would cost approximately six dollars in extra raw materials, energy, and electricity. Since machinery that is currently costing you 4.91 million dollars per year could be used for the new product, selling a million videogames at ten dollars each would reduce your losses to 0.91 million dollars."

"But a ten-dollar price is not as good as a twelve-dollar price," complains the accountant. "I stick by my advice. Sell a million videogames at twelve dollars each, and earn a profit of 1.09 million."

"But if you set the price at twelve dollars and only sell six hundred thousand games, your revenue will be 7.2 million and variable costs will equal 3.6 million; this will result in net revenue of 3.6 million dollars, which, when applied to the 4.91-million-dollar fixed overhead, results in a loss of 1.31 million. Sure, twelve dollars is better than ten, and a hundred is better than twelve. But one must anticipate how much one can actually sell, rather than how much one would like to sell," concludes I. C. Clearly.

"The board of directors and I thank you for your advice," says the president. "We will produce the game on a trial basis, setting the price at ten dollars. But, after we've tested the market for a year, we will raise the price to twelve dollars, or higher, if the market will bear it. If it doesn't show a profit, we will scrap the idea, along with the excess machinery."

"Sound's right by me," replies the accountant. "You've got to break even in the long run. In the meantime, producing videogames might be a good tax shelter."

"I wouldn't know about that. Now, if you will excuse me. Some guy named Hooper wants to consult me on the price of coffee."

Input Availability and Factor Prices

As with development of the household's allocation of purchasing power among commodities, analysis of the firm's selection of input combinations is simplified by making several assumptions. As usual, when any of these assumptions becomes crucial, we will trace the implications of relaxing that proposition. For most of this chapter, and subsequent chapters, we will assume that variable inputs can be purchased at a constant price. There are two realistic contexts in which this assumption is valid: (1) the price of an input is determined in a competitive input market; (2) the firm has signed a contract—such as a collective bargaining agreement—which specifies a constant factor price (e.g., the union wage), although the firm is free to vary employment of that factor.

Violation of the constant factor price assumption occurs when the quantity of the input a firm hires influences the price it pays. In one form of violation, price increases with quantity. This may occur when the firm has few or no competitors in the purchase of a specialized input—say, a particular labor skill or a custom-made machine. If alternative suppliers have different opportunity costs, the firm will have the option of buying from low-priced sellers first. But as the amount of the input purchased increases, the unit cost of services will also increase. If all suppliers must be paid the same price, the **marginal input cost**—the change in factor payments due to the last unit hired—will exceed the input price.[1]

The second violation of the constant factor price assumption occurs when input price falls as the quantity purchased rises. An employer may

---

[1] The total payment for factor i is $w_i v_i$. Thus: $MC_i = \dfrac{d(w_i v_i)}{dv_i} = w_i + v_i \dfrac{dw_i}{dv_i}$

obtain lower insurance premiums by enrolling workers in a group health program once employment has reached a certain level. Industrial users of electricity generally pay lower rates as consumption increases, often because their size makes it feasible for them to generate their own power if rates are too high.

The three patterns for factor prices are illustrated in Figure 6-1. The case of the constant factor price appears in Figure 6-1a. Since the firm pays the same price regardless of how much (or how little) of an input it hires, the marginal input cost (MC_i) equals the factor price—and the average input cost (AC_i)—at all employment levels. Were the price of the input to change, either because its competitive price changed or because the terms of the contract fixing factor prices were changed, the average and marginal costs of the input would change uniformly for all employment levels.

Figure 6-1b shows the case of increasing factor prices, which often occurs when a firm has **monopsony** power, denoting a situation where there is but *one buyer* in the market. If equally productive units of an input are available at different prices, the firm will exhaust low-cost sources before employing higher priced units. If the price paid to all suppliers must be the same, expanding the employment of higher priced units will require raising the price for all units. The marginal input cost will exceed the average input cost.

Figure 6-1c depicts the case of falling factor prices. Large buyers of inputs may acquire leverage with large sellers, thereby obtaining dis-

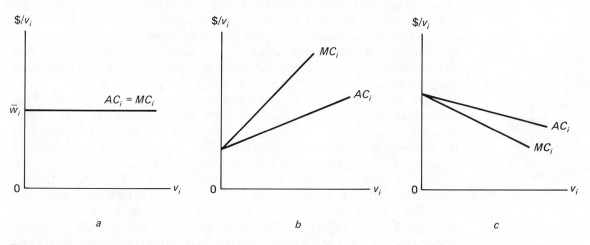

Figure 6-1
Input Price Patterns for (a) Price Taker, (b) Monopsonist, and (c) Quantity Discounts. a, Constant factor price: average input cost equals marginal input cost for all employment levels. b, Increasing factor price: marginal input cost exceeds average input cost after first unit. c, Declining factor price: marginal input cost is less than average input cost after first unit.

counts and rebates. If the price of all units of an input falls as more are purchased, the marginal cost of the input will be lower than its average cost. More likely, as in the case of declining utility and freight rates, cost savings occur only on the last units purchased, so that the MC_i curve would reflect factor prices, while the average input cost would be bouyed up by higher prices for the first units hired.

In addition to the assumption of constant factor prices, we assume that factors of production are homogeneous. This allows us to postpone the troublesome issue of imperfect input substitution until chapter fourteen. As in chapter five, we will continue to treat variations in factor productivity as the consequence of changes in factor proportions, rather than as stemming from the characteristics of individual inputs or their owners.

Economic Efficiency and Optimal Factor Proportions

The assumptions of homogeneous inputs and constant factor prices simplify the identification of economically efficient input proportions. But before the best production technology can be identified, "best" must be defined in realistic terms. Unfortunately, one popular notion of efficiency is incompatible with basic economic realities. "Producing the greatest possible output at the lowest possible cost" implies the absence of scarcity. The lowest possible cost a firm can experience is zero, but zero cost is associated with the lowest possible output, which must be zero, since zero cost implies no input use. It is not clear what the greatest possible output of any commodity would be, but in a world of scarcity, it is surely finite. And since the cost of using inputs to produce one commodity is the sacrifice of other commodities, using all available resources to produce only one commodity would result in opportunity costs of incredible magnitude.

The producer's selection of input services involves *constrained optimization*: the *best* mix of input services must be drawn from the menu of feasible combinations. Just as a consumer's utility is constricted by the limits of the household budget, the firm's use of inputs is constrained by the ability to pay for factor services, either out of owners' wealth or, ideally, revenue received from the sale of output. In household consumption, utility is treated as the goal and the budget the means, but the firm's input decision does not involve such a direct ends-means relation. The firm's hypothetical goal, profit, is expressed as the difference between total revenue and total opportunity cost. Revenue is price times quantity sold; the relationship between output and price varies with the degree of competition in the market. That topic will concern us in part four. Here, we will concentrate on the relation between output and opportunity cost. It makes just as much sense to define production efficiency as producing the maximum output possible for a given opportunity cost as it does to define the ideal input mix as that combination associated with the lowest opportunity cost for producing a target rate of output. What is less obvious is that either approach results in the same rule for input selection. One of the most practical concepts in the theory of cost is the *dual* approach to **economic efficiency**. The input combination that achieves economic efficiency can be identified as the one which produces a *specified rate of output* (i.e., the constraint) at the *minimum opportunity cost* (i.e., the objective). It can also be defined as the combination which produces the *maximum rate of output* (the objective) or a *specified opportunity cost* (the constraint). A competitive firm which minimizes the cost of producing a specified level of output will employ the same factor proportions as one which maximizes output for a specified level of cost.

The geometric development of the dual nature of economic efficiency involves the juxtaposition of the firm's output, represented by the isoquant, and the economic cost of inputs, which can be represented by the **isocost line**. The isocost line represents *combinations of inputs with the same total opportunity cost*. The isocost line for a firm facing constant input prices is depicted in Figure 6-2. As with the household

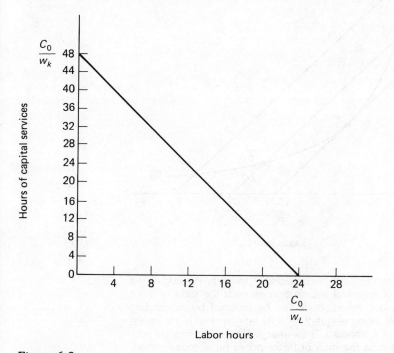

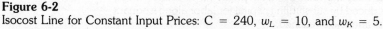

Figure 6-2
Isocost Line for Constant Input Prices: $C = 240$, $w_L = 10$, and $w_K = 5$.

budget line, the isocost line is obtained by graphing the firm's expenditure on inputs, $C = w_L L + w_K K$, where C is the firm's cost of inputs, w_L is the wage rate for labor (which also reflects the opportunity cost of time), and w_K is the rental rate for capital (either what a firm pays to lease a machine or could receive by leasing its own machinery to another firm). By fixing the level of cost at C_0, we can solve the expenditure equation for capital: $K = C_0/w_K - (w_L/w_K)L$. The intercept on the capital axis is the maximum capital services which could be procured for C_0, and the slope of the isocost line equals the reduction in capital services which is necessary to keep cost at C_0 when an extra hour of labor services is hired. A firm which could rent typing equipment (typewriters, word processors, high-speed printers) for $5 per hour or hire typists for $10 per hour would have to reduce capital by two units for each extra hour of labor services employed. (As discussed in chapter

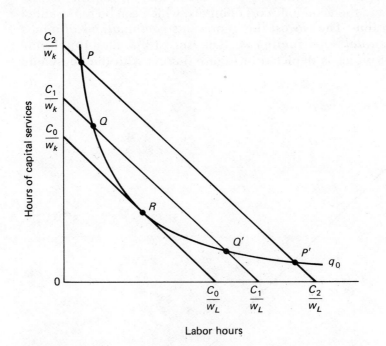

Figure 6-3
Economic Efficiency: Cost Minimization Approach. As long as the marginal rate of technical substitution exceeds the ratio of input prices (in absolute value), costs can be reduced by substituting labor for capital along isoquant q_0 until tangency with the lowest isocost line (C_0) is attained. If the marginal rate of technical substitution is less than the ratio of factor prices (in absolute value), costs can be reduced by substituting capital for labor along isoquant q_0 until isocost line C_0 is reached.

five, measuring heterogeneous capital can be solved by measuring capital in money equivalents. Hence, if one typewriter can be rented for $5 an hour and word processors rent for $20 an hour, a word processor is treated as four capital units.) The isocost line in Figure 6-2 depicts combinations of labor and capital (at the rate of $w_L/w_K = 2$) available for $240.

The producer who wishes to maximize profit must begin by finding the minimum cost technique for each rate of output. Since output determines revenue, profit can never be maximized if it is possible to produce a specified rate of output at a lower cost. A firm can determine whether it is possible to produce a given rate of output at a lower cost by relating the target isoquant to isocost lines. In Figure 6-3, isoquant q_0 intersects isocost line C_2 at point P. Point P is feasible, since it produces the target rate of output, q_0. However, by substituting labor services for capital services along isoquant q_0, lower isocost lines can be attained. At point P, the marginal product of labor relative to the marginal product of capital exceeds the ratio of the price of labor services to the price of capital services. At point Q, isoquant q_0 intersects isocost C_1. While cost has been reduced by moving production from point P to point Q, the fact that isoquant q_0 intersects isocost C_1 (rather than being tangent to it) indicates that lower isocost lines can be attained to the right of point Q.

At point R, isocost line C_0 is tangent to isoquant q_0. At movement along isoquant q_0 in either direction from point R would raise production costs; a movement along isocost line C_0 would cause output to fall below q_0, violating the output constraint. Hence, when the target isoquant, q_0, is tangent to the relevant isocost line, C_0, it is impossible to reduce cost unless output is also reduced.[2]

Since *tangency* means that the isoquant curve and the isocost line are changing at the same rate at their common point, point R is characterized by the equality of the ratio of the marginal products of the two input services (the slope of the isoquant) and the ratio of the two input

---

[2] The chain rule (discussed in appendix A) allows us to employ calculus directly to solve the cost minimization problem. To limit combinations of input services to those which produce the target rate of output, we can tie together the amount of labor and capital used by taking the derivative of cost with respect to labor and requiring that dK/dL, the change in capital services due to the change in labor services, conform to the marginal rate of technical substitution. By setting dC/dL equal to zero, we require that labor be increased (implying that capital be decreased according to $MRTS$) until cost stops falling:

$$\frac{dC}{dL} = w_L + w_K \frac{dK}{dL} = w_L + w_K(MRTS) = w_L + w_K\left(-\frac{MP_L}{MP_K}\right)$$

Setting this derivative equal to zero, we obtain the same tangency solution as in the geometric analysis: $w_L + w_K(-MP_L/MP_K) = 0$ implies $w_L = w_K(MP_L/MP_K)$, or $MP_L/w_L = MP_K/w_K$.

prices (the slope of the isocost line):

$$MRTS = -\frac{MP_L}{MP_K} = -\frac{w_L}{w_K} = \frac{\Delta L}{\Delta K} \quad \text{so that} \quad \frac{MP_L}{w_L} = \frac{MP_K}{w_K}$$

When inputs are used in their economically efficient combination, the marginal product of each input will be proportional to its price.

The alternative approach to reaching the economically efficient combination of input services is presented in Figure 6-4. Producing the maximum rate of output for a specified input cost can be shown by making isocost line C_2 the constraint and finding that point on C_2 associated with the highest attainable isoquant. At point P, isoquant q_0 intersects isocost C_2. Although this point satisfies the cost constraint, the isoquant is steeper than the isocost line here: $-MP_L/MP_K < -w_L/w_K$. Reducing expenditure on capital by w_K allows the firm to employ w_L/w_K additional units of labor. Since the ratio of the marginal product

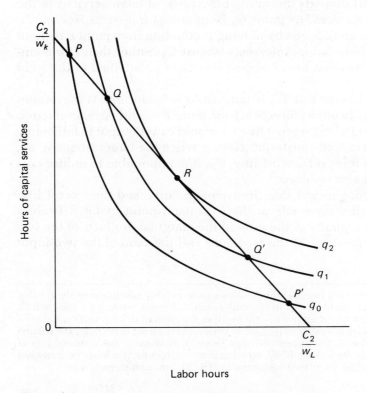

Figure 6-4
Economic Efficiency: Output Maximization Approach. Intersection of isoquant and isocost means that output can be increased if inputs are substituted along the isocost line (C_2) until tangency is reached at point R.

of labor to the marginal product of capital exceeds that price ratio, the output lost by reducing capital is smaller than the output gained by increasing labor. At point Q, the same opportunity cost results in output $q_1 > q_0$, but because the slope of isoquant q_1 is also steeper than the slope of C_2, additional output gains are possible.

At point R, isoquant q_2 is tangent to the constraint line, C_2. Again, equal slopes mean that the marginal rate of technical substitution equals the ratio of factor prices:

$$MRTS = -\frac{MP_L}{MP_k} = -\frac{w_L}{w_k} = \frac{\Delta K}{\Delta L} \quad \text{so that} \quad \frac{w_L}{MP_L} = \frac{w_k}{MP_k}$$

When resources are allocated efficiently, the last dollar spent on each input service results in the same change in output. In fact, efficient resource allocation implies that the cost of increasing the rate of output by one unit would be the same regardless of which input's service was increased.[3]

APPLICATION
Numerical Example of Input Choice

A numerical simulation may help clarify the process of input selection. In Table 6-1 we employ one of the most popular production function formulas, the Cobb-Douglas function (described in chapter five), to estimate the isoquants for 16 units of output. We imagine that output is given by the production function $q = L^{2/3}K^{1/3}$. By fixing the value of $q = 16$, we obtain the following formula for the amounts of labor and capital required to produce 16 units of output: $16 = L^{2/3}K^{1/3}$ or $4{,}096 = L^2K$, so that $K = 4{,}096/L^2$.

Using 8 units of labor and 64 units of capital produces 16 units of output at a cost of \$400. The capital-labor ratio is so great that the marginal product of labor is 16 times the marginal product of capital. Increasing labor by one unit allows capital services to be cut by 13.4 units without a reduction in output. Since one unit of labor costs twice as

---

[3] In a manner similar to that used in the cost minimization problem, the cost constraint means that one input can be increased only if the other input is decreased, such that $dK/dL = -w_L/w_K$. Taking the derivative of the production function, $q = f(L, K)$, with respect to L (with K given by the constant cost requirement), we have:

$$\frac{dq}{dL} = \frac{\partial q}{\partial L} + \frac{\partial q}{\partial K} \cdot \frac{dK}{dL} = MP_L + MP_K\left(-\frac{w_L}{w_K}\right) = 0$$

implies:

$$\frac{w_L}{MP_L} = \frac{w_K}{MP_K} = \frac{\partial C/\partial L}{\partial q/\partial L} = \frac{\partial C/\partial K}{\partial q/\partial K} = \frac{\partial C}{\partial q} = MC$$

much as one unit of capital, substitution of labor for capital reduces cost by \$57.16.

When $L = 9$ and $K = 50.6$, the marginal product of labor is still 11 times the marginal product of capital; substitution of labor for capital results in a cost saving of \$38.04. However, each subsequent increase in labor allows for smaller and smaller reductions in capital. When $L = 16$ and $K = 16$, the marginal product of labor is twice the marginal product of capital; the marginal rate of technical substitution equals the (negative) ratio of the price of labor to the price of capital—the cost-minimizing input combination has been reached. Any further increase in labor would save less than two units of capital per unit of labor; thus total cost would increase.

Table 6-2 holds the input cost at \$240 and demonstrates how output increases can result from factor substitution, using the same production function employed in Table 6-1. With 23 units of labor and only 2 units of capital, the marginal product of labor is only 17 percent of the marginal product of capital. Reducing labor by one unit allows two units of capital to be purchased. Cost remains constant but output increases by 2.27 units. The diminishing marginal rate of technical substitution guarantees that the marginal product of labor increases relative to the marginal product of capital; with $L = 22$ and $K = 4$, $-MP_L/MP_k = -0.364$. Increasing capital and reducing labor in a ratio of 2 to 1 allows output to continue to increase until the maximum output consistent with an input cost of \$240 is achieved. As in Figures 6-3 and 6-4, the cost-minimizing input combination in Table 6-1 is identical to the output-maximizing input combination in Table 6-2. However defined, the economically efficient combination of labor and capital services is achieved when the

TABLE 6-1
Cost Minimization for Given Output Level

Output	Labor Hours	Capital Hours	Input Cost	$-\dfrac{MP_L}{MP_k}$	$-\dfrac{w_L}{w_k}$	ΔC	$\dfrac{C}{q}$
16	8	64.00	\$400.00	-16.0	-2		\$25.00
16	9	50.60	342.84	-11.2	-2	$-\$57.16$	21.43
16	10	40.96	304.80	-8.2	-2	-38.04	19.05
16	11	33.90	279.30	-6.2	-2	-25.54	17.45
16	12	28.44	262.22	-4.7	-2	-17.03	16.39
16	13	24.24	251.18	-3.7	-2	-11.04	15.70
16	14	20.90	244.49	-3.0	-2	-6.69	15.28
16	15	18.20	241.02	-2.4	-2	-3.47	15.06
16	16	16.00	240.00	-2.0	-2	-1.02	15.00
16	17	14.17	240.87	-1.67	-2	$+0.87$	15.05
16	18	12.64	243.21	-1.53	-2	$+2.34$	15.20

TABLE 6-2
Output Maximization for Given Input Cost

Input Cost	Labor Hours	Capital Hours	Output	$-\dfrac{MP_L}{MP_k}$	$-\dfrac{w_L}{w_k}$	Δq	$\dfrac{C}{q}$
$240	23	2	10.19	−0.174	−2		$23.55
240	22	4	12.46	−0.364	−2	2.27	19.26
240	21	6	13.81	−0.571	−2	1.37	17.35
240	20	8	14.74	−0.800	−2	0.90	16.29
240	19	10	15.34	−1.05	−2	0.60	15.64
240	18	12	15.72	−1.33	−2	0.38	15.27
240	17	14	15.93	−1.65	−2	0.21	15.06
240	16	16	16.00	−2.00	−2	0.07	15.00
240	15	18	15.93	−2.40	−2	−0.06	15.06
240	14	20	15.76	−2.86	−2	−0.17	15.22

last dollar spent on each input results in the same change in output:

$$\frac{w_L}{MP_L} = \frac{w_K}{MP_K}$$

Output Expansion and Production Costs

The **output-expansion path** is obtained by connecting the isocost-iso-quant tangencies for a constant set of input prices. Each point of tangency indicates the maximum output for the relevant isocost line; each point of tangency gives the minimum opportunity cost necessary to produce the level of output indicated by the isoquant. The economically efficient combination of inputs can be identified either by moving along an iso-quant to the lowest attainable isocost line (cost minimization) or by moving along an isocost line to the highest attainable isoquant (output maximization). Either method leads to the same set of tangencies.

The expansion path defines a one-to-one relationship between output (the dependent variable of the production function) and cost (the dependent variable of the cost function). Plotting these economically efficient output-cost combinations for the expansion path in Figure 6-5*a* yields the total cost curve in Figure 6-5*b*.

The output-expansion path in Figure 6-5*a* depicts a relationship between a set of parallel isocost lines—constant input prices—and a variable returns-to-scale production function. The most likely explanation for the pattern in the figure is that only two inputs are variable while more than three inputs are required to produce the output. Hence, the intercept of the cost function in Figure 6-5*b* is greater than zero, depicting the invariant cost of nonvariable inputs (e.g., land, management).

Initial increases in labor and capital generate larger and larger increases in output, due to increasing specialization of labor and capital. Up to output level q_0, total cost increases at a decreasing rate. From q_0 to q_1, gains from specialization of the variable inputs are roughly offset by limited availability of the fixed factors. Over this range the total cost function in Figure 6-5*b* shows total cost increasing at roughly a constant rate. Finally, isoquants move farther apart as variable inputs expand beyond L_1 and K_1. The total cost increases at an increasing rate until the maximum possible rate of output, q_2, is reached, causing the total cost curve in Figure 6-5*b* to become vertical.

When all inputs are variable, the total cost curve passes through the origin, since zero output could be produced at zero cost. To keep our diagrams simple, we revert to the assumption that capital and labor are the only inputs necessary for the production of the commodity in ques-

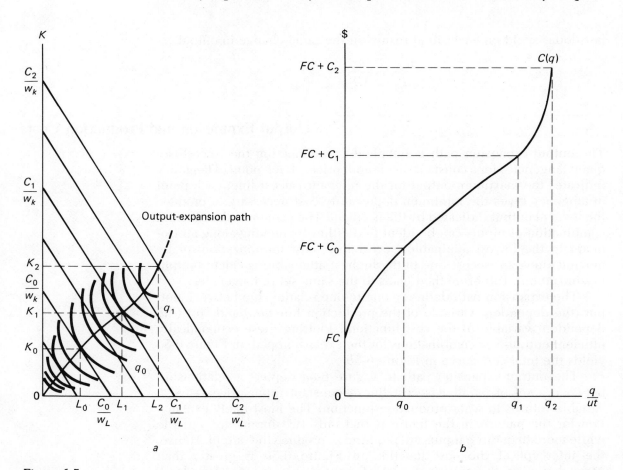

a

b

Figure 6-5
Derivation of (*b*) Total Cost Function from (*a*) Output Expansion Path

tion. A firm which can purchase labor and capital services at constant prices confronts a parallel set of isocost lines, $\Delta K/\Delta L = -w_L/w_K$, regardless of the rate of output produced. Although factor prices might change occasionally, due to market-wide forces, prices paid for input services are assumed to be independent of the quantity of input services hired. If the production function was homogeneous, isoquants would be parallel along any ray, so that all points where the marginal rate of substitution equals $-w_L/w_K$ would occur at the same capital-labor ratio. The combination of parallel isocost lines and parallel isoquants results in a linear expansion path; each planned rate of output would be associated with the same cost-minimizing capital-labor ratio.

As discussed in chapter five, the most likely instance of a homogeneous production function would be the constant returns to scale associated with small-scale, easily replicated production technologies. If a firm finds it efficient to produce 10 pages of documents per hour with one word processor, leased for $10 per hour, and one operator, paid $5 per hour, it is likely that 20 pages of documents per hour could be produced for $30 in outlays. However, when word processors come in different sizes, or when more terminals can be linked into a central computer, varying returns to scale will occur, and output expansion is likely to cause changes in input proportions.

The output-expansion path for a homogeneous production function and parallel isocost lines is depicted in Figure 6-6. Note that output q_0 is associated with the minimum cost input combination (L_0, K_0), purchased for the cost $C_0 = w_L L_0 + w_K K_0$. The assumption of a homogeneous production function means that use of λL_0 hours of labor and λK_0 hours of capital produces $\lambda^b q_0$ units of output per hour. Furthermore, the marginal rate of technical substitution at point $(\lambda L_0, \lambda K_0)$ on isoquant $\lambda^b q_0$ is the same as the marginal rate of technical substitution on isoquant q_0 at point (L_0, K_0). The minimum cost of producing $\lambda^b q_0$ units of output per hour is $\lambda C_0 = w_L(\lambda L_0) + w_K(\lambda K_0)$. Since λ can be any positive number, knowing the least cost combination of labor and capital services for one rate of output is sufficient to determine the minimum cost of producing all rates of output, all input services being variable. Hence, we can set $q_0 = 1$, and define $C_0 = m$; the consequence of constant factor prices and a homogeneous production function generates a total cost function of the form $C = mq^{1/b}$, where b is the degree of homogeneity of the production function.[4]

If the production function exhibits constant returns to scale, the firm which faces constant input prices will confront a cost function which is

---

[4] Let $m = w_L l + w_K k$, where l and k are the minimum cost input services of labor and capital necessary to produce one unit of output per hour. Since $f(\lambda L, \lambda K) = \lambda^b f(L, K)$, the production function can be written as $q = f(q^{1/b}l, q^{1/b}k) = (q^{1/b})^b f(l, k)$. It follows that the cost of producing q units per hour is $C(q) = q^{1/b}(w_L l + w_K k) = q^{1/b}m$.

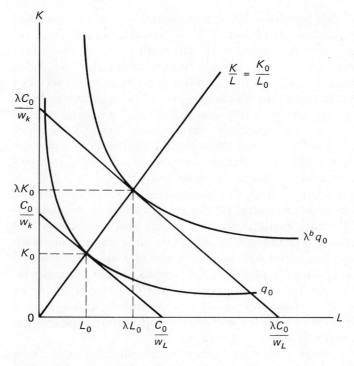

Figure 6-6
Output-Expansion Path for Constant Factor Prices and a Homogeneous Production Function

linear, when all inputs are variable, that is, over the long run. Each planned rate of output, q, could be produced with q "doses" of the labor and capital required for one unit of output per hour. **Long-run marginal cost**, defined as the change in planning costs required to increase the planned rate of output by one unit, all inputs being variable, is equal to m for all planned rates of output. For the same reason, **long-run average cost**, defined as the ratio of planning cost (all inputs variable) to the planned rate of output, would also equal m, the cost of the first planned unit of output per hour. This unique situation, in which long-run marginal cost equals long-run average cost for all rates of output, is depicted in Figure 6-7a.

If increasing returns to scale characterize the homogeneous production function ($b > 1$), long-run total cost will increase with the planned level of output, albeit at a decreasing rate. Long-run marginal cost will decrease as the planned rate of output increases, causing long-run average cost to fall also, although long-run average cost will always remain greater than long-run marginal cost.[5] The cost curves for a firm

---

[5] Given $C(q) = mq^{1/b}$, $dC/dq = (1/b)mq^{1/b-1}$ and $C/q = mq^{1/b-1}$. If $b = 1$, $dC/dq = C/q = m$; if $b > 1$, $C/q > dC/dq$ and $d^2C/dq^2 < 0$; if $b < 1$, $dC/dq > C/q$ and $d^2C/dq^2 > 0$.

with constant factor prices and increasing returns to scale are depicted in Figure 6-7*b*.

Finally, a homogeneous production function which exhibits decreasing returns to scale ($b < 1$) will give rise to a long-run total cost curve which shows the cost of inputs increasing at a faster rate than output, even if factor prices remain constant as the planned level of output increases. In such a case, both long-run marginal cost and long-run average cost will increase as planned output increases, and long-run average cost will lag behind long-run marginal cost, as shown in Figure 6-7*c*.

The combined assumptions of a homogeneous production function and constant factor prices simplify the one-to-one relationship between the planned level of output and the minimum cost of producing that output. However, many economists question whether the simple cost curves in Figure 6-7 represent even approximations of real-world input-output cost experiences. As discussed in chapter five, "returns to scale" is a misnomer except in the special case of constant returns to scale,

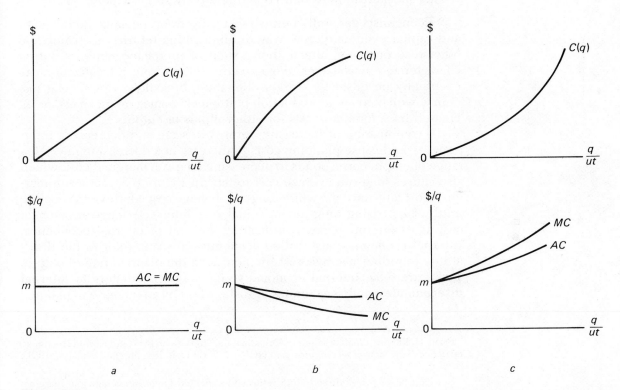

Figure 6-7
Long-Run (Planning) Costs for Constant Factor Prices and a Homogeneous Production Function. *a*, Constant returns to scale and constant factor prices; *b*, increasing returns to scale and constant factor prices; *c*, decreasing returns to scale and constant factor prices.

when a production "module" (one typist, one typewriter, one desk) can be duplicated over a wide output range. Generally, output increases at a faster rate than inputs when labor and capital become more specialized. If one automobile per year can be produced with one mechanic, a tool kit, and a garage, "economies of scale" are realized by constructing an integrated automobile plant, rather than by employing 1,000 mechanics, 1,000 tool kits, and 1,000 garages to produce more than a thousand automobiles per year. Aside from the problems of input measurement, gains from specialization imply a change in factor proportions. As Frank Knight stated:

> A tool or machine is usually much more specialized than a human being can ever be, and its efficiency in a particular task is connected with its specialization. Many things can be done, after a fashion, with a hammer; only one with an automatic printing press or a watch screw machine; but that one thing is done with wonderful precision and speed. Perhaps the very largest single source of gain from the specialization of labor is that it makes possible the development and use of machinery, the effectiveness of which is almost a matter of its specialization to limited and relatively simple operations.[6]

Economists generally believe that gains from specialization of labor and capital eventually give way to diminishing returns "to scale" and other diseconomies[7] after either a short or protracted range of output characterized by constant (average) costs. Gains from specialization can eventually be offset by worker alienation, breakdowns of special machines which create a production bottleneck, management snags, or increased transportation costs for either inputs or outputs.

A combination of increasing returns to scale and decreasing input prices would cause planning costs to increase at a decreasing rate. This range of output corresponds to decreasing long-run marginal cost, which also causes long-run average cost to fall. In Figure 6-8a, long-run marginal cost falls until q_0, while long-run average cost continues to decline until, at q_1, rising long-run marginal cost intersects long-run average cost at its minimum point, indicating the end of internal economies. **Internal economies**, also called **economies of scale**, refer to the firm's ability to reduce average cost by increasing the planned rate of output. In Figure 6-8a, internal economies give way immediately to **internal diseconomies**, or **diseconomies of scale**, whereby an increase in planned

---

[6] Frank H. Knight, "Social Economic Organization," in William Breit and Harold Hochman, eds., *Readings in Microeconomics*, 2nd ed. (New York: Holt, Rinehart and Winston, 1971), p. 13.

[7] Constant factor prices directly link returns to scale and long-run average and marginal costs. Long-run marginal costs and long-run average costs might increase with output because of decreasing returns to scale, because factor prices increase as output increases or because the quality (potential productivity) of inputs decreases as input use increases.

output (varying all inputs) results in increasing long-run average cost. Beyond q_1, $LRMC > LRAC$.

In Figure 6-8b, internal economies cause long-run marginal cost to fall until, at q_0, the cost of producing an extra unit of output with all inputs variable begins to rise. Long-run average cost falls until, at q_1, it equals (rising) long-run marginal cost. Between q_1 and q_2, long-run average cost and long-run marginal cost remain at the same level, and long-run total cost has a constant slope. This is the region of *constant (marginal and average) cost*. For rates of output greater than q_2, long-run marginal cost rises as planned output increases, due to internal diseconomies. Long-run average cost is pulled upward by long-run marginal cost, even though $LRAC < LRMC$. If a researcher observed only

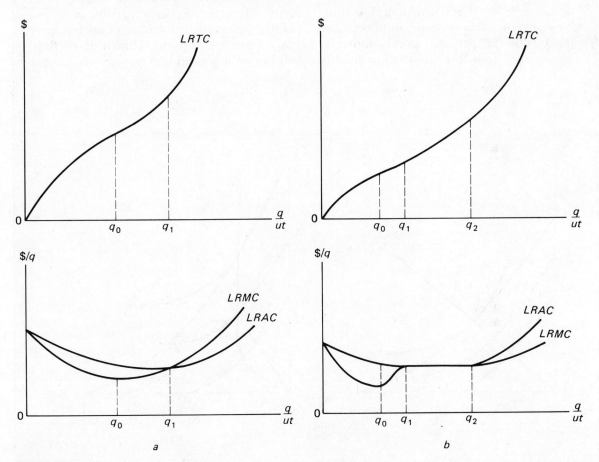

Figure 6-8
Long-Run (Planning) Costs for Variable Returns to Scale. a, Internal economies immediately followed by internal diseconomies; b, internal economies followed by protracted region of constant costs before internal diseconomies occur.

Business Illustration
Production Costs and Plant Location

One planning decision which highlights the problems of nonconstant factor prices and/or nonhomogeneous production functions is where to locate a production facility. In the field of location economics, economists determine the impact of transportation costs and other economic "frictions" associated with space on the location and spatial distribution of economic activity. When raw materials must be transported from their source to the production facility and goods must be transported from the production facility to consumers, production costs will vary with the combination of inputs used and the place where production occurs. Since more tons of coal than iron ore go into producing a ton of steel, it is more than coincidental that steel mills tend to locate closer to coal fields than to iron ore deposits.

The accompanying figure depicts two types of output-expansion paths. Note in both diagrams that isocost lines are bowed-in toward the origin. This reflects the ability of the producer to vary the costs

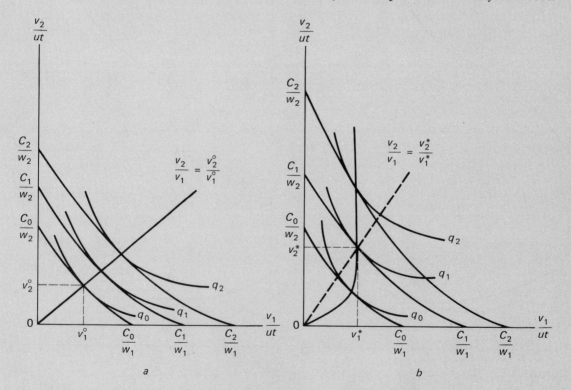

Output-Expansion Paths for Firm with (*a*) Homogeneous and (*b*) Nonhomogeneous Production Function. *a*, Linear expansion path: optimal plant site invariant with respect to planned output. *b*, Nonlinear expansion path: different planned output levels imply different optimal plant sites.

of (delivered) inputs v_1 and v_2 by changing location. Each point on an isocost line represents a different plant site as well as a different combination of inputs.

In panel *a*, the isoquant-isocost tangency points describe the linear output-expansion path v_2^0/v_1^0, indicating that the optimal combination of inputs for any rate of output results in the same input proportions, implying that the optimal plant site is the same for all rates of output. The entrepreneur can build one plant of a given size, then add to it or subtract from production capacity according to the firm's operating experiences.

In panel *b*, the optimal (minimum average cost) input combinations for different rates of output represent different input proportions. This could occur because the marginal rate of technical substitution of v_1 for v_2 changes as both inputs change proportionately or because isocost lines (curves) have different slopes

when inputs are increased or decreased proportionately. Planning the rate of output (forecasting the market demand for the firm's product) plays a crucial role under the nonparallel isoquant or nonparallel isocost generalization of the plant location problem. The plant site chosen to minimize the cost of producing q_1 units of output per period would not be the optimal plant site for producing q_0 units of output or q_2 units of output per period. Hence, complications assumed away (such as transportation costs) in simple theory can be very important when applying the lessons of microeconomics to the real world.

Based on Leon Moses, "Location and the Theory of Production," *Quarterly Journal* of Economics (1958), pp. 259–272; reprinted in Robert D. Dean, W. H. Leahy, and D. L. McKee, eds., *Spatial Economic Theory* (New York: Free Press, 1971), pp. 59–71.

plants with productive capacity between q_1 and q_2, he or she might mistakenly infer that firms in that industry were characterized by constant (average) costs for rates of production less than q_1 or greater than q_2.

APPLICATION
Changes in Input Prices

The concept of long-run costs is more relevant to the strategic and long-range planning activities of a business than to the day-to-day operation of an actual production facility. Planning costs represent a menu of alternative plant sizes, site locations, and combinations of highly specialized machinery which planners have determined would minimize the cost of producing alternative rates of output, *given prevailing or projected relative input prices*. From among these alternative output-cost prospects, a firm must choose one production capacity, which will mean that other rates of output cannot be produced at their minimum long-run cost. Once contracts have been signed, a firm may never again experience simultaneous variability of all inputs and all production costs. Data taken from the actual output and costs experienced by firms will, more often than not, involve input combinations other than the optimal combination for the long run. It is hard to overstate the importance of accurate planning for success in the business world. However, because there is greater flexibility in planning than in actual experience, planning must involve more than extrapolating current cost trends.

Changes in factor prices can cause the reported outlays of firms to diverge from planning costs or the costs confronting newly constructed plants. Long-run costs are forward looking; data available to researchers are, for the most part, reflections of past input decisions. A firm might hire an accountant, an industrial engineer, or a managerial economist to relate various rates of output to payments for inputs. Its purpose would be to determine whether changes in production techniques (say, replacing obsolete machinery before it has been fully depreciated for tax purposes) would be likely to reduce production costs. During the period data were collected, exogenous changes in input prices could have caused actual costs to deviate from anticipated (or planned) costs. Over the past decade, energy prices soared and computer costs plunged; firms in a position to change production techniques fared much better than firms which were "locked into" investments in energy-guzzling machinery.

The complexity of strategic planning can lead into one of two simplistic attitudes, each equally deadly. One is to assume that firms always pick the technology which minimizes short-run average cost, ignoring the fact that the time lag between choosing a production facility and when that facility comes "on line" may leave the firm with a white elephant—a plant which cannot produce as economically as plants that reflect prevailing relative factor prices. The other mistake is to dismiss long-run costs as irrelevant. Despite the uncertainty of future costs, firms which fail to plan ahead will surely expire; those which use the best available information to estimate future costs will stand the best chance of survival.

The effect of a change in relative input prices is developed in Figure 6-9. An increase in the wage rate rotates isocost line C_0 toward the origin along the labor axis. Output q_0 can no longer be produced with an expenditure of C_0. The least-cost input combination for q_0 changes from point P, now on new isocost line C_2, to point Q on new isocost line C_1. As in the case of a change in the price of a consumer good, the effect of a change in the price of an input can be divided into two parts. The input *substitution effect* reflects the influence of the change in relative input prices. The increase in w_L relative to w_k leads the employer to use more capital and less labor. The output-expansion path in Figure 6-9 shifts from OPP' to OQQ'. There is also a *cost effect*. Because of the increase in the money wage, the minimum cost of producing q_0 increases

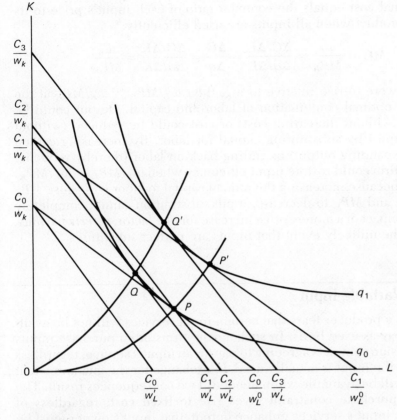

Figure 6-9
Substitution and Cost Effects of Input Price Increase. The increase in the price of labor from w_L^0 to w_L' rotates isocost line C_0 along the labor axis; q_0 can no longer be produced at cost C_0. By substituting capital for labor, the firm minimizes the cost effect of that wage increase.

from C_0 to C_1. Point P is now on isocost line $C_2 > C_1$. The ability to substitute inputs reduces the impact of a factor price increase on the cost of production.

The impact of a change in one input's price on the cost of production can be clarified by investigating how input substitution mitigates the rise in marginal cost in the wake of the increase in one input, other factor prices remaining constant. We have already seen that efficient production planning requires using labor and capital in combinations so that $w_L/MP_L = w_K/MP_K$. The assumption that input prices do not vary as output changes means that each factor's price represents the change in cost resulting from using one more hour's worth of that input. By definition, each input's marginal product is the change in output resulting from using one more hour of that input's services. Simple algebra implies that marginal cost equals the common ratio of each input's price to its marginal product when all inputs are used efficiently:[8]

$$MC = \frac{w_L}{MP_L} = \frac{\Delta C/\Delta L}{\Delta q/\Delta L} = \frac{\Delta C}{\Delta q} = \frac{\Delta C/\Delta K}{\Delta q/\Delta K} = \frac{w_K}{MP_K}$$

If w_L were to rise relative to w_K, then $w_L/MP_L > w_K/MP_K$ at the previously optimal combination of labor and capital. Output could be expanded (without increasing cost) or cost could be reduced (without cutting output) by substituting capital for labor. By increasing capital (thereby expanding output) or cutting back on labor (thereby reducing costs), the firm could restore input efficiency when $w_L'/MP_L = w_K^0/MP_K$. However, because increasing the ratio of capital to labor will cause MP_L to increase and MP_K to decrease, input substitution cannot completely offset the impact of a money price increase for one factor, *ceteris paribus*, except in the unlikely event that inputs are perfect substitutes.

Operating Costs with One Variable Input

Sometimes a producer fears that certain input services will not be available on a pay-as-used basis. In such a case, firms often purchase inputs outright or sign contracts agreeing to pay for an input's service, regardless of whether the input is actually used, in exchange for the guarantee that the input will be available when needed. Two consequences result. The **minimum purchase constraint** gives rise to **fixed cost**; regardless of whether an input's services enhance output, that input's owner must be paid (or the firm will incur opportunity cost in the case of inputs it owns and cannot sell or lease quickly). **Variable cost**, by contrast, refers to cost which changes as output changes. The *limited availability constraint* means that the "fixed" input's services cannot exceed the amount pur-

---

[8] If the firm has an n input production function, long-run marginal cost can be determined as the ratio of the total derivative of input costs, $C = w_1v_1 + w_2v_2 + \cdots + \cdots + w_nv_n$, to the total derivative of the production function, $q = f(v_1, v_2, \ldots, v_n)$:

$$\frac{dC}{dq} = \frac{\frac{\partial C}{\partial v_1} dv_1 + \frac{\partial C}{\partial v_2} dv_2 + \cdots + \frac{\partial C}{\partial v_n} dv_n}{\frac{\partial q}{\partial v_1} dv_1 + \frac{\partial q}{\partial v_2} dv_2 + \cdots + \frac{\partial q}{\partial v_n} dv_n} = \frac{w_1 dv_1 + w_2 dv_2 + \cdots + w_n dv_n}{MP_1 dv_1 + MP_2 dv_2 + \cdots + MP_n dv_n}$$

Picking any input, v_i, we factor its price from the numerator and its marginal product from the denominator:

$$\frac{dC}{dq} = \frac{w_i}{MP_i} \left[\frac{(w_1/w_i)dv_1 + (w_2/w_i)dv_2 + \cdots + (w_n/w_i)dv_n}{(MP_1/MP_i)dv_1 + (MP_2MP_i)dv_2 + \cdots + (MP_n/MP_i)dv_n} \right]$$

Since $w_j/w_i = MP_j/MP_i$ for every pair of inputs i and j, the numerator and denominator cancel, implying $dC/dq = w_i/MP_i$ for all v_i.

chased by contract or the capacity of inputs owned by the firm. As explained in chapter five, it is frequently possible to vary the rate of use of a "fixed" input below its capacity; as we will see presently, being able to use less than the amount of an input available may reduce variable costs for very low rates of output.

Figure 6-10 illustrates the effects of minimum purchase requirement and the **maximum availability constraint** in the **short run**, which is the

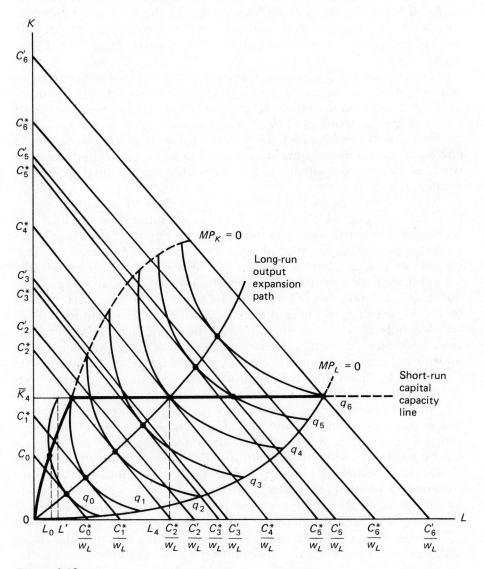

Figure 6-10
Cost Minimization in the Long Run and the Short Run

period when production actually occurs. Imagine that Sparky Electronics has planned to produce q_4 widgets per day. The tangency of isoquant q_4 to isocost line C_4^* in Figure 10-6 implies that the target rate of output can be produced at minimum cost by hiring K_4 machine-hours and L_4 workers per day. To implement the plan, Sparky Electronics builds a plant with the capacity to supply K_4 hours of machine services daily. Once the bank loan has been signed, using the machinery and buildings as collateral, Sparky Electronics must pay a daily machinery cost of $w_K K_4$; if Sparky defaults on its loan payments, the bank will confiscate its collateral. The minimum purchase requirement turns the variable costs of capital in the long run into daily fixed costs (*FC*). Thus, $FC = w_K K_4$.

To keep the analysis simple, we will assume that factor prices remain constant at w_L and w_K. Hence, if Sparky Electronics actually produces q_4 widgets per day, then the optimal quantity of L_4 labor services would be hired and variable costs (*VC*) would equal $VC = w_L L_4$. Each day the firm's short-run total cost (*SRTC*), also called **operating costs**, would also equal the minimum long-run total cost (*LRTC*), also called **planning costs**, as long as output did not deviate from the planned rate of q_4 widgets per day.

If the actual rate of output deviates from the optimal rate of output for the fixed input, which is quite plausible, then the short-run total cost will exceed long-run total cost for the rate of output actually produced. For instance, the least-cost combination of inputs for producing q_5 widgets per day is identified by the tangency of isoquant q_5 and isocost line C_5^* in Figure 6-10. Because only K_4 machine-hours are available per day, the short-run total costs of producing q_5 widgets per day is determined by the intersection of the capital capacity line and isoquant q_5. Labor, which is only an imperfect substitute for the shortfall of capital services, cannot produce the extra widgets as efficiently as the ideal combination of labor and capital; operating costs, C_5', exceed minimum planning costs C_5^*. If Sparky Electronics tried to produce q_6 widgets per day, the short-run total cost, C_6', would deviate even more from long-run total cost, C_6^*, for that rate of output. In fact, since isoquant q_6 intersects the ridge line at the same point that the capital capacity line intersects the horizontal line at K_4, q_6 represents the maximum number of widgets that can be produced with any amount of labor, given the maximum availability of K_4 hours of capital per day. Under the limited availability constraint, short-run (operating) costs exceed long-run (planning) costs for output rates above the planned rate due to diminishing marginal productivity of the variable input (in this case, labor).

Short-run costs also exceed long-run costs when less than the target rate of output, except in this case higher short-run costs are traced to the minumum purchase constraint. Note that the long-run output expansion path, identifying least-cost input combinations when both inputs are variable, intersects isoquants q_0 through q_3 below the capital capacity line, which represents the minimum amount of capital services that must be purchased (although not necessarily the minimum amount that must be used). If capital costs could be reduced by reducing the use of machinery, q_3 widgets per day could be produced at a cost of C_3^*. However, since the firm must pay for K_4 hours of machinery regardless of how much is used, short-run costs are lower by operating where isoquant q_3 intersects the capital capacity line at isocost line C_3'. Similar logic holds for producing q_1 or q_2 widgets per day: as long as the marginal product of capital is positive, short-run costs are lower when all available fixed input services are used. But if the firm wished to produce q_0 widgets per day, short-run costs would be lower if some of the fixed input were left idle. Isoquant q_0 intersects the capital ridge line at point (L_0, K_0): if Sparky Electronics used only K_0 of the available K_1 machine-hours, q_0 widgets per day could be produced with only L_0 hours of labor. If all capital were used, either because of a management error or because K_4 was an integrated production process with all machine-hours operating, L' workers would be required; extra labor costs would be incurred merely to offset the destructive influence of too much machinery for that rate of output.

In Figure 6-11, the long-run (planning) cost curve is drawn by plotting the cost from the isocost lines against the outputs derived from the tangent isoquants along the output expansion path in Figure 6-10. Assuming that fixed cost, FC^*, results from the minimum purchase con-

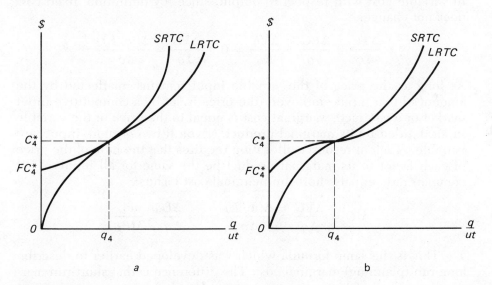

Figure 6-11
Relationship between Short-Run (Operating) Total Cost and Long-Run (Planning) Total Cost. *a*, Use of the limited input variable; *b*, use of the limited input fixed.

straint depicted in Figure 6-10, it follows that short-run operating costs will correspond to long-run planning costs only when L_4 workers are hired to produce q_4 widgets per day. For rates of output exceeding q_4 widgets per day, short-run total cost will exceed long-run total cost because of diminishing marginal productivity of labor. Since capital services for this range of output are less than the cost-minimizing amount, the shape of the short-run total cost curve is unaffected by whether it is possible to use the fixed input below capacity.

Figure 6-11*a* is drawn under the assumption that less than K_4 machine-hours can be used to produce less than q_1 widgets per day (whose isoquant intersects the capital capacity line in Figure 6-10). Since labor services are minimized by expanding output along the capital isoquant in Figure 6-10 until the capital capacity line is reached, the short-run total cost curve gets progressivly steeper as output gets closer to q_4. By contrast, Figure 6-11*b* shows the consequences of using all available fixed input services to produce small rates of output: total operating costs increase much more rapidly as output expands, due to the necessity of hiring extra labor to counteract the negative marginal product of capital. Eventually, increasing marginal productivity of the variable input causes short-run total costs to increase at a decreasing rate, so that when output reaches q_4, short-run costs are the same in Figure 6-11*b* as in 6-11*a*.

Short-run total cost is the sum of fixed cost and variable cost: $TC = FC + VC = w_k K_4 + w_L L$ (in our two-input example). Marginal cost, the change in total cost with respect to output, is also equal to the change in variable cost with respect to output, since, by definition, fixed cost does not change:

$$\frac{\Delta TC}{\Delta q} = \frac{\Delta FC}{\Delta q} + \frac{\Delta VC}{\Delta q} = 0 + \frac{\Delta VC}{\Delta q} = \frac{\Delta(w_L L)}{\Delta q}$$

As long as the price of the variable input remains unaffected by the amount of that input employed (the price is set by a competitive input market or a contract), marginal cost is equal to the price of the variable input divided by its marginal product. (Even if two or more inputs are variable, efficient resource allocation requires that the ratio of the price of each factor to its marginal product be the same for all inputs. That common ratio equals short-run marginal cost.) Thus:

$$MC = \frac{\Delta VC}{\Delta q} = \frac{\Delta(w_L L)}{\Delta q} = w_L \frac{\Delta L}{\Delta q} = \frac{w_L}{MP_L}$$

This is the same formula which was developed earlier to describe long-run (planning) marginal cost. The difference is that short-run marginal cost is a *ceteris paribus* concept, whereas long-run marginal cost is a *mutatis mutandis* concept. In the short run, bottlenecks in one or more fixed inputs cause the marginal product of the one or more variable inputs to decline as output expands. In the planning process, the firm's management can compare the costs of different levels of output by varying (planned) services of all inputs. The marginal product of each input can be kept from declining by increasing all inputs as (planned) output increases. But, once a plant has been constructed and some inputs are fixed, costs will change only in response to changes in variable inputs. For outputs less than the planned rate (the output identified by the isoquant-isocost tangency), the firm will economize on the variable input by using as much of the fixed factor as is consistent with a nonnegative marginal product. *For less than the planned level of output, short-run marginal cost is less than long-run marginal cost.*[9] In the long run, cost would fall to zero if planned output were zero; management would let contracts expire and not renew them. In the short run, cost can fall only to fixed cost and no lower.

Short-run average total cost has two components, average fixed cost and average variable cost: $ATC = TC/q = FC/q + VC/q = AFC + AVC$. **Average fixed cost** is fixed cost divided by the rate of output: as more is produced, fixed cost divided by output approaches (but never reaches) zero. This is what production managers and accountants mean by *spreading overhead.*[10] **Average variable cost** is the ratio of the price of the variable input to its average product:

$$AVC = \frac{VC}{q} = \frac{w_L L}{q} = \frac{w_L}{AP_L}$$

Diagrams of short-run costs depend upon whether inputs subject to maximum availability constraints can be used below capacity. If so, short-run marginal cost will not decline over all levels of output, pulling average variable cost up as diminishing marginal productivity sets in. This pattern, illustrated in Figure 6-12a, corresponds to the short-run total cost curve in Figure 6-11a. If all of a fixed input must be used, variable input requirements will be greater when the marginal product of the fixed input is negative than would have been the case had that input been used below capacity. As the marginal product of the fixed input approaches zero, fewer variable inputs will be needed to compensate

---

[9] That short-run marginal cost can be less than long-run marginal cost may seem like a contradiction; it is not. Our point of reference for calculating the change in cost is not the origin but the tangency point of the long-run and short-run cost curves. Ideally, costs should rise as little as possible for output increases and fall as much as possible for output decreases. That short-run marginal cost is less than long-run marginal cost below the planned rate of output means costs remain higher after any particular output cut in the short run than in the long run.

[10] $\dfrac{d(AFC)}{dq} = \dfrac{d\left(\dfrac{FC}{q}\right)}{dq} = -\dfrac{FC}{q^2}$

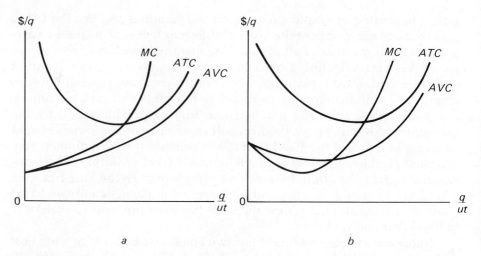

Figure 6-12
Short-Run Marginal and Average Costs. *a*, Variable use of limited input; *b*, fixed use of limited input.

for the overuse of the fixed input; marginal cost will fall as output increases as excess variable inputs are freed for productive work. After the marginal product of the variable input has reached its maximum, (i.e., when marginal product of the fixed input is zero) diminishing marginal productivity of the variable input will cause marginal cost to rise with output. Average variable cost will continue to fall until $AVC = MC$, then marginal cost will pull average variable cost up.[11] The short-run cost curves reflecting invariant use of a fixed input are presented in Figure 6-12*b*. Note that marginal cost increases when $q = q_0$ in both Figure 6-12*a* and *b*; using a fixed input to capacity when its marginal product is negative merely causes the first few units to cost more than they would have if less of the fixed input had been used.

   Average total cost (i.e., total cost divided by output) is obtained by adding average fixed cost to average variable cost for each rate of output. Average fixed cost approaches infinity as output approaches zero ($FC/0$ is undefined) and decreases as output increases. Average total cost is still falling when average variable cost begins to rise in Figure 6-12*b* because its average fixed cost component continues to fall. Average total cost reaches its minimum when $ATC = MC$ and increases when $MC > ATC$. Thus, short-run average total cost is U-shaped in Figure 6-12*a*

---

[11] The change in average variable cost with respect to output is:

$$\frac{d\left(\dfrac{VC}{q}\right)}{dq} = \frac{q\left(\dfrac{dVC}{dq}\right) - VC\left(\dfrac{dq}{dq}\right)}{q^2} = \frac{1}{q}\left(\frac{dVC}{dq} - \frac{VC}{q}\right) \overset{>}{\underset{<}{=}} 0 \text{ as } MC \overset{>}{\underset{<}{=}} AVC$$

and *b*. The U-shaped curve of average total cost indicates why a naive strategy of trying to produce more output to spread overhead often leads to disaster. Regardless of the rate of output, fixed cost is always the same; dividing fixed cost by more units of output does not change fixed cost— but variable cost always increases as output increases. Although average fixed cost becomes inexorably smaller as output increases, diminishing marginal productivity eventually causes average total cost to rise faster and faster.

APPLICATION

Revenge of the Numerical Example

Because confusion can beset students and economists alike when distinguishing planning costs and operating costs, we pause to reconsider the numerical example encountered in Tables 6-1 and 6-2. There, we assumed that output was generated according to a production function with the formula $q = L^{2/3}K^{1/3}$. Further assuming a wage rate of $w_L = 10 and a capital rental rate of $w_k = 5, we discovered that the economically efficient input combination of $L = 16$ and $K = 16$ for producing 16 units of output could be determined either by maximizing output subject to a cost constraint or by minimizing cost subject to an output constraint.

In Table 6-3 the planning (long-run) costs for each rate of output from $q = 1$ to $q = 25$ are compared with the operating (short-run) costs after contracts have generated fixed costs for three planned levels of output. The first five columns of Table 6-3 give information derived from the output-expansion path when $w_L = 10, $w_k = 5, and planned output varies from 1 to 25 units per time period. Given that the slope of the parallel isocost lines is $\Delta K/\Delta L = -w_L/w_k = -2$ and that the marginal rate of technical substitution is $\Delta K/\Delta L = -2(K/L)$, the optimal input combination for each level of output is given by $q = K = L$.[12] This conveniently simple result makes it easy to compare actual operating costs with planning costs when production deviates from the level anticipated when fixed inputs (in this case, capital services) were hired.

Columns 6 through 9 in Table 6-3 relate marginal and average operating costs to each rate of output when capital is fixed at 10 units, presumably because management built a plant to produce 10 units of output per time period. With ten machines available, only about one-third of a unit of labor is needed to produce one unit of output. However,

---

[12] Since the marginal rate of technical substitution is the ratio of the marginal product of labor to the marginal product of capital: $\partial q/\partial L = (2/3)L^{-1/3}K^{1/3}$ and $\partial q/\partial K = (1/3)L^{2/3}K^{-2/3}$, so that $MRTS = dK/dL = -MP_L/MP_k = -([2/3L^{-1/3}K^{1/3}][1/3L^{2/3}K^{-1/3}]) = 2(K^{1/3+2/3}/L^{2/3+1/2}) = -2(K/L)$. The economically efficient input combination is identified as $MRTS = -w_L/w_k = -2$, implying $-2(K/L) = -2$ or $K = L$. Finally, substituting L for K gives $q = L^{2/3}L^{1/3} = L = K$.

TABLE 6-3
Planning Costs and Operating Costs: A Numerical Example

	Planning Costs				$q^* = 10, \bar{K}^* = 10$				$q^* = 15, \bar{K}^* = 15$				$q^* = 20, \bar{K}^* = 20$			
q	L	K	LRMC	LRAC	L	MC	AVC	ATC	L	MC	AVC	ATC	L	MC	AVC	ATC
1	1	1	$15	$15	0.32	$ 3.16	3.16	53.16	0.26	2.58	2.58	77.58	0.22	2.24	2.24	102.24
2	2	2	15	15	0.89	5.78	4.47	29.47	0.73	4.72	3.65	41.15	0.63	4.09	3.16	53.16
3	3	3	15	15	1.64	7.49	5.48	22.14	1.34	6.11	4.47	29.47	1.16	5.29	3.87	37.21
4	4	4	15	15	2.53	8.87	6.32	18.82	2.07	7.24	5.16	23.91	1.79	6.27	4.47	29.47
5	5	5	15	15	3.54	10.05	7.07	17.07	2.89	8.21	5.77	20.77	2.50	7.11	5.00	25.00
6	6	6	15	15	4.65	11.12	7.74	16.08	3.79	9.08	6.32	18.82	3.29	7.87	5.48	22.14
7	7	7	15	15	5.86	12.09	8.37	15.51	4.78	9.87	6.83	17.55	4.14	8.55	5.92	20.20
8	8	8	15	15	7.15	12.99	8.94	15.19	5.84	10.61	7.30	16.68	5.06	9.18	6.32	18.82
9	9	9	15	15	8.53	13.83	9.49	15.04	6.97	11.29	7.75	16.08	6.04	9.78	6.71	17.82
10	10	10	15	15	10.00	14.62	10.00	15.00	8.16	11.94	8.16	15.66	7.07	10.34	7.07	17.07
11	11	11	15	15	11.54	15.36	10.49	15.03	9.42	12.55	8.56	15.38	8.16	10.87	7.42	16.51
12	12	12	15	15	13.15	16.08	10.95	15.12	10.73	13.13	8.94	15.19	9.30	11.37	7.75	16.08
13	13	13	15	15	14.82	16.77	11.40	15.24	12.10	13.69	9.31	15.08	10.48	11.86	8.06	15.75
14	14	14	15	15	16.56	17.43	11.83	15.40	13.53	14.23	9.66	15.02	11.71	12.32	8.37	15.51
15	15	15	15	15	18.37	18.06	12.25	15.58	15.00	14.75	10.00	15.00	12.99	12.77	8.66	15.33
16	16	16	15	15	20.24	18.67	12.65	15.77	16.52	15.25	10.33	15.02	14.31	13.20	8.94	15.19
17	17	17	15	15	22.17	19.27	13.04	15.98	18.10	15.73	10.65	15.06	15.67	13.62	9.22	15.10
18	18	18	15	15	24.15	19.84	13.42	16.19	19.72	16.20	10.95	15.12	17.08	14.03	9.49	15.04
19	19	19	15	15	26.19	20.40	13.78	16.42	21.38	16.66	11.25	15.20	18.52	14.43	9.75	15.01
20	20	20	15	15	28.28	20.95	14.14	16.64	23.09	17.10	11.55	15.30	20.00	14.81	10.00	15.00
21	21	21	15	15	30.43	21.48	14.49	16.87	24.85	17.54	11.83	15.40	21.52	15.19	10.25	15.01
22	22	22	15	15	32.63	21.99	14.83	17.11	26.64	17.96	12.11	15.52	23.07	15.55	10.49	15.03
23	23	23	15	15	34.88	22.50	15.17	17.34	28.48	18.37	12.38	15.64	24.66	15.91	10.72	15.07
24	24	24	15	15	37.18	22.99	15.49	17.58	30.36	18.77	12.65	15.77	26.29	16.26	10.95	15.12
25	25	25	15	15	39.53	23.48	15.81	17.81	32.27	19.17	12.91	15.91	27.95	16.60	11.18	15.18

10 units of capital cost five times the wage rate for labor; saving two-thirds of a variable unit causes short-term marginal cost and average variable cost to fall substantially below their long-run counterparts. However, short-run average total cost exceeds long-run average cost by a factor of 3.5. A firm which plans to produce one unit of output does not intentionally build a plant with an optimal output of 10 units and then use it at only 10 percent of capacity. It is not the low marginal cost which dominates short-run average cost at low levels of output; it is the high level of fixed cost.

As output approaches 10 units, the short-run marginal cost and the short-run average total cost of the q_{10} plant approach long-run marginal cost and long-run average cost, respectively. At $q = 10$, short-run marginal cost equals long-run marginal cost and short-run average total cost equals long-run average cost. Above 10 units, both short-run marginal and average total costs exceed their long-run counterparts due to diminishing marginal productivity of labor, the variable input.

If planned output had been 15 instead of 10 units, short-run marginal cost and average variable cost would have been even less at low levels of output. Lower costs of variable inputs would have been more than eclipsed by higher fixed costs, however. (See columns 10–13 in Table 6-3.) Compared with $53.16 average total cost for the first unit when planned output is 10, average total cost for one unit of output equals $77.58 when a plant is designed to produce 15 units of output. The two-plant capacities result in roughly the same average total cost when 13 units of output are produced in each plant; above 13 units per period, the plant with greater capacity has lower costs.

Building a plant with an optimal output of 20 units results in higher fixed cost and lower marginal and average variable costs at all rates of output, compared to the two plants with smaller capacity (columns 14–17 in Table 6-3). The average total cost for 10 units per period is smaller, the smaller the plant capacity. At 15 units of output per period, the plant designed for 20 units achieves lower average cost than does the plant designed for 10 units. When output exceeds 18 units per period, the plant with a capacity of 20 units of output has the lowest average cost of all three.

Even a simple simulation like that in Table 6-3 demonstrates the importance of accurate forecasts of output prior to the construction of production facilities. If the estimated rate of output is too low, diminishing marginal productivity of the variable input will cause increasing marginal cost to eclipse the advantages from low fixed cost. If too large a facility is built because the output forecast overestimated demand for the product (see the appendix to chapter nine), advantages from low variable costs will be negated by fixed cost of such a great magnitude that the plant will have much higher average costs than plants designed to produce a smaller rate of output.

Policy Illustration
Regulation and the Price of Electricity

The economic approach to production treats costs and prices as separate but related phenomena, whose mutual influences work themselves out through consumer demand, seller attempts to maximize profit, and the impersonal forces of the market. As we shall see in chapter nine, market competition generates an equilibrium relation between market price and the most efficient method of production.

When market forces are very weak, as in the case of monopoly sellers of a basic service which does not have close substitutes, there is no guarantee that prices reflect minimum average production costs. If the demand for the service is price inelastic, as tends to be the case with the demand for electricity, telephone service, and mass transportation, profit maximization would cause prices to rise, at least until demand became price elastic, so that revenue would decline if rates increased further. The specter of skyrocketing utility rates has led most states to regulate the maximum prices utility companies can charge.

State utility commissions cannot set rates capriciously, however. A monopoly seller must still purchase input services. Often, as in the case of financing plant and equipment, utilities must pay factor prices set in competitive input markets. The results of high interest rates of the early 1980s led one consortium of electric companies to publish the following statement in a nationally prominent newsmagazine:

> Future costs and quality of service depend upon the ability of electric utilities to finance new facilities and equipment now. To attract the capital required, utilities must be able earn sufficient amounts to provide a fair return to investors after actual operating costs have been defrayed.

> Unfortunately, the returns permitted by most state regulatory commissions today are below those offered by competitive, relatively safer investments. Actual returns are even lower. As a result, many utilities have had to cut back efforts to increase efficiency, convert to lower cost fuel, and develop new generating technology. When they do undertake such programs, they often must pay premium rates for funds. In either case, the consumer ultimately will pay.*

This all sounds very reasonable, but there is a catch. When utility rates are set to allow for a "fair return" on investment, the cost of production can become a direct cause of price. As long as demand remains price inelastic, a rate increase will increase revenue, even if the higher costs used to justify that rate increase do not provide enhanced services (e.g., the Three Mile Island nuclear plant).

In an attempt to determine the influence of "cost pass-through" on the reward structure for chief executive officers of investor-owned utilities, the author and David Ciscel related the pay of chief executives to the firm's revenue and to ex-

---

* Eugene M. Lerner, "Electricity Users Will Pay for Adverse Regulation," advertisement in *Newsweek*, March 22, 1982, p. 77.

ecutive cost-consciousness.† While transportation firms and nonregulated industrial corporations showed a positive relationship between cost control and executive pay, the salary of the utility executive appeared to decrease as costs fell, holding revenue constant. In 1973 a utility executive who reduced his company's costs by $1 million could expect his salary (plus bonus) to *fall* by $619.

As we shall see in chapter ten, the economic consequences of regulating

monopoly prices by a fair return formula create a policy dilemma. Allowing utilities to earn higher returns on investments gives them an incentive to overinvest in equipment and other sources of overhead cost, even if the investments are not economically efficient. However, allowing these producers to maximize profits, which would eliminate the incentive for wasteful spending, would lead to monopoly utility rates. As the advertisement states, eventually consumers pay for adverse regulation. Deregulation, which might lead to more efficient internal management, would also generate monopoly prices. Do we wish to pay higher rates gradually, or all at once?

---

† Thomas M. Carroll and David H. Ciscel, "The Impact of Administrative Regulation on Executive Compensation in Large Corporations," *Review of Economics and Statistics*, forthcoming.

Compared to the flexibility of production planning, short-run or operating costs represent two liabilities: minimum purchase requirements and limited availability constraints. At small rates of output, average fixed costs are high because more than the optimal quantity of some inputs must be paid for, regardless of whether those services are used to capacity. As long as the cost of *using* fixed inputs is zero, the firm is encouraged to depart from the optimal input combinations for low rates of output by using all of the fixed input it paid for. For higher rates of output than the plant was constructed to produce, bottlenecks in the fixed inputs generate diminishing marginal productivity in the variable inputs, causing marginal cost to rise more rapidly in the short run than would be the case were more of the fixed input available at a constant price.

The Envelope Curve: The Short Run Meets the Long Run

We conclude our discussion of cost by developing the relationship between the lowest possible average cost for each rate of output, long-run average cost (*LRAC*) and each possible short-run average total cost curve (*SRAC*) which would result from selecting a specific output capacity. The long-run total cost (*LRTC*) curve is generated from the output expansion path: the set of isoquant-isocost tangencies for prevailing technology and input prices. Since the long-run total cost curve represents the minimum cost of producing each rate of output, short-run total cost

(*SRTC*) will equal long-run total cost only when the firm produces that rate of output corresponding to the isoquant-isocost tangency identifying fixed input services.

In Figure 6-13, the short-run total cost curve is tangent to long-run total cost at q^*, the optimal rate of output for the fixed inputs. For rates of output less than q^*, short-run total cost is greater than long-run total cost because of the minimum purchase requirement for fixed inputs. For rates of output greater than q^*, short-run total cost is greater than long-run total cost because of diminishing marginal productivity of the variable input(s). There are two relations between short-run and long-run costs when $q = q^*$: (1) short-run average total cost equals long-run average cost, since $LRTC/q^* = SRTC/q^*$, and (2) short-run marginal cost (*SRMC*) equals long-run marginal cost (*LRMC*) at q^*, since *SRTC* has the same slope as *LRTC* at q^*.

The long-run cost curve displayed in Figure 6-13 is atypical: constant long-run marginal cost and long-run average cost result from the crucial assumptions of constant returns to scale and invariant prices for all input services. This special relation between *LRMC* and *LRAC* creates a special equality between short-run average total cost at the point of tangency between the short-run and long-run average cost curves at point q^*:[13]

1. *LRMC* = *SRMC*, since the two total cost curves are tangent at q^*
2. *LRAC* = *SRAC*, since *LRTC* = *SRTC* at q^*
3. *LRAC* = *LRMC*, for this special combination of constant returns to scale and constant factor prices
4. ∴ *SRMC* = *LRMC* at q^*

If either assumption underlying Figure 6-13 is violated—either the

---

[13] Recall from chapter five that $\epsilon = \sum_{i=1}^{m} \epsilon_i$, where ϵ is the returns to scale of the production function and ϵ_i is the output elasticity of input v_i: $\epsilon_i = \dfrac{\partial q/q}{\partial v_i/v_i} = MP_i/AP_i$. When prices of input services are invariant with respect to output, each term to the right of the equality sign can be multiplied by w_i/w_i, since multiplication by 1 does not change an equation:

$$\epsilon = \frac{MP_1}{w_1}\left(\frac{w_1 v_1}{q}\right) + \frac{MP_2}{w_2}\left(\frac{w_2 v_2}{q}\right) + \cdots + \frac{MP_m}{w_m}\left(\frac{w_m v_m}{q}\right)$$

Since $w_i/MP_i = LRMC$, for every input, we can factor out $MP_i/w_i = \dfrac{1}{LRMC}$:

$$\epsilon = \frac{MP_i}{w_i}\left(\frac{w_1 v_1 + w_2 v_2 + \cdots + w_m v_m}{q}\right) = \frac{LRAC}{LRMC}$$

For constant returns to scale ($\epsilon = 1$), $LRAC = LRMC$, and both curves are horizontal; increasing returns to scale ($\epsilon > 1$) implies that long-run average cost exceeds long-run marginal cost: both are decreasing as output increases; and decreasing returns to scale ($\epsilon < 1$) means long-run marginal cost exceeds long-run average cost; both are increasing as output increases.

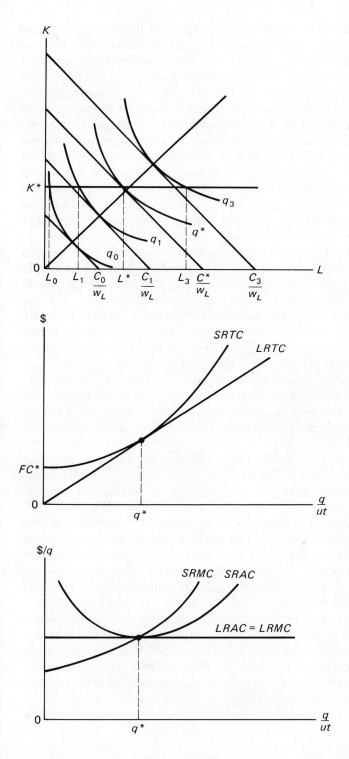

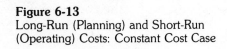

Figure 6-13
Long-Run (Planning) and Short-Run
(Operating) Costs: Constant Cost Case

prices of input services change with the amount of input services purchased, or constant returns to scale do not prevail for all rates of output—the relationship between long-run average cost and short-run average cost becomes more complex. The U-shaped long-run average cost curve is an **envelope curve**, touching one point on each short-run average cost curve, although not necessarily at the minimum point of the latter.

If long-run average cost falls as the planned rate of output increases, either because of increasing returns to scale or decreasing input prices, short-run marginal cost will be less than short-run average total cost at the point of tangency between the short-run and long-run total cost curves. That is because falling long-run average cost means: $LRMC < LRAC$. Since $SRMC = LRMC$ and $SRAC = LRAC$ at the point in question, it follows that $SRMC < SRAC$. In Figure 6-14, long-run average cost is falling at $q = q_0$, so $SRMC$ must intersect $LRMC$ below where $SRAC$ touches $LRAC$. As output expands beyond q_0, both long-run average cost and short-run average total cost would continue to fall, although $LRAC$ would fall faster than $SRAC_0$; the former turns up while the latter is still falling.

As output increases, internal economies frequently give way to internal diseconomies, due to increasing input prices, decreasing returns to scale, or deteriorating input quality (since the firm would attempt to hire the "best" inputs first). At q' in Figure 6-14, long-run marginal cost exceeds long-run average cost due to internal diseconomies. Once again, the relation between $LRMC$ and $LRAC$ determines the relation between $SRMC$ and $SRAC$ at the point of tangency between $LRTC$ and $SRTC'$: $LRMC > LRAC$, combined with the facts that $LRMC = SRMC$ and $LRAC = SRAC$, implies $SRMC' > SRAC'$ at q'.

Note that $q*$ is associated with the minimum point on the U-shaped long-run average cost curve in Figure 6-14. At $q*$, but only at $q*$, $LRMC = LRAC$. So after long-run average cost has stopped declining (because economies of scale have been realized or input prices have stopped declining with input use) but before it has started to increase (due to increasing input prices or decreasing returns to scale), the long-run average cost curve reaches its minimum where long-run marginal cost intersects it. Only at one point in the U-shaped long-run average cost curve—at its minimum point—does the point of tangency with the short-run average total cost curve occur at the minimum point of the latter.

As we will see in chapter nine, the existence of a unique minimum $LRAC$ plant size plays an important role in defining the equilibrium plant size for a perfectly competitive firm. The possibility that the market for a commodity is exhausted before one firm realizes all economies of scale forms the theoretical basis for *natural monopoly* in chapter ten and the controversy over the impact of product differentiation on production efficiency in chapter eleven. The possibility of a protracted range of

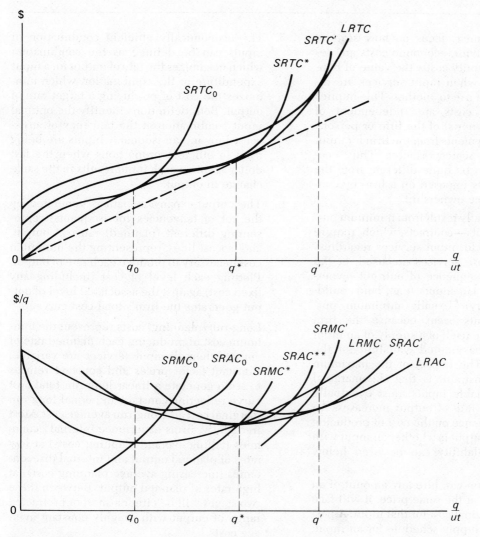

Figure 6-14
Long-Run (Planning) and Short-Run (Operating) Costs: Variable Returns to Scale or
Variable Input Prices

constant long-run average cost, which requires a minimum production
size which results in a few firms in an industry, is one of the underlying
(and controversial) causes of oligopoly, to be discussed in chapter twelve.
So while the relationship between long-run average cost and short-run
average cost may seem abstract at this point in your studies, it will play
a major role in part four of this book.

HIGHLIGHTS

1. Because economists focus on how scarcity influences behavior, economic costs are defined as opportunity costs: the value of benefits sacrificed when input services are diverted from one use to another. This implies that economic costs are independent of whether the owner(s) of the firm or persons who receive payments from the firm for input services own a scarce resource. Thus, economic costs can be quite different from the accounting costs imposed on a firm by contracts or resource ownership.

2. Fixed costs usually result from minimum purchase constraints—contracts which require the firm to pay for input services regardless of whether those services are used, or the equivalent consequence of outright ownership of nonhuman inputs (e.g., land, buildings, machinery). Usually minimum purchase constraints occur because the firm wishes to assure itself of a supply of an input service which has limited availability on the open market. The impact of the maximum availability constraint is that the marginal product of variable inputs must eventually decline as the rate of output increases. An important influence on the cost of producing small rates of output is whether an input with maximum availability can be used below capacity.

3. Whenever a firm can hire any amount of an input's service at the same price, it will face a constant marginal cost for that input. A positively sloped supply schedule for an input, which often reflects monopsony power in an input market, means that the marginal input cost increases as use of that input increases. If the supply curve for an input's services is negatively sloped (e.g., due to quantity discounts) the marginal input cost will fall as more of the input is hired.

4. Constant factor prices result in parallel, linear isocost lines. Isocost curves will be bowed-out when the prices of input services rise as more are hired and bowed-in if the prices of input services fall as more are hired.

5. The economically efficient combination of inputs can be defined as the combination which maximizes the rate of output for a input expenditure or the combination which minimizes the cost of producing a target rate of output. Both definitions identify the optimal input combination at the tangency of an isocost line and an isoquant. Inputs are being used in efficient proportions when the last dollar spent on each input results in the same change in output.

6. The output-expansion path is generated by the set of tangencies for isoquants, representing different (planned) rates of output, and isocost lines, representing the minimum cost necessary to produce each rate of output. Plotting each level of cost (including any fixed cost) against the associated level of output generates the firm's total cost curve.

7. Long-run (planning) costs represent the minimum cost of producing each planned rate of output when all input services are variable. Constant factor prices and constant returns to scale generate a linear long-run total cost curve reflecting constant and equal long-run marginal cost and long-run average cost. Most frequently, firms experience internal economies (falling average planning costs) at low rates of planned output and internal diseconomies (increasing average planning costs) at high rates of planned output. Between these two stages will be either a short or protracted range of output with roughly constant average costs.

8. A change in one input's price, other factor prices being constant, will have a substitution effect: the firm will use more of the input whose relative price has decreased and less of the factor whose relative price has increased. Since different inputs are rarely perfect substitutes, a change in one factor's price will also change the cost of production in the same direction.

9. When only one input's costs are variable, the short-run total cost curve will be dominated

by the influence of diminishing marginal productivity of the variable input. If the firm can avoid stage I of the short-run production function, costs will be smaller for low levels of output than if use of the fixed factor cannot be varied below capacity.

10. Short-run average total cost is made up of average variable cost and average fixed cost. Minimum average variable cost occurs where $AVC = MC$. Minimum average total cost occurs at a higher rate of output than minimum average variable cost, since average fixed cost continues to decline as output increases. Minimum average total cost occurs where $ATC = MC$.

11. The long-run average cost curve forms an envelope curve for the short-run average total cost curves which result from picking different output capacities (different-sized plants). At the point of tangency between the short-run average total cost curve and the long-run average cost curve, short-run marginal cost equals long-run marginal cost. Hence, the relationship between short-run marginal cost and short-run average total cost at that rate of output is determined by whether long-run marginal cost is less than (internal economies), greater than (internal diseconomies) or equal to (constant cost) long-run average cost.

12. The shape of the long-run average cost curve plays an important role in the different market structures encountered in the study of the firm's output decision.

GLOSSARY

Average fixed cost   Fixed cost divided by output: $AFC = FC/q$.

Average total cost   Total cost divided by output: $ATC = TC/q = AFC + AVC$.

Average variable cost   Variable cost divided by output: $AVC = VC/q$.

Diseconomies of scale   See **internal diseconomies**.

Economic efficiency   The condition of producing a specified rate of output at the minimum possible cost or, equivalently, producing the maximum rate of output at a specified input cost. Economic efficiency implies that output can be increased only if cost also increases and cost can be decreased only if the rate of output decreases.

Economies of scale   See **internal economies**.

Envelope curve   The long-run average cost curve, which, when taking on a U-shape because internal economies at low rates of output give way to internal diseconomies at high rates of output, touches each short-run average cost curve at one point, not necessarily the minimum of the latter.

Fixed cost   Cost which does not change with output, usually because of a minimum purchase constraint.

Internal diseconomies   Increasing long-run average cost, due to decreasing returns to scale, increasing input prices, and/or deteriorating input productivity. Also called **diseconomies of scale**.

Internal economies   Reduction in long-run average cost as the planned rate of output increases, due to increasing returns to scale and/or falling input prices. Also called **economies of scale**.

Isocost line   The diagram depicting combinations of input services which have the same total opportunity cost.

Long-run average cost   The minimum cost of producing a rate of output, identified by the isoquant-isocost tangency (all input services variable), divided by that rate of output.

Long-run marginal cost   The increase in the planning cost when planned rate of output is increased by one unit. Long-run marginal cost equals the common ratio of each input's price (or marginal input cost when input prices vary with input use) to its marginal product, when all input services are variable.

Marginal input cost The cost of employing one more unit of factor service. When factor prices are invariant with the amount of services purchased, the marginal input cost equals the factor price. When an input's price increases as more of the input is hired, the marginal input cost will usually exceed the price paid for the last unit of input hired. When input prices fall as more services are hired, the marginal input cost will equal the price of the last unit if savings occur only for incremental units.

Maximum availability constraint When the services of an input cannot be increased in the short run beyond the amount hired under contract or owned by the firm. This gives rise to diminishing marginal productivity of the variable inputs' services.

Minimum purchase constraint The requirement to pay for a factor's services regardless of whether that factor is used, either because the firm has hired a factor under contract, or because the firm owns the input and cannot lease that input's services to others in the short run.

Monopsony Technically, a market with one buyer. Used more generally to refer to a buyer confronting a positively sloped supply schedule of a good or service, such as being able to hire

workers with equivalent productivity at different wage rates.

Operating costs Another name for short-run costs (i.e., marginal cost, average variable cost, average fixed cost, average total cost), emphasizing the fact that production actually occurs when minimum purchase requirements and maximum availability constraints are in force.

Opportunity cost The benefits sacrificed in terms of alternatives foregone when an input is used in one way instead of another way.

Output expansion path The set of tangencies between the isocost lines determined by prevailing factor prices, and their associated isoquants, representing alternative rates of output.

Planning costs A name for long-run average cost and long-run marginal cost which emphasizes the fact that all inputs are variable only when enough time elapses for minimum purchase constraints and maximum availability constraints to expire.

Short run The operating horizon of the firm, generally defined by the duration of minimum purchase or maximum availability constraints, such that cost cannot be reduced below fixed cost and output expansion is hampered by diminishing marginal productivity of variable inputs.

Variable cost Any cost which varies as the rate of output varies.

SUGGESTED READINGS

Alchian, Armen A. "Costs and Outputs." In Moses Abromowitz et al., eds. *The Allocation of Economic Resources*. Stanford: Stanford University Press, 1959. Reprinted in William Breit and Harold Hochman, eds. *Readings in Microeconomics*. 2nd ed. New York: Holt, Rinehart and Winston, 1971, pp. 159–171.

Baumol, William J. *Economic Theory and Operations Analysis*. 4th ed. Englewood Cliffs, New Jersey: Prentice-Hall, 1977, chapter 11.

De Alessi, Louis. "The Short Run Revisited."

American Economic Review (June 1967), pp. 450–461.

Dean, Joel. "Statistical Cost Functions of a Hosiery Mill." *Journal of Business* (1941). Reprinted in Edwin Mansfield, ed. *Microeconomics: Selected Readings*. 4th ed. New York: Norton, 1982.

Dean, Robert D., and Thomas M. Carroll. "Plant Location Under Uncertainty." *Land Economics* (November 1977).

Gold, Bela. "Changing Perspectives on Size, Scale

and Returns: An Interpretive Survey." *Journal of Economic Literature* (March 1981), pp. 5–33.

Mansfield, Edwin, ed. "Statistical Cost Functions." In Edwin Mansfield *Microeconomics: Selected Readings.* 4th ed. New York: Norton, 1982.

Moore, Frederick T. "Economies of Scale: Some Statistical Evidence." *Quarterly Journal of Economics* (May 1959).

Moses, Leon. "Location and the Theory of Production." *Quarterly Journal of Economics* (1958). Reprinted in Robert D. Dean, William

H. Leahy, and David L. McKee, eds. *Spatial Economic Theory.* New York: Free Press, 1971, pp. 59–71.

Stigler, George. "The Economics of Scale." *Journal of Law and Economics* (October 1958), pp. 54–71.

Viner, Jacob. "Cost Curves and Supply Curves." Reprinted in American Economic Association. *Readings in Price Theory.* Homewood, Illinois: Irwin, 1952.

Walles, A. A. "Production and Cost Functions." *Econometrica* (January-April 1966), pp. 1–66.

EXERCISES

Evaluate

Indicate whether each statement is true (agrees with economic theory), false (is contradicted by theory), or uncertain, (could be true or false, given additional information). Explain your answer.

1. Short-run marginal cost may equal but may never be less than long-run marginal cost.
2. The tangency point between an isoquant and an isocost line indicates the maximum output for the minimum cost.
3. At the minimum point on the long-run average cost curve, the sum of the output elasticities for all inputs will equal one.
4. The best site for a plant is one that minimizes total transportation costs.
5. When the ratio of variable input services to available fixed input services corresponds to the input service ratio at the point of tangency between the relevant isoquant and isocost line, the firm is producing at the minimum point of its average total cost curve.
6. An increase in the price of one factor's services will increase payments to owners of that factor only if factor substitution is impossible.
7. The output which minimizes average variable cost is smaller in the short run than in the long run.
8. If one were able to adjust factor prices for inflation accurately, a graph of the firm's historical output costs would correspond to its long-run total cost curve.
9. Producing in stage III of a short-run production function would result in negative marginal cost.
10. Constant returns to scale imply constant long-run marginal cost if and only if factor prices are constant.

Calculate

Answer each of the following questions, showing all your calculations.

11. In question 11 for chapter five, you were given the following five plans for delivering taxi service to the municipal airport:

Plan	Taxis	Mechanics
A	40	2
B	35	3
C	31	4
D	28	5
E	30	6

    a. If a mechanic can be hired for two times the cost of leasing a taxi, which of the technically efficient plans minimizes the cost of the taxi company's compliance with the terms of its contract?
    b. How is your answer to part *a* affected by the information that cab drivers' earnings have just been increased 15 percent per day?

12. Use the following information, supplied with question 12 for chapter five, to calculate the

marginal cost, average variable cost, and average total cost for each level of output, under the assumptions that workers are hired for $40 per day and capital fixed cost is $1,000 per day:

Labor	Output	Capital/Worker
1	5	100
5	40	20
10	100	10
20	180	5
30	240	$3\frac{1}{3}$
40	280	$2\frac{1}{2}$
50	300	2
60	280	$1\frac{2}{3}$

a. At approximately what level of output are marginal cost and average variable cost minimized? Explain.

b. If capital services could be varied and production were characterized by constant returns to scale, what would be the marginal cost and average variable cost of the first 100 units of output?

c. What is the most the entrepreneur would pay for the 101st unit of capital if only 300 units of output were to be produced? Explain your answer.

Contemplate

Answer each of the following in a brief but complete essay.

13. Comment on the following: A firm finds that the optimal combination of inputs for producing 10 units of output involves 10 hours of labor and 20 units of capital. Engineering reports that with 20 hours of labor and 40 units of capital, 20 units of output result. However, although factor prices are constant, the optimal input combination for $q = 20$ is *not* $L = 20$ and $K = 40$. If labor and capital are the only inputs, the firm is experiencing decreasing long-run average cost.

14. Suppose that an input is "inferior" in the sense that fewer input services are used as output expands along the output expansion path. Under what circumstances might a decrease in the relative price of that input cause its use to fall?

15. Two substitute raw materials, A and B, can be used to produce commodity X. Currently the firm uses input A because its price is lower (per unit of output) than input B. During a period of inflation, the price of A increases faster than the average price level, while the price of B increases slower than the average price level (as measured by the producers' price index). What happens to the cost of producing commodity X?

Chapter 7

Linear Programming: Cost Theory and Simple Technology

This chapter presents a nontechnical overview of **linear programming**—computer techniques which solve business resource allocation problems by depicting production as a process involving fixed input proportions. Many commodities, such as chemicals, metals, and even some foods, require that ingredients be used in fixed proportions. Using more of one ingredient in place of another changes the nature of the commodity. Even when input services can be substituted, changing input proportions often means that the production activity is modified. Two lumberjacks can cut down a tree by standing on either side of it and drawing a two-handle saw back and forth. If the two-handle saw is replaced by a power-driven chain saw, attempting to use the old labor-intensive method would result in severe injury to one of the lumberjacks. When more than one process can be used to produce a commodity, different types of machines and different kinds of skills usually come into play.

In this chapter we will explore the nature of simple (fixed-proportion) production process and see how the theory of production and cost is modified when input substitution involves process substitution. We will discover that when only one fixed-proportion process is deemed technically efficient, isoquants degenerate into single points along a ray depicting efficient input proportions. When two technically efficient processes exist, isoquants are negatively sloped lines bounded by linear ridge lines. With three or more processes, the isoquants similar to those encountered in chapters five and six emerge. Hence, viewing input selection as a choice among production processes provides a different and enlightening perspective of the economic nature of production.

Simple Technology and Production Processes

Suppose that the Swifty Typing Service owns 20 electric typewriters and that it hires typists on a day-to-day basis to pound out term papers for students at State University. If the typists' average speed is 50 words per minute, the total number of words typed depends upon the number of typists hired or the number of typewriters used, whichever is less. The *process* of typing a term paper requires one hour of labor for each hour of capital (i.e., typewriter time); output is limited by whichever input is scarcer relative to input requirements. If only 10 typists are hired, production will average 500 words per minute; the availability of labor will constrain output. If 30 typists are hired, output will be limited to 1,000 words per minute, since only 20 typewriters are available.

In general, we can define a **production process** as a fixed proportion production function: $q = \min(L/\alpha, K/\beta)$, where q is the rate of output, L and K are labor and capital services, measured in hours, and α (alpha) and β (beta) are **input coefficients**, the minimum labor and capital services required to produce one unit of output per unit of time.[1]

Suppose that Whatsit Widgets must hire four workers to operate a semiautomatic widget-maker. If the machine, plus labor, can turn out one widget every 2 hours, then $\alpha = 8$ and $\beta = 2$; the production function for this process is: $q = \min(L/8, K/2)$. Table 7-1 displays the rates of output (widgets per hour) for selected combinations of input services. The rates of output along the diagonal in the table determine the technically efficient input combinations; since input substitution is impossible with only one fixed proportion process, there is only one efficient input combination for each rate of output. Since each widget requires 8 hours of labor and 2 hours of capital, the efficient input combinations for all rates of output result in a capital-to-labor ratio of 1 to 4 ($K/L = 0.25$).

If Whatsit hired too many workers for the machinery available—for example, if $L = 24$ and $K = 2$—output is determined by the smaller ratio of labor to its input coefficient, 24/8, and capital to its coefficient, 2/2. Output is one widget per hour; 16 labor hours will be wasted. If $K/L < \alpha/\beta$, labor is the redundant input. If one more worker were hired, output would remain at 1 widget per hour, since 25/8 > 2/2. If labor services were reduced to 23, output would still remain at 1 unit per hour, since 2/2 < 23/8. *For a simple production process in which input substitution is impossible, the marginal product of a* **redundant input** *is zero.*

When labor is the redundant input, capital is called the **binding**

---

[1] For a firm producing many products with many inputs, each process has the form $q_i = \min(v_1/a_{1i}, v_2/a_{2i}, \ldots, v_j/a_{ji}, \ldots, v_m/a_{mi})$, where a_{ji} is the amount of input j required to produce one unit of output i per period.

TABLE 7-1
Input-Output Combinations for Production Process A: $q = \min(L/8, K/2)$

Labor (hours)	Machinery (hours)								
	0	*2*	*4*	*6*	*8*	*10*	*12*	*14*	*16*
0	0	0	0	0	0	0	0	0	0
8	0	1	1	1	1	1	1	1	1
16	0	1	2	2	2	2	2	2	2
24	0	1	2	3	3	3	3	3	3
32	0	1	2	3	4	4	4	4	4
40	0	1	2	3	4	5	5	5	5
48	0	1	2	3	4	5	6	6	6
56	0	1	2	3	4	5	6	7	7
64	0	1	2	3	4	5	6	7	8

constraint on output. The binding constraint, or limiting factor of production is often called the **production bottleneck**. Output cannot be increased beyond 1 widget per hour unless machine services are greater than 2 hours. Suppose another machine is procured, making 3 hours of capital services available; with $L = 24$, output would increase to 1.5 widgets per hour: $q = 3/2 < 24/3$. If capital were reduced to 1.5 hours, output would fall from 1.0 to 0.75 units per hour. *When one factor is the effective constraint on output, increasing that input's services will increase output; its marginal product is the reciprocal of its input coefficient.*

If capital were the redundant factor—for instance, if $L = 24$ and $K = 8$, so that $K/L > 1/4$—labor would constitute the production bottleneck and capital would be the redundant input ($MP_K = 0$). A slight increase or decrease in capital services would have no influence on the rate of production: $\min(24/8, 7/2) = \min(24/8, 8/2) = \min(24/8, 9/2) = 3$. An increase in labor services from 24 to 25 hours would increase output from 3 widgets per hour to $3.125 = \min(25/8, 8/2)$; a reduction in labor services to 23 hours would reduce widget production to $2.875 = \min(23/8, 8/2)$ per hour. When labor is the limiting constraint on output, the marginal product of labor is the reciprocal of its input coefficient: $MP_L = 1/8$.

An ironic result occurs when inputs are being used in their efficient proportions. Suppose $L = 24$ and $K = 6$, so that $q = \min(24/8, 6/2) = \min(3, 3) = 3$. An increase in either factor, holding the other factor constant, makes the increased factor redundant. Note that $q = \min(25/8, 6/2) = \min(24/8, 7/2) = 3$. *When factors are being used in technically efficient proportions, each factor has a zero marginal product for input increases, the other factor remaining constant.*

On the other hand, if either factor's services are reduced below their efficient level, the other factor, whose services are not changed, becomes redundant. If L is reduced from 24 to 23 hours, while K remains constant at 6 hours, q falls from 3 to 2.875 widgets per hour. Since $\Delta q = -0.125$ and $\Delta L = -1$, $MP_L^- = \Delta q/\Delta L = -0.125/-1 = 0.125$, where MP_L^- is read "the marginal product of labor for labor decreases." If L remains at 24 but K is reduced from 6 to 5, output falls from 3 to 2.5; $MP_K^- = \Delta q/\Delta K = -0.5/-1 = 0.5$. Note that the marginal product of capital (or labor) is positive for input decreases, even though it is zero for input increases. (And this is called simple technology!) *When factors are being used in efficient proportions, a reduction in either factor's services will cause that input to become the production bottleneck, and its marginal product will be the reciprocal of its input coefficient.*

The isoquant for a fixed-proportion production function is a right angle, formed by lines parallel to the two input axes, which meet at the efficient input ratio. In Figure 7-1, isoquants for the input combinations in Table 7-1 are represented by dashed lines emanating from the ray $0A$, identified by the equation $K = 1/4\ L$. At the point $(L = 8, K = 2)$, neither

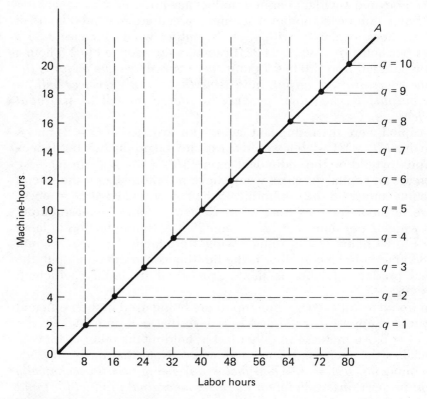

Figure 7-1
Isoquant Map for Fixed-Proportion Process A: $q = \min(L/8, K/2)$

factor is redundant in the production of 1 unit of output per hour. An increase in labor, holding capital constant, would have no impact on output; q would remain 1 unit per hour. To the right of ray $0A$, labor is redundant, so that $MP_L = 0$ for both increases and (small) decreases in labor services. At point $(16,2)$, $q = 1$; but if capital is increased to 3 units, output rises to $\min(16/8, 3/2) = 1.5$. To the right of ray $0A$, the marginal product of capital is 0.5.

Above (to the left of) ray $0A$ are points where capital is the redundant factor. Point $(8,4)$ produces 1 unit of output per hour, just like point $(8,2)$; extra capital services do not increase the rate of widget production. Starting from point $(8,4)$, a point on isoquant $q = 2$ can be reached by adding 8 hours of labor services. The marginal product of labor is 0.125 for points to the left of ray $0A$. The technically efficient points lie along ray $0A$, called the **production ray** or the **process ray**, which separates the points with redundant capital ($MP_K = 0$) from the points with redundant labor ($MP_L = 0$). *With a single production process, the locus of efficient points is also the ridge line for both labor and capital.*

As specified, the simple production process is characterized by constant returns to scale.[2] Given $q_0 = \min(L_0/\alpha, K_0/\beta)$, it follows that $\min(\lambda L_0/\alpha, \lambda K_0/\beta) = \lambda \min(L_0/\alpha, K_0/\beta) = \lambda q_0$. Regardless of whether a point is on the production ray, increasing both inputs by the same proportion will increase the bottleneck input by that proportion, guaranteeing that output will always increase by the common proportion that inputs are increased. This characteristic of simple technologies serves as an important link between linear programming, a computer technique used for real production planning, and neoclassical production theory.

If there is only one process for producing a commodity, there is only one technically efficient input combination—identified by points along the production ray—for producing each rate of output. Since only technically efficient combinations can be economically efficient, that single technically efficient input combination will be the least-cost input combination, regardless of the relative prices of input services.

Two Production Processes: Linear Isoquants

Suppose that Whatsit Widgets, which has been producing widgets with the process $q = \min(L/8, K/2)$, discovers a new process: $q = \min(L/4, K/8)$. For instance, a computerized widget wizard, which requires a rental outlay four times greater than that required for the semiautomatic widget-

---

[2] Increasing or decreasing returns to scale could be generated by specifying the simple technology in the form $q = \min(L/\alpha, K/\beta)^\gamma$, where γ (gamma) is the degree of homogeneity. If $\gamma > 1$, increasing returns to scale would result; decreasing returns to scale would be implied by $\gamma < 1$.

maker of the original process, allows the firm to cut its labor use in half. To distinguish between the two processes, we will call the process $q = \min(L/8, K/2)$ process A and the new technique process B. Table 7-2 relates input services and rates of output for process B. (The use of the relative prices—or the equivalent relative rental rates—of two machines as a common denominator for measuring capital is discussed in detail at the beginning of chapter five.)

The first question the production manager investigates is whether the new process could ever be the least-cost process. Process B requires 8 units of capital per unit of output, or four times as much capital (measured in machine rental rates) as process A. Clearly, process B is not always superior to process A. If workers receive a wage rate less than one and one-half times the machine rental rate, the firm would have lower production costs using process A. However, process B does require less labor per widget, meaning that it might be the least-cost process (i.e., if wage rates were more than 1.5 times the machine rental rate). When there are two processes for producing a commodity, each process will be technically efficient if at least one of its input coefficients is smaller than the corresponding input coefficient for the other process. Process B is technically efficient since its labor coefficient is smaller than the labor coefficient for process A; process A is technically efficient because its capital coefficient is smaller than the capital coefficient for process B. The identity of the least cost process depends upon the relative prices of input services.

The technically efficient combinations of labor and capital services for process B appear along the diagonal in Table 7-2. If $K/L > 2$, capital would be redundant in process B; $MP_L = 0.25$ and $MP_K = 0$. If $K/L < 2$, there is too much labor, relative to available capital, for all of it to be

TABLE 7-2
Input-Output Combinations for Production Process B: $q = \min(L/4, K/8)$

Labor (hours)	Machinery (hours)								
	0	8	16	24	32	40	48	56	64
0	0	0	0	0	0	0	0	0	0
4	0	1	1	1	1	1	1	1	1
8	0	1	2	2	2	2	2	2	2
12	0	1	2	3	3	3	3	3	3
16	0	1	2	3	4	4	4	4	4
20	0	1	2	3	4	5	5	5	5
24	0	1	2	3	4	5	6	6	6
28	0	1	2	3	4	5	6	7	7
32	0	1	2	3	4	5	6	7	8

employed in process B; $MP_L = 0$ and $MP_K = 0.125$ when capital is the binding constraint in process B. If process B were the only known production technique, the ray depicting technically efficient input proportions for process B would be the ridge line for labor and capital (as was ray $0A$ when only process A was known). However, the existence of two technically efficient processes means that input combinations lying between the two process rays are also efficient. Line $0A$ continues to serve as the ridge line for labor, since $MP_L = 0$ when $K < 0.25\ L$; line $0B$ continues to be the ridge line for capital, since $MP_K = 0$ when $K < 2\ L$. Because of the constant returns-to-scale assumption, process A and process B can be operated side by side, producing widgets with an infinite variety of input proportions.

Figure 7-2 illustrates the production possibilities when processes A and B are both available. Suppose that Whatsit Widgets has 12 workers and a capital budget sufficient to rent the equivalent of 10 hours of semiautomatic widget-making machinery. Since $K = 5/6\ L$, there is too

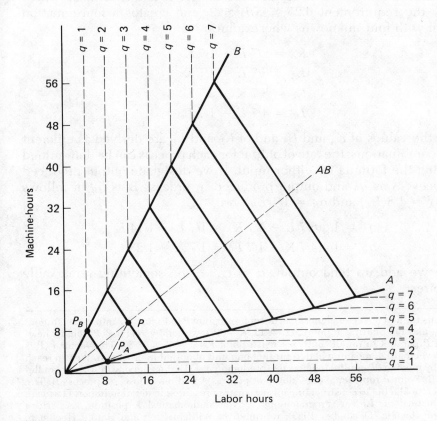

Figure 7-2
Linear Isoquants Generated from Two Efficient Production Processes

much labor for process B (alone) and too much capital for process A alone. However, by using 8 hours of labor with two hours of semiautomatic widget-making machinery, 1 widget per hour can be produced with process A. Money for 8 hours of semiautomatic machinery can be used to purchase enough computerized widget machinery to combine with the remaining 4 hours of labor to produce 1 widget per hour with process B.[3] Using the two processes side by side can be considered as a third process: process AB is identified by the production function q = $\min(L/6, K/5)$, where the input coefficients are the average of those for process A and process B. Assuming that each process can be operated at any rate, an infinite number of processes can be defined by dividing inputs between processes A and B according to the following formulas:

$$L_A + L_B = L, \; K_A + K_B = K, \; K_A = 0.25\,L_A, \text{ and } K_B = 2\,L_B$$

These four relations imply that all available labor and capital are used; neither input is redundant and that inputs are used in efficient proportions. This limits acceptable values for K and L to those which satisfy the requirement $0.25 \leq K/L \leq 2$, and creates a four-equation system with four unknowns whose solution is:

$$K_A = 2/7\,L - 1/7\,K$$
$$L_A = 8/7\,L - 4/7\,K$$
$$K_B = 8/7\,K - 2/7\,L$$
$$L_B = 4/7\,K - 1/7\,L$$

Since the values of K_A and L_A and of K_B and L_B are derived as efficient input combinations, the rate of output for each process can be determined by using the formula for either input. If we designate output produced in process A as q_A and output produced in process B as q_B, it follows that $q_A = 1/8(L_A)$ and $q_B = 1/4(L_B)$, or:

$$q_A = 1/8(8/7\,L - 4/7\,K) = 1/7\,L - 1/14\,K$$
$$q_B = 1/4(4/7\,K - 1/7\,L) = 1/7\,K - 1/28\,L$$

When we add up total output, $q = q_A + q_B$, something remarkable transpires:

[3] Students trained in vector algebra can decompose point P in Figure 7-2 into its constituent parts, P_A and P_B. Starting at point $P(L = 12, K = 10)$, we follow vector $P_A P$ from its head at point P parallel to ray OB until we reach point $P_A(L = 8, K = 2)$. The vector $P_A P$ is equal to vector OP_B, meaning both represent one unit of output in process B. We can reach point P by moving OP_A units along ray OA (producing $q = 1$); then moving OP_B units parallel to ray OB. Point P represents one "dose" of process A and one "dose" of process B. The use of vector algebra to construct linear isoquants is presented in detail in Robert Dorfman, "Mathematical or 'Linear' Programming: A Non-Mathematical Exposition," *American Economic Review* (December 1953); reprinted in William Breit and Harold Hochman, eds., *Readings in Microeconomic Theory*, 2nd ed. (New York: Holt, Rinehart and Winston, 1971), pp. 172–193.

$$q = q_A + q_B = (1/7\,L - 1/14\,K) + (1/7\,K - 1/28\,L)$$

Grouping labor and capital terms for easier solution:

$$q = (1/7\,L - 1/28\,L) + (1/7\,K - 1/14\,K) = 3/28\,L + 1/14\,K$$

Given any combination of labor and capital falling within the range $0.25 < K/L < 2$, the rate of output will be a linear function of the two inputs.[4] Fixing the value of q generates the equation for a **linear isoquant**: $\bar{q} = 3/28\,L + 1/14\,K$. Solving for K yields:

$$1/14\,K = \bar{q} - 3/28\,L \qquad \text{or} \qquad K = 14\bar{q} - 1.5\,L$$

The slope of the isoquant is the marginal rate of technical substitution:

$$MRTS = \left.\frac{\Delta K}{\Delta L}\right|_{\bar{q}} = -1.5$$

As long as the capital-to-labor ratio remains within the limits set by the two production rays, using the two processes side by side allows the firm to reduce capital by 1.5 units for each additional unit of labor services employed.

Clearly, linear isoquants have a negative slope, since $\Delta K/\Delta L = -a/b$, where a and b are the coefficients from the linear production function. Further, from the linear production function $q = 3/28\,L + 1/14\,K$, the marginal products of the two inputs are $MP_L = 3/28$ and $MP_K = 1/14$. Unlike the isoquants encountered in chapters five and six, isoquants have constant slopes when two production processes are combined. But doesn't this violate the law of diminishing returns? The answer is no.

Remember that the linear isoquants in Figure 7-2 are defined only within the range $0.25 \leq K/L \leq 2$. For instance, if beginning at point P ($L = 12$, $K = 10$) in Figure 7-2, Whatsit Widgets adds 1 unit of labor, increasing output from $q = 2$ to $q = 2.107$ widgets per hour. If Whatsit Widgets continues adding labor services until $L = 40$ and $K = 10$, output will increase from 2 to 5 units, and all capital will have been transferred from process B to process A. Any further increase in labor would cause that input to be redundant. Or, beginning at point P, output will increase by $1/14 = 0.0714$ for every unit increase in capital until $L = 12$ and $K = 24$. At that point, all labor will have been transferred to process B,

---

[4] An alternative way of reaching the same result is to specify a linear production function of the form $q = aL + bK$, where a and b are treated as unknowns. Since process A and process B identify the end points for an isoquant, we can substitute known values for q, L, and K in those processes and solve for a and b:

$$2 = 16a + 4b \ \text{(process A) so that} \ b = 1/14$$
$$\underline{2 = 8a + 16b} \ \text{(process B) and} \quad a = 3/28$$
$$\therefore -2 = \quad -28b$$

Policy Illustration
Who Is to Blame for Lagging Productivity?

During recent years, debate has raged over the lagging productivity of workers in the United States relative to workers in other countries, particularly Japan. Are American workers lazy, or is management starving enterprise of capital? How much of the blame accrues to government policies? When it comes to explaining a stagnant economy, blame is not scarce.

Many production technologies provide little leeway for factor substitution once a technique has been installed, although input substitution may be possible in the planning stage by selecting one technology instead of another. A firm typically owns its machinery and faces contractual principal and interest payments to banks and bond holders regardless of whether that machinery is used. If operating below capacity will idle some machinery, management will be reluctant to incur additional capital costs unless it is confident that new equipment will be fully used. Recessions, like those experienced in the late 1970s and early 1980s, are not boons to investment. Old equipment breaks down and workers are idled. Idle workers have low productivity.

While machines may have narrow operating limits—two workers cannot drive the same forklift at the same time—they can be operated quickly or slowly. Workers who fear that excess inventories of manufactured goods will result in layoffs may decide that working faster will eliminate jobs. Few employers in the United States care for redundant workers the way paternalistic Japanese firms do.

There are two other reasons for declining productivity measured as real output per worker-hour. First, among alternative production techniques, energy and capital tend to be complementary inputs, while energy and labor operate as substitutes because capital and labor are substitutes among processes. A process which

and any further increase in capital would have no influence on output. Unlike the marginal rate of technical substitution of conventional isoquants, which gradually goes from $-\infty$ at the capital ridge line to 0 at the labor ridge line, the marginal rate of technical substitution of a linear isoquant changes abruptly when a ridge line is encountered.

Three Processes: Kinked Isoquants

After all the trouble of calculating rates of output resulting from parallel operation of processes A and B, Whatsit Widgets develops a third process, which we will call process C, $q = \min(L/6, K/4)$. An automatic, manually operated widget-maker, leasing for half the rate of the computerized machinery of process B, can produce a unit of output with six workers. Since process C requires only half the outlay on capital as in process B, there are hypothetical situations in which process C would be less expensive than process B. Process C requires more labor per widget than uses less capital (or energy) per unit of output will use more labor per unit of output, relative to another technically efficient process. The combined influence of higher energy costs and high (real) rates of interest encourages the substitution of labor-intensive production for capital-intensive production, resulting in a lower rate of output per production worker.

Second, many capital costs which have been mandated by environmental and safety regulations are not reflected in (and thus not offset by) higher revenue. Although society may be better off when firms are forced to include environmental costs in production planning, and workers receive higher real wages when employers install safety devices, the gross national product does not increase in response to enhanced worker safety or environmental quality.

In conclusion, the troublesome decline in American worker productivity has many possible causes: pessimistic investment expectations, fear of layoffs, higher (relative) capital and energy costs, environmental and safety regulations, and even the desire of workers to enjoy leisure on the job. What most economists care to address is not who should be blamed for lower output per worker but how incentives can be modified to enhance the standard of living of all Americans. One reason investment is high in Japan is that wages take a smaller share of revenue there than in the United States. Over time, Japanese workers may demand a bigger slice of output, a safer workplace, and a cleaner environment. Then Japanese productivity will come to approximate the productivity of American workers.

process B; thus both processes are technically efficient. Process C economizes on labor relative to process A, while process A requires less expenditure on capital per unit of output. All three processes are technically efficient.

However, process AB, which requires six labor units and five capital units per widget, is clearly inefficient relative to process C. For each widget, process C requires the same amount of labor time as process AB, but less capital. In Table 7-3, which gives the input-output combinations for process C alone, we see that process C requires 12 labor hours and the equivalent of 8 capital hours to produce 2 widgets; producing one widget in process A and one widget in process B requires 12 labor hours and the equivalent of 10 capital hours. The introduction of a process whose technically efficient input proportion is less than one process and greater than another process will render combinations of the latter two processes technically inefficient, although it may be efficient to use the new process with either of the older processes.

Figure 7-3 shows how introducing a third efficient process draws

TABLE 7-3
Input-Output Combinations for Production Process C: $q = \min(L/6, K/4)$

Labor (hours)	Machinery (hours)							
	0	4	8	12	16	20	24	28	32
0	0	0	0	0	0	0	0	0	0
6	0	1	1	1	1	1	1	1	1
12	0	1	2	2	2	2	2	2	2
18	0	1	2	3	3	3	3	3	3
24	0	1	2	3	4	4	4	4	4
30	0	1	2	3	4	5	5	5	5
36	0	1	2	3	4	5	6	6	6
42	0	1	2	3	4	5	6	7	7
48	0	1	2	3	4	5	6	7	8

each isoquant toward the origin. For three processes to remain efficient, the process with the intermediate input ratio (here, process C) must economize on inputs relative to *combinations* of the other processes which lie on the new production ray. If Whatsit Widgets begins at ray *0B* and substitutes labor for capital, combining processes B and C will release more capital than will combining processes B and A to produce the same rate of output. When all production has been transferred to process C, further substitution of labor for capital involves combining processes C and A. Each additional hour of labor services now frees less capital than was the case between processes B and C. *With three (or more) production processes, the marginal rate of technical substitution decreases discretely at each production ray.*

To the left of process B, the marginal rate of technical substitution is still $-\infty$, since capital is redundant. Between process B and process C, the marginal rate of substitution can be determined by solving the linear production function $q = a_1L + b_1K$ for a_1 and b_1. Picking the relevant points from process B (8,16) and process C (12,8) for producing 2 units of output, substitution for q, L, and K gives us the following two-equation system:

(Process B) $2 = 8a_1 + 16b_1$ or $\quad 2 = \quad 8a_1 + 16b_1 \quad a_1 = 1/8$
(Process C) $2 = 12a_1 + 8b_1$ $\qquad \underline{4 = \quad 24a_1 + 16b_1} \quad b_1 = 1/16$
$\qquad\qquad\qquad\qquad\qquad\qquad -2 = -16a_1$

Solving the production function $q = 1/8\,L + 1/16\,K$ for K, $1/16\,K = q - 1/8\,L$, or $K = 16q - 2L$.

Between ray *0B*, the capital ridge line, and ray *0C*—that is, for $5/6 \leqq K/L \leqq 2$—the marginal rate of technical substitution is -2. By hiring an additional hour of labor, 2 units of capital services can be saved. When an additional hour of labor is hired, the firm reduces output in process B by 1/2 unit per hour, freeing 2 labor hours and 4 capital hours. In process C the additional labor hour is added to the two released from process B to produce the 1/2 unit lost from process B. Since only 2 units of capital services are required, the addition of 1 labor hour reduces capital requirements by 2 hours.

When process C has absorbed all available capital and labor, further substitution involves transferring production from process C to process A. The linear production function abruptly shifts to a new set of labor and capital coefficients: $q = a_2 L + b_2 K$. Substituting values for q, L, and K from process C and process A, we can solve for the values of a_2 and b_2:

$$\text{(Process C) } 2 = 12a_2 + 8b_2 \text{ or} \quad 2 = \quad 12a_2 + 8b_2 \quad a_2 = 1/10$$
$$\text{(Process A) } 2 = 16a_2 + 4b_2 \quad \underline{\quad 4 = \quad 32a_2 + 8b_2} \quad b_2 = 1/10$$
$$-2 = -20a_2$$

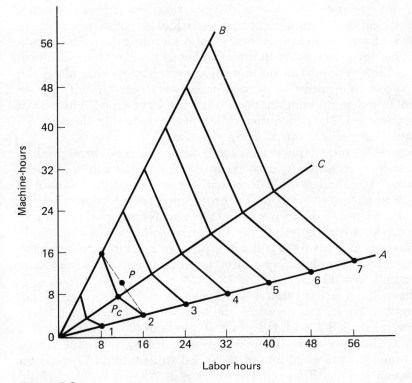

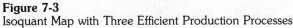

Figure 7-3
Isoquant Map with Three Efficient Production Processes

Solving the production function $q = 1/10\,L + 1/10\,K$ for K, $1/10\,K = q - 1/10\,L$, or $K = 10q - L$. Between process C and process A ($1/4 \leqq K/L \leqq 5/6$), the marginal rate of technical substitution is -1. If an extra unit of labor services is hired, output can be cut by 1/2 unit per hour in process C, freeing 3 hours of labor and 2 units of capital. Since producing that 1/2 unit of output in process A requires 4 hours of labor and 1 hour of capital, capital requirements are reduced by 1 hour. The isoquant for two widgets per hour is "kinked" along process C, where the slope of each isoquant abruptly changes.

Production Costs and Production Processes

In chapter six, identification of economically efficient input combinations involved the equivalent solutions to complementary optimization problems. The tangency between an isocost line and the related isoquant could be discovered by moving along the isoquant—minimizing the cost of a target rate of output—or by moving along the isocost line—maximizing the output from a specified expenditure on input services. When isoquants are generated by a few distinct production processes, the economically efficient input combination is located at a *corner* where two linear sections of the isoquant meet, and identification of this point is called a **corner solution**. As in the continuous isoquant case, the economically efficient point can be identified either by moving along the relevant isocost line until the optimal process is discovered or by substituting planned input combinations until the lowest possible isocost line is encountered. The conceptual difference is that *input substitution* actually involves *process substitution*.

In Figure 7-4 the isoquant map for Whatsit Widgets' three production processes is simplified by displaying only for isoquant for four widgets per hour. We shall assume that workers are equally proficient at operating the machines used in the three processes and that they can be hired at a wage rate of $8 per hour. We also assume that machinery used in process A can be leased for $5 per hour. Since each machine-hour for process B rents for 4 times the price of machinery for process B, an outlay of $288 per hour is required to produce four units in process B ($L = 16$ and $K = 32$ implies $C = \$8 \times 16 + \$5 \times 32 = \$288$).

We have been using relative machine rental rates to add up homogeneous capital. By our measure, the price of labor services relative to capital services is 8/5, with the price of one hour of the machinery in process A as the *numeraire* (French for "unit of measure") for capital services. Since the marginal rate of technical substitution of capital for labor between process B and process C is -2, Whatsit Widgets could reduce production costs by installing process C instead of process B. As

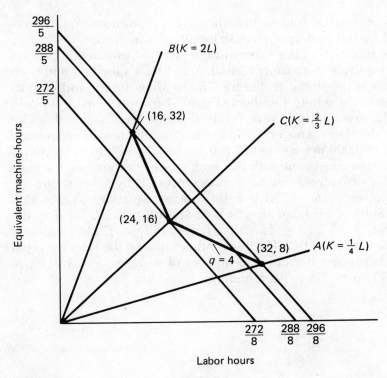

Figure 7-4
Minimizing the Cost of Producing a Given Output: $q = 4$ widgets per hour.

with smooth isoquants, $-w_L/w_K < -MP_L/MP_K$ ($|MRTS| > w_L/w_K$) implies that the cost of the target rate of output can be reduced by substituting labor for capital. While it costs \$288 to produce four widgets in process B, isoquant $q = 4$ meets process ray $0C$ at point ($L = 24$, $K = 16$), requiring an outlay of \$272 on input services ($w_L L_C + w_K K_C = [\$8 \times 24] + [\$5 \times 16] = \$272$).

Once it has been determined that process C is superior to process B in terms of cost, whether or not process C is economically efficient depends on the marginal rate of substitution between process C and process A relative to the negative input price ratio. In this range of isoquant $q = 4$, $MRTS = -1$, which is smaller in absolute value than the input price ratio, $w_L/w_K = 8/5$. Increasing labor by one hour allows a one unit saving of capital services. Since an hour of labor cost 1.6 times what an hour of capital for process A costs, transferring production from process C to process A would increase cost from \$272 to \$296.

Because cost is reduced when process C is installed instead of process B, and since process C costs less than process A per widget, process C gives the lowest cost for producing four widgets per hour. With the assumptions of constant returns to scale and constant input prices, proc-ess C would be the preferred process for all rates of output.

The identification of the economically efficient production process through the equivalent maximization of output for a specified outlay on input services is presented in Figure 7-5. To allow inputs and outputs to be measured in whole numbers, Figure 7-5 represents a 100-fold blowup of the example in Figure 7-4. In this case we imagine that Lee Whositz, production manager for Whatsit Widgets, has been given a budget of \$1,088,000 per week (\$27,200 per hour) and told to maximize the rate of output consistent with that budget. Lee determines the max-imum number of widgets per hour from process B by substituting the efficient input ratio ($K = 2\,L$) into the isocost equation, $\$8\,L + \$5\,K = \$27,200$. Solving for labor results from substituting $2\,L$ for K in the equation: $\$8\,L + \$5(2\,L) = \$27,200$. Hence, $18\,L = 27,200$, and $L = 1,511$, with $K = 2\,L = 3,022$. Dividing either input by the relevant input coefficient for process B yields the number of widgets: $q = 1,511/4 = 3,022/8 = 377.75 = 378$ (with rounding).

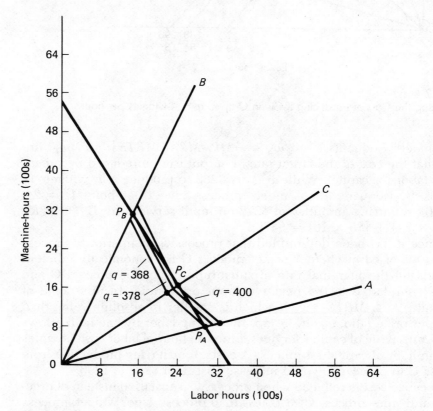

Figure 7-5
Maximizing Output for a Given Budget

Figure 7-5 shows that moving along the isocost line from $P_B(L = 1,511, K = 3,022)$ to P_C on production ray $0C$ allows output to increase. Holding cost constant, each extra worker hired requires a reduction in 1.6 capital units ($w_L/w_K = 8/5$). However, since each extra worker can replace 2 units of capital, the net savings of $2 from each increase in labor can be spent to purchase more inputs. Hiring 2,400 workers leaves sufficient funds to purchase 1600 units of capital, thereby producing 400 widgets per hour (16,000 per week). Point P_C is the only place isoquant $q = 400$ touches the isocost line for $C = \$27,200$. Further transfers of expenditures from capital to labor are not justified, since moving output from process C to process A requires $16 worth of labor for every $10 saving in capital. Hence, had production been planned for point $P_A(L = 2944, K = 736)$, the $27,200 in expenditure would have resulted in 268 widgets per hour. By transferring production to process C, output could have been increased to 400 widgets per hour. No matter where the analysis starts—at point P_B, point P_A, or indeed, at point P_C—and regardless of whether the production manager follows isocost line $C = \$27,200$ or isoquant $q = 400$ widgets per hour, Lee finds the economically efficient solution at the corner where that isocost line meets that isoquant line.

Unit Cost and Production Processes

The assumptions underlying a simple production process—constant factor proportions, constant input prices, and constant returns to scale—make planning costs a linear function of output. Average variable cost, often called **unit cost,** equals the sum of each input coefficient times the price of that input. In our widget example, process C is the least-cost process when $w_L = \$8$ and $w_K = \$5$; unit cost is determined by labor cost per widget, $8(6)$, plus capital cost per unit, $5(4)$: AVC = $68. Since the cost of production equals the cost of one unit times the number of units produced, variable cost in Figure 7-6a is drawn through the origin, with a constant slope: $MC = AVC = m$. Unit costs are represented by the horizontal line with the constant height m in Figure 7-6b.

Most firms, and many plants, produce more than one commodity, and usually have costs which are independent of the rate of output of any particular product. In Figure 7-6, overhead costs such as management, taxes, and the cost of building space, are treated as fixed cost, so that total cost is a parallel displacement of the variable cost line in Figure 7-6a. Average total cost approaches constant average variable cost as output increases, as shown in Figure 7-6b.

When, machinery, or some other input used in a fixed proportion production process is hired under contract or owned outright by the firm, the owner must contend with the consequences of minimum purchase

Business Illustration
Plant Size and Average Cost of Electric Power Generation

One of the most intensively researched issues in applied economics is the technology and cost of electric power generation. Since electric power cannot be stored economically, its production must be varied as the quantity demanded varies—by time of day and by season. Hence, electric companies must have sufficient production capacity to meet peak-load demand. And since most utilities are multiplant operations, empirical estimates of economies of scale must make allowances for two factors: (1) the size of individual plants, defined as the maximum instantaneous rate of output the unit can generate, and (2) the fuel efficiency of individual plants, the amount of fuel the unit requires to produce a given amount of electric energy.

According to John F. Stewart, these two characteristics of a plant are embedded in capital equipment and cannot be varied once a plant has been constructed. Stewart concluded that for a given plant utilization rate, average cost per kilowatt hour decreased with increasing size only for gas turbine plants and actually tended to increase with the size of steam plants. In both cases, however, the impact of size on costs appeared relatively small. On the other hand, average cost declined for all unit sizes as the utilization rate increased. One plant can produce double the kilo-watts per hour of another plant either because it is twice as large and is used at the same rate or because it is used at twice the rate of a plant with the same capacity, or some combination of the two. The analysis of the relationship between size and unit costs of electricity is further complicated by the fact that plant capacity is essentially a long-run decision, while the operating rate of a plant with fixed capacity is a short-run decision. Yet quantity demanded, which is influenced by the price charged for electricity, depends upon the rate the utility commission allows, which usually depends on the average cost of electricity generation!

Perhaps the most striking and perplexing discovery of the Stewart study was that lower costs associated with larger plants appeared to be due, to a large extent, to the relative cost of generating equipment itself. Since capital is usually measured by using the price of equipment as a common denominator, it is possible that the economies of scale in electricity generation represent declining capital prices, rather than increasing returns to scale.

Based on James F. Stewart, "Plant Size, Plant Factor and the Shape of the Average Cost Function in Electric Power Generation: A Nonhomogeneous Capital Approach," *Bell Journal of Economics* (autumn 1979), pp. 549–565.

requirements and maximum availability constraints similar to those faced by a producer with variable input proportion technology. If the cost of capital is fixed, while labor is still hired on a pay-as-used basis, capital

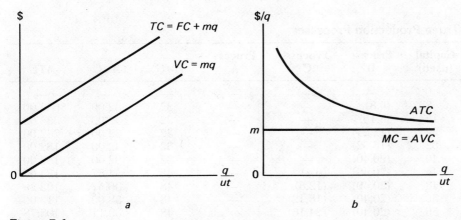

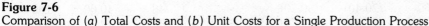

Figure 7-6
Comparison of (a) Total Costs and (b) Unit Costs for a Single Production Process

costs are absorbed in fixed costs in Figure 7-6a, and variable costs reflect only the cost of labor. If either input is available in limited quantities, that input will become a production bottleneck when used to its maximum availability. Qt, the maximum possible rate of output, the marginal cost curve becomes vertical—output cannot be increased at any cost—until the production bottleneck is eliminated.

Once machinery for a specific production process has been installed, the firm's short-run options are limited to the technology available. While this often means that only one process is available, this is not always the case. Machines wear out at different rates, and since relative factor prices frequently change, a plant may replace machinery for one process with machinery used in another process only gradually. At any particular time, a plant may combine two or more processes, each characterized by minimum purchase requirements (fixed capital cost) and maximum machinery capacity.

Table 7-4 presents the plausible case of Whatsit Widgets operating with three technologies, each limited to 40 machine-hours of equivalent capital services. Since other fixed costs will not influence the firm's output decision, they are ignored; Table 7-4 is constructed under the assumption that the only fixed costs are machinery costs.

With the cost of machinery independent of the rate of output, an efficient production manager would try to minimize wage payments for each rate of output. Widgets are first produced through process B, which requires only 4 labor hours for each widget, thereby minimizing marginal cost and average variable cost. But the process which minimizes labor hours per widget also uses the most capital (8 units) per widget; the capital bottleneck for process B is reached when output reaches 5 widg-

TABLE 7-4
Short-Run Costs with Three Production Processes

Output per Hour	Labor (hired)	Capital (used)	Process B	Process C	Process A	MC	AVC	ATC
0	0	0	—	—	—	—	—	—
1	4	8	(4,8)	—	—	$32	$32.00	$632.00
2	8	16	(8,16)	—	—	32	32.00	332.00
3	12	24	(12,24)	—	—	32	32.00	232.00
4	16	32	(16,32)	—	—	32	32.00	182.00
5	20	40	(20,40)	—	—	32	32.00	152.00
6	26	44	(20,40)	(6,4)	—	48	34.67	134.67
7	32	48	(20,40)	(12,8)	—	48	36.57	122.29
8	38	52	(20,40)	(18,12)	—	48	38.00	113.00
9	44	56	(20,40)	(24,16)	—	48	39.11	105.78
10	50	60	(20,40)	(30,20)	—	48	40.00	100.00
11	56	64	(20,40)	(36,24)	—	48	40.72	95.27
12	62	68	(20,40)	(42,28)	—	48	41.33	91.33
13	68	72	(20,40)	(48,32)	—	48	41.84	88.00
14	74	76	(20,40)	(54,36)	—	48	42.29	85.14
15	80	80	(20,40)	(60,40)	—	48	42.67	82.67
16	88	82	(20,40)	(60,40)	(8,2)	64	44.00	81.50
17	96	84	(20,40)	(60,40)	(16,4)	64	45.18	80.47
18	104	86	(20,40)	(60,40)	(24,6)	64	46.22	79.56
19	112	88	(20,40)	(60,40)	(32,8)	64	47.16	78.74
20	120	90	(20,40)	(60,40)	(40,10)	64	48.00	78.00
21	128	92	(20,40)	(60,40)	(48,12)	64	48.76	77.33
22	136	94	(20,40)	(60,40)	(56,14)	64	49.45	76.72
23	144	96	(20,40)	(60,40)	(64,16)	64	50.08	76.17
24	152	98	(20,40)	(60,40)	(72,18)	64	50.67	75.67
25	160	100	(20,40)	(60,40)	(80,20)	64	51.20	75.20
26	168	102	(20,40)	(60,40)	(88,22)	64	51.69	74.77
27	176	104	(20,40)	(60,40)	(96,24)	64	52.15	74.37
28	184	106	(20,40)	(60,40)	(104,26)	64	52.57	74.00
29	192	108	(20,40)	(60,40)	(112,28)	64	52.97	73.66
30	200	110	(20,40)	(60,40)	(120,30)	64	53.33	73.33
31	208	112	(20,40)	(60,40)	(128,32)	64	53.67	73.03
32	216	114	(20,40)	(60,40)	(136,34)	64	54.00	72.75
33	224	116	(20,40)	(60,40)	(144,36)	64	54.30	72.48
34	232	118	(20,40)	(60,40)	(152,38)	64	54.59	72.24
35	240	120	(20,40)	(60,40)	(160,40)	64	54.86	72.00

ets per hour. While marginal cost and average variable cost are $32 for the first five units, and average total cost drops rapidly from $632 to $152 per unit, the capacity in process B is quickly exhausted.

To produce the sixth unit of output, Lee Whositz must pick from the remaining two processes with unused machinery. Process C requires 6 labor hours per widget and process A requires 8 labor hours per widget; the sixth widget is produced in process C. Because marginal cost equals the labor cost of the sixth unit, marginal cost jumps from $32 for the fifth widget to $48 for the sixth. Average variable cost begins to increase as well, but not as rapidly as marginal cost, since the former is held down by the lower variable cost of the first five widgets. When ten widgets are produced in process C, available capital for that process has been used up; average total cost has declined to $82.67 as capital costs are spread over 15 widgets per hour.

Producing the sixteenth widget means that enough labor must be hired to use the machinery for process A. From the sixteenth through the thirty-fifth widget, marginal cost jumps to $64 per widget, while average variable cost continues to climb. Average total cost approaches marginal cost from above. When 35 widgets are being produced per hour, the plant is operating at peak capacity. Until additional capital services can be procured, the cost of producing the thirty-sixth widget per hour is, quite literally, infinite.

Figure 7-7 depicts the step pattern for marginal cost when short-run production involves increasingly labor-intensive processes. Instead of rising smoothly, as in the smooth isoquant model of production, marginal

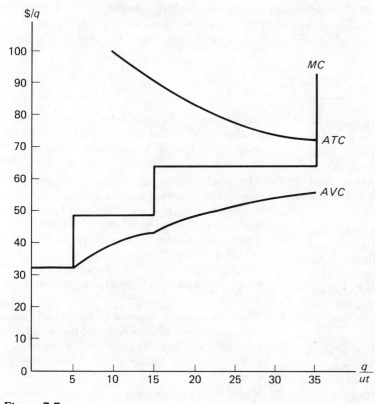

Figure 7-7
Short-Run Average and Marginal Costs with Three Production Processes

cost rises to a new level when the production process used for the last widget changes. Average variable cost equals marginal cost for those rates of output which involve the most capital-intensive technology. After marginal cost has risen to its second plateau (the switch from process B to process C), average variable cost begins to creep upward as output increases. Average total cost, in this case, falls as output rises, until capacity output is reached.

While the example in Table 7-4 and Figure 7-7 is plausible for firms with mixed technologies (i.e., firms not operating exclusively with the economically efficient process), the short-run choice among production processes is more likely to involve a plant which uses some fixed inputs (e.g., machinery, storage space, management personnel) to produce a variety of products. When an input service with a maximum availability constraint is used to produce more than one commodity, opportunity cost, rather than fixed accounting costs, are the relevant consideration in allocating inputs. If an input is being used to capacity, the output of one commodity might be increased by reducing the rate of output of some other commodity which also requires that input. When producing more of one good means sacrificing a number of other commodities, that good will have a steplike marginal cost curve, with each step corresponding to the sacrifice of an increased opportunity cost for the bottleneck input(s).

HIGHLIGHTS

1. By dropping the assumption that inputs can be substituted continuously, we view input use as a production process requiring a fixed proportion of variable input services. Only when one input is redundant can another input have a positive marginal product, equal to the reciprocal of its input coefficient.

2. Assuming constant returns to scale means that a production process is described by a ray emanating from the origin, with an efficient input ratio equal to the ratio of input coefficients. When there is only one technically efficient process for producing a commodity, the production (or process) ray is the ridge line for both labor and capital.

3. If two processes are technically efficient, each uses less of one input per unit of output, relative to the other. If there are two technically efficient processes, the isoquant map is obtained by connecting points representing the same rate of output on the two production rays with straight lines. The resulting linear iso-

quants are characterized by a constant marginal rate of technical substitution between ridge lines, that is, between the two production rays.

4. When there are three technically efficient processes, the isoquant map is pulled in toward the origin along that ray with the intermediate input ratio. The marginal rate of technical substitution equals the slope of the linear segment between adjacent process rays, meaning that marginal rate of technical substitution declines in absolute value at the intermediate process.

5. When there are a number of technically efficient processes to choose from, the economically efficient process is located at the corner of the isoquant touching the lowest isocost line.

6. When short-run production involves only one production process, variable cost is a linear function of output. As long as all inputs used in the process are variable and factor prices

are invariant with respect to input use, the marginal cost and the average variable cost will correspond to a horizontal line, whose height equals the sum of the costs of all inputs required for one unit of output.

7. When machinery for different processes is available, with machinery representing maximum availability constraints for each process,

with capital costs fixed, short-run costs are minimized by minimizing the cost of variable inputs (e.g., labor, raw materials). Each time a more labor-intensive production process is brought into use (because less labor-intensive processes are being used to capacity), marginal cost rises in a steplike fashion, while average variable cost rises gradually as output increases.

GLOSSARY

Binding constraint on output   See **production bottleneck.**

Corner solution   Any diagramatic solution to an optimization problem, such as output maximization or input minimization variants of the economic efficiency problem, in which the solution does not occur at a point of tangency.

Input coefficient   The amount of an input service required to produce one unit of output efficiently. When an input is a production bottleneck, its marginal product is equal to the reciprocal of its input coefficient.

Linear isoquant   An isoquant defined by connecting points on adjacent production rays which represent the same rate of output. When there are only two technically efficient processes, the two production rays are ridge lines, and the marginal rate of technical substitution is constant between ridge lines. When there are three or more technically efficient processes, isoquants are made up of line segments, with the marginal rate of technical substitution declining (in absolute value) as input substitution involves progressively labor-intensive processes.

Linear programming   Computer techniques which solve business resource allocation problems by depicting production as a process involving fixed input proportions.

Process ray   The diagram of technically efficient input combinations for a single production process. The equation of the process ray is

given by the ratio of input coefficients. Also called the **production ray.**

Production bottleneck   A limiting factor of production: the rate of output cannot be increased unless more of this input's services are procured. The marginal product of a production bottleneck input is the reciprocal of its input coefficient: $MP_i = 1/\alpha_i$. Also called the **binding constant on output.**

Production process   An input-output relationship wherein output per unit of time is determined by that input with the smallest ratio to its input coefficient: $q = \min(v_1/\alpha_1, v_2/\alpha_2, \ldots, v_m/\alpha_m)$. For two inputs (e.g., labor [L] and capital [K]), the production process has the form: $q = \min(L/\alpha, K/\beta)$, where α and β are the input coefficients for labor and capital, respectively.

Production ray   See **process ray.**

Redundant input   An input whose available services exceed the amount that can be used efficiently. The marginal product of a redundant input is zero.

Unit cost   The cost of producing one unit of output with a simple production process, since average variable cost equals marginal cost up to capacity of fixed inputs. Use of the term *unit cost* can cause confusion when more than one production process is available, because once output expands through a second process, marginal cost and average variable cost will no longer be equal.

SUGGESTED READINGS

Baumol, William J. *Economic Theory and Operations Analysis*. 4th ed. Englewood Cliffs, New Jersey: Prentice-Hall, 1977, chapters 5, 6, and 12.

———. "Activity Analysis in One Lesson." *American Economic Review* (December 1958), pp. 837–873.

Dorfman, Robert. "Mathematical or 'Linear' Pro-

gramming: A Non-Mathematical Exposition."
American Economic Review (December 1953),
pp. 797–825. Reprinted in William Breit and
Harold Hochman, eds. *Readings in Micro-
economic Theory*. 2nd ed. New York: Holt,
Rinehart and Winston, 1971, pp. 172–193.
———, Paul A. Samuelson, and Robert Solow. *Lin-
ear Programming and Economic Analysis*.
New York: McGraw-Hill, 1958.
Heineke, John M. *Microeconomics for Business*

Decisions: Theory and Application. Engle-
wood Cliffs, New Jersey: Prentice-Hall, 1976,
pp. 90–105, 119–127.
Naylor, Thomas H. "The Theory of the Firm: A
Comparison of Marginal Analysis and Linear
Programming." *Southern Economic Journal*
(January 1966), pp. 263–274. Reprinted in
Richard E. Neel, ed. *Readings in Price The-
ory*. Cincinnati: South-West, 1973, pp. 208–222.

EXERCISES

Evaluate

Indicate whether each of the following statements
is true (agrees with economic theory), false (is contradicted by theory), or uncertain (could be true
or false, given additional information). Explain
your answer.

1. When two factor services have the same
   price, the economically efficient production
   process will use those inputs in equal
   proportions.
2. Linear isoquants, which are characterized by
   constant marginal products for both inputs,
   imply that output could be produced even if
   one of the input's services were zero.
3. If two products share the same inputs, the
   cost of producing more of one good is the
   price of the other good.
4. To be technically efficient, a new process
   must use fewer services of all inputs, relative
   to other processes.
5. If the marginal rate of technical substitution
   between two processes on a linear isoquant
   equaled the slope of the isocost line, either
   process would be economically efficient.
6. If a process is technically efficient, it is also
   economically efficient.
7. Calculating the marginal rate of technical
   substitution between production processes
   is really a planning exercise, rather than the
   physical substitution of homogeneous machinery for homogeneous labor.
8. A firm has purchased 100 units of capital services under contract and requires a minimum
   of 5 units of capital and 10 units of labor for

each unit of output. The marginal product of
labor, the variable input, is 0.20.
9. A firm produces a unit of output with 5 units
   of capital and 10 units of labor. Capital is
   hired under contract, but labor is hired in a
   monopsony market, where the employer can
   hire equally productive workers at different
   wage rates. Both marginal cost and average
   variable cost will be increasing functions of
   output.
10. A new process replaces combinations of two
    existing processes. Therefore, the two earlier
    processes must not have been technically
    efficient.

Calculate

Answer each of the following questions, showing
your calculations.

11. Given: widgets can be produced with any
    of the following three processes: X: $q =
    \min(L/0.25, K/0.5)$; Y: $q = \min(L/0.5, K/0.25)$;
    Z: $q = \min(L, K/0.1)$.
    a. Determine the technically efficient com-
       binations of labor (L) and capital (K) for
       producing $q = 20$ in each process.
    b. Determine the marginal rate of technical
       substitution of capital for labor between
       process X and process Y, and between
       process Y and process Z.
    c. Determine the economically efficient
       process for each of the following factor-
       price ratios of labor services (w_L) and
       capital services (w_K): (i) $w_L/w_K = 2.0$,
       (ii) $w_L/w_K = 0.5$, (iii) $w_L/w_K = 0.25$.

12. Using the three production processes in question 11, suppose that the firm has a binding contract for 10 machine-hours per day (at a rental rate of w_K = $25 per machine-hour), although the firm is free to determine the mix of machinery for process X, process Y, and/or process Z. Assume that workers are equally proficient in the three processes and that labor can be hired at an invariant wage rate of $10 per hour.

   a. What is the firm's daily fixed cost?

   b. What is the cheapest method for producing 20 units of output per day, given that the firm must pay for at least 10 machine-hours per day?

   c. What is the minimum marginal cost for the 21st unit, given the minimum outlay of $250 per day for capital?

   d. What is the marginal cost of the 41st unit of output, given the minimum purchase contract?

13. Continuing with these three production processes, we now assume that the firm is free to hire as much or as little capital as it wants at a constant rental rate of $25 per machine-hour. However, the amount of labor that can be hired varies according to the wage rate paid, as given by the following schedule:

Wage Offer	Maximum Labor Hours Offered
$5.00	5
7.50	10
10.00	15
12.50	20
15.00	25
17.50	30
20.00	35
22.50	40
25.00	45
27.50	50
30.00	55
32.50	60
35.00	65
37.50	70

   a. How much will it cost the firm to produce 5 units of output per day?

   b. If the firm can pay different workers different wage rates (this is called *wage discrimination* and will be discussed in chapter fourteen), how much will it cost the firm to produce 50 units of output per day?

   c. If all workers must be paid the same wage, what will be the cost of producing 50 units of output?

Contemplate

14. Adam Malthus, an economics student, has been advised to supplement his diet with 1,000 units of iron and 800 units of vitamin E each day. The Friendly Drug Store stocks four brands of vitamins; each brand comes in a bottle of 100 tablets and sells for $1 per bottle. Combinations of iron and vitamin E are:

Brand	Iron (units/tablet)	Vitamin E (units/tablet)
A	40	5
B	20	10
C	10	20
D	5	25

   a. Diagram combinations of iron and vitamin E which can be purchased for $5 and for $10 (assume tablets can be purchased at $0.01 each).

   b. What combination of brands will provide Malthus with a 20-day supply of iron and vitamin E at minimum cost?

15. It has been suggested that the smooth isoquants encountered in chapters five and six could be treated as an infinite number of technically efficient processes. How are the following characteristics of smooth isoquants implied by linear technology?

   a. Isoquants do not intersect with each other or with either axis.

   b. Isoquants have a negative slope.

   c. Isoquants are bowed-in toward the origin.

PART FOUR
Theories of Firms and Markets

Part four brings together the theory of consumer choice, which culminates in market demand, and the theory of producer input choice and production costs, which generates market supply, to explain and predict the behavior of output markets. Chapter eight provides a general overview of the firm and the market. Markets require private property rights to operate, but markets themselves are meant to function as a commons, an arrangement which individual participants are free to enter and leave without worrying how other participants are affected. Firms are shown to emerge from attempts to reduce transaction costs by eliminating those which would be incurred if all stages of production involved buying semifinished goods and producing a small amount of value added. Next comes an outline of market types—perfect competition, pure monopoly, monopolistic competition, and oligopoly—which emerge because of the ambiguity between property rights and market openness. The chapter concludes by discussing profit maximization and the goals of managers of firms.

Chapter nine presents the theory of perfect competition, beginning with the profit-maximizing decision of the individual price taker, which leads to a well defined supply curve. The aggregation of individual supply curves, facilitated by the characteristics of a competitive market, generates the market supply curve. We see how market equilibrium price and quantity emerge from the counteracting influences of supply and demand. As additional firms enter an expanding industry and established firms leave a declining industry, consumers reap the ultimate benefit of perfect competition: by pushing price to its lowest sustainable level, perfect competition maximizes consumer surplus in the long run. The chapter concludes with a discussion of long-run supply curves for perfect competitive industries.

The appendix to chapter nine extends the competitive model to emphasize the relevance of the theory of perfect competition to the estimation of supply and demand by business economists. The distinction between shifts in supply or demand curves and movements along those curves is reiterated in the context of the identification problem.

Chapter ten is concerned with the nature of monopoly, both single sellers and cartels. It also develops concepts that will be used in later chapters. How control over price leads to a distinction between price and marginal revenue is discussed in several contexts. We see how revenue maximization corresponds to profit maximization only in the special case of a monopolist with only fixed costs (e.g., a movie theater). The conventional monopoly, with positive marginal cost, is then developed in detail. An extended discussion of natural monopoly reveals that privately owned, publicly owned, and government-regulated monopolies might behave similarly, setting the price at the monopoly level if maximizing profit were treated as the efficient outcome, or setting the price at the normal profit level if break-even analysis were the basis of monopoly pricing. The remainder of the chapter discusses the nature of cartels, collusive monopolies composed of multiple entities, and the reasons behind the instability of price-fixing arrangements.

Chapter eleven investigates monopolistic, or differentiated, competition. While attempting to remain faithful to the spirit of the monopolistic competition theories that emerged from the 1930s, the chapter presents differentiated competition in a way that incorporates both refinements and criticisms of those earlier models. The nature of product differentiation is developed by revising the model of consumer choice by assuming that goods are ranked in terms of their characteristics. This approach allows each seller's demand function to be stated in terms of the commodity's own price, the price of substitute and complementary goods, consumer perceptions of the characteristics of the good, information about the characteristics of competitive products, consumer income, and tastes. In this manner, the economic impact of advertising can be explored. The pursuit of monopoly profits

in the short run is shown to be equivalent to the use of an elasticity-based markup pricing policy. Finally, the impact of new sellers of imperfect substitutes—and the role of trademarks, patents, and brand names in preventing perfect substitutes—is explored in the context of long-run equilibrium. Included in the final section is a balanced discussion of the allocational efficiency of product differentiation.

Chapter twelve presents some of the many models of oligopoly, beginning with classic models of Cournot and Stackelberg which emerge from the attempt to predict a stable equilibrium for a market with a few sellers. Next comes the price rigidity prediction of the kinked demand curve model, which is examined in the context of empirical evidence. The modern models of passive price-leadership and potential-entry pricing models of oligopoly downplay the role of rivalry. Another approach focuses on the incentive for sellers in an oligopolistic industry to collude, although individual oligopolists have an incentive to cheat on price-fixing arrangements. Oligopolistic pricing is shown as a risky decision whereby each seller compares its expected profits if it accepts the cartel price with the expected gains of cheating on the agreement. The economic impact of antitrust law, which prohibits cartel contracts but often permits subtler forms of collusion, is also discussed. The third approach to oligopoly, associated with the work of John Kenneth Galbraith, William Baumol, Herbert Simon, and others, involves an implicit or explicit denial that decision makers for oligopolistic firms attempt to maximize profits. A discussion of whether the oligopoly pricing problem is solved by positing goals of sales maximization, growth maximization, or the pursuit of sub-maximum satisficing outcomes concludes the chapter and part four.

Chapter 8

The Firm and the Marketplace

After so many chapters about inputs, outputs, and costs, it is time to pause for a moment to reestablish our bearings. Often the study of microeconomics gives rise to a dilemma: should the students be given a lay of the land—an overview of topics to be covered so that their way is illuminated, if not enlightened—or should they plod along, mastering each concept before the next is introduced? We have chosen the former path, counting on the students' interest in the subject and familiarity with a few words and ideas to sustain them through a broad description of the economics of the firm before we immerse ourselves in important, but sometimes myopic, detail.

In this chapter we consider some general and paradoxical characteristics of property rights, competitive markets, and firms. We begin by showing how property rights create economic incentives consistent with production and exchange. We also explore why the efficient exchange of property rights requires a competitive market, whose ideal form is a commons. The institutions of property rights and competitive markets are discussed as necessary complements, but also potential rivals. By appreciating how market failure (monopoly) often occurs as an attempt to prevent property failure (external benefits and costs), some of the paradoxical contrasts between perfect competition and monopoly encountered in subsequent chapters will be more easily understood.

The firm itself evolved as a means of reducing the costs of transacting business. By operating a production facility under a command system, the seller can avoid the costly renegotiation of contracts each time changes in input combinations or output characteristics are required.

After a discussion of the nature of economic profit and the role of profit maximization as a motivator of seller behavior, the chapter concludes with a survey of alternative goals of the business firm, particularly the large corporation.

Property Rights

Before an economic system can develop markets, competitive or otherwise, a system of property rights must exist. **Property rights** represent the legal right to exclude others from the use of inputs or commodities. The opposite of a private property system is a **commons**, a system in which no one owns scarce resources. In the nineteenth-century American West, both cattle ranchers and sheepherders defended, often to the death, their right to graze their livestock on the open range. It was a right without responsibility. Lacking incentives to preserve rangeland for next season's livestock, the ranchers and herders let their animals eat plants to the roots. In other words, they acted selfishly because there was no tangible reward for behaving altruistically. Cattle and sheep were private property; owners received the difference in value between a fat animal and a skinny one. Costs seemed to be minimized by consuming the "free" fodder of the open range. Yet scarcity cannot be avoided; the cost of overgrazing was shared by all users of rangeland.

The real "tragedy of the commons," according to Garret Hardin, is that communal rights to scarce resources generate perverse incentives.[1] A commons allows individuals to waste scarce resources without experiencing the full cost of that waste. While society will try to instill a social conscience in individual members, community disapproval is rarely an effective deterrent to selfish action. The livestock owner who allows the herd to overgraze will be confronted with the rhetorical question: "What if everyone behaved like you?" The retort, "Then I would be pretty foolish to behave any other way," will gain the livestock owner the grudging admiration of fellow realists. By contrast, the altruist who sacrifices personal welfare for that of the group may be publicly praised but is often privately scorned for being naive.

According to one version of the genesis of private property, a number of self-interested but reasonable individuals agree that the perpetuation of communal access to scarce resources works to everyone's detriment.[2]

---

[1] Garret Hardin, "The Tragedy of the Commons," *Science* (December 1968), pp. 1243–1248.

[2] Harold Demsetz, "Toward a Theory of Property Rights"; Svetozar Pejovich, "Toward an Economic Theory of the Creation and Specification of Property Rights"; and W. C. Stubbelbine, "On Property Rights and Institutions"; reprinted in Henry Manne, ed., *The Economics of Legal Relationships: Readings in the Theory of Property Rights* (St. Paul: West Publishing Company, 1975).

They unanimously agree to divide the community's resources equitably. Each person is permitted by the others to keep his or her own output and to arrange a mutually advantageous exchange of property rights with anyone else. *The essence of private property is the right to exclude:* each owner can control who uses his or her property. The right to exclude is the foundation of an ability to exchange. Only if you must obtain my permission to use my property (because society will punish you if you take it without my permission) will you be willing to give me something in exchange if I transfer my property right to you. That different people have different tastes and that the value of additional consumption falls with the rate of consumption means that voluntary exchange hurts neither party as long as each is adequately informed.

Another fable from economic mythology is equally plausible and illustrates the superior incentives of property rights over the commons. Members of a band of marauders, operating under the "might makes right" principle of social interaction, eventually discover the flaw of an economic system based on loot and pillage. As long as it seems easier to take what someone else has produced than it is to produce for oneself, the strong will specialize in plunder. The weak, unless they are incredibly stupid, will eventually realize that anything they produce will be taken by someone stronger and that they will lead a hand-to-mouth existence, gathering food that can be immediately consumed. Before long, with the gatherers eating what they produce, the looters will have nothing to plunder.

Imagine a warlord, climbing down from his emaciated horse, calling together his hungry (and wary) troops and the even hungrier (and warier) peasants. "It is the dawning of a new age!" he proclaims. "No longer will a person's property be seized by those stronger than he! From this day forward, a man may keep what he produces with his own property, and everyone, no matter how rich or how strong, must pay to use someone else's property. We will call this system 'free enterprise!'"

The peasants all cheer: "What a wonderful idea! No more starvation! Oh wise lord, return to us our property that we may get back to planting!"

"What do you mean, *your* property?" asks the warlord, with an innocent shrug. "I stole that farmland fair and square under the loot-and-pillage system. We will start the free enterprise system where the old left off. Only now, I will not steal your crops. From now on, we will call it rent."

Not surprisingly, proponents of free enterprise use the first fable to extoll the efficiency gains of private property over the commons, while critics of capitalism cite the unfairness of initial entitlements to challenge the equity of a system which bases a person's share of output on property ownership rather than need or merit. But the efficiency gains of a private-property system do not imply, nor do they depend on, an equitable distribution of property rights. The incentives for efficient resource use created by a system of private property can exist even when the distribution of property is grossly unfair.

The Market as a Commons[3]

There is a paradox latent in the system of *private enterprise* (a less emotional term than *free enterprise*). Although property rights are an essential precondition for the existence of a market, there are many contexts in which property rights and market efficiency are trade-offs. If the essence of property rights is the ability to exclude, the chief characteristic of an ideal market is that no one can be excluded. To operate efficiently, markets must be accessible to all. While it is necessary to eliminate the commons before a market can exist, the essential nature of a market is that of a commons.

With private property but without markets, individuals or households can consume only what they produce. With private property and markets, gains from specialization are possible; what is lost by no longer being self-sufficient is more than offset by the gains from specialization and trade. Markets extend the ability to exclude to the ability to exchange. When exchange is voluntary and traders have many options (because of competition), all parties to a trade are assured of being better off, in their own estimation, after trade than before. Through the interaction of supply and demand, a competitive market assigns an exchange value (i.e., price) to objects traded. Knowledge of this set of prices enables owners of resources to allocate property to its most efficient uses.

While the market establishes value, competition does not guarantee value. The value an object can command in exchange is vulnerable to changes in supply or demand. When the price of a commodity falls, specialized resources used to produce that commodity also decline in value. Another assault on the value of property is the **external effect** of one person's use of property impinging upon the integrity of another's property rights. Two types of **externalities** can occur. **External costs** occur when the owner of property (e.g., a steel foundry) does not bear personal or financial responsibility for the costs he imposes on others (lung diseases caused by air pollution). **External benefits** occur when a property owner (e.g., the owner of a steel foundry) is not able to charge others for the benefits of his property use; consumers of steel would not pay higher prices for steel produced by more expensive techniques designed to prevent air pollution.

External benefits and external costs both constitute **property fail-**

---

[3] This section is based largely on Thomas M. Carroll, David H. Ciscel, and Roger K. Chisholm, "The Market as a Commons: An Unconventional View of Property Rights," *Journal of Economic Issues*, 13 (June 1979), 605–627.

ure—either the benefits or the costs of the use of scarce resources are experienced by *third parties* who are neither buyers nor sellers in the exchange. Sometimes property failure results from the intangible nature of inputs or outputs themselves. Potential users of a valuable idea cannot be prevented from poaching as easily as trespassers can be removed from land with clearly marked boundaries. Trespassers can be evicted; violators of a copyright or patent are not given lobotomies in order to wrest a stolen idea from their possession. Yet if rights to ideas are not protected, might not a commons approach to research reduce the incentive for creative thinking?

It is in the attempt to protect the value of property that the conflict between property and markets emerges. If liability is clearly assigned, and costs of reaching an agreement—transaction costs—are sufficiently small, private negotiations may be able to eliminate an external cost without further public intervention.[4] When transaction costs are high, usually because there are too many interested parties or because private agreements are costly to enforce, government intervention beyond assigning liability may be required to achieve efficient resource allocation. Whether real-world governments—with all their imperfections—are able to improve the performance of real-world markets—with all their imperfections—is much more difficult to determine than it is to show that an ideal market could function without government meddling or that an ideal government could compensate for the flaws in an imperfect market.

Competitive markets function efficiently because new entrants increase output, forcing established firms to cut their price and their margin of profit. Since the price-reducing consequence of market entry is shared by all sellers, new firms take no account of how their entry reduces the revenue and raises the cost for other firms. Adam Smith's **invisible hand** is really an external effect; so many sellers enter an ideal market that transaction costs prevent conspiracies in restraint of trade, and the anonymity of individual sellers makes cheating on price-fixing agreements an irresistible temptation.

The paradox rests at the very heart of the institutions of private enterprise. Efficiency requires that all scarce resources be allocated by buyers and sellers possessing complete property rights. Yet the market, which depends upon the entry of new firms to force exchange rates to reflect relative opportunity cost, must remain always a commons: no one can have the right, *de jure* or *de facto*, to exclude other buyers or sellers from a market. The dividing line between inefficient externalities generated by incomplete property rights and the efficiency generating external effects of a competitive market is blurred indeed. It is precisely

---

[4] This is the "Coase theorem," attributed to Ronald Coase, "The Problem of Social Cost," *Journal of Law and Economics* (October 1960), pp. 1–44.

this haziness about where property rights must be sacrificed to assure market efficiency which gives rise to many causes of and sanctions for monopoly power.

The argument for **patents**, the exclusive right to sell a commodity produced with a particular technology, or having a particular set of characteristics, is based on the inability of an inventor to prevent others from "stealing" an idea. But patents do not make an idea secret; indeed, to receive a patent, the petitioner must publish the idea behind a process or product. Otherwise, innocent use by others could not be deterred. Information and knowledge are not scarce in the usual sense that use by one denies use by others; any number of people may know of an idea without limiting the number who may also learn it. Yet knowledge, like other commodities, does derive its value from its relative scarcity. Instead of giving innovators the right to an idea, a patent constitutes ownership of the market in which the idea is used. Prices of commodities sold under **monopoly**—which constitutes market failure—will be kept artificially high by the ability of the patent holder to exclude competitors or to charge other sellers monopoly royalties for the right to sell the product in question. (The arguments for and against patent monopolies are explored in greater detail in chapter fifteen.)

The behavior of firms depends on how closely the markets in which they buy and sell approximate the competitive ideal. Under **perfect competition**, individual sellers have virtually no control over their environment. The product they sell is homogeneous (standardized or fungible) and therefore market forces generate a unique, market-wide price. New firms are free to enter the market and older firms are often forced to liquidate. The number of sellers is so large that agreements designed to coordinate output prices or input costs cannot be enforced.

The most unrealistic assumption of the competitive model is the assumption of **product homogeneity**. Consumers desire variety in their clothing, food, entertainment, and appliances. Producers respond to consumer willingness to pay higher prices for brand-name products by supplying commodities with a variety of characteristics and a corresponding variety of prices. Relaxing the assumption of product homogeneity means that each firm confronts its own demand schedule, from which the profit-maximizing price-quantity combination is chosen.

Product differentiation creates another conflict between property rights and market efficiency. If a producer is providing a commodity with a set of desirable characteristics, consumers eventually associate those characteristics with the producer's brand name or trademark. Imitators would enter a competitive market and provide the product at a price approximating the minimum production cost, putting downward pressure on the innovator's price. But what is to stop imitators from merely copying the established trademark while substituting an inferior product? To protect the reputation of the product innovator and to save consumers the trouble and expense of sorting out fraudulent imitations, the government grants exclusive rights to use brand names, trademarks, and even combinations of product characteristics. In extending the property rights of the producers of differentiated products, society grants some degree of monopoly power over narrowly defined markets in which the products are sold.

If monopoly power over product characteristics is narrowly limited, many sellers of *close substitutes* can exist; perfect competition will be supplanted by **monopolistic competition**. Under monopolistic competition, each seller has an influence over his or her own price, but each firm faces a highly elastic demand curve. Nearly free entry of imitators tends to eliminate excess (economic) profit, just as free entry under perfect competition does.

When the optimal scale of operation is so large that only a few firms can coexist in a market at a particular time or place, **oligopoly**, or *rivalry among the few*, exists. Firms in an oligopolistic industry lack the individual anonymity of perfect or even monopolistic competition. Any firm's price or output change can send a clearly traceable ripple throughout the industry. The oligopolistic market structure has confounded theoretical and empirical economists with the most perplexing analytical problems. Oligopolies, which recognize their interdependence, have a strong incentive to coordinate their output and pricing decisions. But collusive arrangements are not only illegal (in theory), but tend to be unstable in light of each producer's incentive to break such agreements. In the name of obtaining an orderly market, oligopolies sometimes succeed in promoting government regulation as a means of enforcing pricing or output restrictions which would be illegal (and quite difficult to police) if they were of wholly private origin.

The culmination of property rights occurs with **monopoly**—a polar case of market organization probably as rare as perfect competition. A monopoly, by virtue of either natural or (more likely) legal barriers to market entry, enjoys protection from would-be rivals. Basically, there are two types of monopoly markets which will concern us: single-firm industries, wherein the single seller can ignore retaliation by rivals to any price change, since rivals in the true sense do not exist, and **cartels**, or multifirm, collusive monopolies, whose major concern is to prevent short-sighted greed by individual sellers from breaking a pricing agreement and restoring, quite inadvertently the forces of market competition.

Transaction Costs and the Firm

As effective as they are for coordinating the voluntary activities of consumers, producers, and resource suppliers, markets are never costless and are often time-consuming. **Transaction costs** occur whenever a buyer and a seller negotiate an exchange. When transaction costs begin to hamper production, alternative coordinating mechanisms will be investigated. Business firms often economize on transaction costs relative to markets, since a system of command may allow for more rapid adjustment of production to changes in market conditions, another irony.

Consider Adam Smith's famous example of the manufacture of pins through the specialization of labor:

> The greatest improvement in the productive powers of labor, and the greatest part of the skill, dexterity, and judgement with which it is any where directed, or applied, seem to have been the effects of the division of labor. . . .
>
> To take an example. . . . One man draws out the wire, another straights it, a third cuts it, a fourth points it, a fifth grinds it at the top for receiving a head; to make the head requires two or three distinct operations; to put it on, is a peculiar business, to whiten the pins is another; it is even a trade by itself to put them into the paper; and the important business of making a pin is, in this manner, divided into about eighteen distinct operations, which, in some manufactories, are all performed by distinct hands, though in others the same man will sometimes perform two or three of them. . . . Each person, therefore, making a tenth part of forty-eight thousand pins, might be considered as making four thousand eight hundred pins in a day. But if they had all wrought separately and independently, and without any of them having been educated to this particular business, they certainly could not each of them have made twenty, perhaps not even one pin in a day; that is certainly, not the two hundred and fortieth, perhaps not the four thousand eight hundredth part of what they are at present capable of performing, in consequence of a proper division and combination of their different operations.[5]

The unspoken assumption in Smith's description of the gains from specialization (division) of labor is that the activity of those 10 to 18 workers must be coordinated by an entrepreneur or supervisor. If each worker plied his or her specialized trade as an independent buyer and seller of semifinished pins, coordination problems would soon swamp the efficiency gains from specialization. For example, suppose that one worker takes part of his savings to invest in a spool of wire, which he draws and cuts into strands to sell to a second worker. The second worker, who purchases those strands, sharpens one end of each, and sells the sharpened wire pieces to a third worker, who flattens the other end to receive a head. When the fourth worker has purchased the prepared wire from the third, as well as pinheads from a fifth worker (who pur-

---

[5] Adam Smith, *An Inquiry into the Nature and Causes of the Wealth of Nations* (New York: Random House, Modern Library edition, 1937), pp. 3–5.

chased semifinished heads from still other workers), the painful discovery is made that the heads are the wrong size for the wire pieces. What might have become 12 pounds of pins in a pin factory amounts to 12 pounds of junk because communication was limited to buying and selling minute stages of a simple commodity.

Eventually one or more of the pin-makers will see the benefits of coordinating the various stages of pin manufacturing; production may begin as a putting-out system with an entrepreneur collecting semifinished pins, or workers may organize themselves into a cooperative enterprise. We imagine the latter. Removing the stages of pin manufacture from the market bestows disruptive power on each worker. Before the cooperative was formed, each independent worker-producer was deterred from demanding a higher price by the forces of market competition. Any supplier holding out for a larger share of the value of the final product would be undersold by other suppliers of the same semifinished pins.

Inside a cooperative, specialists are insulated from the market; the advantage of lower transaction costs could be eliminated if individuals threatened to discontinue their work to extort a larger share of co-op revenue. Members of the cooperative could purge disruptive colleagues, offering membership to other suppliers; but the cooperative arrangement was created to avoid the need to seek out suppliers continually in the market. Each worker could learn the jobs of his or her fellows, but such protection from extortion would require a wasteful redundancy of skills, canceling many of the gains from specialization. And as long as a worker's share of the final product was independent of his or her contribution to output, the group would subsidize the leisure of individuals. In the extreme, output could fall to zero as the tragedy of the commons was visited upon the workplace.

If production is to run smoothly, the tension between private incentives and group outcomes must be relaxed. It is the duty of the production supervisor to subordinate the behavior of individuals to the goals of the group. Workers might designate one of their own to supervise production, or hire a professional plant supervisor, as is done under a system of *workers' management*.[6] The supervisor would assure that workers performed their assigned tasks and would have the authority to punish shirkers or extortionists. Since the plant supervisor is removed from direct production, his or her remuneration would be based on the extra output achieved by careful supervision. Revenue remaining after each worker had been paid his or her promised wage (including the supervisor's opportunity wage as a worker) would belong, at least in

---

[6] See Benjamin Ward, *The Socialist Economy: A Study of Organizational Alternatives* (New York: Random House, 1967).

part, to the production supervisor. As **residual claimant**, the supervisor would bear the risk of revenue falling short of promised rewards, but would also have first claim on revenue in excess of cost.

This idyllic version of the genesis of the business firm is sharply contrasted by the Marxian version of the rise of the capitalist system. The enclosure of the commons dispossesses the peasantry, who must turn to factory work. Propertyless, the workers have no recourse but to sell their labor services to the owner of the nonlabor factors of production, the capitalist. The workers give up time and effort in exchange for a wage income that is somewhat better than they could have expected as landless peasants. The difference between the value of what workers produce—under the supervision and with the tools of the capitalist—and what they are paid belongs to the capitalist. Since this surplus is received in the form of profit, the owner of the firm tries to maximize the difference in the value of what workers produce and the wages they are paid.

Despite the opposing sentiments behind these two scenarios, their implications are consistent. The internal organization of the business firm is based on command. A person's decision to work for one employer rather than another is likely to be a voluntary one, albeit under duress of imminent starvation. But the worker's activities on the job will be dictated by the employer. The worker is always free to leave one job and find another, but job search is not a costless process, and the threat of employment termination is a mightly stick to balance the carrot of wage payments. A similar loss of freedom befalls any resource supplier. A landowner who leases his or her land loses power to determine how that land is used (outside limitations written into the lease). A firm's stockholders have a legal claim on the firm's profits, but their ownership rights do not extend to the right to exclude managers from the firm's premises or to interfere with the day-to-day operation of a production facility.

The entrepreneur plays the protagonist's role in the neoclassical drama of the firm. One person originates or finances the development of an idea for a product, risks personal fortune and credit to purchase or lease capital equipment, signs leases, and hires workers, all to make that idea a reality. While the entrepreneur's authority within the firm is un-questioned, the use of that authority is tempered by the single-minded pursuit of economic profit. Outside the firm, the entrepreneur is pow-erless against the forces of competition. The costs of production are dictated by the possibilities of universally known and extensively used technologies and by input prices set in unassailable factor markets. The price of the final product is also set by competitive forces beyond the entrepreneur's control. The only discretion the competitive entrepre-neur has is picking the rate of output; those who produce too much or too little, or whose costs are too high, are ruthlessly eliminated by the invisible hand. The inefficient never know what hits them.

APPLICATION
The Ironic Role of Economic Profit

There is a provocative bumper sticker which proclaims: "Guns don't kill people; people kill people." Perhaps. An economist might paraphrase this slogan: "Firms don't make profit; people make profit." Again, perhaps. Just as guns are instruments people use to kill people, firms are instruments people use to make profits. But despite the disagreement over whether guns should be controlled, there are few who believe that killing should be encouraged. In economics and in society at large, there is considerable disagreement about whether firms should be controlled and about whether profit itself is a good thing.

Most economists subscribe to the philosophy espoused by Adam Smith's invisible hand parable. "By preferring the support of domestic to that of foreign industry, [the individual] intends only his own security; and by directing that industry in such a manner as its produce may be of the greatest value, he intends only his own gain, and he is in this, as in many other cases, led by an invisible hand to promote an end which was no part of his intention."[7] It is not profit which is good; the good is the social welfare which the pursuer of profit inadvertently promotes. An ideal market uses the *profit motive* to eliminate the reality of **economic profit**, total revenue minus opportunity cost. It is the consumer, not the producer, who ends up with the surplus. An ideal market—a perfectly competitive market—uses the promise of economic profit to titillate, to motivate, and ultimately, to frustrate, the seller.

And the moral of Smith's fable does not end with the magical transformation of selfish motives into socially beneficial actions. Do not trust those who claim to promote the social good, says Smith. "By pursuing his own interest [the merchant] frequently promotes that of the society more effectively than when he really intends to promote it. I have never known much good done by those who affected to trade for the public good. It is an affectation, indeed, not very common among merchants, and very few words need be employed in dissuading them from it."[8]

The relevance of the profit maximization assumption to the behavior of the proprietor of a small firm is not particularly controversial among economists. The small-scale firm of today operates under market pressures which approximate the forceful influence of the invisible hand. As a motivation, the maximization of profit by the owner-manager of a competitive firm means that any profit would belong to the decision maker who caused it. Since the only decision the proprietor makes is what rate of output to produce, and since producing too much or too little means disaster, the profit maximization assumption amounts to assuming that the owner of a small firm will attempt to survive in the market.

---

[7] Smith, *The Wealth of Nations*, p. 423.
[8] Ibid.

Policy Illustration
The Inefficiency of Nonprofit Institutions

One of the tenets of *The Wealth of Nations* is that the market guides resources to their most productive use *through* the profit motive, while prices hover about their lowest sustainable levels *despite* the profit motive. When markets cease to be competitive, maximizing profit means monopoly prices: consumers pay tribute to producers in excess of the costs of production.

An alternative mode of resource allocation that is receiving increased attention from economists is the "not-for-profit" institution. Churches, universities, hospitals, and museums are (at least on paper) constituted to provide services (salvation, education, health, or esthetics) at cost. Their legal tax exemptions require that their revenue be exactly equal to expenditures. Perhaps economists are overly cynical, but few accept unmitigated altruism as the sole explanation for the behavior of nonprofit institutions.

One fruitful approach is to view not-for-profit producers as professional syndicates, whose members wish to maximize the sum of income and amenities. This sometimes leads to tensions between the "professionals" and "staff" of such institutions. Well-heeled doctors exploit underpaid and overworked nurses; tenured faculty members hold junior faculty to standards which they themselves could not meet, and both exploit graduate assistants and secretaries. While doctors clamor for the newest and most expensive medical technology, hospital administrators complain about runaway costs—and medical fees soar. Faculty members lobby for smaller teaching loads, better libraries, more sophisticated research facilities, and expanded travel budgets. University presidents and vice-presidents for financial affairs complain about financial exigency. Tuition rises at the same time that student loans dry up.

What morals can be drawn from all this? Clearly, not-for-profit institutions behave much like government bureaucracies or regulated monopolies: budget size or allowable fees depend on cost increasing justifications. The incentive to minimize the costs of production is weak, especially when costs include professional salaries and perquisites. On the other hand, evidence that such institutions are able to cover higher costs with fee increases indicates that demand for their services is price inelastic, which means that prices are less than what a profit-maximizing monopoly would charge. Critics who suggest that not-for-profit institutions should be run in a more businesslike manner would do well to specify whether there would be a sufficient number of sellers to generate price competition. Those who praise such institutions for providing services "at cost" would do well to remember that profits can disappear through cost increases as well as price decreases.

Adapted from Thomas M. Carroll, "The Not-for-Profit Firm as a Managerial Syndicate" (paper delivered at the Southwest Social Science Association Meetings, Dallas, Texas, 1981).

The viability of the profit maximization assumption as the basis for the theory of the entrepreneurial firm is further enhanced by the resilience of the theory to relaxation of that assumption. Entrepreneurs who reveal a preference for goals other than maximum profit (e.g., a taste for the quiet life, a preference for workers of their own race, sex, or religion) can be treated as utility maximizers under a profit constraint. Just as we assumed in chapter three that a wage income is earned 24 hours a day and a worker purchases leisure with foregone income, we can also imagine that an entrepreneur first maximizes profit, then finances amenities by foregoing profit. That economic losses would confront such an entrepreneur in the long run is no more troublesome than the fact that consumption can always be financed out of wealth.

The controversy over the profit maximization assumption begins to heat up as the firms being investigated grow in size and market influence. One of the most articulate critics of the profit maximization assumption in the analysis of the large corporation is John Kenneth Galbraith:

> The separation of ownership from control involves a sharp challenge to the assumption of profit maximization. The pursuit of profit in the neoclassical model is relentless and singleminded. Acquisitiveness, avarice and cupidity (not man's most saintly attributes) are, by a most fortuitous paradox, the source of energy which is the subordinate to the public command of the public good. Yet when ownership is divorced from control, a grievous problem arises. The acquisitiveness, avarice and cupidity that so valuably motivate the system are supplied by the managers—the technostructure—and their fruits go to the owners. The managers are not beholden to the owners. Thus the system works because those who are most acquisitive are also most conscientiously determined to toil on behalf of others. Avarice is philanthropy in the service of others. This is a remarkable contradiction which the modern corporation poses for neoclassical economics. It is a problem which neoclassical theory solves mostly by ignoring it. It resorts to the most useful of intellectual conventions of the economist which is, when inconvenient facts are encountered, to assume them away. In all formal theory and most pedagogy the entrepreneur, uniting ownership and a beneficial stake in profits with active direction of the enterprise, is held to be the important case. The corporate reality is ignored.[9]

There are a number of criticisms of neoclassical theory in Galbraith's statement. First, the separation of ownership from control means that corporation managers can be assumed to maximize profit only if Adam Smith's skepticism about the selfish motives of business people is abandoned. If the self-interest of managers is to remain the basis for the formation of corporate goals, then the profit maximization assumption

---

[9] *Economics and the Public Purpose* (Boston: Houghton Mifflin, 1973), pp. 96–97.

must give way to the assumption that executives attempt to maximize their own income or their own utility. Second, since the modern corporation exercises much more market power than did the entrepreneurial firm depicted by Adam Smith, pursuit of maximum profit by corporations does not imply that corporations would automatically advance the public good. For these reasons, Galbraith challenges the relevance of Adam Smith's invisible hand allegory to the economic impact of the modern, multinational business enterprise.

But Galbraith's challenge of the profit maximization assumption, as applied to the goals of corporate management, allows him to avoid the logical inference that market power must make the corporation irresponsible. To Galbraith, corporations usually act in a socially responsible manner because such behavior is consistent with the alternative goals Galbraith attributes to corporate executives: maintaining a stable, growing market environment. To Milton Friedman, the idea of a corporate executive claiming to run a corporation in a socially responsible manner is as suspect as such behavior was to Adam Smith: "In a free-enterprise, private property system, a corporate executive is an employee of the owners of the business. He has direct responsibility to his employers. That responsibility is to conduct the business in accordance with their desires, which generally will be to make as much money as possible while conforming to the basic rules of the society, both those embodied in law and those embodied in ethical custom."[10]

Galbraith and Friedman seem united in their admiration of the *ideal* outcome of the pursuit of profit, but they are clearly divided on how to reconcile Adam Smith's ideal with the role of profit in the management of the large corporation. Galbraith is consistent with Adam Smith in his skepticism about the altruism of the business executive. If the separation of ownership from control insulates the executive from the power of stockholders, why should executives altruistically maximize someone else's profit? However, in denying that corporate executives seek to maximize profit, Galbraith avoids depicting powerful corporate officials as ravenous wolves run amok among defenseless consumers. Corporate executives are cast as reasonable, highly competent people, the peers of labor leaders and federal government policy makers, whose desire for a secure market position leads them to policies more consistent with public welfare than excessive profits would be.

To Friedman, socially responsible corporate executives are little more than embezzlers, spending their employers' (the stockholders') money on projects with dubious allocational effects. The executive's function is to maximize the stockholder's income, meaning profit. Log-

---

[10] Milton Friedman, "The Social Responsibility of Business Is to Increase its Profits," *The New York Times Magazine* (September 13, 1970); reprinted in Thomas R. Swartz and Frank J. Bonello, eds., *Taking Sides: Clashing Views on Controversial Economic Issues* (Guilford, Connecticut: Duskin, 1981), pp. 29–30.

ically, an executive who cannot be trusted with social responsibility could not be trusted with market power either. It must follow that the behavior of executives is dictated by the power of stockholders and the reality of the invisible hand.

To summarize, the firm emerges as a way of economizing on transaction costs which would otherwise severely limit the advantages of labor specialization. By acting as residual claimant, the proprietor of a small, competitive firm coordinates the actions of specialized workers and machinery, preventing the former from shirking responsibility and disrupting production, while financing the latter and keeping it in good repair. The proprietorship is the simplest form of business organization to analyze, since the goals of the owner are also the goals of the firm. A competitive market forces the owners of small firms to produce efficiently, and thereby, like an invisible hand, allocates resources for the public good. However, as the firm grows, both in absolute size and relative to the market it serves, two challenges to the invisible hand metaphor are encountered. First, market power causes the maximization of profit by firms to diverge from optimal patterns of resource allocation. Second, as firms grow, the unchallenged, if limited, authority of the entrepreneur is displaced by the fragmented goals, but more extensive influence, of the business bureaucracy.

Hence, the following enigma divides economists about the relevance of the profit-maximizing assumption to the modern corporation. If one believes stockholders have very limited control over the day-to-day decisions of corporate management, the characterization of managers as self-interested pursuers of their own gain means that the interests of executives will come before the interests of stockholders. There is no logical reason why executives should maximize corporate profit. However, since maximizing profits of oligopoly firms would not necessarily serve the public interest anyway, Adam Smith's invisible hand gives way to the attitude that corporate executives behave in a socially responsible fashion in accordance with non-profit-maximizing motives. Milton Friedman's restoration of the invisible hand analogy not only requires the belief that stockholders are powerful enough to punish corporation managers who do not maximize profit, but also requires faith in a competitive business environment, in which the large corporation, like Adam Smith's entrepreneurial firm, is powerless to resist the pressure to pursue socially beneficial policies.

The Meaning of Profit Maximization

As discussed in chapter one, assumptions play three distinct but related functions in economic theory: pedagogical, predictive, and prescriptive. This book is intended primarily as a teaching instrument, making the pedagogical role of assumptions preeminent. For the remainder of this book, the assumption that managers of firms attempt to maximize profit will be maintained as a simplifying assumption. When the profit-maximizing assumption becomes a crucial assumption, the predictions of a theory are modified if that assumption is dropped. We will explore two contexts in which nonprofit motives can have an important influence on how firms behave, and, more importantly, on the consequences of that behavior on patterns of resource allocation. In chapter twelve, we will rejoin the debate about the relevance of the profit-maximizing assumption after showing how theory is complicated by maintaining the profit-maximizing assumption in the context of the fragmented management of the oligopoly firm. In chapter fourteen, we will explore non-profit-maximizing goals as one explanation for patterns of racial and sexual discrimination in labor markets.

As a pedagogical device, the model of the profit-maximizing entrepreneur synthesizes the models of utility maximization and resource allocation already developed. Economic profit, symbolized by the Greek letter *pi*, π, is defined as total revenue (price times quantity) minus total opportunity cost: $\pi = pq - C(q)$. All firms, regardless of size or competitive structure, can be considered to have the same objective: to find the rate of output such that the revenue from the last unit equals the cost of producing that unit (subject to the condition that variable costs are covered).[11] The rule is the same for all firms: produce so that marginal revenue equals marginal cost, making sure that losses never exceed fixed costs.[12]

The essential difference between perfect and imperfect competition concerns how the firm relates output changes to revenue changes. Individual wheat farmers face market-determined spot and futures prices for their products; since output will have no influence on the price they receive for their crops, the farmers attempt to produce that amount for which the anticipated price equals the marginal cost of that quantity. The owners of a vineyard who bottle their wine under a distinctive label, realize that the price they receive for each bottle depends upon the quantity offered for sale. Unlike the price-taking farmers, whose only consideration is whether the price will cover the cost of producing the last bushel of wheat, the vintners must determine how much revenue is lost from the first bottles sold when the price of all bottles must be reduced to sell additional ones.

For price takers, marginal revenue is always equal to the market determined price. Control over price by imperfect competitive sellers

---

[11] Formally, $\partial\pi/\partial q = \partial(pq)/\partial q - \partial C/\partial q = 0$ implies $\partial(pq)/\partial q = \partial C/\partial q$, or $MR = MC$; $\partial^2\pi/\partial q^2 < 0$ implies $\partial MR/\partial q < \partial MC/\partial q$. A corner solution results if $p < AVC$.

[12] That is, $\partial(pq)/\partial q = p + q(\partial p/\partial q)$. For price takers, $\partial p/\partial q = 0$, so that $\partial(pq)/\partial q = p$. For sellers of differentiated products, $\partial p/\partial q < 0$, so that $\partial(pq)/\partial q < p$.

means that consumer surplus is seen as a potential source of profit; the market ceases to function as a commons when firms realize that output increases by any one of them may reduce the revenues for all. Yet the incentive for pricing conspirators to cheat still gives the invisible hand at least a supporting role in determining price and output under imperfect competition.

Prolonged internal economies, causing average cost to fall as plant capacity expands, may cause the optimally sized firm to be too large and the number of firms to be too small for firms to remain price takers. When the ownership of firms is transferable, it will generally be less risky and less expensive for a producer to enter a concentrated industry by purchasing an existing firm rather than starting a new one. Oligopoly implies that market entry does not cause the number of firms to increase enough to make each firm's pricing decision an autonomous one. If declining long-run average cost results in an intersection between one firm's cost curve and the market demand curve for its product (e.g., electric power, local print news), the phenomenon of *natural monopoly* is encountered.

APPLICATION
Alternative Goals of the Firm

Although the assumption of profit maximization is analytically convenient, the practical question of whether the profit-maximizing assumption yields accurate predictions remains. A number of alternative goals have been proposed by economists who claim that the models based on these goals yield more accurate predictions of the behavior of large-scale firms in particular. A few of these alternative goals are sales maximization, growth maximization, and the generalized assumption of managerial utility maximization.

According to the sales maximization hypothesis, firms find a profit-maximization objective either impossible or undesirable. If attempting to earn the highest short-run profit leads to highly variable dividend patterns, managers may find themselves in trouble with stockholders. If stockholders do not expect one year's high dividend to continue, they will sell their stock to others who expect high dividends the next year. The next year's stockholders, who already paid high prices for the company's stock, will experience a lower than normal return on their financial investment when the company announces normal dividends. While stockholder revolts and successful takeover bids are rare, they are not unprecedented.

Rather than maximizing short-run economic profit, managers of corporations might attempt to secure their tenure by pursuing a stable growth in sales (or market share) as long as an *acceptable* level of profit (dictated by a stable dividend policy) was attained. Profit becomes the constraint rather than the objective.[13] If the best profit the firm can earn in a particular year is less than or equal to the profit target, the constraint would be binding and management would attempt to get as close to the target as possible by maximizing economic profit. If the realized profit level could exceed the target, the firm would generate the highest revenue consistent with the profit target.

The growth maximization hypothesis is not so much an alternative to the profit maximization assumption, but a variant of it. Because of the double-taxation of corporate dividends (once as corporate income, then as stockholder income), stockholders prefer to receive part of their share of corporate profit as capital gains (increases in the market value of their stock), giving them a lower tax rate and the ability to deter tax payments until their capital gain is realized (the asset is sold). Pursuing a growth maximization objective, managers reinvest a substantial portion of after-tax corporate income into the firm, increasing expected future dividends or capital gains, and thereby increasing the market value of shareholder equity. But if management wishes to maximize the firm's growth, it will also maximize long-run profit and the wealth of its stockholders. And since the larger the net income, the greater the retained earnings (earnings not distributed as dividends), the growth maximization hypothesis can even result in the same short-run output and price as that implied by the profit maximization model.

Armen Alchian has noted the emergence of a theory of management based on the hypothesis that managers are utility maximizers confronted by various institutional constraints.[14] According to Alchian, attributing utility-maximizing behavior to corporate executives is hardly novel; the trick is to specify the nature of the managers' utility functions in empirically testable ways and to explain how utility maximization changes behavior relative to the profit maximization hypothesis.

The proprietor faces a direct trade-off between the firm's profits and other personal goals. Specifying a profit maximization motive does not eliminate the possibility of substituting other goals for maximizing economic profit. However, one would still tend to find that entrepreneurs attempt to achieve the highest economic profit compatible with other goals (e.g., location of one's firm in a city with amenities, hiring employees with agreeable personalities, involvement with civic activities).

For corporation executives, who receive, at most, only a small share

---

[13] A sales (revenue) maximization objective with a profit constraint is stated formally as follows: Maximize pq, subject to $\pi^* \leqq pq - C(q)$. If the profit target were not achievable in a particular year, profit maximization would be substituted for revenue maximization as the firm's goal.

[14] Armen A. Alchian, "The Basis of Some Recent Advances in the Theory of Management of the Firm," *Journal of Industrial Economics* (November 1965), pp. 30–41.

of dividend income, the trade-off between profit and other influences of a manager's utility becomes less pronounced. In one simple model, a manager's utility is a function of his or her own compensation, both in financial and nonpecuniary forms, and corporate profit. Since profit goes to shareholders, increasing profit must indirectly increase managerial utility: through greater job security, more prestige as an officer of a profitable concern, the performance bonus, or other rewards provided by stockholders. It follows that a manager's utility function would be characterized by negatively sloped indifference curves exhibiting diminishing marginal rates of substitution between firm profit and executive reward.

The marginal rate of substitution between profit and executive compensation depends, at least in part, upon how closely stockholders police managerial activity. Managers of corporations with a few powerful owners of large blocks of stock (closely held corporations) would tend to have a greater reluctance to trade stockholder income or wealth for executive compensation than they would if stock ownership were more dispersed.

To a manager's indifference map in Figure 8-1 we have added a transformation curve, showing the relationship between compensation received by executives and the firm's level of profit.[15] Corporations which offer low executive compensation (EC) prospects would tend to attract less skilled executives who would generate lower profits than more able managers. As executive compensation increases, so does realized profit (*ceteris paribus*) until the profit maximum of π_{max} is achieved. Beyond EC', increases in executive compensation would come at the expense of the firm's profit.

A manager would attempt to *maximize* profit, in the strict sense, only if the marginal rate of substitution between profit and compensation were zero at point P in Figure 8-1. This may be plausible for·a proprietorship, but implies that corporate managers are pure altruists if profits are received by others. A typical manager would maximize utility at a point such as Q in Figure 8-1, obtaining compensation of EC^* ($>EC'$), which corresponds to corporate earnings of π^* ($> \pi_{max}$).

Figure 8-1 implies that the profit maximization assumption is not an accurate description of actual management goals. However, the question remains whether theories based on the profit maximization assumption accurately predict changes in resource allocation resulting from changes in profitable opportunities. This question is investigated in Figure 8-2. Suppose that a firm has been realizing a profit of π_0 and managers have

---

[15] The transformation curve, which is explored in more depth in chapter fifteen, shows efficient combinations of two "goods" (in this case, executive compensation and profits) which can be produced with available resources (in this case, the assets of the corporation).

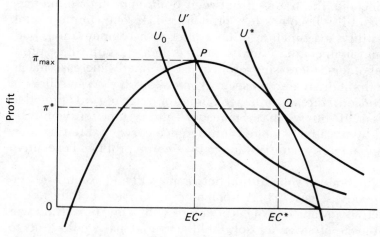

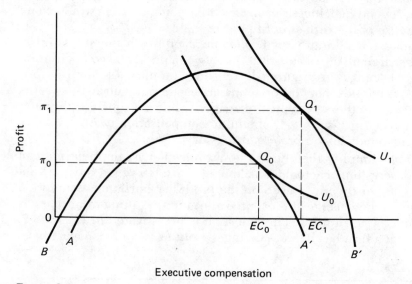

Figure 8-1
The Utility Maximization Model of Executive Behavior. Profit maximization implies that the *MRS* between executive compensation and profit is zero at point *P*; separation of ownership from control implies that the utility maximum will occur at a point like *Q*, where the marginal rate of substitution between profit and executive compensations is negative.

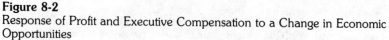

Figure 8-2
Response of Profit and Executive Compensation to a Change in Economic Opportunities

Business Illustration
What Determines Executive Pay

Are chief executive officers of major corporations paid for increasing profits or sales? This controversy has raged in economics journals for twenty years. The author's own research, accomplished with economist David Ciscel, provided a clear answer to this question. The answer is yes.

What a minute! you say. The question is one of either-or not yes-no. But is it? When reporting their sales, most corporations report price times quantity (i.e., revenue); the typical *Fortune* 500 firm sells so many products that its sales are reported in dollar terms. But this measure of sales is also the largest component of profit, which is defined as revenues minus cost. If we see that an executive's salary increases as his firm's revenue increases, does this imply that he has a stronger incentive to increase sales than to increase profit? After all, when revenue increases more than cost, profit increases.

We found that the typical corporate chief executive in 1975 received about $10 more in annual salary for every additional $1 million of revenue his company earned and $159.50 more per year for every $1-million reduction in costs, revenue being constant. That is, in addition to verifying the incentive of executives to increase sales, our research showed that there was a strong incentive to increase profits by reducing costs. Similar correlations were obtained for 1974. However, the incentive to control costs appeared somewhat weaker in 1970–1973 and in 1976. These results are particularly interesting because 1974 and 1975 were recession years, indicating that evidence in favor of the profit maximization hypothesis also supports the hypothesis that firms attempt to maximize sales (or market share) subject to a profit constraint.

The most interesting result was that changes in revenue and changes in cost appeared to account for only about 10 percent of the salary plus bonus of chief executive officers. By far the strongest influence on executive pay appeared to be the market for managers. In 1970 a chief executive's pay, independent of his firm's sales and profit, averaged $185,938.60; in 1976 that "base pay" averaged $349,612.90. Chief executive officers— and, presumably, other corporate officers—are not *pure residual claimants* in the sense that entrepreneurs are assumed to be.* Decision makers for oligopolistic firms receive their opportunity cost (their expected minimum salary) regardless of how their firm performs. Thus, while firm performance (specified as either sales or profit growth) influences executive compensation, it is not the most important influence.

---

* In an earlier study, Ciscel showed how the salary plus bonus of the management team could be used in place of the salary plus bonus of the chief executive without a major change in the results ("Determinants of Executive Compensation," *Southern Economic Journal* [April 1974], pp. 613–617).

Based on David H. Ciscel and Thomas M. Carroll, "The Determinants of Executive Compensation: An Econometric Survey," *Review of Economics and Statistics* (February 1980), pp. 7–13.

been receiving compensation of EC_0 when the firm faces the profit–executive compensation transformation curve AA'. An increase in consumer demand for the product(s) that the firm produces increases both executive compensation opportunities and profit opportunities; the transformation curve shifts from AA' to BB'.

As usual, the increase in opportunities to obtain more of two "goods" shifts the optimal point. In Figure 8-2, the maximum attainable indifference curve is U_1, which is tangent to transformation curve BB' at point Q_1. Compensation of executives increases to EC_1 ($>EC_0$), while stockholders receive dividends (or capital gains) based on profits of π_1 ($>\pi_0$). If opportunities for both executive compensation and profit increase, a positive association between the firm's performance (profit) and executive compensation will be observed.

A feature that many models proposing managerial goals other than profit maximization share with profit maximization models is that "management" is still treated as a monolithic entity, whether decisions are made by an owner-entrepreneur or by an army of corporate bureaucrats. No doubt, models assuming monolithic management provide a simpler explanation of how large firms influence the pattern of resource allocation. However, the model of the complex organization maximizing anything has been attacked by Herbert Simon, winner of the 1978 Nobel Prize in economics for his work in intrafirm decision theory:

> The notion of satiation plays no role in classical economic theory, while it enters rather prominently into the treatment of motivation in psychology. In most psychological theories the motive to act stems from *drives*, and action terminates when the drive is satisfied. Moreover, the conditions for satisfying a drive are not necessarily fixed, but may be specified by an aspiration level that itself adjusts upward or downward on the basis of experience.
>
> If we seek to explain behavior in the terms of this theory, we must expect the firm's goals to be not maximizing profits, holding a certain share of the market or certain level of sales. Firms would try to "satisfice" rather than maximize.
>
> It has sometimes been argued that the distinction between satisficing and maximizing is not important to economic theory. For in the first place, the psychological evidence on individual behavior shows that aspirations tend to adjust to the attainable. Hence in the long run, the argument goes, the level of aspiration and the attainable maximum will be very close together. Second, even if some firms satisficed, they would gradually lose out to the maximizing firms, which would make larger profits and grow more rapidly than the others.
>
> However, the economic environment of the firm is complex and it changes rapidly; there is no *a priori* reason to assume the attainment of long run equilibrium. Indeed, the empirical evidence on the dis-

tribution of firms by size suggests that the observed regularities in size distribution stem from the statistical equilibrium of a population of adaptive systems rather than the static equilibrium of a population of maximizers.[16]

There is no point in denying that the behavior of large firms is more complex than that of small firms. As we shall see in subsequent chapters, ignoring some of these complications as long as possible allows economic theory to be more general. Assuming that firms are guided by managers in pursuit of maximum economic profit provides a benchmark which relates the operation of an ideal, competitive market to an efficient allocation of resources: the best outcome possible in a world of scarcity. Analyzing real firms in less than ideal market environments presents two challenges to Adam Smith's notion of the invisible hand. First, would the attempt by firms to maximize profits result in desirable resource allocation patterns? Second, how sensitive are the predictions of theories of imperfect competition to the profit-maximizing assumption? By maintaining the profit-maximizing hypothesis when confronting the impact of imperfect competition on the firm's price and output decision, we attempt to answer these questions one at a time.

---

[16] Herbert Simon, "Theories of Decision Making in Economics and Behavioral Science," *American Economic Review* (June 1959), pp. 223–83; reprinted in Edwin Mansfield, ed., *Microeconomics: Selected Readings*, 2nd ed. (New York: Norton, 1975), p. 86.

HIGHLIGHTS

1. For a market to exist, economic agents must have property rights, which give them the legally enforceable ability to exclude others from using scarce resources. The opposite of system property rights is the commons, wherein individuals cannot be held accountable for their misuse or waste of scarce resources because no individual can exclude others from the benefits of efficient resource use.

2. The ability to exclude gives rise to the ability to exchange, whereby one property right can be traded for another. Exchange makes gains from specialization possible, which enhances the standard of living that can be squeezed from scarce resources.

3. While a market requires that resources be privately owned, the ideal market is itself a commons—an institution to facilitate exchange from which no would-be buyer or seller can be excluded.

4. When exclusive use of scarce resources cannot be enforced, property failure, or externalities result. An external cost occurs when the use or exchange of property harms a party not involved in the use or exchange. An external benefit occurs when the owner of a scarce resource or commodity cannot exclude nonpayers from benefiting from property use.

5. One of the great ironies of a private enterprise economy is that property failure is often "solved" by the award of monopoly rights, whereby market failure results when would-be sellers are excluded from a market.

6. Between the polar cases of market organization—perfect competition (the market as

a commons) and pure monopoly (the market as property)—are the more complex and controversial economic models of monopolistic competition (many sellers of differentiated products protected by narrowly enforced monopoly rights) and oligopoly (wherein a few firms, usually trying to anticipate one another's behavior, coexist in a market).

7. The business firm has its origins in attempts to reduce transaction costs by organizing productive activity through a command system rather than through market exchange. The pivotal role is played by the supervisor, or residual claimant, who coordinates input services and prevents individual input owners from extorting an unfair share of output.

8. For the small-scale, entrepreneurial firm, the assumption of profit-maximizing behavior by the firm's owner-manager is generally accepted and provides a unifying reference of various types of market organization. This model is traceable to Adam Smith's metaphor of the invisible hand whereby the ideal market causes self-interested behavior to promote social welfare.

9. The assumption of profit-maximizing behavior is more controversial when applied to management inside the large corporation. First, decision makers are not usually owners but employees. Second, market power means that maximizing profit may not result in socially desirable outcomes. Third, there is an empirically testable question of whether predictions based on the assumption of profit-maximizing managerial behavior provides accurate predictions in the case of large firms.

10. Two models that assume alternative goals for the firm—maximization of sales or of growth—may lead to predictions that are not significantly different from those of a model based on the profit-maximizing assumption.

11. If managerial utility is a function of corporate profit and executive compensation, one would not expect non-owner-managers to pursue the maximum possible rate of profit at the expense of their own compensation. However, theories assuming profit maximization might accurately predict the response of managers to new profit opportunities.

GLOSSARY

Cartel A monopoly made up of two or more sellers who conspire to establish an artificial shortage to sustain a higher than competitive price.

Commons An arrangement in which scarce resources are owned by no one, since ownership by everyone is a contradiction.

Economic profit Revenue received from the sale of a commodity minus the opportunity cost of inputs used to produce that commodity.

External effect See **externality**.

Externality A situation in which the use of a scarce resource is not exclusive, so that the welfare of individuals other than the owner (if there is one) is influenced by the use or exchange of that input or output. Also called **external effect**.

External benefit A benefit of an action enjoyed by parties other than the individual(s) who

undertook the action.

External cost A cost of an action incurred by parties other than the individual(s) who undertook the action.

Invisible hand Adam Smith's metaphor for a competitive market as a force to turn self-interested behavior into socially beneficial outcomes.

Market failure The consequence of the legal or physical ability of one or more market participants to exclude others, resulting in monopoly distortion of resource allocation.

Monopolistic competition A market situation in which many sellers of differentiated products have narrowly defined monopoly rights to brand names, trademarks, or product characteristics.

Monopoly A market with one seller; the market as property.

Oligopoly A market with only a few sellers, characterized by each seller's attempts to anticipate the actions and reactions of rivals.

Patent A monopoly license allowing the holder to exclude others from a market if they make use of the protected idea or process.

Perfect competition A market situation in which free entry results in a large number of sellers of a homogeneous product; the market as a commons.

Product differentiation Variety in product characteristics. Consumers reveal preferences for different sellers' products by their willingness to pay higher prices for those with characteristics they consider desirable.

Product homogeneity Standardization in product characteristics; one assumption of the ideal market model. Buyers are indifferent

among the sellers of a standardized commodity and seek out those charging the lowest price, so that a single, market-wide price eventually prevails.

Property failure The failure of legal or social institutions to enforce exclusivity in the use or exchange of scarce inputs or outputs.

Property right The legally enforceable ability to exclude others from using a scarce resource or commodity; a necessary precondition for exchange.

Residual claimant The economic agent who receives any surplus or incurs any shortfall of revenue after owners of inputs, including labor, have been paid.

Transaction costs The economic costs involved in reaching or enforcing a production or exchange agreement.

SUGGESTED READINGS

Alchian, Armen A. "The Basis of Some Recent Advances in the Theory of Management of the Firm." *Journal of Industrial Economics* (November 1965), pp. 30–41.

Baumol, William. *Economic Theory and Operations Analysis.* 4th ed. Englewood Cliffs, New Jersey: Prentice-Hall, 1977, chapter 15.

Calebresi, Guido, and A. Douglas Melamed. "Property Rules, Liability Rules, and Inalienability: One View of the Cathedral." *Harvard Law Review* (1972). Reprinted in Bruce Ackerman, ed. *The Economic Foundations of Property Law.* Boston: Little, Brown, 1975.

Carroll, Thomas M., David H. Ciscel, and Roger K. Chisholm, "The Market as a Commons: An Unconventional View of Property Rights," *Journal of Economic Issues* 13 (June 1979), 605–627.

Ciscel, David, and Thomas M. Carroll. "The Determinants of Executive Compensation: An Econometric Survey." *Review of Economics and Statistics* (February 1980), pp. 7–13.

Coase, Ronald. "The Problem of Social Cost." *Journal of Law and Economics* (October 1960), pp. 1–44.

Cyert, R. M., and J. G. March. *A Behavioral Theory of the Firm.* Englewood Cliffs, New Jersey: Prentice-Hall, 1963, chapter 6.

Furbotn, Eirik G., and Svetozar Pejovich. "Property Rights and Economic Theory: A Survey of Recent Literature." *Journal of Economic Literature* (December 1972), pp. 1137–1162.

Galbraith, John Kenneth. *Economics and the Public Purpose.* Boston: Houghton Mifflin, 1973.

Hardin, Garret. "The Tragedy of the Commons." *Science* (December 1968), pp. 1243–1248.

Held, Virginia. *Property, Profits and Economic Justice.* Belmont, California: Wadsworth, 1980.

Manne, Henry, ed. *The Economics of Legal Relationships: Readings in the Theory of Property Rights.* St. Paul, Minnesota: West Publishing Company, 1975.

Simon, Herbert. "Rational Decision Making in Business Organizations." *American Economic Review* (September 1979).

Smith, Adam. *An Inquiry into the Nature and Causes of the Wealth of Nations.* New York: Random House, Modern Library edition, 1936, books I and IV.

EXERCISES

Evaluate

Indicate whether each of the following is true (agrees with economic theory), false (is contradicted by theory), or uncertain (could be true or false, given additional information). Explain your answer.

1. For markets to work effectively, producers must be able to maximize profit.
2. Property rights encourage individuals to take the public welfare into account when resources are used.
3. Air pollution can be seen either as property failure—polluters misallocate scarce resources—or as market failure—producers are not able to recover the costs of cleaning up the air.
4. The existence of firms, organized on a command basis, gives evidence that exchange relationships are an ineffective means of organizing production.
5. Without markets, property rights could not exist.
6. While both Milton Friedman and John Kenneth Galbraith admire the invisible hand in the abstract, neither really trusts the market to guarantee that corporate executives will behave responsibly.
7. The division of labor ultimately destroys the effectiveness of the entrepreneurial firm, since an effective entrepreneur must be able to monitor all stages of production.
8. Monopoly can be seen as a necessary component of property rights.
9. The economic impact of corporations is fuzzy because the goals a corporation pursues change as different groups within it gain and lose power.
10. By interfering with the property rights of sellers, laws against discrimination in employment reduce the efficiency of resource allocation.

Contemplate

Answer each of the following in a brief but complete essay.

11. Comment on the following: The president of company A, who has been credited with reversing that company's fortunes, is hired by corporation B, which is larger than company A and can afford to pay a higher salary. There is no appreciable change in the value of either company's stock during the following year. Apparently, the president's reputation was a sham.
12. Several years ago, when most countries (including the United States) increased their offshore territorial limits to 300 miles to protect domestic fishermen, newspapers criticized the move as damaging to poor countries which depend on fish for protein. Do you agree with this criticism? Explain your answer.
13. "Since 'collective ownership' is a contradiction, so-called socialist or communist countries are really characterized by bureaucratic stewardship of scarce inputs." Do you believe this statement to be positive or normative? How would your answer change if "stockholder ownership" was substituted for "collective ownership" and "corporations" was substituted for the phrase "so-called socialist or communist countries"? Explain your answer.
14. Comment on the following: "At best, private ownership encourages the user of scarce resources to consider the benefits of his or her heirs for a generation or two. However, private enterprise is an ineffective means of encouraging the preservation of forests, natural beauty and endangered species."
15. Do you agree or disagree with the following statement? "Microeconomic theory is intended to show the benefits of private enterprise, rather than to draw objective conclusions from observation of the real world." Give the reasons for your answer.

Chapter 9
Price Takers and Market Competition

The theory of the firm is something like human locomotion in that a person must master the simple before attempting the complex. First we learn to crawl, then to walk, then to run; similarly, we learn to understand the simplest model of firm behavior, then the increasingly complex. The competitive firm is a *price taker* and as such has the fewest and simplest decisons to make. The market determines the price of its output and the prices of its inputs. The technology it uses is available to all, and the market contains so many sellers that each one can be viewed as passively reacting to market-wide forces beyond its control. In the first part of this chapter, we see how the attempt of the price taker to maximize profit results in a unique output for each market determined price, generating a well-defined supply function.

Market supply is shown to be the consequence of the adjustment of all sellers to a change in the market price. Together with the market demand curve, which reflects the independent behavior of buyers, the competitive supply curve helps determine the price and output of the commodity in question. As in our earlier development of the market demand curve, the important distinction between a change in supply (which upsets the market price) and a change in quantity supplied (which is a reaction to a change in the market price) is emphasized.

Shifting focus from the short run to the long run reveals how competitive firms enter or leave a competitive industry in response to opportunities for economic profit or the prospect of continued losses. The invisible hand of market competition guides the price toward its minimum sustainable level when market entry is free, causing zero economic profit in long-run equilibrium. Entry restrictions generate higher prices without creating sustainable profits; economic profit still tends toward zero as costs rise to absorb transferable entry barriers. The long-run supply curve is developed as a *mutatis mutandis* extrapolation of zero-profit market equilibria.

The appendix to the chapter explains, in nontechnical terms, how economists apply the theory of competitive equilibrium to real markets to calculate the actual equations for supply and demand functions. The importance of knowing whether a curve shifted, thereby upsetting an equilibrium price, or whether two observations lie on the same curve is linked directly to the ability of economists to uncover real supply and demand equations. The appendix ends by contrasting the relative success of economists at uncovering the patterns of commodity markets with their failure (along with everyone else's) to uncover a pattern behind the random walk of the market for financial assets.

The Meaning of Competition

One of the first things which strikes students as odd about the model of **perfect competition** is how little competition there actually is. The word *competition* connotes combat—if not actual warfare at least aggressive team sports, which William James called the "moral equivalent of war." There is about as much combat in a perfectly competitive market as there is in a game of bingo. In bingo, a random series of numbers is called by a neutral person. When, say, B-14 is called, all participants with that letter-number combination on their game cards can mark it. The person who fills his or her card first wins that round of bingo; as long as players pay attention to the numbers that are called, there is little skill involved.

It is a rare loser at bingo who feels vanquished by the winner. Success at bingo is a matter of luck, and cheating is so easily detected that it is rarely attempted. Winning one round of bingo provides no advantage in the next round. Churches, fraternal groups, and other charitable organizations often organize bingo games, charging each player a fee, which, although small, is nonetheless greater than his or her expected winnings. While a few players do win small amounts of money, the real winners of these bingo games are the groups that sponsor them.

In a perfectly competitive market, the caller is the market itself, which many economists have characterized as an auctioneer. Whether a firm's product commands a high or low price is more a matter of luck than the producer's skill or merit. There are so many participants, all responding to the same set of prices, that it is impossible for firms to manipulate the rules of competition or change the outcome. Firms that make a short-run economic profit are soon confounded by the entry of more sellers, who cause prices to fall, reducing economic profit to zero. Winning one round of the production game gives no advantage in the next round under perfect competition. While a few owners of nonreplicable inputs may increase their wealth when profits turn into economic rent (see chapter thirteen), the real winners under perfect competition are consumers. The outcome of perfect competitive markets is the maximization of consumer surplus.

The Assumptions behind Perfect Competition

Just as the outcome of a bingo game follows inevitably from the simple rules of the game, the predictions of the theory of perfect competition follow logically from its assumptions. These are:

1. There is free entry into and exit from the industry; the market is a commons (see chapter eight).
2. Buyers and sellers are so numerous that price is invariant with respect to the actions of any individual buyer or seller. Attempts to fix prices are doomed to failure.
3. All firms in the industry produce a single, homogeneous product. Each producer has access to the same technology and pays the same market determined prices for input services.
4. All firms are owned and managed by proprietors who seek to maximize economic profit.
5. All buyers and sellers have accurate information about prevailing prices. Consumers and firms select trading partners only on the basis of price.

The combined impact of these assumptions is that each competitive seller faces a horizontal demand schedule at the market determined price; each firm can sell all it produces at that price. Figure 9-1a shows how total quantity demanded by all consumers varies inversely with the market price. When the market price equals p_e, consumers attempt to buy more than they would if the price were p_1 but less than they would if the price were p_0. If price p_e is established by the market, all firms that charge this price will sell a share of the total quantity demanded, Q_e. Because of the large number of sellers, Q_e is so large relative to the production capability of any firm that market output would not be noticeably affected if one seller doubled its output or disappeared completely from the industry.

Suppose that one seller unilaterally raised its price above p_e. Since consumers could purchase the identical commodity from other sellers, they would abandon the higher priced seller, whose sales would drop

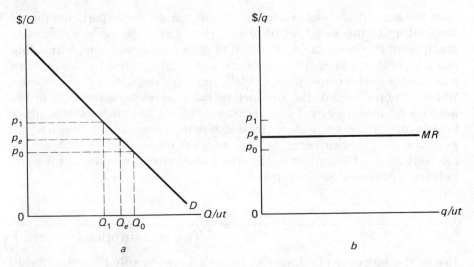

Figure 9-1
Demand under Perfect Competition. *a*, Negatively sloped market demand curve for a homogeneous product; *b*, horizontal demand curve for a price taker's output.

to zero. Except when a **shortage** of a commodity exists—when sellers offer less than buyers wish to purchase at the prevailing price—sellers who raise their price are unable to sell anything.

In Figure 9-1*b*, the intercept of the firm's demand curve is the market determined price. Were the firm to raise its price by even a fraction of a penny above p_e, its product would be priced out of the market. If the firm reduced its price to p_0, even though it could sell all it produced at p_e, the quantity demanded from it would literally run off the page; the units used to measure the firm's output are too small for the entire market demand of Q_0 to be registered in Figure 9-1*b*. The firm's demand curve is horizontal at the market determined price.

As explained in chapter four, the price elasticity of demand measures the percentage change in the quantity of a product demanded due to a 1 percent change in its price, other factors constant. The demand for the output of a competitive firm is infinitely elastic at the market price.[1] Any increase in price above p_e, no matter how small, causes quantity demanded from that firm to fall to zero. Any decrease in price below p_e

---

[1] By definition, $\eta = \partial q/q/\partial p/p = (\partial q/\partial p)(p/q)$. If $\Delta p_i > 0$, $\partial q_i/\partial p_i = -q_i$: if firm i raises its price while the price charged by all producers of a perfect substitute remains constant, its sales will drop to zero. If $\Delta p_i < 0$, $\partial q_i/\partial p_i = Q_d$: if firm i reduces its price below the going rate, quantity demanded from that one seller is the entire quantity demanded at that price, but no individual firm could produce so much. Since q can increase or decrease without a change in p, η has a denominator of zero:

$$\eta = \lim_{\Delta p \to 0} \frac{\Delta q/q}{\Delta p/p} = -\infty$$

increases quantity demanded so much that the firm's production capability is swamped. The individual firm can change its output, and hence the quantity it sells, without changing it price.

For the individual firm, market price is a parameter which is no more subject to its control than is the weather to anyone's control, the prime-time television schedule to a single viewer's control, or questions asked on economics exams to a student's control. The firm's revenue equals the constant market price, $\bar{p}$, times the quantity it sells. **Marginal revenue**, the change in revenue resulting from one additional unit of output, is simply the market price of the output of the perfectly competitive firm.

$$MR = \frac{\Delta(\bar{p}q)}{\Delta q} = \bar{p}\frac{(\Delta q)}{\Delta q} = \bar{p}$$

In addition to the model firm depicted in the theory of perfect competition, other types of firms can be characterized as price takers, thereby increasing the real-world applications of what is admittedly an abstract model. Frequently, large buyers negotiate purchase contracts with smaller firms. Although the price of the commodity involved is not directly determined by market forces, once the contract has been signed, the small supplier discovers that the large buyer will purchase all it can produce at the specified price. During the contract period, the supplier's marginal revenue equals the contract price. Similarly, some firms face regulated prices set by the government. If the regulation is binding, the individual firm will discover that price is invariant with respect to its output. Finally, some models of oligopoly (the subject of chapter twelve) hypothesize formal or informal price leadership. If a small producer has decided to "play along" and allow another (i.e., larger) producer to set the price, the price follower will behave like a price taker.

Short-Run Profit Maximization

The assumption that firms seek to maximize profits generates a cause-effect relationship between the market determined price and the competitive firm's rate of output. Once the pattern of output and price has been established for the price taker, the stage will be set for the drama of imperfect competition to be played out in later chapters.

We begin our investigation of the price taker's output decision with Figure 9-2. Total revenue and total cost are both functions of output. Total profit is also a function of output, since economic profit is the difference between total revenue (whose slope is price) and total cost (whose slope is marginal cost). By plotting the distance between the total revenue and total cost curves at each rate of output, we generate the economic profit function, labeled $\pi(q)$ in Figure 9-2.

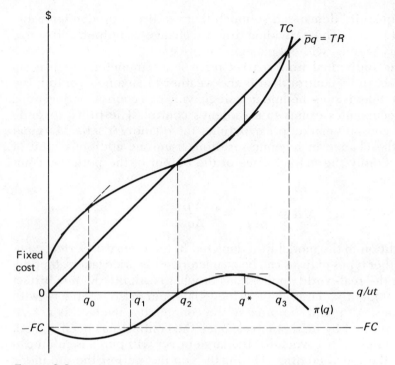

Figure 9-2
Profit Maximization in the Short Run: Profit = Total Revenue − Total
Cost. When output is zero, the firm loses payments on fixed costs (which
must be made in any event). The relevant consideration is whether total
revenue exceeds variable costs.

If a firm produced no output in the short run, all payments for fixed-cost inputs would be lost. Thus profit function has a vertical intercept at the negative value of fixed cost, $\pi(0) = -FC$. As long as the total cost curve is above the total revenue line, the profit curve lies below zero, which is denoted by the quantity axis. If the use of fixed inputs cannot be varied, the first few units of output might actually increase the firm's losses, since variable input services must be hired both to produce output and to counteract the negative marginal product of the fixed inputs. As the output rate increases, fewer and fewer variable inputs will be required per unit of output as their marginal productivity increases, which will cause variable cost (and hence total cost) to increase at a decreasing rate. In Figure 9-2, losses increase until q_0, then begin to decrease as output increases. At q_1, losses again equal fixed costs; past q_1, losses become less than fixed costs.

As output increases beyond q_0, total revenue continues to increase more rapidly than total cost, causing profit to change in the same direction as output: $\Delta\pi/\Delta q > 0$. In Figure 9-2, the total revenue line, *TR*, intersects the total cost curve, *TC*, from below at output q_2. Total revenue has caught up to total cost, although total cost had a head start: $TR = 0$ when $q = 0$, while $TC = FC$ when $q = 0$. Were the rate of output to increase to q_3 per period, the total revenue line once again intersects the total cost curve, this time from above. At q_3, total cost is increasing at a faster rate than total revenue, and profit changes in the opposite direction to the change in output: $\Delta\pi/\Delta q < 0$. The profit-maximizing rate of output, q^*, is identified where total revenue and total cost are both increasing at the same rate. Since the total revenue line and the total cost curve are neither moving apart (which would imply that profit is still increasing as output increases) nor moving together (which would mean that increases in output would reduce profit), the profit-maximizing rate of output is identified where the rate of change of profit is zero: $\Delta\pi/\Delta q = 0$.[2]

Maximizing profit means increasing output until profit can no longer be increased and then producing at that rate so that profit does not fall below the maximum. The perfect competition model assumes that the total cost curve is predetermined by technological possibilities, input prices, and the binding force of minimum purchase contracts and maximum availability constraints for fixed inputs.

Although the product price (marginal revenue) is invariant with respect to the firm's rate of output, market-wide price changes might occur at any time, replacing one total revenue line with another. Figure 9-3 shows three different market prices giving rise to three different total revenue lines. In Figure 9-3a, total revenue equals p_0q. Price p_0 has been determined by the market, allowing the firm to determine its revenue by choosing its rate of output. The way Figure 9-3a is drawn, total revenue is everywhere below total cost and is below variable cost at every output except q_0. At q_0, total revenue exactly equals variable cost, and since the total revenue line is tangent to the variable cost curve (indicating that the two have the same slope at q_0), marginal cost equals price at q_0. Were price less than p_0, causing a flatter total revenue line, total revenue would be less than variable cost at every rate of output; the manager would limit losses to fixed costs by shutting down operations. Hence, p_0 represents the minimum price necessary for the firm to offer output to consumers.[3] For this reason, p_0 is often referred to as the **shutdown price**.

---

[2] Those familiar with calculus will recognize this straightforward maximization problem: $d\pi/dq = d(\bar{p}q)/dq - dTC/dq = 0$ implies $\bar{p} = dTC/dq = MC$. The second-order condition requires that $d^2\pi/dq^2 < 0$ or that $dMC/dq > 0$.

[3] When $p <$ minimum AVC, a corner solution to the profit maximization problem results. Instead of occurring at the local profit maximum, identified where $d\pi/dq = 0$ and $d^2\pi/dq^2 < 0$, the loss-minimizing point occurs at $q = 0$, where $\pi = -FC$. By rewriting the profit equation, $\pi = p \times q - (FC + VC)$, as $\pi = -FC + q(p - AVC)$, we emphasize that $\pi > -FC$ only if $p > AVC$ where $MC = p$. Since minimum AVC is identified where $MC = AVC$, first checking that $p \geqq$ minimum AVC automatically controls for the possibility of a corner solution.

Business Illustration
Break-Even Analysis

It is not unusual for a student to be confused by the different descriptions of the output decision given in accounting, marketing, or management courses and in the profit-maximizing model posited in microeconomic theory. The accompanying figure is presented to clear up some of this confusion. There are three different production decisions in which managers of a firm might use break-even analysis, and most problems arise from confusing one decision with another. The box labeled *Net worth* is the focus of the long-run planning decision: should resources be committed to a production facility, thereby incurring fixed costs that must be paid out of the owners' wealth, regardless of whether fixed inputs are used? Since the present costs of a still nonexistent production facility are zero, the appropriate benchmark for the *long-run* production decision is whether *expected* revenue will at least cover long-run total cost for some rate of output. If the firm's managers do not expect to at least "break even"— that is, to recover long-run costs—the new facility will not be purchased.

If the best evidence at the time of the planning decision indicates that long-run costs could be recovered with expected revenue, acquiring the production facility will involve signing minimum purchase contracts that will create an inexorable drain on the owners' wealth. If management discovers—after it is too late to back out of the contracts—that its commitment of resources to production was based on an erroneous forecast of price or cost conditions, the appropriate responses are to mutter a few invectives, curse fate, kick inanimate objects, enter psychoanalysis, or search for loopholes in minimum-purchase contracts. But fixed costs should not influence the two short-run decisions: whether to produce any output at all (or

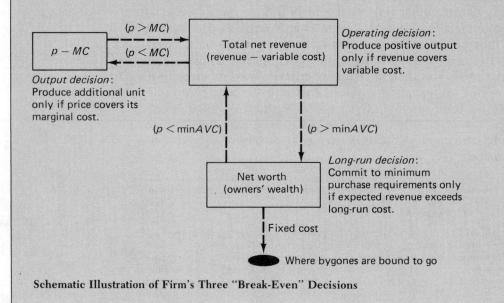

Schematic Illustration of Firm's Three "Break-Even" Decisions

shut down the facility), and if so, what rate of output to produce. As shown in the figure, fixed costs are bygones which have, alas, gone by.

In the short run, the firm's owners will be able to bank any positive difference between total revenue and variable cost (i.e., net revenue). Since nothing can be done about the outflow of fixed cost, the best strategy for maximizing the owners' wealth is to make the flow of *net revenue* as great as possible. First, management must be sure that net revenue is flowing into net worth. If variable costs exceed total revenue for each conceivable rate of output, operating the facility (i.e., producing any positive rate of output) will cause losses to exceed the outflow of fixed cost. The short-run reference point for whether to operate an existing facility is whether net revenue is positive. By ceasing production whenever price is less than the minimum average variable cost ($p < minAVC$), managers avoid creating a secondary drain on the owners' wealth.

Assuming that the prevailing price exceeds the minimum point on the average variable cost curve ($p > minAVC$), the inflow of net revenue is maximized by monitoring the relationship between the market price and marginal cost. As long as price exceeds marginal cost, the last unit produced adds more to revenue than to cost, and net revenue continues to rise. When price equals marginal cost,

management learns that it is no longer profitable to expand output; the ideal rate of output has been found. By breaking even on the last unit produced, output is finely tuned to the market price: if price increases, expanding the rate of output will raise profit; if price decreases, output should be cut in order to minimize the adverse impact of the price decline on owners' wealth.

The moral is an important one: break-even analysis does not yield one unique production decision. If management's goal is to maximize the owner's wealth (since, for small firms, the owner and the manager are often the same person), then care must be taken that the criteria used for the break-even decision are consistent with the options the firm has. In the long run, the firm should commit to a new venture only if management is confident that all costs can be recovered by revenue: the firm must at least break even on long-run cost. Once some costs are fixed, only variable costs are relevant to the operating decision; if price equals or exceeds minimum average variable cost, the firm can at least break even on variable cost and can add something to owners' wealth to counteract (but not eliminate) the drag of fixed cost. Finally, once the decision to produce has been made, the profit-maximizing rate of output is determined when the firm breaks even on the last unit produced, that is, when price equals marginal cost.

In Figure 9-3*b*, the slope of the total revenue line is p_1, which exceeds minimum average variable cost, since $p_1 > AVC = MC$ at q_0. If the price in Figure 9-3*b* prevailed, the producer would clearly be better off by producing output q_0 than by shutting down, and since $p_1 > MC$ at q_0, losses would still be decreasing at that rate of output. In

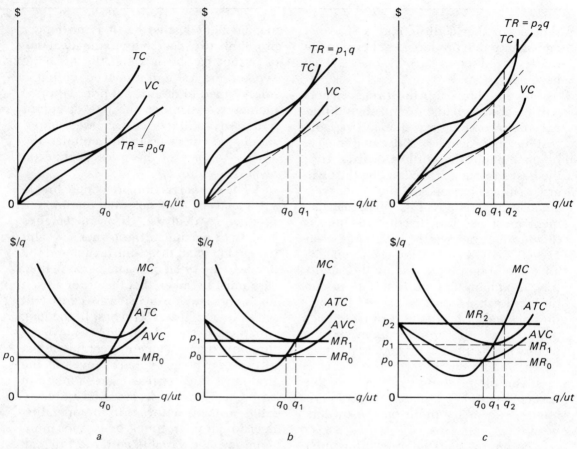

Figure 9-3
Profit-Maximizing Output for Alternative Market Prices

fact, the total revenue line in Figure 9-3b is tangent to the total cost curve at output q_1, which indicates that price (the slope of the total revenue line) equals marginal cost (the slope of the total cost curve) at that rate of output. Price p_1 is often called the **break-even price** because, at the profit-maximizing output, q_1, total revenue exactly equals total cost (zero economic profit). However, since the firm has no influence on the market price, whether the price is less than, equal to, or greater than p_1 is purely a matter of chance from the perspective of one firm. Later we will see that since the cost curves depicted in Figure 9-3 reflect efficient resource use, long-run market forces push the price toward p_1. But this long-run tendency does not change the assumption that the profit-maximizing firm reacts only to the prevailing price.

In Figure 9-3c, price p_2 causes the total revenue line to exceed the total cost curve at output q_1. Prices greater than the break-even price allow competitive firms to realize greater than zero economic profit at q_1, the output that would result in zero profit if price p_1 prevailed. Furthermore, since the total revenue line p_2q is steeper than the p_1q line, it follows that price is greater than marginal cost at q_1 in Figure 9-3c; by expanding output to q_2, profit can be increased. Profit maximization means obtaining the greatest *possible* profit (or incurring the smallest possible losses) for each market determined price. This is done by expanding output as price rises until marginal cost equals price, and contracting output as price falls until marginal cost equals price. As long as price remains above p_0, the portion of the firm's marginal cost curve which lies above its average variable cost curve indicates the best rate of output for each price.

APPLICATION
A Numerical Example of Short-Run Profit Maximization

In chapter six we used an isoquant-isocost tangency example to distinguish long-run planning costs from short-run operating costs. This example is extended in Table 9-1 to illustrate the output selection process for Gadget Inc. The first four columns of Table 9-1 reprise the short-run cost data for a gadget plant with fixed costs of $75 per hour (it has installed 15 machines which are each leased at $5 per hour). Labor, the variable input, is available at a constant wage rate of $10 per hour. Gilda Gadget, the proprietor, must have *expected* a market price of $15 or greater, since that is the minimum average total cost. However, once the contract for capital services has been signed, whether or not fixed costs are covered by revenue will be irrelevant to the firm's output decision. In the short run, only variable costs are under the firm's control. Consequently, only average variable cost and marginal cost are relevant to the short-run production decision.

Unlike the short-run costs depicted in Figures 9-2 and 9-3, those in Table 9-1 reflect diminishing marginal productivity of the variable input after the first unit of output. Accordingly, while $15 may have been the anticipated price, the *minimum price necessary to make producing less costly than shutting down is the minimum average variable cost*—in this case, $2.58. The short-run rate of gadget production is determined by this simple rule: if price exceeds marginal cost, expand production. (Note that in this case marginal cost exceeds average variable cost after the first unit of output. Therefore, the rule that "marginal cost should equal price" subsumes the requirement that price exceed average variable cost.) A price of $2.00 would cause Gadget Inc. to shut down, producing zero output and losing $75.00 per hour. Had one unit of output been produced, variable cost would have exceeded revenue by $0.58, and losses would have been $75.58. At a price of $3.00, one gadget per

TABLE 9-1
Cost and Supply Schedule for Gadget Inc.

q	MC	AVC	ATC	p	q	TR − VC	π
0	–	–	∞	$ 2.00	0	0	− $75.00
1	$ 2.58	$ 2.58	$77.58	3.00	1	$0.42	− 74.58
2	4.72	3.65	41.15	5.00	2	2.70	− 72.30
3	6.11	4.47	29.47	7.00	3	7.59	− 67.41
4	7.24	5.16	23.91	8.00	4	11.36	− 63.64
5	8.21	5.77	20.77	9.00	5	16.15	− 58.85
6	9.08	6.32	18.82	9.50	6	19.08	− 55.92
7	9.87	6.83	17.55	10.00	7	22.19	− 52.81
8	10.61	7.30	16.68	11.00	8	29.60	− 45.40
9	11.29	7.75	16.08	11.50	9	33.75	− 41.25
10	11.94	8.16	15.66	12.00	10	38.40	− 36.60
11	12.55	8.56	15.38	13.00	11	48.84	− 26.16
12	13.13	8.94	15.19	13.50	12	54.72	− 20.28
13	13.69	9.31	15.08	14.00	13	60.97	− 14.03
14	14.23	9.66	15.02	14.50	14	67.76	− 7.24
15	14.75	10.00	15.00	15.00	15	75.00	0.00
16	15.25	10.33	15.02	15.50	16	82.72	7.72
17	15.73	10.65	15.06	16.00	17	90.95	15.95
18	16.20	10.95	15.12	16.50	18	99.90	24.90
19	16.66	11.25	15.20	17.00	19	109.25	34.25
20	17.10	11.55	15.30	17.50	20	119.00	44.00
21	17.54	11.83	15.40	17.75	21	124.32	49.32
22	17.96	12.11	15.52	18.00	22	129.58	54.58
23	18.37	12.38	15.64	18.50	23	140.76	65.76
24	18.77	12.65	15.77	19.00	24	152.40	77.40
25	19.17	12.91	15.91	19.50	25	164.75	89.75

hour would be optimal: total revenue would exceed variable cost by $0.42, and losses would be cut from $75.00 to $74.58. The second gadget, with a marginal cost of $4.72, would not be worth producing at the $3.00 price. If the price were $5.00, the second gadget would be worth producing; revenue from the second gadget would exceed its marginal cost by $0.28. While this may seem like a pitifully small margin (which implies that producing the third unit is likely to be unprofitable at this price), the difference between the price and the marginal cost of the first unit is now $2.42. By producing two gadgets per hour when the price is $5.00, Gilda Gadget receives $2.70 of net revenue, reducing her losses to $72.30 per hour.

For a price taker with given input prices, the higher the price, the more output is cost justified. By comparing price with marginal cost, managers (and economics students) avoid having to cover the same ground with every price change. If the price rose from $5.00 to $7.00, Gilda Gadget would not have to determine whether the first two gadgets should be produced. By comparing that price with the marginal cost of the third unit, she would know that the optimal rate of output was three gadgets per hour. A price increase to $8.00 would justify production of the fourth unit. A price of $9.00 would justify the fifth unit, and so forth. As long as price exceeds minimum average variable cost, (here, the marginal cost of the first gadget) the firm's output decision can be simplified to determine whether the *next* unit of output is profitable. (The example in Table 9-1 *assumes* that marginal cost is known for each rate of output; hence the profit-maximizing output can be identified where price equals marginal cost. If output must vary discretely, and if marginal cost is not known, some guessing about whether to produce the last unit will occur.)

If the price reached $15.00, Gilda Gadget's long-run expectations would be realized. In the short run, the occurrence of the break-even price is fortuitous; nothing the entrepreneur can do will bring about that price. Nor, to the outsider, would the occurrence of the long-run break-even price be distinguished by any perceptible change in the firm's production strategy. A price increase from $14.50 to $15.00 would cause output to increase from 14 to 15 units per hour. As usual, the difference between revenue and variable cost would increase. That net revenue $(TR - VC)$ exactly equaled fixed cost would stop the drain on Gilda Gadget's bank balance, but all an outsider could determine would be that output increased as price rose.

Table 9-1 shows that output would continue to expand as price increased beyond the break-even price. At a price of $15.50, the fifteenth unit of output would return $0.75 more than its marginal cost, encouraging the production of the sixteenth unit, whose marginal cost is $15.25. To repeat, a price increase causes net revenue to increase for output already being produced at the lower price; expanding output then adds to net revenue the difference between the higher price and the marginal cost of additional units of output.

Marginal Cost and the Firm's Supply Curve

Maximizing profit means increasing output until profit cannot be increased any more, then producing at that rate so that profit does not fall below the maximum. This has been stated before, but it bears repeating. In Figure 9-4a and b, the profit-maximizing rate of production is identified at q^* for price p^*. Output is expanded until, at q^*, the last unit generates exactly enough revenue to cover its marginal cost. For the competitive firm, marginal revenue equals price. As long as the market is clearing at the prevailing price, any firm can sell all its owner or manager wishes to produce. To determine the benefit of selling an extra

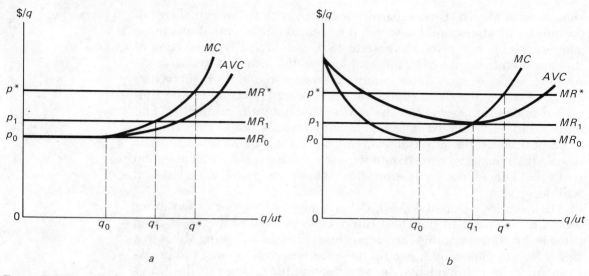

Figure 9-4
Variations in the Competitive Firm's Supply Curve. *a,* Variable use of fixed input(s); *b,* one or more fixed inputs must be used to capacity.

unit, management need only compare the revenue it brings in with the additional cost incurred by producing it. As long as price exceeds marginal cost, more is being added to revenue than is being added to cost; economic profit (revenue minus opportunity cost) must be growing (or losses shrinking), as output expands. If marginal cost exceeds price, the firm has overshot the optimal rate of output and must reduce production to increase profit (or cut losses). By setting the rate of output so that marginal cost equals price, the firm avoids realizing profit levels below the maximum.

Compare the two diagrams in Figure 9-4. An entrepreneur can avoid stage I of the production process if it is possible to prevent the marginal product of any fixed input from becoming negative by using that factor at less than its capacity rate. In Figure 9-4a, the marginal cost and average variable cost curves emanate from the vertical axis and remain at that original level until q_0 units are being produced. Expanding output along the ridge line for any fixed input minimizes the cost of variable inputs for each rate of output, until fixed inputs are used to capacity. Once all fixed inputs are being used, diminishing marginal productivity of the variable input(s) causes both marginal cost and average variable cost to rise as output increases. Marginal cost rises at a faster rate because average variable cost is held down by the lower variable cost of the first few units. The minimum price necessary to generate production is the marginal cost (equals average variable cost) of the first unit.

If use of the fixed input cannot be varied (e.g., an integrated assembly plant as opposed to a typing pool with surplus typewriters), more variable inputs will be required at low rates of output to counteract the negative marginal product of the fixed factor. This situation is depicted in Figure 9-4b, in which the marginal cost and average variable cost curves display a higher common intercept than in Figure 9-4a. However, except for the fact that fixed inputs must be used at capacity in Figure 9-4b, all other assumptions about the prices of input services, and the marginal product of the variable input inside the ridge line for the fixed input are the same for both diagrams. For instance, diminishing marginal productivity of the variable input commences at q_0 units of output in Figure 9-4. Increasing marginal productivity for the variable input in Figure 9-4b means that marginal cost at q_0 is identical in both diagrams. However, because average variable cost does not fall as fast or as far as marginal cost in Figure 9-4b, the minimum average cost in that diagram lies above the intercept of average variable cost in Figure 9-4a.

Recall that the minimum average variable cost (identified by $MC = AVC$) determines the shutdown price of the perfectly competitive seller. The contrasting diagrams in Figure 9-4 show that the ability to use "fixed" inputs below capacity allows a firm to sustain low rates of output at lower prices than could be borne by firms whose fixed inputs always had to be used at capacity. In Figure 9-4a, the shutdown point is (p_0, q_0): if $p = p_0$, total revenue would equal variable cost, and losses would equal fixed cost if the firm produced q_0. Hence, the firm would not produce at prices less than p_0, and would never maximize profit or minimize losses by producing less than q_0 units per period. In Figure 9-4b, average variable cost intersects marginal cost at q_1, identifying a shutdown price of p_1. While the firm depicted in Figure 9-4a would produce while the price was between p_0 and p_1 (since losses would be less than fixed cost by doing so), the firm in Figure 9-4b would produce only when the price equaled or exceeded p_1. When fixed inputs must be used to capacity for small rates of output, the shutdown price is determined by solving for the rate of output at which marginal cost equals average variable cost, then calculating the price that would equal average variable cost.

Minimum average variable cost identifies the lowest point on the supply curve of the perfectly competitive firm. The rule—produce where marginal cost equals price as long as price exceeds average variable cost—identifies a unique rate of output for each market price (prices of input and technology held constant). For prices less than minimum variable cost, the firm's profit-maximizing output is zero. For prices greater than the shutdown price, output is given by the marginal cost equals price rule. At each profit-maximizing rate of output, marginal cost will be increasing and will lie above the average variable cost. Once the shutdown price has been surpassed, the marginal cost curve will intersect the prevailing marginal revenue line (everywhere equal to the market price) only once.

The one-to-one correspondence between price and points on the marginal cost curve above minimum average variable cost indicates the profit-maximizing rate of output for each price. The portion of the firm's short-run marginal cost curve above minimum average variable cost is the firm's *short-run supply curve*. As long as $p > p_{\min} = AVC_{\min}$, then $\Delta q/\Delta p > 0$; an increase in price causes the firm to expand production until marginal cost equals the new price or until the capacity of fixed inputs is reached.[4] Price decreases cause the firm to contract output until marginal cost falls to equal the lower price or, should price drop below the shutdown point, to cease operations.

Having recognized that equalizing marginal cost and price (for $p > AVC$) yields a unique rate of output for each price in the short run, one final step is required before the short-run supply curve of the competitive producer is precisely defined. As in the case of household demand, the price of the product acts as the independent variable and quantity reacts as the dependent variable along the firm's short-run supply curve. Hence, that short-run supply curve is defined by first setting the marginal cost formula equal to price, then solving that equation for the value of q. Since only the upward sloping portion of the short-run marginal cost curve that lies above the average variable cost curve is relevant, solving $p = MC(q)$ for q generates a positively sloped supply function of the form $q = s(p)$,[5] where s stands for "supply function."

APPLICATION

Changes in Supply versus Changes in Quantity Supplied

The firm's **supply curve** indicates the quantity of a commodity it will deliver to the market at each market price during the relevant period of time. As a price taker, the competitive firm reacts to changes in the market price by expanding or contracting output until marginal cost

---

[4] If production is characterized by the type of technology discussed in chapter seven, whereby the marginal product of a variable input is constant for a fixed-proportion technology and then falls to zero when the capacity of fixed inputs is reached, the marginal cost curve will become vertical at the capacity of fixed inputs. If more than one technology is available, the marginal cost curve will be a step function.

[5] In our numerical example, $q = L^{2/3}K^{1/3}$; with $\overline{K} = 15$, $q = 15^{1/3}L^{2/3} = 2.47L^{2/3}$, so that $L = 0.258q^{1.5}$. Since $MC = \partial C/\partial q = \partial C/\partial L/\partial q/\partial L$, MC can be determined as:

$$\frac{w}{MP_L} = \frac{10}{2/3(2.47)L^{-1/3}} = 6.08L^{1/3} = 6.08(0.258q^{1.5})^{1/3}$$

or $MC = 3.87q^{1/2}$. Finally, setting $MC = p$ and solving for q, we have: $p = 3.87q^{1/2}$, implying $q^{1/2} = 0.258p$, so that $q = 0.067p^2$.

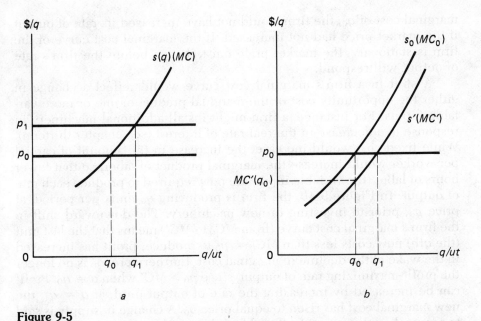

Figure 9-5
Distinction between *a*, Change in Quantity Supplied, and *b*, Change in Supply for Individual Seller in a Competitive Market.

equals the new market price—unless the new market price is less than the shutdown price, in which case production ceases. As long as each variable input's price and marginal product do not change, the firm's supply curve will remain stationary. A change in market price will locate a new profit-maximizing rate of output along the short-run supply curve; a change in the market price will cause a **change in quantity supplied**, *ceteris paribus*.

It is not unusual to hear a merchant proclaim that he or she is in business to serve the public. This is a noble sentiment which probably does little harm, but it does not jibe with the economic theory of the firm. An idea which has survived over two centuries of refinement of economic theory was expressed eloquently by Adam Smith: "It is not from the benevolence of the butcher, the brewer or the baker that we expect our dinner, but from their regard for their own self interest. We address ourselves, not to their humanity but to their self-love, and we never talk to them of our necessities but of their advantages."[6] When consumers desire more output from competitive producers, they signal their increased demand by offering to pay a higher price. In Figure 9-5a, the increase in market price from p_0 to p_1 causes the firm to increase output from q_0 to q_1. Since the previous price, p_0, exactly covered the

[6] *An Inquiry into the Nature and Causes of the Wealth of Nations* (New York: Modern Library edition, 1937), p. 14.

marginal cost of q_0, the firm would not have increased its rate of output if the market price had not increased. If the marginal cost curve of the firm is stationary, the market price must change before the firm's rate of output will respond.

A shift in a firm's marginal cost curve would reflect a change in either the opportunity cost or the marginal product of one or more variable inputs. For instance, a firm might install additional machinery in response to a decrease in the real rate of interest (see chapter thirteen). While fixed cost would increase, the increase in the amount of capital per worker would increase the marginal product of labor, so that fewer hours of labor (the variable input) are now required to produce each rate of output. In Figure 9-4b, the firm is producing q_0 units per period, at price p_0, prior to investing in new machinery. The downward shift in the firm's marginal cost curve (from MC_0 to MC') means that the last unit (the qth) now costs less than $MC_0 = p_0$ to produce; profit has increased in the wake of the decline in marginal cost. Furthermore, q_0 is no longer the profit-maximizing rate of output, since $p_0 > MC'$ when $q = q_0$. Profit can be increased by increasing the rate of output until, at $q = q_1$, the new marginal cost has risen to equal price p_0. **A change in supply** is said to occur when the quantity offered for sale at each market price increases. For the individual competitive seller, a change in supply occurs when its short-run marginal cost curve shifts to the right or the left.

APPLICATION
The I-Can't-Pass-the-Costs-to-Buyers Blues

Figure 9-6 illustrates an important, if painful, lesson about the limited options of the competitive seller. If the cost of production rises, the seller must absorb the cost increase, unless market-wide forces change the product price. Let us return to the mundane adventures of Lee Whositz, production manager for Whatsit Widgets. In the absence of contrary evidence, we assume that widgets are sold in a perfectly competitive market. In Figure 9-6b, a prevailing price of p_0 causes Lee to produce q_0 widgets per day, which is identified by the intersection of marginal cost curve MC_0 with the marginal revenue line p_0, MR_0. In Figure 9-6a, we note that the optimal input combination for q_0 widgets per day is L_0 labor hours and K_0 capital hours, purchased at prices w_L^0 and w_K^0, respectively. Invoking poetic license, this firm just happens to be producing the optimal rate of output for its capital input.

An economic boom in Tinytown, where the Whatsit Widgets plant is located, increases the wage rate for unskilled labor from w_L^0 to w_L', causing the cost of L_0 labor hours and K_0 machine-hours to rise to C_2. As a result, the tangency point for isoquant q_0 and the former isocost line, C_0, is now the intersection point between isoquant q_0 and the new

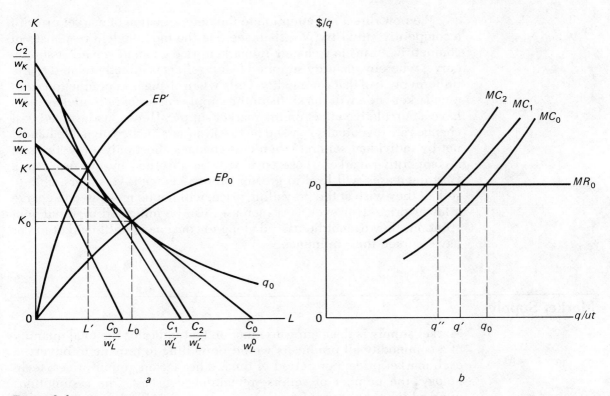

Figure 9-6
Impact of an Increase in the Wage Rate on Profit-Maximizing Output (product price constant)

isocost line C_2. If substitution of capital for labor is impossible in the short run because widget-making machinery must be designed to the specifications of individual plants, the short-run marginal cost curve for Whatsit Widgets jumps from MC_0 to MC_2 in Figure 9-6b. Without an increase in the market price of widgets, the only way to cut costs would be to reduce output; by reducing output to q'', Lee would minimize losses associated with the higher cost of labor.

If input substitution were possible, perhaps because widget-making machinery could be rented by the day, the cost of producing q_0 widgets could be reduced from C_2 to C_1 by reducing labor hours from L_0 to L' per day, while hiring $(K' - K_0)$ capital hours per day. Being able to expand and contract output along the new output expansion path, OEP', allows Lee to hold the cost increase to points along marginal cost curve MC_1 in Figure 9-6b. With the product price constant, the *output effect* of the wage increase equals $(q_0 - q'')$ when input substitution is impossible. Input substitution reduces the size of the output effect to $(q_0 - q')$, meaning that input substitution leads to a smaller decrease in supply (leftward shift of the firm's short-run supply curve).

We now direct our attention to the determination of market price in a competitive industry. We shall see that the independent responses of competitive firms to a change in market price generate a market supply curve, whereby quantity supplied by all sellers is directly related to the uniform price of that commodity. Only when changes in production costs are market-wide will the shifts in the supply curves of individual sellers have a cumulative effect on the market supply. Hence, widespread cost changes are (eventually) passed on to consumers by the "invisible hand," not by individual sellers. When cost changes affect only a few firms in a competitive market, those costs will be absorbed by the firm itself. Cost decreases will lead to greater profits; competitive sellers, able to sell all they wish at the prevailing price, will not be motivated to charge a lower price. However, cost increases can be mitigated by input substitution; they cannot be passed along to consumers until market forces have worked their influence.

Market Supply

Market supply is the aggregate function that indicates the total quantity of a commodity all producers would be willing to provide to buyers at each market price, per period of time, other factors (input prices, technology, the number of sellers) remaining constant. The assumptions upon which the theory of perfect competition is based make it possible to generate a market supply curve by summing the quantity supplied by every firm at each price. First, the assumption of a homogeneous product means that each firm receives the market price for its output. The assumption of many sellers means that each firm is a price-taker: the market price determines the firm's rate of output, rather than firms manipulating their rate of output to change price (as monopolies do). Later we will see that the assumption of free entry (and exit) generates a long-run (*mutatis mutandis*) supply curve, as the number of sellers changes in response to economic profit or loss.

In Figure 9-7, the market supply curve, $S(p)$, is generated by summing the quantity supplied by firms 1 through n at alternative market prices. When price p_0 prevails, firm 1 produces q_0^1 and firm 2 produces q_0^2 and firm n produces q_0^n per period: total quantity supplied at price p_0 is:

$$Q_0 = q_0^1 + q_0^2 + \ldots + q_0^n = \sum_{i=1}^{n} q_0^i$$

using summation notation. When price p_1 prevails, firm 1 produces q_1^1, firm 2 produces q_1^2, and firm n produces q_1^n. The total quantity supplied at p_1 is Q_1, which is the sum of the quantity supplied by all firms at that price. Technically, horizontal summation of all producers' supply curves

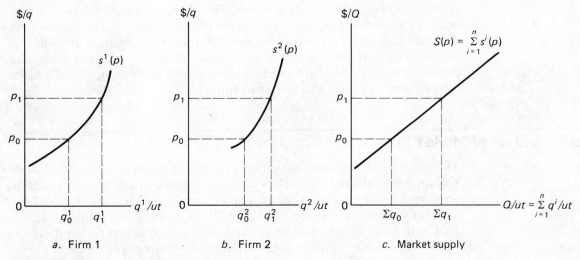

Figure 9-7
Aggregation of Firm Supply into Market Supply

means that the $MC^i = p$ profit maximization condition for all firms $(i = 1, 2, \ldots, n)$ is first solved to make quantity a function of price: $q^i = s^i(p)$. For each value of p, market quantity supplied is determined as $Q = \sum_{i=1}^{n} q^i$ so that $Q = S(p) = \sum_{i=1}^{n} s^i(p)$.

The process of aggregating a large number of individual firms' supply curves to obtain the market supply curve is similar to the procedure, outlined in chapter four, used to generate the market demand curve by the horizontal summation of household demand curves. This process relies on the **law of large numbers** and the *normal curve of error* to bypass the idiosyncrasies of particular firms, thereby focusing only on market-wide influences on supply. If Acme Widgets mistakenly hired only Ph.D. economists as widget welders, Acme's excessive marginal cost could be counterbalanced by Walter Warlock's talent for reducing the marginal cost of Ballistic Widgets by use of psychokinesis. In contrast, a market-wide change in the wage rate would shift the short-run supply (i.e., the short-run marginal cost) curve of each firm in the industry in the same direction; hence, the market supply curve for widgets will shift. Similarly, one firm may enter the industry while another leaves; as long as the number of sellers remains roughly the same, the market supply curve will not shift. However, when there is a systematic increase in the number of firms, particularly in response to the existence of positive economic profit by existing firms, the market supply curve will shift to the right. Similarly, were the number of sellers to decrease systematically, say, in response to prolonged economic losses by members of the industry, the market supply curve would shift to the left.

The distinction between the short-run (operating) and long-run (planning) periods for individual firms is also relevant to the shape and position of the market supply curve. The short-run market supply curve is a *ceteris paribus* curve: the number of firms, the costs of inputs, and the state of technology are all assumed to remain constant. The long-run market supply function, as will be shown below, is a *mutatis mutandis* curve, taking into account predictable changes in the number of sellers (due to entry or exit) and prices of inputs.

Determination of Market Price

Having seen that short-run market supply is a positive relation between the quantity offered by sellers and the market price, we are ready to explore how the interaction of market supply and market demand determines the market price. Being unable to control market price means that individual buyers and individual sellers must adjust their purchases to changes in the market price. Hence, like the market demand curve, the market supply curve actually represents a set of contingent quantities; the relevant quantity supplied is determined by the price that actually prevails. Since they are derived from the process of profit maximization by the firms in the industry, a change in the number of firms or in the position of the representative firm's marginal cost curve will change the production plans (quantity supplied at each price) of sellers. Also, if sellers (or buyers) are unable to carry out their plans (e.g., sellers offer more than buyers wish to purchase at the prevailing price), then market price itself will change.

The magic of a competitive market is that since market price is beyond the control of individual participants, they must adjust their behavior to that price. However, only when the planned purchases of buyers and the planned sales of sellers are the same will the market price be stable; otherwise, the market price will adjust to the response of buyers and/or sellers to the frustration of their intentions. This process might seem circular; it is. The invisible hand is quicker than the eye!

In Figure 9-8, the market equilibrium price and quantity are determined by the intersection of the supply and demand curves. A competitive market is in **equilibrium** if, and only if, at the prevailing price, the *quantity supplied* equals the *quantity demanded*. Given their tastes, incomes, and the prices of complements and substitutes, consumers always prefer lower prices to higher prices. However, because households attempt to purchase more at lower prices than at higher prices (*ceteris paribus*), prices that are below the equilibrium price generate market shortages. This causes prices to rise, which in turn causes buyers and sellers to modify the quantity they wish to buy or sell. Given prevailing technology, the prices of inputs, and the number of firms in the industries, firms always prefer higher prices to lower ones. However, because the attempt to maximize profit causes firms to increase their rate of output

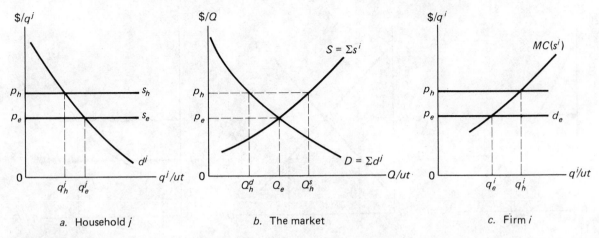

Figure 9-8
Reaction of Quantity Demanded and Quantity Supplied to a Market Surplus

as price rises, prices above equilibrium would cause a surplus of the commodity in question. The surplus would cause the price to fall, which in turn would modify the amount that sellers wished to sell and buyers wished to buy.

In Figure 9-8, the nature of market equilibrium is analyzed through *reductio ad absurdum* logic: we understand why the market price must settle at p_e by working through the forces that would come into play if some other price prevailed. Later, we will see how changes in exogenous variables (e.g., consumer income, input prices) cause market price and quantity to change from one equilibrium to another. However, to simplify the exposition of Figure 9-8, we assume that outside forces remain constant; that is, that neither the demand curve nor the supply curve shifts.

First, suppose that the price were too high for equilibrium; let $p = p_h$. A typical household (i), depicted in Figure 9-8a, would attempt to purchase q_h^j units of the commodity per period of time. At price p_h, households collectively demand quantity $Q_d^h = \sum_{j=1}^{m} q_h^j$, where m is the number of households. A typical firm (j), pictured in Figure 9-8c, would produce q_h^i, causing a total quantity supplied $Q_h^s = \sum_{i=1}^{n} q_h^j$ to exceed the quantity demanded at p_h. Precisely because exchange is voluntary in a competitive market, the desires of consumers would be decisive at price p_h: sellers would be left with unwanted inventories of the commodity, for which production costs had already been incurred. Rather than lose their entire outlay for producing the **surplus** output, sellers would cut their price.

Because of the large number of sellers, sales at price p_h are likely to be spread unevenly among firms. Those who are lucky sell all they

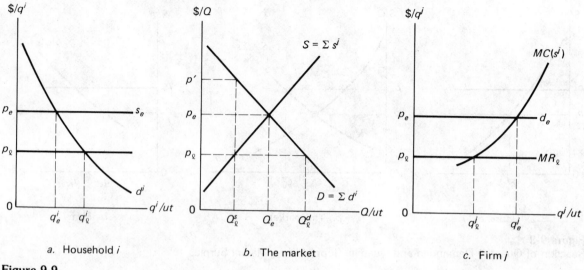

Figure 9-9
Reaction of Quantity Demanded and Quantity Supplied to a Market Shortage

produced; others sell almost nothing. Some of the latter firms will panic, slashing price before bankruptcy occurs. This price-cutting attracts consumers from higher priced sellers. Soon, even those sellers who once sold all they could produce at price p_h find it necessary to cut their prices as well. For a while, the assumption of a uniform competitive price will be violated, but eventually prices will cluster about p_e. Buyers and sellers would react in opposite ways to the price decrease. Households desire to purchase more at p_e than at p_h; the quantity demanded increases along the stationary market demand curve D. For sellers, who cut price in the wake of the shortage, the rate of output falls, both because sales are temporarily made out of inventories, and because, at p_e, it is profitable only to produce q_e^i. After inventories have stabilized, firms have reduced output along the stationary market supply curve, S. When price reaches p_e (equilibrium), the rate of sales would equal the rate of output (i.e., unplanned inventories would be exhausted[7]) and sellers would have no incentive to cut price further. At p_e consumers would be able to buy all they wanted (at that price) and producers would be able to sell all they offered (at that price).

If the price of a commodity was too low for equilibrium, such as p_l in Figure 9-9, a **shortage** would occur. The typical firm would be able

---

[7] The model of perfect competition does not take into account such influences on consumer purchases as seasonal variations, the influence of weather, when workers are paid, and so forth. Many economists earn their incomes by determining a firm's optimal inventory policy: how to distinguish variations in sales due to cycles or seasons from variations due to a change in market conditions.

to sell all it produced, q_f^i, at the prevailing price. However, total quantity demanded, $Q_f^d = \sum q_f^i$, would exceed total quantity supplied, $Q_f^s = \sum q_f^i$. A firm might discover the shortage when inventories began to decline because its rate of sales exceeded its rate of production. Consumers would discover the shortage when the commodity became scarcer (harder to find) at the prevailing price.

When consumers wish to buy more than sellers are willing to supply at the prevailing price, some mechanism must be found to ration the goods available. Many rationing procedures exist: first come, first served (used for underpriced rock concerts and sporting events); nepotism and favoritism (used for dispensing political favors or club memberships when fees are insufficient to reduce the number of applicants to the number of memberships available); and even complicated systems of limiting the opportunity to purchase (e.g., the 1974 gasoline rationing scheme whereby the right to purchase gasoline on a particular day was based on whether the last digit in a car's license plate was even or odd).

Each form of rationing has some (intended or unintended) side effect(s). A first come–first served approach favors consumers with a low valuation of time, who experience the least cost standing in line. The costs to the consumer (the purchase price plus opportunity costs incurred in waiting) exceed the revenue received by the seller. Use of cronyism to allocate scarce goods requires that those who seek favors channel some of their energy into cultivating friendships with influential people, or staying on good terms with relatives who have connections, which can generate high psychic costs and impair digestion. Even a seemingly egalitarian scheme for rationing gasoline (since money prices were frozen) had an unnerving side effect. On the first morning the "odd-even" rationing system was set to go into effect in 1974, the city of Los Angeles experienced a wave of an unprecedented crime—license plate theft. Auto parts stores soon sold out of two commodities: lockable gasoline-tank caps and siphon hoses.

The form of rationing most consistent with the profit-maximizing goal of sellers also is the most effective at relieving the shortage. Confronted with more buyers than they have merchandise to sell, firms hold auctions, raising the price until the market clears. Disgruntled buyers, unwilling to pay high prices, embark on their search for sellers offering lower prices. To their dismay, they find no lower priced sellers. Facing the inevitable, consumers decide that paying a higher (than expected) price is better than doing without, even though they will purchase less at the higher price then they would have at a lower price (an upward movement along the demand curve).

Using price to ration a scarce commodity also encourages sellers to offer more of that commodity. As the price rises, producers expand output along their short-run marginal cost curves. When the price reaches p_e in Figure 9-9, equilibrium has been achieved. Since more is now being produced, the shortage has been elevated while consumers have had to reduce their purchases only by $\Delta Q^d = Q_l^d - Q_e$. Had some other rationing scheme been used, such as the first come–first served system, consumers would have been able to obtain only Q_l^s. When sellers are legally prevented from raising their price (price controls), an illegal market, called a **black market**, will come into being. Because selling a commodity illegally entails risk, the black market price will generally rise higher than what the legal equilibrium price would have been. In Figure 9-9, the black market price associated with quantity Q_l^s would be p' $(>p_e)$ or higher.

The Nature of Market Equilibrium

When a market is in equilibrium, the countervailing forces of supply and demand are in balance. Equilibrium does not mean a suspension of consumer utility-maximizing behavior or producer profit-maximizing behavior. However, when a competitive market is in equilibrium, the downward pressure on price exerted by consumers' utility-maximizing behavior is checked by the success of producers at selling all they choose to offer at the prevailing price, while the upward pressure on price exerted by producers' profit-maximizing behavior is checked by the success of consumers at obtaining all they wish to buy at the prevailing price.

Market equilibrium is a dynamic phenomenon; the opposing forces acting on market price tend to keep price and quantity at the same level over time. In Figure 9-10 (as in Figures 9-8 and 9-9 and other diagrams

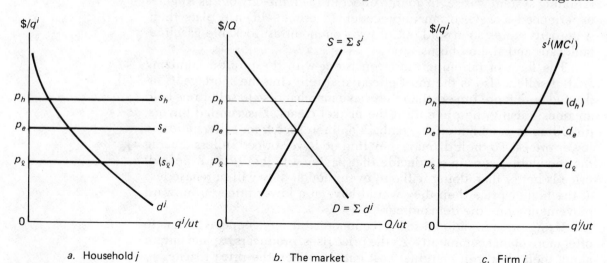

a. Household *j*   b. The market   c. Firm *i*

Figure 9-10
The Nature of Competitive Market Equilibrium

of supply and/or demand curves), the horizontal axis measures quantity per unit of time. Market equilibrium does not refer to a one-time exchange, but a continuous rate of exchange over time. In an important sense, how perfect competition works is revealed not so much in the behavior of a market in equilibrium as in the events that occur when a market is not in equilibrium.

When the price of a commodity is too high for equilibrium, a surplus exists. In Figure 9-10a, the horizontal supply curve labeled s_h indicates that at price p_h each household is capable of buying all that its members wish to purchase at that price. However, in Figure 9-10c the horizontal demand curve labeled (d_h) is an illusion. Some producers will discover that they cannot sell all they wish to offer at p_h. Since costs of production are usually incurred before a product is sold,[8] the normal reluctance of sellers to cut price will be dissolved in the wake of unwanted inventories. Panicky sellers will reduce their prices, hoping to recover some of their expenses. Consumers who periodically sample sellers' prices in the hope of finding bargains will gravitate to the price cutters. Resentment and chagrin will move like a wave through the industry as all producers are forced to match price cuts to avoid financial disaster.

When the price settles at p_e, households face a new horizontal supply curve, s_e, indicating that they can now purchase all they desire at the equilibrium price. Supply curve s_h has melted into irrelevance. Since producers are able to sell all they desire to offer at p_e, there is a realistic horizontal demand curve at the equilibrium price (as opposed to the former illusion of d_h).

The shape of the market supply curve is determined by the shape of the typical firm's marginal cost curve (above minimum average variable cost). The fact that a household is usually a price taker means that, when the market is in equilibrium, any household can purchase all that it wants at the market price. How much a particular household actually purchases is, of course, determined by its negatively sloped household demand curve, which is generated by members' utility-maximizing purchase plans. The shape of the market demand curve is determined by the shape of the typical household demand curve. The fact that a competitive firm is a price taker means that, when the market is in equilibrium, any firm can sell all it chooses to produce. How much a particular

---

[8] Incurring a cost obligation does not imply immediate payment. For instance, workers' paychecks usually reflect payment for past work. This practice became more prevalent as real wages rose, eventually ending the wages fund controversy which raged in the late eighteenth and early nineteenth century. If workers were paid before their output was sold, the argument went, the employment level would be determined by the stock of wage goods in society, just as any employer would be able to hire only up to the level of his wages fund (i.e., money with which to pay labor before output is sold). Seeing production as a continuous process, however, workers who are paid after work is performed can be paid out of revenue; and since workers spend their earnings slowly, inventories can be monitored to adjust output to changes in demand.

competitive firm actually produces depends on its profit-maximizing rate of output at the equilibrium price.

When the price of a commodity is too low for equilibrium, as is p_l in Figure 9-10, firms can nevertheless sell all they wish at that price. Consumers, however, face a horizontal supply curve (s_l) that is really an illusion. If they look for sellers charging p_l or less, some will be frustrated, since less is offered by firms than consumers wish to buy. Rather than do without, some buyers will overcome their normal aversion to higher prices and pay more for the commodity.

A market shortage neutralizes the downward pressure on prices normally exerted by consumers, thereby giving rein to the upward pressure on prices stemming from producers' profit-maximizing behavior. As the price rises, however, consumers' downward pressure on prices begins to reassert itself. The quantity demanded by consumers falls; each market transaction results in a smaller quantity exchanged than would have been the case at a lower price. Further, as the price increases, so does the firm's profit-maximizing rate of output. Equilibrium is established at p_e. Sellers now respond to the horizontal marginal revenue curve d_e; the willingness of consumers to purchase at price p_l is ignored. But each household now faces an actual (as opposed to an illusory) horizontal supply curve; at p_e the household can purchase all its members desire at that price. Consumers no longer have an incentive to offer a higher price.

APPLICATION
Changes in Supply and Demand in the Short Run

Market equilibrium, which involves the balance of counteracting forces, is analogous to the concept of inertia in the physical sciences: a market in equilibrium tends to remain in equilibrium, unless position of the supply curve or the demand curve is shifted by outside forces. Those outside forces are, of course, those variables held constant by the *ceteris paribus* assumptions underlying those two curves. As long as consumer tastes, consumer income, the prices of substitutes and complements (which determine the position of the demand curve), and input prices, technology, and the number of sellers (which determine the position of the supply curve) remain constant, the equilibrium price and quantity will also repeat their pattern each period. In this section, we explore the process by which a competitive market adjusts to a shift in either the short-run demand curve or the short-run supply curve.

In Figure 9-11, we encounter the market for generic oatmeal, initially in equilibrium at a price of $1.00 per pound, with the Smith family, a typical household, consuming 16 pounds of oatmeal per month. Typical

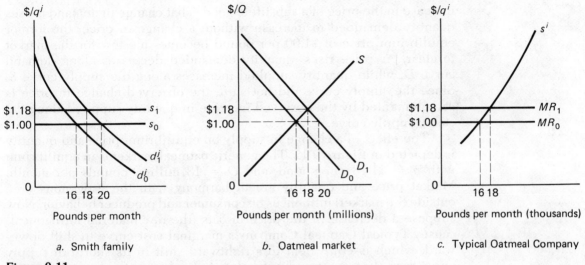

Figure 9-11
Increase in the Demand for Generic Oatmeal: Price and Quantity Increase.

Oatmeal Company, a representative producer, maximizes profit by producing 16,000 pounds of oatmeal per month. We now imagine that the price of cornflakes increases from $1.05 to $1.25 per box; the Smiths, being typical, reduce their consumption of cornflakes and decide to buy 20 pounds of oatmeal instead. The increase in demand from d_0^j to d_1^j for the typical household is reflected in a rightward shift in the market demand curve from D_0 to D_1 in Figure 9-11*b*. At the prevailing price of $1 per pound, consumers wish to purchase 20 million pounds of oatmeal, while producers offer only 16 million pounds at that price. The shortage of 5 million pounds of oatmeal causes the price of oatmeal to rise.

When the price reaches $1.18 per pound, producers have increased the total output of oatmeal to 18 million pounds per month; Typical Oatmeal Company, in Figure 9-11*c*, is now producing 18,000 pounds of oatmeal per month. As the price rises, the Smith family reduces its intended consumption of oatmeal from 20 pounds to 18 pounds per month. The cumulative reduction in quantity demanded means that consumers have reduced their intended consumption to 18 million pounds of oatmeal per month. However, since households were unable to buy the 20 million pounds of oatmeal they wanted at the $1.00 price, a market observer would notice only two points: 16 million pounds of oatmeal were sold at $1.00 per pound; 18 million pounds are now sold at $1.18 per pound.

The distinction between a change in demand and a change in quantity demanded has a concrete relevance to the order of events when one market equilibrium is replaced by another. A change in demand occurs in response to a change in an exogenous variable—in this case, an increase in the price of a substitute good. That change in demand causes quantity demanded to increase without a change in price; the former equilibrium price of $1.00 per pound becomes too low for the market to clear. As price rises, quantity demanded decreases along demand curve D, while quantity supplied increases along the supply curve S. Since the supply curve did not shift, the observed change in price is complemented by the observed increase in quantity supplied along the stable supply curve.

The effect of a change in supply on equilibrium price and quantity is depicted in Figure 9-12. The generic oatmeal market is in equilibrium with p = $1.18 per pound, and Q = 18 million pounds per month. Market price and quantity are in harmony with the exogenous (i.e., outside the market) influences on consumer and producer behavior. Now suppose a decrease in the price of oats (the raw material for oatmeal) causes Typical Oatmeal Company's marginal cost curve to shift downward, which is equivalent to a rightward shift in its short-run supply curve from s_0^i to s_1^i. At each market price (including the prevailing one), each firm offers more pounds of oatmeal per month: the market supply curve shifts to the right, from S_0 to S_1. Typical Oatmeal Company now produces 22,000 pounds of oatmeal per month, which it stores in its warehouse until sales are made. But without a decrease in price, consumers will continue to purchase 18 million pounds of oatmeal per month: a surplus of 4 million bushels per month cancels sellers' usual resistance to price decreases.

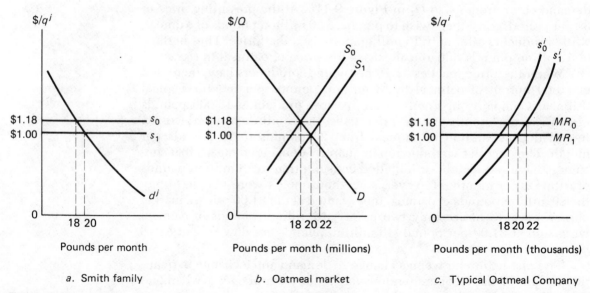

a. Smith family   *b.* Oatmeal market   *c.* Typical Oatmeal Company

Figure 9-12
Reaction of Equilibrium Price and Quantity to a Change in Supply of Generic Oatmeal

As inventories build up, some firms cut their price, which forces all other firms to cut their price as well. As price falls, the Smiths, and other families, increase their consumption of oatmeal. When the price settles at $1.00 per pound, the Smith household has increased its consumption of oatmeal to 20 pounds per month, and total quantity demanded has increased to 20 million pounds per month. The representative oatmeal producer has cut output to 20,000 pounds per month, since the last 2,000 pounds, which were profitable at $1.18 per pound, are no longer worth producing. The increase in supply has reduced the equilibrium price; since the demand curve did not shift, the two price-quantity equilibria both lie on that demand curve.

Long-Run Competitive Equilibrium: The Invisible Hand Points the Way

In the short-run model of supply and demand, the number of firms operating in the competitive market and the production capacity of the representative firm are treated as constants; a change in either variable would cause the short-run market supply curve to shift, and the restoration of market equilibrium would then be traced along the stable demand curve. In the long-run model of perfect competition, both the number of firms in the industry and the production capacity of each are **endogenous variables**; that is, these variables are now determined within the model. The *short-run* supply function is a *ceteris paribus* function: the relationship between price and quantity is defined by holding all other variables constant. The long-run supply curve is a *mutatis mutandis* function: predictable changes in the number of firms in the industry, and in the plant size or input prices for typical firms, are taken into account in tracing through the path of long-run responses to demand changes.

In Figure 9-13c, the long-run and short-run average and marginal cost curves are added. To add some drama to a less-than-spell-binding adventure, Typical Oatmeal Company is shown as operating on the increasing portion of its long-run average cost curve. Typical Oatmeal is in short-run equilibrium, since its output of q_0^i corresponds to the intersection of its short-run marginal cost curve and the horizontal marginal revenue line MR_e. To his chagrin, Rolly Dotes, the entrepreneur, is earning zero economic profit—also called *normal profit*—since the accounting profits of this firm are what Rolly's resources (his labor, land, and financial assets) could earn in another competitive industry. When he built the Typical Oatmeal plant, he obviously expected price to equal p_1, given by the intersection of the long-run and short-run marginal cost curves. Instead, price p_0 prevails, which by amazing coincidence (except

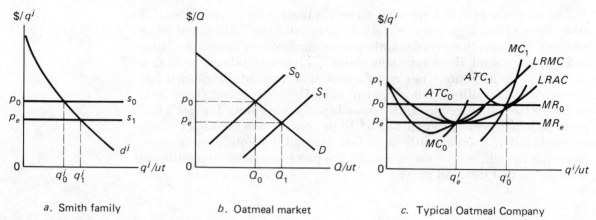

a. Smith family   *b.* Oatmeal market   *c.* Typical Oatmeal Company

Figure 9-13
Long-Run Competitive Equilibrium

for a textbook example), just happens to intersect SAC_1 at its minimum point (i.e., where $SAC_1 = MC_1$).

At price p_0, Typical Oatmeal produces q_0^i, since that is where MC_1 intersects MR_0. Although Rolly Dotes cannot make a positive economic profit at price p_0, firms with plants constructed for smaller rates of output could escape the diseconomies of scale experienced by Typical Oatmeal. Firms with production capacity characterized by short-run average cost curve ATC_0 will be attracted to the oatmeal industry. As entry occurs, the short-run supply curve creeps toward S_1, generating a surplus at price p_0. Market price begins to erode along market demand curve D. When price reaches p_e, a firm with a plant characterized by ATC_0 would be producing q_0 pounds of oatmeal per month; its total revenue ($p_e \times q_0$) would exactly equal its total economic costs ($ATC_0 \times q_0$).

As efficient-sized firms enter the industry, firms of inefficient size begin to experience economic losses. If internal diseconomies are reversible, Typical Oatmeal will reduce plant size (e.g., by selling off excess machinery and laying off management and production workers) until it can produce oatmeal at the minimum long-run average cost. If internal diseconomies are not reversible, firms like Typical Oatmeal will either be driven from the business or the net worth of Rolly Dotes will deteriorate to the resale value of the Typical Oatmeal plant. Considered as a return on the current value of an inefficient plant, Rolly's net revenue will constitute a normal return on assets. And once old firms are receiving zero economic profit, the incentive for entering the industry will have been eliminated.

As discussed at the beginning of this chapter, the ultimate beneficiaries in the perfectly competitive model are consumers. This result can be seen by tracing the long-run reaction of a competitive market to an autonomous change in consumer demand. In Figure 9-14, we assume that the oatmeal market is in long-run equilibrium with a price of p_e. Because of, say, an increase in population (adding more household demand curves like the one in Figure 9-14a), market demand for oatmeal increases. For simplicity, each household's demand curve (represented by the Smith household diagram) is assumed to remain stationary.

The increase in market demand from D_0 to D_1 creates a shortage of $Q_2 - Q_0$ at price p_e. In the short run, price increases to p_1 and intended consumption falls to Q_1, where the new market demand curve intersects the short-run supply curve S_0. Because fixed inputs cannot be increased immediately, Typical Oatmeal Company expands output along its short-run marginal cost curve. Price exceeds short-run average total cost at output level q_1^i, where short-run marginal cost equals price p_1 for the typical firm operating with the minimum long-run average cost plant. Established firms are earning enough revenue to cover all variable costs and all fixed costs, with something extra left over—positive economic profit. Owners of optimally sized plants such as Rolly Dotes may *plan* to expand into the region of internal diseconomies to equate long-run marginal cost to the price of p_1. If they are lucky, the long-run adjustment process due to market entry by additional optimally sized firms will begin to erode economic profit before short-sighted entrepreneurs sign contracts for fixed inputs resulting in excessive long-run average cost.

The prospect of short-run economic profit attracts additional producers to the industry. As the number of sellers increases, the short-run supply curve shifts to the right until, when the market price has been driven back down to p_e, the possibility of positive economic profit has been eliminated. As the price fell toward the long-run equilibrium level,

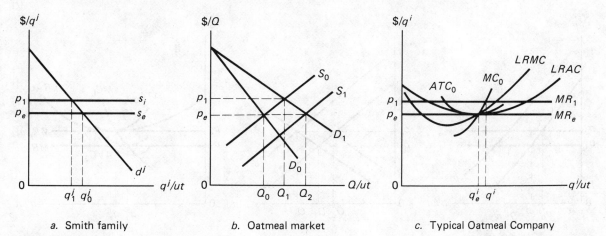

a. Smith family   b. Oatmeal market   c. Typical Oatmeal Company

Figure 9-14
Long-Run Response to an Increase in Demand. Consumers get everything they want at the long-run price—if they are patient.

the Smiths increased their consumption. At p_e a typical household is again consuming q_0^i, resulting in a total consumption of Q_2. While the competitive price had to increase in the short run to accommodate additional households, the long-run reaction of the market, through the entry of new firms, eventually provided the amount which the new households wished to purchase without imposing permanent sacrifices on the original households.

The short-run economic profit, which attracted new producers to the industry, was transitory. Ultimately, consumers were able to purchase oatmeal at a price equal to minimum long-run average cost. Consumption could increase to the level where the marginal utility the Smiths obtained from the commodity (the benefit that would have been derived from spending scarce purchasing power on other commodities) equaled the marginal cost of resources necessary for that good's production (which reflected the value consumers placed on alternative commodities that could have been produced with those resources).

The long-run reaction of a competitive market to a decrease in demand also works to the benefit of consumers, although the logic at first may seem ironic. In Figure 9-15, we again assume that an industry is operating in long-run competitive equilibrium with a price of p_e. Typical Oatmeal Company, depicted in Figure 9-15c, is earning zero economic profit, producing q_e^i pounds of oatmeal per period at the price just sufficient to cover average total cost.

Suppose that the typical family gets tired of oatmeal and shifts the demand curve of the representative household to the left, resulting in a decline in market demand from D_0 to D_1 in Figure 9-15b. At the long-run equilibrium price, p_e, consumers now wish to buy less (Q_0) than

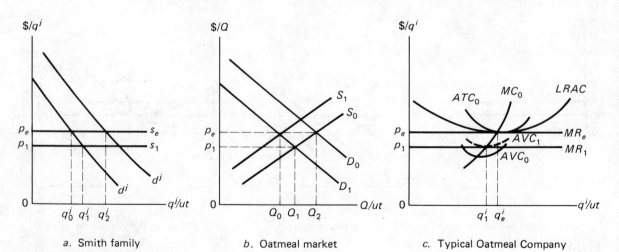

Figure 9-15
Long-Run Response to a Decrease in Demand. The Typical Oatmeal Company bites the dust.

firms are producing (Q_z). Price falls as firms sell off their excess inventories. At price p_1, the market has achieved a short-run equilibrium; quantity demanded and quantity supplied both equal Q_1. Typical Oatmeal is producing q_1^i, where short-run marginal cost MC_0 equals price p_1. Since $ATC_0 > p_1 > AVC_0$ at q_1^i, Rolly Dotes is incurring economic losses, although he is able to cover more than his outlays for variable inputs.

Over time, Rolly's contracts begin to expire, causing some fixed costs to become variable again. In Figure 9-15, this is depicted as an upward shift in average variable costs from AVC_0 to AVC_1. Note that average total costs remain constant, although discretionary costs have risen while fixed costs have fallen. When average variable costs equal p_1, Rolly decides to look at other industries for a better return on his (now discretionary) funds. As firms leave the industry, market supply shifts to the left, creating a shortage, which raises price. When the short-run supply curve reaches S_1, the short-run equilibrium price has returned to p_e, the long-run equilibrium price. Surviving firms (i.e., those whose contracts did not expire before long-run equilibrium was restored) are again producing q_e^i. They are fewer in number, but their owners are again earning sufficient revenue to cover the opportunity cost of all inputs. Since economic profit is again zero, there is no longer an incentive for established firms to leave the market. Households are now consuming Q_0 pounds of oats per month, exactly the amount they were consuming at p_e immediately after the demand decrease.

One might wonder how an *increase* in the price from p_1 to p_e would benefit consumers. The long-run equilibrium price, p_e, is the *lowest sustainable* market price: at this price, firms are covering the opportunity costs of inputs necessary for producing this commodity with the optimally sized plant. When market demand falls, consumers are demonstrating their wish that less of this commodity be produced and resources be transferred to the production of some more highly valued commodity. Immediately after the decrease in demand, too many scarce resources are being used to produce oatmeal and too few resources are being devoted to the production of other goods (e.g., Krispy Krackles). To placate consumers until enough time has passed for the orderly transfer of resources, market signals between consumers and firms have to be coordinated.

By pushing the market price below its long-run equilibrium level, the market confronts firms with losses. The longer these firms continue producing a commodity whose price is below minimum long-run average cost, the greater their losses will be. By leaving the industry as soon as the opportunity presents itself (as soon as average variable cost exceeds price), the firms' owners minimize losses.

Until resources have been transferred from the declining industry to the expanding one, the relative prices of the two goods will reflect the productive capacity of those industries. (How relative prices and quantities in different industries converge on their long-run equilibrium values is explored in general equilibrium theory in chapter fifteen.) In the declining industry, the abnormally low price encourages consumers to purchase what is produced by loss-minimizing firms. In the expanding industry, both price and economic profit remain above their long-run equilibrium levels, holding back consumption until enough firms have entered the industry (in response to positive economic profit) to produce the quantity demanded at the long-run equilibrium price.

Because of the binding contracts their owners have signed, firms in the declining industry will experience economic losses until long-run equilibrium is restored (or until some other exogenous variable sets the market on a different adjustment track). Ultimately, consumers are confronted with relative prices which reflect the opportunity costs of all inputs. While consumers may benefit from the misfortune of entrepreneurs in the short run,[9] they can hardly expect producers to subsidize their consumption by incurring avoidable losses.

APPLICATION
Long-Run (*Mutatis Mutandis*) Supply

In Figures 9-14 and 9-15, the effect of entry or exit of firms in response to short-run economic profits or losses was to return the market to the same long-run equilibrium price. A change in the number of firms in the industry did not change the minimum price necessary to cover the opportunity costs of inputs, what we have called the *minimum sustainable price*. Since the minimum sustainable price is equal to (and determined by) the lowest point on the efficient producer's long-run average cost curve, the existence of a unique long-run equilibrium price (independent of the magnitude of equilibrium quantity) identifies a **constant-cost industry**. Given sufficient time for adjustment, a short-run deviation in the equilibrium price of a constant-cost industry, due to a change in market demand, will result in a tendency for the market price to return to its former (long-run equilibrium) level, as long as remaining exogenous variables (e.g., input prices, technology) do not change.

The series of events leading to the restoration of long-run equilibrium in a constant-cost industry can be represented by a horizontal long-run supply curve, such as the line labeled S_{LR} in Figure 9-16. **Long-run**

---

[9] Actually, some consumers who prefer the substitute good when prices in the expanding and contracting industries reflect opportunity costs will be indifferent between these commodities when the price in the declining industry is below long-run equilibrium (and the price in the expanding industry is above long-run equilibrium). However, some consumers who actually prefer the commodity in the declining industry when prices are equal to opportunity costs will probably be better off in the short run but worse off in the long run.

Policy Illustration
Agricultural Price Supports

The perennial favorite of economists for showing a real-world counterpart of the competitive market model is agriculture, wherein a large number of producers of homogeneous commodities must accept prices wholly beyond their individual control. However, the prices of many agricultural products are not determined by a free market but by a market distorted by government intervention. The United States Department of Agriculture has intervened in agricultural markets for half a century, guaranteeing minimum prices. Paradoxically, it is by understanding the nature of a competitive market that we

can appreciate both the motives behind and the inefficiencies which result from agricultural price supports.

The accompanying figure illustrates the premise behind farm price supports. The family farm, depicted as producing q_0 in diagram a, comprises too few acres and too little capital to achieve the economies of larger-scale operations. If prices were not maintained at p_o, the market would ruthlessly eliminate the small farm in favor of the larger corporate farm, shown producing along ATC^* in diagram a. Free entry of optimally sized farms (e.g., through consolidation of smaller holdings) would shift the short-run supply curve from S_0 to S_1 in diagram b. Instead of approximately 3 million family

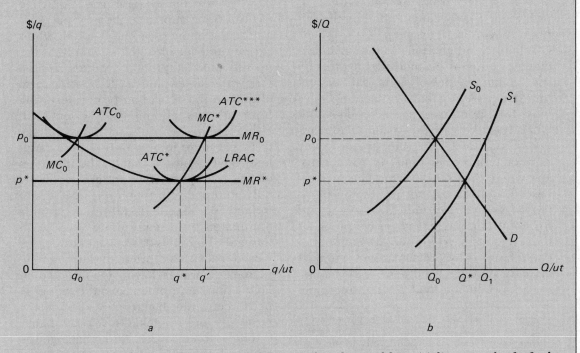

Economic Impact of Agricultural Price Supports. Concern for suboptimal farms (*a*) distorts market for food products (*b*).

farms each surviving with price p_0, perhaps only 50,000 corporate farms would survive at price p^*.

During the New Deal era of the 1930s, sympathy for the small farmer led to an attempt to sustain the suboptimally sized farm through minimum price guarantees. If the price of a covered commodity (e.g., tobacco, peanuts) fell below the support price,* the Department of Agriculture would buy surplus crops, keeping the price at, say, p_0. This practice, if continued, creates an embarrassing problem: the higher price reduces the quantity of food bought by households (i.e., Q_0 instead of Q^*), increasing the price increases output (i.e., from Q^* to Q_1). Consumer-taxpayers are fleeced twice by agricultural price supports: the outlay of $p_0 (Q_1 - Q_0)$ from tax collections (or printing money) is augmented by the implicit excise tax of $(p_0 - p^*)Q_0$.

Public indignation over such inefficiency seems to be mollified a little by the strange practice of paying farmers not to produce. A moment's reflection shows why this perverse incentive does not work. It is likely that the majority of readers of this text, like the author, grow neither tobacco, peanuts, nor soybeans. Yet when was the last time you or I received a check for not producing these crops? Aha, you say, only *farmers* get paid for not producing. Okay, so we proclaim ourselves farmers. You say we cannot become farmers by proclamation? We must actually produce food to receive money for not producing food? Delightful logic!

---

* Support price was defined as a percentage of parity, a measure of the relative price of agriculture goods in terms of nonfarm goods during World War I.

As we shall see in chapter ten, greater than competitive prices for a homogeneous product sold under erstwhile competitive conditions can only be sustained by erecting a barrier to entry. You and I do not share in price supports because we do not own acreage allotments, which constitute land officially approved for growing a protected crop. Since growers can be fined for marketing crops not grown on approved land, price supports reward those who do produce, rather than those who do not produce.

How can this practice continue? Are congressional representatives and senators all economically incompetent? Are they scheming to undermine the free enterprise system with the intent of confiscating our property? Paradoxically, the main excuse for preserving the practice of farm price supports, thereby perpetuating inefficiency in the United States agricultural sector of the economy, is the preservation of property values. In the long run, land values will be bid up to eliminate the economic profits resulting from acreage allotments; farmers will either pay higher rents, or they will have to invest more money to buy their farmland. Two generations after the initiation of price supports, farmers are receiving only a normal return on their investment in land. Were agricultural price supports eliminated by discontinuing acreage allotments, a competitive market price would cause the price of farmland to plummet. Farmers, having mortgaged their land to buy equipment, would suddenly be forced into bankruptcy, and many farms would be taken over by banks through foreclosure. And that, gentle reader, is where this story began.

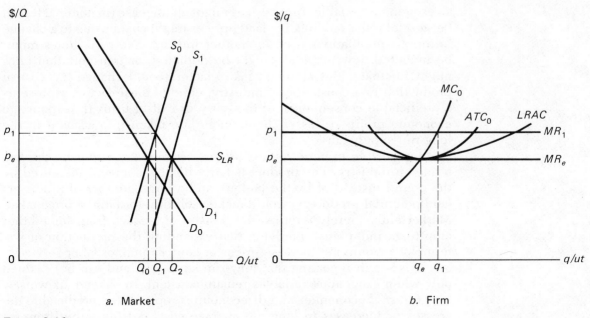

Figure 9-16
Long-Run (*Mutatis Mutandis*) Supply for a Constant-Cost Industry

supply is a *mutatis mutandis* concept, linking long-run equilibrium price
and quantity combinations by treating the number of (optimally sized)
firms in the industry as an *endogenous variable* in the model of the
perfectly competitive industry.

Because economic theory does not attempt to account for changes
in consumer tastes, and since other influences on household demand
(or market demand) are determined in other markets (e.g., income, prices
of complements and substitutes), we will treat changes in demand as
unexplained phenomena and drop the diagram of the household from
the remaining illustrations in this chapter. In Figure 9-16, an increase
in demand for a competitively supplied product is depicted by the shift
from D_0 to D_1. The shortage equal to $Q_2 - Q_0$ causes the price to rise
from p_e to p_1, and quantity produced to increase to Q_1 along the short-
run supply curve S_0. The existence of temporary economic profit when
a representative firm is producing q_1 causes new firms, with optimally
sized plants, to enter the industry. As this happens, the short-run supply
curve shifts to the right until, when supply curve S_1 intersects demand
curve D_1, long-run equilibrium is restored at price p_e. If the entry of
new firms does not cause a predictable change in the price of inputs,
economic profits will again equal zero when p_e is restored.

For a constant-cost industry, the minimum long-run average cost is an exogenous variable. Input prices might all increase (in nominal terms) because of inflation. Relative factor prices might change due to a change in input combinations used in another industry. New machines might be invented, raw materials might be depleted, or transportation rates might fluctuate. But although many factors could change the cost of production in a constant-cost industry, none of these factors represents a predictable consequence of the entry or exit of firms in response to economic profits or losses; hence none are taken into account in the long-run supply curve.

A plausible example of a constant-cost industry might be the watermelon industry. The product is fairly homogeneous (if measured by the pound instead of by the melon), and a large number of producers (and potential producers) would make each firm (or farm) a price taker. Market entry merely requires the transfer of acreage from some other crop (e.g., pumpkins), implying that expanding the production of watermelons would not increase prices of land, capital, or labor services.

It is worth repeating that long-run supply is (and can be) defined only when exogenous variables remain constant. In chapter six we saw how *internal* economies and diseconomies represented predictable decreases or increases in long-run average costs, arising either from increasing or decreasing returns to scale or from decreasing or increasing input prices as planned production was increased. By similar logic, a nonhorizontal (i.e., a positively or negatively sloped) long-run supply curve is generally traceable to *external* diseconomies or economies. An *external diseconomy* occurs when the expansion of industry output causes the minimum average total cost of a typical firm to increase. The most likely cause of an external diseconomy is a positively sloped supply curve for one or more inputs used within a competitive industry. Thus while every firm in the industry would (by assumption) pay the same factor price at any given time, expansion of industry demand for that input would raise its price for all firms in the industry.

The model of an **increasing-cost industry** which results from external diseconomies is presented in Figure 9-17. Once again, our analysis begins with the industry in long-run equilibrium at p_e; the typical firm is making zero economic profits producing q_e. We assume that an unexplained increase in demand from D_0 to D_1 produces a shortage at price p_e, causing price and output to increase along the short-run supply curve S_0 to p_1 and Q_1, respectively. Since the typical firm is now earning a positive economic profit by producing q_1, the stage is set for the entry of new firms and the restoration of long-run equilibrium.

As usual, the entry of additional firms shifts the short-run supply curve to the right. Only in this case, the increase in the number of firms causes the price of one or more inputs to increase, which increases the long-run (and associated short-run) average cost curve of every firm in the industry. When the short-run supply curve reaches S_1, the typical

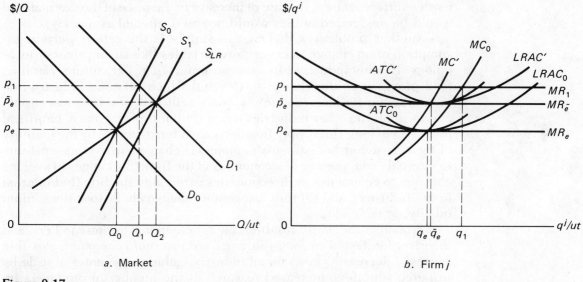

Figure 9-17
Long-Run (*Mutatis Mutandis*) Supply for an Increasing Cost Industry

firm's long-run average cost curve has shifted to *LRAC′*. In this case, economic profits are squeezed between the pressures of falling price (due to the increase in market supply) and rising costs (due to external diseconomies). The new long-run equilibrium price is $\tilde{p}_e$ ($>p_e$). With the likelihood that relative factor prices are changing as well as the factor price level, it is entirely possible that the minimum average cost point on *LRAC′* will occur at a different level of output from q_e; in Figure 9-17, the new minimum average planning cost occurs at $\tilde{q}_e$. Connecting the two long-run equilibrium points, (p_e,Q_0) and ($\tilde{p}_e,Q_2$), generates a positively sloped long-run supply curve, S_{LR}.

One point of contention among economic theorists is whether or not external diseconomies are reversible. In some cases, they seem to be. For instance, if a competitive industry used a special type of capital good, it is possible that the price of the good would vary directly with the size of the industry. As the industry expanded, the increase in demand for the capital good would cause its price (for both new and replacement equipment) to increase. If the industry began to contract, price competition among producers of the capital good, plus a glutted market in used machinery, would cause the price of the good to fall.

In other cases, external diseconomies are not reversible. Suppose that an industry used a particular raw material which had to be mined. As demand for the input increased, deeper and deeper mines would have to be dug and the price of the input would rise. However, if the industry began to contract, ore would not suddenly appear closer to the earth's surface; at best, the rate of increase in the price of the raw material would be moderated (mines would not be deepened as quickly).

Another problem with long-run supply is the *ceteris paribus* assumption of no change in **exogenous variables** like factor prices or technology. If many industries use similar inputs (e.g., agriculture, canning, food processing), the change in demand which sets one industry into motion along its long-run supply curve will shift the long-run supply curves in all the other industries using similar inputs. Hence, empirical estimates of long-run supply functions are often distorted by the inability of the researcher to distinguish among (1) changes in average cost due to internal economies or diseconomies of the firm, (2) changes in average cost due to economies or diseconomies external to the firm (but internal to the industry), and (3) truly exogenous changes in factor prices, input quality, or technology.

Probably the most troublesome phenomena for researchers and theorists interested in long-run costs are *external economies*. Possible causes of decreasing costs for an industry include economies of scale by resource suppliers, increased research as the number of producers increases, and agglomeration economies, or reductions in transaction costs occurring when complementary activities cluster together in space. In the first two cases—economies of scale experienced by input suppliers or cost savings resulting from increased research—the possibility of an imperfectly competitive input market complicates the analysis.[10] (This topic will be explored in detail in chapter thirteen.) Further, in the case of research, external economies are probabilistic rather than certain—more resources devoted to research do not guarantee that cost-reducing innovations will follow. We will return to these issues presently.

In Figure 9-18, the shift in the market demand curve from D_0 to D_1 causes the now familiar shortage, with the consequent increase in price and output along the short-run supply curve S_0. As before, the existence of short-run economic profit for the typical firm producing q_1 and selling that output at p_1 encourages the entry of new firms. Additional firms increase supply, causing price to fall. With external economies, however, the typical firm's long-run average cost curve would be shifting downward as more firms entered the industry. In fact, when the short-run supply curve reached S_1, the market price would be back at its former long-run equilibrium value, p_e. In this case, economic profits would still be possible for new entrants, given the decrease in the minimum long-run average cost due to external economies. The number of firms would

[10] For an argument that imperfect competition is not a major problem in dealing with external economies, see George J. Stigler, "The Division of Labor Is Limited by the Extent of the Market," *Journal of Political Economy* (June 1951); reprinted in William Breit and Harold Hochman, eds. *Readings in Microeconomics*, 2nd ed. (New York: Holt, Rinehart and Winston, 1971), pp. 140–148.

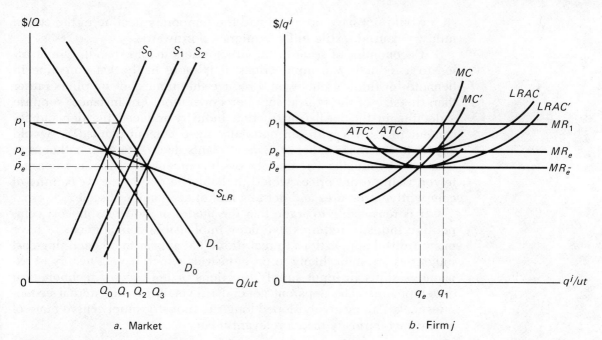

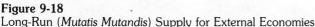

Figure 9-18
Long-Run (*Mutatis Mutandis*) Supply for External Economies

continue to grow until, at total output Q_3, the typical firm was earning zero economic profits at the lower equilibrium price $\tilde{p}_e$.

Connecting points (p_e,Q_0) and ($\tilde{p}_e,Q_3$) creates the appearance of a negatively sloped long-run supply curve, S_{LR}. But for this curve to reflect appropriate *mutatis mutandis* logic, we must be able to reverse the process and argue that a contraction of the industry would cause long-run equilibrium price and quantity to change in opposite directions: as output declined, price would rise. It is not likely that technological discoveries resulting from increased research and development during an industry's growth will somehow be forgotten with industry decline. Technological change is, for our purposes, more plausible as an exogenous force, whose impact is traced through *ceteris paribus* analysis, than an endogenous variable, which determines the shape of the long-run supply curve.

For similar reasons, **agglomeration economies** gained during an industrial expansion are not likely to be lost if not all of the clustered activities are in declining industries. For instance, when textile mills began substituting synthetic fibers for cotton, their migration to the sunbelt continued; apparently the cotton industry itself was given a second life by the development of cotton-synthetic blends. Certainly this last step would not have occurred had the temporary decline in the cotton industry caused textile mills to migrate northward.

If economies of scale for input suppliers to an expanding industry led to a reduction in input prices, it is more likely that a decline in demand for those inputs would reduce the number of suppliers rather than the size of the typical supplier's operation. For instance, suppose a decline in the local construction industry reduced the demand for cement in a town with ten optimally sized cement plants. We would expect to see the number of cement plants decline to nine, rather than each plant reducing its capacity by 10 percent. As suppliers became fewer, rising input prices would probably be due to the weakening of competitive pressures and not to a loss of economies of scale.

It is reasonable to argue that the model of a decreasing-cost competitive industry requires too many implausible coincidences to have many fruitful applications to real life. What appear to be declining-cost industries are more likely to be industries which have a history of exogenous shifts in input supply functions or unexpected technological developments. The apparent general irreversibility of external economies makes a negatively sloped long-run industry supply curve more of an abstract curiosity than a relevant theory.

HIGHLIGHTS

1. The competitive firm is a price taker. It can sell as little or as much output at the market determined price as its owner wants to supply at that price. The competitive firm maximizes profit by producing that level of output at which marginal cost equals price (which is also marginal revenue), as long as price exceeds average variable cost at that rate of output.

2. When price is less than minimum average variable cost, the competitive firm should shut down operations, thereby limiting its losses to fixed cost.

3. A change in quantity supplied occurs when the firm modifies its output in reaction to a change in price. A change in supply occurs when the firm offers more (or less) for sale at each market price.

4. The short-run supply curve for a competitive industry is determined by the horizontal summation of individual producers' supply curves—that portion of each firm's marginal cost curve lying above the shutdown price (minimum average variable cost).

5. A market is in equilibrium when quantity supplied equals quantity demanded at the prevailing price. When the price is too high for equilibrium, sellers offer more than buyers wish to purchase at that price; the surplus causes the market price to fall. When the price is too low for equilibrium, sellers offer less than buyers wish to purchase at that price; the shortage causes the market price to rise.

6. When market demand changes while supply remains constant, the new equilibrium price and quantity will lie on the original supply curve. When market supply changes while demand remains constant, the new equilibrium price and quantity will lie on the original demand curve.

7. In the long run, the existence of opportuni-

ties for economic profit will cause additional firms to enter a competitive industry until price reaches its lowest sustainable level, given by minimum long-run average cost.

8. When economic losses are being incurred, firms will tend to leave a competitive industry when expiring contracts cause their average variable costs to exceed the market price. When the market price equals the minimum long-run average cost, no further change in the number of firms will occur.

9. The long-run market supply curve is a *mutatis mutandis* supply function in which the number of firms in the industry is treated as an endogenous variable. When firms can enter or leave an industry without causing predictable changes in the minimum long-run average cost, a constant-cost industry exists. Such an industry has a horizontal long-run supply curve.

10. When an increase in the number of firms leads to external diseconomies, the long-run supply curve is positively sloped. External economies lead to a negatively sloped long-run supply curve. Considerable difference of opinion exists among economists over whether the concept of long-run supply can be meaningfully applied to real-world markets.

GLOSSARY

Agglomeration economies Mutual reductions in production or selling costs when complementary producers (e.g., coal mines and steel mills) locate in close proximity.

Black market An illegal market in which commodities are bought and sold when the legal market is prevented from reaching an equilibrium price, usually due to government intervention. Also called a *secondary market*.

Break-even price The price associated with the firm's minimum average total cost. When the break-even price prevails, the competitive firm produces the rate of output given by the equality of marginal cost and average total cost, thereby receiving zero economic profit (i.e., by suffering no losses).

Change in quantity supplied A change in the amount offered to buyers resulting from a change in market price, other factors being constant. A movement along a stable supply curve.

Change in supply A change in the amount offered to buyers at every market price, resulting from a change in one or more exogenous variables (e.g., technology, factor prices, the number of sellers, prices of alternative products). A change in supply causes a change in the market equilibrium price and/or quantity, due to the displacement of the supply curve.

Constant-cost industry A competitive industry in which the entry or exit of sellers in response to changes in economic profit tends to return the market price to the same equilibrium level, input prices and technology remaining constant. A constant-cost industry is characterized by a horizontal long-run supply curve.

Endogenous variable A variable whose value is determined within a theoretical or market framework. The equilibrium price and quantity are endogenous variables in a competitive market, as is the number of firms in the industry in the long-run supply curve of perfect competition.

Equilibrium A condition in which opposing forces are in balance. A competitive market is in equilibrium if, and only if, at the prevailing price, quantity supplied equals quantity demanded. At that point, the downward pressure on price resulting from consumers' utility-maximizing behavior is counterbalanced by the upward pressure on price stemming from profit-maximizing behavior of sellers.

Exogenous variable A variable whose value is determined outside a theoretical or market framework. An exogenous variable is treated as parameter when charting an adjustment path or determining the value of endogenous variables.

Increasing-cost industry   A competitive industry in which the long-run equilibrium price varies directly with equilibrium quantity, exogenous factors remaining constant. An increasing-cost industry has a positively sloped long-run supply curve.

Law of large numbers   The principle of statistics and probability theory which states that small, random variations in individual behavior can be ignored when dealing with aggregate (e.g., market-wide) phenomena.

Long-run supply   A *mutatis mutandis* supply function in which the number of sellers adjusts to move price to its lowest sustainable level, namely, the price associated with zero economic profit.

Marginal revenue   The revenue obtained from the sale of an additional unit of output: $MR = p + q(\Delta p/\Delta q)$. Under conditions of perfect competition, marginal revenue equals the market determined price.

Market supply   The aggregate function that indicates the total quantity all producers would be willing to sell per period of time, at alternative market prices, *ceteris paribus*.

Perfect competition   The ideal model of market organization characterized by a large number of firms selling a homogeneous product, un-restricted entry and exit of firms, and a large number of accurately informed consumers.

Shortage   A market situation in which quantity demanded exceeds quantity supplied at the prevailing price, causing consumers to bid up prices (or not resist producer price increases by switching patronage) until equilibrium is established at a higher price.

Shutdown price   The price associated with the minimum average variable cost of a competitive firm. When the price falls below the shutdown price, the firm ceases operations, cutting its losses to fixed cost.

Supply curve   A diagram relating the quantity of a commodity offered to consumers and the market determined price. The competitive firm's supply curve is derived from the portion of its marginal cost curve lying above its average variable cost curve. The market supply curve is generated by aggregating the quantity supplied by all firms at each prevailing price.

Surplus   A market situation in which quantity supplied exceeds quantity demanded at the prevailing price. The unsold output $(Q_s - Q_d)$ shows up as unintended additions to inventories and generates a downward pressure on market price until equilibrium is reached at a lower price.

SUGGESTED READINGS

Baumol, William. *Economic Theory and Operations Analysis.* 4th ed. Englewood Cliffs, New Jersey: Prentice-Hall, 1977, pp. 393–401.

Gold, Bela. "Changing Perspectives on Size, Scale and Returns: An Interpretive Survey." *Journal of Economic Literature* (March 1981), pp. 5–33.

Knight, Frank H. *Risk, Uncertainty and Profit.* Boston: Houghton Mifflin, 1921, chapters 5 and 6.

Machlup, Fritz. *Economics of Seller's Competition.* Baltimore: Johns Hopkins Press, 1952, pp. 79–125.

Marshall, Alfred. *Principles of Economics.* 9th ed. Book 5, chapters 1–3.

Robinson, Joan. "What Is Perfect Competition?" *Quarterly Journal of Economics* (1934), pp. 104–120.

Sraffa, Piero. "The Laws of Returns Under Competitive Conditions." *Economic Journal* (December, 1926), pp. 535–550.

Stigler, George. "Perfect Competition, Historically Contemplated." *Journal of Political Economy* (February 1957), pp. 1–17.

EXERCISES

Evaluate

Indicate whether each of the following statements is true (agrees with economic theory), false (is contradicted by theory), or uncertain (could be true or false, given additional information). Explain your answer.

1. A firm which experiences a negatively sloped portion of its short-run marginal cost curve may actually produce more of a commodity as its price falls, *ceteris paribus*.
2. The short-run shutdown point for a competitive firm corresponds to the level of output at which the average product of a variable input is maximum.
3. Any firm which is paying out more money than it is taking in should shut down operations immediately.
4. A price increase will not necessarily increase a competitive firm's profit, since, at a higher rate of output, that firm would also be incurring a higher marginal cost.
5. Short-run minimum average variable cost for an efficiently operating firm is the lowest possible short-run equilibrium price in a competitive market.
6. If all firms in a competitive industry produce under conditions of constant returns to scale, the industry supply curve is horizontal.
7. Time is money. Therefore, it makes no difference to consumer welfare whether time (e.g., standing in line, waiting in a physician's office, waiting for orders to be filled) or money is used to ration output during a shortage.
8. Because the demand curve in a competitive industry has a negative slope, an excise tax can never raise the price of a competitively produced commodity by as much as the tax itself.
9. When firms are leaving a competitive industry, rents paid for preferred locations by firms remaining in that industry will decline.
10. A competitive firm uses two inputs, L and K;

a reduction in the price of L will lead to an increase in employment of both L and K.

Calculate

Answer each of the following questions, showing all your calculations.

11. Suppose that 1,000 identical firms each have fixed costs of $500 per day and marginal cost curves given by the formula $MC = 5 + 2q$.
   a. What is the minimum price necessary for any firm to produce?
   b. When $p = \$45$, what is the output of each firm?
   c. Calculate each firm's profit when $p = \$40$. (Hint: $TC = 500 + 5q + q^2$.)

12. Given the data in question 11:
   a. What is the supply equation for each firm? (Hint: solve $MC = p$ in terms of q.)
   b. What is the formula for the industry supply curve?
   c. Given a market demand curve of $Q^d = 27,500 - 100p$, what is the industry equilibrium price and quantity?
   d. At this price and quantity, will firms be encouraged to enter or leave the industry? Explain.

Contemplate

Answer each of the following in a brief but complete essay.

13. In 1923 the town of Curliques, Ohio, began licensing its barbershops. One hundred licenses were issued in 1923 and none has been issued since. All the original owners of these licenses have died. Their heirs, who inherited the barbershop licenses, were free to open their own shops or sell their licenses to the highest bidder. Although the town's population has tripled since 1923, the owners of barbershops today are receiving only a normal return on their investments. Why?

14. Compare the impact on equilibrium price and quantity of the entry of firms into a competitive industry if (a) new firms are able to duplicate the cost curves of established firms, and (b) new firms have higher marginal and average costs than established firms.

15. Evaluate the following: Even if no industry met the conditions of perfect competition, the theory of perfect competition would be useful in explaining attempts by producers to limit entry into their industries and why such attempts are often frustrated.

APPENDIX TO CHAPTER 9

Applications of Supply and Demand to the Business Environment

This appendix applies the theory of perfectly competitive markets to the estimation of supply and demand equations by business and research economists. In dealing with real market data, economists are confronted by the identification problem. Only the prevailing price and quantity exchanged are observed and recorded. If the market was in equilibrium at the time, observed price and quantity identify the intersection of a demand curve and a supply curve. The practical distinction between a change in quantity demanded (or in quantity supplied) and a change in demand (or in supply) is the key to whether the series of price and quantity data can be deciphered. When only one curve shifts, the former and new equilibrium observations lie on the other curve, which is said to be identified. Whether either curve can be estimated when both curves shift at the same time depends on whether that shift was merely coincidental or both supply and demand responded to the same exogenous variables.

Estimating Empirical Supply-and-Demand Equations

After students have mastered the basics of supply and demand, they are often surprised to learn how difficult it is to estimate supply and demand equations for real-world markets. Figure 9A-1 shows a typical market datum. At best, one can observe the quantity of a good exchanged and the prevailing price for one time and place. The dashed lines labeled S_0 and D_0 in Figure 9A-1 represent phantom supply and demand curves which generated p_0 and Q_0. However, too little information is obtained from one observation to estimate either the supply or the demand equation.

If the researcher is lucky, the observed price-quantity pair will be an equilibrium price and quantity, identifying the intersection of a supply curve and a demand curve. Unless exogenous variables change, market information will consist of repetitions of that price-quantity datum. Since the point of intersection alone does not indicate the shape of the two curves, more than one observation is necessary to estimate the supply and demand equations that gave rise to the observed price and quantity.

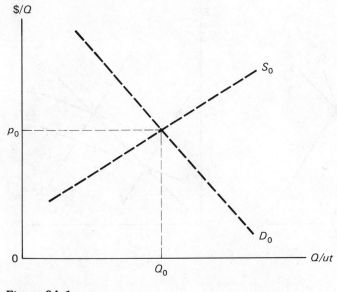

$/Q

p_0

0

Q_0

Q/ut

S_0

D_0

Figure 9A-1
The Identification Problem

A change in market conditions creates a pattern of price-quantity data that may give a researcher enough information to sort out the underlying supply and demand equations. In Figure 9A-2, the new combination (p_1, Q_1) represents an increase of both price and quantity relative to (p_0, Q_0). Economic theory assures us that except in the highly unlikely cases of a Giffen good or a Veblen good, the two points in Figure 9A-2 do not lie on the same demand curve.[1] As long as (p_0, Q_0) and (p_1, Q_1) are both market equilibria, two possibilities exist. First, both points are located on the same supply curve; (p_1, Q_1) was generated by an increase in demand (from D_0 to D_1), which upset equilibrium at (p_0, Q_0), thus causing price and quantity supplied to increase along S until equilibrium was reestablished. Second, both curves could have shifted: an increase in demand was coincidental with a change in supply. In Figure 9A-2a, an increase in supply from S_0 to S_1 is pictured; in Figure 9a-2b, an unseen supply decrease is depicted. When both curves shift, ignoring the change in supply would make quantity supplied seem to be more responsive or less responsive to a change in price than was in fact the case. Just as the responsiveness of quantity demanded to a change in price is measured by the elasticity of demand, the responsiveness

---

[1] The Giffen good and the Veblen effect, discussed in chapters two and four, respectively, are particularly unlikely occurrences because verification would contradict the theory of competitive markets. For instance, to observe a price increase along a demand curve, the supply curve must shift to the left. If price increase led to an increase in consumption, where did the extra quantity come from? Without a decrease in quantity, the market price would never have increased, unless, of course, an increase in demand (shift in the demand curve) had initiated the price increase.

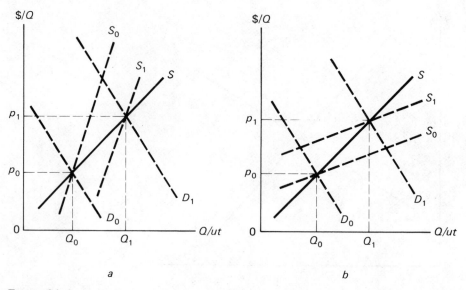

Figure 9A-2
Potential Identification of Supply Curve. *a*, Possibility of supply increase; *b*, possibility
of supply decrease.

of quantity demanded to a change in price is measured by the elasticity of
supply:

$$\eta_s = \frac{\Delta Q_s/Q_s}{\Delta p/p} = \frac{\Delta Q_s}{\Delta p} \times \frac{p}{Q_s}$$

For all positively sloped supply curves, η_s is a positive number; the more elastic
the supply, the smaller the price increase necessary to cause a specified change
in quantity supplied. In Figure 9A-2*a*, if an increase in supply from S_0 to S_1 was
responsible for part of the increase in observed quantity, the estimation of a
single supply function (e.g., S) would imply a greater elasticity of supply than
was in fact the case.

If a price increase was instigated by a simultaneous increase in demand and
a decrease (i.e., leftward shift) in supply, equilibrium would be restored only
when quantity demanded had decreased along D_1 and quantity supplied increased along S_1 in Figure 9-2*b*. Since the increase in quantity would start at
a quantity less than Q_0, the observed change in quantity would understate the
responsiveness quantity supplied along the new supply curve (S_1). If the supply
curve S in Figure 9A-2*b* were estimated, when supply had actually decreased
from S_0 to S_1, the elasticity of supply would be underestimated.

In Figure 9A-3, the observed price and quantity have moved in opposite
directions; quantity decreased as price increased. Clearly, as long as (p_0,Q_0) and
(p_1,Q_1) are observations of equilibrium price and quantity, they do not lie on
the same short-run supply curve. They may identify the demand curve D; or

they may be on different demand curves. Mistaking a shift in both the supply curve and the demand curve for a change in quantity demanded would cause an erroneous estimate of the responsiveness of quantity demanded to a change in price. In Figure 9A-3*a*, the possibility of a simultaneous increase of both supply and demand are shown. The demand curve drawn through (p_0, Q_0) and (p_1, Q_1), indicated as D, would overstate the absolute value of price elasticity of demand along D_1 if the latter were the true demand curve. In Figure 9A-3*b*, an increase in supply from S_0 to S_1 could have been accompanied by a decrease in demand from D_0 to D_1. Since quantity demanded at price p_0 would be less than Q_0 after the decrease in demand, the observed change in quantity would understate the responsiveness of quantity to price along the true demand curve D_1.

Figures 9A-2 and 9A-3 show that empirical demand curves, like any results of a statistical analysis, must be interpreted carefully and with healthy skepticism. Living in a world in which markets reach equilibrium quickly relative to the frequency of data collection means that the contingencies along supply and demand curves, except for equilibrium points, are not observed. In fact, if observed price-quantity pairs were the results of disequilibrium exchanges—either shortages or surpluses—the alert researcher would have to delete those data, lest supply or demand curve estimates be biased. Hence, statistics always involve a degree of guesswork. The careful use of theoretical insights, however, replaces speculation with an educated guess.

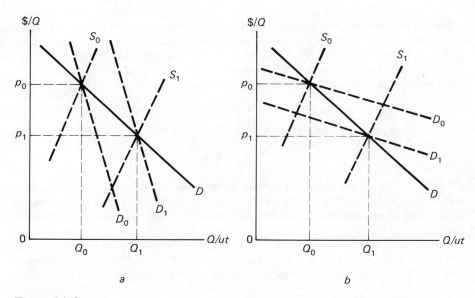

Figure 9A-3
Potential Identification of Demand Curve. *a*, Possibility of demand increase; *b*, possibility of demand decrease.

Identification of Supply and Demand Curves[2]

Figure 9A-4 shows the process by which an empirical demand curve could be identified from the independent shifts of the market supply curve. We imagine that the demand function contains only the two endogenous variables, price, p, and quantity demanded, Q^d. Actually, statistical techniques used to estimate supply and demand equations isolate the influence of each exogenous variable, thereby simulating the pattern of Figure 9A-4. For simplicity, we are assuming that all of the exogenous influences on demand (e.g., income, tastes, price of substitutes and complements) remain constant over the period the data are collected, so that those variables are absorbed by the constant term of the demand equation. We also assume that the supply equation contains one exogenous variable, the wage rate for production workers in the industry in question w. As long as workers in this industry consume an insignificant proportion of the commodity, changes in w need not shift the demand curve.

In Figure 9A-4 we begin with a market in equilibrium with price p_0^* and quantity Q_0^*. An increase in the wage rate from w_0 to w_1 shifts the supply curve from S_0 to S_1, thus reducing quantity supplied at price p_0^* from Q_0^* to Q_0^s and creating a shortage at price p_0^*. Because Q_0^s is a disequilibrium quantity, it is doubtful that this quantity would be observed at price p_0^*. In all likelihood, only points (p_0^*, Q_0^*) and (p_1^*, Q_1^*) would be available for the estimation of the underlying equations. Since quantity supplied immediately after the wage increase (Q_0^s) would not be observed, only one point on S_0 and one point on S_1 would be observed, and data would be insufficient to estimate the slope of the supply curve.

Because a change in w causes a shift in the supply function without causing a shift in the demand function, we say that the demand function is *identified by the change in the wage rate*. Given a supply function, $Q^s = -\alpha_0 + \alpha_1 p - \alpha_2 w$, and a demand function, $Q^d = \beta_0 - \beta_1 p$, market equilibrium means $Q^s = Q^d = Q^*$. This allows us to set the supply and the demand equations equal to each other and to solve for equilibrium price, p^*:

$$-\alpha_0 + \alpha_1 p^* - \alpha_2 w = \beta_0 - \beta_1 p^*$$

$$(\alpha_1 + \beta_1)p^* = \beta_0 + \alpha_0 + \beta_2 w$$

$$\therefore p^* = \frac{\beta_0 + \alpha_0}{\alpha_1 + \beta_1} + \frac{\alpha_2}{\alpha_1 + \beta_1} \times w$$

When the supply equation contains one exogenous variable (often called a *shift parameter*) and the demand function contains only the two endogenous variables, equilibrium price is completely determined by the value of the exogenous variable.

Having specified the supply and demand equations so that all coefficients are positive (i.e., the minus signs on α_2 and β_1 pick up the inverse relationship between Q^s and w and between Q^d and p), we know that $\alpha_2/\alpha_1 + \beta_1 > 0$; an

---

[2] A classic, nontechnical exploration of statistical demand functions is E. J. Working's "What Do Statistical Demand Curves Show?" *Quarterly Journal of Economics* (1927); reprinted in Edwin Mansfield, ed., *Elementary Statistics for Economics and Business: Selected Readings*, 2nd ed. (New York: Norton, 1981).

$/Q

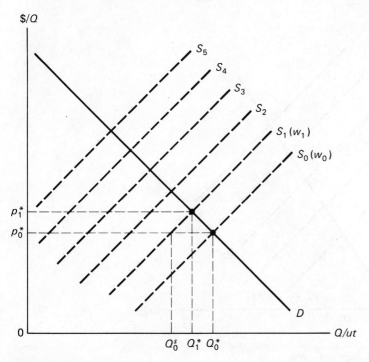

Figure 9A-4
Identification of a Demand Curve

increase in the wage rate will increase the equilibrium price, *mutatis mutandis*. By substituting the formula for p^* into either the demand equation or the supply equation, we obtain an expression for the equilibrium quantity, Q^*, also as a function of the shift parameter, w. Using the demand equation, we have:[3]

$$Q^* = \beta_0 - \beta_1 p^* = \beta_0 - \beta_1 \left(\frac{\beta_0 + \alpha_0}{\alpha_1 + \beta_1} + \frac{\alpha_2}{\alpha_1 + \beta_1} w \right)$$

$$= \frac{\beta_0 \alpha_1 + \alpha_0 \beta_1}{\alpha_1 + \beta_1} - \frac{\beta_1 \alpha_2}{\alpha_1 + \beta_1} w$$

Every time w changes, the supply curve shifts and p^* reacts in the same direction as w. Since the observed quantity Q^* responds in the opposite direction as the change in w (i.e., $-\beta_1 \alpha_2 / [\alpha_1 + \beta_1] < 0$), the observed change in quantity will be inversely related to the observed change in price: $\Delta Q^* / \Delta p^* < 0$. In fact, the

---

[3] Substituting for p^* in the supply function:

$$Q^* = -\alpha_0 + \alpha_1 p^* - \alpha_2 w = -\alpha_0 + \alpha_1 \left(\frac{\beta_0 + \alpha_0}{\alpha_1 + \beta_1} + \frac{\alpha_2}{\alpha_1 + \beta_1} w \right) - \alpha_2 w$$

$$= \frac{\alpha_1 \beta_0 - \alpha_0 \beta_1}{\alpha_0 + \beta_0} - \frac{\beta_1 \alpha_2}{\alpha_1 + \beta_1} w$$

which is the same result as substituting for p^* in the demand equation.

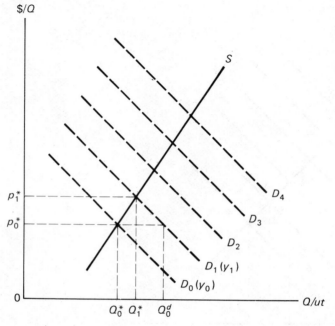

Figure 9A-5
Identification of a Supply Curve

ratio of the observed change in quantity to the observed change in price serves as an estimate for the slope of the demand curve: $\Delta Q^*/\Delta p^* = \hat{\beta}_1$.[4]

Figure 9A-5 shows data from which only the supply curve can be identified. We now assume that the supply equation contains only the two endogenous variables, price and quantity (supplied). We also assume that the demand function contains one exogenous variable, real per capita income, y. The equation system becomes: $Q^s = -\alpha_0 + \alpha_1 p$, $Q^d = \beta_0 - \beta_1 p + \beta_2 y$, with equilibrium requiring that $Q^s = Q^d = Q^*$ when $p = p^*$. Assuming that the commodity is a normal good, market demand will increase (shift to the right) whenever real per capita income increases. By assumption, y has no influence on Q^s. Thus an increase in y will create a shortage at the former equilibrium price. The market price will rise until quantity demanded decreases and quantity supplied increases to restore equilibrium.

In Figure 9A-5, we imagine that an increase in real per capita income shifts the demand curve from D_0 to D_1. The former equilibrium price, p_0^*, is now too low for consumers to obtain all they wish to purchase. The shortage causes price to increase to p_1^*, where $Q^d = Q^s = Q_1^*$. Since a disequilibrium quantity de-

---

[4] Actually, equations estimated statistically contain an "error term," so that the statistical supply function would have the form: $Q^s = \alpha_0 + \alpha_1 p - \alpha_2 w + \epsilon$, and the demand function would have a similar form: $Q^d = \beta_0 - \beta_1 p + \upsilon$, where ϵ and υ are error terms, each with an expected value of 0 and a constant variance. For this reason, the estimated value of β_1 has a circumflex to indicate that it is actually an approximation of β_1.

manded (Q_0^d) would not usually be observed, only one point on D_0 and one point on D_1 were observed. Therefore, the pattern of equilibrium price and quantity indicates nothing about the slope of any demand curve in Figure 9A-5.

As with identification of the demand curve, the pattern of Q^* and p^* caused by changes in y can be discerned by setting $Q^s = Q^d = Q^*$ and solving for the equilibrium price, p^*:

$$-\alpha_0 + \alpha_1 p^* = \beta_0 - \beta_1 p^* + \beta_2 y$$

$$(\alpha_1 + \beta_1)p^* = \alpha_0 + \beta_0 + \beta_2 y$$

$$p^* = \frac{\alpha_0 + \beta_0}{\alpha_1 + \beta_1} + \frac{\beta_2}{\alpha_1 + \beta_1} y$$

Since $\beta_2/\alpha_1 + \beta_1 > 0$, the equilibrium price will be positively related to real income, *mutatis mutandis*. Substituting the formula for p^* into the supply function, we discover that equilibrium quantity is also a positive function of the exogenous variable, y. Using the supply function:

$$Q^* = -\alpha_0 + \alpha_1 p^* = -\alpha_0 + \alpha_1 \left(\frac{\alpha_0 + \beta_0}{\alpha_1 + \beta_1} + \frac{\beta_2}{\alpha_1 + \beta_1} y \right)$$

$$= \frac{\beta_0 \alpha_1 - \alpha_0 \beta_1}{\alpha_1 + \beta_1} + \frac{\alpha_1 \beta_2}{\alpha_1 + \beta_1} y$$

The final pattern, wherein a supply curve and a demand curve shift simultaneously, is presented in Figure 9A-6. Suppose that the demand function contains one exogenous variable, per capita real income, while the supply function contains a different exogenous variable, the wage rate for workers in that industry. It will be possible to sort out the independent influences of price on quantity demanded and quantity supplied only if y and w change independently of each other.

In Figure 9A-6, an increase in per capita income increases demand for a certain commodity; the demand curve shifts to the right. At the same time, an increase in the industry wage shifts the supply curve to the left. Restoring equilibrium requires a substantial increase in price and results in only a small increase in quantity exchanged. The chance of the two equilibrium points—(p_0,Q_0) and (p_1,Q_1)—lying on the same demand curve is nil. If both points were on the same supply curve, supply would be very inelastic: a substantial price increase would appear to be required to obtain a small increase in quantity supplied.

If supply decreased at the same time demand increased, neither the quantity demanded nor the quantity supplied at the outset of the shortage would have been observed. Both the increase in real income, Δy, and the increase in the wage rate, Δw, contributed to the shortage at p_0. The equilibrium price, p^*, is a positive function of both y and w:

$$p^* = \frac{\beta_0 + \alpha_0}{\alpha_1 + \beta_1} + \frac{\alpha_2}{\alpha_1 + \beta_1} w + \frac{\beta_2}{\alpha_1 + \beta_1} y$$

Equilibrium quantity, on the other hand, might increase, decrease, or remain the same when p^* increased, depending on the relative magnitude and influence

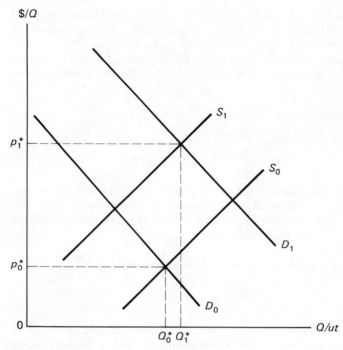

Figure 9A-6
Simultaneous Shift in Supply and Demand Curves

of Δw and Δy:

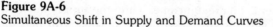

$$Q^* = -\alpha_0 + \alpha_1 \left(\frac{\beta_0 + \alpha_0}{\alpha_1 + \beta_1} + \frac{\alpha_2}{\alpha_1 + \beta_1} w + \frac{\beta_2}{\alpha_1 + \beta_1} y \right) - \alpha_2 w$$

$$= \frac{\alpha_1 \beta_0 - \beta_1 \alpha_0}{\alpha_1 + \beta_1} + \frac{\alpha_1 \beta_2}{\alpha_1 + \beta_1} y - \frac{\beta_1 \alpha_2}{\alpha_1 + \beta_1} w$$

The problem of *multicollinearity* is encountered in statistical estimation of demand and supply curves when two nominally independent variables appear to move together, either because both variables change in response to a third variable left out of the system (e.g., the change in the average price level due to inflation) or simply because coincidental changes in those variables happened to be observed. In the case of multicollinearity, statistical techniques used to isolate the influence of each variable on observed price and quantity would be unsuccessful. Sometimes, parallel behavior of two variables can be removed by replacing one variable (or both) with an instrumental variable (i.e., a synthetic variable created to remove the parallel change with the other variable). Despite problems of measurement, real wage rates and real per capita income could be used to avoid the multicollinearity of nominal wage rates and nominal per capita income.

If the problem of multicollinearity is not severe or can be resolved by the use of instrumental variables, the investigator first determines the relationship between *each* of the endogenous variables, p^* and Q^*, and *all* the exogenous variables. The estimated equations will have the following form:

$$p^* = \hat{\gamma}_0 + \hat{\gamma}_1 y + \hat{\gamma}_2 w$$
$$Q^* = \hat{\delta}_0 + \hat{\delta}_1 y + \hat{\delta}_2 w$$

By comparing these equations with the *reduced form* (or equilibrium) equations for p^* and Q^*, we see that:

$$\frac{\hat{\delta}_1}{\hat{\gamma}_1} = \hat{\alpha}_1 \quad \text{and} \quad \frac{\hat{\delta}_2}{\hat{\gamma}_2} = \hat{\beta}_1$$

Even if exogenous variables change at the same time, their separate influence on price, as well as the independent influence of a price change on quantity demanded and quantity supplied, can be indirectly estimated.[5] However, as we shall see in the next section, there are some instances when it is obvious that the independent influence of a price change on quantity demanded and quantity supplied cannot be discovered, given the nature of the market involved. In such cases, knowing that a task (e.g., predicting the stock market) is impossible at least gives the trained economist time to find a new job before being fired for failing to do the impossible.

Supply, Demand, and Predicting Stock Prices: If We're So Smart, Why Aren't We Rich?

The need to observe independent shifts in supply and demand curves in order to estimate those curves may help explain the failure of economists (and everyone else) at consistently predicting the stock market. There are several types of traders in corporate securities: individual stockholders, institutional investors (mutual funds, pension funds, insurance companies), brokers, and by far the smallest group, corporations themselves. What is most significant about these traders is that every buyer of a security is a potential seller and every seller is a potential buyer.

A demand function for a particular corporation's common stock would include the following: (1) the current price of the stock itself, p_1, the expected dividend, r_1, and the expected future price of the stock, ρ_1; (2) the present prices, p_2 through p_n, of all other corporate securities, the expected dividend of each, r_2 through r_n, and the expected future price of each, ρ_2 through ρ_n; (3) the expected yields from other financial and nonfinancial investments; (4) the current and expected future term structure of interest rates; (5) the current and expected future state of the economy; and (6) what Joan Robinson has called the "animal spirits" of investors. With all the financial assets traded in the world

---

[5] The equations in this example are called exactly identified, since the reduced form equations provide exactly one estimate of each of the two slope coefficients. When an equation system is over-identified, the coefficients on p in the demand and supply equations are estimated using instrumental variables, $\hat{p}$ and $\hat{Q}$, which are predicted values of p and Q using the results of the reduced form estimates. This is called two-stage least squares, whereas the procedure outlined in the text is called indirect least squares.

every day, this is clearly a massive data requirement. But in a world in which financial data are readily available, and in which high-speed computers can handle a vast amount of data, the data requirements alone are not the problem.

If we specified the supply function for the same corporation's common stock, we would find exactly the same list of variables enumerated for the demand function. That is the rub; one person can buy a share of stock only if someone else is willing to sell it. The willingness of individuals, institutions, brokers, and even corporations to sell shares of stock depends on (1) the present price, expected future price, and expected dividend rate of the stock itself; (2) the same variables for all other corporate securities; (3) the expected yields of other financial investments; (4) the prevailing and expected future structure of interest rates; (5) the state of the economy and its expected future state; and (6) "animal spirits."

Out of the phenomenal amount of financial information generated every day, there is no conceivable way of cracking the jumble of prices and volume of shares traded to deduce the formulas of the underlying demand and supply curves. Both the supply curve and the demand curve for each share traded will shift together; this will not be a coincidental shift which can be sifted by statistical techniques, but a shift caused by the presence of the same variables in both equations. There is no reliable way to employ demand and supply analysis to predict where the market is going, because there is no pattern to where it has been. Now that is a random walk.

Chapter 10

Monopoly: Single Sellers and Cartels

After developing the theory of perfect competition, we now veer to the opposite extreme and consider pure monopoly. Whereas the monopolist has a more complex profit maximization problem than the price taker, monopoly price and output decisions are less troublesome than those under imperfect competition. Although its price varies with output, the monopolist need not worry about multiple imitators as monopolistic competition must nor rivals as oligopolists must. The first part of the chapter is devoted to a pragmatic definition of a monopoly as a market with one seller confronting a stable, albeit negatively sloped, demand curve.

The contrast between the monopoly and perfect competition theories of price is developed through a fable about how a sole owner of an industry would go about monopolizing a competitive market. More abstract discussions are devoted to the monopoly seller who attempts to maximize revenue (the zero marginal cost case) and the pricing decision of the conventional monopolist with increasing marginal costs. The ironic reasons why monopoly profits are just as elusive as competitive ones are also explored.

The controversial natural monopoly is considered next. The assumption that competition with potential entrants would waste resources has been rarely tested since most "natural" monopolies enjoy government franchises. Further, similar price and output decisions are shown to result under private, unregulated ownership, public ownership, and government regulation of natural monopolies.

Cartels and multiplant monopolies are revisited with an exploration of the problems of collusive pricing in structurally competitive industries. The chapter concludes with a discussion of price discrimination.

Defining Monopoly

The economic model of monopoly is the logical opposite of the model of perfect competition. Perfect competition involves independence of buyer and seller behavior; price is determined by the impersonal forces of the market. The entry of new sellers in response to economic profit pushes price toward its lowest sustainable level. The market price of a commodity produced under competitive conditions will tend to cover only the opportunity cost of the most efficient combination of inputs.

Strictly speaking, a **monopoly** exists when a firm or person produces and/or sells the entire quantity of a commodity. Hence, the words *monopoly seller* and *monopoly market* can be used interchangeably. However, *monopoly* is often employed in a much broader context, denoting any deviation from perfect competition. *Monopolistic competition* means a market characterized by a mixture of monopoly and competitive features. Considerable emotion is bound up in the term; to be labeled a monopolist implies that the firm exploits its consumers by charging artificially high prices. We will proceed by first examining the behavior of a single-firm industry, wherein the seller can pick any price-quantity combination along the market demand curve for that commodity. Then we will extend that narrow model to encompass attempts by groups of sellers to behave *as if* price was determined and enforced by an autonomous entity. In the end we will find that extending a concept to multiple uses often blurs its precise meaning.

Although all sellers confront consumer resistance to price increases, lack of direct competition means another seller will not undercut a monopolist's price. A stable demand curve for its product allows the monopolist to anticipate consumer response to a price change when specifying the market price. Monopoly prices usually exceed the minimum production costs. However, if monopoly power arises from internal economies, a monopoly seller may experience lower production costs than would smaller competitive firms trying to serve the same market. Monopoly power is the ability to set price without unleashing price-reducing market forces. Yet, since the ability to manipulate price does not guarantee that revenue will exceed costs, not even a monopolist is immune from the risk of economic misfortune.

Monopoly power rests on the ability to exclude rivals from the market. Since property rights entail the ability to exclude, monopoly power is equivalent to ownership of the market.[1] Monopoly power may be acquired when economies of scale dictate that only one firm will serve a market. More likely, monopoly power is obtained through the grant of a government license or franchise, so that would-be rivals are liable to legal sanctions if they try to enter the monopolized market.[2] Monopoly power can also be acquired and maintained through illegal means, either by violating antitrust statutes or through the monopolization of already illegal activities, as in the case of organized crime.[3] (Antitrust policy will be covered in chapter twelve.)

The analytical advantages of the monopoly model can be lost if the relevant market is defined either too narrowly or too broadly. If monopoly is defined too narrowly, then the economic model of monopoly ceases to have relevance to actual events. One ploy of those who advocate the theory of perfect competition for all markets is to define monopoly as a case where there is only one seller of a commodity with no substitutes. The theory of consumer choice is then invoked to show that every good can serve as a substitute for any other good, both in the household's utility function and in its budget. Therefore, the argument goes, since there is no good that has no substitutes, there can be no monopoly markets. Such a narrow definition of monopoly in no way implies that all industries are characterized by free entry of small-scale producers of a homogeneous commodity. The narrow definition of monopoly merely creates a void in microeconomic theory that the model of perfect competition cannot fill. Hence, as nature abhors a vacuum, so does the careful theorist. We will abandon the narrow definition for a more operational one.

If the monopoly model were meant for all firms facing a negatively sloped demand curve, it would have to account for all firms outside of the polar case of perfect competition. As we shall examine in more detail in chapter twelve, the consequence of rivalry among differentiated **oligopoly** firms (rivals facing negatively sloped demand curves) is that a reduction in price by one seller often causes other sellers to cut their prices, resulting in a shift of the original price cutter's demand curve (due to the reduced prices of substitutes). Since we will find it useful to determine how a negatively sloped demand curve affects a seller's behavior without getting into the more complex *mutatis mutandis* logic of simultaneous price changes and demand curve shifts, we will limit

---

[1] See Thomas M. Carroll, David H. Ciscel, and Roger K. Chisholm, "The Market as a Commons: An Unconventional View of Property Rights," *Journal of Economic Issues*, 13 (June 1979), 605–627; this theme was introduced in chapter eight and will be expanded further in chapter fifteen.

[2] See Sam Peltzman, "Toward a More General Theory of Regulation," *Journal of Law and Economics* (August 1976), pp. 211–240.

[3] See Thomas Schelling, "The Economics of Criminal Enterprise," *Public Interest* (spring 1967), pp. 61–78.

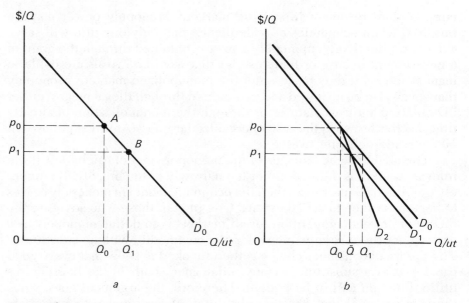

Figure 10-1
Comparison of (a) *Ceteris Paribus* Demand Curve in Monopoly and (b) *Mutatis Mutandis* Demand Curve in Oligopoly. The lack of rivalry means a monopoly firm can move from one point to another along a stable demand curve. Because market share depends on relative price (among other things), an oligopoly firm which lowers its price will, by causing other firms to lower their prices, also cause its demand curve to shift.

real-world applications of the monopoly model to firms confronting stable demand curves.

Figure 10-1a presents the demand schedule of a utility company that is the sole supplier of electric power to a well-defined geographic area. If this seller reduces its price, quantity sold will increase. If demand were price elastic, revenue would increase (rectangle Op_1BQ_1 is larger than rectangle Op_0AQ_0 in Figure 10-1a).[4] This would imply that consumers were decreasing their expenditures on other goods.[5] But because of the lack of any pattern in how consumers reduced their other expenditures, no other seller would have an incentive to retaliate by reducing the price of its product. Hence, although the demand for electricity would depend on the prices of other commodities contradicting the narrow definition of monopoly, there would be no shift in the demand

---

[4] Later in the chapter we shall see that the demand for electricity tends to be price inelastic because regulation keeps the price lower than managers would like to charge, and not because of any intrinsic quality of the demand for electricity per se.

[5] Given the budget constraint $Y = \sum_{i=1}^{n-1} p_i q_i + p_n q_n$, where the nth good is the monopoly good, $\eta_{nn} < -1$ implies $\partial(p_n Q_n)/\partial p_n < 0$, so that $\sum_{i=1}^{n-1} p_i q_i$ changes in the same direction as p_n, behaving as would a substitute for product n.

curve for electricity after the rate change because no other seller would be noticeably affected by the change in household expenditure patterns.

Figure 10-1*b* depicts the demand schedule of an oligopoly producer (one of a few producers of a class of commodities), such as an automobile manufacturer. Although Chrysler is a monopoly in the very narrow sense that it has the legally enforceable right to exclusive use of the name "Dodge," apparently consumers of Dodge products are sensitive to the price changes of Fords and Chevrolets. Demand curve D_0 in Figure 10-1*b* is drawn under the usual *ceteris paribus* assumption of constant prices of substitutes. Suppose this firm reduces the price of its product from p_0 to p_1 with the aim of increasing the quantity sold from Q_0 to Q_1. A large proportion of the expected increase in quantity sold (say $Q_1 - \tilde{Q}$ of the total increase from Q_0 to Q_1) would occur at the expense of rival sellers of substitute commodities. Affected rivals therefore reduce their prices to protect their market shares. The firm's demand curve shifts to the left (from D_0 to D_1) as prices of substitute goods fall. After predictable changes in the prices of substitutes, the firm's attempt to reduce the relative price of its product will have caused a reduction in every seller's nominal price, so that relative prices have not changed.

To repeat, the definition of monopoly we shall use is based on the pragmatic assumption of a stable demand curve: the monopoly seller can change sales by changing price and need not worry about the reaction of other sellers to its price change. As we shall see in the next chapter, the monopoly definition can be the basis of a short-run analysis of the way producers of differentiated products select their rates of output and prices, since there are too many sellers for any price cutter to be identified. In this chapter, the monopoly model will be developed under the assumption that entry barriers exclude would-be rivals from the monopolized market.

APPLICATION
Monopoly and Competition

It is often easiest to introduce a new concept by contrasting it with a familiar one. Therefore, before we examine the monopoly pricing strategy in detail, we will explore how monopolization of a once competitive market changes the prevailing price and quantity produced. And rather than confront the complications of enforcing monopoly discipline on colluding firms, we will examine a simple fable in which one entrepreneur comes to own all plants in a competitive market. Table 10-1 is the cost profile of a hypothetical widget producer—one of a hundred identical producers in a competitive market. At $q = 4$, $MC = AVC = \$40$, which is also the minimum average variable cost. The short-run shutdown price is thus $40. For convenience, marginal cost increases by

TABLE 10-1
Output and Cost Schedules for a Hypothetical Firm

Output	Total Cost	Marginal Cost	Average Variable Cost	Average Total Cost
0	150	–	–	∞
1	200	$ 50	$50.00	$200.00
2	240	40	45.00	120.00
3	270	30	40.00	90.00
4	310	40	40.00	77.50
5	360	50	42.00	72.00
6	420	60	45.00	70.00
7	490	70	48.57	70.00
8	570	80	52.50	71.25
9	660	90	56.67	73.33
10	760	100	61.00	76.00
11	870	110	65.45	79.09
12	990	120	70.00	82.50
13	1,120	130	74.62	86.15
14	1,260	140	79.29	90.00
15	1,410	150	84.00	94.00

$10 for each unit of output past the third: $MC = 10q$ for $q \geq 3$. Each firm's profit-maximizing output selection implies $10q = p$, or $q_s = 0.10p$. Assuming 100 identical firms means that industry supply is given by $Q_s = 100q_s = 100(0.1p) = 10p$.

Table 10-2 presents the market supply and demand schedules for the widget industry. Widgets would be priced out of the market at p = \$140, while quantity demanded increases by 10 units for every \$1

TABLE 10-2
Revenue and Cost Schedules for a Competitive Industry (100 firms)

Price	Quantity Supplied	Quantity Demanded	Point Elasticity	Industry Revenue	Industry Cost
$140	1,400	0	– ∞	0	$126,000
130	1,300	100	– 13.00	$13,000	112,000
120	1,200	200	– 6.00	24,000	99,000
110	1,100	300	– 3.67	33,000	87,000
100	1,000	400	– 2.50	40,000	76,000
90	900	500	– 1.80	45,000	66,000
80	800	600	– 1.33	48,000	57,000
70	700	700	– 1.00	49,000	49,000
60	600	800	– 0.75	36,000	42,000
50	500	900	– 0.56	25,000	36,000
40	400	1,000	– 0.40	16,000	31,000
30	0	1,100	– 0.27	0	15,000

reduction in price. Stating this relationship in the usual form, with quantity demanded as the dependent variable, we first determine that consumers would demand 1,400 units when $p = 0$, yielding a demand equation of:

$$Q_d = 1,400 - 10p$$

The equilibrium price at $p = \$70$ is obvious from Table 10-2. Equilibrium can also be determined by specifying that $Q_d = Q_s = Q_e$, then solving for the equilibrium price. $Q_d = 1,400 - 10p = Q_e = 10p = Q_s$ yields:

$$1,400 - 10p = 10p$$
$$1,400 = 20p$$
$$p = 70$$

Therefore:

$$Q_e = 1,400 - 10(70) = 10(70) = 700$$

By construction, average total cost equals $70 when $q = 7$ for each firm. Since this is the lowest point on the short-run average total cost curve (i.e., $MC = ATC = \$70$ at $q = 7$), the industry is in a normal profit equilibrium. It is not unrealistic to suggest that the 100 producers would like to find a means of achieving positive economic profits. Table 10-2 shows why individual response to the market price makes improvement of the firm's profit position impossible. If price exceeded $70, firms would collectively produce a market surplus; total costs for all sellers would exceed their total revenue at the above-equilibrium price. The specter of unsold inventories would drive the price back down to the equilibrium level. (Actually, with 800 units produced, price would sink to $60, keeping revenue at $48,000. The shortage in the next production period, however, would restore the $70 price.)

In desperation, the 100 producers gather at a moderately sized, seedy bar to discuss their options. After much complaining and even more drinking, a lottery is proposed. Each owner will sign the deed to his or her plant and place it in a hat. The person whose deed is subsequently drawn at random will win all 100 plants, becoming sole owner and residual claimant of the widget industry. The former owners of the other 99 plants will be retained by the monopolist as salaried plant managers, subject to employment termination at the discretion of the widget magnate.[6]

After considerable delay, the drawing is held and the winner announced. The monopolist surveys her options. According to Table 10-2,

---

[6] Even if all 100 entrepreneurs were risk averse, a lottery with monopoly power as a prize would have a positive expected value, especially if losers were retained as managers at a salary equal to their former share of normal profits.

TABLE 10-3
Profit Opportunities for a Monopolist Restricting Output (100-plant producer)

Quantity Supplied	Price	Total Revenue	Total Cost	Monopoly Profit	Marginal Revenue	Marginal Cost
0	$140	0	$15,000	− $15,000		
					$130	$50
100	130	$13,000	20,000	− $ 7,000		
					110	40
200	120	24,000	24,000	0		
					90	30
300	110	33,000	27,000	$ 6,000		
					70	40
400	100	40,000	31,000	9,000		
					55	45
450	95	42,750	33,500	9,250	(50)	(50)
					45	55
500	90	45,000	36,000	9,000		
					30	60
600	80	48,000	42,000	6,000		
					10	70
700	70	49,000	49,000	0		
					− 10	80
800	80	48,000	57,000	− $ 9,000		

the equilibrium price of $70 appears to be the best available. Was the lottery nothing but a charade?

Just then an economist enters the bar and orders whiskey with a Shirley Temple chaser. "If my honor did not bind me to encourage competition, I could tell you how to increase profits," he says, apparently to his own reflection in the mirror behind the bar. "Of course, my fee for such advice would not be unsubstantial—if my conscience would permit it, that is," he continues, still maintaining his aloof demeanor.

The monopolist-designate slaps a $500 bill onto the bar in front of the wide-eyed economist. Regaining his composure, he jots down the information in Table 10-3 on the back of a cocktail napkin.

"The only thing which keeps a group of competitors from raising price is that their independent reactions to a price increase cause a surplus and corresponding price cut. This is what Adam Smith meant by the invisible hand," says the economist somberly.

"What?" asks one of the losers, drowning his sorrows in beer.

"Something about somebody named Smith. No doubt an alias. Sounds like some sort of con artist; you know, hand quicker than the eye and all of that," his companion volunteers.

"As I was saying," continues the economist, glaring at the disturbance, "once all industry output is under the control of a single producer, a surplus can be prevented by anticipating the tendency of consumers to buy less as the price rises. Instead of producing 800 units at a price of $80, produce only 600. That way, although revenue would fall by $1,000, costs could be cut by $7,000." The economist is now addressing the monopolist directly, his earlier aloofness forgotten in his enthusiasm for an attentive audience.

"I see," says the monopolist, "that would mean more profit by producing less. But of course! If 600 units can be sold for $80 each, selling 700 units at $70 each means the last hundred units only bring in $10 each. Since each costs $70, this is like throwing $60 away. But let's see, if I could sell 500 units for $90 each, then I could earn $45,000 revenue. In exchange for a revenue loss of only $3,000 (that's $30 per unit), I could cut costs by $6,000. Why, that's another $3,000 in profit. You know, being a monopolist just might be fun after all."

"Now notice how cutting output from 500 to 400 units appears to keep profit constant at $9,000," continues the economist. The monopolist nods. "That implies a balance between the change in revenue and the change in cost. So maximum profit occurs somewhere in between. If we, excuse me, if *you* were to cut output by just 50 units, instead of 100, you could raise your price to $95. That means a $45 loss in revenue against a $55 reduction in cost for each unit not produced. Any further cutback would cause the revenue loss to exceed the cost reduction. Profit will be maximum at 450 units, when the added cost of the last unit exactly equals the added revenue."

"So are you saying I should raise my price by cutting output to the level where marginal revenue equals marginal cost?" asks the monopolist.

"Far be it from me to tell you what to do. We economists must keep our objectivity. However, if you need additional financing for your enterprise, I know where you can get very good terms."

"Thanks, but my financial adviser will be handling all that now that you've shown me how to maximize profits. What is your name, anyway?" The monopolist turns away for a moment, and when she looks back, he is gone. On the bar is a little silver calculator.

"Who was that fast talker anyway?" murmurs a drunk in the corner.

"I don't rightly know his real name," says his companion, "but I've heard him called the Loan Arranger."

The process of profit maximization for a monopoly firm involves a contrived shortage of the product. Unlike the competitive firm, which is given the price by an impersonal market, the monopolist raises price by selling less. In balancing revenue gains against costs as output expands, the monopolist takes into account the willingness of consumers to pay a higher price for the inframarginal units (all units except the last) purchased at the market clearing price.

Monopoly Price and Marginal Revenue

A monopoly is sometimes characterized as a firm whose owner can charge any price he or she wants. But this is hardly a distinguishing characteristic of monopoly. In a private enterprise economy, exchange is voluntary; either party to a transaction can veto the terms of trade. However, a monopoly seller has considerably more leverage than a competitive seller due to the lack of *close substitutes* for the monopolist's product. The firm facing a horizontal demand schedule loses all its business if its price rises even a penny over the equilibrium price. Under monopoly, and imperfect competition in general, quantity demanded falls *gradually* as price rises and increases *gradually* as price falls.

If the monopoly seller knew the demand for the firm's product, the direct relationship between revenue and output could be determined. In Figure 10-2, a monopolist is selling output Q_0 at its market clearing price, p_0. If more output were offered to consumers, the price of all output would ordinarily be reduced as a consequence.[7] For instance, if output were increased to Q_1, price would have to fall to p_1 for the additional output to be sold. Revenue from the additional sales, rectangle $p_1(Q_1 - Q_0)$, would be partly offset by revenue lost on the first Q_0 units, which used to sell at a higher price, $Q_0(p_0 - p_1)$. Net revenue from the additional output would equal $p_1(Q_1 - Q_0) - Q_0(p_0 - p_1)$, the shaded area in Figure 10-2.

Labeling $(Q_1 - Q_0)$ as ΔQ and $(p_0 - p_1)$ as $-\Delta p$, the net change in revenue resulting from the increase in output is:

$$\Delta TR = \Delta(pQ) = p_1\Delta Q - Q_0(-\Delta p) = p_1\Delta Q + Q_0\Delta p$$

Dividing ΔTR by ΔQ yields the formula for **marginal revenue,** the change in total revenue divided by the change in output:[8]

$$MR = \frac{\Delta TR}{\Delta Q} = p_1 + Q_0\frac{\Delta p}{\Delta Q}$$

Factoring the price term out of this expression reveals a close relationship between marginal revenue (MR) and the price elasticity of demand (η) for the monopoly product:

$$\frac{\Delta TR}{\Delta Q} = \frac{\Delta(pQ)}{\Delta Q} = p\left(1 + \frac{\Delta p/p}{\Delta Q/Q}\right) = p\left(1 + \frac{1}{\eta}\right)$$

---

[7] The exception is the price-discriminating monopolist, who can sell the same product to different consumers at different prices. The behavior of the discriminating monopolist will be studied later in the chapter.

[8] Those familiar with calculus know that the derivative of total revenue with respect to output can be obtained by imagining that the change in quantity approaches zero. This derivative shows how total revenue is *changing* at each level of output:

$$MR = \frac{dTR}{dQ} = \lim_{\Delta Q \to 0}\left(p + Q\frac{\Delta p}{\Delta Q}\right) = p + Q\left(\lim_{\Delta Q \to 0}\frac{\Delta p}{\Delta Q}\right) = p + Q\frac{dp}{dQ} = p\left(1 + \frac{1}{\eta}\right)$$

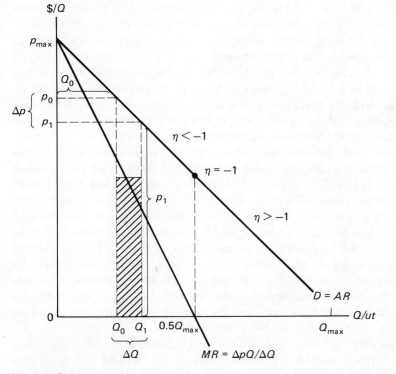

Figure 10-2
Price (Average Revenue) and Marginal Revenue for Nondiscriminating
Monopolist. If output is expanded from Q_0 to Q_1, the market clearing
price falls from p_0 to p_1. The net change in revenue is the difference
between the revenue from the additional output ($p_1 \Delta Q$) and the revenue lost from output previously sold at a higher price ($Q_0 \Delta p$).

If demand is price elastic ($\eta < -1$), the reciprocal of η is a number
between zero and negative one ($-1 < 1/\eta < 0$); this makes the ($1 +
1/\eta$) component of marginal revenue, $MR = p(1 + 1/\eta)$, a positive num-
ber. When demand is price elastic, total revenue increases as output increases: marginal revenue is positive. If demand is price inelastic ($-1 <
\eta < 0$), the reciprocal of η is smaller than negative one ($-1 > 1/\eta$),
and the ($1 + 1/\eta$) expression is negative. When demand is price inelastic,
total revenue decreases as output increases: marginal revenue is negative. And when demand has unitary price elasticity ($\eta = -1$), revenue
does not change with output, since ($1 + 1/\eta$) = 0 when $\eta = -1$. For the
linear average revenue equation, marginal revenue falls exactly twice
as fast as price when output increases; total revenue is maximized at the
midpoint of the average revenue function, the point where the elasticity
of demand is unitary.

To understand the relevance of marginal revenue to the firm's output decision, we will concentrate on the special case of a monopoly with zero marginal cost. Examples include a movie theater or a sports stadium; once the event is being staged, additional patrons can be seated without increasing the costs of the entertainment. Since all costs are fixed, profits will be maximized when the positive difference between total revenue and fixed costs is maximum—that is, when total revenue is maximum. (We are ignoring the possibility that a monopolist might wish to trade lower ticket revenue, by setting the ticket price in the inelastic region of the demand curve, for more revenue from refreshment sales.)

In Figure 10-3, the monopoly theater faces the horizontal cost function *FC*. During any performance, costs are invariant with the number of patrons (tickets sold). Starting at the price intercept on the average revenue (inverse demand) curve (Figure 10-3*b*), the proprietor reduces the ticket price until the point of unitary elasticity is encountered, or until all seats are filled, whichever implies a smaller number of tickets.

In Figure 10-3, a monopoly theater with a capacity for Q_0 patrons per performance would maximize revenue (and, in this case, profit) by selling tickets at price p_0, thus selling Q_0 tickets per performance. As Figure 10-3*a* shows, total revenue would still be increasing with Q_0 sales per performance. However, selling more than that number of tickets would either violate fire laws or constitute fraud.

If the facility had seating capacity for Q_1 persons, setting the ticket price at p_1, which would sell all seats available, would not maximize revenue. At price $p = 0.5p_{max}$, the elasticity of demand is unitary; increasing sales beyond $Q = 0.5Q_{max}$ (requiring $p < 0.5p_{max}$) would cause marginal revenue to become negative. Anyone who has sat in a half-empty movie theater watching an unpopular movie or shivered in an autumn rain watching two mediocre football teams sloshing in the mud before a few diehard (or foolhearty) fans may have wondered why ticket prices were not lowered to increase patronage. One possible explanation is that the ticket price was set at roughly the point of unitary elasticity, so that selling more tickets would have reduced revenue.

Profit Maximization under Monopoly Conditions: The Influence of Positive Marginal Cost

If a monopolist's costs vary with output, maximization of total revenue will not constitute maximization of profit. Total revenue maximization implies expanding sales (output) until the net revenue obtained from the last unit produced is zero. If marginal cost is positive, maximizing revenue would cause the monopolist to incur a loss on the last unit produced. Profit maximization will require that output expand only until the revenue gained from the last unit is balanced by the cost of producing that unit.

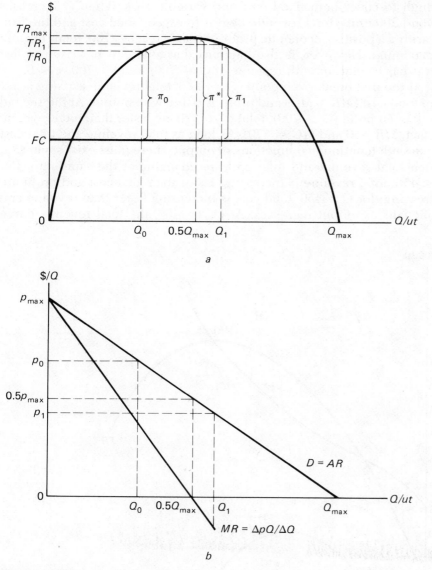

Figure 10-3
Output Decision for Monopolist with Invariant Costs

Returning to our example of the 100-plant widget monopoly, Figure 10-4 reprises the total cost and total revenue information in Table 10-3. If nothing were produced, the monopolist would lose fixed cost. Note that the profit function, $\pi(Q)$, begins at $\pi = -\$15,000$. Like the competitive firm, the monopoly firm can only generate revenue if it produces output and incurs variable costs. At $Q = 200$, total revenue has risen enough to cover both fixed cost and variable cost. When Q increases beyond 200 units, total revenue begins to exceed total cost and the firm is earning a positive economic profit. When Q reaches 700, total revenue is maximum. However, it also happens that total cost has risen so fast that it has caught up with revenue at $Q = 700$; for $Q > 700$, $\pi < 0$.

At the first break-even point ($Q = 200$), total revenue is rising faster than total cost ($MR > MC$) and profit is rising with output. At the second break-even point ($Q = 700$), total cost is rising faster than total revenue (in fact, $MR = 0$ and $MC = \$70$). As long as total revenue and total cost are smooth (continuous) functions of output, there must exist some Q at which total revenue and total cost are changing at the same rate. For $Q < 450$, total revenue is increasing faster than total cost and profit are increasing; for $Q > 450$, total cost is increasing faster than revenue and profit falls as output increases. At $Q_m = 450$, the total revenue curve

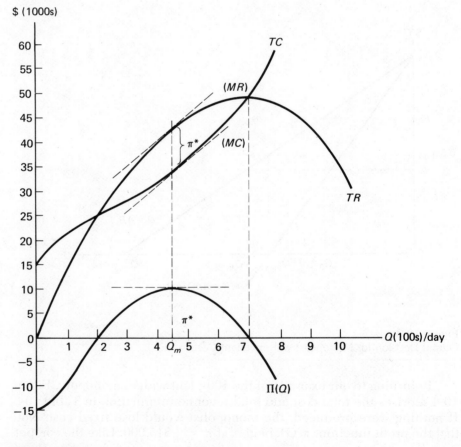

Figure 10-4
Output Decision for Monopolist with Variable Costs

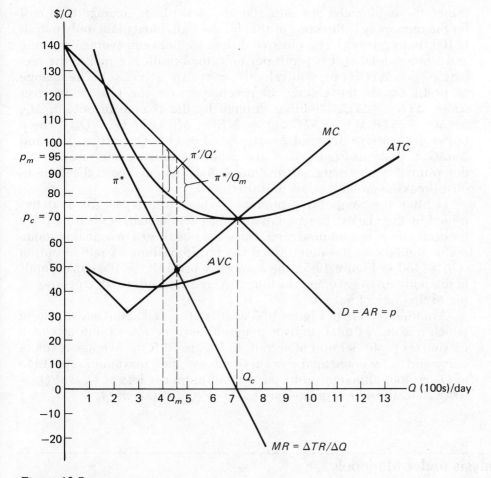

Figure 10-5
Monopolization of a Competitive Market

has achieved its maximum separation from the total cost curve; profit is maximum.[9]

Figure 10-5 contains the same information as Figure 10-4, but on a per unit basis. The two break-even rates of output, $Q = 200$ and $Q = 700$ (which would be market quantity under competition, i.e., $P_c = \$70$ and $Q_c = 700$), are identified by the intersection of the market demand (average revenue) curve and the monopoly's average total cost curve.

---

[9] This result is known as *Rolle's theorem* in calculus, which is reviewed in appendix A. If $\Pi(Q)$ is a function which is continuous over the closed interval $Q\epsilon(a,b)$ and differentiable over the open interval $Q\epsilon(a,b)$, and $\Pi(a) = \Pi(b) = 0$, there exists some $Q = c$, such that $a < c < b$ and $\Pi'(c) = 0$ at $Q = c$, where $\Pi'(Q)$ is the derivative of Π with respect to Q: $\Pi'(Q) = d\Pi/dQ$.

(Since the monopolist operates 100 identical plants, average total cost for the monopoly is the same as that for the individual plant, only output is 100 times greater.) The positive difference between average revenue and average total cost is profit per unit; total profit is equal to the rectangle $(p - ATC)Q$ or, equivalently, $\pi = (AR - ATC)Q$. The change in profit equals the change in revenue minus the change in cost: $\Delta\pi = \Delta TR - \Delta TC$. Dividing through by the change in output, ΔQ, $\Delta\pi/\Delta Q = \Delta TR/\Delta Q - \Delta TC/\Delta Q = MR - MC$. For $Q < Q_m$ (where $Q_m = 450$), $MR > MC$ and $\Delta\pi/\Delta Q > 0$. For $Q > Q_m$, $MR < MC$, and $\Delta\pi/\Delta Q < 0$. As in Figure 10-4, the profit-maximizing rate of output is determined where marginal revenue equals marginal cost: the monopolist breaks even on the last unit produced.

Unlike the competitive producer, whose price ($p = 70$) is determined by the market, the monopolist must set the market clearing price for each rate of output produced. Once the equality of marginal revenue and marginal cost has determined the profit-maximizing rate of output ($Q_m = 450$ in Figure 10-5), the monopoly price ($P_m = 95$) corresponds to the point on the average revenue (inverse demand) curve corresponding to that rate of output.

Another feature of Figure 10-5 worth noting is that the rate of output which maximizes total profit is generally *not* the rate of output which maximizes profit per unit of output. In Figure 10-5, the average revenue curve and the average total cost curve achieve their maximum separation at $Q' = 400$; although profit per unit of output is less at Q_m ($\pi'/Q' > \pi^*/Q_m$), total profit is greater at Q_m: $Q'(\pi'/Q') < Q_m(\pi^*/Q_m)$.

APPLICATION
Break-Even Analysis under Monopoly

Just as the price taker would do better to shut down when price is insufficient to cover average variable cost, the monopolist must determine whether total revenue is sufficient to cover variable cost. When starting up a new product, all costs of the potential monopolist are variable. Typically, an attempt will be made to forecast demand and cost conditions prior to signing contracts or constructing a production plant. Figure 10-6 shows two possible demand and cost profiles confronting the potential monopolist. In Figure 10-6a, minimum long-run average cost at Q_1 seems to imply a long-run break-even price of $p_{\min}$. According to Figure 10-6a, however, charging price $p_{\min}$ would result in a quantity demanded of Q_0, which occurs while long-run average cost is still falling. Unlike the competitive firm, which need only determine whether the expected price exceeds the long-run break-even price, the monopolist must compare the expected demand curve with the long-run average cost curve. The long-run prospects confronting the potential monopolist

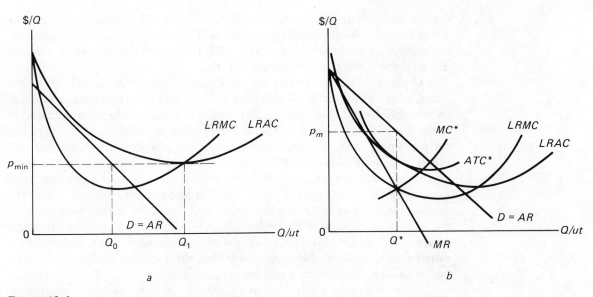

Figure 10-6
Long-Run Break-Even Analysis for a Monopoly, with All Costs Variable. *a*, Expected economic profit negative; *b*, expected economic profit positive.

in Figure 10-6*a* indicate that purchasing the required inputs (and other expenses[10]) would result in a negative (expected) economic profit. Either the would-be monopolist should reduce his or her offer or, if minimum average cost cannot be reduced, the would-be captain of industry should forego dreams of monopoly power and purchase a business in an industry where a normal return could be earned. (Of course, a person might want to own a monopoly—a sports franchise or daily paper—as a source of personal diversion.)

In Figure 10-6*b*, the potential monopolist discovers a *range of output* over which expected revenue exceeds expected cost. The budding robber baron can thus expect a positive economic profit from market entry—say, using a patent. In such a case, plotting the estimated demand schedule against the estimated planning cost schedule not only indicates that entry is warranted but also that long-run (expected) profit will be maximized by building the optimally sized plant to produce output Q^*, that is, a plant associated with ATC^* and MC^*. Note that the long-run expected profit-maximizing rate of output is indicated by the intersection of the long-run marginal cost curve and the (estimated) marginal revenue curve. In this case, the ideal rate of output is considerably below the

---

[10] As we will see in the next section, if monopoly power is transferable, any economic profit existing in the short run would be capitalized in the long run in the market value of the firm's assets. In such a case, a potential purchaser of a monopoly license should calculate the maximum bid price.

output identified by the intersection of the (still decreasing) long-run average cost schedule and the (expected) average revenue curve, as well as below that point where $LRMC = LRAC$. We will return to this anomaly when we discuss natural monopoly.

Once a monopolist has entered into agreements which fix some costs, whether revenue is sufficient to cover *all* costs is no longer relevant to whether or not the firm should produce a positive level of output. As with the competitive firm, the *short-run* break-even decision depends on whether or not revenue at the profit-maximizing rate of output will cover the resulting *variable cost*. Figure 10-7a depicts a monopolist whose average revenue curve lies everywhere below the average total cost curve. No matter what price is selected from the demand curve, the market clearing quantity for that price will generate insufficient revenue to cover fixed cost plus variable cost. A well-meaning accountant might suggest that price should be increased to cover overhead, but an economist would remind the monopolist that the negatively sloped demand curve means raising price reduces quantity sold.

Note in Figure 10-7a that marginal cost equals marginal revenue at two rates of output: first at Q_0, where MC intersects MR from above, and again at Q_m, where MC intersects MR from below. Naturally, marginal

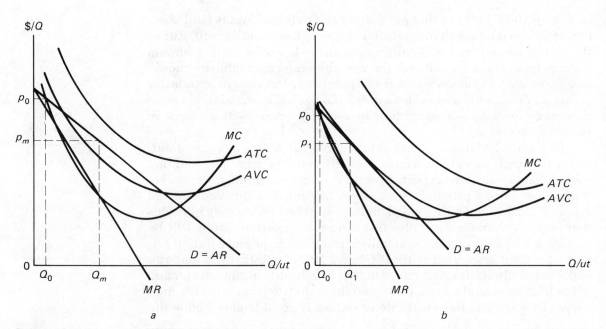

Figure 10-7
Short-Run Break-Even Analysis for a Monopoly: Some Costs Fixed. *a*, Demand curve above portion of average variable cost curve: produce Q_m for price p_m ($\pi > -FC$). *b*, Demand curve everywhere below average variable cost curve: shut down ($\pi = -FC$).

revenue is decreasing at both Q_0 and Q_m: marginal revenue is a decreasing function of output for all firms except price takers. However, marginal cost is also decreasing with output at both Q_0 and Q_m.[11] Unlike the case of the price taker, it is not necessary that marginal cost be increasing at the monopolist's profit-maximizing rate of output. What is necessary for a profit maximum under monopoly conditions is that marginal revenue be decreasing at a faster rate than marginal cost at the rate of output identified by $MC = MR$.

It should be obvious that output Q_0 in both Figure 10-7a and b could never represent the profit maximum (or loss minimum). For $Q < Q_0$, marginal cost exceeds marginal revenue; the first few units of output cost more to produce than the net revenue they generate. If output were set at Q_0, the monopolist would lose not only fixed costs but also the difference between variable costs and revenue. Losses are maximum at output Q_0 because marginal revenue is less than marginal cost up to Q_0. This implies that p_0, the market clearing price for output Q_0, must be less than average variable cost at that rate of output. (Given $\pi = -FC + Q(p - AVC)$, $\pi < -FC$ implies $p < AVC$.) Like the price taker, the monopolist would be better off (minimize losses) shutting down than producing at a rate of output for which average variable cost exceeds price. However, before shutting down, the monopolist has another point to check.

At Q_m in Figure 10-7a, profit is at a local maximum rather than at a local minimum; not only does marginal revenue equal marginal cost at Q_m, but marginal revenue is decreasing at a faster rate than marginal cost at Q_m. Furthermore, although p_m, the market clearing price for Q_m, is less than average total cost for that rate of output, p_m is greater than average variable cost; by producing Q_m and selling at price p_m, the monopolist is able to cover a portion of fixed costs. By contrast, although output Q_1 in Figure 10-7b is also a local profit maximum, which means that losses are smaller at Q_1 than for any other positive rate of output, the best option for this firm is to shut down entirely. Since p_1, the market clearing price for Q_1, is less than average variable cost at Q_1, producing that rate of output would result in loss of more than fixed cost.

As with the competitive firm, the requirement that price exceed average variable cost subsumes the requirement that marginal cost must not be falling faster than marginal revenue. That is, at Q_0 in both diagrams, $p_0 < AVC$, implying that Q_0 could not be a profit maximum. The lesson comes as a shock to would-be monopolists; the ability to manip-

---

[11] Those familiar with calculus may recognize the concern for the relative rates of change of *MR* and *MC* as the second-order condition for a local profit maximum. The first-order condition requires that the derivative of π with respect to Q equal zero: $d\pi/dQ = dTR/dQ - dTC/dQ = 0$ implies $MR = MC$. The second-order condition requires that the second derivative of profit with respect to quantity be negative where the first derivative is zero: $d^2\pi/dQ^2 = d^2TR/dQ^2 - d^2TC/dQ^2 = dMR/dQ - dMC/dQ < 0$.

ulate price never guarantees economic profit, since profit is the result of the difference between unrelated phenomena: consumer demand and production cost. Hence, the prudent monopolist, like the alert price taker, must double-check that where the difference between total revenue and total cost is the greatest, revenue at least covers variable cost.

The Capitalization of Monopoly Profit: The Sleight of the Invisible Hand?

In chapter nine we saw that entry and exit of firms, due to the economic profit or loss of incumbent firms, bring about a zero-economic-profit long-run equilibrium under perfect competition. It is fascinating to see a parallel tendency by which short-run monopoly profit disappears (zero economic profit) in the long run, even though additional firms are barred from the market. The only way that entry into a monopoly industry can occur is through the transfer of monopoly power; while the identity of the seller may change, there remains only one seller in the industry. As we shall see, this transfer of economic power tends to transform monopoly profit into artificial opportunity cost, called the **capitalization** of economic profit.

Suppose that the monopoly depicted in Figure 10-8 maximizes profit by producing Q_m units of output per year. Note that p_m exceeds average total cost ATC_0 at the profit-maximizing level of output. Each year the monopolist receives an income supplement equal to $\pi_m = (p_m - ATC_m)Q_m$ in addition to the normal opportunity cost income from its scarce resources. Suppose that since leisure is a normal good, the monopolist decides to join the jet set and looks around for a buyer for his monopoly power. Not surprisingly, the monopolist is swamped with offers to purchase fixed inputs at their replacement cost, since the monopoly dominance of the market means that those inputs are earning a higher return than they would in a competitive market. If the monopolist sells out to the highest bidder, the business could sell for as much as the present value of all expected monopoly profits, over and above the present value of normal returns to fixed inputs. (If the value of the monopoly is V_m and the monopoly power does not depreciate, a normal return on investment would imply that $\pi_m = iV_m$; it is simple to show that $V_m \leqq \pi_m/i$, where i is the relevant rate of interest. (See chapters three and thirteen for a further discussion of present value.)

If the monopoly is sold for a price equal to the present value of its expected returns, the income stream which formerly constituted monopoly profit of π_m per period now is required for a "normal return" on the purchase price of the business. If the owner decides not to sell, the opportunity cost of continuing to operate the monopoly must now reflect the return on wealth, which is equal to the (foregone) market value of the monopoly power. Whether the monopolist sells or not, the average

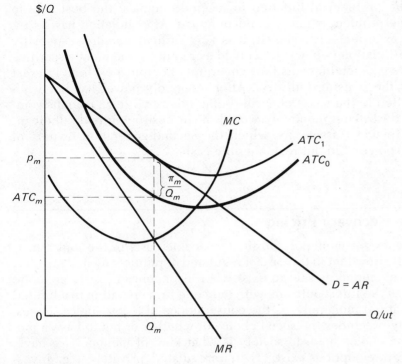

Figure 10-8
Capitalization of Monopoly Profit

total cost curve in Figure 10-8 shifts from ATC_0 to ATC_1. The new
average total cost curve, which includes the capitalized value of monopoly profit, is tangent to the average revenue curve at point (p_m, Q_m).
Only by continuing to charge the monopoly price can the second-generation monopolist earn a normal return on the investment in the business or could the original owner accumulate the same wealth that selling
would have generated.

The consequence of extending property rights to encompass the
right to exclude from a market is that markets tend to develop for transferable sources of monopoly power. In New York City, where the number
of taxis is kept artificially low by requiring each cab to display a city-
issued medallion, the price of a medallion (paid to a cab operator leaving
the market) is higher than the price of a new cab. Farmland sells for a
price which includes the present value of its acreage allotment. In states
which tie liquor licenses to location, rents or lease options include the
capitalized value of monopoly profits which accrue only to the original
owners of the monopoly power.[12]

The problem of monopoly in microeconomics is somewhat analo-

---

[12] See Carroll et al., "The Market as a Commons," p. 612.

gous to the problem of inflation in macroeconomics: the best way to "solve" the problem is never to encounter it. After inflation has set in, as recent experience has shown, it is very difficult to cure, especially when anti-inflation policy is perceived as requiring too great a sacrifice by a few (e.g., spending cuts hurt government employees, high interest rates hurt the housing industry). After monopoly power has been bestowed, often in the name of curing some other evil (e.g., ruinous competition), destroying monopoly would mean destroying real, albeit intangible, financial assets, for which the second-generation owners of monopoly power laid out real, tangible cash.

APPLICATION
Natural Monopoly and Cost Recovery Pricing

The tendency for monopoly profits to become costs in the long run is particularly prevalent in the case of regulated or publicly owned utilities. A **natural monopoly** is said to exist when economies of scale generate a survival of the fittest outcome with only one firm operating in a limited market. Natural monopoly, as the consequence of technological forces, supposedly precludes the social choice of whether or not to have a monopoly; the choice open to society is what kind of monopoly to have. Generally, three options exist: (1) an unregulated, privately (e.g., investor) owned monopoly; (2) a publicly owned monopoly; and (3) a government regulated monopoly. Despite the emotional arguments which permeate the debate over whether private enterprise or government should deliver electricity, water, and communications services, we will see that the outcomes of these three approaches tend to be quite similar, at least in the United States, where prevailing attitudes favor running government monopolies like private ones.

In Figure 10-9, the market demand curve for electric power intersects the long-run average cost curve of a single producer at an output rate below the output necessary for achieving minimum long-run average cost. By growing, a single firm could underprice smaller rivals; whichever producer first achieved internal economies would win the market for itself. Natural monopoly supposedly prevents the costly duplication of large-scale plants. But this argument ignores the duplication of production facilities during the battle of the titans for monopoly power. In fact, most utilities operate under a government franchise, which the government awards to itself when utilities are publicly owned (e.g., the Postal Service, municipal bus services) or to private-sector monopolies for their acquiescence to rate regulation. The long-term stability of natural monopoly, in the absence of government enforcement of barriers to competition, has rarely been subjected to a market test. (One of the very few cases of a utility *duopoly* exists in Lubbock, Texas, where

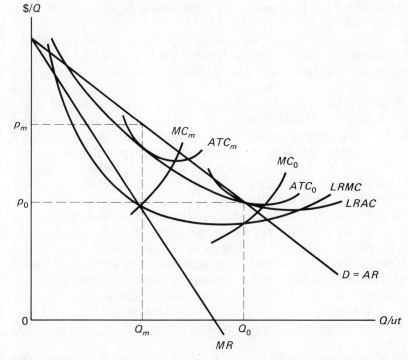

Figure 10-9
Natural Monopoly: Profit-Maximizing and Entry-Preventing Prices

households have a choice of purchasing electricity from a large investor-owned utility or from a smaller city-owned utility. See the work of economist Walter Primoux.)

If the monopoly in Figure 10-9 were allowed to maximize economic profit, its planned rate of output would be Q_m, where the long-run marginal cost curve intersects the (expected) marginal revenue curve from below. The monopoly would set price at p_m, which, by necessity, would be located in the elastic region of the market demand curve for electricity. Note that constructing a plant to produce Q_m would leave potential economies of scale unrealized. Some economists have suggested that in the absence of government protection from the entry of rivals, a monopoly producing only Q_m would be constantly threatened by the entry of larger producers. A nonfranchised monopoly might erect a plant to produce output Q_0, identified by the intersection of the long-run average cost curve and the (expected) demand curve. By operating the plant with the short-run cost curve ATC_0, an unprotected monopoly would be producing a price-quantity combination earning approximately zero economic profit. Barring a drastic, unanticipated shift in demand or a wealthy entrepreneur with pronounced risk preferences (see chapter three), entry would be deterred by the elimination of prospects for economic profit.

An alternative approach to natural monopolies is public ownership and operation of the production facilities. In many countries, utilities, communications, and transportation networks are owned and operated by the national government. In the United States, public ownership of utilities generally takes the form of municipal ownership, with obvious exceptions being the Postal Service, the Tennessee Valley Authority, and Amtrak.[13] The prevalence of "urbanization" of natural monopolies in the United States probably stems from its lower population density relative to Western European countries and Japan. Nevertheless, "creeping municipalism" does not appear to foment the angry rhetoric instigated by the threat of creeping socialism.

Figure 10-10 depicts the economic environment of a publicly owned utility. It is entirely possible that a government might milk its monopoly franchise for electrical service to obtain enough revenue to cover all the costs of power generation as well as to supplement general government revenues. Whether characterized as monopoly profits, taxation, or "good fiscal management," the price which generates the greatest net revenue (above the opportunity cost of inputs) is p_m, the monopoly price, determined by the intersection of the marginal revenue and long-run marginal cost curves.

Although politicians might stand for reelection on the basis of the sound management practice of charging p_m, their opponents might challenge that practice by promising to maximize the benefits from the publicly owned monopoly. According to economic theory, the appropriate price for electric power would be p_e, identified by the intersection of the market demand curve and the long-run marginal cost curve. (According to welfare economics, the topic of chapter fifteen, efficient allocation of resources implies that price equal marginal cost for all products, regardless of whether this allows fixed costs to be recovered.) At output Q_e, households' evaluation of the last unit produced equals the opportunity cost of inputs necessary to produce it. Note that Q^* would not be the optimal output level, even though long-run average cost would be minimum. Society's evaluation of that output is less than the opportunity cost of resources its production would require.

The political problem associated with setting the utility price at p_e is that $p_e Q_e$ is less than the total cost of Q_e; thus funds from some source other than the price of electricity are required to make up the deficit.

---

[13] The influence of government provision of goods and services on allocational efficiency is studied in the field of public finance or public economics. For the most part, governments provide public goods: commodities (e.g., national defense) from whose use or benefits nonpayers cannot be excluded.

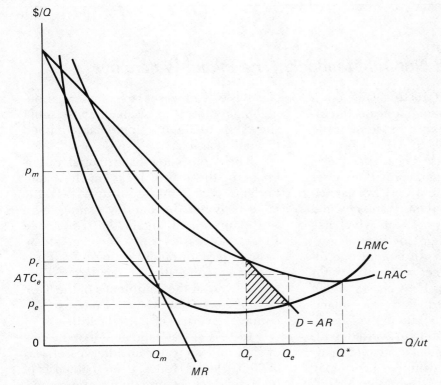

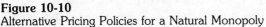

Figure 10-10
Alternative Pricing Policies for a Natural Monopoly

Although many ways could be found to finance the deficit (e.g., an annual "hookup charge" to utility users independent of the rate of usage or higher than marginal cost pricing for initial kilowatt-hours[14]), politicians who favor marginal cost pricing of utility services may be vulnerable to charges of fiscal mismanagement.

If the rate were set at the usual regulated price, p_r, identified by the intersection of the demand curve and the long-run average cost curve (i.e., the entry-preventing price under private ownership), total revenue from utility customers would equal the total cost of electricity. Ironically, amid praise for sound financial management and loss-prevention prac-

---

[14] Price discrimination against customers with the least elastic demand for electric power is often used to reduce the price to a level close to marginal cost for those with more elastic demand (e.g., industrial users who include negotiations for lower utility rates as part of their location decision). Generally, residential users pay a rate much higher than marginal cost on their few thousand kilowatt-hours, while the rate paid for several hundred thousand kilowatt-hours is much lower.

Policy Illustration
Government and Natural Monopoly: The Inland Waterways

One of the most interesting, and often overlooked, natural monopolies is the inland and coastal waterway system of the United States. The U.S. Army Corps of Engineers constructs dams and locks, dredges channels, and provides other services to make these waterways navigable, free of charge to the privately owned barge lines and pleasure boats which use them. The justification for federal government expenditures to benefit one industry (which competes with railways for freight business) is a 1796 law in which Congress proclaimed that the inland waterway system "shall be forever free." Congress was attempting to avoid the difficulties of the European system of riparian rights, whereby a shipper had to pay a toll every time he passed through a different principality. At the same time, Congress was not able to repeal economic scarcity; by avoiding tolls on waterway users, Congress merely passed the costs on to the public at large.

Aside from the equity issue, there is evidence that financing waterway improvements out of general revenues leads to a misallocation of resources. First, allowing "free" use of costly services means that services are not provided on the "willingness to pay" basis. As an extreme example, the Cordell Hull Lock and Dam on the Cumberland River was completed in 1976 at an estimated cost of $97.2 million. The purpose of that facility was to open up the Cumberland River east of

Nashville, Tennessee, to commercial development. As the accompanying table shows, in 1976 not a single barge passed through that lock.

The table shows substantial differences in the use of locks on the Cumberland and Tennessee rivers. Traffic is so heavy at the Barkley Dam, where the Cumberland enters the Tennessee River, that vessels wait an average of one hour to pass through the lock. Traffic is nearly as congested at the larger Kentucky Dam, at the confluence of the Tennessee and Ohio rivers. Free use encourages overuse of these facilities.

In 1976 it was estimated that the cost of fuel and crew for an idle vessel was $200 per hour. Hence, even if all costs of lock and dam construction, maintenance, and the crew to process vessels are considered as fixed costs (and hence not the basis of an efficient user's fee), charging each vessel for the congestion it creates would have two effects. First, it would use the price system to monitor use of facilities. Some facilities (the Kentucky, Barkley, and Pickwick dams) could be enlarged. Others might be abandoned if usage was minimal. Second, forcing vessel operators to pay a congestion charge might encourage development of alternative routing. For instance, if recreational vessels were charged $200 each for using the Barkley Lock, it is likely that a local entrepreneur would find a way of using a boat trailer to take pleasure

Estimated Congestion Costs Due to Free Passage Through Locks on the Tennessee and Cumberland Rivers in 1976

Lock	Commercial Lockages	Recreational Lockages	Congestion per Lockage[a] (minutes)	Dollar Equivalent Congestion Cost
Cumberland River				
Barkley	1,125	622	59.3	$197.67
Cheatham	1,002	503	17.1	57.67
Old Hickory	387	1,435	7.1	23.64
Cordell Hull	0	187	–	–
Tennessee River				
Kentucky	5,623	507	42.9	$143.06
Pickwick	1,828	889	51.8	172.67
Wilson	1,987	975	20.1	67.02
Wheeler	1,588	1,466	15.5	51.68
Guntersville	1,225	1,886	12.4	41.33
Nickajack	1,243	797	33.8	112.67
Chickamauga	1,613	1,753	10.4	34.49
Watts Bar	569	1,604	13.6	45.42
Fort Loudoun	318	1,094	19.3	64.18

[a] Congestion per lockage is the estimated total delay time for all vessels in the lockage queue when one more vessel shows up. Hence, if it takes 20 minutes per lockage (recreational vessels can be processed two or three at a time) and an average of three boats are waiting, congestion per lockage will be one hour. Results are based on data obtained from the U.S. Army Corps of Engineers, giving the number of vessels, arrival time, and lockage time for all locks on the Cumberland and Tennessee rivers in 1976.

boats *around* the lock at a fraction of the cost.

The moral: While citizens are usually concerned when monopolies charge prices which exceed marginal cost, it is also important to avoid the allocational inefficiency that results from government provision of services at prices below marginal cost.

Based on Thomas M. Carroll, "The Use of a Lockage Fee as a Congestion Toll for Financing the Inland Waterway System" (Paper presented at the Annual Meeting of the Southwest Social Science Association, Houston, Texas, April 15, 1978).

tices, politicians, newspapers,[15] and voters may overlook the fact that the increase in customers' bills for the Q_r units of service under break-even pricing, namely $(p_r - p_e)Q_r$, is always greater than the subsidy required for marginal cost pricing.

The shaded triangle, whose area equals $(p_r - p_e)(Q_e - Q_r)/2$, represents the consumer surplus which is lost when break-even pricing is used instead of marginal cost pricing for utility services. As long as taxpayers and utility consumers are roughly the same group, managing a government-owned utility in a "businesslike" manner often makes those taxpayer-consumers worse off than they need be. Government ownership of a natural monopoly is likely to result in the same kind of pricing policy that would prevail under private, unregulated monopoly. A challenge from a reform ticket of office seekers *may* prevent monopoly exploitation of citizen-consumers (charging p_m) much the same as the fear of entry *might* cause a nonfranchised monopoly to charge p_r instead of p_m. However, the danger of having their motives misunderstood (or misrepresented) probably prevents municipal officials from setting the marginal cost-price of p_e.

The fallacy of equating zero economic profit with efficient allocation of resources may help explain the peculiarities in pricing postal services and other government-operated (so-called) natural monopolies. In Figure 10-11 a natural monopoly is constructed so that the average total cost curve is everywhere above the market demand curve for the product. The efficient price implied by economic theory would be p_e, where the market demand curve intersects the marginal cost curve. Consumers would purchase Q_e units of service, requiring an outlay of $(ATC_e)Q_e$, of which $(ATC_e - p_e)Q_e$ is made up out of general revenues. For instance, Americans might pay \$0.08 to mail a first-class letter, spending \$80 billion to mail 1 trillion (that is, $1,000 \times 10^9 = 10^{12}$) first-class letters. But since the total cost is \$140 billion, \$60 billion must be made up from other sources.

The attempt to do away with the U.S. postal deficit gave rise in the 1970s to a quasi-autonomous postal corporation which has an obligation to pay its own way. In our example, the price of a first-class stamp is raised to \$0.14 (p_0), but the price increase causes a reduction in quantity demanded to Q_0. But average total cost increases when quantity falls; once again a rate hike is required. Since $ATC > p$ for each rate of output,

---

[15] Newspapers themselves may function as natural monopolies in small and medium-size metropolitan areas. After a daily paper is written (high fixed costs), its marginal cost is little more than the cost of paper and ink and delivery, which is the approximate price of home delivery. Fixed-cost payments and profit are covered by revenue from local print advertising, which is monopolized, and from national or regional advertising, which is competitive. Often a morning and an evening paper are owned by the same publisher; to the extent that circulation depends on editorial policy, a publisher may obtain greater revenue by allowing the two papers to represent opposing philosophies. Monopolizing editorial policy would reduce revenue from monopolizing local print (e.g., classified) advertising.

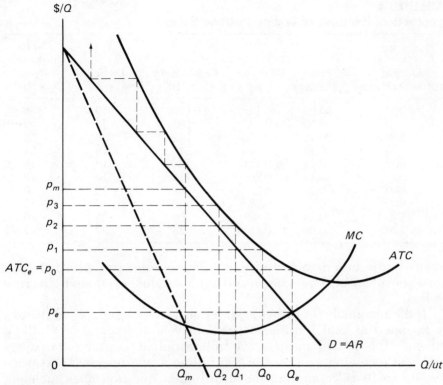

Figure 10-11
Consequences of Break-Even Pricing of an Unprofitable Natural Monopoly

every time the price is raised, quantity demanded falls and losses persist. Even at Q_m, where $MR = MC$, total costs would exceed total revenue, although losses would be minimized by charging p_m. The futile attempt to raise price to cover overhead will cause price and quantity to ricochet between the demand curve and the average total cost curve until, as in Figure 10-11, the price approaches infinity and the quantity demanded approaches zero.

Since the government monopoly is clearly not working out as planned, why not give the private sector a chance? After all, private-sector managers are assumed to have a stronger incentive to reduce costs and increase revenue than do government bureaucrats. Table 10-4 is a hypothetical revenue and cost schedule for postal services designed to provide one possible answer. As in Figure 10-11, a nondiscriminating monopolist, whether operating in the public sector or the private sector, would lose $10 billion per year at the best possible price-quantity combination (p_m = $0.18). If these were real costs (i.e., not a return on an investment in monopoly power), the minimum loss would eventually bankrupt a private-sector firm. So why not let the market work and the

TABLE 10-4
Hypothetical Example of Pricing Postage Stamps

Output (10⁹ letters/year)	Price ($/letter)	Average Cost	Total Value to Consumers ($ × 10⁹)	Deficit ($ × 10⁹)	Net Consumer Surplus ($ × 10⁹)
1,000	$0.08	$0.14	$170	$60	$30
900	0.10	0.147	162	42	30
800	0.12	0.155	152	28	28
700	0.14	0.166	140	18	24
600	0.16	0.18	126	12	18
500	0.18	0.20	110	10	10
400	0.20	0.23	92	12	0
300	0.22	0.28	72	18	−12
200	0.24	0.38	50	28	−26
100	0.26	0.68	26	42	−42

monopoly die in a dignified manner? Supposedly, as Table 10-4 indicates, consumer-taxpayers are receiving a surplus, even after covering the loss.

If the marginal cost of $0.08 per letter were charged, postal patrons are assumed to mail 1 trillion letters per year and spend $80 billion. Although this would mean a $60-billion deficit, consumer-taxpayers would be receiving a surplus of $22 billion at the marginal cost price (see Table 10-4).[16] Ignoring the distribution question for a moment, society would be ahead by $22 billion with marginal cost pricing and deficit financing of postal services. Raising the price of stamps, however, is not an efficient means of financing the deficit for two reasons: (1) a price of $0.14 implies charging consumers more than the cost of the last unit produced; (2) the increase in price reduces quantity demanded, so that the $60-billion fixed costs are spread over fewer units, meaning that some of the loss remains.

Being reasonably confident that federal taxpayers and Postal Service patrons are roughly the same people and firms, a case exists for subsidizing marginal cost pricing of that natural monopoly, whether it is publicly or privately operated. In concluding this discussion, we will show how regulation of privately owned natural monopolies often leads to the same perverse incentives that we have just catalogued for publicly owned natural monopolies.

---

[16] To calculate consumer surplus, multiply the maximum price that would be paid for each increment to output, then subtract total expenditure (in this case, price times quantity plus tax payments to cover the deficit). Since the first 100 billion letters are valued at $0.26 each, the second 100 billion at $0.24 each, and so forth, total consumer benefit from 1,000 billion (1 trillion) letters per year equals: ($0.26 × 100 billion) + (0.24 × 100 billion) + (0.22 × 100 billion) + ⋯ + (0.08 × 100 billion) = (0.26 + 0.24 + 0.22 + 0.20 + 0.18 + 0.16 + 0.14 + 0.12 + 0.10 + 0.08) 100 billion = $170 billion. Subtracting the total cost of $140 billion yields consumer surplus of $30 billion.

APPLICATION
Regulation of Natural Monopolies

Government regulation of natural monopolies represents a tacit denial of faith in the entry prevention theory of private monopoly pricing. If governments grant monopoly franchises to privately owned firms in exchange for cooperation with the regulatory process, the issue of entry prevention pricing becomes moot.

Regulation of utility rates usually involves the stipulation of a price ceiling—the maximum rate the monopoly can legally charge for its product. In order for the rate ceiling to change the behavior of the utility, it must be set *below* the profit-maximizing price. If the utility commission set a maximum price at p' in Figure 10-12, the price would still be set at p_m. For output less than Q', marginal revenue would equal p', since charging a higher price is legally prevented. At Q', the utility would have to reduce price below p' to sell additional output, causing marginal revenue to slip to the line labeled MR for $Q > Q'$. Since $MR > LRMC$ at Q', the monopoly would increase output and reduce price until $MR = MC_0$ at Q_m and p_m, respectively, assuming the plant associated with ATC_0 had been constructed.

The regulatory commission cannot ignore the market demand for the product in setting the maximum allowable rate. Suppose that the commission, enamored by the idea of minimum long-run average cost,

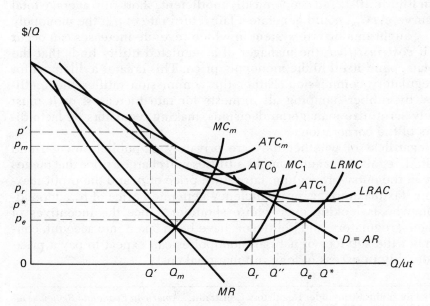

Figure 10-12
Alternative Ceiling Prices for a Natural Monopoly

set the maximum rate at $p*$, since $LRMC = LRAC$ at $Q*$. Unaware of market demand, the utility builds a plant to deliver $Q*$ units of output, only to discover that only Q'' units can be sold at price $p*$. The utility commission would have to grant a rate increase, not only to cover higher *long-run* average costs than anticipated in setting $p*$, but also to cover the excessive fixed costs of a generating plant with excessive production capacity.

Because nonsubsidized private-sector firms must cover their total costs, utility commissions adopt a *fair return* rule for setting the maximum rate utilities may charge for their products. Since long-run average costs include the opportunity cost of investment funds, following the fair return rule implies setting the allowable rate at the point on the demand curve where the long-run average cost curve intersects it. This price is designated as p_r in Figure 10-12, and production occurs along ATC_1.

There is a paradox when the fair return formula implies a regulated price in the inelastic portion of the market demand curve ($MR < 0$). To guarantee, say, a 12 percent rate of return on investment, a utility commission would have to allow an automatic pass through of costs; any investment expenditure, whether economically justified or not, would become part of the *rate base*. Conversely, any decrease in the cost of production would imply a rate decrease. Economists H. Averch and L. L. Johnson, among others, have noted the tendency of regulated firms to have more capital-intensive production methods than justified by efficiency considerations.[17]

In Figure 10-12, an economically inefficient (short-run) average total cost curve, ATC_m, could generate a fair return rate of p_m, the monopoly price. Caught in a bizarre system in which revenue increases can occur only if *cost justified*, the manager of a regulated utility finds that the firm can spend itself to the monopoly price. This creates a dilemma for the regulatory commission. Either the commission ratifies the inefficiency by rubber-stamping all requests for rate increases, or it must actively scrutinize managerial decisions, making regulators de facto directors of the corporation.

Regardless of whether they are privately or publicly owned and operated, regulated or autonomous, utilities will charge a price that ranges between the entry-preventing, fair return price of p_r and the profit-maximizing, tax-maximizing, or inefficiency-generated price of p_m, depending on who is looking over whose shoulder. Once the incentives of managers, regulators, and politicians have been taken into account, consumers of the services of natural monopolies can expect to pay a price considerably in excess of long-run marginal cost.

---

[17] "Behavior of the Firm under Regulatory Constraint," *American Economic Review* (December 1962), pp. 1052–1069.

Cartels and Multiplant Monopolies

We open this chapter with a fable about transforming a competitive industry into a one-owner monopoly. In this section, we examine the more likely case of a **cartel**, which is a monopoly composed of more than one firm. The Organization of Petroleum Exporting Countries (OPEC) is probably the best-known cartel, but others include trade associations, producer cooperatives, the medical profession,[18] and labor unions in general (see chapter fourteen).

As we have often repeated, the essence of a competitive market is the ability of additional sellers to enter, until price falls to the minimum long-run average cost of an efficient firm. Price cuts result only from a market surplus, but once some producers cut price, all are forced to follow suit. To sustain an artificially high price, a monopolist must cut industry output to the rate determined by the equality of industry-wide marginal cost (given by the industry supply curve) and industry-wide marginal revenue. The essence of monopoly is that the price changes which result from output changes are treated *as if* they were changes in the costs of production. The cartel problem emerges when group discipline is imperfectly enforced upon individual sellers. As noted in chapter eight, what would be inefficient behavior in the commons generates efficient outcomes in the market.

To highlight the problems faced by a collusive agreement among independent sellers, we reprise the pricing and production decisions of a multiplant, single-firm monopoly like the one in Tables 10-1 and 10-2. In Figure 10-13, a single firm acquires ownership of a competitive industry in long-run equilibrium at price p_c and output Q_c. The monopolist decides to increase profit by cutting output to Q_m, where industry marginal cost (identified by the horizontal summation of individual plant marginal cost curves) equals marginal revenue (derived from the market demand curve). Output is then allocated among the various plants so that marginal cost for each plant equals industry-wide marginal revenue.[19]

---

[18] See the classic article by Reuben A. Kessel, "Price Discrimination in Medicine," *Journal of Law and Economics* (October 1958), pp. 20–53.

[19] The multiplant monopolist wishes to maximize $\pi = p \left(\sum q_i \right) - C(\sum q_i)$, where q_i is the output produced in the ith plant. Taking the partial derivative of π with respect to each q_i:

$$\frac{\partial \pi}{\partial q_i} = \left(p + Q \frac{\partial P}{\partial Q} \right) \frac{\partial Q}{\partial q_i} - \frac{\partial C}{\partial q_i} = 0$$

for all $i = 1, \ldots, n$. Since $\partial Q / \partial q_i = 1$ for all $i = 1, \ldots, n$, this rule requires that production be allocated so that marginal cost for each plant is equal to industry-wide marginal revenue. Of course, if average variable cost were less than p_m for any plant, that plant would be closed and its fixed costs written off.

Business Illustration
The Strange Incentives under Regulation

Despite considerable disagreement over the proper role of government in mitigating imperfect competition, it is generally acknowledged that government regulation is intimately related to monopoly. Ironically, governments tend to set maximum prices below the equilibrium level in markets which are dominated by natural monopolies, hence (in theory) removing some of the sting of monopoly structure. However, when governments set minimum prices above the equilibrium level, the regulations are responsible for monopoly distortions which the market, left to its own devices, would tend to eliminate.

To determine the impact of maximum and minimum price regulation on incentives confronting chief executive officers (CEOs) of regulated corporations, the author and David Ciscel related the salary plus bonus for the CEO of company i, EC_i, to that company's sales, S_i, and its residual profit, $\tilde{\pi}_i$ (profit purged of the influence of total revenue*), estimating the equation: $EC_i = \hat{\beta}_0 + \hat{\beta}_1 \tilde{\pi}_i + \hat{\beta}_2 S_i + \hat{\epsilon}_i$. Data were obtained for 46 privately owned utilities (which faced maximum rate regulations set by different state and federal regulatory commissions) and 23 transportation firms (whose minimum rates were enforced by federal regulatory commissions prior to deregulation after the period covered by the data).

As in a previous study,[†] the intercept term, $\hat{\beta}_0$, was interpreted as the CEO's base pay: that portion of executive pay independent of the firm's performance. In every year, the base pay of utility executives was lower than that estimated for nonregulated firms. From 1970 through 1973, base pay for transportation executives paralleled that of utility executives, but from 1974 through 1976, base pay for transportation executives was not materially different than that estimated for nonregulated firms. Apparently the combined impact of higher fuel prices and recession reduced the revenue of transportation firms so much that managing such firms was as risky as managing corporations whose prices were set in an environment of rivalry (see chapter twelve). This explains why transportation firms apparently became disenchanted with minimum rate regulations and did not fight deregulation very vigorously.

The coefficient on residual profit, $\hat{\beta}_1$, was positive and significant (meaning a miniscule chance that $\beta_1 \leqq 0$) for transportation firms in all years, while there is little evidence that executive compensation increased as sales increased in

---

* What we call "residual profit" approximates the concept of "X-efficiency," coined by Harvey Leibenstein to refer to the internal efficiency of resource allocation (i.e., within the firm, rather than between firms). See Harvey Leibenstein, "Allocative Efficiency versus 'X-Efficiency,'" *American Economic Review* (June 1966), pp. 392–415.

† David H. Ciscel and Thomas M. Carroll, "The Determinants of Executive Compensation: An Econometric Survey," *Review of Economics and Statistics* (February 1981), pp. 7–13.

Determinants of Executive Compensation

Year	$\hat{\beta}_0$	$\hat{\beta}_1$	P(error)	$\hat{\beta}_2$	P(error)	R^2
Transportation Firms						
1970	99,707.06	0.4711	(0.004)	0.0660	(0.005)	0.4001
1971	98,847.10	0.2616	(<0.001)	0.0571	(0.023)	0.4288
1973	102,104.38	0.8494	(<0.001)	0.0875	(0.006)	0.4955
1974	233,588.03	0.6393	(0.008)	0.0139	(0.856)	0.3024
1975	223,360.80	0.7134	(0.002)	0.0163	(0.814)	0.4485
1976	330,388.44	1.1403	(0.005)	0.0223	(0.707)	0.3169
Utility Companies						
1970	99,653.60	−0.0535	(<0.001)	0.0356	(<0.001)	0.5510
1971	112,310.80	−0.3120	(0.003)	0.0270	(<0.001)	0.5730
1973	113,669.50	−0.6190	(<0.001)	0.0383	(<0.001)	0.5846
1974	130,137.71	−0.2945	(<0.001)	0.0250	(<0.001)	0.5222
1975	113,794.00	−0.5639	(<0.001)	0.0391	(<0.001)	0.6301
1976	96,754.60	−0.4445	(<0.001)	0.0312	(<0.001)	0.6477

$EC_i = \beta_0 + \beta_1 \bar{\pi}_i + \beta_2 S_i + \epsilon_i$, where EC_i = salary plus bonus of CEO of company i; $\bar{\pi}_i$ = residual profit (net of revenue) for company i; S_i = sales revenue of company i; and ϵ_i = statistical error term.

1974–1976. These results reinforce the conclusion that prohibition of price competition among transportation firms made it extremely difficult for them to increase revenue, forcing executives to become increasingly cost conscious.

By contrast, there is clear evidence that executives of utilities are rewarded for increasing sales much the same as executives of nonregulated firms are. For utility firms facing maximum rate constraints, the quirk is that increasing sales *revenue* means raising rates, since "fair return" regulation places the maximum rate in the inelastic region of the monopoly's demand curve. Since the maximum rate is related to the average total cost of generating the amount of service demanded by customers, a rate hike requires cost increases not covered by revenue at the old rate. The perverse incentives of maximum rate regulation, associated with the Averch and Johnson effect, show up as an inverse relationship between cost control and the executive's salary.

Adapted from Thomas M. Carroll and David H. Ciscel, "The Effects of Regulation on Executive Compensation," *Review of Economics and Statistics* (August 1982), pp. 505–509.

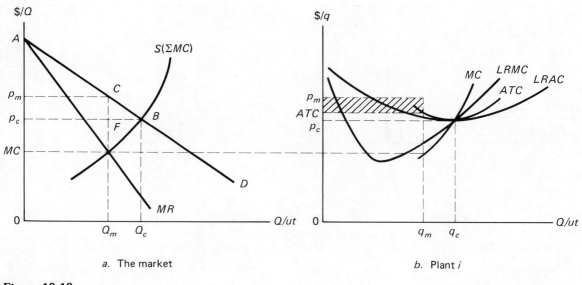

a. The market

b. Plant *i*

Figure 10-13
Multiplant Monopoly

Figure 10-13 shows that the monopolization of a previously competitive market results in a higher price and less output for the industry and for the representative plant. In the short run, the monopoly possesses excess capacity; the typical plant is generating profit equal to $(p_m - ATC)q_m$, which is considerably less than the increase in consumers' expenditures for the first q_m units: $(p_m - p_c)q_m$. The net profit of the monopolist, roughly $n(p_m - ATC)q_m$, is less than the total harm suffered by consumers. Monopolization of a market is an economically inefficient method of transforming consumer surplus into producer surplus. (This proposition is demonstrated in considerably more detail in chapter fifteen, which is devoted to welfare economics.)

Under competitive equilibrium, each household breaks even on the last unit of a commodity purchased. At the margin, the consumer benefit gained from the last unit of the commodity purchased is the same as the utility which would have been obtained from spending that money on some other commodity.[20] However, since marginal utility decreases with consumption, *ceteris paribus*, the household receives more utility from each dollar spent on inframarginal units than it would have received from spending that money on any other commodity. This bonus, known

---

[20] As shown in chapter two, utility is maximized (subject to the budget constraint) when the ratio of marginal utility to price is the same for all commodities the household purchases: $MU_i/p_i = MU_j/p_j$, so that $MU_i = (p_i/p_j) MU_j$. The opportunity cost of purchasing any commodity is the utility sacrificed by not purchasing some other commodity.

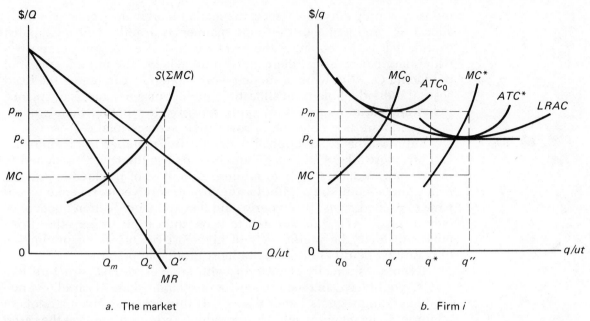

a. The market   *b.* Firm *i*

Figure 10-14
The Cartel Problem

as *consumer surplus* (see chapter two) is roughly equal to the area of triangle ABp_c in Figure 10-13*a*.

Imposition of the monopoly price causes consumer surplus to shrink to the area of triangle ACp_m. The excess burden of monopoly to society is the lost consumer surplus which does not become producer surplus, equal to at least triangle CFB in Figure 10-13*a*.[21] The monopolist reduces output to Q_m in order to increase price to p_m. Although no costs are incurred in producing the $Q_c - Q_m$ units of output (freeing these resources for alternative, supposedly lower priority uses), there are no direct revenue gains to the producer from the output not produced. The consumer surplus on the $Q_c - Q_m$ units that would have been generated under perfect competition is simply lost to consumer and monopolist alike.

If monopolization of a market involves the formation of a cartel, the individual firms must reach agreement on the industry-wide price to be charged, and how the profits and output implied by that price will be divided among participants. In Figure 10-14, total profit for the cartel would be maximized by producing output to Q_m, where the short-run

---

[21] If the industry is a constant-cost industry, long-run marginal cost will remain at p_c, so that $(p_m - p_c)q_m$ will represent producer surplus. Otherwise, producer surplus will be less.

industry supply curve intersects the market marginal revenue curve. By allocating production in the same manner as a multiplant monopolist would, that is, by equating the marginal cost of each firm to industry-wide marginal revenue, the cartel would achieve the minimum cost of producing Q_m. But while a single-owner monopoly can ignore the fixed costs of individual plants in allocating production among its many plants, individual cartel members are quite sensitive to whether their production quotas are large enough to cover their average total costs.

Suppose that a suboptimally sized cartel member has a short-run cost structure like ATC_0 in Figure 10-14b. If output were assigned to individual producers so as to minimize the cost of producing Q_m, this firm's quota would be q_0. But for the firm to survive, its revenue would have to exceed $p_m q_0$. Its owner would demand a production quota of q' (where $p_m = ATC_0$) or threaten to leave the cartel. Either other firms must subsidize the inefficiency of high-cost producers, or production quotas must be diverted from the most profitable pattern.

Even an optimally sized firm, with an average cost structure like ATC^*, would have an incentive to obtain a larger share of cartel revenue by demanding a quota larger than q^*. If this firm was given a quota of q^* (or less), its owner would try to produce and sell q'' units at the cartel price of p_m. Even after quotas are assigned, production by cartel members must be carefully policed. Cartels have a tendency to disintegrate, either because initial agreements over output or profit quotas cannot be made, or because, after quotas are assigned, individual members try to produce where their marginal cost equals the monopoly price. If some members produce more than their quotas, other members must reduce output more or else the surplus will cause price to fall. Indeed, in the face of the 1981 oil glut, OPEC ministers met to decide how much Saudi Arabia should cut its output!

In a private enterprise society, parties to a legal agreement are prevented from cheating by legally enforced contracts. The significance of antitrust law (discussed in chapter twelve) is that, at the very least, the courts refuse to abet the "conspiracies in restraint of trade" which constitute formal cartel agreements. Further, the attempt by a cartel to have the courts enforce such an agreement would be self-incriminating. But, as we shall also see in chapter twelve, government cannot always deter informal pricing conspiracies.

Price Discrimination

The ultimate in monopoly power is the ability to charge different prices to different consumers of the same commodity. Movie theaters typically charge half the adult price for children's tickets, airlines charge lower fares to students than to business travelers, and auto repair shops charge more to insurance companies than to car owners paying out of their own pockets. Is this because children are small enough to fit two to a theater seat, thus costing the theater operator only half what it costs to accommodate adult patrons? Do students get reduced fares on airlines because they eat less, thereby requiring less fuel to lift off the ground than an overfed corporate traveler? Does the added expense of paperwork really justify the higher price of insurance-company–financed auto repairs?

In each of the cases mentioned, attributing differences in price to different costs of production is dubious. What all three cases have in common is that the demand for the service tends to be much less elastic for the group paying the higher price. Baby-sitters provide an excellent substitute for children's movie tickets; for adults, the ticket price is usually a small fraction of the opportunity cost of time spent watching a movie. Business travelers have a higher opportunity cost of time than students. People whose insurance company is paying for auto repair work tend to be less sensitive to price than those who must pay their own expenses. A monopolist who recognized that some customers had highly elastic demand while others had less elastic demand would face a dilemma if all customers were to pay the same price. A price rise intended to increase expenditure by consumers with inelastic demand would reduce the revenue from consumers with elastic demand. If the price were reduced to increase revenue from those with elastic demand, revenue would be lost from those with inelastic demand.

Price discrimination is the practice of charging different prices for commodities which are technically the same. By dividing the market according to the sensitivity to price of different categories of consumers, the monopoly seller can raise price where demand is price inelastic, while maintaining or even reducing price where demand is price elastic. Not only must such a seller have no competitors who can undercut the higher price, but **arbitrage**, which is the practice of buying at a low price and reselling at a higher price, must also be infeasible. With arbitrage, a price discriminator would receive only the lowest price it tried to charge. Consider, for instance, the impact of arbitrage on the practice of international dumping. It has been alleged that Japanese companies sell steel in the American market for prices below average total cost. If Japanese steel could be purchased at the United States price in Honolulu and then shipped back to Japan and resold at the Japanese price, a profit could still be made, even after deducting the transportation charges. Only because of Japan's trade restrictions against importing steel—including Japanese steel—into Japan can arbitrage be prevented. This state of affairs has led to partial protection of American steel against "unfair" competition from Japan. What is overlooked is the fact that Japanese consumers, rather than American consumers, are the ones being exploited by price-discriminating Japanese firms. A competitive world steel market would lower the price the Japanese pay; regulations and protectionism raise the prices Americans pay.

If OPEC tried to sell oil at different prices to different countries, the attempt at price discrimination would fail. Poor Caribbean countries like Jamaica have much lower per capita incomes than the United States or Canada, yet much higher gasoline prices (as high as $5 per gallon in 1978) because all oil must be imported. Essentially, only taxis, cars rented by tourists, and buses crammed with Jamaicans use gasoline—an indication that demand for gasoline is highly price elastic. Yet while the demand for gasoline was becoming more price elastic in the United States at the beginning of the 1980s, it is still likely that a price increase in this country would increase revenues by foreign and domestic sellers of petroleum.

It might seem strange that OPEC did not raise the price of oil for rich countries like the United States while reducing the price for poor countries like Jamaica, thereby increasing revenue by rerouting oil from markets with inelastic demand to markets with elastic demand. The reason it did not is that oil is a fungible commodity; it is difficult to determine whether a buyer is a consumer or a broker. If the U.S. price of OPEC oil were, say, $50 per barrel and the Jamaican price $25, Jamaica would become the oil broker for the Western Hemisphere, and OPEC would only sell $25/barrel oil.

By contrast, few parents send their children to the movies on their behalf, settling for a description of the plot from their offspring instead of seeing the film themselves. Few insurance companies have been able to convince policy holders to bargain for lower rates at hospitals or auto repair shops. Airlines usually require discount passengers to make reservations well in advance, or to fly standby, on the premise that business trips will be last-minute decisions too crucial for ticket price to be an issue in choosing which airline to use. However, the behavior of some standby passengers has produced instability in the discount patterns used by airlines to segment their market. The problem is caused by standby passengers who book flights for nonexistent football teams or church groups, thus guaranteeing themselves a seat when the fictitious group fails to show up. Airlines have therefore resorted to overbooking their flights, with sad results for the business traveler, not to mention trouble for the airlines when a well-known consumer advocate was bumped from an overbooked flight.

To understand the influence of price discrimination on monopoly profit, let us return to the movie theater example introduced earlier in the chapter. Recall that when the marginal cost of serving additional patrons is zero, as is the case when a movie theater has empty seats for a performance, maximizing revenue is equivalent to maximizing profit. Table 10-5 provides hypothetical information on ticket demand for a movie theater with a seating capacity of 1,200. Supposedly, an operator of an actual movie theater could obtain information like that in Table 10-5 by monitoring patrons' responses to changes in ticket prices.

TABLE 10-5
Numerical Example of Price Discrimination

Price	Q_a	p_aQ_a	η_a	Q_c	p_cQ_c	η_c	TR	η_t
$6.00	300	$1,800.00	−2.00	0	0	−	$1,800.00	−2.00
5.50	350	1,925.00	−1.57	0	0	−	1,925.00	−1.57
5.00	400	2,000.00	−1.25	0	0	−	2,000.00	−1.25
4.50	450	2,025.00	−1.00	0	0	−∞	2,025.00	−1.00
4.00	500	2,000.00	−0.80	100	$ 400.00	−4.00	2,400.00	−2.00
3.50	550	1,925.00	−0.64	200	700.00	−3.50	2,625.00	−1.40
3.00	600	1,800.00	−0.50	300	900.00	−2.00	2,700.00	−1.00
2.50	650	1,625.00	−0.39	400	1,000.00	−1.25	2,625.00	−0.71
2.25	675	1,518.75	−0.33	450	1,012.50	−1.00	2,531.25	−0.60
2.00	700	1,400.00	−0.29	500	1,000.00	−0.80	2,400.00	−0.50

If the operator charged both children and adults the same price, revenue would be maximized by setting the price at $3.00 per ticket, selling 900 tickets per showing, and receiving $2,700 in revenue. When all tickets sell for $3.00, the elasticity of demand for all tickets is unitary. However, at that price, demand for tickets by adults is price inelastic ($\eta_a = -0.5$), while demand for children's tickets is price elastic ($\eta_c = -2.0$). If the proprietor can charge adults and children different prices, he or she should raise the adult price until demand became unit elastic ($\eta_a = -1.0$ when $p_a = \$4.50$), while lowering the price of children's tickets until demand for them also reached unit elasticity ($\eta_c = -1.0$ when $p_c = \$2.25$). Price discrimination would increase revenue to $3,037.50. This is a gain of $337.50 in both revenue and profit, since the cost of policing the system (printing different color tickets for children and adults and hiring a ticket-taker with minimal depth perception) would be virtually zero.

For the producer with positive marginal cost, price discrimination requires that marginal revenue in each market be set equal to the common marginal cost of production. In Figure 10-15, a product sells in two monopoly markets. If the markets cannot be separated, the seller aggregates the quantity demanded at each price in the two markets, then derives the marginal revenue schedule, MR_t from the integrated market demand schedule, $\sum D$. In Figure 10-15, the single-price policy results in output Q_m and a price of p_m in both markets.

With price discrimination, the seller aggregates the output associated with the same marginal revenue in each market $\sum MR$. The first unit is sold in the market with the highest price intercept (Figure 10-15b), and additional sales in that market will cause marginal revenue to fall faster than price. When marginal revenue in market 2 equals the price intercept for market 1, output is sold in both markets, divided in such a way that marginal revenue remains the same in the two markets.

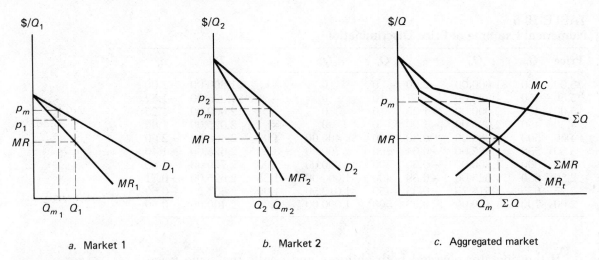

a. Market 1   b. Market 2   c. Aggregated market

Figure 10-15
Monopoly Price and Output: With and Without Price Discrimination.

When marginal revenue in *each* market, $\sum MR$, equals their common marginal cost, monopoly profit is maximized. The market clearing price in each market is then determined by finding the price in that market corresponding to the common marginal revenue $\overline{MR}$.[22]

Figure 10-15 shows that price discrimination results in a higher price (and less quantity) in the market with the less elastic demand (market 2) and a lower price (and higher quantity) in the market with

---

[22] Mathematically, the price-discriminating monopolist maximizes $\pi = \sum_1^n p_i Q_i - C(Q)$, where $Q = Q_1 + Q_2 + \cdots + Q_n$. The separation of markets means a change in the price in one market has no impact on the price received in any other market. Taking the partial derivative of π with respect to each Q_i:

$$\frac{\partial \pi}{\partial Q_1} = p_1 + Q_1 \frac{\partial p_1}{\partial Q_1} - \frac{\partial C}{\partial Q}\left(\frac{\partial Q}{\partial Q_1}\right) = 0 \text{ implies } MR_1 = MC$$

$$\frac{\partial \pi}{\partial Q_2} = p_2 + Q_2 \frac{\partial p_2}{\partial Q_2} - \frac{\partial C}{\partial Q}\left(\frac{\partial Q}{\partial Q_2}\right) = 0 \text{ implies } MR_2 = MC$$

.

.

.

$$\frac{\partial \pi}{\partial Q_n} = p_n + Q_n \frac{\partial p_n}{\partial Q_n} - \frac{\partial C}{\partial Q}\left(\frac{\partial Q}{\partial Q_n}\right) = 0 \text{ implies } MR_n = MC$$

Since $\partial Q/\partial Q_1 = \partial Q/\partial Q_2 = \cdots = \partial Q/\partial Q_n$, the price-discriminating monopolist would maximize profit by dividing total output among the different markets so that the marginal revenue in each market equaled the common marginal cost.

the more elastic demand (market 1).[23] Price discrimination results in higher profits for the monopolist, with an increase in consumer surplus in market 1 at the expense of part of the consumer surplus in market 2.

As stated at the outset of this chapter, the model of monopoly is the polar complement of the model of perfect competition. Each model is an abstract version of the real world, which works reasonably well for explaining some phenomena but not so well for explaining others. The next two chapters fill in part of the gap between the extremes of perfect competition and pure monopoly. Neither the theory of monopolistic competition nor any one of the plethora of models of oligopoly is universally popular or accepted by economists. I have attempted to present these theories and criticisms of them in a manner which allows readers to draw their own conclusions.

---

[23] Recall that $MR = p(1 + 1/\eta)$, where η is the price elasticity of demand. If $p_2 > p_1$, then $p_1(1 + 1/\eta_1) = p_2(1 + 1/\eta_2) = MC$ implies that $-1 > \eta_2 > \eta_1$ if $MC > 0$, and $-1 = \eta_2 = \eta_1$ if $MC = 0$.

HIGHLIGHTS

1. A monopoly is a market in which there is only one seller. For practical purposes, this means that a monopolist can pick the most advantageous price-quantity combination from the market demand curve for the monopoly product and that there will be no retaliation by rivals if the monopolist changes price.

2. A monopolist takes into account consumer response to a price change; this internalizes the change in revenue due to a change in output. For a monopolist, marginal revenue is the price of the last unit minus the revenue lost (due to the price decrease) on all units except the last.

3. There are two steps to the monopolist's output decision. First, set output where marginal revenue equals marginal cost. Second, determine the market clearing price for that output, making sure that the monopoly price exceeds average variable cost.

4. Maximizing profit corresponds to maximizing revenue (unit elastic demand) only for a monopolist whose costs are all fixed. When

marginal cost is positive, a profit-maximizing monopolist will attempt to produce in the price-elastic region of the demand curve.

5. As long as monopoly power can be transferred from one owner to another, the market value of the monopoly firm will absorb, or capitalize, expected monopoly profit.

6. A natural monopoly supposedly occurs when economies of scale select for one seller. This proposition has rarely been tested due to the widespread practice of granting franchises to utility and transportation suppliers.

7. The profit-maximizing monopoly price tends to occur when a private natural monopoly is protected from market entry by would-be rivals, when a publicly owned utility attempts to maximize its operating surplus, or when regulated firms are able to "spend" their way to the monopoly price through inefficient investments.

8. The zero economic profit price tends to result when a private natural monopoly attempts to reduce the probability of entry by rivals to

zero, a government-owned utility attempts to set fees to exactly cover costs, or regulated utilities are prevented from making unjustified investments (to increase their rate base).

9. According to economists, the ideal price for a natural monopoly is identified by the intersection of the market demand curve and the long-run marginal cost curve. At this price consumer surplus would be maximized, as long as the monopoly's deficit was financed in a way which did not redistribute wealth or raise price.

10. A cartel would maximize total profit by setting output where the industry marginal revenue curve intersects the market supply curve, then allocating output among producers so that marginal cost for each equaled the industry marginal revenue.

11. Cartels face two problems. First, individual members wish to obtain production quotas as large as possible (up to the level of output where marginal cost equals the monopoly price). Second, individual cartel members have an incentive to produce more than their quotas, generating a surplus.

12. The ultimate monopoly power is the ability to practice price discrimination, which involves charging higher prices to customers with relatively inelastic demand and lower prices to customers with relatively elastic demand.

13. Successful price discrimination requires that arbitrage be prevented; otherwise, only sales at the lowest price would be made. This explains why price discrimination tends to be more prevalent in service industries than in the sale of tangible, and especially fungible, commodities.

GLOSSARY

Arbitrage   The practice of buying a commodity at a low price and reselling it for a higher price.

Capitalization   The process by which monopoly profit is absorbed into the market value of the monopoly license, franchise, or other transferable source of monopoly power.

Cartel   A monopoly made up of more than one individual or firm, whereby output is artificially reduced to maintain a higher than competitive price.

Monopoly   A market with only one seller.

Marginal revenue   The net change in revenue due to selling one more unit of output. Under imperfect competition, marginal revenue equals price minus revenue lost on infra-marginal units: $MR = \Delta(pQ)/\Delta Q = p + Q(\Delta p/\Delta Q) = p(1 + 1/\eta)$.

Natural monopoly   A market in which one firm survives due to protracted economies of scale, which cause that firm's long-run average cost curve to intersect the relevant market demand curve at an output smaller than the output associated with minimum long-run average cost.

Oligopoly   A market with only a few sellers, each of whom tends to anticipate the reaction of rivals to price and quantity changes.

Price discrimination   The practice of charging different prices to consumers with different elasticities of demand for a technically homogeneous commodity.

SUGGESTED READINGS

Averch, H., and L. Johnson. "Behavior of the Firm under Regulatory Constraint." *American Economic Review* (December 1962), pp. 1052–1069.

Carroll, Thomas M., David H. Ciscel, and Roger K. Chisholm. "The Market as a Commons: An Unconventional View of Property Rights." *Journal of Economic Issues*, 13 (June 1979), 605–627.

Fisher, Franklin. "Diagnosing Monopoly." *Quarterly Review of Economics and Business* (summer 1979), pp. 7–35.

Harberger, Arnold C. "Monopoly and Resource Allocation." *American Economic Review* (May

1954), pp. 77–87. Reprinted in Edwin Mansfield, ed. *Microeconomics: Suggested Readings.* 4th ed. New York: Norton, 1982.

Hicks, J. R. "Annual Surveys of Economic Theory: The Theory of Monopoly." *Econometrica* (1935). Reprinted in Edwin Mansfield, ed. *Microeconomics: Suggested Readings.* 4th ed. New York: Norton, 1975.

Kessel, Reuben. "Price Discrimination in Medicine." *Journal of Law and Economics* (October 1958), pp. 20–53.

Lerner, Abba P. "The Concept of Monopoly and the Measurement of Monopoly Power." *Review of Economic Studies* (June 1943). Reprinted in William Breit and Harold Hochman, eds. *Readings in Microeconomics.* 2nd ed. New York: Holt, Rinehart and Winston,

1971, pp. 207–223.

Mansfield, Edwin. *Monopoly Power and Economic Performance.* 3rd ed. New York: Norton, 1974.

Patinkin, Don. "Multiplant Firms, Cartels and Imperfect Competition." *Quarterly Journal of Economics* (February 1947). Reprinted in William Breit and Harold Hochman, eds. *Readings in Microeconomics*, 2nd ed. New York: Holt, Rinehart and Winston, pp. 262–281.

Posner, Richard. "The Social Costs of Monopoly and Regulation." *Journal of Political Economy* (August 1975), pp. 807–827.

Robinson, Joan. *The Economics of Imperfect Competition.* New York: St. Martin's Press, 1969.

EXERCISES

Evaluate

Indicate whether each of the following statements is true (agrees with economic theory), false (is contradicted by theory), or uncertain (could be true or false, given additional information). Explain your answer.

1. If a monopolist has a positively sloped marginal cost curve at the profit-maximizing output, setting a legal price ceiling at the intersection of the market demand curve and the monopolist's marginal cost curve would increase output but reduce profit.

2. If a cartel wants to maximize the total income of its members, output should be allocated among members in such a way that each firm has the same average variable cost.

3. A monopoly movie theater discovers that the demand for snacks is very inelastic, but that the elasticity of demand for snacks increases as their prices are increased. Hence, it might pay the monopolist to set the price of tickets in the inelastic region of the demand curve in order to sell more popcorn and soda.

4. An increase in the property tax imposed on a monopolist would increase price and decrease output, *ceteris paribus.*

5. If the elasticity of demand for a monopolist's product is −2.0 at the prevailing price, and if price is exactly twice marginal cost, the monopolist is maximizing profit.

6. As long as monopoly power can be transferred, monopolists can continue to receive monopoly profit in the long run.

7. An increase in demand for a monopolist's product will always result in an increase in price and quantity sold.

8. Allowing monopolists to practice price discrimination increases consumer welfare.

9. Arbitrage and price discrimination are incompatible.

10. Defining a monopolist as a producer of a product with no substitutes implies that monopolists do not maximize profit.

Calculate

Answer each of the following questions, showing all your calculations.

11. A monopoly sells its output in two markets, from a plant located on the boundary between market 1 and market 2. An econometrician

has estimated the average revenue function for market 1 to be $p_1 = 100 - 2Q_1$, and for market 2 as $p_2 = 80 - Q_2$. Assuming the cost of production is $10 per unit for both markets:

a. Write the formula for the marginal revenue in each market. (Hint: $\Delta p_1/\Delta Q_1 = -2$; $\Delta p_2/\Delta Q_2 = -1$.)

b. What is the profit-maximizing output and price for each market? What is the price elasticity of demand in each market? (Hint: $\Delta Q/\Delta p$ is the reciprocal of $\Delta p/\Delta Q$.)

c. If the monopolist's total costs are $C = 100 + 10Q_1 + 10Q_2$, what is the total profit from both markets?

12. Continuing with the situation outlined in question 11, suppose that a method is discovered whereby the monopolist's product can be shipped from either market and resold in the other market at a cost of $5 per unit:

a. What would be the initial profit per unit from arbitrage? What would happen to the monopolist's sales in the two markets if nothing were done to anticipate resale of the commodity? (Remember, the monopolist can sell at the same cost in either market because of the location of the plant.)

b. Let p_h be the price in the market with the less elastic demand and p_L be the price in the market with the more elastic demand. If the monopolist redefines the price in the less elastic market as $p_h = p_L + 5$ (so that arbitrage no longer pays), what is the new profit-maximizing price and quantity for each market?

Contemplate

Answer each of the following in a brief but complete essay.

13. A book publisher sells two economics books, one an advanced treatise on mathematical theory which sells for $25.00 in a limited market of third-year Ph.D. students, and the other a principles text which sells for $12.50 and is purchased by college freshman. Each book costs the publisher $5.00 for paper, ink, shipping, sales commissions, and royalties. Make a brief case for the argument that since the prices in the two markets obviously reflect different elasticities, the publisher must be a price discriminator. Then try to formulate a plausible argument that since the contents of the two books are different, the publisher is not practicing price discrimination. Which argument appeals to you more? Explain your answer.

14. Back in the era of "cheap" foreign oil, the price of oil produced from wells in the United States was twice the world price. This price was supported by limitations on oil imports.

a. Why was it in a company's interest to import as much foreign oil as possible, given that total imports were limited to 10 percent of domestic oil sales?

b. If the government auctioned licenses to import foreign oil, what would be the approximate equilibrium price of a license?

c. If, as was the case, a company's import quota depended on its domestic market share, how might these import restrictions have contributed to the United States' vulnerability to OPEC?

15. Without government, there could be no monopoly, since monopoly requires de facto ownership of the market, and only the government can protect property rights without the system degenerating into "rule by the strong" and the "tragedy of the commons." Hence, if government allowed the free enterprise economy to operate unhindered, monopoly would cease to be a problem. Do you agree or disagree with this statement? Explain your reasoning.

Chapter 11

Monopolistic Competition: Variety at a Price

So far we have studied the two extremes of market organization: perfect competition—wherein all firms are price takers and unrestricted market entry tends to drive price to its lowest sustainable level—and monopoly—wherein market entry is precluded, so that price is manipulated by a single seller or a collusive group of sellers. For some economists, these two models are enough, but many economists feel that limiting the theory of the firm to these extreme models can lead to dangerous distortions when analyzing real-world firms which operate in markets where crucial assumptions of both models are violated. For instance, if we are able to show that entry into an industry is possible and that collusive arrangements are not enforceable, is it necessarily true that all sellers in that industry must charge the same price, which will tend toward minimum long-run average cost? Alternatively, if we can show that a firm is able to pick its price from a negatively inclined demand curve, does it follow that the firm can ignore the prices other firms charge and that price can remain permanently above long-run average cost?

There are two approaches to these questions—one ideological and the other practical. This chapter attempts a pragmatic exploration of one type of market lying between the polar cases of perfect competition and pure monopoly. Appropriately, this model is dubbed *monopolistic competition.* The monopolistic aspect rests on the assumption that consumers perceive differences among the products offered by sellers, so that sellers' demand curves are negatively sloped. The competitive feature is the assumption that entry is relatively simple, allowing new firms to offer close, albeit imperfect, substitutes for commodities sold by established firms.

We begin with an analysis of product differentiation itself. Commodities are perceived as combinations of various characteristics. To be successful, a new product must offer a combination of ingredients at a price which consumers believe to be a bargain relative to other commodities or combinations of commodities. The tendency of consumers to identify product characteristics and product quality with brand names and trademarks leads to real, although very narrowly enforced, impediments to new sellers offering duplicates of successful products.

The short-run profit-maximizing strategy of a producer of a differentiated product involves the same rule as the output-price choice of a pure monopolist: produce where marginal cost equals marginal revenue, then set price in accordance with market demand. Of particular relevance for business students is the similarity between the profit maximization rule—that marginal revenue is equal to marginal cost—and the widespread practice of markup pricing.

Market entry by imitators is shown to result in the tendency for price to equal average cost in the long run. However, not only does product differentiation cause long-run equilibrium under monopolistic competition to differ from long-run equilibrium under perfect competition, but the process of achieving that equilibrium differs as a consequence of how established firms react to new producers. The chapter concludes with a discussion of the controversy surrounding the allocative effects of product differentiation.

Between Competition and Monopoly

The models of perfect competition and monopoly present neat, orderly pictures of the business world. This is hardly surprising; it is what theories are designed to do. However, like all good things in a world of scarcity, neatness and order are not free. Many economists feel that economic models should also have other attributes, including accuracy of predictions, realism of explanations, and applicability to real-world problem solving.

In the first third of the twentieth century, microeconomics (then called "value theory") was limited almost exclusively to the models of perfect competition and monopoly. In 1933 two books challenged the two-model basis of the theory of markets. Joan Robinson's *Economics of Imperfect Competition* presented a continuum of market types spanning the simple models of monopoly and competition, and Edward

Chamberlin's *Monopolistic Competition* offered an equilibrium model involving a large number of sellers of close but imperfect substitutes. Today, the original distinction of these titles remains: **imperfect competition** refers to all market types between perfect competition and monopoly (no competition), while **monopolistic** (or **differentiated**) **competition** usually refers to the particular case of a large number of sellers of differentiated products.

Just as 200 years have witnessed considerable refinements in the model of ideal competition envisioned by Adam Smith, 50 years of criticism and research have modified the theories proposed by Joan Robinson and Edward Chamberlin. This chapter attempts to capture the spirit of the original Robinson and Chamberlin models, while incorporating criticisms of monopolistic and imperfect competition. We begin with an analysis of product differentiation itself, following the lead of Kelvin Lancaster, who showed how product differentiation could occur through changes in the bundles of characteristics commodities possess.[1] We will also show that the monopolistic element in monopolistic competition does not result solely from the demand for product differentiation, but also from the creation of such legal devices as trademarks, brand-name registration, and patents thought necessary to assure the supply of differentiated commodities.

The Demand for Product Differentiation

We have been treating household preferences as if utility resulted from the purchase of commodities, rather than from the consumption of commodity services. We have also treated the marginal rate of substitution as a trade-off among commodities, rather than a willingness to consume commodity characteristics in different proportions. Some people prefer coffee with cream; some sweeten their coffee with sugar, others with a sugar substitute; others prefer black coffee. Because coffee, cream, and sugar are purchased separately, people can produce the kind of beverage they desire. Frequently, however, product characteristics (taste, color, calories, vitamins, status) are purchased in fixed proportions under various brand names and associated with endorsements by well-known actors and athletes. The demand for particular commodities is really a derived demand for the characteristics those commodities have or are thought to have.

Consider, for example, consumer demand for toothpaste. As toothpaste ads inform us, some brands render teeth impervious to decay,

---

[1] Kelvin Lancaster, *Consumer Demand: A New Approach* (New York: Columbia University Press, 1971).

while others make a person irresistible to the opposite sex. Some sellers claim their toothpaste provides both services, although presumably either with muted intensity or at a higher price. By analyzing commodities according to their characteristics, we can treat each product as a process, analogous to production with simple technology. Just as substituting labor for capital often involves changing production processes (see chapter seven), so the substitution of decay prevention for white teeth involves changing brands or the combination of brands.

In Figure 11-1 we imagine a consumer's preferences for two characteristics of toothpaste: decay prevention (traditionally measured as cavities per checkup) and whitening power (which might be measured as romantic experiences per month), plotted on the horizontal and vertical axes, respectively. Overlaid on the consumer indifference map in Figure 11-1 are two vectors (rays) which represent the proportions of characteristics available from two brands of toothpaste. (A *vector* is a relationship between two or more variables, involving magnitude and direction. The vector of product characteristics in Figure 11-1 means that as the ounces of toothpaste increase, decay prevention and whitening power increase proportionately.) Preppydent contains a high proportion of whitening power relative to decay prevention: in whitening

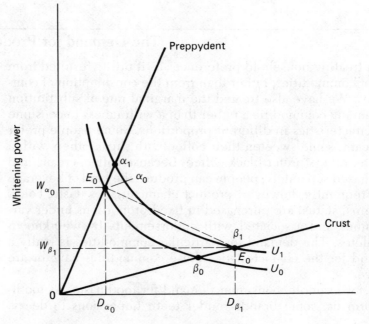

Figure 11-1
Indifference Map Showing the Derived Demand for Competing Brands of Toothpaste

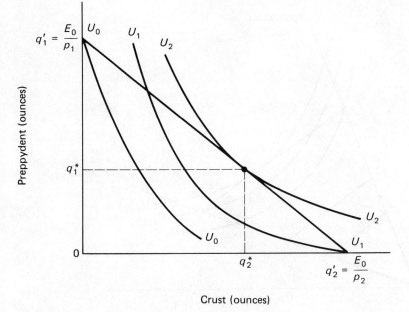

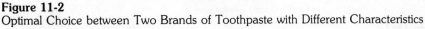

Crust (ounces)

Figure 11-2
Optimal Choice between Two Brands of Toothpaste with Different Characteristics

teeth, this brand scrapes away the enamel, promoting tooth decay. Crust protects teeth from cavities but leaves a green film, which often impedes romance.

If only these two brands could be purchased, the consumer would require some criterion for choosing between them. As in the conventional theory of consumer choice, we assume that the consumer compares the marginal rate of substitution—in this case, for product characteristics—with the relative prices of those characteristics. In Figure 11-1, the consumer, Denny Friss, is indifferent between point α_0 on the ray for Preppydent and point β_0 on the ray for Crust. He calculates that the combination of decay prevention and whitening power indicated by point α_0 would require an expenditure of $E_0 = p_1 q_1'$, where p_1 is the price per ounce of Preppydent and q_1' is the number of ounces needed for D_{α_0} units of decay prevention and W_{α_0} units of whitening power. Denny prefers Crust to Preppydent because the expenditure of E_0 (= $p_2 q_2'$) allows him to purchase combination β_1 on the Crust ray. Here p_2 is the price per ounce of Crust, and q_2' is the number of ounces necessary to obtain D_{β_1} units of decay prevention and W_{β_1} units of whitening power.

While we gain insight into the nature of product differentiation by assuming that commodities are desired for their characteristics, it is also true that insights are clearer when we use an already familiar vantage point. Figure 11-2 reproduces the consumer choice problem of Figure

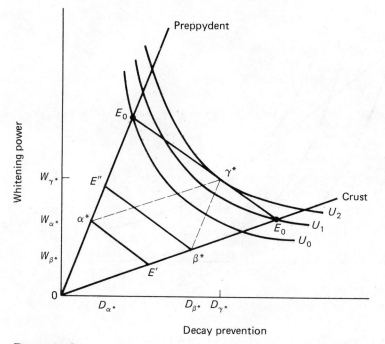

Figure 11-3
Utility Maximization by Purchasing a Combination of Brands

11-1 in the more familiar form of defining utility as the consequence of consuming quantities of two commodities. Point α_0 in Figure 11-1 translates as the vertical intercept of the budget line E_0/p_1, E_0/p_2. We can avoid the untenable premise that satisfaction depends only on the brand of toothpaste consumed by assuming that the demand for toothpaste is unit elastic: the consumer has budgeted E_0 to spend on toothpaste and attempts to find the optimal combination of decay prevention and whitening power available for that expenditure. If E_0 were spent exclusively on Preppydent, q_1' ounces could be purchased, resulting in satisfaction associated with indifference curve U_0.

Point β_1 in Figure 11-1 corresponds to the horizontal intercept of the budget line E_0/p_1, E_0/p_2 in Figure 11-2. An expenditure of E_0 on Crust would result in consumption of q_2' ounces and a satisfaction level of U_1. While Figures 11-1 and 11-2 imply that the consumer would prefer spending E_0 on Crust to spending that amount on Preppydent, satisfaction can be increased by purchasing q_2^* ounces of Crust and q_1^* ounces of Preppydent. As toothpaste ads tell us, if no one brand gives the preferred combination of characteristics, a combination of brands may be purchased. (Figures 11-1 through 11-4 are drawn under the assumption that each brand of toothpaste can be purchased at a constant price per ounce. The practice of selling "economy size" tubes at a lower price per ounce than "regular size" tubes would bow the budget line toward the origin.)

The consequence of dividing expenditure E_0 between the two brands is reprised in Figure 11-3, which illustrates how the optimal combination of decay prevention (D_{γ^*}) and whitening power (W_{γ^*}) is obtained by purchasing combination D_{α^*}, W_{α^*}, corresponding to q_1^* ounces of Preppydent, and combination D_{β^*}, W_{β^*}, resulting from q_2^* ounces of Crust. It is conceivable that a marketing research firm would observe a latent demand for a toothpaste with the combination of characteristics associated with point γ^* in Figure 11-3.

Figure 11-4 shows how the introduction of a new brand of toothpaste might entice consumers away from Preppydent and Crust. To simplify the analysis, we assume that Amen toothpaste ("The last word in toothpaste!") offers decay prevention and whitening power in the same proportions as point γ^* in Figure 11-3. Although Amen has the combination of ingredients many consumers have been purchasing, whether the new brand succeeds (how much consumers purchase) will depend on the price of Amen relative to the prices of Preppydent and Crust. Suppose that an expenditure of $E_0 = p_3 q_3{}'$ results in the purchase of combination γ_0 on the ray for Amen toothpaste in Figure 11-4. The consumer's response would be to continue buying combination γ^*, resulting from q_1^* ounces

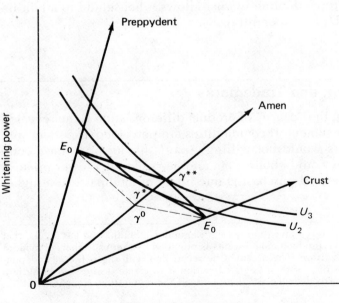

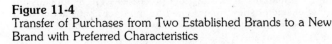

Figure 11-4
Transfer of Purchases from Two Established Brands to a New Brand with Preferred Characteristics

of Preppydent and q_2^* ounces of Crust. *For a new product to succeed in capturing sales from established brands, consumers must perceive that it provides the preferred combination of ingredients for a lower (or at least no greater) expenditure than combining existing brands.*

If the budget line (isocost line) for decay prevention and whitening power passed through point γ^* on the Amen ray, the consumer would be indifferent between Amen toothpaste and purchasing the designated amounts of Preppydent and Crust. However, were it possible to attain point γ^{**} on the Amen ray, the new product would succeed in capturing some of the market of established brands. Of course, households with a smaller marginal rate of substitution of decay prevention for whitening power might continue to buy Preppydent, perhaps in combination with Amen. Households with a greater marginal rate of substitution of decay prevention might continue to buy Crust, also possibly in combination with Amen. Ultimately, consumer preferences for product characteristics lie outside the scope of microeconomics,[2] and as long as consumers continue to have different marginal rates of substitution for product characteristics, multiple brands can coexist in the toothpaste (or breakfast cereal, or cosmetic, or soap) market. What we have been able to show is that the successful introduction of a new brand will tend to cause the isocost line for product characteristics to bow outward.[3] Being able to buy Amen toothpaste at a price which is less than the price of the optimal combination of Preppydent and Crust allows a household to attain indifference curve U_3 for expenditure E_0.

APPLICATION

Consumer Information, Advertising, and Trademarks

For the economist, the "cause" of product differentiation is the revealed preferences of consumers. If commodities are perceived as perfect substitutes, consumers would not willingly pay a higher price for a commodity which they could obtain from another seller at a lower price. If a consumer is observed purchasing one brand of toothpaste at a higher

---

[2] A vocal dissenter from this convention is John Kenneth Galbraith, who has argued that the "direct link between production and wants is provided by the institutions of modern advertising and salesmanship. These cannot be reconciled with the notion of independently determined desires, for their central function is to create desires—to bring into being wants that previously did not exist" (*The Affluent Society* [Boston: Houghton Mifflin, 1958]).

[3] In chapter seven, the introduction of a third efficient production process caused the two-process isoquant to bow in; combinations of two distinct processes were technically inefficient. In this case, product characteristics are assumed to "produce" satisfaction, and new products succeed when the resulting isocost line bows out to encompass higher indifference curves.

price than another brand sitting next to it on the supermarket shelf, we can infer that those brands are perceived as having different characteristics.

Product differentiation alone is not sufficient to generate imperfectly competitive markets, however. Brussels sprouts are different from asparagus, but most economists would treat growers of those vegetables as price takers in different markets. The essence of monopolistic competition is the close identification between seller and product, an identification which is subject to such legal protections as brand-name and trademark registration, copyrights, and patents, and which may be strengthened by expenditures on advertising and other marketing techniques.

Imagine an entrepreneur who discovers a formula for a delicious brown liquid, which he markets as Eco-Cola. Another entrepreneur perceives the higher than normal profits earned by the bottler of Eco-Cola and decides to enter that market. Since consumers cannot determine the taste of the beverage until after it has been purchased, the second producer decides to fill empty Eco-Cola bottles with a solution of brown dye, soap (for bubbles), and water. Because these ingredients cost less, the second seller is able to undercut the price of Eco-Cola. Consumers begin to stock up on "Eco-Cola" at the bargain price, but then they taste it. Both sellers eventually leave the market: the second by fast freight in the dead of night, the first in shocked despair.

It is doubtful that such fraud constitutes an improvement in the pattern of resource allocation. Allowing new producers to duplicate the outward appearance of a commodity without also guaranteeing product quality makes both the consumer and the original seller worse off.

In the name of consumer protection, society grants exclusive licenses to trademarks and brand names and often grants patents to unique combinations of product characteristics.[4] Each seller becomes a mini-monopoly, not because of consumer desires for product differentiation per se, but because legal protection of producers' reputations leads to de facto ownership of narrowly defined markets. The monopolistic aspect of monopolistic competition results more from imperfections in consumer information and the blur between property rights and markets than from the mere fact that commodities have different characteristics (see chapters eight and fifteen).

The degree of competition in monopolistic competition depends on how broadly or narrowly monopoly power is protected. When a seller is granted an exclusive franchise or when cartel contracts are legally enforceable, competition is indeed remote: the seller confronts the buyer

---

[4] Another argument for patents is that without exclusive rights to sell a commodity embodying technological discoveries, innovators could not recover their research and development costs, thereby impeding technological and economic progress. This argument is explored in detail in chapter fifteen.

with a "take it or leave it" option. However, the right to exclusive use of the name "Eco-Cola," which does not extend to the right to exclude other sellers of "cola," even those whose name starts with *E*, would not guarantee that the entrepreneur's market remained free of poachers.

This perspective on monopolistic competition also illuminates the controversial issue of whether advertising increases or decreases consumer welfare. Product homogeneity makes advertising a futile gesture by individual sellers in a perfectly competitive market; since all receive the same price, advertisers cannot recover selling costs. The presence of advertising is often used as one indicator that the crucial assumption of product homogeneity underlying the theory of perfect competition, is violated. But using advertising as an indicator of imperfect competition does not imply that advertising, per se, *causes* imperfect competition.

As with many issues in microeconomics, economists attempt to judge how advertising influences resource allocation by inferring preferences from actual behavior of consumers and producers. If one producer in an industry perceives a willingness of consumers to pay a higher price for a combination of characteristics not currently available, he can only cash in on that demand by communicating the characteristics of his product to consumers. Advertising is often a necessary cost of doing business for a vendor of a new commodity. Economists, of course, cannot say whether advertising has the effect of merely informing consumers with preexisting desires about the characteristics of goods or whether advertising actually changes tastes. This is a direct consequence of leaving the explanation of tastes to other disciplines.

The economic effects of advertising are complicated by the hybrid nature of information as a commodity. When the mass media (e.g., newspapers, periodicals, radio, television) are used to advertise a product, any number of persons can "consume" the same message without reducing the amount of information available to others. But while information is not scarce in the usual sense—what one person consumes another cannot consume—scarce resources must nevertheless be allocated to the production, verification, transmission, interpretation, and storage of information. It is frequently in the interest of the advertiser to minimize the effort of consumers in recognizing and remembering the message. This leads to so-called **persuasive advertising**, which is generally associated with television commercials and slick ads in magazines. By providing entertainment along with the intended message, the seller is able to attract the attention of otherwise disinterested consumers. By contrast, **informative advertising**, which refers to messages aimed at consumers who have an interest in purchasing, tends to be straightforward and unembellished. Examples of informative advertising are classified ads and catalogs.

Like the competitive market itself, many of the beneficial side effects of advertising are unintentional. Supermarkets differ in location, brands

Policy Illustration
An Economic Approach to Deception in Advertising

Advertising is a big business and a controversial business. In the United States, advertising allows daily newspapers to sell for prices which barely cover the cost of paper, ink, and delivery. Mass media advertising brings commercial television into tens of millions of homes. We can watch the world series or the super bowl without bothering to buy the automobiles or razor blades whose manufacturers subsidize our entertainment. Ultimately, advertising may help us communicate with extraterrestrial life. A sphere of television programs, approximately 35 light-years in radius, is delivering *The Milton Berle Show*, *I Love Lucy*, and *Gilligan's Island*, complete with commercials, to far-flung corners of our galaxy. Someday, other beings may better understand our culture, based on underarm deodorants, mouthwash, and light beer.

The passage of the Wheeler-Lea Act in 1938 gave the Federal Trade Commission (FTC) the major responsibility for preventing deceptive advertising. Until the late 1960s, deceptive advertising was controlled through the use of cease-and-desist orders. Since the early 1970s, the FTC has used affirmative disclosure orders. Formerly, advertisers were made to stop deceptive claims for products. Today they can be forced to correct misinformation in their future ads. The criticism of cease-and-desist orders is that they may take effect only after the offending ad campaign has run its course and thus do not deter deception by other advertisers. Affirmative disclosure is criticized as being an interference with advertisers' rights of free speech.

Some economists have argued that once consumers understand that some ads are deceptive, they will seek out more reliable sources of information. Teresa Gaines McLendon has pointed out that both honest and deceptive advertisers would be penalized by such a consumer reaction. Hence, the real victims of deceptive advertising are other advertisers. McLendon has suggested that deceptive advertising be handled as a civil wrong. Under this approach, injured parties could not only sue for cessation of the deceptive advertising but could also be rewarded damages. Optimal fines would be high enough to deter deception but low enough so that advertising "bounty hunters" were not encouraged.

The advantage of this approach is that it would encourage advertisers to police themselves *through the courts*. Too often, extralegal organizations for policing intraindustry behavior serve as a means of price collusion. By treating deceptive advertising as a civil wrong, criticisms of the FTC for interference in business decisions could be avoided. Of course, leaving the policing of advertising to other advertisers is not likely to satisfy those who believe all advertising is persuasive and, consequently, deceptive. But if we got rid of advertising, how would we communicate with extraterrestrial beings?

Source: Teresa Gaines McLendon, "An Economic Approach to Deceptive Advertising: Definitions and Remedies," *The American Economist* (fall 1981), pp. 49–54.

of products available, prices of specific items, and so forth. One supermarket, advertising its wares and prices, could expect to attract considerable business away from competitors. When all supermarkets advertise, their relative sales may be approximately the same as they would be in the absence of advertising; the real beneficiary is the consumer, who can learn of prices by opening the morning paper. And although advertising may be an indicator of imperfect competition, it is essentially a means of competition. Banning advertising is one of the many ways in which cartels attempt to prevent outbreaks of price competition.

Short-Run Pricing of a Differentiated Commodity

The major pedagogical advantage of the theory of monopolistic competition is that the firm's short-run profit-maximizing decision can be treated as a variation of monopoly pricing, while in the long run, economic profit approaches zero, as it would under perfect competition. After developing the model of monopolistic competition, we will consider whether there should be a theory of monopolistic competition (i.e., whether the model is relevant to real-world events).

We begin by focusing on a seller confronting a negatively sloped demand curve. A producer of a differentiated commodity will sell a greater quantity per unit of time the lower the price, *ceteris paribus*. The existence of a large number of sellers of imperfect substitutes means that each seller enjoys pricing autonomy; any firm can change its price, the characteristics of its product (save for infringing on another's trademark, brand name, or patent), or information about its product without fearing direct retaliation from other firms. The producer can influence its sales and profit by changing price, modifying the mix of characteristics of its good, or by advertising.

We write the firm's demand equation as:

$$q_d^1 = f[p^1, p^2, \ldots, p^n; k(z^1), k(z^2), \ldots, k(z^n); y, t]$$

where p^1 is the price of good 1, the firm's product, p^2 through p^n are the prices charged by the $n - 1$ other sellers, z^1 stands for the variable characteristics of good 1, and $k(z^1)$ stands for perceptions of those characteristics, with a similar meaning for the other $n - 1$ products. The variables y and t, indicating consumer income and tastes, respectively, are treated as beyond the control of any seller.[5] Treating other prices, other products' characteristics, knowledge of those characteristics, con-

---

[5] This may be a controversial assumption for those who believe, along with Galbraith and others, that sellers are able to manipulate consumer tastes. For our purposes, consumers may be manipulated through deceptive advertising: $k(z^i)$ may not correspond to the true characteristics of product i.

sumer tastes, and consumer income as given, the firm's profit maximization decision involves manipulating three variables, p^1, z^1, and $k(z^1)$, which together determine q^1, output, and C, the firm's cost of production:

$$\pi^1 = p^1 q\, [p^1,k(z^1)] - C(q^1,z^1,k)$$

Figure 11-5 shows the profit-maximizing price and quantity when product characteristics and advertising are treated as constants. Advertising, for instance, may be treated as a fixed cost which determines the position of the firm's demand curve but remains fundamentally fixed at various rates of output. Product characteristics are likely to be embodied in the firm's production process, packaging, and labeling and can also be treated as fixed in the short run. As with the pure monopoly seller, the producer of a differentiated product determines the short-run profit-maximizing rate of output where marginal revenue equals marginal cost. Price is then determined by the market clearing price for that output, q^*.

The two diagrams in Figure 11-5 illustrate the importance of covering average variable cost in the short run. In Figure 11-5a, the profit-maximizing price, p^*, exceeds average variable cost at q^*, meaning that the firm will be able to cover some of its fixed costs by producing. If the firm depicted in Figure 11-5b produced q^* units of output per period and charged price p^*, total revenue would fall short of average variable cost. That seller would be better off shutting down, limiting its loss to fixed cost. Producing any other rate of output or charging any price other

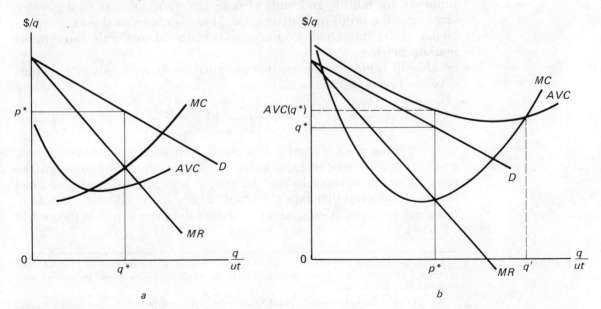

Figure 11-5
Short-Run Output and Price Decision for Two Producers of Differentiated Commodities. *a*, Produce where $MC = MR$ ($p^* > AVC$); *b*, shutdown ($p^* < AVC$).

than p^* would only make matters worse. For instance, since the demand curve lies everywhere below the average variable cost curve, the seller could not survive by raising price to cover average variable cost. As price rose, quantity sold would fall; price and quantity would carom between the demand curve and the average variable cost curve until the product was priced out of the market and the firm sold zero output.

Economic theory does not predict what a particular firm will actually do. Economics explains the requirements for profit maximization or loss minimization. When a situation like that depicted in Figure 11-5b is unavoidable,[6] economists advise the entrepreneur to shut down operations until conditions change or a new product can be tried; producers who tough it out will only incur greater losses than those who heed economists' advice.

APPLICATION
Markup Pricing

Before we consider changes in product characteristics or advertising as short-run strategies, we will take a short detour to relate the economic model of commodity pricing to noneconomic accounts. According to some observers, small firms set prices by adding a markup factor to the variable cost of a good to cover overhead and profit. Economic theory does not predict what the price will be for all products,[7] since entrepreneurs are fallible and often change price a number of times before arriving at the profit-maximizing one. However, we can show the equivalence of the "marginal revenue equals marginal cost" rule and optimal **markup pricing**.

Recall from chapter ten that marginal revenue equals price minus revenue lost on inframarginal units:

$$MR = \frac{\Delta TR}{\Delta q} = \frac{p(\Delta q)}{\Delta q} + \frac{q(\Delta p)}{\Delta q} = p\left(1 + \frac{\Delta p/p}{\Delta q/q}\right) = p\left(1 + \frac{1}{\eta}\right)$$

where η is the price elasticity of demand. As discussed in chapter seven, producing with simple technology causes marginal cost to equal the constant average variable cost for output up to the capacity of fixed inputs. Producing that rate of output, where marginal cost is equal to marginal revenue, is equivalent to setting the price equal to the cost of

---

[6] That is, we assume that the firm cannot change its advertising strategy or product characteristics and achieve a new demand-cost profile whereby losses would be smaller than its prevailing fixed costs.

[7] This gives the lie to George Bernard Shaw, who once quipped that an economist is one who "knows the price of everything and the value of nothing." There are many economists who do not know the price of some things.

producing that last unit times a markup factor. Economic theory enhances the analysis of markup pricing by relating the optimal markup
to what the market will allow, rather than to fixed cost or profit targets.
$MR = MC$ implies:

$$MC = p\left(1 + \frac{1}{\eta}\right) \qquad \text{or} \qquad p = MC\left(\frac{\eta}{1 + \eta}\right)$$

This result is shown in Figure 11-6. At q^*, where $MR = MC$, $p^* = MC$
$(\eta^*/1 + \eta^*)$, where η^* is the elasticity of demand at q^*. Since MC
$(\eta^*/1 + \eta^*) = MC - MC/(1 + \eta^*) = MC + (MC/|1 + \eta^*|)$; under
imperfect competition, price exceeds marginal cost by a markup factor
equal to marginal cost divided by the absolute value of one plus price
elasticity of demand.

Since $\eta < 0$, $\eta/(1 + \eta) > 0$ if and only if $\eta < -1$. Like the pure
monopoly firm, the monopolistically competitive firm which prices a
commodity in the inelastic portion of its own demand curve would not
be maximizing profit. The more elastic the demand for a commodity, the
smaller the optimal markup will be. For instance, jewelry stores typically
use markups of 100 percent and more; bookstores use markups of 20
percent over publishers' book prices; and grocery stores place retail
prices about 10 percent above wholesale. Merely stating that sellers use
some markup does not tell us how much that markup should be. Economic theory shows that the optimal markup depends on a good's price

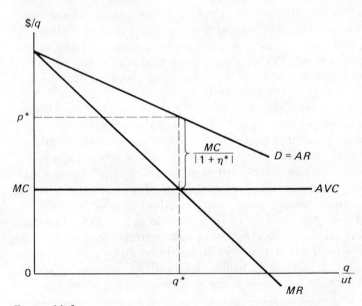

Figure 11-6
Equivalence of Profit Maximization and Optimal Markup Pricing

elasticity. If the elasticity of demand is roughly constant across firms in a differentiated industry (e.g., publishing, grocery stores), small firms may approximate their profit-maximizing prices by adopting the markup used by industry leaders. It would not be surprising to learn that the original markup factor was determined by an entrepreneur trained in economics or by an economic consultant retained by an industry leader.

Variations in Product Quality or Sales Effort

The short-run profit-maximizing strategy outlined in the two previous sections emphasized the similarity between monopoly pricing and the pricing of differentiated products. This analysis has led some critics to condemn product differentiation per se as a source of monopoly distortion of resource allocation. Others have condemned the model of monopolistic competition as a slander of free enterprise. Let us try to cut through the obstinacy of inflexible opinion by engaging in a thought experiment. What would happen to consumer welfare if a competitive firm successfully differentiated its product?

The drama unfolds in Figure 11-7, which reveals the A-Typical Oatmeal Company to be in long-run competitive equilibrium, selling generic oatmeal at its lowest sustainable price, p_0 (where MC_0 intersects ATC_0 at q_0). Differentiation of breakfast food requires expenditures on raisins, nuts, and honey; bright yellow, atypical oatmeal boxes; and 30-second advertising spots during cartoon shows. Since there is no a priori reason to expect differentiation to generate either economies or diseconomies of scale, we assume that the new (negatively sloped) demand curve for A-Typical Oatmeal passes through the minimum point on the higher average cost curve (ATC_1) at q_0, the original equilibrium output.[8] Hence, continued production of q_0, whose market clearing price is now p_1, would result in zero economic profit.

As one might expect about a highly controversial issue, Figure 11-7 is ambiguous about the impact of product differentiation on allocational efficiency. First, it is fairly clear that the price increase from p_0 to p_1 would be cost justified: the opportunity cost of resources used to produce q_0 boxes of embellished oatmeal is clearly higher, and consumers are willing to purchase q_0 units at price p_1. However, the negative slope of the demand curve means that by reducing production to q_m boxes, where $MR = MC$, price can be raised to $p_m > ATC$. Potential consumer surplus ABC, $\simeq 1/2(\Delta p)(\Delta q)$, is lost entirely, and part of the increased revenue on the first q_1 units will be absorbed in higher average total costs. Unlike perfect competition, monopolistic competition does not appear to maximize consumer surplus, at least in the short run.

---

[8] If advertising adds more to fixed costs than to variable costs, the minimum point on ATC_1 will be to the right of q_0 and greater than p_1.

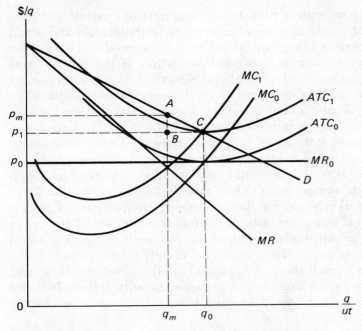

Figure 11-7
Impact of Differentiation on the A-Typical Oatmeal Company's Price and Quantity

We must be careful to avoid unwarranted inferences from Figure 11-7. Under perfect competition, long-run equilibrium price and quantity maximize consumer surplus. Under monopolistic competition, particularly in the short run, consumer surplus could be increased if price were decreased (e.g., from p_m to p_1 in Figure 11-7). Nevertheless, this does *not* imply that monopolistic competition reduces consumer surplus below what it would be under perfect competition. When buyers reveal their preferences for differentiated products, it is possible that the consumer surplus on the first q_m boxes of A-Typical oatmeal is greater than the consumer surplus for q_0 boxes of generic oatmeal sold at price p_0. As long as consumers buying A-Typical oatmeal have the option of buying generic oatmeal at price p_0, their actions indicate that they are at least as well off consuming the differentiated product.

Economic Profit and Market Entry

As in the case of perfect competition, the opportunity for positive economic profit will attract new sellers to a monopolistically competitive industry. Analysis of the process of market entry by producers of differentiated products is more complex than the description of market entry into a perfectly competitive industry. Uniqueness of location, personal relationships with customers, legal protections of trademarks and brand names, and imperfect consumer information about product characteristics and quality all provide a limited insulation of incumbent firms against the encroachment of new sellers. Nevertheless, as under perfect competition, the number of sellers of similar commodities will tend to increase as long as new entrants believe they can make a positive economic profit. It is entirely possible that new entrants will be experiencing economic losses at the same time that established firms continue to receive revenue in excess of the opportunity cost of all inputs.[9]

The vagueness of the definition of the industry or product group creates another complication. Product differentiation means that there is no unique market price for the commodity; a spectrum of prices, reflecting different consumer tastes for different combinations of product characteristics, prevails under monopolistic competition. Because a firm may find it efficient to produce a number of closely related commodities, a producer with a small share of a narrowly defined industry (e.g., nail polish) may have such a large output in a more broadly defined industry (e.g., cosmetics) that it would constitute an oligopolist (see chapter twelve).

Despite these complications, microeconomic theory can suggest some long-run tendencies for monopolistically competitive industries. First, as under perfect competition, the entry and exit of firms will change the number of producers, causing economic profit to approach zero. Like entry under perfect competition, entry into a monopolistically competitive industry is fundamentally different from "entry" into a monopolized market, or even into many oligopoly markets, which involves the transfer of ownership of an operating business or displacement of one firm by another.

Second, the long-run equilibrium price-output combination for a monopolistically competitive producer will be identified by the tangency of the firm's demand curve and long-run average cost curve. However, as long as the firm's product is distinguished in the minds of consumers, so that its demand curve is negatively sloped, the long-run equilibrium price will not equal the lowest point on its long-run average cost curve, and long-run equilibrium output will not usually be associated with minimum long-run average cost.[10]

---

[9] Since entry into a monopolistically competitive industry is risky—one must guess whether or not a new set of characteristics will attract enough customers at a high enough price to cover costs—the number of firms would stabilize with a positive expected profit level if entering entrepreneurs were risk averse, whereas entering firms would have negative expected profits if new entrepreneurs were risk lovers.

[10] Harold Demsetz and others have dissented from this conclusion; their arguments will be dealt with later in the chapter.

Third, as with monopoly, short-run economic profits which are protected by entry impediments (e.g., patents which cover a range of product characteristics) or the uniqueness of inputs (e.g., location) will be capitalized in the market value of the firm or in transferable patents, brand names, trademarks, and so on. There will be a tendency for the economic profit of monopolistically competitive firms to approach zero, even when market entry is impeded. However, only when the number of firms is free to increase, will market entry tend to increase consumer welfare.

The consequences of market entry on an established firm's demand curve are depicted in Figure 11-8. Recall the variety of arguments in the demand equation for a differentiated product:

$$q_d^1 = f[p^1, p^2, \ldots, p^n; k(z^1), k(z^2), \ldots, k(z^n); y, t]$$

The entry of new sellers will be heralded by new combinations of product characteristics (changing a z^i, $i \neq 1$), advertising campaigns, and/or lower prices of close substitutes for the goods sold by incumbent firms. Such changes in exogenous variables will shift the demand curves of established firms to the left.

The impact of market entry on the price and output of established firms depends, in part, on their reaction to the new competition. Figure 11-8 depicts a *passive price-cutter*. With demand curve D_0, the firm was receiving a positive economic profit, selling q_0 units of output per period

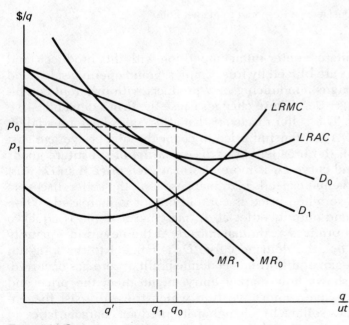

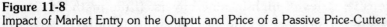

Figure 11-8
Impact of Market Entry on the Output and Price of a Passive Price-Cutter

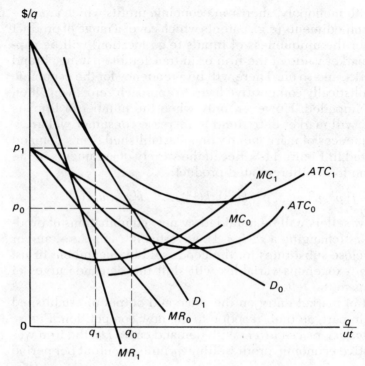

$/q

p_1

p_0

MC_1 ATC_1

ATC_0

MC_0

D_0

D_1

MR_0

q_1 q_0

MR_1

0

$\dfrac{q}{ut}$

Figure 11-9
Upgrading Product Quality as a Response to Market Entry

at price p_0. As imitators enter into competition with this producer (and others), consumers are blitzed by free samples, grand opening sales, and advertising campaigns announcing new products with different combinations of characteristics. These changes cause the firm's demand curve to shift to the left. The seller discovers that at p_0, sales have now fallen to q', where $p_0 < ATC$. Raising price to cover the higher average cost would be suicidal; the broadening of the spectrum of substitute goods means that demand curve D_1 is more elastic at each price than D_0 was. Since marginal revenue exceeds marginal cost at q', the seller discovers that losses decrease when price is cut and output is increased. When price reaches p_1 and output settles at q_1, marginal revenue is equal to marginal cost and profit is again maximized. At the new price-quantity combination (p_1, q_1), the demand curve D_1 is tangent to the long-run average cost curve: an equilibrium economic profit of zero has occurred.

Figure 11-9 shows how market entry might affect the price and output of an aggressive, innovative firm which tries to resist the encroachment of new sellers by changing its product characteristics to satisfy expensive tastes of high-income buyers. If the methods chosen to counteract new rivals reduce the absolute value of price elasticity of demand, market entry might actually increase the price charged by some incumbents, although at least part of that price increase would result from the new product's higher production and marketing costs. For expository convenience, demand curve D_1 in Figure 11-9 passes through the previous profit-maximizing price-quantity combination (p_0, q_0) but is less elastic than D_0 at each rate of output. Increases in marginal cost shift MC_0 to MC_1, and since fixed cost (e.g., advertising, custom-designed machinery) are likely to increase as well as variable cost, the minimum point on ATC_1 is to the right of the minimum point on ATC_0.

The tangency between demand curve D_1 and ATC_1, the average total cost curve reflecting higher production and advertising costs of the more expensive product, results in a higher price in Figure 11-9. The firm in Figure 11-9 now earns a normal profit; if a positive economic profit were still being earned, this firm would still be enticing imitators into the market. If new firms could not duplicate the combination of inputs this firm used, ATC_1 would absorb the capitalized value of patents, ideal location, and other transferable entry impediments.

The entry of new firms would usually increase the price elasticity of demand for established brands; this increased elasticity, along with the leftward shift of the demand curves of established sellers, encourages lower prices. However, at this stage in the development of monopolistic competition theory, most economists are reluctant to conclude that the entry of new sellers always reduces the prices of differentiated products, *ceteris paribus*.

Economic Loss and the Exit of Sellers

Sometimes the zero economic profit equilibrium condition under perfect competition and monopolistic competition is misinterpreted to mean that efficient producers are guaranteed zero economic profit. This is not true in either model. As under perfect competition and monopoly, comparing the profit-maximizing price to average variable cost of the associated rate of output, determines whether the firm operates in the short run. Comparing that price to average total cost determines whether imitators are attracted to or repulsed from that market,[11] and whether the firm remains in the industry in the long run.

Figure 11-10 depicts the two firms which experience economic losses at the short-run equilibrium quantity and price (i.e., $ATC > p_0 >$

---

[11] To emphasize the riskiness of introducing a differentiated product, a new producer or potential producer would calculate its expected profit by weighting each observed profit level $(\pi_1, \pi_2, \ldots, \pi_n)$ by the subjective probability of achieving that profit: $E(\Pi) = \rho_1\pi_1 + \rho_2\pi_2 + \ldots + \rho_n\pi_n$. Hence, a firm with a positive economic profit will increase the expected profit of would-be entrants, and a firm with a negative economic profit will reduce the expected profit of would-be entrants.

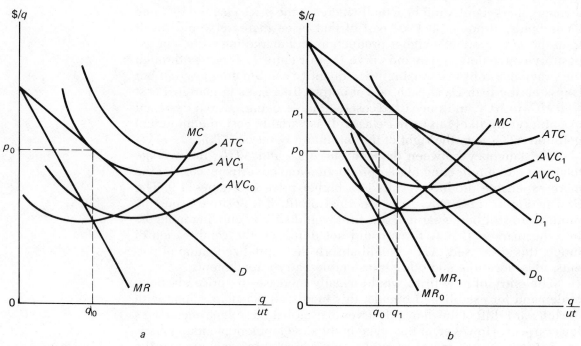

Figure 11-10
Exit and Survival under Monopolistic Competition. *a*, Firm leaves industry when average variable costs reach AVC_1; *b*, remaining firm survives when new demand curve (reflecting fewer substitutes) allows zero economic profit where D_1 is tangent to *ATC*.

AVC_0). As the time horizon expands, fixed-cost contracts will expire and can be renegotiated; the longer the time horizon, the greater the proportion of total costs that will become variable costs. Assuming no change in factor prices or the characteristics of the two commodities, both average total cost curves will remain unchanged.[12] The increase in average variable costs from AVC_0 to AVC_1 represents an increase in variable cost reflected in an equal decrease in fixed cost, so that total costs do not change. The firm pictured in Figure 11-10*a* leaves the industry when its average variable cost curve reaches AVC_1; economic losses equal fixed cost and the firm has no reason to remain in business. At the same time, the firm in Figure 11-10*b* remains and waits for its contracts (with later termination dates) to expire.

---

[12] When there is more than one fixed factor, the average total cost curve may change due to factor substitution. Hence, Figure 11-10, which shows the *ATC* curve as stationary over time, is something of a simplification.

The exit of firms producing similar products causes an increase in the demand for the commodities sold by the remaining producers; former customers of defunct firms must now combine products of surviving firms to obtain the mix of commodity characteristics they desire. In Figure 11-10b, the rightward shift of the firm's demand curve from D_0 to D_1 allows the firm to survive with zero economic profit. Eventually the firm is able to sell q_1 units of output at price p_1, which results in an equality of price and average total cost at the profit-maximizing rate of output.

There is no reason for concluding that surviving firms fare better than firms which leave the industry—quite the contrary. When the firm in Figure 11-10a left because $AVC_1 = p_0$, the firm depicted in Figure 11-10b was still experiencing an economic loss; revenue covered only a fraction of fixed costs, causing the wealth of the owner of the latter firm to deteriorate further. Resources released from the industry by firm exit presumably earned a normal return elsewhere in the economy while the firm in Figure 11-10b was still incurring an economic loss. Hence, other things remaining the same, short-term fixed-cost obligations will be preferred to minimum purchase requirements with later expiration dates.

Business Illustration
Barriers to Entering the Soft Drink Industry

As in the theory of perfect competition, free entry under monopolistic competition makes possible an increase in the number of sellers when incumbents are receiving positive economic profit. A larger number of sellers means a greater variety of products and, usually, lower prices. However, because economic profit will tend to zero when entry barriers are transferred, one cannot infer that zero economic profit by producers means enhanced consumer welfare.

One might expect the soft drink industry to epitomize the model of monopolistic competition. Not so, according to a recent paper by Professor Barry L. Duman of West Texas State University.

While there were 2,400 bottling plants in the United States that bottled soft drinks in 1975, most of the soft-drink syrup was and is manufactured by a handful of parent companies for nationally known brands. Each bottler, who turns the syrup into soda, has an exclusive franchise with one or more parent companies. Each local market constitutes an oligopoly among Coca-Cola, Pepsi-Cola, Seven-Up, Royal Crown Cola, Dr. Pepper, and a few other bottlers. Under the exclusive market system, the number of bottling plants cannot grow; in fact, it has been declining steadily. Between 1965 and 1975, the number of bottling plants in operation in the United States declined by 38 percent; at the same time, the amount of soda sold increased by 78 percent.

The simultaneous decrease in the number of bottling plants and increase in the volume of soft drinks sold contradicts the predictions of the monopolistic competition model. The most obviously violated assumption of that model is ease of entry by imitators of successful sellers. Exclusive franchises insulate established bottlers from new entrants; new bottlers must either manufacture both syrup and bottled soft drinks for new, unknown brands (requiring substantial advertising outlays) or pick up a franchise if a parent company drops its agreement with an established bottler. However, the parent companies, particularly "Big Coke" and "Big Pepsi," have been taking over their own bottling plants. This gives them greater control over the demand for syrup. A local bottler, facing weak competition from other brands, might reduce output to raise the price of soda. Since this would reduce its use of syrup, the parent company would seek to thwart this strategy.

In 1971 the Federal Trade Commission (FTC) decided to challenge the practice of exclusive franchising of soda bottlers. But the wheels of regulation turn slowly. An administrative-law judge ruled in favor of the soft drink industry after holding hearings in 1975. It was 1978 before the FTC, having overruled the judge, moved against exclusive franchises. To counter the FTC, the industry turned to Congress, which passed the Soft Drink Interbrand Competition Bill (Public Law 96-308); it was signed into law by President Carter on July 9, 1980. The bill had had 75 co-sponsors in the Senate and over 300 co-sponsors in the House of Representatives.

The effect of the bill was to perpetuate the practice of exclusive franchises by defining competition as interbrand competition (e.g., Coca-Cola versus Pepsi-Cola) instead of intrabrand competition (e.g., price wars between two Coca-Cola bottlers). In addition, the burden of proof was placed on plaintiffs or the government in allegations of anticompetitive behavior. Soft drink bottlers and their parent companies became less vulnerable to the punishment of triple damages, and the time during which private civil suits could be filed against soft drink firms was limited to four years after the alleged violation took place.

The advantages of the act to parent companies and large bottlers are more obvious than the benefits to small bottling companies. Bottlers with small territories tend to be squeezed out of dealings with large wholesalers that have warehouses outside the bottler's territory or that ship outside that territory. Company-owned bottlers' plants, of course, face no such restrictions. Duman concluded: "What is not quite so clear is why many small independent bottlers agreed to support this legislation when all evidence pointed to the ultimate elimination of that group of competitors. . . . [T]he most compelling reason may have been that inasmuch as small bottlers knew that they were a fast disappearing group, their only and best motivation might have been one of guarding the capitalized value of their real estate and franchises."

Source: Barry L. Duman, "A New Legal Environment for the Soft Drink Industry and the Case of the Small Independent Bottler" (paper presented at Southwest Social Science Meetings, San Antonio, Texas, March 18, 1982).

APPLICATION
Allocative Efficiency and Product Differentiation

The negatively sloped demand curve of the monopolistically competitive firm has been cited as a source of economic inefficiency. The monopolistically competitive equilibrium is characterized by the profit maximum for the firm, so that marginal revenue equals marginal cost, and by normal profits for representative firms, so that price equals average total cost. Since product differentiation implies $p > MR = MC$, the $p = ATC$ normal-profit equilibrium implies $ATC > MC$ at the long-run equilibrium rate of output. This syllogism led Edward Chamberlin to conclude:

> It may be seen that the effect of monopoly elements on the individual's adjustment (barring the possibility of advertising, to be considered later) is characteristically to render his price higher and his scale of production smaller than under pure competition. No matter in what position the demand curve is drawn, its negative slope will define maximum profits at a point further to the left than if it were horizontal, as under pure competition. This means, in general, higher production costs and higher prices.[13]

In Figure 11-11, a perfectly competitive firm in long-run equilibrium is compared with a similarly situated producer of a differentiated commodity. Both long-run equilibria involve a tangency between the firm's long-run demand curve (due to market entry) and its long-run average cost curve. As shown in chapter nine, long-run equilibrium under perfect competition (Figure 11-11a) occurs at the minimum point on the firm's long-run average cost curve. Since the firm produces where its horizontal demand curve, $D_{LR} = p_e$, is tangent to its long-run average cost curve, it is forced to produce at the lowest sustainable price: $p_e = LRAC = LRMC$.

The negatively sloped demand curve resulting from the entry of imitators, D_{LR}, gives the monopolistically competitive firm a long-run equilibrium output to the left of the minimum point on its long-run average cost curve. Given identical long-run average cost curves (a heroic assumption in light of the higher production and selling costs resulting from product differentiation), a monopolistically competitive firm appears to produce a smaller level of output, and to charge a higher price, in long-run equilibrium than would be the case were the firm perfectly competitive. Although the increase in the number of monopolistically competitive sellers in response to the prospect of positive economic profit would reduce expected economic profit to zero, product differentiation appears to be associated with resource use that leads to greater

[13] Edward Chamberlin, *The Theory of Monopolistic Competition: A Reorientation of the Theory of Value*, 7th ed. (Boston: Harvard University Press, 1956), pp. 77–78. The impact of selling costs on long-run equilibrium is discussed on pp. 171–172.

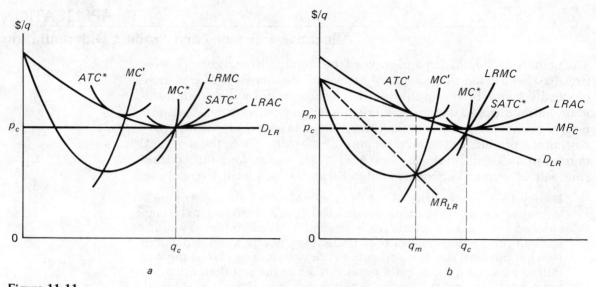

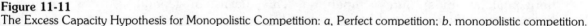

Figure 11-11
The Excess Capacity Hypothesis for Monopolistic Competition: *a*, Perfect competition; *b*, monopolistic competition.

than minimum long-run minimum average cost. As shown earlier, monopolistic competition does not appear to maximize consumer surplus in the short run. Figure 11-11*b* implies that consumer surplus would not be maximized in long-run equilibrium for the monopolistically competitive firm.

Adding advertising expenditures and other selling costs means that the equilibrium price under monopolistic competition is not comparable with that of perfect competition, wherein selling costs are assumed to be zero. In Figure 11-12, the average cost curve *PP'* is the analogue of the long-run average cost curve under perfect competition which includes only the opportunity costs of inputs used to produce a homogeneous output. Product differentiation means that the seller can increase quantity sold at each price by expenditures to modify product characteristics and to communicate those characteristics to consumers. Optimal selling costs would occur when the marginal revenue from additional output (price constant) equaled the marginal cost of selling efforts.[14] In Figure 11-12, curve *FF'* is the *mutatis mutandis* average cost curve, which reflects optimal selling costs for each price. Since some selling

---

[14] A similar analysis is developed by Harold Demsetz in "The Nature of Equilibrium in Monopolistic Competition," *Journal of Political Economy* (February 1953), pp. 21–30, and in "The Welfare and Empirical Implications of Monopolistic Competition," *Economic Journal* (September 1964), pp. 623–641. Despite their critical tone, these two articles reinforce Chamberlin's conclusion that the average cost of production becomes ambiguous when selling costs are included in the analysis of equilibrium under monopolistic competition.

costs would be fixed costs, the minimum point on curve FF' is to the right of the minimum point on curve PP'.

In Figure 11-12, we contrast long-run equilibrium for the passive price-cutter and the aggressive innovator, overlaying the conventional average cost curve (PP') and the *mutatis mutandis* average cost curve (FF'), which is adjusted for selling and product innovation costs. Obviously, Figure 11-12 is contrived since the zero profit equilibrium for the *mutatis mutandis* average cost curve, FF', is tangent to the (advertising stimulated) demand curve D' at output q_1, the minimum average cost output for the conventional average cost curve, PP'. The diagram is meant to be illustrative: once selling costs and product differentiation costs are included in the calculation of long-run equilibrium, there is no reason to expect "excess capacity" in the sense of unrealized economies of scale. This was a conclusion Chamberlin himself reached:

> The conclusions are different, however, when comparison is made, not with pure competition, but with conditions as they would be without advertising. It is now seen that although, similarly, the scale of production *may* be either larger or smaller with selling outlays than without them, it is much more likely to be larger. If the slope

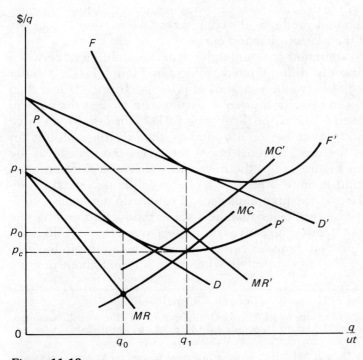

Figure 11-12
Long-Run Equilibria Compared: Without Selling Costs (p_0, q_0) and with Selling Costs (p_1, q_1).

of the demand curve is unaffected by the selling outlays, its point of tangency with the average cost curve which includes advertising costs is bound to lie to the right of its point of tangency with the average cost of production curve . . . . Prices (although inevitably higher than under pure competition), may be either higher or lower than they would be without advertising.[15]

We may conclude, then, that whether monopolistically competitive equilibrium can be considered economically efficient depends on how one perceives the price differential $p_1 - p_c$ in Figure 11-12. In describing a slightly different variation of the analysis we have outlined in Figure 11-12, Harold Demsetz advanced the following argument: "[O]ne can argue that consumers are willing to pay a higher price for more expenditure on differentiation-producing costs (location, quality, and promotional costs). Therefore, consumers derive some utility from these cost expenditures, and they (the costs) are properly included in the welfare economist's marginal cost curve."[16]

We have come full circle: given the choice of homogeneous or differentiated products, consumers willing to pay a higher price for one seller's product are revealing their preferences. They must be better off in their own estimation as long as higher prices for differentiated products are voluntarily paid. And how can we guarantee that higher prices paid for differentiated products are voluntary? One answer lies in the development of the plateau demand curve.[17]

Suppose, the argument goes, enough buyers are indifferent between the wares of allegedly differentiated sellers. In Figure 11-13, a seller can sell any amount between q_0 and q_1 at price p_0. If price is less than p_0, more than q_1 can be sold; if price is greater than p_0, less than q_0 can be sold. In Figure 11-13, marginal revenue (MR_0) falls faster than price up to q_0, is equal to price between q_0 and q_1, then declines rapidly for $q > q_1(MR_1)$. If the marginal cost curve intersects the plateau of the demand curve in Figure 11-13, the erstwhile seller of a differentiated product might find it more profitable to behave like a perfectly competitive seller. Hence, the argument goes, if sellers do not behave competitively, it must be true that consumers value product differentiation.

The argument, while suggestive, is not decisive. Figure 11-13 demonstrates that a plateau demand curve might encourage a producer to ignore a large number of consumers who are indifferent about product

[15] Chamberlin, *Theory of Monopolistic Competition*, pp. 166–167.

[16] Harold Demsetz, "The Welfare and Empirical Implications of Monopolistic Competition," *Journal of Political Economy* (September 1964); reprinted in Richard E. Neel, ed., *Readings in Price Theory* (Cincinnati: South Western, 1973), p. 342.

[17] Attributed to A. J. Nichol, "The Influence of Marginal Buyers on Monopolistic Competition," *Quarterly Journal of Economics* (1934–1935), pp. 121–135; see also G. Warren Nutter, "The Plateau Demand Curve and Utility Theory," *Journal of Political Economy* (December 1955), pp. 525–528.

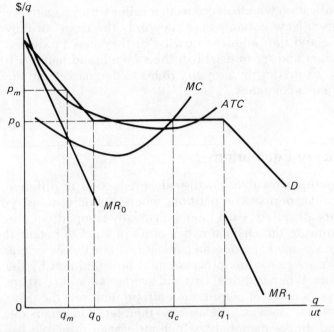

Figure 11-13
Plateau Demand Curve with Multiple Potential Profit Maxima

characteristics and concentrate on the higher prices some consumers are willing to pay. Below q_0, it is possible that the marginal revenue curve intersects the marginal cost curve, so that two candidates for profit-maximizing output exist: q_m, in the negatively sloped portion of the plateau demand curve, and q_c, where the marginal cost curve intersects the horizontal section of the demand curve. The diagram is drawn in a way that both p_m, q_m and p_c, q_c encourage market entry. If q_c is produced, one market entrant could also produce q_c, causing a surplus at price p_0. But the theory of perfect competition assumes that no firm can influence price. When one firm can change the price of an undifferentiated product, competitive equilibrium will not be stable.

If price is raised to p_m to take advantage of the willingness of some buyers to pay a higher price, market entry will tend to generate the tangency solutions of Figure 11-12, as long as the integrity of differentiated products is legally protected. If firms are allowed to copy or closely imitate brand names or trademarks, so that sellers become anonymous, perfect competition may emerge. But would consumers be better off if fraudulent products flooded the market?

The issue of product differentiation and allocational efficiency involves a trade-off between property rights and market efficiency. A firm's reputation for quality may be identified with its brand name or trademark, an identification which confronts that seller with a negatively sloped demand curve. New entrants may copy only the name, or they may copy the name and the product's quality, or they may produce a higher quality product and try to establish their own brand name. Ultimately, free entry would destroy property rights to the market and the market would become a commons.

Differentiated Competition and Industry Equilibrium

Monopolistic competition involves small-scale production of differentiated products. Unlike perfect competition, where a single industry-wide price confronts all sellers, each monopolistically competitive producer must communicate the characteristics of its product to potential customers, then pick a market price and quantity from the emerging demand curve.[18] We saw how this process could be simplified by the use of markup pricing. When marginal cost and average variable cost are roughly constant over a range of output, the entrepreneur sets the price according to his estimate of demand elasticity, then lets consumers determine output. And unlike monopoly, which at least in principle has a stable demand curve, the demand for the monopolistic competitor's product is continually buffeted by gales of creative destruction: changes in the characteristics of other goods, in price, and in information (and images) due to advertising.

The greatest success, and the greatest potential, for the model(s) of monopolistic competition is in the application of microeconomic analysis to the operation of a small business. By indicating the necessary conditions for the success of a new product, by relating markup pricing and profit maximization, and by predicting how an increase in the number of firms influences the firm's economic profit, the model of monopolistic competition offers the economics student one bridge between theory and practice. At the same time, whether because of a sense of ethics or fear of the consequences of deception, it is important for economists to include the bad news of the monopolistic competition model along with the good. Yes, we can tell the owner of a small business, economics can help you market a product; in fact, economics brings together insights from engineering (production theory), accounting (cost theory), management (output selection), and marketing (product differentiation, pricing, and advertising). However, you should also know that market forces

---

[18] George Stigler, in *Theory of Price*, 3rd ed. (New York: Macmillan, 1966), pp. 2–3, shows how imperfect information and the economics of consumer choice predict that the standard deviation of prices in real-world markets is inversely related to the average price in that industry. However, a crucial assumption of this model is that consumers treat products by alternative sellers as perfect substitutes.

will tend to reduce your economic profit to zero and entry barriers will become artificial costs.

It is important for economists to communicate to entrepreneurs, consumers, and our colleagues in other business disciplines that product differentiation, per se, does not promise, or even imply, positive economic profit. As we have seen, passive firms which are forced to cut their price in the wake of competition from anonymous new sellers will tend to achieve a tangency between an elastic (although negatively sloped) demand curve and the negatively sloped portion of their long-run average cost curve. Moreover, firms which change their product characteristics or finance advertising campaigns to resist entry will also tend toward normal profit, although their demand curves will be tangent to *mutatis mutandis* average cost curves which include selling costs. Once selling costs are taken into account, the so-called excess capacity theorem (i.e., that monopolistically competitive sellers fail to achieve all potential internal economies) becomes hazy. The only clear-cut conclusion is that product differentiation means higher long-run equilibrium prices than would occur under perfect competition.

Consumer behavior reveals a preference for product differentiation. The plateau demand curve, despite its problems, predicts that perfect competition will result if enough consumers are indifferent among producers. Monopolistic competition springs from consumers'/willingness to pay more for differentiated products than for generic goods. If monopolistic competitors behave as passive price cutters, they will not realize all potential economies of scale. Whether the benefits of product variety and the consumer protection afforded by patents, brand names, and trademarks are worth the cost of "inefficiency" in production is unclear. If monopolistic competitors attempt to sustain their markets by vigorous advertising or product innovation, they will still receive zero economic profit in the long run and equilibrium prices will be higher under monopolistic competition on two accounts. Selling costs result from communicating product differences to consumers. Price will exceed marginal cost in long-run equilibrium because of the ability of the seller to raise price by limiting output. In contrast to perfect competition, monopolistic competition does not *maximize* consumer surplus in long-run equilibrium; it is nevertheless possible (perhaps likely) that the consumer surplus from product differentiation is greater than if product homogeneity were somehow forced on consumers by making it impossible for innovators to protect the link between their brand name and product characteristics.

What is missing from the model of monopolistic competition is the neat synthesis of the behavior of the firm and the behavior of the market which is a feature of both the theory of perfect competition and pure monopoly. In both models, changes in consumer demand change a well defined *market* demand curve, leading to predictable changes in price and quantity (in the short run) augmented by predictions of the number of producers and the profit level for the typical firm (in the long run). Under monopoly, the long-run implications are either trivial (entry is barred and profit is capitalized) or identical to perfect competition (the breakup of cartels). No such neatness characterizes monopolistic competition.

The long-run equilibrium for the imperfectly competitive firm occurs at a tangency between some sort of demand curve, of which little is known save its negative slope, and some sort of average cost curve, which may or may not reflect an efficient allocation of scarce resources. Further, by the very nature of product differentiation, it is difficult to determine where one industry begins and another ends. So, unless economists wish to explain demand changes—the works of Lancaster and Galbraith represent exceptions to that general reluctance—the model of monopolistic competition will remain incomplete and, in the minds of some economists, not quite a theory. Milton Friedman contends: "The theory of monopolistic competition offers no tools for the analysis of an industry and so no stopping place between the firm at one extreme and general equilibrium on the other. It is therefore incompetent to contribute to the analysis of a host of important problems: the one extreme is too narrow to be of great interest; the other, too broad to permit meaningful generalizations."[19]

One can respond to such a sentiment only by stipulating the obvious: Friedman is entitled to his opinion about what economic theories ought to do. The author's sentiments lie more with those of Paul Samuelson: "Chicago economists can continue to shout until they are blue in the face that there is no elegant alternative to the theory of perfect competition. If not, the proper moral is 'So much the worse for elegance.'"[20] Ultimately, microeconomic theory is like the market itself: a commons wherein ideas are free to enter but differentiated ideas are viewed with some suspicion. The reason for this uneasy feeling is that one can never be sure whether consumers of microeconomic theory are made better off when they are allowed to match theories with their tastes and preferences.

---

[19] Milton Friedman, "The Methodology of Positive Economics," in *Essays in Positive Economics* (Chicago: University of Chicago Press, 1966).

[20] Paul Samuelson, "The Monopolistic Competition Revolution," in Edwin Mansfield, ed., *Microeconomics: Selected Readings*, 4th ed. (New York: Norton, 1982), p. 359.

HIGHLIGHTS

1. Monopolistic competition theory originated in the 1930s with the work of Edward Chamberlin and Joan Robinson, who sought to overturn the perfect competition–pure monopoly dichotomy which characterized value theory up until that time. Today, monopolistic competition refers to a market containing a large number of producers of differentiated products.

2. Product differences ultimately reflect con-

sumer willingness to pay higher prices for some sellers' products than others. By viewing commodities as different combinations of characteristics, the necessary condition for the successful introduction of a new product is that consumers believe they can obtain a desired combination of product characteristics at lower cost by purchasing the new product than by combining existing products.

3. Product differentiation alone is not sufficient for monopolistic competition; legal restrictions on product duplication—patents, brand names, and trademark registration—prevent new firms from offering perfect substitutes of successful commodities. This means that the differentiated seller confronts a negatively sloped demand curve.

4. The short-run profit-maximizing output and price for a monopolistically competitive seller is determined in the same manner as in the monopoly model: produce where marginal cost equals marginal revenue, after checking that price exceeds average variable cost.

5. Using a markup formula equal to the ratio of elasticity to one plus elasticity is equivalent to maximizing profit by the $MR = MC$ rule, especially for the producer with a horizontal average variable cost (= marginal cost) curve.

6. As under perfect competition, the expectation of positive economic profit will attract additional sellers to a monopolistically competitive industry. If an established firm passively cuts price in the wake of increased competition, long-run equilibrium price and quantity will be determined by the tangency of the firm's negatively sloped demand curve and its average total cost curve. Since this tangency occurs while average total cost is still falling, some observers have suggested that monopolistically competitive industries have too many sellers and too small an output per seller.

7. When established firms vary their sales effort through product innovations and/or increased advertising, the equilibrium price and quantity consistent with zero economic profit will correspond to a higher than competitive price, since the firm's demand curve will be tangent to the *mutatis mutandis* average total cost curve which includes selling costs. However, there is no necessary relationship between the level of output and decreasing average total *production* costs.

8. As in perfect competition, firms will exit a monopolistically competitive industry when price is less than average variable cost—that is, when a sufficient proportion of average total costs have become variable due to expiring contracts. The sooner a firm is able to exit and escape fixed cost, the sooner its owner will be able to receive a normal income in another market. After a sufficient proportion of firms have left the industry, remaining firms will again experience zero economic profit.

9. Because consumer willingness to pay higher prices for differentiated products is a requirement for the negatively sloped demand curve under monopolistic competition, the higher long-run equilibrium price under monopolistic competition can be interpreted as what consumers pay for variety. While consumer surplus is not maximized under monopolistic competition, it is possible that consumers are better off under differentiated competition than when producers are unable to differentiate their products.

10. There is a problem in defining the industry to which the monopolistically competitive model is supposed to apply. This arises from the fact that consumer tastes determine multiple long-run equilibrium prices. Because consumer tastes are largely treated as an exogenous force in microeconomic theory, economists cannot predict the pattern of prices under monopolistic competition.

GLOSSARY

Differentiated competition See **monopolistic competition.**

Imperfect competition The general name for market types between perfect competition and pure monopoly.

Informative advertising Advertising that presents straightforward information about product price and product characteristics, in contrast to persuasive advertising.

Markup pricing The practice of setting product price equal to the cost of variable inputs, with an "add-on" factor to cover overhead and profit. For the producer with simple technology (for whom $MC = AVC$), markup pricing is equivalent to profit maximization when $p = [\eta/(1 + \eta)]MC$, where η is the price of elasticity of demand.

Monopolistic competition The market type characterized by a large number of producers of differentiated commodities, in which producer-product identification is maintained through patents and/or trademark or brand-name protection. Also called **differentiated competition.**

Persuasive advertising Advertising which changes consumer tastes, in contrast to informative advertising.

SUGGESTED READINGS

Baumol, William. "Monopolistic Competition and Welfare Economics." *American Economic Review* (May 1964), pp. 44–55. Reprinted in Ingrid Rima, ed. *Readings in the History of Economic Thought.* New York: Holt, Rinehart and Winston, 1970, pp. 202–209.

Bishop, Robert L. "Monopolistic Competition after Thirty Years: The Impact on General Theory." *American Economic Review* (May 1964), pp. 33–44. Reprinted in Ingrid Rima, ed. *Readings in the History of Economic Theory.* New York: Holt, Rinehart and Winston, 1971, pp. 235–247.

Buchanan, Norman S. "Advertising Expenditure: A Suggested Treatment." *Journal of Political Economy* (August 1942). Reprinted in William Breit and Harold Hochman, eds. *Readings in Microeconomics.* 2nd ed. New York: Holt, Rinehart and Winston, 1971, pp. 235–247.

Cassels, John M. "Excess Capacity and Monopolistic Competition." *Quarterly Journal of Economics* (May 1973). Reprinted in William Breit and Harold Hochman, eds. *Readings in Microeconomics.* 2nd ed. New York: Holt, Rinehart and Winston, 1971, pp. 224–234.

Chamberlin, Edward. *The Theory of Monopolistic Competition: A Reorientation of the Theory of Value.* 7th ed. Boston: Harvard University Press, 1956.

Das, Satya P. "Long Run Behavior of a Monopolistically Competitive Firm." *International Economic Review* (February 1981), pp. 159–165.

Demsetz, Harold. "The Nature of Equilibrium in Monopolistic Competition." *Journal of Political Economy* (February 1953). Reprinted in William Breit and Harold Hochman, eds. *Readings in Microeconomics.* 2nd ed. New York: Holt, Rinehart and Winston, 1971, pp. 253–261.

———. "The Welfare and Empirical Implications of Monopolistic Competition." *Journal of Political Economy* (September 1964). Reprinted in Richard E. Neel, ed. *Readings in Price Theory.* Cincinnati: South Western, 1973.

———. "Barriers to Entry." *American Economic Review* (March 1982), pp. 47–57.

Lancaster, Kelvin. *Consumer Demand: A New Approach.* New York: Columbia University Press, 1971.

———. *Introduction to Modern Microeconomics.* 2nd ed. New York: Rand-McNally, 1974, pp. 253–256.

Nelson, Phillip. "Advertising and Ethics." In Richard T. DeGeorge and Joseph A. Pichler, eds. *Ethics, Free Enterprise and Public Policy.* New York: Oxford University Press, 1978,

pp. 187–188.
Nutter, G. Warren. "The Plateau Demand Curve and Utility Theory." *Journal of Political Economy* (December 1955), pp. 525–528. Reprinted in William Breit and Harold Hochman, eds. *Readings in Microeconomics.* 2nd ed. New York: Holt, Rinehart and Winston, 1971, pp. 248–252.

Robinson, Joan. *Economics of Imperfect Competition.* New York: St. Martin's Press, 1969.
Samuelson, Paul. "The Monopolistic Competition Revolution." In Robert Kuenne, ed. *Monopolistic Competition Theory.* New York: Wiley, 1967. Reprinted in Edwin Mansfield, ed. *Microeconomics: Suggested Readings.* New York: Norton, 1982.

EXERCISES

Evaluate

Indicate whether each of the following statements is true (agrees with economic theory), false (is contradicted by theory), or uncertain (could be true or false, given additional information). Explain your answer.

1. The existence of a long-run equilibrium price which results in normal profits for all firms in an industry is unique to perfect competition.
2. The fact that many consumers are willing to pay higher prices for differentiated products indicates that no inefficiency results from charging prices higher than marginal costs.
3. Introduction of a new product with slightly different characteristics might actually shift the demand curve of some established firms to the right.
4. A producer can make a profit by introducing a new commodity which is perceived to contain the same characteristics as combinations of other products on the market only if the new product sells for a lower price than the unit cost of combinations of existing brands which result in the same set of characteristics.
5. Informative advertising increases consumer surplus, while persuasive advertising reduces consumer surplus, *ceteris paribus.*
6. Since a monopolistically competitive seller's price must cover selling costs as well as production costs in long-run equilibrium, whether production costs themselves are minimized in equilibrium cannot be determined a priori.
7. Monopolistically competitive firms are competitive to the extent that they do not create contrived shortages the way pure monopolies do.
8. Monopolistic competition models illustrate the ambiguity between ideal property rights and ideal market efficiency.
9. Markup pricing illustrates the basic irrelevance of the marginal-cost-equals-marginal-revenue rule to real-world output and price decisions.
10. As long as some consumers purchase only the brand with the lowest price, perfectly competitive outcomes will prevail under alleged conditions of monopolistic competition.

Calculate

Answer each of the following questions, showing all your calculations.

11. Mom's Pizza Parlor is one of fifty independently owned pizza shops in a medium-sized city. Mom's daughter, an economics major, has determined that the daily demand for Mom's pizzas is $q_D = 40\bar{p} - 20p_i$, where $\bar{p}$ is the average price of pizzas in town and p_i is the price Mom charges.
    a. Determine the formula for Mom's average revenue. (Hint: solve p_i in terms of $\bar{p}$ and q.)
    b. What is the equation for Mom's marginal revenue (remember: $MR = p + q[\Delta p/\Delta q]$)?
    c. If $\bar{p} = \$10$ and $MC = \$3$ for all pizzas produced, at what price should Mom sell her pizzas? How many will she sell a day?
    d. If Mom's fixed costs are $500 per day, what is her daily rate of profit?
12. Given your answer to question 11:
    a. Will Mom's experience in the pizza business tend to attract other firms to, or repel them from, the pizza business?

b. Suppose that price competition in the pizza industry drops the average price ($\bar{p}$) to $6 per pizza. What happens to Mom's daily output and the price of pizza? What happens to her profit?

Contemplate

Answer each of the following in a brief but complete essay.

13. Suppose it were somehow possible to obtain an infinite number of combinations of two measurable product characteristics (e.g., vitamin C and calories). The existence of a large number of brands, each with slightly more of one characteristic and slightly less of the other, would confront the consumer with an isocost curve which was bowed-out from the origin. Explain how this conclusion was reached.

14. If sellers of the differentiated products in question 13 attempted to practice price discrimination by charging lower prices only for the marginal quantities as package sizes increased (e.g., $1.00 for 8 oz., $1.90 for 16 oz., $2.70 for 24 oz., etc.), how would the equilibrium number of sellers be influenced by this practice? Would this practice be likely to continue if there were no cost savings in selling the product in larger packages? Explain.

15. Briefly explain why television networks and the advertising industry suffered a greater reduction in profits because of the ban on cigarette advertising than tobacco producers apparently did. What was the effect of this ban on (a) the incidence of smoking, (b) cigarette advertising in other media, and (c) the price of cigarettes?

Chapter 12

Oligopoly: Rivalry among the Few

Few topics in microeconomic theory generate as much controversy as oligopoly. Dealing with **oligopoly**, a market with a few sellers, involves a conflict between the desire for simple theories and the need for realism when proposing solutions to actual business problems. Economists take their heritage seriously; like Adam Smith, they strive to explain—even to praise—the virtues of private enterprise to a skeptical public and a meddlesome government. On the other hand, firms willing to pay most handsomely for economists' practical insights are rarely the atomistic price takers lauded in the theory of perfect competition. The same economist may write speeches in praise of the corporation's contribution to consumer welfare while advising management how to extract more consumer surplus. Sometimes it pays to be schizophrenic.

    In this chapter we confirm a menu of models which constitute oligopoly theory—if such a variety of approaches can really be called a theory. We begin by exploring how market size and internal economies combine to generate rivalry. When the optimally sized firm must be so large that it has a noticeable impact on the price other firms charge, while diseconomies of scale prevent a single seller from serving the whole market, each seller's profit maximization problem is significantly more complex than those of monopoly as well as either perfectly or monopolistically competitive sellers.

The nature of rivalry unfolds in the investigation of the classical models of Augustin Cournot and Heinrich von Stackelberg, who attempted to devise simple theories of equilibrium price and quantity under duopoly: a market with two sellers. Ironically, by uncovering the shortcomings of these early attempts, we appreciate the complexity of the oligopoly environment. A closer inspection of the oligopoly pricing problem leads to the kinked demand curve model, which was first developed during the later 1930s. We will see how three assumptions—that sellers are aware of rivalry, attempt to maximize short-run profit, and do not collude—predict a rigidity in oligopolistic prices and output. We will briefly review the conflicting empirical evidence about whether oligopolistic prices actually change less frequently than prices generated under other types of markets (e.g., pure monopoly and perfect competition). We will argue that although the kinked demand curve model might be at odds with empirical evidence, it is logically consistent. That is, contradiction of the rigid price prediction means that at least one of the assumptions of the kinked demand curve model is incorrect or inappropriate.

Relaxing each of the three assumptions of the kinked demand curve model leads to the three major versions of modern oligopoly theory. Variations of classical duopoly themes represent attempts to generate stable equilibrium price and output solutions for markets with a few sellers by downplaying the role of rivalry on the individual firm's output choice. The dominant firm price-leadership model assumes a powerful firm pursuing a pricing strategy that is inimical to its long-run interests; this model predicts that competitive price and output patterns will emerge from homogeneous oligopoly in the long run. A more sophisticated variation on classical themes relates economies of scale to the entry-prevention price for an oligopoly market.

The second approach drops the assumption that firms do not collude, thereby exploring the problems confronting oligopoly cartels; while total profit for all firms is maximized by setting a monopoly output and price for the industry, each seller is tempted to increase its profit by selling below the cartel price. The output and price decision is based upon maximizing expected profit—that is, determining if the extra profit from breaking the cartel agreement is worth the expected costs of punishment. Analysis of oligopoly collusion in the United States is further complicated by inconsistencies in government policies toward monopoly behavior.

The third approach emerges from the work of John Kenneth Galbraith on the one hand and that of the managerialist school of industrial organization on the other. This variation rejects the proposition that managers of large corporations are motivated to maximize short-run profit. To Galbraith, the inability of stockholders to control day-to-day decisions causes executives to pursue stable growth in sales and dividends instead of the more disruptive and less rewarding practice of restricting output and raising price to maximize short-run earnings. To members of the managerialist school, the complexity of the oligopoly environment makes maximization of any objective impossible. We will investigate how alternative goals, like sales maximization under a minimum profit constraint, generate nonprice competition among a few sellers. Finally, we will consider whether satisficing models, offered as alternatives to the optimizing models of neoclassical theory, might really constitute a complementary set of insights.

Economies of Scale and Oligopoly

Oligopoly presents a problem of perspective. The typical oligopoly firm—a member of the *Fortune* 500 and a multinational corporation—is generally much larger in terms of assets and geographic scope than the typical natural monopoly—say, the local power and light company. It seems obvious that a firm which dominates its market would be larger than one which shares a market with a few rivals. However, it is the size of the market, not the absolute size of the firm, which determines whether that market is a monopoly or an oligopoly.

Because crude oil and refined petroleum products can be transported at a much lower cost (relative to the selling price of the product) than can electricity or water, the petroleum industry is oligopolistic (albeit cartelistic) while local electricity service is almost always available from only one seller. Although there are more utility companies than petroleum corporations, the market for petroleum products is global, whereas the market for electricity is local.

Most cities with populations of less than a million have only one local newspaper publisher, who uses the same printing presses to put out both a morning and an evening paper. The fixed costs of a daily paper include writing and editing the copy, composing the type, and overhead. Marginal costs are limited to paper, ink, and delivery costs. The price of a local newspaper is roughly its marginal cost; the publisher's fixed costs are covered by advertising revenue. Local advertisers find the most receptive audiences among the readers of local newspapers; competition from television, radio, and junk mail tends to be remote. Because they cannot afford 30-second commercial spots on radio, classified advertisers normally pay the highest rate per square inch of newspaper space. Access to large circulation newsmagazines, which often publish regional editions for advertisers in different parts of the country, means that advertisers with large markets pay lower rates for local newspaper space. Although the market for national newsmagazines is oligopolistic, Newsweek and Time-Life each have a greater circulation than the Memphis Publishing Company or Dayton Newspapers, publishers of the only daily newspapers in Memphis, Tennessee, and Dayton, Ohio, respectively.

Figure 12-1 contrasts the market conditions leading to natural monopoly and oligopoly. In Figure 12-1a, the market demand curve for a commodity intersects the long-run average cost curve of a single producer to the left of the minimum point on its long-run average cost curve. Operating the plant associated with ATC_1 to produce Q_1 and at price p_1, one firm could discourage potential rivals from entering its market. Ironically, the monopolist would maximize profit by operating the plant associated with ATC_0, restricting output to Q_0 in order to charge p_m. As shown in chapter ten, it is doubtful that natural monopolies charge prices which embody their potential economies of scale, since franchises protect firms from would-be rivals, and inelastic demand in the neighborhood of output Q_1 encourages increasing cost to justify a higher regulated price.

In contrast to natural monopoly, oligopoly "naturally" results when one firm would experience diseconomies of scale if it tried to dominate its market, while the minimum size of an efficient firm is too large for it to remain a price taker. In Figure 12-1b, the market demand intersects a firm's long-run average cost curve to the right of its horizontal range. If a firm with a short-run cost curve ATC_1 tried to serve the entire market, a price of p_1 or greater would be required to cover all costs. A second firm constructing a smaller plant (say, that associated with ATC_0) would

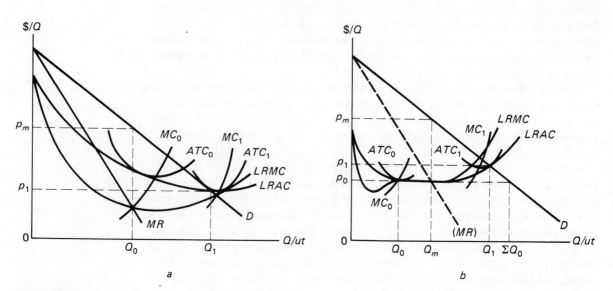

a

b

Figure 12-1
Contrast Between (*a*) Natural Monopoly and (*b*) Oligopoly. Economies of scale determine firm size while market demand determines the number of firms.

be able to preempt the would-be monopolist by charging a price as low as p_0. Zero economic profit, resulting from price p_0, would require more than one producer. But since firms would enter the market with production capacity of Q_0 or greater, only a few firms would be needed to produce the entire quantity demanded (ΣQ_0) at the zero profit price (p_0). The maximum number of firms, $n = Q_0/\Sigma Q_0$, would be too small to guarantee that price competition led to the lowest sustainable price, p_0. **Rivalry**—competition among a few firms—makes price collusion more attractive than when many competitors share the market.

A group of firms operating in an oligopolistic industry might restrict output to Q_m in order to charge the cartel price of p_m. Entry might be deterred (although not absolutely barred) by fear of a price war and the difficulty of obtaining financing for a new firm in an oligopolistic industry. Economies of scale do not deter entry, but they may set an upper limit on the number of producers.

In contrast to monopolistic competition, wherein producers of differentiated products can be treated as monopolists in the short run, product differentiation within an oligopolistic industry does not eliminate the pricing interdependency of firms. A few producers of close substitutes consider how rivals react to price changes; a price reduction, which causes rivals to reduce their prices, can cause an oligopolist's demand curve to shift to the left. Furthermore, the typical oligopoly produces many commodities, selling goods which are joint products in production (e.g., gasoline and petrochemicals), complements in consumption (e.g., television sets and video recorders), or similar products designed to appeal to different consumers (e.g., subcompacts, family-sized and luxury automobiles). Product differentiation increases the difficulty of entry by new sellers who must produce, sell, and advertise in many markets at the same time.

Classical Duopoly Theories

The first formal theory of oligopoly was offered by the nineteenth-century French economist Augustin Cournot. Cournot began by asking what happens if a second seller enters a previously monopolized market: is it possible for a **duopoly**—an industry with two sellers—to attain a stable price-quantity outcome? If so, one could add a third seller, then a fourth, and so on, until a logical bridge was constructed between monopoly (one seller) and competition (many sellers). As we shall see, it is more difficult to predict price and quantity for a market with a *few* sellers than for a market with only one seller or for a market with many sellers.

Cournot assumed a market with two sellers of a homogeneous product. As with pure competition, homogeneous oligopoly requires that both sellers charge the same price; otherwise, only the seller offering the lower price would sell anything. The assumption of a homogeneous product makes market price (average revenue) a function of the combined output of both sellers. To simplify calculations, we will assume that market price is a linear function of total output: $p = a - b(Q_1 + Q_2)$, where Q_1 and Q_2 are the outputs of seller 1 and seller 2, respectively. We will also assume that each seller has a horizontal marginal cost curve: $MC = k$, where k is a constant.

The Cournot theory depended on what we might characterize as a myopic view of the market: each seller is aware of the market demand and the other seller's current rate of output. Each firm calculates its impact on market price by assuming that the other seller will not change its output, believing that its marginal revenue changes only when its own output changes. In Figure 12-2a, seller 1 estimates its average revenue function as $p = (a - bQ_2^*) - bQ_1$, expecting seller 2 to hold its output to Q_2^*. Since $(a - bQ_2^*)$ is treated as a constant, seller 1 calculates its marginal revenue function as:[1]

$$MR_1 = p - \frac{\Delta p}{\Delta Q_1}Q_1 = (a - bQ_2^*) - bQ_1 - bQ_1 = (a - bQ_2^*) - 2bQ_1$$

Setting $MR = MC = k$, firm 1 supplies Q_1^* units of output. The market clearing price of Q_1^*, given Q_2^*, is $p^* = a - bQ_2^* - bQ_1^*$.

At the same time firm 1 is making its output decision, firm 2 determines its output by maximizing profit, given the output it *expects* seller 1 to produce. Expecting seller 1 to produce Q_1^0, seller 2 defines its average revenue function as $p = (a - bQ_1^0) - bQ_2$, so that:

$$MR_2 = p + Q_2\frac{\Delta p}{\Delta Q_2} = (a - bQ_1^0) - 2bQ_2$$

Figure 12-2b shows firm 2 producing Q_2^0, whose market price will be p^0 if firm 1 produces the output seller 2 expects.

Equilibrium price and output occur in Cournot's duopoly model *if and only if* each seller's output corresponded to what its rival expected, that is, if $Q_1^* = Q_1^0$ and $Q_2^0 = Q_2^*$, so that $p^0 = p^*$. There is no problem in the Cournot model *if* the market starts in equilibrium: each firm maintains its rate of output (ratifying the other's expectation) until either demand or cost conditions changed. However, if the duopoly were not in equilibrium, there are contradictions in the Cournot description of how equilibrium would be achieved.

Let us return to the premise that the market is initially a monopoly one, so that $Q_2^* = 0$ in Figure 12-2a. Acting as a monopolist, seller 1 sets

---

[1] Given $\partial p/\partial Q_1 = \partial p/\partial Q_2 = -b$, each marginal revenue function is estimated by substituting $(a - [bQ_1 - bQ_2])$ for p and $-b$ for $\partial p/\partial Q_i$, $i = 1, 2$.

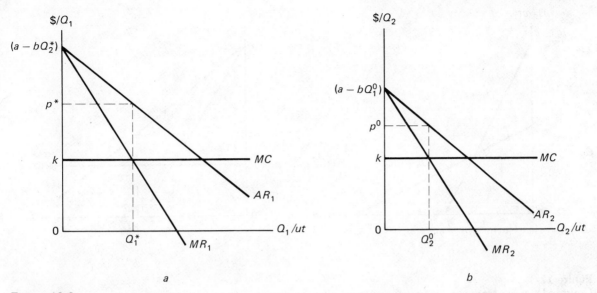

Figure 12-2
Cournot's Duopoly Model of Independent Pricing: Output and Expected Price of (*a*) Seller 1 (the Former Monopolist) and (*b*) Seller 2 (the Market Entrant).

output where $MR_1 = MC$, that is, where $a - 2bQ_1 = k$, so that $Q_1 = (a - k)/2b$ and $p = a - b[(a - k)/2b] = \frac{1}{2}a + k$. Seller 2 will enter the market only if total revenue for firm 1 exceeds its total cost. Since $VC_1 = kQ_1 = (1/2b)(ak - k^2)$ and $TR_1 = (\frac{1}{2}a + k)[(a - k)/2b] = (1/2b)(a^2/2 + ak/2 - k^2)$, seller 2 is predicted to enter only if $FC_1 \leq (1/4b)(a^2 - ak)$.[2]

Cournot simplified the analysis by assuming zero fixed costs for both sellers; at any price above marginal cost, the second seller would have an incentive to enter the market. But entry by a second seller contradicts the expectations of the former monopolist. Figure 12-2 is constructed so that $p^0 < p^*$: expecting seller 1 to maintain monopoly output at $Q_1 = (a - k)/2b$, seller 2 would define its marginal revenue function as $MR_2 = (\frac{1}{2}a + k) - 2bQ_2$, setting output so that $MR = MC$, or $(\frac{1}{2}a + k) - 2bQ_2 = k$, yielding $2bQ_2 = \frac{1}{2}a$, or $Q_2 = a/4b$. When the second seller's output is added to that of the erstwhile monopolist, market price must fall. The first seller's expectation of monopoly price has been contradicted and its output must be adjusted accordingly.

---

[2] The result is obtained as follows. Economic profit for seller 1 means $\pi = pQ_1 - (VC + FC)_1 \geq 0$, or $pQ_1 - VC_1 \geq FC_1$. Substituting the monopoly values for Q_1 and p, we have $pQ_1 = (\frac{1}{2}a + k)[(a - k)/2b] = a^2/4b - ak/4b + ak/2b - k^2/2b = (a^2 + ak - 2k^2)/4b$. $VC_1 = kQ_1 = (1/2b)(a - k)k = (2ak - 2k^2)/4b$. It follows that $pQ_1 - VC_1 \geq FC_1$ only if $FC_1 \leq (a^2 - ak)/4b$.

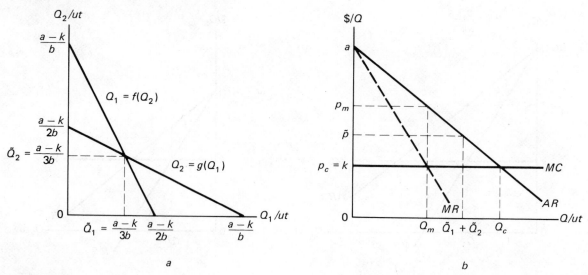

Figure 12-3
Cournot Duopoly Model. *a*, Duopoly reaction function and Cournot "solution"; *b*, monopoly, competition, and duopoly output, and prices.

In the Cournot model, the adjustment of output to unexpected changes in market demand (due to the other seller's not producing its expected output) defines the **reaction function** of each seller. The reaction function of seller 1 is derived from its $MR_1 = MC$ profit maximization rule, solving for Q_1 in terms of Q_2: $(a - bQ_2) - 2bQ_1 = k$ implies $Q_1 = (1/2b)(a - k - bQ_2)$. When $Q_2 = 0$, $Q_1 = (1/2b)(a - k)$, the monopoly output. However, market entry causes the first seller to reduce output by one-half unit for each unit of output produced by seller 2: $\Delta Q_1/\Delta Q_2 = (1/2b)(-b) = -1/2$.

When the first seller changes its output, the second seller will be given a new profit-maximizing rate of output, according to its reaction function, derived by solving its $MR_2 = MC$ output rule for Q_2: $(a - bQ_1) - 2bQ_2 = k$ implies $Q_2 = (1/2b)(a - k - bQ_1)$. Since $\Delta Q_2/\Delta Q_1 = (1/2b)(-b) = -1/2$, the second seller will increase its output by one-half unit for each one-unit decrease in the output of seller 1.

This process of each seller adopting its rate of output to the other's change in output, total output, and the resulting price is supposed to converge on a stable equilibrium.[3] The graphical solution of the Cournot duopoly is presented in Figure 12-3*a*.

---

[3] Given $Q_1 = (1/2b)(a - k - bQ_2)$ and $Q_2 = (1/2b)(a - k - bQ_1)$, we have:

$$2Q_1 + Q_2 = \frac{a - k}{b} \qquad \therefore \tfrac{3}{2}Q_1 = \frac{a - k}{2b}$$

$$\tfrac{1}{2}Q_1 + Q_2 = \frac{a - k}{2b} \qquad Q_1 = Q_2 = \frac{a - k}{3b}$$

The equal marginal cost and homogeneous product (equal price) assumptions mean that the equilibrium rate of output would be the same for each duopolist. Further, as Figure 12-3*b* illustrates, the Cournot duopoly price, $\tilde{p}$, is less than the monopoly price but greater than the marginal cost (competitive) price.[4] As long as each seller faithfully adjusts its rate of output to the other's output change, while faithfully believing that no further output adjustments will be necessary, the Cournot equilibrium will eventually emerge. This adjustment process led American economist William Fellner to comment:

> It was Augustin Cournot's great achievement to have discovered the distinctive feature of the oligopoly problem. He also showed in 1838 that on certain assumptions a determinate equilibrium solution is obtained for the duopoly problem and that this solution could be extended from duopoly to oligopoly. It seems to us that the determinateness of Cournot's solution is the *least* significant feature of his analysis. In fact, it may be argued that truly significant insights arise in connection with legitimate criticisms of the Cournot solution. But this is another way of saying that we have to start by considering how the determinate solution is obtained. A realistic approach to oligopoly problems cannot be based on Cournot's theory. Yet now, after more than a century, it is still difficult to see what is involved in an oligopoly theory without showing how the theory is related to Cournot's basic construction.[5]

Attempting to improve on Cournot's behavioral assumptions, German economist Heinrich von Stackelberg developed a variation of the

---

[4] If seller 1 and seller 2 colluded, the monopoly price would require limiting output to where industry marginal revenue equals (common) marginal cost. $MR = MC$ implies $a - 2bQ = k$, or $Q = (a - k)/2b = Q_1 + Q_2$, and:

$$p_m = a - b\left(\frac{a - k}{2b}\right) = \frac{a + k}{2}$$

If output (and hence profit) were divided equally between the two firms, $Q_1 = Q_2 = (a - k)/4b$. Inserting this output into either firm's reaction function shows that the monopoly outcome is not a Cournot equilibrium:

$$Q_i = \frac{1}{2b}(a - k - bQ_j) = \frac{1}{2b}\left(a - k - b\frac{a - k}{4b}\right) = \frac{3(a - k)}{8b} > \frac{a - k}{4b}$$

If one seller produces its output under the monopoly solution, the other seller produces more than its cartel quota, lowering price below the monopoly price.

Under the Cournot equilibrium, the duopoly price, $\tilde{p}$, is determined by substituting total industry output into the average revenue function for the industry:

$$\tilde{p} = a - b\left(\frac{2a - 2k}{3b}\right) = \frac{2k + a}{3}$$

which is less than p_m and greater than marginal cost as long as $a > k$, which must be true if either seller is to cover variable cost.

[5] William J. Fellner, *Competition among the Few*, rev. ed. (Fairfield, New Jersey: Augustus M. Kelley, 1965), p. 56.

duopoly model based on **price leadership**. One seller, the price leader, sets its output only after correctly anticipating the follower's reaction. The follower's belief in the stability of the leader's output is reinforced by the latter's perfect foresight.

In Figure 12-4a, seller 2 behaves like a Cournot duopolist, assuming that the observed output of seller 1 will not change. Figure 12-4a is a replica of Figure 12-2a: one seller sets its output, assuming that only its output will affect price. Figure 12-4b shows seller 1, the leader, stabilizing the behavior of the follower by pricing its optimal output in anticipation of the other's response. The leader's foresight generates a *mutatis mutandis* marginal revenue function which takes into account predictable adjustments in output resulting from the follower's *ceteris paribus* logic. Aware of how its output affects the marginal revenue function of seller 2, seller 1 produces Q_1^* units of output per period in Figure 12-4b. When the follower responds by producing its predicted Q_2^*, a market price of p^* results.

Under our assumptions of equal and constant marginal costs for both producers of a homogeneous product and a linear (market) demand, the Cournot solution results when either seller acts as the price leader.[6] If both act as followers, the Stackelberg model is indistinguishable from the Cournot model. As soon as the assumption of identical costs is abandoned, the symmetry of the outcomes breaks down, and each firm could make higher profits by acting as the leader than as the follower. The weakness of the Stackelberg model is the asymmetric behavior of the duopolists:

> There is another peculiarity in the leader-follower type of model, a convenient asymmetry. The leader is a very clever fellow, but the follower is an extremely naive and blind person. One knows exactly, correctly, how his rival behaves, while the other makes the most patently false and silly assumption about his rival. Unless and until solid empirical evidence is marshalled to prove the descriptive accuracy of such a model, it must be regarded as a trivial ad hoc variation on the Cournot theme.[7]

---

[6] The follower sets output according to the $MR_2 = MC$ rule, given the leader's output, Q_1: $MR_2 = (a - bQ_1) - 2bQ_2 = k$ implies $Q_2 = (1/2b)(a - k - bQ_1)$. The leader generates its *mutatis mutandis* marginal revenue curve by substituting the follower's reaction function for Q_2:

$$MR_1 = a - bQ_2 - 2bQ_1 = a - b\left[\frac{1}{2b}\left(a - k - bQ_1\right)\right] - 2bQ_1 = \frac{a + k}{2} - \frac{3b}{2}Q_1$$

$MR_1 = MC$ means $(a + k)/2 - (3b/2)Q_1 = k$, or $(3b/2)Q_1 = (a - k)/2$, so that $Q_1 = (a - k)/3b$. Hence,

$$Q_2 = \frac{1}{2b}\left(a - k - b\frac{a - k}{3b}\right) = \frac{a - k}{3b} \quad \text{and} \quad p^* = a - b\frac{2(a - k)}{3b} = \frac{a + 2k}{3}$$

[7] James W. Friedman, "Cournot, Bowley, Stackelberg and Fellner, and the Evolution of the Reaction Function," in Bela Balassa and Richard Nelson, eds., *Economic Progress, Private Values and Public Policy: Essays in Honor of William Fellner* (Amsterdam and New York: North Holland Press, 1977), p. 115.

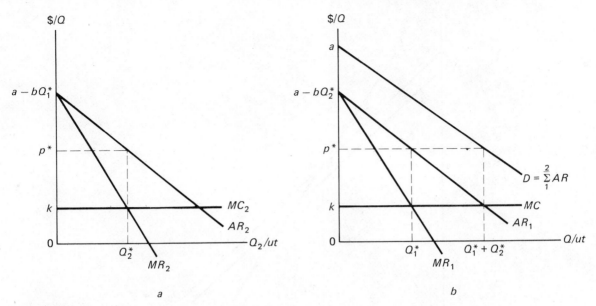

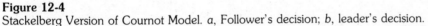

Figure 12-4
Stackelberg Version of Cournot Model. *a*, Follower's decision; *b*, leader's decision.

The Oligopoly Pricing Problem

What is lurking in the classical models of oligopoly is the uncomfortable recognition that *rivalry* is much more complex than either competition or monopoly. In chapters ten and eleven, the theory of monopoly was applied to two distinct forms of market organization. In one case, the firm and the industry are identical; the price maker (sometimes called the "price searcher") need only anticipate the reaction of consumers to a price change in setting industry output. In the other case, atomistic producers of differentiated products, narrowly protected by trademarks, brand registration, or patent laws only consider their own price and output because the large number of products and the ease of market entry make competition an irresistible force. The monopolistic competitor might as well maximize its profit in the short run if market entry will inevitably increase the number of sellers whenever positive economic profits are possible.

The predictable response of rivals to an oligopoly firm's own price can cause an oligopolist's demand curve to shift. In Figure 12-5, a seller reduces the price of its product from p_0 to p_1, hoping to increase revenue from p_0Q_0 to p_1Q_1. Demand curve D_0 is constructed under the usual *ceteris paribus* assumptions: constant consumer income and tastes, constant prices of substitute and complementary goods. By now it should be clear that these *ceteris paribus* conditions mean that consumer income, tastes, prices of complements, and prices of substitutes are as-

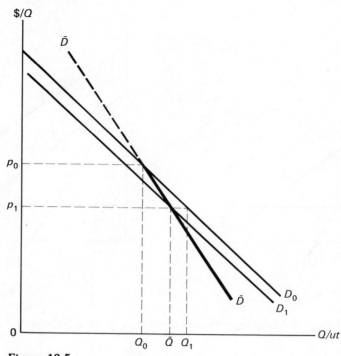

Figure 12-5
Ceteris Paribus and *Mutatis Mutandis* Demand Curves under Oligopoly

sumed to be independent of the price the firm charges for its product. All of the models of seller behavior up to this point have assumed that firms could change output and price without worrying about *causing* their own demand curves to shift. Indeed, this assumption characterized the Cournot and Stackelberg models of duopoly. What we call the *oligopoly pricing problem* stems from the fact that a seller's own experience under oligopoly market conditions contradicts this assumption that the price and output of rivals are independent of the price they set.

In Figure 12-5, we imagine that $Q_1 - \tilde{Q}$ of the increased quantity demanded because of the price decrease from p_0 to p_1 occurs at the expense of rivals. If those other firms reduce their prices to recapture their lost sales, the price of substitute goods for this seller's product will fall, causing a leftward shift in demand from D_0 to D_1, and reducing the actual increase in quantity demanded to $\tilde{Q} - Q_0$.

The demand curve labeled $\tilde{D}$ in Figure 12-5 is the *mutatis mutandis* demand curve, generated by a specific expectation about how rivals will react to price changes. Prior to cutting price from p_0 to p_1, the seller expects rivals to cut their prices enough to reduce quantity sold from Q_1 to $\tilde{Q}$ at price p_1. When, as in Figure 12-5, rivals are assumed to cut their prices only enough to regain their lost business, the seller can accomplish a modest reduction in its relative price, gaining all additional sales for the industry. If the seller expected rivals to match price cuts, relative prices would remain constant for different nominal prices and the *mutatis mutandis* demand curve would be less elastic than $\hat{D}$ in Figure 12-5.[8] Even worse, rivals might be expected to punish price cutting by retaliating with a larger percentage decrease. Such a prospect would tend to deter price cuts except in times of economic distress, since the ensuing price war could cause losses for all sellers.

The *mutatis mutandis* demand curve in Figure 12-5 is shown as a dashed line for prices greater than p_0 because a seller is likely to be less confident that rivals will match its price increases, particularly when other firms are known to have excess capacity. A price increase by this firm would shift the demand curves for rivals' products to the right; those rivals may prefer to have the extra business at their prevailing prices rather than join in the price gouging. Then again, they might follow along; but then the laws against pricing conspiracies come into play.

The reaction of rivals to a price change cannot always be predicted; this is the essence of the oligopoly pricing problem. Will firms react to a price decrease by matching it, so that each firm sells more output while market shares remain relatively constant? Or will rivals attempt to deter future price cuts by starting a punitive price war? Or will the firm's timing be just right, so that a cost-saving technological development, occurring when other firms are operating at or near capacity, allows the price cutter to pick up a substantial increase in market share? Similar questions must be asked prior to a price increase. Under what conditions will a price increase be matched by rivals, and when will other sellers be content to keep their prices constant and reap the larger market shares which a unilateral price increase bestows upon them? Further, if a price increase were matched by rivals, would coincidental price changes result in prosecution for price fixing? If the firm were prosecuted, would its officers be able to defend themselves?

---

[8] Using calculus, the percentage change in an oligopoly seller's revenue due to a 1 percent change in its own price is:

$$\frac{dR_i/R_i}{dp_i/p_i} = \frac{1}{Q_i} \cdot \frac{d(p_iQ_i)}{dp_i} = \frac{1}{Q_i}\left[Q_i + p_i\frac{\partial Q_i}{\partial p_i} + p_i\left(\sum_{j=1}^{n} \frac{\partial Q_i}{\partial p_j} \cdot \frac{dp_j}{dp_i}\right)\right]$$

$$= \frac{Q_i}{Q_i}\left[1 + \frac{\partial Q_i/Q_i}{\partial p_i/p_i} + \left(\sum_{j=1}^{n} \frac{\partial Q_i/Q_i}{\partial p_j/p_j} \cdot \frac{dp_j/p_j}{dp_i/p_i}\right)\right]$$

$$= 1 + \eta_{ii} + \sum_{j=1}^{n} \eta_{ij}\theta_{ji}$$

where $\theta_{ji} = (dp_j/p_j)/(dp_i/p_i)$. Under perfect competition, monopoly, and monopolistic competition, the reaction of other sellers to a price change is assumed to be zero ($\theta_{ij} = 0$), so that cross elasticity of demand between products does not enter into the firm's output-price decision.

We almost expect this string of questions to be followed by an announcer saying, "Tune in tomorrow...," over the theme music of a television soap opera. Just when Fay is trying to determine whether Alice knows about her affair with Gerald, and Alice is trying to decide whether Fay knows that she knows, the oligopoly pricing problem involves so much second guessing that the plot becomes mired in conjecture. And just as some people dislike soap operas for not being "high drama," some economists dislike oligopoly models for not being "elegant theory." Furthermore, just as a viewer can follow the plot of a soap opera only by watching the program loyally, an observer can apply economic analysis to large corporations only by keeping informed with the latest data from the relevant industry. This type of research does not appeal to all theorists, who like simple predictions which apply to many different firms in differing industries.

The Kinked Demand Model

During the 1930s Harvard economist Paul Sweezy offered the following explanation for the apparent price rigidity in industries with only a few sellers:

> The most important consideration in this connection seems to me the obvious fact that rivals react differently according to whether a price change is upward or downward. If producer A raises his price, his rival producer B will acquire new customers. If, on the other hand, A lowers his price, B will lose customers. Ordinarily the reaction to a gain in business is a pleasurable feeling calling for no particular action; the reaction to a loss in business, however, is likely to be some alarm, accompanied by measures to recoup the loss. If the cause of the loss is obviously a rival's price cut, the natural retaliation is a similar cut. From the point of view of any particular producer, this means simply that if he raises his price he must expect to lose business to his rivals (his demand curve tends to be elastic going up), while if he lowers his price he has no reason to believe he will succeed in taking business away from his rivals (his demand curve tends to be inelastic going down).[9]

Sweezy's prediction can be developed formally by making the following assumptions:

1. Each firm in an oligopolistic industry will anticipate the reaction of rivals *before* changing price or quantity.

---

[9] Paul Sweezy, "Demand Conditions under Oligopoly," *Journal of Political Economy* (June 1939), pp. 568–573. Credit for proposing the kinked demand model is also shared by R. L. Hall and C. J. Hitch, "Price Theory and Business Behavior," *Oxford Economic Papers* 2 (1939), 12–45.

2. Firms do not collude in their output and price decisions.
3. Each firm attempts to maximize short-run profit by expanding output whenever marginal revenue exceeds marginal cost and by reducing output whenever (or not producing so much output that) marginal cost exceeds marginal revenue.

The logical consequence of these assumptions is the **kinked demand curve** model of oligopolistic price rigidity, presented in Figure 12-6. We assume that Acme Products is producing Q_0 widgets per month, charging a market clearing price of p_0. Two demand curves intersect at point (p_0, Q_0): demand curve D_0 is the *ceteris paribus* demand curve, constructed under the assumption of constant prices for substitute goods; demand curve D_1 is a *mutatis mutandis* demand curve, constructed under the assumption that rivals match price changes so that relative prices of widgets remain constant.

Because a change of Acme's price would constitute a relative price change along the *ceteris paribus* demand curve, D_0, this demand curve is more elastic at each rate of output than demand curve D_1, the *mutatis*

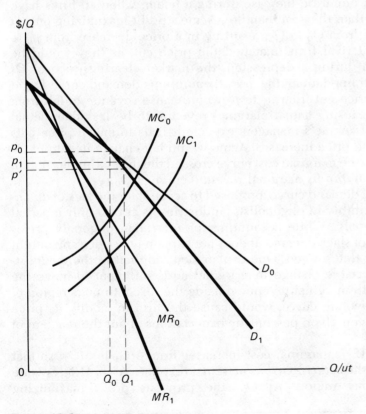

Figure 12-6
The Kinked Demand Curve Model of Oligopolistic Pricing

mutandis demand curve with constant relative prices. Therefore, the marginal revenue curve associated with the *ceteris paribus* assumption, namely MR_0, reflects a greater responsiveness of quantity demanded to a (unilateral) price change than does MR_1, associated with the *mutatis mutandis* demand curve, D_1. An output increase would mean a smaller revenue gain under demand curve D_1 (MR_1 has a steeper slope than MR_0). An output decrease would mean a smaller revenue loss if Acme's rivals matched its price increase than if that price increase were unilateral.

The kinked demand model predicts the worst alternative for price increases and for price decreases.[10] Demand will tend to be *relatively inelastic* for output expansions, since price cuts (necessary to sell more output) are expected to be matched by rivals. For output decreases (associated with price increases), demand is more price elastic.

Sweezy was writing during the Great Depression, a period of falling production costs depicted as the downward shift from MC_0 to MC_1 in Figure 12-6. If management believed that a price reduction would *not* be matched (as might be the case during a boom, when all firms have more business than they can handle), Acme's profit-maximizing output would increase from Q_0 to Q_1, resulting in a price decrease from p_0 to p_1. However, if rival firms matched the price cut, as they would be expected to do during a depression, the market clearing price of Q_1 would be determined along the *mutatis mutandis* demand curve D_1, at $p' < p_1$. The price cut from p_1 to p' would cause revenue to fall from $p_1 Q_1$ to $p' Q_1$, causing actual marginal revenue to be less than actual marginal cost. If Acme's managers expected rivals to match price cuts and not to match price increases, Acme would not change its output (or price) as long as the marginal cost curve crossed the discontinuous region of the *mutatis mutandis* marginal revenue curve at Q_0.

The kinked demand curve, proposed to account for the lack of *downward* price flexibility in oligopolistic industries, is at best only a partial model of oligopoly. While accounting for *inertia* in oligopoly prices during periods of slack demand, it does not explain how price and output were originally determined. One explanation, implicit in the model itself, is that a sizable change in marginal cost, sufficient to move the intersection with marginal revenue outside the discontinuous region of the marginal revenue curve, would cause the firm to modify its price and quantity, even given pessimistic expectations about the reaction of rivals.

In Figure 12-7, marginal cost increases from MC_1 to MC_2, so that MC_2 intersects the *ceteris paribus* marginal revenue curve, MR_0, outside its discontinuous region. At Q_0, the previous profit maximizing

---

[10] In terms of the calculus formula in footnote 8, the model assumes that $\theta_{ji} = 1$ if $dp_i < 0$ and that $\theta_{ji} = 0$ for $dp_i > 0$.

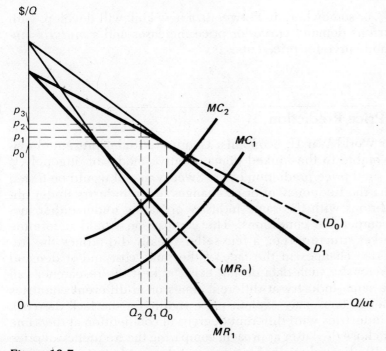

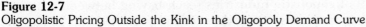

Figure 12-7
Oligopolistic Pricing Outside the Kink in the Oligopoly Demand Curve

rate of widget production, marginal cost now exceeds marginal revenue. The firm would increase profit or cut losses by reducing output to Q_1 and raising price to p_1. According to the assumptions underlying *ceteris paribus* demand curve D_0, Acme's management expects rivals to maintain their prices, as would be the case if only Acme experienced increased marginal cost. But if all widget producers experienced similar marginal cost increases, the *ceteris paribus* logic underlying demand curve D_0 would be contradicted. Each seller's unilateral price increase would represent a price increase for a substitute for its rivals' products. If prices of substitute goods increase in response to an increase in one firm's price, the *ceteris paribus* demand curve, D_0, is replaced by the *mutatis mutandis* demand curve D_1. In Figure 12-7, the market clearing price of O_1 Acme widgets is p_2 (which exceeds p_1).

The indeterminacy of the kinked demand curve model recurs in the inferences sellers draw from the unexpected simultaneous increases in all their prices. Would Acme's executives be emboldened enough to reduce output to Q_2, where the *mutatis mutandis* marginal revenue curve, MR_1, intersects the higher marginal cost curve? If so, would all other sellers reduce their output, allowing the market clearing price to reach p_3? Regardless of where the new price and quantity settle (at p_2,

Q_1, at p_3, Q_2, or somewhere in between), a new kink will develop, with a *ceteris paribus* demand curve for price increases and a *mutatis mutandis* demand curve for price cuts.

APPLICATION
Empirical Tests of the Rigid Price Prediction

Shortly after World War II, economist George J. Stigler presented evidence unfavorable to the kinked demand curve model of oligopoly.[11] Ideally, the rigid price prediction of the Sweezy model would be tested by comparing the frequency of price changes for an industry under oligopoly conditions with the same industry operating under either monopoly or competitive conditions. The comparison would determine whether market structure (i.e., a *few* sellers) really did reduce the frequency of price changes in the face of the same cost and/or demand changes. Obviously, such data do not exist; at best the researcher can compare the same industry at different times or in different countries (where "other factors" may explain price rigidity or the lack thereof), or different industries with different degrees of competition at the same time. Stigler chose the latter approach, comparing the frequency of price changes for 19 oligopolistic industries (each having between 2 and 12 firms) and two monopolies, using data for the years 1929 to 1939—the period during which Sweezy claimed to have observed price rigidity under oligopolistic market conditions.

Stigler concluded (1) that prices in his sample of monopoly industries were more rigid than those in the oligopoly industries, (2) that industries with more than two firms changed prices more frequently than duopolies, and (3) that price leadership tended to be associated with less frequent price changes. He then argued that since no known theory predicted rigid prices under monopoly, the frequency of price changes under oligopoly must not be abnormally low. Hence, there was no empirical support for the rigid price prediction: "Is this adverse conclusion really surprising? The kink is a barrier to changes in prices that will increase profits, and business is a collection of devices for circumventing barriers to profits. That this barrier should thwart businessmen—especially when it is wholly of their own fabrication—is unbelievable."[12]

In 1972 economist Gardiner C. Means, an economic consultant and an early advocate of the rigid price hypothesis, offered his own empirical support in favor of his theory of **administered prices**:

[11] George J. Stigler, "The Kinky Demand Curve and Rigid Prices," *Journal of Political Economy* (October 1947), pp. 432–447.
[12] Ibid., p. 447.

Basically, the administered-price thesis holds that a large body of industrial prices do not behave in the fashion that classical theory would lead one to expect. It was first developed in 1934–35 to apply to the cyclical behavior of industrial prices. It specifically held that in business recessions administered prices showed a tendency not to fall as much as market prices while the recession fall in demand worked itself through a fall in sales, production and employment. Similarly, since administered prices tended not to fall as much in a recession, they tended not to rise as much in recovery while rising demand worked itself out primarily in a rising volume of sales, production and employment.[13]

There is a subtle distinction between the administered price hypothesis and the kinked demand curve explanation of rigid prices. The kinked demand curve predicts inertia in both output and prices during periods of slack demand, due to awareness of rivalry and the absence of collusion; the administered price hypothesis suggests an artificial control over oligopoly prices which allows output to contract without a fall in price. Nevertheless, Means's challenge of Stigler's refutation of the rigid price prediction followed a report by Stigler and James K. Kindahl which concluded that the administered price hypothesis could not be supported by data on price changes over the business cycles of the late 1950s and early 1960s.[14]

Using the data employed in the Stigler-Kindahl study, Means showed that 69 percent of the price changes in concentrated industries were consistent with the administered price hypothesis and therefore contradicted the neoclassical theory of price adjustment for competitive markets. He went on to demonstrate that when the prediction of *rigid* prices was replaced with the prediction that the magnitude of price changes would be smaller for oligopolistic than for competitive industries, evidence in favor of the administered price hypothesis was even stronger:

> In the two contractions, the eighteen indexes which showed no tendency either way dropped an average of 2.0 percent compared with a 6.7 percent average drop for the thirteen market-dominated indexes in the NB sample. In the two recoveries, the eighteen neutral indexes showed an average *drop* of .8 percent compared with a 3.5 percent average rise for the thirteen market-dominated indexes. Thus, while the new data give strong support for the truncated thesis, they give even greater support for the full administered-price thesis.

---

[13] Gardiner C. Means, "The Administered Price Thesis Reconfirmed," *American Economic Review* (June 1972), pp. 292–293.

[14] George J. Stigler and James K. Kindahl, *The Behavior of Industrial Prices* (New York: National Bureau of Economic Research, 1970).

Only to a nonsignificant extent did the administration-dominated prices fail to conform to the administered-price thesis.[15]

If the requirement of price rigidity is replaced with that of relatively small price changes for oligopolistic compared with competitive industries, Means's evidence would seem to support rejecting the null hypothesis that oligopoly prices are not rigid. When Stigler tested the rigid price prediction, the burden of proof rested on the hypothesis he was trying to refute; when Means tested a similar prediction, the burden of proof rested on the hypothesis he was trying to support. From this point of view, the rigid price prediction has not so much been disproved as defamed.

Alternatives to the Kinked Demand Curve Model

Even if the rigid price prediction were contradicted by empirical evidence—a proposition which is subject to debate—the kinked demand model can serve a heuristic purpose as a unifying point of reference for the diverse modern approaches to oligopoly theory. The kinked demand curve prediction of rigid price and quantity is the logical consequence of assuming that sellers (1) take the anticipated response of rivals into account when setting price and output, (2) do not collude, and (3) try to maximize short-run economic profit. If evidence fails to support the rigid price prediction, it is likely that one of the crucial assumptions of the Sweezy model is wrong.

The *classical* approach to oligopoly is associated, as we saw, with attempts to define stable equilibrium price-quantity patterns in markets with a few sellers. These models essentially ignored the impact of rivalry on pricing and output decisions, resulting in implausible behavior by duopolists. These classical models, which ignored rivalry, ironically highlight the influence or rivalry in oligopolistic pricing. Modern variants of the classic theme concern the influence of market entry or potential entry on the divergence between oligopoly prices and minimum long-run average cost.

The *neoclassical* approach focuses on the incentive of oligopoly sellers to collude in their price-output decisions. Price leadership and other methods may be used to set cartel-like prices, which then erode as individual sellers cheat on the agreement. In this context, government plays an ironic role; it is both an opponent of collusion (through antitrust prosecution) and an abettor of collusion (through pro-monopoly regulation).

The *managerialist* approach argues that the complex behavior of giant corporations cannot be characterized by simplistic models of profit

---

[15] Means, "Administered Price Thesis Reconfirmed," p. 296.

maximization. On the one hand, John Kenneth Galbraith points to the control the large corporation is able to exercise over its environment, manipulating markets, consumers, and governments almost at will. On the other hand, Herbert Simon and William Baumol emphasize the inherent complexity of the oligopolistic environment, arguing that corporate executives seek to achieve satisfactory resolution of problems, because maximizing profit or any other objective may be impossibly complicated.

APPLICATION
Potential Entry and Maximum Oligopoly Prices

A modern version of the Stackelberg price-leadership model is the dominant-firm, residual-monopoly model. In Figure 12-8, we imagine an industry containing one large producer of a homogeneous product (e.g., aluminum, steel, or copper) whose marginal cost curve, MC_l, reflects a significant share of total industry production capacity. The industry also contains a number of smaller producers, whose collective productive capacity gives rise to their aggregate supply curve, $\sum MC_f$. The cost curves for a typical follower, depicted in Figure 12-8b, indicate a shutdown price of p_{min}, identified by the minimum point on the firm's average variable cost curve. The intersection of the collective marginal

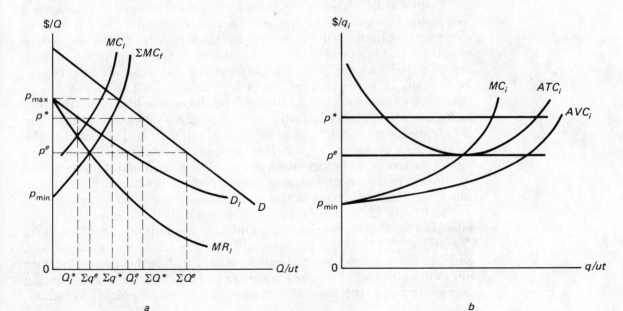

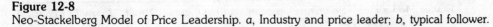

Figure 12-8
Neo-Stackelberg Model of Price Leadership. *a,* Industry and price leader; *b,* typical follower.

cost curve for followers, $\sum MC_f$, and the market demand curve, D, indicates that if $p \geqq p_{max}$, small firms would produce the total quantity demanded. Hence, the price leader could set a price below p_{max}, since only for $p \leqq p_{max}$ would followers produce less than the total quantity demanded, leaving part of the market for the leader.

By anticipating the amount followers would produce, the price leader defines its residual demand curve, D_l, subtracting the quantity produced by followers from the quantity demanded by consumers at each price. The price intercept of the residual demand curve is p_{max}, where followers produce total quantity demanded (at prices greater than p_{max}, a surplus would exist). The residual demand curve merges with the market demand curve at p_{min}, where the typical follower would cease production entirely.

In Figure 12-8a, the leader's residual marginal revenue curve (MR_l) intersects its marginal cost curve (MC_l) at Q_l^*. The price leader sets price p^*, which generates $\sum q^*$ output from followers, so that total output is $\sum Q^* = Q_l^* + \sum q^*$. Note that Figure 12-8b is constructed so that $p^* > \min(ATC_i)$; the leader's short-run profit-maximizing price would encourage market entry by small firms. With unrestricted entry, the price leader has the dubious choice of setting the entry-preventing price of p^e and producing $Q_l^e = \sum Q^e - \sum q^e$ or earning short-run profits and watching market entry erode the optimal price toward the long-run competitive equilibrium, p^e.

Critics of this passive price-leadership model argue that assuming free entry by small firms ignores **internal economies**, which tend to characterize oligopoly in the first place. It is not hard to reach competitive results by making competitive assumptions. A more sophisticated analysis of potential entry and oligopoly pricing was presented by Franco Modigliani in his review of works by Paolo Sylos-Labini and Joe S. Bain.[16] A *new* (that is, an *additional*) producer would contemplate entering an oligopolistic industry only if positive economic profit were anticipated after output and price in that industry had adjusted to the newcomer's presence. Figure 12-9 presents the simpler version of the model, wherein a homogeneous commodity is assumed. Later we will consider whether complications introduced by product differentiation cause significant changes in the results demonstrated in Figure 12-9.

In Figure 12-9a, which reprises Figure 12-1b, the minimum efficient rate of output, Q_0, represents a significant proportion of total quantity demanded, $\sum Q_0$, when price equals minimum long-run average cost, i.e., when $p = p_0$. A potential entrant would realize that producing with minimum efficient plant size (or greater capacity) would increase output and lower price. It follows that price p_0 would deter potential entrants,

---

[16] Franco Modigliani, "New Developments on the Oligopoly Front," *Journal of Political Economy* (June 1958), pp. 215–232.

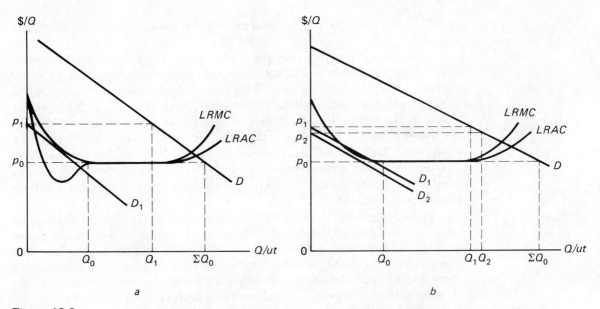

Figure 12-9
Potential Entry, Oligopoly Price, and Economies of Scale. *a*, Entry-preventing price leaves room for less than one optimally sized plant; *b*, entry-preventing price identified by tangency of residual demand to *LRAC*.

just as the long-run equilibrium price discourages entry under perfect competition. However, while p_0 is the lowest sustainable price, it is not necessarily the maximum sustainable price under oligopoly. Under perfect competition, insignificant size by each producer implies entry whenever established firms are earning a positive economic profit. Under oligopoly, minimum efficient size resulting from internal economies implies that price can exceed minimum long-run average cost without the number of producers increasing. In Figure 12-9, entry is deterred by the prospect of economic losses following output adjustment to the greater number of firms. Ironically, to the extent that potential entrants can have different assumptions about price reactions to their productions, the issue of rivalry cannot be completely ignored, even in a model designed to ignore it!

One resolution of this dilemma is to model the consequences of a fairly optimistic assumption about the price reaction to the entry of an additional seller, since more pessimistic assumptions would tend to lead to higher entry-preventing prices. So, believe it or not, we are looking for the *minimum* maximum sustainable price: the greatest difference by which the price of a homogeneous product sold in an oligopoly market could exceed the minimum long-run average cost. (See why economists yearn for the serenity of perfect competition and pure monopoly?) If a potential entrant expected established firms to merely cut price to accommodate the output of the new seller (obviously an optimistic attitude), entry would still be deterred by the prospect of total output in excess of $\sum Q_0$.

In Figure 12-9a, its assumption of constant output and passive price-cutting by established firms causes the potential entrant to view all potential sales below the prevailing price as its residual demand curve. If price were p_1 and total sales were Q_1, such that $Q_1 > \sum Q_0 - Q_0$, entry by an optimally sized firm would cause price to fall below p_0, resulting in losses by the new producer and established firms. Furthermore, note that the residual demand curve, identified by line $p_1 D_1$ in Figure 12-9a, lies everywhere below the declining portion of the firm's long-run average cost curve, which also discourages entry by a suboptimally sized producer.[17]

In Figure 12-9b, the residual demand curve $p_1 D_1$ passes below point (p_0, Q_0), indicating that increasing market output by Q_0 would cause price to fall below p_0, *ceteris paribus*. However, by operating a less than optimally sized plant, a new firm might expect to survive the passive response of established firms with greater than normal profits. Under these conditions, p_1 would *not* be an entry-preventing price. To find the entry prevention price, the intercept of the residual demand curve is reduced along the price axis, the intercept of each new residual demand curve being the price charged by established firms. Residual demand curve $p_2 D_2$ lies everywhere below the long-run average cost curve of a representative firm: if established firms set price p_2, entry could be prevented. Note the similarity between the zero profit equilibrium under monopolistic competition and the entry prevention price under the assumption of passive price cutting in a **homogeneous oligopoly**. In both models, the solution involves the tangency between the firm's negatively sloped demand curve and long-run average cost curve.

Despite the similarity of outcomes, the issue explored in Figure 12-9 is different from long-run equilibrium under monopolistic competition. First, the entry-preventing model assumes a homogeneous commodity, so that all sellers charge the same price, whereas monopolistic competition, by definition, presupposes product variety. Second, under differentiated competition, market equilibrium implies normal profits for all firms, new and old alike; under the assumptions in Figure 12-9, the prospect of zero economic profit deters entry, even if economic profit would remain above zero for established firms. What is similar about the two models is the assumption of passive price cutting in the face of market entry. The moral of Figure 12-9 is that if one makes the reasonable assumption that potential oligopoly sellers anticipate their own impact on the common price charged by all firms, one can predict

---

[17] If the maximum size of the market is given by $S = \sum Q_0/Q_0$, then $Q_1 \simeq \sum Q_0 - Q_0 = \sum Q_0(1 - Q_0/\sum Q_0) = \sum Q_0(1 - 1/S)$. Since $LRMC = LRAC = p_0$ at Q_0, and denoting the elasticity of demand as η, then $p_1 \simeq p_0(1 + 1/S \times \eta)$.

that oligopoly price, *at best*, will resemble the price charged under monopolistic competition rather than under pure competition.

If the simplifying assumption of homogeneous oligopoly is dropped for the more plausible hypothesis that different consumers prefer the product of one seller over another, the impact of potential entry on the oligopolistic price structure becomes more complex, but the process outlined above remains essentially the same. With oligopoly sellers facing negatively sloped demand curves for differentiated products, the "residual demand" confronting potential entrants would be *fragmented* among the demand curves served by different sellers. If the commodity (e.g., automobiles, appliances, computers) can be differentiated by changing quality and the mix of product characteristics, there may be inadequate "room" for another producer of any narrowly defined commodity (e.g., subcompact cars), even though each oligopolist sets price above minimum long-run average cost (e.g., using markup pricing).

This explains why **differentiated oligopoly** is usually associated with product differentiation *within firms* as well as between firms. Economies of scale may dictate minimum plant size for producing, say, automobiles, while product differentiation means that the market for automobiles is fragmented among small economy cars, family-sized cars, luxury cars, and high-performance sports cars. Some components (e.g., engines, chassis) may be interchangeable (indeed, General Motors got in trouble a number of years ago for not telling buyers of Oldsmobiles that they were getting Chevrolet engines). Although automobile firms once specialized in one type of car, this practice ceased long ago. Fragmenting the market for potential entrants has eliminated the possibility of survival by the specialized producer of consumer durables or business machines. Ironically, entry into American oligopolistic industries has involved incursion by efficiently sized foreign producers, who are accused of dumping extra output.

This leads us to one other controversy, which we can discuss only briefly at this stage. Does product differentiation, per se, constitute a barrier to market entry, or does it merely accentuate other barriers (e.g., economies of scale) which exist for technical reasons? While this issue has rarely been addressed in these terms, it would appear that the answer is yes, that is, at least one of those alternatives is true. As shown in chapter eleven, legal restrictions in the form of patents, brand names, and trademarks, which tend to accompany product differentiation, are monopoly licenses, although they are usually narrowly enforced. Hence, were these restrictions broadly interpreted to give property rights over a broad spectrum of product characteristics, it is conceivable that product differentiation, per se, could limit the number of sellers in similar markets. However, many economists would disagree with the product differentiation "cause" of oligopoly.

It seems more plausible to argue that product differentiation magnifies the impact of entry barriers due to economies of scale. For instance, where manufacturers maintain their own or franchised dealerships, a new producer may find it virtually impossible to market its product without a large outlay for its own dealerships. Economies of scale in advertising may enhance the economies of scale in manufacturing a differentiated product. In short, by reducing the cross elasticity of demand among producers, and by accentuating the role of economies of scale in limiting the number of sellers, product differentiation increases the difference between the entry-preventing price under oligopoly, and the minimum long-run average cost.

Oligopoly Cartels

The neoclassical approach to oligopoly rejects the noncollusion assumption of the kinked demand curve model. Awareness of rivalry means that industry profit can be maximized if sellers coordinate their pricing and output decisions. However, the incentive to collude tends to be thwarted by two factors: (1) individual sellers can increase their own profits, at the expense of other cartel members, by secretly selling below their assigned price or producing more than their assigned output; and (2) in the United States (although not in all private enterprise countries), cartel contracts will not be enforced and evidence of such contracts will result in prosecution for conspiracy in restraint of trade.

Figure 12-10 depicts a duopoly whose members have marginal cost curves MC_1 and MC_2; once again the simplifying assumption of a homogeneous product is invoked. Figure 12-10a reprises the price-leadership model of Figure 12-8: firm 2, the high-cost producer, allows firm 1 to set the price. Expecting firm 2 to produce where MC_2 equals the (leader's) price, firm 1 generates a residual demand function, p_hD_1, where p_h is the price at which firm 2 produces all market output. Equating its own marginal cost and residual marginal revenue (MR_1), the leader sets its output at Q_1. Market price is set at p_1, and the follower produces Q_2, determined where $MC_2 = p_1$.

The price leader obtains little benefit from its cost advantage when the follower behaves like a price taker and produces where its marginal cost equals the administered price. Since the follower produces as much as it wants (i.e., where $MC_2 = p_1$), while the price leader absorbs the cost of restricting output, each seller has an incentive to allow the other to lead! In fact, the way Figure 12-10a is constructed, a residual demand curve of $p_h'D_2$ would result in approximately the same collusive price. However, firm 1, as follower, would be able to use its advantage as low-cost producer to sell $\sum Q - Q_2'$ at that price, which would result in profits considerably higher than when it acts as price leader.

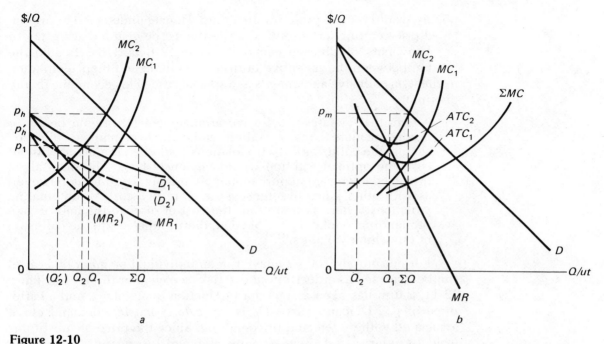

Figure 12-10
Alternative Models of Price Leadership. *a*, Laissez-faire attitude toward follower; *b*, cartel discipline imposed on follower.

Figure 12-10*b* shows the joint profit-maximizing solution when the price leader attempts to restrict the output of the follower. If firm 1 were a two-plant monopolist, output would be set at $\sum Q$, identified by the intersection of the aggregate marginal cost curve, $\sum MC$, and the industry marginal revenue curve, MR. Total output would be divided between plants so that $MC_1 = MC_2 = MR$, leading to production quotas of Q_1 and Q_2 for the low-cost plant and the high-cost plant, respectively. A two-plant monopolist would be only mildly concerned that the revenue generated by the high-cost plant $(p_m Q_2)$ just covered total costs of that plant, since a handsome return would have been earned on production in plant 1.

In the case of a duopoly cartel, the division of output between plants would initially determine the distribution of profit between firms. The low-cost firm would fare considerably better under the joint profit maximum than as passive price leader (Figure 12-10*a*). The high-cost producer could increase its profit by producing more than its quota, Q_2, if it could count on the low-cost firm to cut its output to maintain the cartel price. (Each time OPEC oil ministers meet in Geneva, they try to decide how much Saudi Arabia should cut its oil exports!) Yet any production pattern which deviates from the optimal pattern for a multiplant monopoly would reduce profit for the group. Hence, undetected or unpunished price cutting (or output expansion) must be guarded against.

University of Chicago economist Gary S. Becker has treated the tension between the incentive of firms to collude and their temptation to cheat on collusive agreements as a special case of his economic theory of crime:

> A firm that violates a collusive arrangement by pricing below or producing more than is specified can be said to commit an "offense" against the collusion . . . . If violations could be eliminated without cost, the optimal solution would obviously be to eliminate all of them and to engage in pure monopoly pricing. In general, however, as with other kinds of offenses, there are two costs of eliminating violations. There is first of all the cost of discovering and of "apprehending" violators. . . . Second, there is the cost to the collusion of punishing violators."[18]

For our purposes, the behavior of an individual member of a cartel can be analyzed as a decision under risk (see chapter three). In Figure 12-11, a firm has been assigned a production quota of Q_m and a cartel price of p_m. Demand curve D_0 is the *ceteris paribus* demand curve associated with undetected price cutting. Since the price of substitutes (sold by other cartel members) are assumed to remain constant, the cheater's demand curve would be highly elastic.

The gain from cheating equals the difference between the firm's profit with undetected cheating, π_1, and the firm's assigned share of cartel profit, π_m. In Figure 12-11, profit with successful cheating equals the area of rectangle p_1EFG, and the firm's assigned share of cartel profit is p_mABC. The greater the difference between these payoffs, the greater will be the temptation for the firm to break the agreement, *ceteris paribus*.

On the other hand, if the firm is caught cheating, it will pay some form of penalty. One obvious, if limited, deterrent is the expectation that other firms will discover the cheating and cut their prices to protect their market shares. This prospect replaces the *ceteris paribus* demand curve with the *mutatis mutandis* demand curve D_1. Output Q_1, identified by the intersection of MR_0 and the (long-run) marginal cost curve, would have a market clearing price of p_1 if the price cut could be kept secret. If the price cut were detected and other sellers reduced their prices, the market clearing price of Q_1 would fall to p_2. Detected price cutting would result in profit equal to p_2HFG, which is clearly less than p_mABC, since $MC > MR_1$ at Q_1. The kinked demand curve appears as the minimum deterrent to cheating on an "understanding" to maintain cartel

---

[18] Gary S. Becker, "Crime and Punishment: An Economic Approach," in *The Economic Approach to Human Behavior* (Chicago: University of Chicago Press, 1978) pp. 39–85; quote from p. 76.

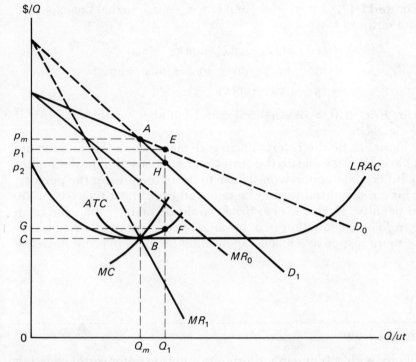

Figure 12-11
The Cartel Problem under Oligopoly: To Cheat or Not to Cheat?

output, lest all firms suffer when failure of the cartel causes market-wide price cutting.

According to Becker, firms can perceive probabilities that price cutting will be detected ranging anywhere from zero to 100 percent, and penalties which range from ill will among peers, to price matching, to all-out price wars and beyond. As a general principle, risk neutral oligopoly sellers would attempt to maximize the **expected profit** from cartel membership versus cartel cheating:

$$E(\pi) = (1 - \rho)G + \rho L$$

where G is the gain from undetected cheating, L is the loss (penalty) if cheating is detected, and ρ is the probability of discovery.[19] If each seller attempts to maximize expected profit, there will be some probability of detection at which cheating will be deemed profitable, given the expected penalty if caught.

---

[19] As shown in chapter three, a risk averse decision maker would cheat only if he or she received a risk premium, $E(\pi) > 0$, while a risk lover might cheat even if forced to pay some risk premium, $E(\pi) < 0$.

In Figure 12-11, $G = \pi_1 - \pi_m$ and $L = \pi_2 - \pi_m$, so that the expected profit from output Q_1 is:

$$E(\pi) = (1 - \rho)(\pi_1 - \pi_m) + \rho(\pi_2 - \pi_m)$$
$$= \pi_1 - \pi_m - \rho\pi_1 + \rho\pi_m + \rho\pi_2 - \rho\pi_1$$
$$= (\pi_1 - \pi_m) - \rho(\pi_1 - \pi_2)$$

Solving for $E(\pi) \geq 0$, a risk neutral cartel member would cut price if $\rho < (\pi_1 - \pi_m)/(\pi_1 - \pi_2)$.

The more elastic the *ceteris paribus* demand curve (for undetected cheating) and the less elastic the firm's marginal cost curve, the higher the probability of detection would have to be, or the greater the penalty, in order for a risk neutral firm to be deterred from cheating. (Given the expected penalty, ρf, risk averse firms would be more responsive to an increase in f and a reduction in ρ, holding ρf constant, while risk lovers would be more responsive to a compensating increase in ρ and decrease in f.)

APPLICATION

Cartel Contracts and Antitrust Law

The difficulty with relying on uniform price cuts to deter cartel cheating is that failure of the deterrent could spell the end of the cartel. If all firms cut their prices in retaliation to the actions of an overly optimistic (or just unlucky) cartel cheater, a new kink would develop in the demand curve, at point (p_2, Q_1) in Figure 12-11. The documented failure of the collusive arrangement would discourage firms from raising their prices to p_m (or returning to the former structure of prices if product differentiation were a factor). Further price cuts would be of little deterrent value when cartel members were already charging prices barely above minimum long-run average cost.

Becker argues that fines would usually minimize the cost of enforcing any agreement. Risk neutral oligopolists would be deterred from cheating on cartel understandings if fines levied on discovered offenders, f, and the probability of detection, ρ, caused the expected cheating, $E(\pi)$, to become negative: $E(\pi) = \pi_1 - \pi_m - \rho f < 0$ implies $f > (1/\rho)(\pi_1 - \pi_m)$, where ρf is the expected fine. Since the idea behind deterring price cutting is that the price cutter's gain is exceeded by the losses suffered by other cartel members, risk averse and risk neutral oligopolists would be deterred by an enforcement mechanism that required "convicted" cheaters to compensate other cartel members for *all* losses due to price cutting by both convicted cheaters and those who escaped punishment. (If the average price cut cost the cartel $1 million in profit, and if an average of one in three cheaters were punished, the optimal fine for deterring risk-neutral potential offenders would be to charge convicted firms triple damages of $3 million.)

As Becker has noted: "The most favorable situation is one in which fines could be levied against violators and collected by the collusion. If fines and other legal recourse are ruled out, methods like the predatory price cutting or violence have to be used, and they hurt the collusion as well as violators."[20] Whatever other criticisms may be levied at its effectiveness, the Sherman Antitrust Act of 1890 is resoundingly clear about the use of American courts to enforce cartel contracts. The law declares illegal "every contract, combination in the form of a trust or otherwise, or conspiracy, in restraint of trade." By denying cartels their most efficient means of enforcing collusive agreements, the government encourages cartel members to cheat on price-setting arrangements. Section II of the act closes an obvious loophole by declaring "every person who shall monopolize, or attempt to monopolize, or combine or conspire with other person or persons, to monopolize any part of trade or commerce" to be guilty of a misdemeanor. If a number of sellers cannot sign a contract to monopolize a market, they also cannot merge into a single firm for the same purpose.

Understanding the problem of enforcing cartel discipline in an environment in which cartel contracts cannot be enforced may clear up some of the confusion which seems to surround various interpretations of antitrust law. So-called **predatory pricing** has been treated as a violation of Section II of the Sherman Act, that is, as an attempt to monopolize a market by destroying smaller rivals. Figure 12-12 shows why trying to capture a market by pricing below the average (variable or total) cost of smaller rivals is a dubious practice.

Figure 12-12*a* shows the market demand curve for a commodity produced under oligopolistic conditions; Figure 12-12*b* shows the short-run cost curves for the typical small firm in an industry. By construction, p_1 is equal to minimum average total cost, and p_0 is equal to minimum average variable cost; these represent the long-run and short-run shutdown prices for the small producer. Supposedly, by cutting price below p_0, a price leader could drive small firms from the industry. Then, after achieving monopoly status, the "predator" produces where industry marginal revenue equals its own marginal cost, raising price to p_m.

The obvious flaw in this argument is that p_m exceeds p_1, the price necessary for a normal return on the investment in a small plant. The plants of firms driven from the market would still exist, although ownership might have changed. Unless the predator had purchased that productive capacity, another entrepreneur could enter the industry in response to a price greater than minimum average total cost. Predatory pricing, as a means of monopolizing a market, would make a poor in-

---

[20] Becker, "Crime and Punishment," p. 76.

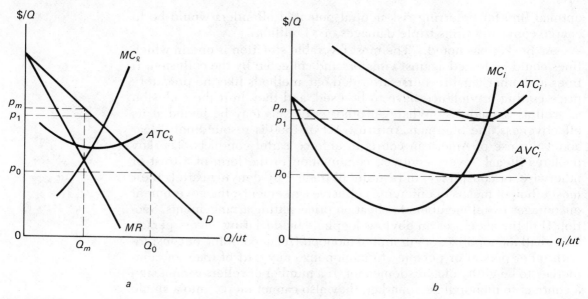

Figure 12-12
Economic Consequences of Predatory Pricing. *a*, The predator; *b*, the victim.

Policy Illustration
Price Leadership in the Steel Industry

The author has argued in another context that industry-wide collective bargaining which results in equivalent cost increases for all producers in an oligopoly may provide a legally defensible means of price leadership.* If antitrust prosecutors lack a signed contract or other tangible evidence of a price-fixing conspiracy, the simultaneous change in prices in an industry, or other circumstantial evidence of cartel pricing, must be judged according to the rule of reason. In other words, corporations, as legal persons, enjoy the rights of due process; the burden of proof lies with the prosecution in antitrust matters. Since across-the-board cost increases would raise the prices of all producers under competition, such a price increase could be defended under oligopoly.

The need for a "cost justified" defense to counter circumstantial evidence of collusion is illustrated in the unsuccessful attempt by U.S. Steel and other

---

* See Thomas M. Carroll, "Achieving Cartel Profits through Unionization: Comment," *Southern Economic Journal* (April 1981).

producers to raise the price of steel in 1962. In April 1962, U.S. Steel announced a price increase of $6 per ton. Other large producers soon followed. On April 11, 1962, President John F. Kennedy opened a press conference by announcing: "The simultaneous and identical actions of United States Steel and other leading steel corporations increasing steel prices by some $6 a ton constitute a wholly unjustifiable and irresponsible defiance of the public interest."†

Kennedy went on to note that the steel industry's profit margins were reasonable for an industry operating (as steel was then) at two-thirds capacity. Further, said Kennedy, the wage contract recently negotiated by the United Steelworkers did not raise the cost of producing steel, since wage increases were matched by productivity increases. He concluded:

In short, at a time when they could be exploring how more efficiency and better prices could be obtained, reducing prices in this industry in recognition of lower costs, their unusually good labor contract, their foreign competition and their increase in production and profits which are coming this year, a few gigantic corporations have decided to increase prices in ruthless disregard of their public responsibilities.

The Steelworkers Union can be proud that it abided by its responsibilities in this agreement, and this Government also has responsibilities which we intend to meet. The Department of Justice and the Federal Trade Commission are examining the significance of this action in a free, competitive economy.

And I am informed that steps are under way by those members of the Congress who plan appropriate inquiries into how these pricing decisions are so quickly made and reached, and what legislative safeguards may be needed to protect the public interest.

Although the chairman of U.S. Steel defended the price increase, the latent threat of antitrust prosecution, a reevaluation of defense contracts, and congressional investigations drove a wedge between the large firms which had already raised their prices and the smaller firms which had not yet done so. U.S. Steel and the other large producers could have lost a share of their market to smaller rivals offering lower prices. On April 13, 1962, U.S. Steel rescinded its announced price increase, as had all the other large steel firms by that time.

The moral of the story: while they may not represent complete deterrents to informal price arrangements, antitrust laws do represent constraints which must be accommodated in such arrangements. In 1962 the uniform price increase by large steel producers stood naked in the absence of a competitive justification for higher steel prices. One may still believe that oligopolistic producers attempt to coordinate pricing and output decisions, perhaps so much that they violate the spirit of antitrust laws. But such coordination may be legally defended if it *looks like* the market response to a common cost change. When even a modest defense is lacking, circumstantial evidence can lead to public embarrassment and legal penalties.

† From "Kennedy vs. U.S. Steel," in Arthur MacEwan and Thomas E. Weisskopf (eds.), *Perspectives on the Economic Problem; A Book of Readings on Political Economy* (Englewood Cliffs, N.J.: Prentice-Hall, 1970), pp. 227–228.

vestment. After sustaining losses while charging a price less than p_0 and having to serve the entire market by producing Q_0, the predator must either purchase the productive capacity of bankrupt firms or keep its price at or below p_1, which could have been done anyway without predation.

As a violation of Section I of the Sherman Act—part of a conspiracy to restrain trade—predatory pricing is more plausible. Under the passive price leadership model, the price leader suffers a reduced market share by allowing rivals to produce where their marginal cost equals the administered price. To enjoy long-lasting monopoly power, the price leader will force other firms to reduce their rate of output below their own profit-maximizing optima. As Becker argues, punishing cheaters when the leader's threat is challenged imposes cost on the collusion in general, and on the leader in particular. Predatory pricing may represent a necessary evil for the cartel unable to find more efficient means of enforcing its agreement.

Administered Prices and Nonprofit Goals

So far we have investigated whether oligopoly firms can maximize short-run economic profit without encountering the inertia of the kinked demand curve. Ignoring rivalry, as shown in the classical models, leads to models with dubious behavioral assumptions. Even asking what the highest sustainable price is when economies of scale specify minimum size by new firms requires some speculation about how potential entrants anticipate the reaction of potential rivals. When allowances are made for collusive pricing in concentrated industries, the kinked demand curve recurs as a deterrent to unilateral price cutting. We now consider the implications of dropping the assumption that firms attempt to maximize short-run economic profit.

At the risk of oversimplification, the argument made by John Kenneth Galbraith, William Baumol, Herbert Simon, and others can be summarized as follows. The kinked demand curve arises from attempts by large corporations operating in global markets to maximize short-run profit while anticipating the reactions of rivals. Drop the assumption that corporations attempt to maximize economic profit, and the problems posed by the kinked demand curve melt into oblivion.

While similar in approach, the insights provided by Galbraith, Baumol, and Simon spring from radically different behavioral premises. As noted in chapter eight, Galbraith's rejection of the profit-maximizing assumption rests largely on the separation of corporate ownership from corporate control. Unless corporate executives, who receive a very small share of dividends, are altruistically inclined—a premise Adam Smith rejected for merchants in general—then the profit-maximizing assumption must be replaced with goals more consistent with managerial interests. Once these alternative goals are understood so is the pricing process:

> Growth is the more important affirmative purpose of the technostructure. Accordingly, prices will be set at the level which, while ensuring the necessary level of earnings, has the primary effect of sustaining and expanding sales. The word primary must be emphasized; the level of prices which would reconcile maximum sales with necessary minimum of earnings may be further adjusted by the need to show an increase in earnings. . . .
>
> The prices that are so set—that reflect the affirmative purposes of the technostructure—will almost always be lower, and on occasion much lower, than those that would maximize profits over some period of relevant managerial calculation. The buyer cannot, at one and the same time, be attracted by prices that expand sales and repelled by those that maximize profit.[21]

According to Galbraith, oligopolistic prices are kept in line by a community of interests—"the technostructure"—rather than by the explicit monopoly collusion posited by Becker and Stigler. To foster a congenial oligopoly environment, prices can be set to avoid the temptations for price competition generated by cartel pricing. At the same time, oligopoly firms can compete by less harmful means:

> The elimination of price competition as part of the protective purposes of the technostructure does not similarly eliminate other forms of rivalry between firms. Competition in product development, advertising, salesmanship and public ingratiation continues. Unlike price competition the effects of such rivalry are limited. Price cutting may plunge all firms into disastrous loss. Other forms of rivalry, although they can be expensive, have no similar potential for damage. On the contrary . . . each firm's selling efforts do something to sell the products or services of the industry as a whole and to affirm the happiness which derives from consumption in general. In price competition there is damage for all; in other forms of competition there can be benefit for all.[22]

Not all economists who criticize the assumption of profit maximization share Galbraith's view of managerial goals or accept his reasons for the lack of downward price flexibility under oligopoly. According to members of the managerialist school—such as William Baumol, Herbert Simon, Richard Cyert, and James March—the increased discretion over price, input costs, and consumer demand, which results from the size

---

[21] John Kenneth Galbraith, *Economics and the Public Purpose* (Boston: Houghton Mifflin, 1973), p. 125.

[22] Ibid. p. 128

of oligopoly firms, makes profit maximization an impossible goal.[23] A vast amount of information is required to identify the greatest profit opportunity. Realistic managers strive for satisfactory, achievable goals, such as a particular rate of return on investment or a specific market share, rather than trying to maximize profit per se.

Unfortunately (or happily, depending on one's perspective), Galbraith avoids diagrams, making it somewhat difficult to integrate his ideas directly into a neoclassical framework. Nevertheless, we will attempt to capture the spirit of Galbraith's thought in the following sections as we consider the nature of sales maximization with a profit constraint, the possibility that nonprice competition may lead to a kinked demand type inertia in advertising for market shares, and how "satisficing" might be more appropriately considered a search strategy than a decision strategy.

APPLICATION

Sales Maximization under a Minimum Profit Constraint

In Figure 12-13, a firm's total revenue is given by TR, while its total cost curve is TC. The firm's expected revenue increases until Q_{max}, where its demand is unit elastic. The firm's profit target is π^*. In Figure 12-13a, the function $\Pi(Q)$, defined by the distance between the revenue and cost curves, intersects the target profit line π^* at two outputs, Q_0 and Q_2. Maximum profit could be achieved at Q_1, where the slope of the total revenue curve equals the slope of the total cost curve. The revenue maximization hypothesis predicts that the firm will produce Q_2 units of output, receiving total revenue of TR_2; this is the highest revenue which is consistent with the profit constraint.

In Figure 12-13b, no output or revenue level satisfies the profit constraint. In this case, managers will try to come as close to the profit target as possible. By producing Q_1, which is associated with total revenue TR_1, the firm maximizes profit—that is, equates marginal revenue and marginal cost. Thus, the revenue-maximizing model actually includes profit maximization as a special case.

It has been suggested that revenue maximization—as an analogue of market share maximization or growth maximization—is actually a special case of profit maximization. If a firm foregoes an increase in profit this year in order to increase its share of the market, it simply means that the present value (see chapters three and thirteen) of future profits anticipated from the greater market share exceeds the foregone profit.

---

[23] See William J. Baumol, *Economic Theory and Operations Analysis*, 4th ed. (Englewood Cliffs, New Jersey: Prentice-Hall, 1977), p. 360; Herbert Simon, "Rational Decision Making in Business Organizations," *American Economic Review* (September 1979); Richard M. Cyert and James M. March, *A Behavioral Theory of the Firm* (Englewood Cliffs, New Jersey: Prentice-Hall, 1963).

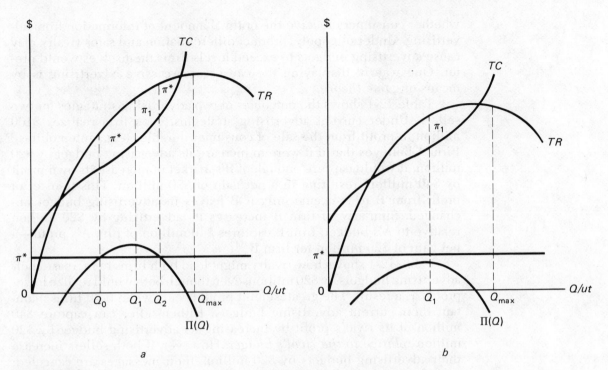

Figure 12-13
Sales Maximization with a Minimum Profit Constraint. *a*, Sales maximum with profit constraint satisfied; *b*, profit maximum with profit constraint unsatisfied.

Growth maximization or sales maximization is the equivalent of long-run profit maximization.

Strategies other than short-run profit maximization mean patterns of resource allocation which differ from those arising under the marginal-revenue-equals-marginal-cost rule. The issue is not whether decision makers pursue profits, but how this pursuit of profit influences product price and quantity produced. A small number of producers attempting to maintain a target level (or rate) of profit in a growing industry may be able to avoid price wars by pursuing larger market shares by other means. But, as we shall see directly, avoiding the worst consequences of price competition (from the producers' perspective) may simply lead to other forms of frustration.

Game Theory Applied to Advertising

As discussed in chapter eleven, advertising can increase consumer welfare by providing low cost—if not always reliable—information about product characteristics and relative prices. Economists are still debating whether consumers receive the optimal amount of information from advertising. Under oligopoly, product differentiation and sales rivalry may cause advertising budgets to exceed levels firms themselves would prefer. One way of displaying the causes of excessive advertising is by means of *game theory.*

Table 12-1 shows the outcomes of two advertising strategies for two sellers. Under current advertising strategies, each firm realizes $100 million in profit from the sale of consumer durables (e.g., automobiles). Firm A believes that if it were to increase its advertising budget by $20 million, it would capture enough of B's market to increase its own profit by $40 million, resulting in a net gain of $20 million. This transfer of profit from B to A occurs only if B leaves its advertising budget unchanged. Similarly, if firm B increases its advertising by $20 million relative to A's budget, firm B captures $40 million of firm A's profit—a net gain of $20 million for firm B.[24]

Table 12-1 shows how rivalry might lead both firms to increase their advertising budgets by $20 million, even though both would realize lower profits as a result. The greatest joint profit occurs when both firms maintain their current advertising budgets. Either seller can capture $40 million of its rival's profit by increasing its advertising budget by $20 million *relative to the rival's budget.* However, if both sellers increase their advertising budgets by $20 million, their messages are canceled; each firm ends up financing $20 million of ineffective advertising out of profit. Yet neither seller dares cut advertising back to its original level, since the other firm could capture $40 million of its profit by *not* reducing its advertising.

If both sellers determine their advertising budgets independently (that is, the sellers do not collude in their advertising decision), the least desirable joint outcome is the most likely. Regardless of the advertising

---

[24] We can define the firm's advertising elasticity as $\eta_{iA_i} = (\partial Q_i/\partial A_i)(A_i/Q_i)$ and the cross advertising elasticity as $\eta_{iA_j} = (\partial Q_i/\partial A_j)(A_j/Q_i)$. Therefore, the percentage change in revenue for firm i due to a 1 percent change in its own advertising budget (price constant) is:

$$\frac{d(p_iQ_i)/p_iQ_i}{dA_i/A_i} = \frac{P_i(dQ_i)}{dA_i} \cdot \frac{A_i}{p_iQ_i}$$

$$= \frac{A_i}{Q_i}\left(\frac{\partial Q_i}{\partial A_i} + \sum_{j=1}^{n} \frac{\partial Q_i}{\partial A_j} \cdot \frac{dA_j}{dA_i}\right)$$

$$= \frac{\partial Q_i}{\partial A_i} \cdot \frac{A_i}{Q_i} + \sum_{j=1}^{n} \frac{\partial Q_i}{\partial A_j} \cdot \frac{A_j}{Q_i} \cdot \frac{dA_j/A_j}{dA_i/A_i}$$

$$= \eta_{iA_i} + \sum_{j=1}^{n} \eta_{iA_j}\theta_{A_jA_i}$$

where $\theta_{A_iA_j} = \dfrac{dA_j/A_j}{dA_i/A_i}$

TABLE 12-1
Oligopoly Nonprice Competition: Profit from Advertising Strategies

Seller B's Advertising Strategy	Seller A's Advertising Strategy	
	Maintain current budget	*Increase budget by $20 million*
Maintain current budget	A = $100 million B = $100 million	A = $120 million B = $ 60 million
Increase budget by $20 million	A = $ 60 million B = $120 million	A = $ 80 million B = $ 80 million

strategy adopted by firm B, firm A is better off by increasing its advertising budget by $20 million. If seller B maintains its current budget, seller A increases its profit by $20 million; if seller B increases its budget, seller A reduces its loss by $20 million. A similar set of expectations confronts seller B: whether seller A increases its advertising or not, seller B is better off by increasing its own advertising expenditures. Only by collusion could advertising budgets be held to their current levels, leaving both sellers with their maximum *joint* profit.

Ironically, competition by nonprice means can arrive at the same impasse as the classical duopoly models. Awareness of rivalry in the absence of collusion can lead firms to advertising expenditures in excess of the amount that would maximize cartel profits. Similar results can be projected for variations in product quality. A price war, of course, benefits consumers (at least in the short run) at the expense of sellers; that is precisely the function that the invisible hand is supposed to perform. The extent to which consumers benefit from "advertising wars" depends on whether the advertising is informative or persuasive and whether "free" television and low-priced magazines provide sufficient social benefit to justify the costs advertisers incur.

Satisficing: Suboptimal Goals or Incomplete Information?

The classical models of Cournot and Stackelberg defined equilibrium outcomes for duopoly by making unrealistic assumptions about seller behavior. The cartel approach to oligopoly sacrifices equilibrium outcomes by stressing the instability of collusive arrangements that are costly to enforce. The challenge to the managerial approach is to develop realistic models of managerial behavior which generate testable predictions about how resources are allocated in oligopolistic industries. An approach offered by Herbert Simon, Richard M. Cyert, and James G.

March is based on the notion that the complexity of the oligopoly environment makes it impossible to maximize anything: profit, sales, or market share.[25] Instead, they suggest, achievable goals are defined. These **satisficing** models then provide a basis for a more realistic *behavioral theory* of the firm.

The criticisms of profit-maximizing models advanced by satisficing theorists are hard to dismiss out of hand. The elaborate simplifications made in the Stackelberg and Cournot models, which are necessary (but not sufficient) to reach predictable outcomes, mean that these models have little relevance in explaining or predicting the behavior of multibillion dollar corporations which must contend with rivals as large as themselves. Maximizing behavior requires knowledge of outcomes of a decision prior to taking action. Since the outcome of an oligopoly's decision depends on what its rivals do, and since rivals may respond in a number of different ways, the oligopoly environment must be classified as risky; one can, at best, maximize the expected value of an objective under risk. But objective probability estimates of rivals' responses to a firm's policy change may not exist, and subjective estimates may be very difficult to calculate.

When satisficing theorists maintain that profit maximization models are too simplistic for oligopoly, they mean that the decision environment of oligopoly is uncertainty. Multiple possible outcomes for the firm's actions exist, and management must employ subjective probability estimates. For our purposes, we wish to know to what extent "realistic" theories of oligopoly are compatible with the other aspects of microeconomics.

The contrast between satisficing and optimizing models of executive behavior suggests that these may be complementary rather than contradictory tools in understanding the impact of large firms on their environment. A decisive test for the satisficing model could be made if evidence indicated that executives were indifferent among alternatives predicted to have different expected payoffs. Such evidence does not exist, and from the perspective of satisficing theorists, begs the question. How were the firm's options discovered, and how were they evaluated? Information can be sought, and sometimes found; or information can be encountered serendipitously—and its value sometimes appreciated. When a course of action is discovered, information about its expected payoff will be sought until the option is rejected as unsatisfactory or accepted as satisfactory. When search is sequential, that is, when only one option is considered until it proves to be acceptable or unacceptable, the firm will probably accept the first satisfactory alternative that pre-

---

[25] Herbert Simon, "Theories of Decision Making in Economics," *American Economic Review* (June 1959), and "Rational Decision Making"; Cyert and March, *A Behavioral Theory of the Firm.*

sents itself. However, when search is more thorough, many alternatives will be considered at once, and more than one alternative is likely to be found acceptable. In this case, the firm typically selects the option with the highest expected payoff.

An example of optimistic search behavior is the neoclassical entrepreneur who enters that industry in which resources are earning a higher than normal return. If corporation managers were to ignore rivalry in allocating resources, they would allocate them according to the *highest possible* return they could receive. Indeed, the normal return definition of zero economic profit provides a satisfactory outcome; the optimistic producer attempts to maximize but actually satisfices.

From the literature on game theory comes the pessimistic strategy of search. When I play a game of chess, I expect my opponent to counter every move I make by selecting that move which minimizes my advantage. An optimistic chess player soon loses, since he expects that the other player will always make the worst move possible. A pessimistic chess player takes a long time contemplating each move because he first determines the worst thing his opponent can do to him. A chess game is won, of course, when every move open to the opponent results in the loss of his king.

If business were like a game of chess, many possible courses of action would be rejected until one acceptable option was found—one course of action whose worst possible outcome exceeded the target outcome. Like the optimistic search strategy, which rejects options whose best (possible) outcome is unacceptable, the pessimistic strategy is sequential. If an option is rejected (because its lowest possible outcome is unacceptable), the next alternative is identified and considered. If an option's lowest possible outcome is acceptable, no further search is deemed necessary. The highest valued option is chosen; the chosen option also happens to be the only viable one.

For all their pedagogical simplicity, the extreme forms of optimism and pessimism are not the only approaches to search. Another is the Bayesian approach.[26] Every manager starts with some information from experience or hunches suggesting that some outcomes are more likely than others. As information is gathered, prudent managers modify their "prior" probability estimates in the light of new evidence. Ultimately, enough information is collected so that the management team is willing to take responsibility for a decision. Once again, satisficing screens out alternatives with expected outcomes that fall short of the target. However, when all outcomes attributable to a course of action are used to calculate its expected payoff, more than one acceptable option is likely to survive the search process. Management then chooses that option with the highest expected payoff.

---

[26] See Carroll and Dean, "A Bayesian Approach," pp. 81–89.

Business Illustration
Plant Location by the Large Corporation

The complementarity of satisficing as a search strategy and the attempt to achieve the highest expected profit from *known* alternatives is illustrated in the plant location (or plant closing) decision of a large corporation. Unlike search problems of a simpler variety—such as the price search by consumers, where each store (alternative) is associated with only one price (outcome)—the plant location problem involves numerous (sequential) alternatives and outcomes. Management must determine the best region for a plant, the optimal number of potential sites to investigate within the chosen region, and the relative impact of each of many plant site characteristics. Furthermore, the expected profit from a new plant depends on some variables the firm cannot control (what will technological change or future economic recessions do to the plant's viability?) and other variables the firm can influence (what concessions can be negotiated with communities hungry for the new jobs a plant would bring?).

Since information collection and eval- uation requires time and other scarce resources, the ideal search would identify the profit-maximizing plant site at the lowest search cost. From this perspective, all search is backward and therefore inefficient. We normally find something in the last place we look; if we looked in the last place first, think of the time and effort that could be saved! All we have to do is know where to look. But that is assuming away the problem.

The plant location problem is really two optimization problems in one: (1) each alternative must be accepted or rejected on the basis of available evidence, and (2) the right amount of information must be collected on each alternative. A *satisficing search strategy* specifies a *target outcome* the plant site must be expected to achieve; as potential sites are uncovered, investigators must determine whether available evidence warrants additional information collection about each. By screening out sites which are not expected to achieve the target rate of profit (or sales), information costs are reduced. However, since many

To summarize, the satisficing approach to corporate decision making is not necessarily in conflict with the optimizing theories of neoclassical microeconomics. Instead of assuming that decision makers have perfect knowledge about alternatives and their outcomes, satisficing theory provides an insight into the search for and evaluation of alternatives. By emphasizing the uncertainty inherent in the oligopolistic environment, satisficing theory helps explain why managers sometimes achieve less than the highest possible payoff. However, satisficing behavior need not contradict maximization models of behavior. Once options have been identified and their payoffs estimated, management will tend to pick the known alternative with the highest expected payoff.

sites will be rejected on the basis of incomplete (or even erroneous) information, it is possible that the ideal site may not be selected. Indeed, it may never be found.

Since the expected profit from a plant location will depend (in a probabilistic fashion) on identifiable characteristics, search will tend to follow a regional hierarchy of plant site characteristics. Whole regions might be rejected on the basis of unacceptable climate or political conditions, or because the company already has a plant adequately serving that area, or because rivalry is thought too great. Within acceptable regions, communities will be compared on the basis of their transportation networks, labor availability, and mix of government services and taxes. If two or more communities are equally acceptable on the basis of characteristics that rank further up on the geographical hierarchy, the corporation may encourage competition between them for tax concessions, exemptions from environmental regulations, or the provision of government services (e.g., highway networks).

While the desire of chambers of commerce or city governments for additional industry is understandable, this approach suggests prudence in granting concessions for plant location. Assuming industry is desired for the jobs and tax revenues it brings, the impact of new plants will depend on how well they fit with the economic profile of the area and the net taxes they pay. A community which is strongly preferred may not have to grant any concessions to attract a firm which is ideally suited to its environment; tax concessions would only reduce the benefits to be reaped. A community which offers concessions not only may give away benefits a new plant might otherwise have bestowed, but may cause resources to be misallocated by diverting location from the pattern dictated by economic factors.

Based on Robert D. Dean and Thomas M. Carroll, "Plant Location under Uncertainty" *Land Economics* (November 1977), pp. 423–444, and Thomas M. Carroll and Robert D. Dean, "A Bayesian Approach to Plant Location Decisions," *Decision Sciences* (January 1980), pp. 81–89.

If nothing else, this chapter has explained why there are so many approaches to pricing and output decisions under oligopoly. The kinked demand curve model was presented as a point of reference: the three major approaches to oligopoly were derived by relaxing, in each case, a different assumption of Sweezy's model. Ignoring rivalry lies behind the classical models of Cournot and Stackelberg, as well as more modern models of passive price leadership and the impact of potential entry on pricing in a homogeneous oligopoly in the long run. Dropping the assumption that oligopoly sellers do not collude led to the various models of oligopoly cartels and the problems of making and enforcing cartel agreements in a hostile legal environment. Finally, the reactions of John Kenneth Galbraith and members of the managerialist school were based on a rejection of profit maximization as a model of managerial behavior in a concentrated market.

Those who are disturbed by the richness of approaches to oligopoly should reflect a moment on the purpose of economic theory. In studying consumer behavior, we emphasized that economics does not predict exactly what a person will consume or why different people have different consumption habits. The purpose of consumer theory, as of all microeconomic theory, is to predict how individuals are likely to respond to changes in their economic incentives.

Awareness of rivalry complicates the firm's output and price decision. Firms in a concentrated industry will attempt to find some informal means of collusion, or individuals or groups will develop other goals which allow them to avoid the consequences of the kinked demand trap.

Successful cartelization of an oligopoly requires some efficient method for policing the agreement. Explicit cartel contracts are outlawed by the Sherman Act and subsequent antitrust legislation. The success of informal collusion depends on timing of price changes to make collusive behavior appear reasonable.

Whether firms attempt to maximize profit or set other goals to ensure industrial tranquility is partly a matter of semantics. When corporations exercise control over price, input costs, and perhaps even consumer demand, profit maximization clearly involves more than setting marginal revenue equal to marginal cost while ignoring rivals.

HIGHLIGHTS

1. Oligopoly, a market with only a few sellers, is one of the most complex and controversial topics in modern microeconomic theory. While minimum efficient size is required for survival in a concentrated industry, diseconomies of scale prevent one firm from dominating the market. Additional complications arise because the typical oligopoly seller (e.g., a member of the *Fortune* 500) is considerably larger in terms of assets than the typical natural monopoly (e.g., a local utility).

2. The classical model of Augustin Cournot generates an equilibrium price-quantity solution to the duopoly pricing problem by an unrealistic set of behavioral assumptions. The Stackelberg variant of this model allows one seller to act as price leader and the other as follower; it has also been criticized for lack of behavioral realism.

3. The kinked demand curve model of oligopolistic pricing rests on three assumptions: (a) individual sellers attempt to predict the response of rivals to price and/or output changes; (b) each seller attempts to maximize short-run profit; and (c) sellers do not collude in setting prices or quantities. The kinked demand curve model predicts that price adjustments will be sluggish in oligopolistic industries, since the asymmetric response of rivals creates a discontinuous marginal revenue curve.

4. While contradictory evidence about the accuracy of the rigid price prediction exists, the kinked demand curve model still highlights alternative models of oligopoly pricing. Relaxing each of the assumptions on which the kinked demand model is based gives rise to three types of oligopoly theories: (a) the classical models which essentially ignore rivalry,

(b) neoclassical theories of oligopolistic collusion, and (c) managerial models which drop the assumption of short-run profit maximization as the goal of managers.

5. The modern variant of the classical model combines price leadership by a dominant firm with free market entry by price followers, so that oligopoly price and quantity outcomes converge on the competitive solution. Assuming a minimum necessary size for new entrants gives rise to another approach which ignores rivalry, not as a behavioral assumption, but in order to ask the technical question of the degree to which the oligopoly price can exceed minimum long-run average cost, assuming a homogeneous product and no artificial barriers to market entry.

6. The second approach to oligopolistic pricing focuses on the contradictory incentives for collusive behavior. Oligopolistic sellers as a group have an incentive to collude in setting the industry price, but individual sellers have an incentive to break the agreement, since undiscovered price cutting would result in a highly elastic demand for their product. Ironically, when discovered cheating is punished by matching the price cut, the result is a kinked demand curve for individual colluders.

7. From this perspective, the impact of antitrust statutes is to raise the transaction costs of enforcing a cartel agreement. However, in the absence of an explicit cartel contract, oligopolistic price collusion may be legally defensible.

8. The third approach to oligopoly pricing is to deny the behavioral objective of short-run profit maximization. If firms pursue other goals, price changes may be easier to accommodate. One model assumes that firms attempt to maximize sales (revenue), constrained by the achievement of a minimum profit target. However, nonprice competition may result in the same type of outcomes as the kinked demand curve model. For instance, noncollusion and awareness of rivalry may result in an excessive amount of advertising among differentiated oligopolists.

9. Finally, the alleged dichotomy between optimizing behavior and satisficing strategies can be resolved by recognizing that satisficing may be a better description of search behavior than of decision making per se.

GLOSSARY

Administered prices Prices set by price leadership or other quasi-manipulation of market forces, rather than by the free play of supply and demand.

Differentiated oligopoly A concentrated industry (e.g., automobiles, computers, appliances) in which the products of rival sellers are treated as close but imperfect substitutes by buyers.

Duopoly A market with only two sellers.

Expected profit The weighted average of profits attributed to prospects in a risky environment, where the weights are the conditional probabilities of outcomes if different options are chosen.

Homogeneous oligopoly A concentrated industry (model) in which the products of rival sellers are treated as perfect substitutes by buyers, so that the lowest price charged attracts all buyers.

Internal economies Decline in long-run average cost due to increasing production capacity, usually stemming from enhanced specialization of labor and particularly of capital goods.

Kinked demand curve A *mutatis mutandis* demand curve based on the assumption that rivals will match price cuts but ignore price increases. The abrupt change in slope of the demand curve above and below the prevailing price causes a discontinuous marginal revenue curve at the prevailing output level. The alleged price rigidity occurs because a change in marginal cost would not change the profit-maximizing price and output if the new marginal cost curve remained in the discontinuous region of marginal revenue.

Oligopoly   A market with only a few sellers, wherein any firm can significantly influence the market price (or cause noticeable shifts in the demand curves of rivals) by changing its own price and/or output.

Predatory pricing   The alleged practice of setting price below average cost to drive rivals from the market to create a monopoly. While predation is a dubious means of monopolizing a market, such behavior may indicate that a price leader is attempting to enforce cartel discipline by making an example of a detected price cutter.

Price leadership   A form of implicit collusion whereby one firm sets the price (or markup) for a group of rivals as well as itself.

Reaction function   A formula relating the price and/or output of a firm to the price and/or output of one or more rivals.

Rivalry   As distinguished from competition, which is treated as an impersonal force in economic theory, rivalry involves identification of the seller responsible for the industry price change or for the demand shift experienced by others.

Satisficing   A decision or search strategy concerned with the identification of courses of action which satisfy a managerial objective, in contrast to attempts to maximize or minimize the managerial objective. The alleged dichotomy between optimizing and satisficing tends to disappear when (expected) information costs are taken into account.

SUGGESTED READINGS

Bain, Joe S. *Industrial Organization.* 2nd ed. New York: Wiley, 1968.

Baumol, William J. *Economic Theory and Operations Analysis.* 4th ed. Englewood Cliffs, New Jersey: Prentice-Hall, 1977, chapters 15, 16, and 18.

———. "Contestable Markets: An Uprising in the Theory of Industry Structure." *American Economic Review* (March 1982), pp. 1–15.

Calvani, Terry, and John Siegfried, eds. *Economic Analysis and Antitrust Law.* Boston: Little, Brown, 1979.

Cyert, Richard M., and James M. March. *A Behavioral Theory of the Firm.* Englewood Cliffs, New Jersey: Prentice-Hall, 1963.

Fellner, William J. *Competition among the Few.* rev. ed. Fairfield, New Jersey: Augustus M. Kelley, 1965.

Galbraith, John Kenneth. *Economics and the Public Purpose.* Boston: Houghton Mifflin, 1973.

Machlup, Fritz. *The Economics of Sellers' Competition.* Baltimore: Johns Hopkins Press, 1952.

Means, Gardiner C. "The Administered Price Thesis Reconfirmed." *American Economic Review* (June 1972), pp. 292–306.

Modigliani, Franco. "New Developments on the Oligopoly Front," *Journal of Political Economy* (June 1958), pp. 215–232.

Posner, Richard A. *Antitrust Law: An Economic Perspective.* Chicago: University of Chicago Press, 1976.

Reid, Galvin C. *The Kinked Demand Curve Analysis of Oligopoly.* Edinburgh: Edinburgh University Press, 1981.

Simon, Herbert. "Rational Decision Making in Business Organizations." *American Economic Review* (September 1979).

Stigler, George J. "The Kinky Demand Curve and Rigid Prices." *Journal of Political Economy* (October 1947), pp. 432–447.

———. "A Theory of Oligopoly." *Journal of Political Economy* (January/February 1964), pp. 44–61.

———. "The Literature of Economics: The Case of the Kinked Oligopoly Demand Curve." *Economic Inquiry* 16 (1978), pp. 185–204.

Sweezy, Paul. "Demand Conditions under Oligopoly." *Journal of Political Economy* (June 1939), pp. 568–573.

EXERCISES

Evaluate

Indicate whether each of the following statements is true (agrees with economic theory), false (is contradicted by theory), or uncertain (could be true or false, given additional information). Explain your answer.

1. An oligopolistic firm in an industry without legal restrictions on entry will operate a plant which is characterized by minimum long-run average cost.
2. Price leadership generates a *mutatis mutandis* demand curve for all prices.
3. When firms are aware of rivalry, any seller can be a price leader for price cuts.
4. The assumption that managers of oligopoly firms maximize sales (revenue) allows for an awareness of rivalry which does not result in a kinked demand curve.
5. Product differentiation is not, per se, a barrier to market entry; however, product differentiation does magnify the effectiveness of other barriers, such as economies of scale.
6. As long as sellers can enter an oligopolistic industry by purchasing the assets of existing firms, a competitive outcome will prevail for price, output, and profit.
7. If the market price of an oligopolistically supplied commodity were found to be in the inelastic region of the industry demand curve, sellers were not successfully colluding to cartelize the industry.
8. There is really no such thing as long-run equilibrium under oligopoly.
9. Out of all oligopoly models, price will range between the ideal cartel price and the minimum long-run average cost.
10. The failure of economists to agree on a single model of oligopoly points out a fundamental weakness of neoclassical economic theory.

Calculate

Answer each of the following questions, showing all your calculations.

11. Consider a duopoly facing an average revenue function of $p = 100 - 2(Q_1 + Q_2)$, where Q_1 and Q_2 are the outputs of sellers 1 and 2, respectively. Each seller's cost function is $C_1 = 100 + 10Q_i$, $i = 1, 2$ (i.e., $MC_i = 10$).

    a. Derive the marginal revenue function for each seller under the Cournot assumption that the other seller does not change output.
    b. Derive the quantity reaction function for each seller in terms of the (given) output of the other seller.
    c. Determine the equilibrium output and price for the Cournot model.
    d. Compare the profit for each seller under the Cournot equilibrium with the profit each would receive under collusive monopoly, each receiving one-half the cartel profit.

12. Assume the following demand functions for a differentiated duopoly: $Q_1 = 88 - 4p_1 + 2p_2$, and $Q_2 = 56 + 2p_1 - 4p_2$.

    a. Calculate the formula for the cross elasticity of demand for each seller in terms of its own output and the rival's price.
    b. Calculate the impact of each firm's price change on its own revenue, including the anticipated effect of the price response of the rival; that is, derive an expression of the form:
    $$\frac{\Delta(p_i Q_i)}{\Delta p_i} = Q_i + p_i \left[\frac{\Delta Q_i}{\Delta p_i} + \frac{\Delta Q_i}{\Delta p_j} \left(\frac{\Delta p_j}{\Delta p_i} \right) \right]$$

    c. Revise your answer to part *b* so that the percentage change in firm *i*'s revenue with respect to a 1 percent change in its own price is given as a function of its own price elasticity, the cross elasticity between its sales and the rival's price, and the percentage change in the rival's price due to a 1 percent change in its own price.
    d. Show that each firm's total revenue is more responsive to a 1 percent change in its price when the rival's reaction is zero than when the other firm matches price changes.

13. An industry is composed of ten firms which produce a homogeneous product. The market demand (average revenue) curve is given by

the formula $p = 100 - 0.5Q$, where $Q = \sum q_i$. Each firm's costs are given by the formula $C = 100 + 5q_i^2$, so that $MC_i = 10q_i$.

a. Derive an expression for the common industry marginal cost curve. (Hint: solve $MC_i = 10q_i$ in terms of q_i, then replace $10q_i$ with Q.)

b. Determine the cartel price and output by setting industry marginal cost equal to industry marginal revenue, $MR = 100 - Q$.

c. Determine each firm's cartel profit under the assumption that each produces 10 percent of industry output.

d. Suppose one firm decides to cheat, believing that price will fall by only 50¢ for each extra unit it produces. Determine the firm's *ceteris paribus* marginal revenue equation and its profit-maximizing price and output.

e. Compare the cheater's profit when cheating is undetected and when all other producers match its output, with the firm's share of cartel profit. At what probability of detection would a risk neutral firm consider cheating a good gamble?

Contemplate

Answer each of the following in a brief but complete essay.

14. The failure of empirical tests to indicate the existence of a kinked demand curve in concentrated industries indicates that oligopolistic pricing is not materially different from pricing in less concentrated industries (e.g., perfect and monopolistic competition). Do you agree or disagree? Explain your answer.

15. In *Economics and the Public Purpose*, John Kenneth Galbraith states: "That price increases follow wage increases shows, more than incidently, that profit maximization is not the purpose of the technostructure. If revenues could be increased after a wage increase, they could, obviously, have been increased well before." Comment on the accuracy of this statement if (a) total revenue, rather than merely price, actually did increase after a wage increase, and (b) Galbraith is using "revenue" as a synonym for "price."

PART FIVE
Income Distribution and Economic Welfare

We now turn our attention to factor markets, where households are sellers of the services of factors of production and firms are buyers of those services. At this point, we are reaping the benefits of the details which engaged us in earlier chapters. Much of the theory of factor markets can be derived easily from the interplay of profit maximization by firms and utility maximization by households—topics already developed for product markets. Another bonus is that the mixture of theory and application can now tilt heavily in favor of the latter. And, as befits an area of such crucial concern as the determination of wages, rents, and profits, many of the topics which will be discussed are quite controversial.

Chapter thirteen develops the supply and demand of factor services for ideal (i.e., competitive) input markets, although a few impediments to pure competition among sellers (e.g., incomplete property rights to raw materials, patents of specific capital goods) are also discussed. The culmination of chapter thirteen is the marginal productivity theory of income distribution, which relates the price of each factor's services to the value of its contribution to total output.

We will close the chapter by clarifying some of the mistaken notions about modern income distribution theory.

Chapter fourteen considers the determination of wages and employment in imperfectly competitive labor markets. Two major themes are pursued throughout the chapter: (1) the impact of labor associations on employment, wages, and profits, and (2) the economic causes and consequences of discrimination, whether unequal pay for equal work, or unequal access to work itself. Labor unions are viewed as cartels—monopolistic associations of sellers. Yet the impact of these cartels on wages and employment depends heavily upon the extent of competition among employers. When wages and employment are competitively determined, the introduction of labor monopoly raises wage rates but reduces employment in the affected market, often resulting in discrimination as a means of job rationing. On the other hand, industrial unions that bargain collectively with a few employers can raise wages and employment together, and thus have an incentive to avoid discrimination. With similar irony, competitive employers who discriminate on the basis of race or gender are penalized by market forces. The invisible hand waves the banner for equal opportunity.

The final chapter ties together the diverse theories developed throughout the text. Chapter fifteen asks how well an ideal market system would advance the economic welfare of individual participants. We derive an important theorem of *welfare economics,* which states that perfect competition in all input and output markets would produce a general equilibrium that would minimize the sting of scarcity. In an ideal economic system, it would be impossible to improve the economic well-being of any

participant without harming some other participant, since all such improvements should have already been made. We also consider why real-world economies fall short of this ideal outcome. We do not encounter easy answers. On the frontiers of economic research looms a troubling question: can a system guard individual liberties—composed in part of the right to property—and at the same time deny market power to any individual or group, so that markets remain beyond the influence of all save the invisible hand? But we give away too much of the plot. Read on.

Chapter 13

Income Determination Through Ideal Input Markets

The standard of living of a household usually depends more on the prices of inputs it sells than on the price of any commodity it buys. Postponing income distribution until the end of the book requires some justification. By honing our understanding of the interaction of households and firms through commodity markets, we have laid a solid foundation upon which to construct an economic analysis of income distribution. Although the topics encountered in the determination of income are controversial, the logic of economics allows us to understand the arguments used on both sides of hotly disputed issues.

In this chapter we will see that the competitive theory of income distribution has a largely deterministic flavor. Firms hire input services of land, labor, and capital according to the market value of the marginal product of each. Workers and the owners of capital and land compare their income prospects from alternative uses of their inputs and select the option that generates the highest income or contributes the most to utility. It is easy to forget that the real world is often less than ideal, and that one's income often depends on being in the right place at the right time. If our view of events is too mechanical, we easily miss much of the paradox, and indeed the charm, of life.

The Competitive Firm's Demand for Variable Inputs

When we move from product markets to input markets, households and firms exchange roles, while their basic motivations remain largely the same as those ascribed to them in theories of product markets. We assume that households attempt to maximize utility as sellers of input services, and that firms attempt to maximize profits while purchasing those services in competitive factor markets. The demand for input services, therefore, depends on the contribution of inputs to profit; the supply of input services (as briefly previewed in chapter three) depends on the psychic rewards and money income from alternative employment prospects. The ideal input market in neoclassical microeconomics is a mirror image of the ideal commodity market: by harnessing the egoistic motives of participants, the market generates socially efficient results as unintended side effects of selfish behavior.

Recall from chapter six that a competitive firm attempts to hire input services so that the price of each factor is proportional to its marginal physical product. We also saw that this common ratio of each input's price to its marginal contribution to output generated the firm's marginal cost in the output market:

$$MC = \frac{\Delta C}{\Delta q} = \frac{\Delta C/\Delta L}{\Delta q/\Delta L} = \frac{w_l}{MP_l} = w_l \times MI_L$$

$$MC = \frac{\Delta C/\Delta K}{\Delta q/\Delta K} = \frac{w_k}{MP_K} = w_k \times MI_K$$

where w_l and w_k are the prices (wage and rental rates) of labor and capital services, respectively, and $MI_i = 1/MP_i$ represents the **marginal input services** needed to produce one more unit of output.

According to the theory of perfect competition, each firm sets its output where marginal cost equals the market-determined price of the commodity it sells. Simple algebra transforms the marginal-revenue-equals-marginal-cost-rule into a profit-maximizing rate of employment for input services: $p = MC$ implies $p = w_i/MP_i$, so that $p \times MP_i = w_i$ for each variable input v_i. A competitive producer will hire each variable input's services so that the last unit hired produces exactly enough revenue (output price times marginal product) to cover that factor's price. Each buyer of an input used to produce a commodity sold under competitive conditions is motivated by the desire to maximize the difference between what factor owners must be paid and the revenue obtained from selling the output those factors produce. Hence, more input services are hired at lower prices than would be hired at higher prices, *ceteris paribus*. Economists call this the *derived demand* for inputs.

Table 13-1 reprises the short-run production example introduced in chapter five. As before, we assume that the Typical Oatmeal plant has fixed land and capital capacities and that individual workers are equally skilled: they can be hired in any order without changing the relation between the quantity of labor and the rate of output. At low rates of output, the marginal product of labor rises as employment expands, due to gains from specialization. Ultimately, the impact of diminishing marginal productivity sets in as more workers are added to fixed land and capital. The **value of labor's marginal product,** VMP_L, is calculated as the price of the commodity times the marginal product of labor: $VMP_L = pMP_L$. In the last two columns of Table 13-1, the value of labor's marginal product is calculated for two market-determined oatmeal prices, $0.50 and $0.75 per pound. We see that a higher commodity price increases the value of each worker to the firm, even though the marginal physical product associated with each employment of labor remains the same as long as available capital and land (and the characteristics of workers) do not change.

Because important issues like variable worker effort and differences in worker characteristics have been assumed away, Table 13-1 implies that the value of labor's marginal product is dependent on two factors wholly beyond a worker's control: the price of the output (determined by a competitive market) and the number of workers hired (determined by the employer's attempt to maximize profit). In its abstract form, the theory of labor demand by the competitive firm is completely divorced from notions about any worker's merit or need.

TABLE 13-1
Marginal Productivity and Value of Labor's Marginal Product for Typical Oatmeal Company

Number of Labor Hours	Total Output (per hour)	Average Product of Labor	Marginal Product of Labor	Value of Marginal Product of Labor	
				$p = \$0.50$	$p = \$0.75$
0	0	—	—	—	—
1	10	10.0	10	$ 5.00	$ 7.50
2	25	12.5	15	7.50	11.25
3	45	15.0	20	10.00	15.00
4	70	17.5	25	12.50	18.75
5	90	18.0	20	10.00	15.00
6	105	17.5	15	7.50	11.25
7	115	16.4	10	5.00	7.50
8	120	15.0	5	2.50	3.75
9	120	13.3	0	0.00	0.00

Note that regardless of the price of oatmeal, the value of a ninth worker would still be zero. This is because that worker is assumed to have a zero marginal product and, hence, adds nothing to the firm's revenue at either product price. There is no presumption of laziness on that worker's part or poor management on the employer's part. Rather, it is assumed that no more than 120 pounds of oatmeal can be produced per hour and that plant capacity is reached when the eighth worker is hired. As we saw in chapter five, hiring more than eight workers would imply producing in stage III of the short-run production function, a contradiction of the profit maximization assumption. Note further that hiring between one and four workers would involve producing in stage I, implying a negative marginal product for land and/or capital. Regardless of the product price or the wage rate, the quantity of labor services hired will never involve a negative marginal product for any variable or fixed input.

Figure 13-1 presents the familiar short-run profit maximization problem of the competitive firm in a different light: cost and revenue are both depicted as functions of labor services. Assuming that the wage rate is determined by forces beyond the firm's control makes labor costs a linear function of the amount of labor employed. As in Table 13-1, revenue depends on output and price; two possible prices are depicted. Assuming that labor is the only variable input means that maximum revenue always occurs when $L = L_{max}$ (eight worker-days in Table 13-1), regardless of the price of the commodity. When the marginal product of labor equals zero, no more output can be produced unless plant capacity is expanded.

As depicted in Figure 13-1, the profit maximization problem involves maximizing the distance between the total revenue curve, pq (whose slope is the value of labor's marginal product, pMP_L), and the variable cost line, wL (whose slope is the constant wage rate). The minimum amount of labor that would be hired is identified by the shutdown condition: total revenue must exceed variable cost. Since variable cost is now a linear function of output, the shutdown wage rate is identified by the variable cost line which is tangent to the relevant total revenue curve. Note that dashed line $W_0^{max}L$ is tangent to total revenue curve p_0Q at the same amount of labor, L_{min}, which is also associated with the tangency of $W_1^{max}L$ to p_iQ. This is more than coincidence. Using the information from Table 13-1, a price of $0.50 per pound ($p_0$) would support a wage rate no higher than $9.00 per hour ($w_0^{max}$); a price of $0.75 per pound ($p$) would allow the firm to pay a wage rate as high as $13.50 per hour ($w^{max}$) before excessive variable costs would force the plant to close. However, at both prices for oatmeal, the least amount of labor hired would be five workers (L_{min}).

Staying with the data in Table 13-1, imagine that the wage rate were $7.50 for blue-collar workers in food processing. Since this is less than

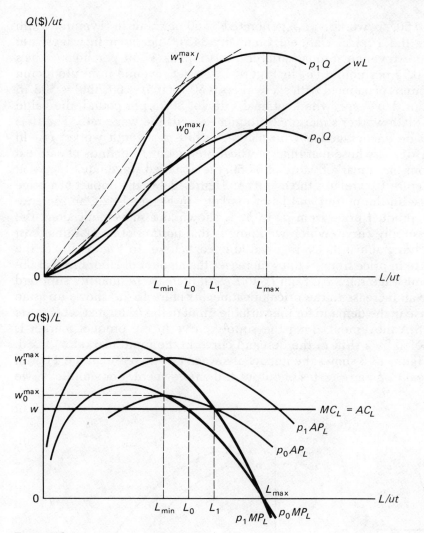

Figure 13-1
Short-Run Profit Maximization: The Labor Side.

the shutdown wage for either price, we can compare the optimal quantity of labor services for the alternative output prices. If $p = \$0.50$ (i.e., p_0 in Figure 13-1), the sixth worker (L_0 in Figure 13-1) would produce enough revenue to pay his or her wage, since the value of that worker's marginal product would exactly equal the wage rate. Since total revenue (price times output) can be calculated as $p \times q = p \times q/L \times L = p \times AP_L \times L$, net revenue (revenue minus variable cost) equals the difference between the market value of the average product of labor and the marginal product of labor, times the number of workers hired. When

$p = \$0.50$, six workers ($L_0$) generate $52.50 per hour in revenue, while costing the Typical Oatmeal Company $45.00 per hour in wages: net revenue (revenue minus variable cost) equals $7.50 per hour. When $p = \$0.75$ per pound (p_1 in Figure 13-1), net revenue from producing 105 pounds of oatmeal with six workers is $0.75(105) - 6(\$7.50) = \$33.75$ per hour. However, when oatmeal sells for $0.75 per pound, the value of the sixth worker's marginal product exceeds the wage rate. The firm would be encouraged by the market to hire a seventh worker (L_1 in Figure 13-1), whose marginal physical product of 10 pounds of oatmeal per hour has a market value of $7.50, the assumed wage rate.

Figure 13-2 relates the events of Figure 13-1 to the impact of a price increase in the output and labor markets. In Figure 13-2*a*, an increase in the product price from p_0 to p_1 is shown as a movement along the firm's supply curve, which we know is that portion of its marginal cost curve lying above its average variable cost curve. In Figure 13-2*b*, the increase in price from p_0 to p_1 increases the amount of labor hired at the constant wage rate, w_0, from L_0 to L_1. An increase in quantity supplied due to an increase in the price of oatmeal (Figure 13-2*a*) shows up as an increase in the demand for the variable input in the factor market (Figure 13-2*b*). A movement along the supply curve in the product market is paralleled by a shift in the demand curve in the input market.

Figure 13-3 shows the impact of a wage rate increase on the Typical Oatmeal Company's rates of output and employment. For simplicity, we

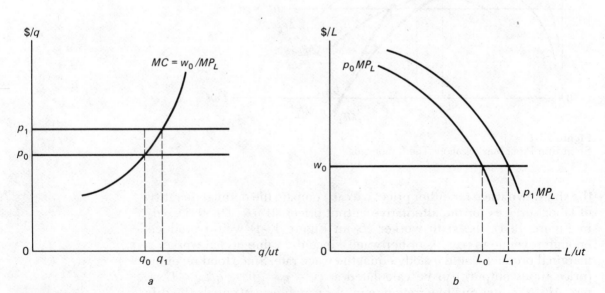

Figure 13-2
Impact of Output Price Increase on (*a*) Output and (*b*) Employment

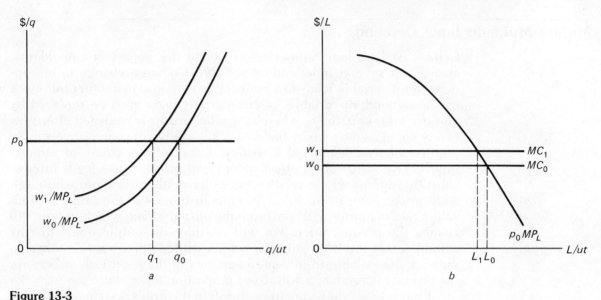

Figure 13-3
Impact of Factor Price Increase on (a) Output and (b) Employment

assume that the wage increase for workers in food processing is due to local conditions (e.g., the opening of a cannery in Littleberg, where Typical Oatmeal's plant is located), so that a change in the firm's rate of output will not be associated with a change in the price of oatmeal. In Figure 13-3b, an increase in the wage rate from w_0 to w_1—the price of oatmeal and the marginal product schedule for labor being constant— reduces the quantity of labor demanded from L_0 to L_1. With fewer workers employed, Typical must have reduced its production of oatmeal; since (by assumption) the price of oatmeal did not change, the reduced rate of output must have resulted from a leftward shift of the firm's short-run supply curve.

Figure 13-3a shows that the increase in the wage rate caused an upward shift in the Typical Oatmeal Company's marginal cost curve. If the price of the product does not change, the firm must reduce its rate of output until the higher marginal cost curve, w_0/MP_1, intersects the constant marginal revenue, p_0. In Figure 13-3a, output falls from q_0 to q_1 per hour. If due solely to local influences, an increase in the price of a variable input cannot be passed on to consumers through a higher price. Unless there is a perceptible change in market-wide output, localized cost increases must be absorbed by competitive firms or those firms will probably go out of business. In the real world, expanding job prospects for workers can have brutal side effects for competitive employers.

Mutatis Mutandis Input Demand

Ceteris paribus logic allows us to isolate the impact of coincidental changes in several independent variables. When a change in one independent variable leads to a predictable response in another influence on the dependent variable, *ceteris paribus* logic must be replaced by *mutatis mutandis* logic, whereby a relationship is analyzed after necessary changes have been made. Our knowledge of competitive supply predicts likely reactions to a change in the relative prices of variable inputs. The *substitution effect* of an input price change leads firms to substitute inputs whose relative prices have fallen for those whose relative prices have risen. In addition, adjustments in the profit-maximization rate of output will constitute the *output effect,* which in turn will change the product price. We will consider the output effect first by assuming that input substitution is impossible, either because other inputs are unavailable in increased amounts in the short run, or because the product is produced with fixed proportion technology.

Figure 13-4a shows an upward shift in the firm's marginal cost curve (from MC_0 to MC_1), which is proportional to the increase in the wage rate when input substitution is impossible. With product price constant at p_0, the firm would reduce its rate of output from q_0 to q', *ceteris paribus.* However, Figure 13-4b shows that an *industry-wide* wage increase would shift the market supply curve from S_0 to S_1, creating a shortage of $Q_0 - Q'$ at the prevailing price p_0. This shortage would raise price to p_1, causing the typical firm to increase output to q_1. In Figure 13-4c, we see that the typical firm, which had planned to reduce em-

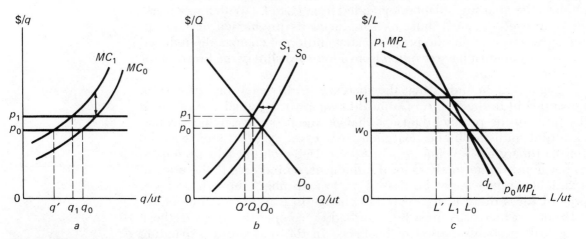

Figure 13-4
Mutatis Mutandis Demand for Labor. Wage increase causes upward shift of each firm's marginal cost curve (a), leads to decrease in supply and increase in price (b), tracing out the *mutatis mutandis* demand for labor, d_2, in the factor market (c).

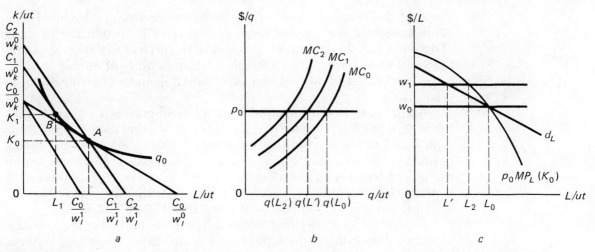

Figure 13-5
Impact of Wage Rate Increase. *a*, Input substitution; *b*, output effect; *c*, *mutatis mutandis* labor demand.

ployment from L_0 to L', discovers that the price increase has justified the employment of L_1 workers, where $L_0 > L_1 > L'$.

Let us review the logical connection between the three diagrams in Figure 13-4. If the change in the price of the variable input has no perceptible impact on market-wide output, the individual firm varies employment of input services along the *ceteris paribus* value of marginal product schedule $p_0 MP_L$ in Figure 13-4c. If the change in price of variable input services causes a shift in the market supply curve of the commodity, the response to that input price change will be mitigated (but not eliminated) by a counteracting change in the price of the product. After the industry-wide price repercussions are accounted for, the firm will change its use of input services along the *mutatis mutandis* input demand curve, d_L, in Figure 13-4c.[1]

In Figure 13-5 we drop the simplifying assumption that labor is the only variable input to examine the impact of factor substitution on the

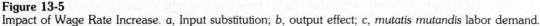

[1] The full impact of a factor price change on factor employment can be determined by taking the partial derivative of profit with respect to the wage rate, then solving for $\partial L/\partial w$, the change in employment due to a unit increase in the wage rate:

$$\frac{\partial \pi}{\partial w} = \frac{\partial pq}{\partial w} - \frac{\partial wL}{\partial w} = \frac{\partial (pq)}{\partial L} \cdot \frac{\partial L}{\partial w} - L = 0$$

implies:

$$\left(p \frac{\partial q}{\partial L} + q \frac{\partial p}{\partial q} \cdot \frac{\partial q}{\partial L} \frac{\partial q}{\partial L} \right) \frac{\partial L}{\partial w} - L = p \quad \text{or} \quad \frac{\partial L}{\partial w} = L \left(p \frac{\partial q}{\partial L} + q \frac{\partial p}{\partial q} \frac{\partial q}{\partial L} \right) - 1$$

Since $\partial p/\partial q = 0$ if the wage change is isolated and $\partial p/\partial q < 0$ if the wage change is market-wide, the absolute value of $\partial L/\partial w$ will be greater in the case of the isolated wage change.

shape of the firm's demand curve for labor services. In Figure 13-5a, point A depicts the optimal input combination for producing q_0 units of output when the ratio of the price of labor services to the price of capital services is w_l^0/w_k^0. The variable cost of q_0 units of output is $C_0 = w_l^0 L_0 + w_k^0 K_0$, as identified by isocost line C_0, tangent to isoquant q_0 at point A.

An increase in the wage rate from w_l^0 to w_l^1 creates a steeper isocost line: the labor intercept for cost C_0 slides back along the horizontal axis from C_0/w_l^0 to C_0/w_l^1. Without input substitution, the cost of producing q_0 units would increase to $C_2 = w_l^1 L_0 + w_k^0 K_0$. If the same rate of output can be produced with more capital and less labor, the cost of producing q_0 units rises only to $C_1 = w_l^1 L_1 + W_k^0 K_1$, identified by isocost line C_1, which is tangent to isoquant q_0 at point B in Figure 13-5a.

Figure 13-5b shows that factor substitution mitigates the increase of marginal cost due to the higher price of one input's services. Without input substitution, MC_0 shifts to MC_2; the total reduction in the quantity of labor services demanded would be due to the output effect. Because the capital input is assumed fixed at K_0, the reduction in labor services from L_0 to L_2 is traced along the stationary value of marginal product schedule $p_0 MP_L(K_0)$ in Figure 13-5c. The substitution effect of a wage increase (Figure 13-5a) reduces the magnitude of the output effect in Figure 13-5b, so that MC_0 shifts only to MC_1. However, with input substitution, the quantity of labor services demanded falls from L_0 to L'. In Figure 13-5c, the substitution effect causes the *mutatis mutandis* demand curve, d_L, to show a greater responsiveness to a factor price change than does the *ceteris paribus* demand curve in Figure 13-4c, which reflects only the output effect.

The possibility of input substitution also complicates the market price effect of an industry-wide rate change. If most employers are able to substitute inputs, the output effect of a wage rate increase will be smaller than it would be if most firms could not substitute inputs. Since price adjustment serves to *reduce* the response of the quantity of labor services demanded to a wage increase, the *mutatis mutandis* demand curve reflecting both input substitution and output price adjustment will be more elastic the greater the magnitude of the substitution effect of a change in relative prices of input services.

To summarize, in an ideal market with homogeneous input services and perfectly competitive employers, the demand for input services is a *derived demand*. The *ceteris paribus* input demand curve is identical to the factor's value of marginal product curve, with output price and the quantity of other inputs being constant. When an input price change leads to market-wide price repercussions, the *mutatis mutandis* input demand curve will be less responsive than the *ceteris paribus* value of marginal product schedule. When input substitution occurs, the *mutatis mutandis* input demand curve will be more responsive to an input price change than when input substitution is not possible.

Input Demand by Differentiated Producers

Our earlier discussions of monopoly, monopolistic competition, and oligopoly showed that firms confronting negatively sloped demand curves produce less output and charge higher prices than they would if marginal revenue equaled the price for all rates of output. Table 13-2 presents the plausible case of a pizza parlor with a negatively sloped demand curve for its differentiated product, while the firm can hire as much labor as desired at the market-determined wage rate. The first two columns in Table 13-2 show that Mom's Pizza Parlor, with a fixed production capacity, experiences increasing marginal productivity of labor for the first two workers (Mom and her son); then the marginal product declines as more workers are hired until maximum output of 95 pizzas per day is reached with six workers.

The third column in Table 13-2 indicates that price falls from a maximum of $10 (the price intercept of the demand curve) at the rate of 5¢ per pizza. The value of labor's marginal product is the price of pizza times the marginal physical product of labor. The automatic downward price adjustment as output expands indicates that this value of marginal product schedule is a *mutatis mutandis* relation. However, it is characteristic of profit-maximizing sellers that changes in output are valued only at the marginal revenue they generate. Hence, the services of an additional worker are valued according to the **marginal revenue product**, MRP_L, of that worker. Because marginal revenue is less than price, the contribution of an additional worker to revenue will be smaller than the value of his or her marginal product: $VMP_L = pMP_L > MRP_L = MR(MP_L)$.

Suppose that kitchen help could be hired at the rate of $25 per day. If pizzas were a homogeneous commodity whose price was set by a

TABLE 13-2
Employment, Output, and Marginal Revenue Product for Mom's Pizza Parlor

Workers per day	Pizzas per day	Price ($p = $10 - 0.05q$)	Value of Labor's Marginal Product	Total Revenue	Marginal Revenue Product
0	0	$10.00	—	0	—
1	20	9.00	$180.00	$180.00	$180.00
2	45	7.75	193.75	348.75	168.75
3	65	6.75	135.00	438.75	90.00
4	80	6.00	90.00	480.00	41.25
5	90	5.50	55.00	495.00	15.00
6	95	5.25	26.25	498.75	3.75
7	95	5.25	0.00	498.75	0.00

competitive market at, say, \$5.25 each, Mom would hire six workers and produce 95 pizzas per day, since the value of marginal product of the sixth worker is \$26.25. Net revenue would be $TR - wL = \$498.75 - \$150.00 = \$348.75$. However, because of the negatively sloped demand curve for Mom's pizza, the marginal revenue product of the sixth worker is only \$3.75. This worker would not return his or her pay to a producer of a differentiated commodity, even though a perfectly competitive producer would hire the sixth worker. Indeed, the fifth worker, whose marginal product is worth \$55.00 would not be hired, because his or her marginal revenue product is only \$15.00. By limiting employment to four workers, Mom is able to charge \$6 per pizza. Total revenue falls to \$480.00 (i.e., the demand for pizza is price elastic), but variable (labor) costs fall to \$100.00. Net revenue rises to $480 - \$100 = \$380$.

Since imperfect competition in the product market causes a firm to restrict output to where $MR = MC$, the firm hires fewer variable input services than it would if production expanded until $MC = p$. In Figure 13-6, product market and factor market conditions are juxtaposed for a monopolistically competitive seller, like Mom's Pizza Parlor. The negatively sloped average revenue curve ($D = AR$) in Figure 13-6a shows the adjustment of commodity price to changes in output. The profit-maximizing rate of output, q_m, is identified by the intersection of the marginal revenue and marginal cost curves, where marginal cost is the price of each variable factor divided by its marginal product: $MR = MC$ implies $MR = w/MP_L$. Multiplying both sides of that equation by the marginal product of labor, we have $w = MR(MP_L)$. Unlike the perfectly competitive producer, who would hire the services of each variable input in quantities that caused the value of that factor's marginal product to equal the price of its services, the imperfectly competitive producer hires variable input services only to the point where the marginal revenue product of that factor equals its market-determined price.[2]

In Figure 13-6b, a monopolistically competitive seller, facing a constant wage of w_0, hires L_m workers per day, identified by the intersection of the marginal revenue product curve, MRP_L, and the horizontal marginal cost of labor line, $MC_L = w_0$. By contrast, a competitive seller in the product market would have hired L_c workers per day to produce q_c units of output per day. For the competitive firm, marginal revenue equals price, so that the marginal revenue product of a variable input equals the market value of that input's marginal product ($MRP_L = VMP_L$).

---

[2] Maximizing $\pi = pq(L) - wL$ with respect to L (assuming labor is the only variable input) implies:

$$\frac{d\pi}{dL} = \left(p + q\frac{dp}{dL}\right)\frac{dq}{dL} - w = 0$$

so that $w = MR(MP_L)$.

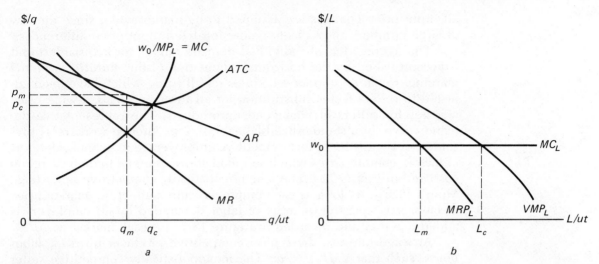

Figure 13-6
Input Demand by Imperfect Competitor Operating as (a) Monopolistic Competitor in Output Market and (b) Price Taker in Input Market.

For the imperfectly competitive seller, price exceeds marginal revenue, so that the marginal revenue product of each variable input is less than the market value of its marginal product ($MRP_L < VMP_L$).

Market Demand for Labor

To derive the market demand curve for the services of a variable input, we sum the quantity demanded by each firm for each market price. To simplify the aggregation process, economists usually make a number of simplifying assumptions, which will be relaxed in chapter fourteen. First, we assume that individual input units (e.g., worker-hours, machine-hours, acres of land, tons of iron ore) are perfect substitutes for one another. That is, it doesn't matter which worker is hired, since workers are assumed to be equally productive; it doesn't matter which machine is used, because individual machines are assumed to be in an identical state of repair. This assumption of homogeneous input services allows us to define the marginal product of one input in terms of the amount of that input used and the proportion of that input (e.g., labor) relative to other inputs (e.g., capital, land). Second, we assume that employers are indifferent about input characteristics which do not affect productivity (e.g., a worker's race, or gender, the brand name of machinery, the amenities in the town where the plant is located). Third, all input price changes are assumed to be market-wide, since the law of large numbers allows us to ignore localized input price differences.

The aggregation of individual demand curves for a variable input is accomplished by the horizontal summation of the *mutatis mutandis* marginal revenue product schedules for all firms, which have been adjusted to reflect factor substitution for all firms and market-wide price changes for sellers of homogeneous products. The representative demand curve for a standardized labor skill (e.g., kitchen workers) is presented in Figure 13-7a for competitive employers (e.g., school cafeterias or factory commissaries which sell food at prices equal to their marginal cost) and in Figure 13-7b for a monopolistically competitive seller (e.g., Mom's Pizza). As long as each employer cannot affect the market price of labor services, the quantity of labor demanded by all employers is added together and recorded in Figure 13-7c for each market wage.

At wage rate w_0, the typical competitive producer hires L_{c_0} labor hours, such that $VMP_{L_0} = w_0$. The monopolistically competitive seller hires L_{m_0}, identified by the condition that $MRP_{L_0} = w_0$. The corresponding quantity of labor services demanded by all employers at wage rate w_0 is ΣL_0 in Figure 13-7c. At the higher wage rate w_1, the perfectly competitive producer hires L_{c_1}, and the monopolistically competitive seller hires L_{m_1}, resulting in the aggregate quantity demanded of ΣL_1. The shift in the *ceteris paribus* demand curve for the competitive producer reflects the combined effects of input substitution (making employment changes more sensitive to wage rate changes) and market-wide product price adjustments (which slightly mitigate the impact of wage changes on the hours of labor services demanded). Since the marginal

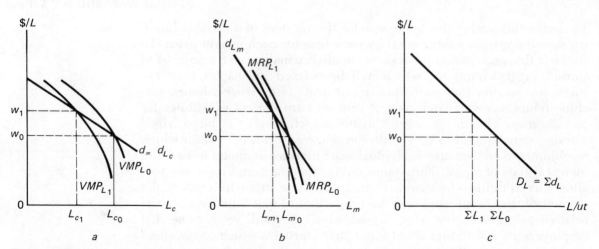

Figure 13-7
Aggregation of Individual Demand to Obtain Market Demand for Input Services. *a*, Perfectly competitive firm; *b*, monopolistic competitor; *c*, market demand.

revenue product curve of an imperfectly competitive producer already reflects the impact of output changes on the firm's revenue, the shift from MRP_{L_0} to MRP_{L_1} reflects only the impact of input substitution.

Given the negatively sloped demand curve for all firms employing the services of an input sold in a competitive factor market, it follows that market demand for that input will also have a negative slope. However, it is prudent to keep in mind that while *mutatis mutandis* demand curves were treated as special cases in the aggregation of consumer demand for goods and services, they are the rule with market demand for inputs. Our knowledge of the process of profit maximization means that many more side effects of a factor price change, such as input substitution and product price adjustment, can be predicted; careful use of logic requires that input demand curves be aggregated only *after* necessary changes have been made.

APPLICATION
Factor Price Elasticity of Demand

The relative importance of input substitution, output price changes for competitive producers, and the elasticity of demand for imperfectly competitive producers will determine the responsiveness of employment changes to a change in the price of a variable input. Like price elasticity of demand in the product market, **factor price elasticity of demand** measures the percentage change in the quantity of an input demanded due to a 1 percent change in the price of that input. And factor price elasticity can similarly be employed to predict how a factor price change will affect total payments to suppliers of factor services.

In Figure 13-8, a wage rate of w_0 results in employment of L_0 workers, meaning a total wage payment of w_0L_0 per period, which is represented by the rectangle with length Ow_0 on the vertical (wage rate) axis and width OL_0 on the horizontal (labor) axis. An increase in the wage rate to w_1 reduces the quantity of labor demanded to L_1. Whether total payments to workers in this market will increase, decrease, or remain the same depends on the relative size of wage gains for workers still employed ($L_1\Delta w$) compared with wage losses due to the employment reduction ($w_0\Delta L$).

Algebraically, the change in wage payments equals:

$$\Delta(wL) = L_1\Delta w + w_0\Delta L$$

Dividing by the change in the wage rate, Δw, and suppressing the subscripts on w and L for generality, we have:

$$\frac{\Delta(wL)}{\Delta w} = L + w\frac{\Delta L}{\Delta w} = L(1 + \xi_L)$$

where $\xi_L = (\Delta L/L)/(\Delta w/w)$.

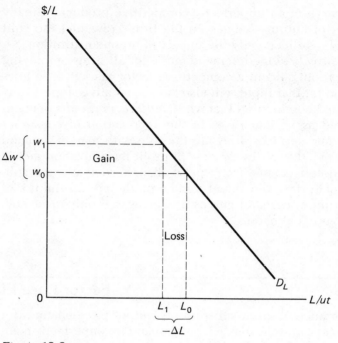

Figure 13-8
Geometric Interpretation of Factor Price Elasticity of Demand

The factor price elasticity of demand (represented by ξ, the Greek letter *xi*) equals the percentage change in the quantity of input services demanded divided by the percentage change in the factor's price. Since market demand for factor services is an inverse relation between quantity of services demanded and the factor's price (*ceteris paribus*), the factor price elasticity of demand for labor, ξ_L, or for any input, is a negative number. Elastic demand, $\xi_L < -1$, means that the percentage change in labor services demanded more than offsets the percentage change in the wage rate; wage payments and the wage rate change in opposite directions. Factor price *inelastic* demand, $0 > \xi_L > -1$, means that the quantity response to a wage rate change is too weak to prevent wage payments and the wage rate from moving in the *same* direction. Finally, if the demand for labor is *unit elastic*, $\xi_L = -1$, the percentage change in the wage rate is exactly offset by the percentage change in employment; wage payments *will not change*.

Alfred Marshall listed four "laws" (or tendencies) of elasticity of demand for an input.[3] The demand for a factor's services are more elastic:

---

[3] Alfred Marshall, *Principles of Political Economy*, 9th ed. (London: Macmillan & Co., 1961), section 2, mathematical note XV.

1.   the greater the importance ("indispensability") of the factor in the production of a commodity[4]
2.   the more price elastic the demand for the final product
3.   the greater share of the factor in total costs
4.   the greater price of complementary factors (e.g., machinery and energy).

Market Supply of Labor

In chapter three the individual's supply of labor *time* was the consequence of the household's allocation of time between leisure (or household production) activities and income-earning activities. To simplify the analysis, the assumption was made that work activity itself provided no utility, so that the labor-leisure choice was based wholly on the wage rate offered and not on nonpecuniary aspects of different jobs.

Now, in exploring the motives behind the market supply of labor, we must note that the amount of labor time an individual offers in exchange for a wage depends in part on the satisfaction or dissatisfaction that alternative jobs provide. Jobs differ in prestige, fulfillment, danger, fellowship, and opportunities for goofing off. A worker is often willing to accept a lower rate of pay to enter an occupation which provides greater satisfaction than the higher paying job he or she holds. Workers also accept lower rates of pay when entering professions which offer the prospect of advancement; a higher wage would be required to fill what is considered a dead-end job. Yet dead-end jobs often pay less because workers who fill them have few attractive alternatives.

Careers which differ in rates of pay and degrees of satisfaction also require different skills, which in turn are acquired through the investment of differing amounts of time and effort. Jobs which require a high-school education generally pay less than those which require a college degree, *ceteris paribus*. Many individuals will sacrifice four years of income or leisure to obtain a college degree only if they believe they will receive higher income as a result.

The supply of labor services is affected by the worker's allocation of time between work and leisure, by the number of workers who are qualified for a particular job, and by the *reservation wages* of different

---

[4] The elasticity of substitution is the characteristic of a production function which relates the percentage change in the ratio of factor services to the percentage change in the marginal rate of technical substitution, which is equal to the factor price ratio when factor services are used efficiently:

$$\sigma = \frac{[\partial(K/L)]/(K/L)}{\partial MRTS/MRTS} = \frac{[\partial(K/L)]/(K/L)}{[\partial(MP_L/MP_K)]/(MP_L/MP_K)} = \frac{[\partial(K/L)]/(K/L)}{[\partial(w_l/w_k)]/(w_l/w_k)}$$

See the business illustration on pp. 536–537.

Business Illustration
The Elasticity of Substitution

The ability of a firm to substitute inputs in the wake of a relative input price change depends on (1) the extent of minimum purchase contracts and maximum availability constraints, and (2) the technological aspects of production itself. The *elasticity of substitution* is a feature of a production function which relates the percentage change in the ratio of input services to the slope of the isoquant. This may seem an esoteric concern. But remember, for a price taker in all input markets, the optimal input combination is identified where the ratio of marginal products for any two (variable) inputs equals their price ratio:

$$\sigma = \frac{\dfrac{\Delta(K/L)}{K/L}}{\dfrac{\Delta MRTS}{MRTS}} = \frac{\dfrac{\Delta(K/L)}{K/L}}{\dfrac{\Delta(MP_L/MP_K)}{MP_L/MP_K}}$$

$$= \frac{\dfrac{\Delta(K/L)}{K/L}}{\dfrac{\Delta(w_l/w_k)}{w_l/w_k}}$$

For the price taker in all input markets, the elasticity of substitution measures the sensitivity of input proportions to changes in relative factor prices.

A fixed-proportion production function, discussed in chapter seven, is characterized by a rigid ratio of factor services. Input substitution is impossible when only one production process exists, and hence $\sigma = 0$. If two technically efficient processes exist, isoquants are character-ized by constant slopes: $MP_L/MP_k = b$, so that $MRTS = -b$. Since the marginal rate of technical substitution does not change, $\sigma = \infty$ when K/L does change. If a firm is using a relatively labor-intensive process because $w_l/w_k < b$, any relative price change which caused $w_l/w_k > b$ would cause a drastic change in factor proportions (since the capital-intensive process would become the economically efficient process).

The business relevance of the elasticity of substitution is easy to see. If factor substitution is difficult, that is, if $0 \leq \sigma < 1$, the share of factor payments to owners will increase as the relative price of a factor increases. For instance, an increase in the union wage rate would reduce the quantity of union workers employed in competitive labor markets, but if the elasticity of substitution is less than one, total payments to the union would increase. On the other hand, if $\sigma > 1$, a factor's share of revenue will decrease as its relative price increases. A highly elastic response of optimal input proportions to a change in relative factor prices would severely limit the ability of a labor union to increase total wage payments.

For empirical studies, economists have made wide use of the *Cobb-Douglas production function*, whose form, $q = AL^\alpha K^\beta$, simplifies its statistical estimation. Unlike fixed-proportion and linear production functions, the Cobb-Douglas function exhibits diminishing marginal productivity for both inputs. The drawback is that regardless of the relative shares of labor and capital (given by α and β, which are the respective output elasticities of labor and capital), the elasticity of substitution for a Cobb-Douglas function is always one.

While some evidence exists that factor shares are relatively constant over time, assuming a Cobb-Douglas production function merely assumes constant factor shares and does not test that proposition. A more general production function is the *constant elasticity of substitution* (CES) production function, which has the form:

$$Q = A[\alpha L^{-\rho} + (1 - \alpha)K^{-\rho}]^{-1/\rho}$$

where $\sigma = 1/(1 + \rho)$. When $\rho = 0$, the CES production function becomes the Cobb-Douglas production function.

Using the CES formula, J. R. Moroney estimated the elasticity of substitution for nineteen broadly defined manufacturing industries using data for 1956, 1957, and 1958.[*] His 1957 results showed one industry (nonelectrical machinery) wherein the null hypothesis of $\sigma = 0$ could not be rejected, three industries (pulp and paper, rubber and plastics, and stone, clay, and glass) wherein the null hypothesis of $\sigma = 1$ could not be rejected, and fifteen industries wherein both null hypotheses could be rejected, giving the statistically reliable estimate that $0 < \sigma < 1$. In no case was the elasticity of substitution significantly greater than one.

Moroney's results seem to call into question the practice of *assuming* a unitary elasticity of substitution as a means of explaining relatively constant factor shares. It is possible than combinations of inelastic response of factor proportions and imperfections in factor markets (discrimination, monopoly, and monopsony) may account (in yet unexplored ways) for this regularity.

However, the Moroney results have not gone unchallenged. Roger Waud tested the sensitivity of production man-hours in manufacturing to wage rate changes and estimated an average elasticity of -0.926, which seems to support the assumption of a unitary elasticity of substitution.[†] Unlike the Moroney study, the Waud study used time series data, which has the advantage of allowing for changes in the capital stock. At the same time, the data in the Waud study were more aggregated. It seems reasonable to conclude that the Moroney study showed that factor proportions tend to be somewhat unresponsive to relative factor price changes in the short run, while Waud's results imply a long-run elasticity of substitution closer to unity. Moroney's results emphasize the importance of testing one's assumptions, rather than building crucial assumptions into the formulas of empirical estimates.

---

[*] J. R. Moroney, *The Structure of Production in American Manufacturing*, Chapel Hill, N.C.: University of North Carolina Press, 1972, pp. 36–65.

[†] Roger N. Waud, "Man-Hour Behavior in U.S. Manufacturing: A Neoclassical Interpretation," *Journal of Political Economy* (May/June 1968), pp. 407–427.

workers. The **reservation wage** is the minimum wage a worker must receive (or expect) in order to offer labor services in a particular market.

Figure 13-9a depicts the short-run labor supply for a skilled occupation, say, secretarial services. At very low wage rates, most people qualified for secretarial jobs pursue other careers which may or may not take advantage of skills in typing, shorthand, or office management. As wage rates for secretaries rise, the reservation wage of more workers will be surpassed. Those already working as secretaries may seek full-time instead of part-time employment; others will return to secretarial careers. At some wage, the reservation wage of those in jobs offering lower nonpecuniary rewards than secretarial work will have been surpassed; larger and larger wage increases will be required to increase the number of persons offering secretarial services. People in occupations which provide more satisfaction—executive assistants, managers, editors—would require a substantial pay increase to switch to a lower status secretarial job.

Figure 13-9b shows that, in the long run, there tends to be a greater responsiveness of quantity supplied to a change in the factor price. If most qualified workers have been attracted to a profession at wage rate w_0, additional labor services can be obtained in the short run only by encouraging those already employed to substitute income for leisure and by attracting a few more workers from jobs with preferred nonpecuniary characteristics. In the long run, however, students can take courses which prepare them for a secretarial career; workers in other fields can also enroll in secretarial school. Given more time for adjustment, higher wage rates will attract additional workers into an occupation. At wage rates below w_0, workers trained for secretarial careers would be inclined to develop alternative job skills, thereby reducing the amount of labor

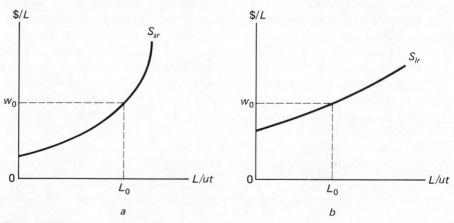

Figure 13-9
Labor Supply (a) in the Short Run and (b) in the Long Run

supplied in the long run below that supplied in the short run. The supply of an input is likely to be *more elastic* in the long run than in the short run.

Elasticity of Supply of a Variable Input

The **elasticity of supply of input services** measures the percentage change in the number of units of a variable input offered divided by the percentage change in the factor price:

$$E_{Ls} = \frac{\Delta L_s / L_s}{\Delta w / w} = \frac{\Delta L_s}{\Delta w} \left(\frac{w}{L_s} \right)$$

Since the supply curve for an input is normally assumed to be positively sloped, an increase in the factor's price will increase payments to factor owners. Major interest actually lies in the reciprocal of supply elasticity. By what percentage would a factor's price have to be increased to generate a 1 percent increase in the quantity of factor services offered?

When workers have different job opportunities, varying preferences for income and leisure, and a range of tastes for the nonwage aspects of various jobs, the market supply of labor will be positively sloped. Elastic supply means that a 1 percent increase in the market wage rate results in more than a 1 percent increase in the amount of labor services offered. Inelastic supply means that employers must raise wage offers by more than 1 percent to increase the amount of labor offered by 1 percent.

Figure 13-10 demonstrates how the elasticity of supply can be measured. Figure 13-10*a* depicts a linear supply of labor which passes through the origin. Such a supply curve has an elasticity which equals one at every point.[5]

Figure 13-10*b* depicts a nonlinear supply curve of labor services. The elasticity of supply can be measured by finding the slope of a line tangent to the supply curve at the point of interest. The line tangent to S_L at point $A(L_0, w_0)$ passes through the origin; the elasticity of supply at point A is one. At point B, the tangent line intersects the horizontal (labor) axis; the ratio of L_1 to w_1 is greater than the rate of change of labor services supplied due to a change in the wage rate. The supply of labor is inelastic at point B.

Figure 13-11*a* shows the supply of labor schedule for a price taker in a competitive market. A horizontal supply curve implies an infinitely elastic supply of input services. If a competitive firm offered less than the market wage, workers would leave that firm for jobs with other

---

[5] A linear equation passing through the origin is described by $w = bL$, so that $\Delta L / \Delta w = 1/b$. The elasticity of supply, accordingly, is $E_{Ls} = \Delta L / \Delta w (w/L) = 1/b(bL/L) = 1$.

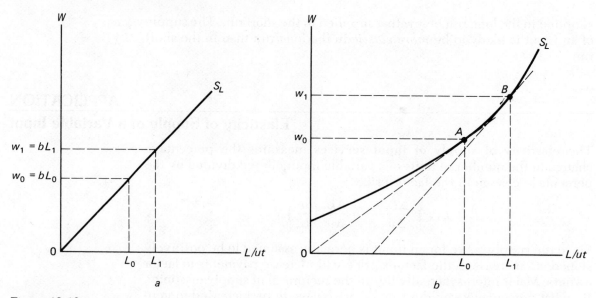

Figure 13-10
Geometric Interpretation of Elasticity of Supply for (a) Linear Supply Curve and (b) Nonlinear Supply Curve

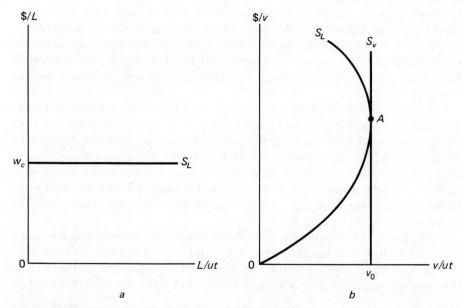

Figure 13-11
Extreme Cases: (a) Perfectly Elastic and (b) Perfectly Inelastic Input Supply Curves

employers; if an employer who had signed a collective bargaining agreement offered less than the contract wage, workers would go on strike. On the other hand, an infinitely elastic labor supply means an employer can hire as many hours of labor services as desired at the prevailing (market or contract) wage without having to offer a higher wage.

In Figure 13-11*b*, supply curve S_v represents the opposite extreme of zero elastic input supply: the same quantity of input services is offered at all prices for those services. Curve S_v is not a plausible supply curve for labor, since workers are expected to substitute leisure for work at low wage rates; S_v might be a plausible supply curve for land, however. The backward-bending supply curve of individual labor services might be mirrored in the market supply schedule if natural (e.g., inherited talents) or artificial (e.g., occupational licenses) barriers kept workers from entering the industry in response to higher wage rates. At point *A*, the backward-bending supply of labor schedule, S_L, has a zero elasticity of supply, with $E_{Ls} > 0$ for lower wage rates and $E_{Ls} < 0$ for higher wage rates. As we will see in chapter fourteen, when a tendency by individual workers to substitute leisure for work at high wage rates cannot be offset by the entry of additional workers into that occupation, the market supply of labor might actually take on a configuration like S_L in Figure 13-11.

Competitive Input Markets: Land

The zero elastic supply curve has been used to depict the aggregate supply of land, which may be defined as a nonproduced, nonlabor input. The nineteenth-century American economist and social reformer Henry George proposed that the fairest means of financing government services would be a single tax on land rent, since the quantity of land supplied to the economy could not change in response to the net (after-tax) rent received. When alternative uses of land are considered, however, the supply of land for one particular use (e.g., residential housing) depends on the rent that could have been earned in its next best use (e.g., agriculture). Hence, the supply of land services to alternative users is likely to have positive price elasticity up to that rental rate at which all available land has been bid away from alternative uses.

As we have seen, the demand for productive inputs depends on the net revenue (gross profit) generated by an extra unit of input service. Production is a flow concept, measured as output or revenue per unit of time. The relevant price for nonlabor inputs is the *rental rate* (e.g., dollars per acre per year), which makes nonlabor input prices comparable to the wage rate paid for labor services. A firm that leases land, equipment, or even money pays a periodic rental rate specified by the lease contract. A firm that owns productive property must make periodic payments on loans for which that property serves as collateral, but its opportunity cost equals the income that input would receive in its next best use. Even a firm which leases property may experience a divergence between the contractual payment and an input's opportunity cost. A business paying rent of $500 per month for land another company would sublease for $1,000 a month will sacrifice $1,000 per month by using that property itself.

We begin our analysis of a competitive market for a nonproduced factor of production with the determination of the rental rate for land in one industry—say, wheat growing. The demand for land is determined by the competitive equilibrium condition that the market value of land's marginal product equals the rent paid for the period during which the land's marginal product was measured. The supply of land is dependent on the rent the land could earn in alternative uses (e.g., growing corn or staging rock concerts). The productivity of land within the industry in question is reflected in the demand curve for land; the productivity of land in other industries is mirrored in its supply curve.

In Figure 13-12, the competitive rental rate for wheat land equals R_0, where the market demand curve D_0 intersects market supply curve S_0. All land for which productivity is higher in wheat growing and for which the marginal product is at least equal to R_0 would be used in wheat production. All land for which the opportunity cost exceeds R_0 or for which the marginal product is valued at less than R_0 would be used in another industry or remain idle. With demand curve D_0 and supply

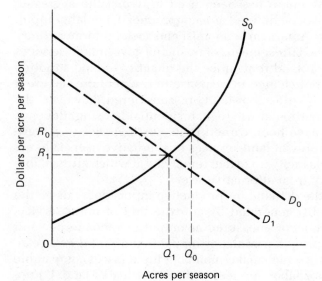

Figure 13-12
Competitive Determination of Land Rent

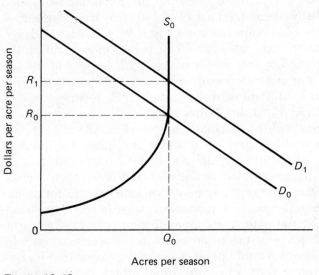

Figure 13-13
Land Rent Becomes Economic Rent

curve S_0, rental rate R_0 causes the market to clear with Q_0 acres. Higher rental rates would create a surplus; more land would be offered to wheat farmers than they would be willing to lease. Competition among landowners would then lower the rent being asked. If the rental rate fell below R_0, a shortage of wheat land would occur, and competition among farmers would raise bids for land use to grow corn.

At the equilibrium rental rate, the last acre hired just pays its own way: the value of land's marginal product in wheat production is exactly what it would have earned in the next best alternative use. Acreage which would have been offered at rents higher than R_0 will be used in other industries. Some land, the *inframarginal* acreage, will receive rent R_0 even though this exceeds the rent necessary to keep that land in wheat production. A leftward shift in the demand for wheat land, due, say, to a reduction in the market demand for wheat, would cause the equilibrium rent to fall. Land no longer earning its opportunity cost ($Q_0 - Q_1$ in Figure 13-12) would be shifted to alternative uses, while land whose marginal product at the lower wheat price still covers its rent would remain in wheat production at R_1. When the elasticity of supply of an input is greater than zero but less than infinity, a change in factor demand will result in a change in both the equilibrium price and the equilibrium quantity in the same direction.

In Figure 13-13, the aggregate supply of land in a particular location is all bid into a particular use (e.g., residential construction) when the market determined rent reaches R_0. A rightward shift in the demand for residential land from D_0 to D_1 cannot cause the amount of land supplied to increase once all the available land has been bid away from alternative uses. When the supply of an input becomes perfectly inelastic ($E_{Ts} = 0$ where T = terra), further increases in factor prices merely ration the available quantity among buyers. Factor payments in excess of the opportunity cost of an input are called **economic rent**. In Figure 13-13, the last acre of residential land employed (Q_0) at rental R_0 receives an economic rent equal to $R_1 - R_0$ at the higher rate.

The term *economic rent* (or Marshallian rent, after Alfred Marshall, who popularized the term) is perhaps unfortunate, given the popular association between "rent" and payments for the use of land. Not all payments for land are necessarily economic rent, as Figure 13-12 shows. Nor are all forms of economic rent payments for land: any factor owner who receives more than the factor's opportunity cost is receiving some economic rent. Finally, the extent of economic rent is largely a matter of perspective. At the level of the price taker in a factor market, who confronts a perfectly elastic supply of an input at the prevailing market rate, there is no economic rent, since any input which the firm might employ could also be employed by a competitor. When a factor market is in competitive equilibrium, only the last unit employed earns no economic rent; inputs which would be supplied to the same industry at lower prices are receiving an economic rent equal to the difference between the prevailing price and that minimum price.

APPLICATION
Raw Materials and Intermediate Goods

The equilibrium prices of intermediate goods and raw materials are determined in much the same way as the rental rate for land. The major difference is a conceptual one: whereas land is an input which is neither produced nor destroyed, raw materials and intermediate goods are delivered at the beginning of the production cycle and transformed into part of the final product. For instance, agricultural land actually contains raw materials—the nutrients in the soil and the topsoil itself—which can be exhausted unless replenished by crop rotation or the use of fertilizer. The demand for raw materials and intermediate goods depends on their marginal revenue products, as usual. The supply of these inputs depends on their production or extraction cost or the value of the input in its next best use, whichever is greater.

If the input is extracted or manufactured under competitive conditions, the positively sloped supply curve reflects the cost of delivering one more unit to the user. However, as discussed in chapter eight (and later in chapter fifteen), conflict between optimal specification of property rights and the ideal amount of competition in the market may blur the definition of the ideal market price.

Consider the costs associated with an extractive industry. Discovery and drilling costs are, quite literally, sunk costs. The relevant cost consideration for a competitive oil producer (if there is such a thing) would be the cost of pumping and transporting oil, as well as the present value of revenue foregone by not keeping the oil for some future sale. The higher today's price relative to the present value of the expected price tomorrow, the more oil would be offered for sale in the present.

Property failure can occur when two or more wells (or mines) are sunk into the same deposit. Each operator expects others to pump oil (or extract minerals) from that common source; no operator has an incentive to consider foregone future revenue as a cost, since each expects rivals to extract as much as possible. The market price would be little more than pumping costs if common oil pools were widespread. Market failure would occur if the entire source of a raw material or intermediate good fell under the control of a single seller or a cartel. As was shown in chapter ten, a monopoly seller internalizes the "lost revenue" from inframarginal units of output when price must be reduced on all quantities sold in order to sell the marginal unit. Because monopoly sellers of an input equate the marginal revenue from an input with its marginal (opportunity) cost, market failure generates an artificially high price for the raw material or intermediate product.

The real tension between property failure and market failure occurs when the source of supply is not divisible or use of the input is not exclusive. Whales, elephants, and jungle cats are endangered species, while trout, cattle, and minks are not endangered. The former species are "bred in the wild." Hunters have little incentive to limit their harvest of these animals because some other hunter can be expected to kill the game any hunter leaves behind. No one owns these animals; no one has an incentive to assure that enough adult pairs are left alive to continue the species. In contrast, trout farms and cattle and mink ranches allow sellers to compare the value of animals as breeders with the immediate revenue from butchering them.

Pollution occurs because scarce air and water resources are not exclusive. Users of air and water are not assessed a fee equal to the cost of cleaning up the pollution they cause. Also, producers who do not pollute the air or water cannot recover their higher production costs; steel produced without polluting the air sells for the same price as steel produced with pollution. Optimal input use requires that a divisible input be exchanged in competitive markets. Few environmentalists would advocate awarding ownership rights to air and water resources to chemical and steel producers. While chemicals and metals might be produced more efficiently, consumers of air and water would be more happy paying monopoly prices for these necessities of life.

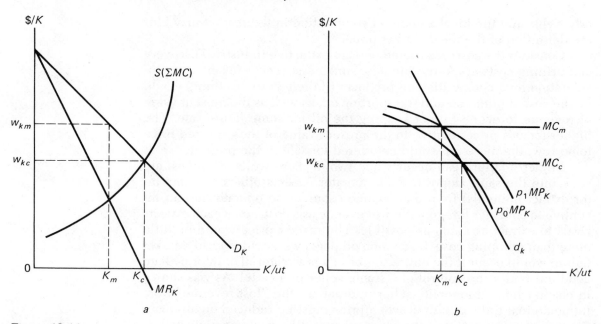

Figure 13-14
Contrast Between Competitive and Monopoly Capital Rentals. *a*, Producer(s) of capital; *b*, buyers of capital (services).

Capital Goods: Commodities Which Produce Other Commodities

Capital has been defined as a "commodity which produces other commodities."[6] In the short run, the rental rate paid for machine services is determined by the marginal revenue product of capital for buyers and the (opportunity) cost of providing machine services for the owners of that machinery. The profit-maximizing quantity of machine services for a competitive firm is determined by the number of machine-hours for which the value of capital's marginal product equals its market-determined rental rate. At competitive rental rate w_{kc}, the user in Figure 13-14*b* would hire K_c machine-hours per period. In Figure 13-14*a*, that competitive rental rate is identified by the intersection of the market demand curve for capital services, D_k, and the market supply curve, which reflects the variable costs of providing machine services.

This concept of a competitive market for capital services is complicated by the nature of capital goods as embodied technology. Years of research and development costs usually precede the introduction of a

---

[6] Piero Sraffa, *The Production of Commodities by Means of Commodities* (Cambridge, England: Cambridge University Press, 1960).

new capital good on the market. These research and development costs are risky investments because expenditures of scarce time and resources will receive a positive return only if the firm is (1) successful at developing a marketable machine and (2) able to prevent others from copying the design of the machine. Were free entry allowed in the capital goods market, some sellers (leasors) could poach on the ideas of others: buying a single machine, they could copy the design at much lower cost than the research and development costs. The tragedy of the commons would result if all firms waited around to copy ideas no seller had an incentive to develop by itself.

This potential property failure is avoided by the granting of patents—transferable licenses which award an inventor or innovator exclusive rights to the *use* of an idea for a specified number of years. Since patents are monopoly licenses, the monopolization of the supply of a *type* of capital good causes the producer to reduce services to K_m, where the marginal revenue from leasing capital equals the marginal cost of capital services. The resulting rental rate of w_{km} in Figure 13-14 causes the competitive lessee to reduce the use of capital to the point where the value of capital's marginal product (after the upward adjustment of the output price) equals the higher marginal cost of capital.

The second analytical complication is also implied by the heterogeneous nature of capital goods. Because capital is a durable good, a machine or building will provide a stream of services over time, until the capital wears out or becomes obsolete. Capital goods can provide services only after they have been produced—someone in society must *invest* scarce resources in the production of capital goods in anticipation of the future revenue the stream of capital services will generate. If the capital good must be tailor-made to the specifications of a producer of a differentiated product, the firm may find that long-run costs are lower if it invests directly in machinery and buildings, rather than leasing the services of machines owned by another firm.

The *investment* decision is based on the same temporal considerations outlined in chapter three in connection with the household saving-borrowing decision. Given the existence of financial markets which allow savers to earn an interest income while requiring borrowers to make interest payments on consumption loans, a firm will prefer to receive a dollar today rather than a dollar a year from now. The interest rate represents the opportunity cost of committing a dollar to an investment project. If the firm uses borrowed funds to finance an investment project, the interest payments will be an explicit, albeit a fixed, cost. If the project is financed by an entrepreneur's wealth or the retained earnings of stockholders, the interest cost is the opportunity cost of foregone interest income.

Recall that if a firm leases capital, optimal employment is given by the equality of the marginal revenue product of capital and the rental rate. For a price taker in the product market, $p = MR$, so that $w_k = pMP_K$.

A firm would find it advantageous to purchase the capital good outright if the present value of the future rentals that would be saved exceeded (or at least equaled) the present cost of the investment:

$$p_{kt} \le \frac{w_{kt+1}}{(1 + i_{t+1})} + \frac{w_{kt+2}}{(1 + i_{t+2})^2} + \cdots + \frac{w_{kt+n}}{(1 + i_{t+n})^n}$$

where w_{kt+j} is the rental rate the investor expects to pay j years in the future, i_{t+j} is the real rate of interest (adjusted for risk) that is expected to prevail in that year, and p_{kt} is the purchase price of a machine (or building) today.

We can simplify this relation between the rental rate, w_k, and the purchase price of capital, p_k, by imagining that the rental rate and the rate of interest are expected to remain constant n years into the future. This allows us to drop the temporal subscripts on w_k and i. Now the firm's optimal investment occurs when it purchases the amount of machinery such that its price equals the present value of rentals saved:

$$p_k = \frac{w_k}{(1 + i)} + \frac{w_k}{(1 + i)^2} + \cdots + \frac{w_k}{(1 + i)^n}$$

Multiplying both sides of this expression by $(1 + i)$, then subtracting the original equation, we have:

$$p_k(1 + i) = w_k + \frac{w_k}{1 + i} + \frac{w_k}{(1 + i)^2} + \cdots + \frac{w_k}{(1 + i)^{n-1}}$$

$$-p_k \qquad\qquad -\frac{w_k}{1 + i} - \frac{w_k}{(1 + i)^2} - \cdots - \frac{w_k}{(1 + i)^{n-1}} - \frac{w_k}{(1 + i)^n}$$

$$\overline{ip_k \qquad\quad = w_k - \frac{w_k}{(1 + i)^n}}$$

Since the long-run equilibrium lease rate would cover the cost of replacing machinery as it wore out, the replacement cost of capital is implicit in the firm's equipment purchase decision. This allows us to assume that the firm replaces its machinery as it wears out, making n a very large number. But as n increases, $1/(1 + i)^n$ approaches zero, so that we can drop the last term. This implies that a company would buy its own equipment when:

$$i \le \frac{w_k}{p_k} = \frac{p_0 MP_k}{p_k}$$

so that $p_k \le p_0 MP_k / i$.

Ignoring the complications of uncertainty, technological change, and market imperfections, the price of a machine will equal the present value of its future marginal revenue products. In deciding the optimal allocation of inputs, the firm should use the rental rate for capital $(w_k = ip_k)$ when comparing the "price" of capital services with the "price" of labor services (the wage rate) and the "price" of land services (the rental rate).

Wage Competition and the Ideal Labor Market

Neoclassical theory, in its search for generality and simplicity, treats the *ideal* labor market as an analogue of the competitive market for non-human inputs. A large number of buyers and sellers of a homogeneous commodity—labor services—reach a bargain so that, at the market wage, the quantity of labor supplied equals the quantity of labor demanded. Like the model of the perfectly competitive product market, the theory of wage competition is based on a set of simplifying assumptions. The crucial[7] assumptions are the following:

1. There are so many employers and so many workers that no individual participant in the labor market can have a perceptible impact on the market wage.
2. Workers possess identical skills, which have been acquired prior to the employment decision. All workers are paid the same market-determined wage rate.
3. Employers are profit maximizers who hire labor only on the basis of the value of labor's marginal product relative to the market wage rate.
4. Real wages are freely flexible to rise during periods of labor shortage and to decline during times of a labor surplus in an industry or occupation.
5. There are no artificial barriers to entry for either workers or employers. Workers need only possess the requisite skills to offer labor services, while employers can hire labor merely by paying the equilibrium wage.

These assumptions imply that a competitive labor market cannot be in equilibrium if (1) there are workers who wish to supply more labor time than employers will hire at the going wage rate, or (2) there are firms which cannot hire as much labor as their managers wish at the prevailing wage. In Figure 13-15*a*, the market clearing competitive wage is identified by the intersection of the market demand curve for labor, based on the *mutatis mutandis* marginal revenue product of labor in the firm (Figure 13-15*b*), and the market supply curve of labor, which depends on the number of workers who are qualified for the job, the distribution of wage offers for other jobs, and workers' tastes for leisure and

---

[7] As discussed in chapter one, a *crucial* assumption is an assumption upon which the results of a theory depend sensitively; if the assumption is modified, so are the predictions of the theory.

Policy Illustration
Minimum Wage Laws, Employment, and Income

A frequent criticism of competitive labor markets is that they may fail to provide an adequate living for the families of workers whose skills command low wage rates. The function of a competitive labor market is to establish wage rates for different types of labor skills so that the quantity which employers wish to hire equals the amount labor workers wish to supply, given the distribution of skills and job opportunities. There is no objective basis for arguing that the wage rates determined by market forces are fair or just. Nevertheless, the model is useful for showing the side effects of mandating higher-than-equilibrium wage rates, as with minimum wage rates, set by amendments to the Fair Labor Standards Act, originally enacted in 1938.

Figures *a* and *b*, respectively, depict the impact of a minimum wage law on a firm's output and the competitive price, and on the market-wide quantity of labor demanded and supplied. We assume that the wage rate would be set at w_c and employment would equal L_c in the absence of a mandatory minimum wage, resulting in competitive price p_0 and output q_0 for

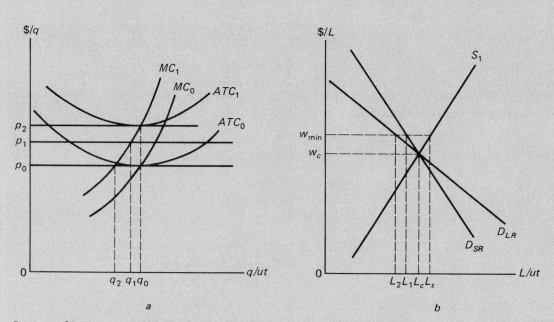

Impact of Minimum Wage Law on *a*, Output and Price, and *b*, Employment.

the typical firm. A minimum wage of $w_{min} > w_c$ would reduce employment to L_1 along the short-run market demand curve for labor D_{SR}, which reflects adjustments for input substitution and the increase in the price of the product, but not the exit of firms. The price adjustment is shown in figure b, where the minimum wage rate shifts the firm's short-run marginal cost curve from MC_0 to MC_1, reducing output at p_0 to q_2. The resulting market-wide shortage raises the price to p_1, which lies below the higher average total cost curve, ATC_1, at output q_1.

In the short run, the beneficiaries of the mandated minimum wage rate are the L_1 workers still employed at that wage rate, since their earnings exceed what they would receive under competitive equilibrium. Other beneficiaries include owners of capital, as well as skilled workers whose productivity already resulted in wage rates greater than the minimum, since demand for substitute inputs will increase. Victims include firms, which incur short-run losses; consumers, who pay higher prices; workers who lose their jobs as a result of the higher wage ($L_c - L_1$ in figure b); and workers who want to work for the higher wage but are not hired ($L_s - L_c$ in figure b). In the long run, further input substitution and the exit of some firms will raise the price to p_2, where the typical firm is again experiencing zero economic profit. In addition, employment decreases in the long run along the long-run *mutatis mutandis* labor demand curve, D_{LR} to L_2.

Empirical evidence supports the argument that raising the minimum wage rate, or increasing the number of workers covered by mandated federal minimum wages, reduces the employment of unskilled and inexperienced workers, particularly teenagers.* At the same time, those studies generally estimate the elasticity of demand for teenage workers from -0.1 to -0.3, meaning that higher minimum wage rates probably increase wage payments to that group assumed to bear the brunt of the unemployment effects of minimum wage laws.

Nevertheless, economists generally discourage the use of mandated minimum wage rates as a means of eliminating low wage rates. Those who oppose income redistribution on principle use the experience with minimum wage rates to argue that a majority of the poor are hurt by these laws—a result which is inconsistent with the evidence of inelastic demand for teenage and unskilled workers. Those who favor some minimum income guarantee usually oppose legislation which ignores the side effects of interfering in competitive labor markets. These economists tend to favor training programs which increase labor productivity or transfer programs, like the negative income tax (discussed in chapter three), which supplement family earnings without unduly distorting beneficial consequences of competition in labor markets.

---

* Charles Brown, Curtis Gilroy, and Andrew Kohen, "The Effect of the Minimum Wage on Employment and Unemployment," *Journal of Economic Literature* (June 1982), pp. 487–528.

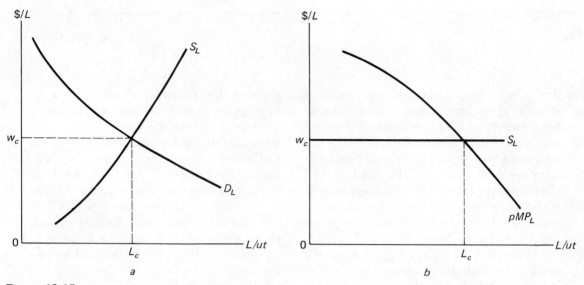

Figure 13-15
Equilibrium Wage and Employment in a Competitive Labor Market. *a*, The market; *b*, the firms.

the nonpecuniary aspects of jobs. At wage rate w_c employers wish to hire L_c labor hours per time period, and L_c labor hours are offered by workers per time period. Were the wage rate higher than w_c, more labor hours would be supplied than demanded; wage competition among workers would reduce the wage rate to its equilibrium value. Were the wage rate less than w_c, a shortage of workers would result; competition among employers would raise the wage to w_c, eliminating the labor shortage.

The operation of a competitive labor market generates an efficient allocation of labor services which corresponds to the competitive equilibrium in the product market. Each firm produces that output for which marginal cost equals market price. This solution in the output market is mirrored in the factor market by the equality of the wage rate and the value of the marginal product of labor.

Multiple Labor Market Equilibria: Compensating Differentials

According to the competitive model of labor markets, the equilibrium wage rate for a labor skill is determined by the intersection of the market demand and supply curves for that labor service. Employers are assumed to care only about the marginal revenue product of labor; workers are assumed to compare wage rates offered for different labor skills they possess and pick that job (and offer that amount of labor time) which maximizes utility. Because the supply of labor in each labor market depends, in part, on the wage rate workers could receive in other markets, the wage competition process suggests an explanation of wage differences.

Figure 13-16 depicts unequal equilibrium wage rates for two labor markets; market A pays a higher wage rate than market B. If both labor markets are competitive—that is, qualified workers are free to apply for jobs in either market—the wage differential must compensate workers in the higher paid market for resource or psychic costs (or lower nonpecuniary rewards) in that occupation. For instance, suppose market A is the market for assistant professors of finance, and market B is the market for assistant professors of economics. Since it is not unusual for a finance professor to have a doctorate in economics, while it is unusual for an economics professor to have a doctorate in finance, higher pay for beginning finance professors would attract some individuals with Ph.D.'s in economics. According to the model of perfectly competitive labor markets (which is, at best, only an approximation of entry-level academic markets), persistently higher pay for assistant professors of finance would indicate that the lower paid economics professors were receiving enough nonmoney income in the form of job satisfaction to offset lower money income. Put another way, economists who migrate to finance departments apparently require higher money income to compensate for lower psychic income or higher psychic costs in those departments.

Suppose that the demand for assistant professors of finance increases, while the demand curve for assistant professors of economics

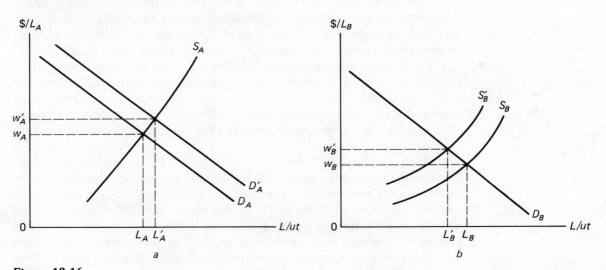

Figure 13-16
Impact of Change in Labor Demand in One Industry on Equilibrium Wage Differences: *a*, market A; *b*, market B.

remains stationary. An initial shortage of beginning finance professors at w_A causes universities to offer higher wages for faculty members with Ph.D's in finance or economics willing to teach finance. As wages for fledgling finance professors begin to rise, some economists are induced to apply for positions in finance departments. This shows up as a leftward shift of supply curve S_B to S_B' in Figure 13-16b. Wages for economics professors now rise to stem the migration. If migration stops when wage rates $w_{B'}$ and $w_{A'}$ have been reached, a new compensating differential has been established. A **compensating differential** is an equilibrium wage differential which reflects psychic or financial costs associated with the higher-paying occupation.

There are many possible causes of compensating wage differentials. We expect the guy who gets shot out of the cannon to be paid more than the assistant who lights the fuse, given the greater danger associated with the former occupation. According to the 1980 salary survey reported by the National Association of Business Economists, the median salary for business economists working in New York City was $44,000, while the median salary for business economists in the rest of the country was $37,000. It is plausible that the higher salary compensated New York economists for higher costs of consumer goods and housing. On the other hand, male business economists had a median salary of $38,200 per year outside New York City, while female business economists reported median earnings of $27,600. Although the disparity in salaries for male and female economists might be explained by the lower average age and experience of female economists or by sex discrimination, it would *not* constitute a compensating differential.

As defined here, and as the term is ordinarily used, compensating wage differentials reflect voluntary decisions by suppliers of labor services and thus do not directly reflect influences on demand, such as worker productivity. For instance, young men and women who decide to pursue acting careers might have sold vacuum cleaners door-to-door instead. Hence, if vacuum cleaner salespeople earn higher average wages than actors and actresses, we might consider this difference in *expected* wage rates a compensating differential; most people are more attracted by the nonfinancial aspects of acting than of selling vacuum cleaners.

Once we drop the simplifying assumptions of homogeneous labor, free mobility between jobs, and no discrimination or other barriers to market entry, we must take care in determining when wage differences are compensating differences. The crucial test is whether or not a wage difference for different types of labor skills could be eliminated by migration of workers from one job to another. If the answer is yes, then any wage difference which persists through time would appear to stem from voluntary decisions on the part of workers in the lower paying jobs. If the answer is no, it is still possible that workers in the lower paying jobs are receiving sufficiently higher psychic income (relative to what they would receive in the other jobs) that the wage difference qualifies as a compensating differential. However, objective evidence would not allow us to reject the alternative explanation: that workers in the higher paying jobs are receiving economic rent due to natural or artificial restrictions on labor mobility.

<hr>

APPLICATION
Human Capital Investments

One source of persistent wage differences which has attracted considerable attention from theorists and applied economists is the return on investments in **human capital**. Human capital has been defined as:

> The skills, capacities, abilities possessed by an individual, which permit him to earn income. We can thus regard income he derives from supplying personal services (as opposed to lending money, letting property) as the return on the human capital he possesses. We can regard a period of formal or informal training and acquisition of these skills as a process of creating human capital, just as the construction of machinery, buildings, etc., creates physical capital."[8]

As an illustration, let us return to Figure 13-16, this time assuming that market A represents the supply of and demand for economists with a master's degree and market B represents the supply of and demand for baccalaureate economists. Upon graduation, Lee Ann can take a job as a management trainee in market B and receive wage rate w_B, or she can spend (we assume for simplicity) one extra year in school and receive a master's degree in economics, allowing her to enter market A. The cost of her master's degree will include tuition payments plus wages (or the equivalent value of leisure time) sacrificed, here w_B. If an economics education is neither inherently enjoyable nor odious, and if jobs for bachelor's degree and master's degree economists differ only in their wage prospects, Lee Ann will turn down a job in market B and undergo training for employment in market A only if:

$$\frac{E(w_A - w_B)_{t+1}}{(1 + i)} \geqq i(T + w_B)_t$$

where $E(w_A - w_B)_{t+1}/(1 + i)$ is the present value of the expected wage difference next year (after training), i is the market rate of interest, and T is the nonwage cost and w_B the foregone wage cost of one year's education. Just as investment in machinery means diverting resources

<hr>

[8] G. Bannock, R. E. Baxter, and R. Rees, *A Dictionary of Economics* (Harmondsworth, Middlesex, England: Penguin Books, 1972).

from consumer goods to producer goods, education or other training diverts time and resources from producing current income (or leisure) in order to enhance expected future income.

Figure 13-17 reprises the intertemporal consumption decision presented in chapter three. Lee Ann's consumption prospects in the present (C_t) and one year hence (C_{t+1}) are given by line EF if she accepts a job in market B at wage rate w_B. As in chapter three, maximum consumption next year, point E, is next year's wage, w_B, plus this year's wage times one plus the interest rate, $w_B(1 + i)$. Maximum (hypothetical) consumption this year, point F, is this year's wage, w_B, plus the present value of next year's wage, $w_B/(1 + i)$. If continued employment at this year's wage were her only prospect, Lee Ann would maximize her utility by consuming at point D. For simplicity, point D is set at the balanced-budget point on consumption possibility line EF.

Line GH represents Lee Ann's present and future consumption possibilities if she invests an extra year in schooling. Because human capital cannot serve as collateral for a loan, investment in education requires a real sacrifice of current consumption. Figure 13-18 is drawn so that consumption possibility line GH passes below the balanced-budget

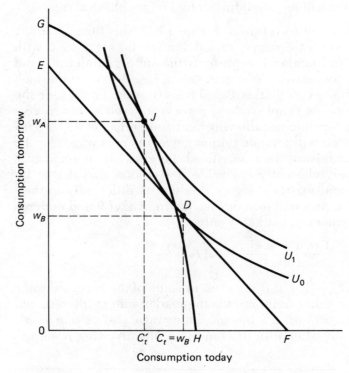

Figure 13-17
Human Capital Investment and Consumption Prospects

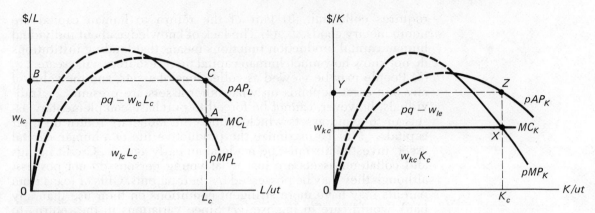

Figure 13-18
Marginal Productivity Theory of Distribution: *a*, Labor as the variable input; *b*, capital as the variable input.

point D on line EF. By reducing consumption from $C_t = w_B$ to C_t' in the present, Lee Ann can increase next year's income from w_B to w_A. By enrolling in school, Lee Ann moves to point J, where her indifference curve U_1 is tangent to consumption possibility line GH.

There is some debate among economists about whether returns to human capital investments (which also include on-the-job training, relocation, and certain health expenditures) constitute compensating differentials. Those who consider wage differences for workers with different educational attainment as equivalent to compensating differentials tend to emphasize the analytical insights from the human capital concept:

> The failure to treat human resources explicitly as a form of capital, as a produced means of production, as the product of investment, has fostered the retention of the classical notion of labor as a capacity to do manual work requiring little knowledge or skill, a capacity with which, according to this notion, laborers are endowed about equally. This notion of labor was wrong in the classical period, and it is patently wrong now.[9]

Critics of the notion that differences in earnings for workers with different educational attainment constitute compensating differentials point out flaws in the "market" for human capital investments:

> Capital markets for investment in human capital are imperfect for several reasons. (1) Capital markets in general are imperfect.... (2) Human capital may not be held as collateral, although borrowing

---

[9] Theodore W. Schultz, *Investment in Human Capital* (New York: The Free Press, 1971), pp. 28–29. Schultz, of the University of Chicago, is largely credited with popularizing the term *human capital*. Other pioneers include Gary Becker, Mark Blaug, Mary Jane Bowman, W. Lee Hansen, Lester Thurow, and Burton Weisbrod.

requires collateral. (3) Part of the return to human capital are nonmonetary goods. . . . (4) The lack of knowledge about individual human capital production functions means that lending institutions do not know how much human capital their resources will create. . . . (5) People may be viewed as collections of assets, and the value of any one asset depends on what other assets are present. . . . Individuals, however, cannot be forced to purchase complementary assets or to avoid assets which reduce the monetary return on their capital. . . . (6) To maximize the productive life of a human capital asset, investments must be made at an early age. . . . Credit ratings and collateral assets are just what young persons do not possess, although they may be possessed by their parents. Gifts or loans from parents may have more stringent conditions on their use than any bank would care to impose. (7) Since variations in the returns to human capital are very large, lending institutions may have only a vague idea of the rate of return a particular human capital asset will earn for a particular individual.[10]

In a fable published while he was a graduate student, the author argued that tastes for education tend to be formed by early childhood educational experiences, so that many students continue through college or drop out of high school because education is, on the whole, pleasurable for the one group and disagreeable to the other. After the fact, educated workers earn more because their learning makes them more productive. However, as a return on inherited abilities and tastes formed early in life, the return on educational attainment may have more in common with economic rent than with a return on investment.[11]

As with many ideas encountered in microeconomics, the problems with the concept of human capital involve differences in value judgments rather than differences over objective facts. Merely to note that education increases earnings does not indicate the extent to which education is pursued for economic motives, so that higher pay is necessary to attract workers away from jobs (or leisure) to improve their skills, and the extent to which education is essentially a consumption activity (financed by parents and government), which nevertheless bestows an enhanced earning capacity on those who enjoy education.

Marginal Productivity Theory of Income Distribution

We have seen that an ideal competitive input market would set the price of a factor's services, and the quantity of services employed, according to the demand and supply curves, representing the behavior of input

---

[10] Lester C. Thurow, *Investment in Human Capital* (Belmont, California: Wadsworth, 1970), pp. 77–78.

[11] Thomas Carroll, "Education and Income: An Analysis by Fable," *The American Economist* (Fall 1972), pp. 81–88.

buyers and input sellers, respectively. We have also seen that as long as inputs are free to move between alternative uses, differences in factor payments will tend to reflect the combined influences of the value of the marginal product of the factor (the demand side) and alternative income (and utility) prospects for the input owner. Particularly with respect to mobile labor, productivity differentials which result in pay differentials will persist only if the cost of acquiring that differential productivity exceeds the return on that "investment." Otherwise, failure of markets to eliminate payment differentials would indicate that productivity differences could not be eliminated through human capital investments (e.g., where natural talent determines worker eligibility) or that other barriers to mobility exist.

We now return to the demand side of factor price determination and investigate conditions under which total revenue earned by employers will be just enough to pay each factor owner the market value of that factor's marginal product. According to the **marginal productivity theory of distribution,** perfect competition in the product market and in all factor markets would return to each owner the market value of the marginal product of that input when all markets are in long-run equilibrium. Furthermore, since long-run equilibrium in the product market results in zero economic profit, each firm's revenue would be just sufficient to pay all input owners for input services.

Figure 13-18 presents the short-run pattern of input payments when labor and capital are the only inputs and one of them is fixed. In Figure 13-18a, labor is assumed to be the variable input. The firm maximizes short-run profit by hiring L_c workers at wage rate w_{lc}. Total wage payments, $w_{lc}L_c$, are indicated by rectangle $Ow_{lc}AL_c$—the market value of the marginal product of labor times the number of workers employed. Total revenue is given by rectangle $OBCL_c = (pq/L_c)L_c$. Total revenue minus wage payments, rectangle w_cBCA, represents the net revenue to offset fixed (capital) costs, in whole or in part.

In Figure 13-18b, capital is the variable input, and the firm hires K_c units of capital services per period at rental rate w_{kc}. Total payments to the owners of capital, $w_{kc}K_c$, equal the area of rectangle $Ow_{kc}XK_c$. Total revenue—measured geometrically as the value of capital's average product times the amount of capital services employed—equals the area of rectangle $OYZK_c$. With labor as the fixed input, net revenue remaining after the payment for capital services—rectangle $w_{kc}XYZ$—represents funds which can be applied to labor costs.

When the competitive firm is in long-run equilibrium, total revenue is exactly sufficient to pay each factor the value of its marginal product. In terms of Figure 13-18, the net revenue after one factor's marginal product has been remunerated would exactly equal the amount necessary to compensate owners of the other factor with the market value of its marginal product times the amount of that factor's services employed:

$$pq - pMP_L(L) = w_kK \quad \text{and} \quad pq - pMP_K(K) = w_lL$$

This can be true only if $w_l = pMP_L$ and $w_k = pMP_K$, so that

$$pq = pMP_L(L) + pMP_K(K)$$

Dividing both sides of this equation by p, total revenue will exactly equal the sum of competitively determined factor payments if the output is exhausted by the sum of each input times its marginal product:

$$q = MP_L(L) + MP_K(K)$$

If we divide this expression by output, we find a familiar relationship:

$$1 = \frac{q}{q} = MP_L \frac{L}{q} + MP_K \frac{K}{q} = \frac{MP_L}{AP_L} + \frac{MP_K}{AP_K}$$

In chapter five, we verified that the ratio of a factor's marginal product to its average product is its output elasticity, and the sum of all output elasticities gives the returns to scale of a production function: $\epsilon = \epsilon_L + \epsilon_K$. When a production function exhibits constant returns to scale, total output is just sufficient to pay each factor owner the market value of that factor's marginal product.[12] This result, named for a mathematical proposition developed by Swiss mathematician Leonhard Euler (pronounced *oi-ler*), is known as **Euler's theorem**.[13]

While Euler's theorem implies that a competitive firm in long-run equilibrium will exhaust its revenue paying each factor the value of its contribution to output, the converse—that a firm that exhausts its revenue on factor payment is paying each factor the value of that input's marginal product—is not necessarily true. In Figure 13-19a, two possible normal profit equilibria are shown for a competitive firm. Free market entry drives the price down to p_0, so that $p_0 = MC = ATC_0$ at output

---

[12] The chain rule provides a proof of this result. Constant returns to scale implies $F(\lambda L, \lambda K) = \lambda F(L, K)$ for any positive constant λ. The partial derivative of this expression with respect to λ yields:

$$\frac{\partial F(\lambda L, \lambda K)}{\partial \lambda} = \frac{\partial F(\lambda L, \lambda K)}{\partial \lambda L} \cdot \frac{\partial \lambda L}{\partial \lambda} + \frac{\partial F(\lambda L, \lambda K)}{\partial \lambda K} \cdot \frac{\partial \lambda K}{\partial \lambda} = \frac{\partial \lambda F(L, K)}{\partial \lambda}$$

so that:

$$\frac{\partial F(L, K)}{\partial L} \cdot L + \frac{\partial F(L, K)}{\partial K} \cdot K = F(L, K), \text{ Q.E.D.}$$

[13] See Joan Robinson, "Euler's Theorem and the Problem of Distribution," in William Breit and Harold Hochman, eds., *Readings in Microeconomics*, 2nd ed. (New York: Holt, Rinehart and Winston, 1971), pp. 399–410.

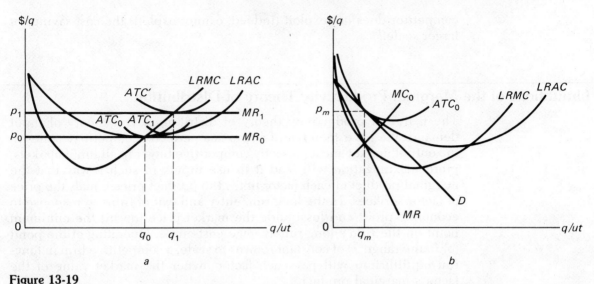

Figure 13-19
Factor Payment Exhaustion under (a) Perfect Competition and Capitalized Cartel Profit and (b) Monopolistic
Competition

q_0. Since q_0 corresponds to the minimum point on the long-run average
cost curve, that rate of output is characterized by constant returns to
scale, with increasing returns to scale for $q < q_0$ and decreasing returns
to scale for $q > q_0$. But suppose that a transferable licensing system
prevented the number of firms from increasing, so that price remained
at p_1 in the long run. As shown in chapter ten, transferable barriers to
entry will be sold for a price which approximates the present value of
expected monopoly profit. This would increase short-run average cost
from ATC_1 to ATC'. Hence, the firm would be earning normal profits,
but price would have remained above its lowest sustainable level (p_0).
Total revenue would exceed the sum of the value of the marginal products of necessary inputs, although excess revenue would be absorbed
by an artificial input (the license).

Figure 13-19*b* shows the exhaustion of factor payments for a monopolistically competitive firm in long-run equilibrium. Since price exceeds marginal revenue, factor owners receive less than the market value
of each input's marginal product. Because long-run equilibrium occurs
in the range of increasing returns to scale, there would be insufficient
revenue to pay each factor owner the market value of the input's marginal
product. The passive price-cutting monopolistic competitor receives
only enough revenue in long-run equilibrium to pay each factor owner
the marginal revenue product of that factor. The "savings" in factor
payments to the entrepreneur are absorbed because the monopolistic

competitor does not exploit (indeed, cannot exploit) the cost savings of larger scale.[14]

Limitations of the Marginal Productivity Theory of Distribution

The marginal productivity theory of distribution is a theory of input demand. We have seen that if a firm is a perfectly competitive seller in the output market and a perfectly competitive buyer in all input markets, profit maximization will lead it to use inputs in such a way that the marginal product of each factor times the product price equals the price of factor services. In the long run, entry and exit of firms in response to economic profit and loss guide the market price toward the minimum point on the firm's long-run average cost curve. Operating at the point (or in the range[15]) of constant returns to scale, a competitive firm in long-run equilibrium will pay each factor owner the market value of the factor's marginal product.

The marginal productivity theory of distribution predicts the pattern of income distribution emerging from a perfectly competitive economy. By showing how factors of production would be rewarded if all resources were allocated efficiently, the theory predicts how imperfect competition in product markets will change the outcome in input markets. We have seen how barriers to entry in erstwhile competitive product markets may allow firms to produce in the output range of decreasing returns to scale. Since payment of factors according to the value of their marginal products would not exhaust total revenue, we were able to show that capitalization of economic profits in the source of the entry restriction still results in "normal" profits. We also have seen how long-run equilibrium in the output range of increasing returns to scale under monopolistic competition allows total revenue to be exhausted on factor payments, even though factor owners receive less than the full market value of each factor's marginal product.

In the next chapter, we will trace how imperfections in factor mar-

---

[14] Marginal revenue can be written as $MR = p(1 + 1/\eta)$, where η is the price elasticity of demand. Since total revenue is exhausted by paying each factor owner that input's marginal revenue product, $pq = p(1 + 1/\eta)MP_L \cdot L) + p(1 + 1/\eta)MP_K \cdot K) = w_L \cdot L + w_K K$. Dividing by pq, p cancels in each term, while the last term for each input becomes its output elasticity:

$$1 = \left(1 + \frac{1}{\eta}\right)\left(\frac{MP_L}{AP_L} + \frac{MP_K}{AP_K}\right) = \left(1 + \frac{1}{\eta}\right)(\epsilon_L + \epsilon_K)$$

Since $(1 + 1/\eta)$ is less than one, $(\epsilon_L + \epsilon_K)$ must be greater than one for their product to equal one.

[15] In chapters six and twelve, oligopolies are presented as having a considerable range of output characterized by constant long-run average cost.

kets affect price and output in product markets. We have already seen how monopoly power of producers of capital equipment, which results in capital goods prices or rental rates in excess of opportunity cost, nevertheless generates a competitive employment level which equates the value of capital's marginal product to its (monopoly) rental rate. We will also see how labor unions—which function as cartels—can have either a detrimental or a beneficial effect on resource allocation, depending on how closely the market on the employers' side conforms to the conditions of competition.

This discussion will reject the view that marginal productivity theory provides a standard of economic justice. That firms are earning normal returns does not necessarily mean that factor owners are receiving the market value of their inputs' marginal products. Nor does the observation that a factor's price equals the value of its marginal product always imply that the factor is being sold at a competitive price. These who judge the appropriateness of market-generated income patterns solely on the distribution produced by an ideal system must somehow transcend the disparity between the ideal and the real. For those who resist casting marginal productivity theory as an ethical norm, this synthesis of product market theory and input market theory provides a limited, but highly useful, guide to the functioning of real-world markets despite their imperfections.

HIGHLIGHTS

1. An employer who is a price taker in both the product market and the input market hires a factor of production until the value of the factor's marginal product equals the price of its services.

2. The firm's demand for input services requires modification for input substitution and market-wide changes in output price. This modification means that the *mutatis mutandis* demand curve for input services differs from the *ceteris paribus* demand curve, given by the value of the input's marginal product.

3. If an employer is an imperfect competitor in the product market, factor services will be hired only to the point at which the price of an input's services (assuming a price-taking employer in the input market) equals its marginal revenue product. When price is greater than marginal revenue in the output market,

   a factor's marginal revenue product is less than the value of its marginal product.

4. The market demand for an input is obtained by adding the total quantity of factor services demanded by all firms at each market-determined factor price, assuming that factors are treated as homogeneous by employers and that all factor owners are paid the same price.

5. The factor price elasticity of demand equals the percentage change in the quantity of factor services demanded divided by the percentage change in the price of those services. The demand for a factor's services will be more price elastic the greater the elasticity of demand for the final good, the larger the factor's share in the cost of production, the more easily inputs can be substituted, and the higher the price of complementary factors.

6. The major determinant of input supply is the

opportunity cost of input use. To bid factor services away from other uses, employers collectively must offer higher and higher prices as more services are hired.

7. Land rent is determined by the value of land's marginal product (the demand side) and the opportunity cost of taking land out of other types of production (the supply side). When all available land has been bid out of alternative uses, increases in demand cause land rent to include economic rent—payment for factor services in excess of the amount necessary to bid those services away from alternative uses.

8. Markets for produced means of production (intermediate and capital goods) often involve a trade-off between property rights and market efficiency. When inventions and ideas are not exclusive, the incentive to innovate is compromised. When rights to market a capital good are limited by patents or other restrictions intended to reward invention and innovation, the price of the capital good (or the equivalent rental rate) will reflect monopoly distortions.

9. The optimal investment capital occurs when the present value of rental payments saved by owning a productive commodity equals the price of the equipment. Rental payments themselves reflect the value of the marginal product of capital in the production of goods by price takers.

10. In an ideal labor market characterized by wage competition, the equilibrium wage rate will be established where the quantity of labor services supplied by qualified workers equals the quantity of labor services demanded by competitive employers.

11. Compensating wage differentials between two competitive labor markets indicate that workers whose reservation wages equal the market wages in the two industries perceive economic or psychic costs associated with moving from the lower paying job to the higher paying job. Of particular interest to economists are wage differences due to investments in human capital, which many consider to be compensating differentials.

12. Euler's theorem indicates that firms in long-run competitive equilibrium would have just enough revenue to pay all factor owners the market value of each factor's marginal product. However, when total revenue equals total factor payments, it is not necessarily true that all factors are being rewarded according to the value of their marginal products, due to the capitalization of economic profit in transferable barriers to market entry and the possibility of long-run zero profit equilibrium for producers of differentiated products.

GLOSSARY

Compensating (wage) differential An equilibrium wage difference for two competitive labor markets. Compensating wage differentials indicate that marginal workers in the higher paid occupation are being recompensed for economic or psychic costs associated with their careers.

Economic rent A payment for factor services in excess of the minimum amount necessary to bid that factor away from its next best use.

Elasticity of supply of input services The percentage change in the quantity of factor services supplied divided by the percentage change in the factor's price.

Euler's theorem The mathematical formula showing that output produced by a production function exhibiting constant returns to scale equals the sum of each factor's marginal product times the amount of services supplied. Euler's theorem is the basis of the observation that a firm in long-run competitive equilibrium would receive just enough revenue to pay each factor owner the market value of the factor's marginal product.

Factor price elasticity of demand   The percentage change in the quantity of factor services demanded divided by the percentage change in the price of those services.

Human capital   The present value of wage differentials due to investment-like activities (e.g., education, worker-financed on-the-job training, migration).

Marginal input services   The amount of an input's services necessary to increase output by one unit, equal to the reciprocal of the input's marginal product: $MI_i = 1/MP_i$.

Marginal productivity theory of distribution   The theory linking the price of each factor of production to the value of the marginal product of that factor.

Marginal revenue product   The change in revenue due to the last unit of factor services hired:

$$MRP_i = \frac{pq}{\Delta v_i} = \left(p + q\frac{\Delta p}{\Delta q} \right) \frac{\Delta q}{\Delta v_i}$$

For price takers in the product market ($\Delta p/\Delta q = 0$), a factor's marginal revenue product is the same as the market value of its marginal product. For an imperfectly competitive seller in the product market ($\Delta p/\Delta q < 0$), the marginal revenue product of each factor is less than the market value of its marginal product.

Reservation wage   The lowest wage rate at which a worker will accept a job offer or supply labor services.

Value of labor's marginal product   The output price times the marginal product of the relevant input's services.

SUGGESTED READINGS

Becker, Gary S. *Human Capital: A Theoretical and Empirical Analysis, with Special Reference to Education*. rev. ed. Chicago: University of Chicago Press, 1980.

Bronfenbrenner, Martin. "A Reformulation of Naive Profit Theory." *Southern Economic Journal* (April 1960), pp. 300–309.

Cain, Glenn C. "The Challenge of Dual and Radical Theories of the Labor Market." *American Economic Review Proceedings* (May 1975).

Cartter, Allan M. *The Theory of Wages and Employment*. Homewood, Illinois: Irwin, 1959, ch. 2–4.

Dewey, Donald J. "The Geometry of Capital and Interest: A Suggested Simplification." *American Economic Review* (March 1963), pp. 134–139. Reprinted in William Breit and Howard Hochman, eds. *Readings in Microeconomics*. 2nd ed. New York: Holt, Rinehart and Winston, 1971, pp. 423–426.

Kaldor, Nicholas. "Alternative Theories of Distribution." In Ingrid Rima, ed. *Readings in the History of Economic Theory*. New York: Holt, Rinehart and Winston, 1970, pp. 262–281.

Mincer, Jacob. "The Distribution of Labor Incomes: A Survey with Special Reference to the Human Capital Approach." *Journal of Economic Literature* (March 1970), pp. 1–26.

Robinson, Joan. "Euler's Theorem and the Problem of Distribution." In William Breit and Harold Hochman, eds. *Readings in Microeconomics*. 2nd ed., New York: Holt, Rinehart and Winston, 1971, pp. 399–410.

———. "Capital Theory Up to Date." *Canadian Economic Journal* (May 1970), pp. 309–317.

Schultz, Theodore W. "The Concept of Human Capital." *American Economic Review* (March 1961).

Solow, Robert W. "The Economics of Resources and the Resources of Economics." *American Economic Review Papers and Proceedings* (May 1974), pp. 1–14.

Thurow, Lester C. *Generating Inequality: Mechanisms of Distribution in the U.S. Economy*. New York: Basic Books, 1975.

Wessell, Robert. "A Note on Economic Rent." *American Economic Review* (December 1967), pp. 1221–1226.

EXERCISES

Evaluate

Indicate whether each of the following statements is true (agrees with economic theory), false (is contradicted by theory), or uncertain (could be true or false, given additional information).

1. A firm earning zero economic profit is paying owners of inputs the market value of the factors' marginal products.
2. Input substitution increases the factor price elasticity of demand.
3. If individual workers substitute leisure for income at higher wage rates, the market supply curve for labor will bend backward.
4. Factor A is a major input in the production of commodity B. A price ceiling on A below equilibrium would reduce the equilibrium price of B.
5. Industry A uses more capital per worker than industry B; hence wages must be higher in industry A than in industry B.
6. Labor-saving technological change in the computer industry has led to an increase in employment of labor in that industry. This result is inconsistent with microeconomic theory.
7. A competitive firm uses two factors, labor (L) and capital (K). A reduction in the wage rate will lead to an increase in the employment of both factors.
8. In a competitive labor market, the derived demand curve for labor is identical to labor's marginal product curve.
9. The ratio of wages in competitive occupation A to wages in competitive occupation B is 2. After a payroll tax of 10 percent, the equilibrium wage ratio will increase.
10. Community A has a preferred set of government services relative to community B. Both communities finance their local services entirely by property taxes. Since property tax rates will be higher in community A, property values will be higher in community B.

Contemplate

Answer each of the following in a brief but complete essay.

11. Occupation A requires a college degree and occupation B requires only a high-school diploma. A person would be indifferent between the two occupations if the present value of the absolute earnings differential between A and B after the investment period equals the full costs of a college education. If government subsidies pay the costs of tuition and books, would the absolute earnings differential between A and B fall to zero? Explain your answer.
12. Suppose there is an excess demand for watchmakers. Explain how a rise in watchmakers' wages will help reachieve equilibrium. What will be the effect of that wage increase on (a) the market price of watchmaking machinery (which can be operated by unskilled labor) and (b) the market price of new watches? Explain your answer.
13. Which of the following are compensating wage differentials? Briefly justify your answer for each.
    a. The average annual salary for a Ph.D. economist is $42,500 in business and $25,000 in academia (source: 1980 salary survey by the National Association of Business Economists).
    b. Assistant professors of economics earn higher salaries than assistant professors of English.
    c. Certified public accountants earn a higher annual income than accountants who are not certified.
    d. The guy who is shot out of a cannon gets paid more than the guy who lights the fuse.
    e. Naval captains are paid more than army captains.
    f. Executive assistants (males) are paid more than executive secretaries (females).
14. According to one critic of the 1981 Reagan administration tax and spending cuts: "According to the Administration, the poor don't work because they are paid too much while the rich don't work because they are paid too little." Under what circumstances might tax cuts stimulate work effort? Under what circumstances might tax cuts deter work effort? (See chapter three for review.)

15. Suppose that you were hired by a Marxist government to determine the economic consequences of redistributing income according to the formula: To each according to his need; from each according to his ability. Write a brief essay (a) justifying positive prices for nonlabor factors of production and (b) explaining the consequences of breaking the connection between work effort and consumption.

Chapter 14

Wages and Employment under Imperfect Competition

This chapter balances the perfectly competitive theory of income by examining two major imperfections of labor markets: monopsony power of employers and monopoly power of workers. These show up as wage and job discrimination, occupational licensing, wage inequality, labor unions, and collective bargaining.

The chapter begins with a review of the assumptions of the ideal labor market. We then investigate employer monopsony—the absence of wage competition due to one or a few employers' dominance of the market for a specific labor skill. The impact of monopsony on wages and employment is applied to the volunteer army–military draft controversy. Monopsony power leads an employer to sustain a labor shortage in the market where it buys labor services. The federal government is different from other employers because it can remedy a shortage of military personnel by the draft. Other employers must abide by the rules of private enterprise.

In contrast to the unique solution to the "failure" of the volunteer army, private-sector monopsonists often attempt to hold down wages by practicing wage discrimination. By paying male and female workers different wage rates for the same work, for example, the monopsonist hopes to reduce the marginal cost of labor, thereby increasing profit. More prevalent than wage discrimination is **job discrimination**—the refusal to hire some workers because of personal characteristics that are irrelevant to productivity (e.g., race, sex, religion). Job discrimination by competitive employers creates a cartel problem, made more difficult by civil rights legislation that takes the government out of the practice of legislating in favor of discriminating employers.

Another distortion of labor market competition arises from uncertainty about worker qualifications, which gives rise to occupational licenses, which in turn encourages labor cartels. We contrast the response of wages and employment to an increase in the demand for labor in an open profession (economics) and a closed one (medicine). Turning to labor unions which operate in erstwhile competitive labor markets, we find that job discrimination often serves as a means of rationing union jobs whose pay exceeds what a competitive market would generate. By contrast, bilateral monopoly—collective bargaining between an industrial labor union and a monopsonistic employer—can lead to wage and employment outcomes closer to what a competitive market would generate than would occur under either unchallenged employer monopsony or unchallenged labor monopoly. The chapter concludes with a numerical example of the ironic results of bilateral monopoly in labor markets.

Competitive Labor Markets Revisited

Before we investigate the effects of imperfect competition on labor markets, let us review the assumptions of the competitive labor market model explored in chapter thirteen:

1. There are so many employers and so many workers that no individual participant in the labor market has a noticeable impact on the market wage.
2. Workers possess identical skills, which they have acquired prior to their employment decision. All workers are paid the same market determined wage rate.
3. Employers attempt to maximize profit by hiring workers only on the basis of their marginal revenue product and the market wage.
4. Real wages are freely flexible to rise during periods of labor shortage and decline when there is a surplus of qualified workers in an industry or occupation.
5. There are no artificial barriers to market entry for either workers or employers. Workers need only possess the requisite skills to offer labor services, while employers can hire workers merely by paying the equilibrium wage.

The operation of a competitive labor market is illustrated in Figure 14-1. Firms wish to hire L_0 workers at a wage rate of w_0 per hour. The last worker hired by each firm generates enough revenue to cover the

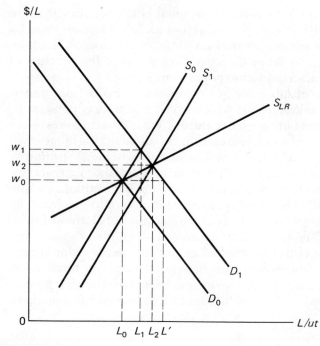

Figure 14-1
Short-Run and Long-Run Adjustments to an Increase in Labor Demand

worker's wage. Workers supply L_0 hours of labor at wage rate w_0 because the reservation wage for that amount of labor services is less than or equal to w_0.

Now suppose that an increase in the demand for labor, due, say, to an increase in demand for the industry's product, shifts the market demand curve for labor from D_0 to D_1, while the supply of labor curve remains stationary at S_0. After the increase in demand, firms wish to hire L' labor hours at wage rate w_0, but workers continue to offer only L_0 hours at that wage. The shortage of labor puts upward pressure on the market wage. Some employers offer a higher wage rate in order to expand output. Workers migrate from lower-wage jobs to higher paying ones. Ultimately, both workers entering the labor market and those already employed in that industry receive the higher wage. In Figure 14-1, the wage rate and employment level follow the short-run supply curve S_0 until a new short-run equilibrium is reached at wage rate w_1 and employment level L_1.

If wage rate w_1 represents a higher than normal return on a worker's investment in human capital, additional workers will apply for jobs at that wage after they have acquired the needed training. As more workers become qualified, the short-run supply of labor curve shifts to the right, and the entry of additional workers exerts a downward pressure on the market wage. When the wage rate has fallen to w_2, due to an employment increase to L_2, the last worker employed is receiving a normal return on his or her investment in training. The curve labeled S_{LR} is the *mutatis mutandis* labor supply curve, representing employment levels corresponding to long-run equilibria for human capital investments.

A competitive labor market, by virtue of its characteristics, succeeds because it frustrates the goals of participants. Employers, attempting to hire more workers at *prevailing* wage rates, are eventually forced to pay higher wages to all workers, including those formerly employed at the lower wage. Individual workers, moving from one job to another in response to wage differences, tend to decrease wage differentials until they compensate workers for financial or psychic costs of different occupations. The system works because no employer has either the ability or the inclination to consider how offering higher wage rates affects the labor costs of other firms. However, when there are few buyers of a specific labor skill, employers become aware of how offering higher wages to additional workers affects the wage rate paid to workers already employed. On the other hand, when selling labor is controlled by a labor union or professional association, the tendency of quantity of labor supplied to increase as wage rates increase is thwarted.

When workers finance their own training or acquire labor skills outside their place of employment, there is always a danger that a *labor cartel* will place artificial restrictions on the number of workers trained. When an unanticipated demand increase causes a rapid rise in wage income for those already qualified for jobs, the subsequent increase in competitive labor supply and erosion of wage gains requires that workers' associations are unable to restrict access to training. When workers themselves provide training and certify qualifications—as is the case in professional schools and union apprenticeships—the assumption of free access to job markets may be called into question.

When employers provide on-the-job training, veteran workers who instruct the fledglings must be assured that trainees will not threaten their job security or earnings. A pattern of rapid wage increases followed by falling wages when newly trained workers ease the labor shortage will disrupt the harmonious environment needed for successful on-the-job training. More likely, wage rates will rise steadily during a worker's career, with employment and wage expansion gradually moving along the long-run supply curve, such as S_{LR} in Figure 14-1. When a **wage structure** must be maintained to assure good worker morale, successful job training, and productivity growth, wage rates for specific jobs will react sluggishly to temporary labor shortages or surpluses.

Monopsony

The first labor market imperfection we consider is **monopsony**, a market dominated by one buyer—in this context, by one employer. Like the monopoly model, the model of monopsony is the polar opposite of the model of perfect competition. Except for certain jobs in government and the vanishing phenomenon of one-company towns, instances of pure monopsony are rare. More likely are occurrences of **oligopsony**, where a few rivals hire similar labor skills and are mutually wary of their influence on wage rates. Two centuries ago, Adam Smith saw employer collusion to depress wages as the likely consequence of fewness among employers:

> We rarely hear, it has been said, of the combination of masters, though frequently of those of workmen. But whoever imagines, upon this account, that masters rarely combine, is as ignorant of the world as of the subject. Masters are always and every where in a sort of tacit, but constant and uniform combination, not to raise the wages of labour above their actual rate. To violate this combination is everywhere a most unpopular action, and a sort of reproach to a master among his neighbors and equals. We seldom, indeed, hear of this combination, because it is the usual, and one may say, the natural state of things which nobody ever hears of. Masters too sometimes enter into particular combinations to sink the wages of labour even below this rate. These are always conducted with the utmost silence and secrecy, till the moment of execution, and when workmen yield, as they sometimes do, without resistance, though severely felt by them, they are never heard of by other people. Such combinations, however, are frequently resisted by a contrary defensive combination of workmen; who sometimes, too, without the provocation of this kind, combine of their own accord to raise the price of their labour. Their usual pretences are, sometimes the high price of provisions; sometimes the great profit which their masters make by their work. But whether their combinations be offensive or defensive, they are always abundantly heard of.[1]

Developing a theory of oligopsony requires explaining how the mutual awareness of their impact on the market wage influences the hiring practices of a few employers. Like oligopoly, oligopsony is a complex market most economists avoid and many ignore. By concentrating on the less typical case of monopsony, we hope to simplify matters, not to distort them.[2]

---

[1] Adam Smith, *An Inquiry into the Nature and Causes of the Wealth of Nations* (New York: Random House, Modern Library, 1937), pp. 66–67.

[2] For a discussion of collusive oligopsony, see Thomas M. Carroll, "Achieving Cartel Profit Through Unionization: Comment," *Southern Economic Journal* (April 1981), pp. 1152–1161.

Monopsony and the "Failure" of the Volunteer Army

One market which comes very close to that of pure monopsony involves the volunteer enlistments into the United States military. For the most part, the armed services recruit privates and second lieutenants, promoting soldiers through the ranks as they become more experienced and are deemed ready for greater responsibility. While many civilian applications of skills are taught in military service, much of a soldier's training is specific to the armed forces. A commercial airline may hire a retired air force pilot, but (we hope) the pilot's skills in bombing and aerial combat will go unused by his new employer.

In Table 14-1, we imagine that the first 200,000 military recruits can be "hired" at a wage rate of $5,000 per year. If more personnel were to be recruited from civilian jobs, the wage offer would have to be increased—generally speaking for all enlistees, including those willing to serve for less pay. The **marginal cost of labor** (often called the **marginal input cost**) for a monopsonist equals the wage rate paid for the last worker plus the wage increase implied for those who would be willing to work for less, but who must be paid the same wage as the last recruit:

$$MC_L = \frac{\Delta(wL)}{\Delta L} = w + L\frac{\Delta w}{\Delta L} = w\left(1 + \frac{\Delta w/w}{\Delta L/L}\right) = w(1 + E_{L_s})$$

where $\Delta w/\Delta L$ is the wage increase needed to attract one more worker and E_{L_s} is the elasticity of the supply of labor. In Table 14-1, the marginal cost of each trainee from 200,001 through 400,000 is $7,000: a $6,000 wage, plus a $1,000 raise for each of the 200,000 people who would have enlisted for $5,000 per year.

TABLE 14-1
Consequences of Hypothetical Volunteer Army under Alternative Wage Offers (without Draft)

Wage Offer (per year)	Labor Supplied (millions)	Marginal Taxpayer Benefit	Total Taxpayer Benefits ($ billion)	Total Wage Payments ($ billion)	Marginal Cost of Labor	Taxpayer Surplus ($ billion)	Economic Rent ($ billion)	Total Net Benefits ($ billion)
$ 5,000	0.2	$17,000	3.6	1.0	$ 5,000	2.6	0.0	2.6
6,000	0.4	15,000	6.8	2.4	7,000	4.4	0.2	4.6
7,000	0.6	13,000	9.6	4.2	9,000	5.4	0.6	6.0
8,000	0.8	11,000	12.0	6.4	11,000	5.6	1.2	6.8
9,000	1.0	9,000	14.0	9.0	13,000	5.0	2.0	7.0
10,000	1.2	7,000	15.6	12.0	15,000	3.6	3.0	6.6
11,000	1.4	5,000	16.4	15.4	17,000	1.0	4.2	5.2
12,000	1.6	3,000	17.2	19.2	19,000	-2.0	5.6	3.6

One problem in simulating the market for military personnel is the inability of the government, or any other seller, to exclude nonpaying beneficiaries from consuming the services of what economists call a pure public good.[3] If the chief function of the military is to deter aggression and to protect a nation's citizens in the event of attack, all citizens will consume the services produced by military recruits. Hence, since national defense is financed by tax payments rather than direct sale, the appropriate proxy for the demand for military recruits is marginal social benefit, defined as the value citizens place on each level of military service. In fact, the requirement of a nationwide tax to finance national defense (which only the federal government can levy) gives rise to the monopsony market in the first place.

According to Table 14-1, the 200,000th military trainee, whose marginal cost is $5,000, is valued at $17,000 per year. Assuming an average value of $18,000 per recruit for the first 200,000 (i.e., the vertical intercept of the marginal social benefit schedule is $19,000), taxpayers receive benefits of $3.6 billion while spending only $1.0 billion on military trainees. There is a **taxpayer surplus** of $2.6 billion. Such a large difference between the value of military personnel and their cost encourages the recruiting of personnel whose reservation wage exceeds $5,000. By offering $6,000, the military attracts an additional 200,000 volunteers.

The second 200,000 recruits are valued less than the first 200,000, due to the combined influences of diminishing marginal productivity of labor and diminishing marginal utility from national defense. Nevertheless, benefits are assumed to rise from $3.6 billion to $6.8 billion, while wage payments increase from $1.0 billion to $2.4 billion. The surplus enjoyed by taxpayers rises to $4.4 billion. In addition, each of the first 200,000 recruits, who would have enlisted for $5,000 a year, receives economic rent equal to $1,000 per year, for a total economic rent of $0.2 billion. Adding the taxpayer surplus and economic rent, a volunteer army with 400,000 enlistees generates total net benefits of $4.6 billion per year.

Increasing pay from $6,000 to $7,000 a year attracts an additional 200,000 recruits, implying a marginal cost of labor equal to $9,000 ($1,000 in wage increases for each of the first 400,000 persons recruited, adding $2,000 to the marginal cost of the last 200,000). Since the marginal taxpayer benefit is assumed to be $13,000, taxpayer surplus increases again, to $5.4 billion. Furthermore, adding $2,000 of economic rent for each of the first 200,000 recruits (paid $7,000 although their reservation wage

---

[3] The classic article on the difficulty of measuring demand for public goods is Paul Samuelson, "Diagrammatic Exposition of a Theory of Public Expenditure," *Review of Economics and Statistics* (November 1955), pp. 550–556. This topic is discussed further in chapter fifteen.

is $5,000) and $1,000 of economic rent for each of the second 200,000 recruits (who would have enlisted for $6,000 per year) gives a total social surplus of $6.0 billion. A further pay increase to $8,000 increases the number of recruits to 800,000, with the first 600,000 recruits receiving a total economic rent of $1.2 billion. With employment of 800,000 recruits, taxpayers receive national defense labor services they value at $12.0 billion but for which they pay only $6.4 billion (a surplus of $5.6 billion). The taxpayer surplus plus the economic rent means a total social surplus of $6.8 billion.

At this stage the economic consequences of monopsony emerge. Note that the labor services of an additional 200,000 workers would be valued at $9,000 for the last recruit (marginal benefit), who would also be paid $9,000. However, the 800,000 individuals willing to enlist for $8,000 per year (or less) would also be paid $9,000 each. If 1 million volunteers were recruited, the marginal cost of labor, equal to $13,000, would exceed the marginal benefit to taxpayers, assumed to be $9,000. Taxpayer surplus would be only $5.0 billion, or $600 million less than it would have been had pay been held to $8,000 per year. However, since a $9,000 wage would result in $2.0 billion in economic rent, an increase of $800 million over economic rent at the $8,000 wage, total social surplus would still increase, to $7.0 billion. In sum, total social surplus will be greatest at the wage rate determined by the intersection of the supply schedule for recruits (traced out by voluntary enlistments at each wage offer) and the marginal benefit (proxy demand) schedule for taxpayers.

If Congress takes as its responsibility pleasing a majority of the population, budgets will be set to maximize taxpayer surplus (determined where the marginal benefit of government services equals their marginal cost), rather than total social surplus. Holding pay for recruits at $8,000 per year instead of raising it to $9,000 per year would "destroy" $800 million in economic rent that might never be missed while increasing the taxpayer surplus by $600 million, a plum for which voters might show their appreciation at election time.

Despite the maximization of taxpayer surplus with 800,000 recruits paid $8,000 each, there would be a nagging feeling that the volunteer army had "failed" to provide an adequately staffed military establishment. If additional personnel could be recruited at the $8,000 wage rate (a possible outcome of an increase in the national unemployment rate), society would prefer a military with 1.1 million trainees, since the marginal social benefit of 1.1 million recruits would be $8,000. The shortage of military recruits (in healthy economic times) occurs because increasing the number of recruits requires a higher rate of pay for all. If the market for military personnel were competitive, as much as $11,000 would be offered for 800,000 recruits, and competition would raise the

TABLE 14-2
Consequences of Hypothetical Volunteer Army–Draft Combination under Alternative Wage Offers

Wage Offer (per year)	Labor Supplied (millions)	Labor Demanded (millions)	Draftees (millions)	Explicit Taxes ($ billion)	Minimum Implicit Taxes ($ billion)	Total Taxes ($ billion)
$5,000	0.2	1.4	1.2	7.0	4.20	11.20
6,000	0.4	1.3	0.9	7.8	2.45	10.25
7,000	0.6	1.2	0.6	8.4	1.20	9.60
8,000	0.8	1.1	0.3	8.8	0.35	9.15
9,000	1.0	1.0	0.0	9.0	0.00	9.00

wage for all. Nevertheless, the marginal cost of recruits would equal the market wage as long as there were a large number of competitive employers.

Except for the rare nihilist, most of us feel more secure knowing there is only one employer of military personnel in our country. Yet it is the monopsonistic nature of the market for recruits which causes the wage rate to remain below the market clearing level. The monoponist creates its own shortage of labor to keep wages low, much the same as a monopolist causes an artificial shortage to raise its selling price.

But the government, as maker of rules, need not be constrained by the rules of markets. By returning to conscription, the labor services offered by volunteers could be augmented by 300,000 young men[4] whose desire to remain out of prison would overwhelm their reservation wage[5]. Suppose taxpayers support an annual enlistment of 1.1 million recruits, composed of 800,000 volunteers and 300,000 draftees. For $8.8 billion, taxpayers (except for draftees themselves) seem to get a larger military establishment at a lower cost (to them) than the market clearing wage rate of $9,000 would have generated.

Table 14-2 shows that a draft armed forces includes a hiddent **implicit tax** on draftees. Assuming that 200,000 men (and women) would volunteer at a wage rate of $9,000 and another 100,000 would volunteer for $9,500, drafting 300,000 persons and paying them a wage of $8,000

---

[4] According to a recent poll, 47 percent of the women questioned favored a return to draft registration and an equal percentage were opposed (*Newsweek*, February 18, 1980). Only 42 percent of the men questioned favored returning to draft registration, with 53 percent opposed. When asked whether young women should also register, 58 percent of the female respondents were opposed, while 61 percent of the male respondents favored female registration. As long as an individual is not personally liable for the draft, conscription can reduce his or her tax liability at someone else's expense.

[5] In 1967 Walter Y. Oi estimated that 36.7 percent of military enlistees were "reluctant volunteers," who, along with draftees, accounted for 47.8 percent of new military trainees ("The Economic Cost of the Draft," *American Economic Review* [May 1967], pp. 39–62).

per year would result in a *minimum* implicit tax of $350 million. Since the Selective Service System, which used birthday lotteries and allowed hardship and occupational exemptions, did not rank potential draftees by reservation wages, the data in Table 14-2 understate the likely implicit taxes paid by draftees. Although it strikes many as unegalitarian, the practice of allowing draftees to hire replacements would effectively make the implicit tax on draftees explicit. As long as replacements remained strictly voluntary, such a system (used during the Civil War) would reduce the social cost of military manpower.

If politicians were less sensitive to the implicit taxes paid by draftees (young adults vote with less frequency than middle-aged and senior citizens), pay for recruits could be set so low that the majority of military manpower would be raised by conscription. In our example, a wage offer of $5,000 would attract only 200,000 recruits, resulting in a personnel shortage of 1.2 million. Drafting 1.2 million men would hold expenditures to $7.0 billion, while imposing an implicit tax of (at least) $4.2 billion on draftees. Note that the wage rate of $9,000, which would result in an all-volunteer army, would minimize the total of explicit and implicit taxes. By taking advantage of its unique ability to draft additional labor services, the federal government would exploit a minority of its citizens (military trainees) on behalf of the majority. Not only are draftees, who are paid less than their reservation wage, exploited by the draft; volunteers, while being paid their reservation wage, receive less than the social value of their labor services.

Monopsonistic Wage Discrimination

It should be obvious that the federal government is unique in its ability to relieve monopsony-induced personnel shortages by confiscating (or selectively taxing) labor services at wage rates below the worker's reservation wage. Other labor monopsonies, such as the markets for municipal government employees and professional athletes (prior to the rise of the "free agent" in baseball), involve employers who have no alternative to paying a worker his or her reservation wage.[6] On the other hand, when monopsony power is limited to a small area, as in the one-company town, the employer of a unique labor skill (e.g., the only manufacturing plant) may mitigate (although not eliminate) labor shortages by practicing **wage discrimination**—paying equally productive workers different wage rates for doing essentially the same work.

---

[6] See John H. Landon and Robert N. Baird, "Monopsony in the Market for Public School Teachers," *American Economic Review* (December 1971), pp. 966–971; and Simon Rottenberg, "The Baseball Players' Labor Market," in William Breit and Harold Hochman, eds., *Readings in Microeconomics*, 2nd ed. (New York: Holt, Rinehart and Winston, 1971), pp. 427–443.

Why would an employer pay a man a higher salary than a woman would require to perform the same job? Phrasing the issue of unequal pay for equal work in this fashion may seem perverse, but this question underscores the economic approach to wage discrimination. We have seen that a profit-maximizing firm which is a price taker in all input markets will hire inputs so that the ratio of factor price to marginal product is the same for all factors. An employer who does not exploit an opportunity to substitute low-wage female workers for (relatively) high-wage male workers must (1) believe that men are more productive than women at the particular job, (2) be pursuing goals other than maximum profits, or (3) face a positively sloped supply curve for labor services, so that the marginal cost of labor exceeds the wage rate paid the last worker hired. Under the third explanation, the ability to separate the labor market according to the elasticity of supply of labor services allows the employer to equalize the marginal cost of male and female workers by paying unequal wages.

A simulation of supply conditions confronting a wage-discriminating monopsonist is presented in Table 14-3. The monopsonist in this example is an imperfect wage discriminator; although the employer knows that on the average, women have lower reservation wages than men due to fewer job opportunities, there is no way to determine the reservation wage of any individual man or woman. In this example, only women will apply for jobs at less than $6.00 per hour. After 10 women have

TABLE 14-3
Hypothetical Supply of Male and Female Labor Confronting a Monopsonist

Wage Offer	Women Hired (L_f)	Wages for Women (wL_f)	Marginal Cost of Female Labor (MC_f)	Elasticity of Supply of Female Labor (E_f)	Men Hired (L_m)	Wages for Men (wL_m)	Marginal Cost of Male Labor (MC_m)	Elasticity of Supply of Male Labor (E_m)
$ 4.00	10	$ 40	$ 4.00	8.00	0	0	—	—
4.50	20	90	5.00	4.50	0	0	—	—
5.00	30	150	6.00	3.33	0	0	—	—
5.50	40	220	7.00	2.75	0	0	—	—
6.00	50	300	8.00	2.40	10	$ 60	$ 6.00	12.00
6.50	60	390	9.00	2.17	20	130	7.00	6.50
7.00	70	490	10.00	2.00	30	210	8.00	4.67
7.50	80	600	11.00	1.88	40	300	9.00	3.75
8.00	90	720	12.00	1.78	50	400	10.00	3.20
8.50	100	850	13.00	1.70	60	510	11.00	2.83
9.00	110	990	14.00	1.64	70	630	12.00	2.57
9.50	120	1,140	15.00	1.58	80	760	13.00	2.38
10.00	130	1,300	16.00	1.54	90	900	14.00	2.22

been hired at $4.00 per hour, the marginal cost of labor will equal $5.00 for the eleventh through the twentieth female worker. (To keep the arithmetic simple, we are assuming that 10 additional workers apply for jobs for every $0.50 wage increase.) Although 20 women can be hired for $4.50 per hour, those hired (or who would apply) at a wage rate of $4.00 per hour will have to be given a raise of $0.50 per hour. Otherwise, those first hired would quit and reapply for the higher wage.

As more women are hired, a divergence between their wage rate and the marginal cost of labor becomes progressively greater. When 30 women have been hired, the marginal cost of labor is $6.00 per hour, even though each is only paid $5.00 per hour. Hiring 40 women implies paying each a wage of $5.50 per hour, meaning a marginal cost of $7.00 per worker. It is at this point that the monopsonist would perceive the benefits of wage discrimination.

In Table 14-3, the lowest reservation wage for a male worker is $6.00 per hour. If male workers could be employed at higher wage rates than females (e.g., women demanding higher wages would be replaced by men), the firm would be able to hire 30 women and 10 men for a total wage bill of $210 per hour ($150 for women, $60 for men) per hour, whereas hiring 40 women would require a labor outlay of $220 per hour (40 × $5.50). After the 10 men willing to work for $6.00 per hour had been hired, hiring either more women or more men would be associated with a marginal cost of $7.00 per labor hour, despite the fact that men would receive a wage of $6.50 per hour while equally productive women would receive $5.50 per hour.

The advantages of wage discrimination for the monopsonist can be seen by comparing the data in Tables 14-4 and 14-5. In Table 14-4, we assume that the monopsonist hires only women up to a wage rate of $5.00 per hour, then hires men and women at different wages so that the

TABLE 14-4
Profit-Maximizing Employment and Wage Rates for Wage-Discriminating Monopsonist

Workers Hired	Marginal Cost of Labor (MC_L)	Wage Offer to Women (w_f)	Female Workers (L_f)	Female Wages ($w_f L_f$)	Wage Offer to Men (w_m)	Male Workers (L_m)	Male Wages ($w_m L_m$)	Marginal Revenue Product (MRP_L)	Total Revenue (TR)	Gross Profit (Π_g)
10	$ 4.00	$4.00	10	$ 40	—	0	0	$18.00	$ 180	$140
20	5.00	4.50	20	90	—	0	0	17.00	350	260
30	6.00	5.00	30	150	—	0	0	16.00	510	360
40	6.00	5.00	30	150	$6.00	10	$ 60	15.00	660	450
60	7.00	5.50	40	220	6.50	20	130	13.00	930	580
80	8.00	6.00	50	300	7.00	30	210	11.00	1,160	650
100	9.00	6.50	60	390	7.50	40	300	9.00	1,350	660
120	10.00	7.00	70	490	8.00	50	400	7.00	1,500	610

TABLE 14-5
Profit-Maximizing Employment and Wage Rate for Nondiscriminating Monopsonist

Wage Offer (w)	Total Labor Hired (L)	Female Workers (L_f)	Male Workers (L_m)	Total Wages (wL)	Marginal Cost of Labor (MC_L)	Marginal Revenue Product (MRP_L)	Total Revenue (TR)	Gross Profit (Π_g)
$4.00	10	10	0	$ 40	$ 4.00	$18.00	$ 180	$140
4.50	20	20	0	90	5.00	17.00	350	260
5.00	30	30	0	150	6.00	16.00	510	360
5.50	40	40	0	220	7.00	15.00	660	440
6.00	60	50	10	360	7.00	13.00	930	570
6.50	80	60	20	520	8.00	11.00	1,160	640
7.00	100	70	30	700	9.00	9.00	1,350	650
7.50	120	80	40	900	10.00	7.00	1,500	600

marginal costs of male and female labor remain equal. The assumption that men and women are equally productive is embodied in the marginal revenue product schedule: the marginal revenue product of labor (MRP_L) is assumed to fall by $1.00 for each 10 additional workers hired (regardless of gender). Since the marginal revenue product of labor is the change in total revenue divided by the change in labor services, total revenue (TR) is obtained simply by summing the marginal revenue products for all workers employed at each point.

In Table 14-4, the marginal cost of labor and the marginal revenue product of labor are equal when 100 workers (60 women and 40 men) have been hired. Although the marginal cost of both male and female workers is $9.00 per hour, women are paid $6.50 per hour while men are paid $7.50 per hour.[7] In contrast, Table 14-5 shows the consequences of denying the monopsonist the ability to practice wage discrimination, say, because of a discrimination suit won by women employees. Note that the inability to practice discrimination does not change the monopsonist's optimal employment decision (this would not usually be the case), since 100 workers are still associated with a marginal cost of $9.00 per hour. However, instead of hiring men at $6.00 an hour when the

---

[7] Treating labor as the only variable input, profit is maximized by setting the partial derivatives of $\Pi_g = pQ - (w_m L_m + w_f L_f)$ with respect to L_m and L_f and setting the results equal to zero:

$$\frac{\partial \Pi_g}{\partial L_m} = \left(p + Q\frac{\partial p}{\partial Q}\right)\frac{\partial Q}{\partial L_m} - \left(w_m + L_m\frac{\partial w_m}{\partial L_m}\right) = 0 \quad \text{implies} \quad MRP_m = w_m\left(1 + \frac{1}{E_m}\right)$$

$$\frac{\partial \Pi_g}{\partial L_f} = \left(p + Q\frac{\partial p}{\partial Q}\right)\frac{\partial Q}{\partial L_f} - \left(w_f + L_f\frac{\partial w_f}{\partial L_f}\right) = 0 \quad \text{implies} \quad MRP_f = w_f\left(1 + \frac{1}{E_f}\right)$$

Equal productivity means $MRP_m = MRP_f$; thus $w_f < w_m$ means $E_f < E_m$.

marginal cost of labor reaches $6.00 (i.e., when 30 women have been hired), a wage offer of $5.00 per hour is followed by a wage offer of $5.50 per hour. The marginal cost of labor when 40 workers are hired is now $7.00, rather than $6.00. However, this is the only change in the marginal cost schedule. Employment of 100 workers is now associated with a gross profit of $10 less than when wage discrimination was allowed.

In our example, doing away with discrimination but leaving monopsony power otherwise intact raises female wages by $0.50 per hour and female employment by 10 workers, while males see their wage rate decline by $0.50 per hour, causing 10 men to seek alternative employment. Supposedly, *marginal workers* of both genders would break even with the equal wage outcome; female workers with a reservation wage of $7.00 per hour would be bid out of other jobs they considered equally rewarding, while male workers whose reservation wage equaled $7.50 would find equally agreeable jobs elsewhere. However, men whose reservation wage was $7.50 would each lose $0.50 in economic rent (total loss of $15), while women with a reservation wage below $6.50 would gain economic rent of $0.50 per hour (total gain of $30). This redistribution of economic rent helps explain why wage discrimination, already conducive to monopsony profit, may also forestall unionization if higher paid workers fear the loss of benefits. We will return to this issue later.

APPLICATION
Employer Discrimination and Civil Rights

In the absence of monopsony power, discrimination by employers tends to increase production costs. According to economist Gary S. Becker of the University of Chicago, employer discrimination in a competitive industry constitutes a deviation from profit-maximizing behavior.[8] Lester C. Thurow of the Massachusetts Institute of Technology has developed a similar model, wherein the employer's taste for discrimination involves the desire for "social distance" rather than "physical distance" from workers with particular characteristics.[9] (According to Thurow, white males who desire "social distance" would hire women as secretaries and blacks as blue-collar workers, but would balk at hiring either as managers.) In either case, refusal to hire workers because of their race, sex, or any other characteristic independent of productivity will result in higher cost for discriminators.

In Figure 14-2*b*, a short-run market equilibrium at p_0, Q_0 results in

---

[8] Gary S. Becker, *The Economics of Discrimination*, 2nd ed. (Chicago: University of Chicago Press, 1971).

[9] Lester C. Thurow, *Poverty and Discrimination* (Washington, D.C.: The Brookings Institution, 1969).

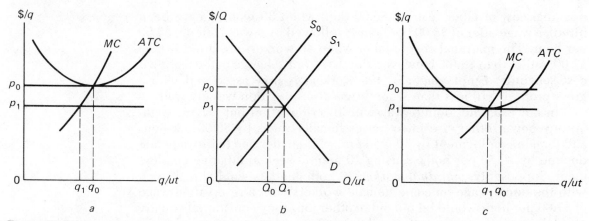

Figure 14-2
The Effect of Free Market Entry on Discrimination in a Competitive Industry: *a*, Discriminating firm; *b*, the market; *c*, nondiscriminating firm.

zero economic profit for a firm whose owner prefers to hire only white males (Figure 14-2*a*). If such discrimination is widespread, disadvantaged workers will have lower reservation wages than equally productive white male workers would have. Nondiscriminating firms, which attempt to hire workers with the required skills for the lowest possible wage, would have lower costs, such as those depicted in Figure 14-2*c*. Market equilibrium at p_0 would generate economic profits for nondiscriminating firms, who would be encouraged to enter the market until price fell to p_1. Discriminating employers would have to incur larger and larger losses to sustain their desire to discriminate. If discrimination is like other commodities, its "consumption" by employers should decrease as its relative price (in the form of economic losses) increases.

The persistence of employer discrimination in otherwise competitive, nonunion jobs implies that firms or privileged workers are able to retard the forces of market competition. Many of the "Jim Crow" laws which were nullified by the civil rights legislation of the mid-1960s can be viewed as government impediments to market entry by nondiscriminating firms. By prohibiting the normal functioning of a market, prodiscrimination laws not only caused lower earnings for women, blacks, and other minorities but also resulted in a lower standard of living for consumers as a whole. One of the more significant impacts of the 1964 Civil Rights Act was that the blessing of the federal government was withdrawn from cartels of discriminating employers and discriminating sellers. Forced to bear the cost of their inefficient allocation of resources, competitive producers with a taste for discrimination must either learn to overcome their prejudices, or else they will ultimately be displaced by lower cost, nondiscriminating producers. Both Becker and Thurow conclude that employer discrimination is more prevalent in imperfectly competitive product markets. This often means that women and minority workers are underrepresented in capital-intensive, high-paying industries, resulting in their overcrowding into labor-intensive, low-productivity industries.

Worker Certification and Labor Cartels

Neoclassical theory of competitive labor markets is based on the simplifying assumption that both employers and workers have perfect knowledge of worker productivity. In some jobs, to be sure, worker qualifications can be measured easily: how many words can be typed per minute, how many pounds can be lifted. In most occupations, however, a worker's job performance can be determined only after that person has been employed for some time. In some professions—medicine and law, for instance—prediction of a practitioner's qualifications prior to employment is an important source of consumer protection. As we shall see, certification of worker qualifications can also be an impediment to the functioning of a competitive labor market.

To dramatize the choice between protecting consumers from unqualified professionals and preserving a competitive labor market, let us consider the medical profession. In a competitive market for medical care, a person's knowledge of and skill at healing would be demonstrated in his or her success in treating patients. Anyone could offer medical services, but after a time those who had established poor reputations

Policy Illustration
A Simple Test of the Job-Crowding Hypothesis

As discussed in chapter one, the first step in the development of an economic theory involves the statistical test of a simple hypothesis. The job-crowding hypothesis—that victims of employment discrimination are overrepresented in labor-intensive, low-paying industries—can be tested by determining whether the percentage of jobs held by women and/or minority workers in comparable industries accurately predicts lower pay in those industries, *ceteris paribus*. In order to isolate the impact of the percentage of females (PCF) and blacks (PCB) holding jobs in a manufacturing industry on the average pay in that industry, other influences must be taken into account statistically. The proportion of jobs in production ($PCPW$) is used as a proxy for the labor intensity of a manufacturing industry, since the greater the ratio of capital to labor, the more supervisory and white-collar workers there would be per blue-collar worker, and the smaller the pro-

Statistical Test of the Job-Crowding Hypothesis

$$PRW_{it} = \beta_0 + \beta_1 VAW_{it} + \beta_2 PCPW_{it} + \beta_3 PCF_{it} + \beta_4 PCB_{it} + \beta_5 PU_{it}$$

Year	β_0	β_1	β_2	β_3
1978	20,667 ($\rho < 0.01$)	0.0518 ($\rho < 0.01$)	-117.94 ($\rho < 0.01$)	-72.83 ($\rho < 0.01$)
1979	19,950 ($\rho < 0.01$)	0.0388 ($\rho < 0.01$)	-90.91 ($\rho < 0.05$)	-80.50 ($\rho = 0.02$)

Year	β_4	β_5	R^2
1978	-35.99 ($\rho = 0.31$)	84.15 ($\rho < 0.01$)	0.9159
1979	-85.77 ($\rho < 0.26$)	103.19 ($\rho < 0.01$)	0.8743

PRW_{it} = payroll per worker in industry i, in year t.
VAW_{it} = value added per worker in industry i, in year t.
$PCPW$ = percent of jobs in production.
PCF = percent of jobs held by women.
PCB = percent of jobs held by blacks.
PU = percent of workers who belong to unions.
ρ = probability that null hypothesis is true (i.e., that coefficient does not have the predicted sign).
R^2 = proportion of variation in PRW attributed to explanatory variables.

Sources: U.S. Department of Commerce, *Survey of Manufacturers* (Washington, D.C.: U.S. Government Printing Office, 1978, 1980). U.S. Equal Opportunity Employment Commission, *1978 Report: Job Patterns for Women and Minorities in Private Industry*, Vol. 1, and *1979 Report: Job Patterns for Women and Minorities in Private Industry*, Vol. 1 (Washington, D.C.: U.S. Government Printing Office, 1980, 1981). U.S. Department of Labor, *Labor Handbook* (Washington, D.C.: U.S. Government Printing Office, 1980).

portion of total product going to labor. The proportion of workers in unions (*PU*)—which are likely to be industrial unions in manufacturing industries—also predicts higher earnings, regardless of the race or gender of workers. Value added per worker (*VAW*) measures the average product of labor, while payroll per worker (*PRW*) is the variable used to measure average earnings.

The statistical analysis of the relevant data for nineteen manufacturing industries is presented in the accompanying table, which reports the regression of *PRW* on the five explanatory variables (*VAW, PCPW, PCF, PCB,* and *PU*).* Regression is the statistical technique used to estimate the *ceteris paribus* relationship between the dependent variable (*PRW*) and each of the explanatory variables:†

$$PRW = \beta_0 + \beta_1 VAW + \beta_2 PCPW + \beta_3 PCF + \beta_4 PCB + \beta_5 PU$$

A successful test of the crowding hypothesis requires that each coefficient have its predicted sign (β_0, β_1, and $\beta_5 > 0$; β_2, β_3, and $\beta_4 < 0$) and that the probability of the result being due to mere chance (ρ) be very small (which makes the result *statistically significant*).

---

* The nineteen industries are: food; textile mills; apparel; lumber and wood products; furniture and fixtures; paper; printing and publishing; chemicals; petroleum and coal; rubber and plastics; leather; stone, clay, and glass; primary metal products; fabricated metal products; nonelectrical machinery; electrical and electronic equipment; transportation equipment; instruments; and miscellaneous industries.

† It can be argued that the proportion of workers in unions also increases as the average wage rate increases; this issue is explored in the business illustration on pp. 598–600.

The accompanying table shows a strong negative association between the average wage rate and the proportion of jobs held by women: $\beta_3 = -72.83$ means that if industry *i* had 1 percent more jobs held by women than industry *j* in 1978, annual wages in industry *i* were $72.83 lower than in industry *j*, *ceteris paribus* (in 1979, industry *i*'s average earnings would be $80.50 less than industry *j*'s). Also, as predicted, payroll per worker increases with the value added per worker and with the proportion of workers who belong to unions, while declining as the labor intensity of the industry increases. With these factors taken into account, the statistical support for the job-crowding hypothesis with respect to black employment is, at best, weak. While β_4 has the predicted negative sign in both years, the likelihood that this result is spurious is greater than one in four in both cases.

In conclusion, national data for manufacturing industries in 1978 and 1979 appear to support the job-crowding hypothesis with respect to women, although evidence is weaker with respect to black workers. One explanation is that black youths, who often suffer from unequal educational opportunities prior to entering the job market, are victims of "noneconomic" discrimination; the market merely translates their lower productivity, resulting from unfair training opportunities, into lower pay. Women, on the other hand, are paid less because they have less access to industries where their skills could earn the highest returns. In other words, while blacks tend to be crowded into low-paying occupations within industries, women tend to be crowded into those industries in which pay for all occupations is lower.

would be forced to lower their fees to attract (risk-loving) patients away from more qualified physicians. Eventually, the least qualified would change careers when their earnings as physicians fell below their expected earnings in an alternative occupation (e.g., taxidermy).

Attainment of a competitive salary and employment equilibrium in medicine would extract a very high—and probably socially unacceptable—cost of patient welfare. Individual victims of medical malpractice have little incentive or opportunity to communicate their experiences to other patients. Accusing a physician of malpractice could become a legal form of extortion if allegations about physician qualifications were not subject to legal restrictions. Furthermore, widespread medical malpractice would harm the reputations of competent as well as incompetent physicians. Displaying a diploma from a medical school would not reassure patients if anyone could obtain a forged diploma certifying medical training which never occurred. Ultimately, both patients and physicians would demand minimum guarantees of professional competence, including accreditation of medical schools, formal internship programs, and medical licensing. Since physicians themselves would be the most qualified to specify the minimum standards for professional licenses, a cartel of physicians would tend to develop.

The ability to deny a license to the unqualified, coupled with authority to establish the standards for competence, gives the medical profession effective control over the supply of labor.[10] As in the granting of patents for inventions, the attempt to create property rights to an abstract resource (here the reputation of qualified physicians) actually results in "ownership of the market"; the attempt to prevent property failure causes market failure (see chapters eight and fifteen).

The adverse consequence of a labor cartel based on occupational licensing is that an increase in the demand for labor will not automatically lead to an increase in the quantity of labor supplied, even when wage rates rise. The labor supply curve for a *closed profession* will tend to be very inelastic in the short run. Furthermore, if professional training is controlled by the profession itself, there is no guarantee that the number of qualified individuals will increase in response to a higher than normal return to investments in professional training. In Figure 14-3, an initial equilibrium wage of w_0 is upset by an increase in the demand for labor from D_0 to D_1. Both the wage rate and employment increase along the short-run supply curve, S_0, until a new short-run wage-employment equilibrium has been established or until all licensed professionals have been attracted into the expanding market. For instance, a short-run in-

---

[10] See Reuben A. Kessel, "Price Discrimination in Medicine," *Journal of Law and Economics* (October 1958), pp. 20–53. Reprinted in William Breit and Harold Hochman (eds)., *Readings in Microeconomics*, 2nd ed. (New York: Holt, Rinehart and Winston, 1971), pp. 370–396.

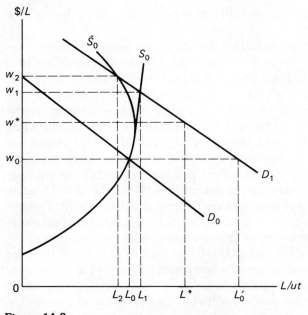

Figure 14-3
Possible Wage Adjustment Paths in a Closed Profession

crease in physicians' fees might cause some doctors to leave retirement, research, or teaching to enter (or return to) private practice. If, as in Figure 14-3, all available licensed professionals have entered the market before equilibrium has been reestablished, further increases in the quantity of labor supplied will depend on a substitution of income for leisure by licensed professionals. As shown in chapter three, there is no guarantee this will occur.

Suppose that all qualified, licensed professionals are supplying labor services at wage rate w^* in Figure 14-3. A shortage of labor services still exists at that wage. The two possible paths which employment and the wage rate could follow are represented by S_0, the familiar positively sloped short-run supply curve, and $\tilde{S}_0$, an unusual **backward-bending labor supply curve**. The positively sloped supply curve would result if the substitution effect of a higher wage rate increased the hours of work enough to blunt the tendency of higher incomes to increase the consumption of leisure (see chapter three). If the income effect of higher fees was stronger than the substitution effect, wages and employment could follow the backward-bending supply curve, $\tilde{S}_0$. With the positively sloped labor supply curve, the new equilibrium is w_1, L_1; consumers' desire for more of the profession's services did create a small increase in those services, albeit at a huge increase in professional fees. In the case of the backward-bending labor supply curve, a wage increase from

w_0 to w_2 results in a smaller quantity of services than were being supplied at the lower wage.

It is important to emphasize that the backward-bending market supply curve in Figure 14-3 is the consequence of the income-leisure choice made by individual licensed professionals. Usually, any tendency of individuals to reduce the number of hours worked (i.e., to increase the consumption of leisure) in response to a higher wage is offset by the addition of more workers to an *open* labor market. A backward-bending market supply curve for labor would occur only when the number of entrants into a profession is restricted, so that the relative strength of the income effect and the substitution effect of wage increases on the supply of labor time by individual workers determines the shape of the market supply curve. Individuals with scarce natural abilities, such as entertainers and sports stars, may also exhibit a backward-bending labor supply schedule at high wage rates. For instance, after his salary was increased by an estimated 50 percent, Johnny Carson decreased his time on the *Tonight Show* from four and a half hours (three 90-minute shows) to four hours (four one-hour shows) a week.

For comparison, let us now consider an *open profession*: economics. There is no licensing authority, dominated by economists or kindred spirits, which controls enrollment in economics courses, restricts the number of students in graduate programs in economics, or administers a licensing exam. Since quacks cannot be prosecuted for "practicing economics without a license," those who are educated in economics must demonstrate their superiority over self-proclaimed experts by their success in the marketplace. When one economist commits a logical error, makes an incorrect prediction, or twists economic theory to conform to his or her own or some client's prejudice, all economists may be tainted.

An increase in the demand for economists—whether in business, government, or academia—will lead to increased earnings for trained economists and those who claim to be economists. However, in an open profession like economics, higher salaries, and the market sorting of successful and untrained economists, will encourage more students to enroll in economics courses and to obtain degrees in economics. In the short run, as indicated in Figure 14-4, an increase in the wage rate from w_0 to w_1 will be accompanied by a small increase in the number of competent economists (along supply curve S_0). Eventually, early wage gains will begin to dwindle as more trained economists graduate and enter the market, increasing competition.

Ultimately, economics departments will react to growing enrollments by hiring more (or better) faculty members and by raising entrance or graduation requirements. Even schools which once had a hard time attracting graduate students will grow. In terms of Figure 14-4, the short-run labor supply curve for economists will shift from S_0 to S_1, eroding the initial rise in economists' salaries and establishing a new equilibrium

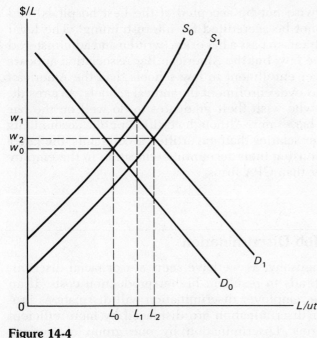

Figure 14-4
Wage Adjustment in an Open Profession

at w_2, L_2. With no licensing board to set uniform "quality standards" for economists, the profession will always encompass a range of talent, reflecting various combinations of educational rigor and philosphical perspective.

An indication of how well the market for economists works can be gleaned from the biannual salary survey published by the National Association of Business Economists. According to its 1980 report, economists with a Ph.D. degree earned a median salary of $42,500 per year in business, while economists who had completed all the coursework but not the dissertation required for a Ph.D. degree earned median salary of $37,500 per year in business. A business economist who took one year off to complete a dissertation (it usually takes longer) would receive a return of approximately 13 percent on the opportunty cost of the time invested. The closeness of this return to prevailing rates of interest in 1980 reflects a market at work. Contrast this market judgment with the plight of an A.B.D. ("all but dissertation") in academia, where a Ph.D. degree is a minimum requirement for tenure.

Economics and medicine may be considered extreme cases of open and closed professions. Many professions .seem to operate as imperfect cartels. According to Reuben Kessel, control over internship programs gives the medical profession direct control of medical schools (whose graduates might otherwise not be accepted at the best hospitals) and hospitals (which may not be accredited for intern training). The legal profession requires entrants to pass a bar exam (written and administered by attorneys) to practice law, but the American Bar Association appears to have less control over enrollment in law schools than the American Medical Association has over enrollment in medical schools. As a result, deans of law schools, who wish their graduates to do well on the bar exam, lobby for easier bar exams. Although certified public accountants (CPAs) command higher salaries than uncertified accountants, the latter are not prevented from using their accounting education in the employ of establishments other than CPA firms.

APPLICATION
Labor Cartels and Job Discrimination

In the absence of monopsony, as we have seen, sex or racial discrimination by employers tends to result in higher production costs. If an industry is competitive, employer discrimination will dissipate as producers with a taste for discrimination are displaced by more efficient (nondiscriminating) firms. Discrimination by one group of workers against another group of workers, on the other hand, often occurs as a side effect of the cartelization of a competitive labor market. Figure 14-5 shows a competitive labor market in equilibrium at wage rate w_0

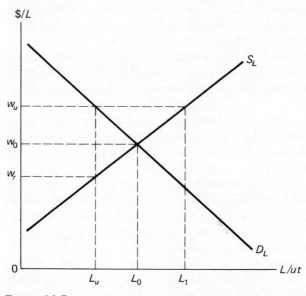

Figure 14-5
Upsetting a Competitive Labor Market and the Costs of Discrimination for a Labor Cartel

and employment L_0. Any increase in the wage rate above w_0 would require either an increase in labor demand (which workers ordinarily cannot influence) or a reduction in the labor supply. We have already seen how occupational licensing can enable professional associations to restrict entry into their markets. Other means of restricting market entry include union control over apprenticeship and other training programs, closed-shop contracts (which require union membership *before* employment), and even violence and intimidation.

In Figure 14-5, an increase in the wage rate from w_0 to w_u requires a reduction in employment from L_0 to L_u. The higher than competitive wage rate creates a surplus of workers applying for jobs; thus the available jobs (L_u) must be rationed among the overabundant applicants (L_1). One method, suggested by Becker, is the use of kickbacks and bribery of union officials by job applicants whose reservation wage is less than the union wage.[11] A worker would presumably offer up to the difference between the union wage, w_u, and his or her reservation wage, w_r (indicated by the distance between the supply curve and the horizontal axis). *Price rationing* would result in a maximum bribe of $w_u - w_r$ in Figure 14-5, where w_r is the reservation wage of the last worker hired (e.g., admitted to the union apprenticeship program). If such blatant extortion were legal, those who auctioned off jobs would have an economic incentive to avoid racial or sex discrimination. Applicants with the fewest alternatives would generally have the lowest reservation wages and therefore would be the ones willing to pay the highest bribes. (If, as has been alleged, medical schools accept only a fraction of qualified candidates (i.e., only those who "know someone" or are sufficiently overqualified), allowing them to charge market clearing tuition would be equivalent to the kickback scheme suggested by Becker. Of course, if medical schools could charge, say, $50,000 tuition per year, presidents of universities with medical schools would attempt to admit as many students as possible, conceivably disrupting the AMA's control over medical school enrollments.)

Since extortion and bribery are generally illegal means of filling jobs, other screening devices must be used when wage rates are pushed above competitive levels. One method is to set entry requirements for professional education, or performance standards on licensing exams, higher than necessary to ensure competence. When occupational licenses are created as a means of consumer protection, professional cartels may find that rigorous educational requirements or very difficult licensing exams are a socially acceptable means of job rationing. In union jobs, it has been argued that higher than equilibrium wage rates cause employers to hire the most productive workers, thereby minimizing

---

[11] *Economics of Discrimination*, pp. 64–74.

(although not eliminating) the impact of high union wages on production costs.[12]

Limiting employment to the "most productive" workers may not be the rationing mechanism preferred by individual members of a labor cartel, however. Nepotism allows a member of a closed profession or a craft union to pass along a valuable asset to his children—access to a job which pays a higher than competitive wage. Although nepotism may be motivated by benevolence toward relatives and friends, discrimination in favor of some implies discrimination against others. When parents use influence to gain admission of their son to medical school, this may prevent admission of the (equally qualified) daughter of a couple who do not have connections. If whites sponsor their friends for union membership and those friends are also white, blacks and other minority workers will encounter restricted job prospects. If a group of union workers or professionals share a taste for discrimination (which may have been an inadvertent side effect of their training), using personal characteristics to ration jobs in closed occupations will allow the favored group to evade the economic costs of discrimination.

The incidence of job discrimination will be higher when discriminators are insulated from market forces. Discrimination by professions or craft unions does not, per se, cause higher wages. Higher than competitive rates of pay in an otherwise competitive occupation result from manipulation of the source of labor supply. Discrimination—whether a result of prejudice or a consequence of nepotism—represents one means of rationing jobs in a closed occupation. As long as society tolerates labor cartels, some (potentially or actually) qualified workers will be excluded from cartelized occupations. The difficult issue that must then be faced is who shall those victims of discrimination be?

This perspective sheds new light on the Bakke reverse discrimination suit of a few years ago. According to Alan Bakke, affirmative action by the University of California, Davis, medical school resulted in discrimination against him, a white male. Since the affirmative action admittees graduated at approximately the same rate as others, the standards which precluded Bakke's admission must have been set higher than necessary. In essence, medical schools have double standards for admission: one set for qualified candidates with connections (e.g., sons of physicians) and another for candidates without connections, who must meet higher admission standards than the former group. By placing minority applicants in the favored category, the Davis medical school reduced the probability of admission for those remaining in the "over-

---

[12] John S. Pettengill, "Labour Unions and the Wage Structure: A General Equilibrium Approach," *Review of Economic Studies* (October 1979), p. 675; Lung-Fei Lee, "Unionism and Wage Rates: A Simultaneous Equations Model with Qualitative and Limited Dependent Variables," *International Economic Review* (June 1978), p. 432.

qualified" category. Although the Supreme Court found in favor of Bakke, it also ruled that Harvard Medical School's affirmative action program was legally sound. The possible reason, not mentioned by the Court, was that Harvard had not discriminated against Alan Bakke, and that each affirmative action—reverse discrimination suit must be decided on its own merits. For, short of finding the medical profession in violation of antitrust laws, there is no way of avoiding some form of discrimination in medical school admissions.

Collective Bargaining and Bilateral Monopoly

After our extended, and largely negative, analysis of labor cartels, a reader might infer that economic analysis proves that labor unions always misallocate resources. This is not true. One of the most ironic, and controversial, predictions of microeconomic theory is that while labor unions impair economic efficiency when they overturn the wage established in a competitive labor market, a union may bring about an improvement in economic efficiency when it represents workers in a market dominated by a monopsonistic employer or collusive oligopsonists.

At the beginning of this chapter, we encountered Adam Smith's observation on the tendency of employers to conspire to maintain or establish subcompetitive wages. Another luminary in the development of economic theory, Alfred Marshall, commented:

> The want of reserve funds and of the power of long withholding their labor from the market is common to nearly all grades of those whose work is chiefly with their hands. But this is especially true of unskilled laborers, partly because their wages leave very little for saving, partly because when any group of them suspends work, there are large numbers who are capable of filling their places. And, as we shall see presently when we come to trade combinations, it is more difficult for them than for skilled artisans to form themselves into strong and lasting combinations; and so to put themselves into something like terms of equality in bargaining with their employers. For it must be remembered that a man who employs a thousand others, is in himself an absolutely rigid combination to the extent of one thousand units among buyers in the labour market.[13]

As we saw earlier, monopsony power allows the employer to select any quantity of labor services by offering the wage rate which causes that number of (qualified) workers to apply for jobs. An employer's leverage over workers can also be enhanced when the training workers receive is specific to one firm. Gary Becker separated the types of on-

---

[13] Alfred Marshall, *Principles of Economics*, 9th ed. (New York: Macmillan, 1961), p. 568.

the-job training workers could receive by who would reap the benefits of an increase in a worker's productivity. When a worker's training enhances potential productivity at many establishments, such as the skills of an artisan, an employer must increase the worker's pay after training is completed, lest the worker take a job with another firm. Since the employer could not recapture an investment in *general* worker training, workers themselves usually bear the cost of such training. But when there is only one employer (or a few geographically dispersed employers) of a particular labor skill (e.g., automobile assembly plants), the firm could recover an investment in a worker's specific training by paying the worker less than his or her marginal revenue product. As we shall see, this is exactly the consequence of the monopsonist's profit-maximizing employment and wage decision.

As with imperfect competition in product markets, the question of monopsony power in an input market is one of degree. Buyers of labor services may have no influence on wages (individual clients of physicians, lawyers, and accountants) or, at the other extreme, complete freedom from wage competition (the military). Whether a person favors the model of perfect competition or pure monopsony for predicting wage rates in the absence of labor unions is partly a matter of taste or ideology and partly a matter of the purpose for which the model is being employed. In this chapter, it is our intent to present both the labor cartel and bilateral monopoly models of labor unionism and allow the student to draw his or her own conclusions. The model of bilateral monopoly (one employer dealing with a union) enjoys less popularity among economists today than the cartel model (which sees unions as impediments to an otherwise ideal market), but this attitude is likely to change as the demand for prounion economists increases.

In Figure 14-6, we imagine a monopsonist who maximizes profit by hiring L_m workers, since that is the level of employment which causes the marginal cost of labor (MC_L) to equal the marginal revenue product of labor (MRP_L). The last worker hired appears to "cost" the employer a wage of w^*, even though that last worker, like all those hired previously, receives a wage rate of only w_m. Had the last worker not been hired, the employer would have saved that worker's wage plus the additional pay which had to be given to the ($L_m - 1$) workers who would have been willing to work for a lower wage. Aware of the effect of employment expansion on the wage paid to all workers, the nondiscriminating monopsonist earns a surplus equal to the difference between the marginal revenue product of the last worker hired and the monopsony wage, a difference which Joan Robinson dubbed *monopsony exploitation*.[14] In Figure 14-6, the monopsony surplus, Π_L, is equal to the area of the shaded rectangle $L_m(w^* - w_m)$.

---

[14] *The Economics of Imperfect Competition* (New York: St. Martin's Press, 1969).

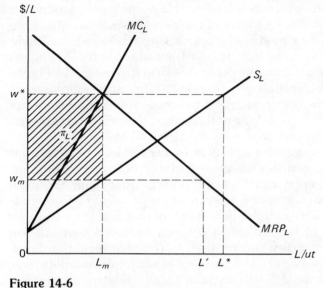

Figure 14-6
Representative Bargaining Range for a Nondiscriminating
Monopsonist and an Industrial Union

Suppose that workers in the monopsonist's plant suspect that their employer, using the "divide and conquer" strategy, is paying them less than they are worth. No individual worker dares to demand a higher wage, lest he or she be fired to serve as a deterrent to others. However, collective action may succeed when individual action is futile. If all L_m workers demanded a higher wage, the employer would be unable to replace them with equally productive workers willing to work for the monopsony wage. Under the nonunion monopsony employment equilibrium, the market clears on the employees' side: all workers who are qualified and willing to work for a wage of w_m (or less) have already been hired. The market does not clear on the employer's side: the firm is unable to hire as much labor as desired at the monopsony wage. To hire L' workers (where the marginal revenue product of labor equals the monopsony wage, w_m) would not only require a higher wage to attract additional workers but would also mean a higher wage for the L_m workers already employed. Wages do not rise in the wake of the labor shortage caused by monopsony, as they would in a competitive labor market, because the monopsonist realizes that paying higher wages for additional workers would also increase wages paid to workers already employed at the prevailing wage.

Now suppose that all L_m workers combine into an **industrial union** (a union representing all production workers in the plant) and try to obtain a wage rate higher than w_m by threatening to withhold their labor services. The wage rate which results from bargaining will depend on their bargaining power relative to that of their employer. In a bargaining environment, both parties begin with unrealistic positions; each side offers less and demands more than it is willing to settle for, hoping to extract greater concessions from the other side than it gives up. In Figure 14-6 the L_m workers prefer their current jobs to alternative employment as long as the wage is w_m or greater, and the monopsonist will continue to employ at least L_m workers as long as the marginal cost of labor remains at w^* or less.

We can take the range of wage rates in Figure 14-6 between the monopsony wage, w_m, and the marginal cost of labor in the preunion monopsony, w^*, as an approximation of the **bargaining range** for wage negotiations. The actual contract wage cannot be predicted without additional information—for example, how much output had the employer stored in anticipation of the strike? how much money is there in the union strike fund? how many substitutes are available for union labor or for the monopsonist's output? The outcome of **bilateral monopoly** (one buyer confronting one seller) will depend on the relative bargaining strength and ability of the two sides. By studying the relative cost to each side of a failure of negotiations (a strike or lockout), individual collective-bargaining outcomes can sometimes be estimated more precisely.

The range of possible collective bargaining wage and employment outcomes is summarized in Figure 14-7. Beginning with monopsony preunion wage and employment levels at w_m and L_m, respectively, employment would expand along the supply of labor curve as the contract wage attracted more workers to the firm (industry). Although the quantity of labor services demanded would fall as the wage rose, actual employment would rise due to the increase in the quantity of labor supplied. If the contract wage happened to correspond to w_c, the quantity of labor demanded would equal the quantity of labor supplied, L_c.

Wage rates in excess of w_c would result in employment levels less than L_c. Nevertheless, employment would be greater than it was before unionization as long as the contract wage was set below w^*, the marginal cost of labor for the nonunion monopsony. If the union was so strong that wage rates in excess of w^* were enforced, employment would fall below L_m. Such high contract wage rates would require that some workers stand ready to strike in order that other workers receive higher wages, although those workers would lose their jobs. This outcome is not consistent with worker solidarity, which is a crucial ingredient in the credibility of the union's strike threat.

The possibility of bilateral monopoly reaching a higher monopsony level of employment, and hence greater output and lower consumer prices, means that the economic impact of unions depends on the structure of the labor market prior to unionization. Assuming that labor mar-

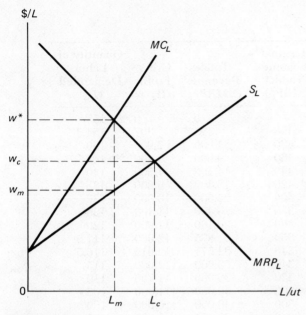

$/L

Figure 14-7
Range of Possible Wage and Employment Outcomes of Collective Bargaining

kets would be competitive in the absence of unions simplifies the analysis of how unions affect wage rates, since union-nonunion wage differences give an approximation of the wage gains achieved by unionized workers. However, allowing for the possibility that unions counteract employer monopsony calls into question the universal applicability of the competitive labor market assumption.

APPLICATION
The Last Numerical Example

Because of the ironic result of the bilateral monopoly model—that collective bargaining could raise employment while forcing an employer to pay a higher-than-monopsony wage—one last numerical example is in order. Table 14-6 presents the employment and gross profit consequences of alternative wage offers by Whatsit Widgets, the only employer of skilled widget workers in Tinytown. Lee Whositz, the plant manager, announces a wage of $190 per week and then sits around drawing a salary, waiting for job applicants who never materialize. Afraid of what the home office will think, she increases the wage offer to $191; only Ed Collins, tired of working overtime for Mr. Crank, applies for a job. Whositz offers $192 per week and attracts only two job applicants, one

TABLE 14-6
Alternative Wage Offers of Monopsony Firm

Wage Offer (w)	Job Applicants (L_s)	Total Wages (wL)	Marginal Cost of Labor (MC_L)	Marginal Revenue Product (MRP_L)	Total Revenue (ΣMRP_L)	Gross Profit (Π_g)	Quantity of Labor Demanded (L_d)
$190	0	0	–	–	0	0	155
191	1	$ 191	191	$498	$ 498	$ 307	154.5
200	10	2,000	210	480	4,900	2,900	150
210	20	4,200	230	460	9,600	5,400	145
220	30	6,600	250	440	14,100	7,500	140
230	40	9,200	270	420	18,400	9,200	135
240	50	12,000	290	400	22,500	10,500	130
250	60	15,000	310	380	26,400	11,400	125
260	70	18,200	330	360	30,100	11,900	120
265	75	19,875	340	350	31,875	12,000	117.5
267	77	20,559	344	346	32,571	12,012	116.5
270	80	21,600	350	340	33,600	12,000	115
280	90	25,200	370	320	36,900	11,700	110
290	100	29,000	390	300	40,000	11,000	105
300	110	30,000	300	300	40,000	10,000	100
310	120	29,450	310	310	38,475	9,025	95
320	130	28,800	320	320	36,900	8,100	90
330	140	28,050	330	330	35,275	7,225	85
340	150	27,200	340	340	33,600	6,400	80

Business Illustration
Union Membership and Manufacturing Earnings

The relationship between the extent of union membership and the wage level (i.e., the average wages for union and nonunion workers) depends upon whether unions raise wages in otherwise competitive labor markets (the labor cartel model) or above subcompetitive monopsony levels (the bilateral monopoly model). In the former case, higher wage rates for union workers imply lower wages for nonunion workers in similar jobs—a variation on the crowding hypothesis. Hence, we would expect to find no systematic relationship between the proportion of a state's labor force that belonged to unions and the average wage rate for manufacturing workers in that state if all manufacturing industries were characterized by competitive labor markets in the absence of unions. On the other hand, if higher wage rates won through collective bargaining caused workers to move from nonunion manufacturing jobs to union manufacturing jobs, we would expect to find a positive association between union membership and average wages for manufacturing workers.

The table on page 600 relates the average hourly wage rate for manufacturing workers (*AHW*) to three regional variables (*NE, S,* and *MW* for the Northeast, South, and Midwest, respectively): value added per production worker-hour (*VAPH*), the proportion of the state's labor force in manufacturing (*PCM*), and the proportion of workers who belong to unions in that state (*PU*).* As in the policy illustration presented in this chapter, the viability of the bilateral monopoly model of unionism depends upon the sign of the coefficients of the regression equation (*ceteris paribus* slopes) and the probability that the observed relationships are due to chance (implying that the labor cartel model is true).

In this case, being in the southern or northeastern part of the United States has a negative impact on the average wages of manufacturing workers. This is important, because the southern region has a low proportion of workers in unions while the Northeast has a high proportion of workers in unions; controlling for regional influences on wage rates prevents attributing those influences to variations in union membership. While generally negative, the midwestern regional indicator is not reliably different from zero. As expected, higher value added per production worker-hour results in higher wage rates. Since greater output per worker can result from capital-intensive manufacturing, which can also be conducive to monopsony, controlling for value added per worker helps eliminate misattributing productivity factors to union influence. Including the proportion of workers in manufacturing helps control for the possibility that manufacturing unions displace workers from manufacturing entirely. While the coefficient on *PCM* is negative in early years, the statistical reliability of this result is weak. For 1976 and 1978 we could reject the null hypothesis that $\Delta AHW/\Delta PCM < 0$; there is little support for the proposition that higher wages in manufacturing result from reducing the number of manufacturing jobs (the labor-cartel theory).

For our purposes, the most impressive result is the consistent positive relationship between the average hourly wage rate for blue-collar manufacturing workers and the proportion of workers who belong to unions. In every year there is less than a 3 percent chance that the real value of β_6 is zero or negative. When we explicitly allow for the possibility of bilateral monopoly in the determination of manufacturing wages through collective bargaining, it appears that unions do raise the average wage for manufacturing workers. This result is at odds with the work of other economists, but for the most part, other statistical studies hypothesize a competitive market in the absence of unions, and rarely allow for the possibility of imperfect competition among employers.

---

* Because workers join unions in search of higher wages, *PU* is predicted to increase as *AHW* increases; hence, *PU* is not really an independent variable. To correct for this, the procedure of two-stage least squares was used, replacing the actual *PU* variable for each state with a predicted value of *PU* based on another regression equation not included here.

Based on Thomas M. Carroll, "Right to Work and Labor Earnings: A Reconsideration of the Evidence," paper presented at the Southwest Social Science Meetings, San Antonio, Texas, March 1982.

Determinants of Average Hourly Wage for Production Workers in Manufacturing

$$AHW_i = \alpha_0 + \beta_1 NE + \beta_2 S + \beta_3 MW + \beta_4 VAPH_i + \beta_5 PCM_i + \beta_6 PU_i$$

Year	α_0	β_1	β_2	β_3	β_4	β_5	β_6	R^2
1964	1.48	−0.213 ($\rho = 0.014$)[a]	−0.327 ($\rho < 0.001$)	−0.087 ($\rho = 0.13$)	0.100 ($\rho < 0.001$)	−0.002 ($\rho = 0.82$)	0.016 ($\rho = 0.016$)	0.8218
1966	1.55	−0.259 ($\rho = 0.016$)	−0.320 ($\rho < 0.001$)	−0.184 ($\rho = 0.029$)	0.086 ($\rho < 0.001$)	−0.001 ($\rho = 0.60$)	0.022 ($\rho < 0.001$)	0.7815
1968	1.82	−0.251 ($\rho = 0.014$)	−0.288 ($\rho = 0.005$)	−0.136 ($\rho = 0.07$)	0.063 ($\rho < 0.001$)	0.003 ($\rho = 0.65$)	0.028 ($\rho < 0.001$)	0.8101
1970	1.82	−0.250 ($\rho = 0.022$)	−0.315 ($\rho = 0.006$)	−0.147 ($\rho = 0.085$)	0.085 ($\rho < 0.001$)	0.003 ($\rho = 0.27$)	0.029 ($\rho < 0.001$)	0.8004
1972	1.66	−0.291 ($\rho = 0.017$)	−0.326 ($\rho = 0.013$)	−0.059 ($\rho = 0.31$)	0.107 ($\rho < 0.001$)	0.007 ($\rho = 0.126$)	0.030 ($\rho < 0.001$)	0.7911
1974	2.23	−0.332 ($\rho = 0.073$)	−0.454 ($\rho = 0.026$)	−0.022 ($\rho = 0.14$)	0.081 ($\rho < 0.001$)	0.011 ($\rho = 0.184$)	0.030 ($\rho = 0.022$)	0.6665
1976	2.20	−0.504 ($\rho = 0.002$)	−0.495 ($\rho = 0.002$)	−0.031 ($\rho = 0.42$)	0.100 ($\rho < 0.001$)	0.016 ($\rho = 0.006$)	0.036 ($\rho < 0.001$)	0.8560
1978	2.2	−0.612 ($\rho = 0.002$)	−0.474 ($\rho = 0.013$)	—[b]	0.117 ($\rho < 0.001$)	0.053 ($\rho < 0.001$)	0.043 ($\rho = 0.003$)	0.7754

[a] ρ = probability that the null hypothesis is true.
[b] Coefficient could not be calculated.

of whom is Ed Collins. The marginal cost of labor exceeds the wage rate paid to the last worker hired by the implied wage increases for workers willing to work at lower wage rates.

A wage offer of $200 per week draws 10 job applicants, well short of the 150 workers desired at that wage. Since the marginal revenue product of the tenth worker is $480, while the marginal cost of labor is $210, Lee Whositz continues to offer higher wages. At $260 per week, 70 workers can be hired, at a marginal cost of $330 per week. Although the marginal revenue product of labor has fallen to $360, profit can still be increased by expanding employment, even though hiring one more worker always means paying more to workers already hired. A wage offer of $265 increases job applications to 75, and the marginal cost of labor, equal to $340, is quite close to the marginal revenue product of labor, at $350. Whositz discovers that profits are maximized when 77 workers are hired at a wage rate of $267 per week.[15]

Notice that the profit-maximizing wage rate of $267 is a market-clearing wage on the supply side of this monopsony labor market, since all 77 workers who apply for jobs at that wage rate are hired. However, the employer confronts a labor shortage of its own making; given that the marginal revenue product of labor falls by $2 for each additional worker hired, MRP_L would not fall to the current wage rate until 116.5 workers were hired. While Lee Whositz would hire nearly 40 more workers at the prevailing wage, marginal cost of labor would exceed the marginal revenue product of labor if the wage rate was increased to attract more labor.

Before we proceed to the impact of collective bargaining on the profit and employment of a profit-maximizing monopsonist, we pause briefly to consider how a sales-maximizing monopsonist, subject to a minimum profit constraint, might ignore its increasing marginal cost of labor schedule and hire that amount of labor consistent with its minimum profit constraint. Suppose that the Whatsit Widgets plant represents a weekly fixed cost of $10,000 for plant and equipment. If the home office desires a 10 percent rate of return on investment, Lee Whositz would be instructed to maximize sales revenue, as long as total revenue exceeds labor costs by at least $11,000 per week. Since the monopsony profit-maximizing employment rate of 77 workers exceeds the target gross profit, Whositz continues to hire labor until, with a wage rate of $290

---

[15] Lee Whositz could have saved considerable time by hiring an economic consultant (like I. C. Clearly) to estimate the marginal cost of labor and the marginal revenue product formulas, so that the profit-maximizing wage rate could be set at the outset of the plant opening. Since the wage formula is $w = \$190 + L$, total wages equal $wL = 190L + L^2$, $MC_L = d(wL)/dL = 190 + 2L$. Also, $MRP_L = 500 - 2L$; thus, $MC_L = MRP_L$ implies that $190 + 2L = 500 - 2L$, which implies that $4L = 310$, or $L = 310/4 = 77.5$. Setting $L = 77.5$ in the wage equation shows $w = 190 + 77.5 = \$267.50$. If the reader overlooks the fact that the author made up these equations, one has to marvel at how close the trial-and-error method brought Lee Whositz to the profit-maximizing outcome!

per week and 100 workers, gross profit equals $11,000 per week. Any more employment would cause gross profit to fall below the target. Hence, the employment and wage distortions of monopsony may be avoided by the substitution of nonprofit goals.[16]

Returning to our assumption of profit maximization, setting employment at 77 workers by offering a wage of $267 per week means that output will be lower, and prices correspondingly higher, than if employment were determined by competitive forces (or, perhaps, nonprofit goals). Recognizing this, Ed Collins calls a meeting of his fellow workers and suggests that they are getting a raw deal: Whatsit Widgets is receiving excessive profits by paying workers less than their contribution to revenue. To back up his findings, he turns the podium over to I. C. Clearly, who (among other things) earns a living advising unions in their collective bargaining strategy.

"As I see it," announces Clearly, "Whatsit Widgets workers produce marginal revenue on the order of $346 each at the prevailing employment level. This means that wages could rise by as much as $79 per week without layoffs occurring. However, if you demand more than $346 per week, some of you will lose your jobs."

"There you have it, gang!" shouts Ed Collins, hoping to awaken the sleeping workers in the back of the hall. "I say we call in the International Brotherhood of Widget Workers to represent us in collective bargaining!"

As I. C. Clearly slips unnoticed out the back door, the assembled workers vote overwhelmingly to contact the National Labor Relations Board to hold a union representation election.

Meanwhile, Lee Whositz has heard the rumblings among the workers and called in a consultant for advice on how to approach the coming union vote and the possible onset of collective bargaining.

"There is really not a lot you can do legally to forestall a representation election," reports I. C. Clearly, who (among other things) advises employers on collective bargaining strategy. "But remember, your workers volunteered for employment: there is no place else in Tinytown where they prefer to work at existing wages, or they would not be working for you. I suggest that you hang tough, keep to your current wage offer, and try to wear down their negotiator. But be wary of empty threats;

---

[16] According to John Kenneth Galbraith:

> When prices are fully under control, they can be raised to offset increases in costs that are not similarly under control. Wages are the most important example of an uncontrolled cost. The ability to offset wage increases with price increases is of great importance to the protective purposes of the technostructure.
>
> That price increases usually follow wage increases shows, more than incidentally, that profit maximization is not a purpose of the technostructure. If revenues can be increased just after a wage increase, they could, obviously, have been increased well before (*Economics and the Public Purpose* [Boston: Houghton Mifflin, 1973], p. 128).

if you try mass firings or a punitive wage reduction, you will create a situation in which some workers have nothing to lose by a strike."

After consulting with the home office, Lee Whositz decides to follow I. C. Clearly's advice. After an overwhelming vote in favor of unionization, the IBWW negotiator, U. R. Struck, meets with the Whatsit Widgets representative, I. U. Snumbers, an accountant pirated from Sparky Electronics. The initial union demand of $346 per week is countered by a "Let's forget the whole thing" offer of $267 per week. As the strike deadline approaches, the union reduces its wage demand to $344, while Whatsit Widgets raises its offer to $268 per week. It is clear that mediation is necessary to forestall a plant closure, which would hurt both sides. Both sides agree to bring in an arbitrator, I. C. Clearly, who (among other things) earns a living as an unbiased consultant on collective bargaining problems.

I. C. Clearly suggests a compromise wage settlement of $305.50 per week, which the union negotiator readily accepts, but which Snumbers snubs. So Clearly suggests a compromise of $286.25, which Snumbers approves, but Struck rejects. Finally, after long lectures by Clearly (and a little poetic license by the author), both sides agree on a wage rate of $290. The contract is signed and Lee Whositz returns to Whatsit Widgets with the intention of determining the optimal number of workers to lay off in the face of the higher labor cost.

To her amazement, Lee Whositz discovers that the profit-maximizing employment rate is actually greater than it was before unionization. The data Whositz used are shown in Table 14-7. The union wage contract causes the marginal cost of labor to equal $290, as long as additional workers are willing to work at that wage. Since this is much greater than the reservation wages of the 77 workers hired under the monopsony solution, gross profit under collective bargaining is lower than under monopsony. However, the marginal cost of the 77th worker is now $290 per week, where it had been $346. Although profit has fallen, the profit-maximizing rate of employment has actually risen. Indeed, if employment remained at 77 workers per week, gross profit would fall from $12,012 per week to $10,241. However, since the marginal revenue product of the 77th worker now exceeds his or her marginal cost (i.e., the union wage rate), profit can be increased until 100 workers have been hired. By expanding employment, the decline in profit is held to just slightly over $1,000.

Since this result seems to contradict what common sense and her accountant dictate, Whositz consults I. C. Clearly, who, to maintain good will, occasionally helps his clients with their problems free of charge.

"You see," Clearly explains, "the union wage represents a constant marginal cost of labor, whereas the marginal cost of labor hired under monopsony increases faster than the wage. If you recall, you actually wished to hire about 116 workers at the pre-union wage, but you could

TABLE 14-7
Employment and Profit Consequences of Union Wage: $w_u \geqq \$290/\text{week}$

Union Wage (w_u)	Workers Hired (L)	Total Wages (wL)	Marginal Cost of Labor (MC_L)	Marginal Revenue Product (MRP_L)	Total Revenue (ΣMRP_L)	Gross Profit (Π_g)	Quantity of Labor Demanded (L_d)
$290	10	$ 2,900	$290	$480	$ 4,900	$ 2,000	105
290	20	5,800	290	460	9,600	3,800	105
290	30	8,700	290	440	14,100	5,400	105
290	40	11,600	290	420	18,400	6,800	105
290	50	14,500	290	400	22,500	8,000	105
290	60	17,400	290	380	26,400	9,000	105
290	70	20,300	290	360	30,100	9,800	105
290	77	22,330	290	346	32,571	10,241	105
290	80	23,200	290	340	33,600	10,400	105
290	90	26,100	290	320	36,900	10,800	105
290	100	29,000	290	300	40,000	11,000	105
291	101	29,391	392	298	40,298	10,907	104.5
292	102	29,784	394	296	40,595	10,811	104
293	103	30,179	396	294	40,890	10,711	103.5
294	103	30,282	294	294	40,890	10,608	103

hire only 77 workers because of the increasing marginal cost of labor. Increasing the wage rate to $290 did reduce the quantity of labor you demand to 105 workers. Your demand for labor is still inversely related to the wage rate. However, by taking away your ability to hire labor at less than $290 per week, the union contract causes employment to expand along the labor supply schedule. You will notice that you still face a small shortage of labor. You have hired 100 workers (the 77 original union members plus another 23 workers whose reservation wages are greater than $267 but less than $291), while you would actually like to hire 105 at the union wage."

"But I can hire more labor only by paying $291 or more; the union would never stand for my paying new workers more than the contract wage, unless all workers are paid the higher wage. Besides, if management is to remain credible in the negotiations that will occur when this contract expires in three years, I can't go paying more than the contract wage today," replied Lee Whositz, incredulously.

"Precisely," said Clearly, distinctly. "I think I will take my leave now. I have a lot of clients, you know."

"While we are on that subject," interrupted Whositz, sternly, "How can you justify working both sides of the street in a labor negotiation?"

"I'm glad you asked," lied Clearly. "Achieving a collective bargaining wage outcome which approximates the competitive outcome requires balanced bargaining strength and accurate information on both sides.[17] By advising both sides, I was able to increase the efficiency of resource allocation, which, as everyone knows, is the ultimate goal of every economist."

"Still, by understanding both sides of the collective bargaining process, you are able to sell your services to the highest bidder, sometimes selling the same information to more than one party!" snarled the plant manager.

"Hmm," mused I. C. Clearly, "that is true."

Beyond Numerical Examples

If there is any conclusion we can confidently draw about the allocational effects of labor unions, it is that microeconomic theory, objectively considered, will support neither unqualified condemnation nor unqualified praise of the efficiency effects of labor unions. Judging the impact of labor unions on employment and output requires an assessment of the competition among employers. A typical statement in praise of the economic impact of labor unionism emphasizes the distortions generated by monopsony power:

> Not often has the power of one man over another been used more callously than in the American labor market after the rise of the large corporation. As late as the early twenties, the steel industry worked a twelve hour day and a seventy-two hour week, with an incredible twenty-four hour stint every fortnight when the shift changed.
>
> No such power is exercised today for the reason that its early exercise stimulated the counteraction that brought it to an end. In the ultimate sense it was the power of the steel industry, not the organizing abilities of John L. Lewis or Philip Murray, that brought the United Steel Workers into being. The economic power that the worker faced in the sale of his labor—the competition of many sellers dealing with few buyers—made it necessary that he organize for his own protection.[18]

On the other hand, a statement implying an adverse impact of labor unions is typically based on the assumption that labor markets would be competitive in the absence of unions; that is, that employers have no

---

[17] To find the employment-maximizing wage rate, we substitute the wage equation, $w = 190 + L$, for the marginal cost of labor expression, and set that formula equal to the marginal revenue product of labor: $w = MRP_L$ implies $190 + L = 500 - 2L$, so that $3L = 310$, or $L = 103.33$, which we can round out to 103. Hence, the employment-maximizing wage rate is $190 + 103 = \$293$.

[18] John Kenneth Galbraith, *American Capitalism: The Concept of Countervailing Power* (Boston: Houghton Mifflin, Sentry Edition, 1962), p. 115.

power—individually or through collusion—to resist the forces of a competitive labor market:

> The power of unions, as of any other monopoly, is ultimately limited by the elasticity of the demand curve for the monopolized services. Unions have significant potential power only if this demand curve is fairly inelastic at what otherwise would be a competitive price. Even then, of course, they must also be able to control either the supply of workers or the wage rate employers will offer workers.[19]

It is ironic, but nonetheless true, that the logic of both John Kenneth Galbraith, author of the first quotation, and Milton Friedman, author of the second, is valid. The implications of each statement are consistent with the assumptions on which it is based. That both attitudes may be correct, depending on whether unions increase wages to competitive levels or beyond (already prevailing) competitive levels, was recognized by that great defender of individual freedom and competitive markets John Stuart Mill:

> It is a great error to condemn, *per se* and absolutely, either trade unions or the collective actions of strikes. I grant that a strike is wrong whenever it is foolish, and it is foolish whenever it attempts to raise wages above that market rate which is rendered possible by demand and supply. But demand and supply are not physical agencies, which thrust a given amount of wages into a labourer's hand without the participation of his own will and actions. The market rate is not fixed for him by some self-acting instrument, but is the result of bargaining between human beings—of what Adam Smith calls the "higgling of the market"; and those who do not "higgle" will long continue to pay, even over the counter, more than the market price for their purchases. Still more might poor labourers who have to do with rich employers, remain long without the amount of wages which the demand for their labor would justify, unless, in vernacular phrase, they stood out for it; and how can they stand out for terms without organized concert? . . . I do not hesitate to say that associations of labourers, of a nature similar to trade unions, far from being a hinderance to a free market, are the necessary instrumentality of that free market; the indispensable means of enabling the sellers of labour to take due care of their own interests under a system of competition.[20]

As we have emphasized more than once in this text, it is usually more difficult for people to recognize their own biases than to recognize the biases of others. Nevertheless, as the last numerical example was

---

[19] Milton Friedman, "Labor Unions and Economic Policy," in Bowen and Ashenfelter, *Labor and the National Economy*, p. 30.

[20] John Stuart Mill, *Principles of Political Economy*, vol. II, 5th ed. (London: D. Appleton & Company, 1896), p. 553.

intended to show, there is often a financial incentive for understanding both sides of controversial issues: the economist can sell his or her services to whichever side is willing to pay higher fees and can sometimes work both sides of the street at once.

HIGHLIGHTS

1. The model of the ideal labor market depends on five crucial assumptions: (1) many employers and many workers, (2) homogeneous labor, (3) profit-maximizing (nondiscriminating) employers, (4) freely flexible wages, and (5) free market entry and exit.

2. Monopsony power causes the employer to be aware of and take into account the inframarginal impact of wage increases designed to attract additional workers. The marginal cost of labor exceeds the wage rate by the amount the monopsonist must raise the wages of workers already employed when extra workers are hired: $MC_L = w + L(\Delta w/\Delta L)$.

3. The volunteer army "fails" because the Defense Department's monopsony power produces a predicted shortage of labor. Arguments for a return to conscription stress the tax saving that would result, but conscription benefits the majority by exploiting a minority (the draftees), that is, by confiscating the difference between a draftee's reservation wage and military pay.

4. A private-sector monopsonist maximizes profit by first determining the amount of labor for which the marginal revenue product equals the marginal cost, then setting the wage rate at the minimum necessary to attract that number of (qualified) job applicants. Wage discrimination is consistent with profit maximization for a monopsonist who hires, say, male and female workers such that their marginal cost equals the marginal revenue product of labor, even though one group receives a higher wage than the other.

5. Job discrimination by competitive employers can be traced to a taste for discrimination, whereby the employer acts as if there were a psychic cost of hiring workers with particular characteristics. Because employer discrimination, in the absence of monopsony, means a departure from economic efficiency, a competitive market will tend to eliminate such discrimination in the long run.

6. Worker cartels develop when a craft union or professional association obtains direct control over the supply of labor. One of the chief sources of such control is occupational licensing, which usually arises because consumers demand protection from unqualified providers of an important service (e.g., medical care, legal representation). Giving members of an occupation the right to determine requirements for licenses provides them with the ability to monopolize that labor market.

7. Unlike employer discrimination in a competitive industry, employee discrimination—whereby one group of workers excludes others from jobs—may benefit the discriminators. Other methods of job rationing include auctioning off union membership or professional accreditation (generally illegal) and setting requirements for entry into a profession at artificially high levels.

8. Bilateral monopoly exists when one employer or a group of colluding employers (buyer) deals with one labor union (seller). Although the precise wage and employment outcome of collective bargaining cannot be predicted without information about the bargaining strength of the two sides, it is likely to be closer to the competitive solution under bilateral monopoly than under unchallenged employer monopsony or labor monopoly.

GLOSSARY

Backward-bending labor supply curve For individuals, a supply curve reflecting a decline in the hours of labor services offered as the wage rate increases, due to the dominance of the income effect of a wage increase, which encourages the consumption of leisure, over the substitution effect, which encourages workers to trade leisure for income. A backward-bending market supply curve will occur only if the number of individuals offering labor services is restricted, so that any tendency of individuals to offer fewer labor hours as the wage rate rises cannot be offset by an increase in the number of persons offering labor services.

Bargaining range The set of wage rates determined by the employer's initial wage offer (e.g., the monopsony wage) and the union's initial wage demand (e.g., the precontract marginal cost of labor). If the wage settlement is within this range, collective bargaining will tend to increase both the wage rate and the employment level.

Bilateral monopoly A market characterized by only one buyer and only one seller.

Implicit tax In the draft of military personnel, the monetary equivalent to the draftee's reservation wage for military service minus the wage rate paid to draftees.

Industrial union A labor organization which represents all production workers in an industry, regardless of skill. Industrial unions usually operate in labor markets characterized by a few employers (oligopsony).

Job discrimination The practice of denying access to jobs to workers with characteristics either employers or other workers consider undesirable. Job discrimination increases producer costs and so is more likely to occur as a job-rationing technique of a labor cartel.

Marginal cost of labor The change in wage payments due to hiring one more unit of factor services. In a competitive labor market (or after collective bargaining), the marginal cost of labor equals the market (or contract) wage. Under monopsony, the marginal cost of labor equals the wage rate paid to the last worker hired plus the extra pay implied for workers who would have received less had the last worker not been hired. Also called the **marginal input cost**.

Marginal input cost See **marginal cost of labor**.

Monopsony A market dominated by one buyer; also used to characterize collusive oligopsony.

Oligopsony A market characterized by a few buyers.

Taxpayer surplus The imputed value of a level of service provided by government minus tax payments for that service. Taxpayer surplus is analogous to consumer surplus, although the fact that nonpayers cannot be excluded from consuming a public good makes the demand for the good (or service) virtually impossible to estimate.

Wage discrimination The practice of paying different wages to equally productive workers. A monopsonist would pay unequal wages to equate the marginal cost of workers with identifiably different reservation wages.

Wage structure A set of equilibrium compensating wage differences for workers of varying productivity or in closely related jobs, required for good worker morale and successful on-the-job training.

SUGGESTED READINGS

Ashenfelter, Orley, "Racial Discrimination and Trade Unions," *Journal of Political Economy* (May/June 1972), 435–462.

—— and George E. Johnson, "Unionism, Relative Wages and Labor Quality in U.S. Manufacturing Industries," *International Economic Review* (October 1972), 488–508.

Becker, Gary S. *The Economics of Discrimination.* rev. 2nd ed. Chicago: University of Chicago Press, 1971.

Bowen, William G., and Orley Ashenfelter, eds. *Labor and the Nation Economy.* rev. ed. New York: Norton, 1975.

Carroll, Thomas M. "Achieving Cartel Profits through Unionization: Comment." *Southern Economic Journal* (April 1981), pp. 1152–1161.

Galbraith, John Kenneth. *American Capitalism: The Concept of Countervailing Power.* Boston: Houghton Mifflin, Sentry Edition, 1962.

Lewis, H. Gregg. *Unionism and Relative Wages in the United States.* Chicago: University of Chicago Press, 1963.

Oi, Walter Y. "The Economic Cost of the Draft." *American Economic Review* (May 1967), pp. 39–62.

Rees, Albert. "The Effect of Unions on Resource Allocation." *Journal of Law and Economics* (October 1963), pp. 69–78. Reprinted in William Breit and Harold Hochman, eds. *Readings in Microeconomics.* 2nd ed. New York: Holt, Rinehart and Winston, 1971, pp. 444–451.

Robinson, Joan. *Economics of Imperfect Competition.* New York: St. Martin's Press, 1969, Books VI–IX.

Sowell, Thomas. "Affirmative Action Reconsidered." *Public Interest* (Winter 1970).

Thurow, Lester C. *Poverty and Discrimination.* Washington, D.C.: The Brookings Institution, 1969.

EXERCISES

Evaluate

Indicate whether each of the following statements is true (agrees with economic theory), false (is contradicted by theory), or uncertain (could be true or false, given additional information). Explain your answer.

1. Military conscription which allowed draftees to hire replacements would exploit the poor.

2. If a craft union has pushed wages above competitive equilibrium, a collusive agreement by employers to resist the wage increase may improve the pattern of resource allocation.

3. If male workers demand a wage premium when required to take orders from female managers, women will be hired as managers only at a lower salary than male managers receive.

4. If an employer hires black and white workers at different wages for the same job, we may conclude that the employer is a monopsonist.

5. Immigration laws, which restrict the right of employers to hire foreign workers, constitute a form of monopolization of U.S. labor markets.

6. If a union succeeds in raising wages in an industry, labor costs will rise by a larger proportion if the employers' side of the market is characterized by monopsony rather than competition, *ceteris paribus.*

7. If a monopsonist were able to practice perfect wage discrimination, paying each worker his or her reservation wage, the wage rate of the last worker hired would equal the value of his or her marginal product.

8. By raising wage rates, labor unions increase consumer prices.

9. During the first half of the twentieth century, the wages of domestic servants rose faster than the wages of construction workers. Since construction workers are highly unionized and domestic servants are rarely unionized, we may infer that unions are unable to raise the wage level of members.

10. The employed members of a newly formed

union will always earn enough from acting as monopolists to be able, if they wish, to compensate fully those thrown out of work by the union, given a positively sloped labor supply curve in that market.

Calculate

Answer each of the following questions, showing all your calculations.

11. Consider again the numerical example of the wage-discriminating monopsonist:

w_f	L_f	w_m
$5.00	30	$6.00
5.50	40	6.50
6.00	50	7.00
6.50	60	7.50
7.00	70	8.00

L_m	MC_L	MRP_L
10	$ 6.00	$15.00
20	7.00	13.00
30	8.00	11.00
40	9.00	9.00
50	11.00	7.00

a. If the union required that men and women be paid the same wage, approximately what wage rate would maximize employment? (Hint: For both men and women, $\Delta L/\Delta w = 40$ and $\Delta MRP_L/\Delta L = -0.1$.

b. What would be the net gain or loss in economic rent for women? for men? for both?

12. Suppose that the demand for plumbers in a large city is $L_d = 50{,}000 - 100w$, and the competitive supply is $L_s = -10{,}000 + 50w$, where w = weekly wage rate.

a. What is the competitive equilibrium wage and employment level? (Hint: set $L_d = L_s$ and solve for w, then find L.)

b. If a worker's reservation wage is given by the inverse supply function, $w_r = 200 + 0.02L$, and the market wage is given by the inverse demand function, $w = 500 - 0.01L$, so that the marginal revenue *to* plumbers is $MR_L = 500 - $

$0.02L$, what level of employment would maximize economic rent? (Hint: set $MR_L = w_r$ and solve for L.)

c. If a plumbers' union sought to maximize economic rent for members, what wage should be set?

d. If union membership were auctioned off, what would a union plumber's *net* (after "dues") weekly pay equal if "kickbacks" to the union were maximized?

Contemplate

Answer each of the following in a brief but complete essay.

13. Comment on the following: When a large manufacturing plant is built near a small town, the average wage rate in that town increases. Hence, employers in one-company towns do not exploit labor.

14. Since a minimum wage law confronts employers, including monopsonists, with a horizontal labor supply curve, it might be argued that minimum wage laws *could* result in higher employment in monopsonized industries. Why, then, would collective bargaining, which takes account of the supply and demand conditions in the industry, still be preferable to minimum wage laws for eliminating monopsony distortions in labor markets?

15. Comment on the following: "Government enforcement of union-negotiated conditions upon all employees in a bargaining unit insulates the union from competition in the labor market. If employees were free to reach individual agreements with employers that depart from union-negotiated terms, the union's economic power could be reduced and open-market solutions emerge. The cartel behavior of trade unions also results in the institionalization of mediocrity in that very productive workers, whose output justify higher wages than negotiated by the

union, cannot, by law, be paid according to their productivity."* How does this argument square with the usual argument that higher than competitive wage rates cause employers to upgrade employment requirements? Does this statement assume a competitive employer or a discriminating monopsonist?

---

* James T. Bennett and Manuel H. Johnson, "Free Riders in U.S. Labour Unions: Artifice or Affliction?" *British Journal of Industrial Relations* (May 1978), pp. 161–162.

Chapter 15

General Equilibrium and Economic Welfare

It is traditional to conclude a text in microeconomic theory with a chapter that pulls together all the ideas which have been developed in the book, and so this chapter shall. It is somewhat rare for a course actually to get this far, unless some topics have been sacrificed along the way. But believing that the student and instructor are best suited to decide which topics to study, the last chapter is presented with a few more innovations than traditionally seen in a chapter nobody is thought to read.

We begin with a discussion of the difficulties encountered in devising a basis for judging the performance of an economic system. Variations on the theme of "the greatest good for the greatest number" are explored and rejected, either because of their lack of realism (violations of scarcity) or their inability to gain a consensus. The Pareto criterion is ultimately selected for pragmatic reasons: whenever it is possible to make a noncontroversial improvement in resource allocation, the situation is inefficient—that improvement should have already been made.

Most of the chapter is concerned with deriving the conditions under which a private enterprise system would achieve a Pareto optimum, whereby it would be impossible to improve the welfare of one participant without diminishing the welfare of another. The character of such an outcome is developed by exploring the interaction of property and markets in a two-person, two-good, two-factor environment. We then show how perfect competition in all markets would lead to such an ideal outcome in a multiple-person, multiple-commodity environment.

We introduce a snake into our Garden of Eden by reprising the trade-off between property failure (externalities) and market failure (monopolies). The general theory of the second best shows what little consensus remains about economic welfare beyond the ideal world of universal competition. The chapter—and the text—concludes by showing that perfect monopoly would lead a market right back to where it supposedly began: the commons.

Welfare Economics: Son of the Invisible Hand

Over two centuries ago, Adam Smith proclaimed that the superiority of a "free market" economy to mercantilism—the economic philosophy that sought to regulate economic activity in the name of national interest—lay in the ironic ability of a free market to achieve the goals of mercantilism better than mercantilist policy. By pursuing self-interest, said Smith, merchants would be guided, as if by an invisible hand (the market), to further the national interest. Today economists are also fascinated by the principle of the invisible hand. However, the issue involved is subtly different from the point Adam Smith made. Today the debate concerns whether an unregulated market—what we have called "the market as a commons"[1]—can further the interests of citizens, both individually and collectively, better than an economy regulated by a democratically elected government "of the people, by the people, and for the people."

We have already noted the disagreement among economists over the proper role for government in dealing with macroeconomic problems. Will a market economy automatically stabilize at ideal levels of output, employment, and price? If not, could government monetary or fiscal policies cause the economy to operate closer to the ideal, or achieve ideal outcomes more quickly? And if an "ideal" government policy might work, is this sufficient reason to give less than ideal bureaucrats and legislators authority to attempt such improvements? Is there really a trade-off between unemployment and inflation, or is the government's attempt to solve one problem responsible for the other?

As has been the case throughout this text, macroeconomic policy will not directly concern us. The concepts needed to develop a balanced analysis of competing macroeconomic theories require more attention than they can be given here. We will focus our attention on the microeconomic manifestations of the invisible hand metaphor. Even if there were no problems of aggregate economic stability (or these problems

---

[1] Thomas M. Carroll, David H. Ciscel, and Roger K. Chisholm, "The Market as a Commons: An Unconventional View of Property Rights," *Journal of Economic Issues* (June 1979), pp. 605–627.

could be costlessly eliminated), would a free market economy achieve the "best" allocation of resources possible, or could selective government intervention achieve "better" results?

Stating the issue in these terms makes **welfare economics** unavoidably normative. Welfare economics is "that branch of economics concerned firstly with defining economic efficiency, secondly with evaluating the economic efficiency of particular systems of resource allocation, and finally with analyzing the conditions under which economic policies may be said to have improved social welfare."[2] As soon as we ask what *ought* to be the composition of economic institutions, we are asking for a value judgment. The problem with value judgments is that disagreements about them cannot be resolved by objective means, such as a statistical analysis or even an ideal controlled experiment. Yet economists can hardly hope to remain relevant (and thereby earn a living) unless they occasionally make a judgment call.

If making a value judgment is unavoidable, we can at least try to pick a criterion for success which is universally acceptable. A value judgment with unanimous acceptance is still normative, but unanimity postpones the inevitable squabbles until basic principles—necessary to define the limits of the debate—have been established. A criterion must be operational: objective research should be able to determine whether it is satisfied. We might all agree that the best policy is one that is better than all other policies, but this definition is not very useful for judging actual economic events.

The difficulty of selecting (or defining) a practical standard for economic performance is demonstrated in the deficiencies of that popular utilitarian maxim "the greatest good for the greatest number." As stated, the goal is unattainable. The greatest good, at least in terms of material consumption, is bliss, a state in which a person is sated with all commodities. The greatest number is the present population of the world, plus all future generations. For everyone to be sated with everything would mean that scarcity no longer existed. This might be a reasonable characterization of the reward in some afterlife, but it will not be attained in this vale of tears. Would an ideal market achieve heaven on earth? No. Would an ideal government be able to? No.

To be practical, "the greatest good for the greatest number" must be transformed into an achievable goal. We could specify a constrained optimization goal. How about "the greatest good for a given number"? Next, we must specify what that number will be. How about one person, say the author of this book? Surely the best minds in economics, engineering, physics, chemistry, and the entertainment arts ought to be able to satisfy completely the humble needs of one textbook writer. Even poetic license cannot invoke unanimous assent to "the greatest good for

[2] Graham Bannock, R. E. Baxter, and Ray Rees, *A Dictionary of Economics* (Harmondsworth, Middlesex, England: Penguin Books, 1972), p.,423.

Tom Carroll." And specifying any given number or population segment would upset those excluded.

Instead, we could try "a given good for the greatest number," sort of a variation on "necessities for all before luxuries for any." Should we take the present standard of living in the United States as our constraint, holding back consumption here and in other rich countries until poorer countries have achieved our standard of living? Why not use the standard of living in Bangladesh instead? That way we could have a larger world population. Obviously, maximizing the number of people with a given standard of living does not imply the same type of economic system as maximizing the standard of living for a given number of people. Unlike the duality theorem for efficient input selection (see chapter six), our two specifications of the constrained maximization of economic welfare do not imply equivalent solutions.

Consider a third variation on the utilitarian theme: An ideal society will achieve the maximum total utility from available resources and known technology. This has a nice ring to it; why, we can even draw a diagram. In Figure 15-1a, population, n, is plotted on the horizontal axis, while total utility is measured along the vertical axis. We assume that the total happiness of all people, or total utility, TU, is an increasing function of total (nonhuman) resources, $\bar{R}$, and that it increases with population until some maximum is achieved. With limited resources and known technology, the relationship between population and total utility resembles a short-run total product curve. (After fourteen chapters in which similar diagrams recur regularly, is this a surprise?)

Figure 15-1a shows total utility increasing at an increasing rate until population n_0 is achieved. The range of increasing marginal utility reflects increasing output per capita due to labor specialization. Total utility increases at a decreasing rate from n_0 to n_2, where total utility is maximized, then begins to decrease as population increases still further. Figure 15-1b exhibits the condition (by now familiar in other contexts) that total utility will be maximized when the last person born can add nothing to total satisfaction ($MU = 0$ when $n = n_2$). But could a society be ideal if the last person born were indifferent between living and never having been born? If the last person is to be less wretched, others will have to reduce their happiness to accommodate a positive level of utility for this last person. Maximizing total utility seems to imply that population should expand until at n_2, the utility gained by the last person born equals the total amount lost by everyone else.

Unless society is composed of pure altruists, utility gained by another would not mean as much as utility lost by oneself. If society is a club whose size expands only if "original members" permit it,[3] popu-

---

[3] James Buchanan, "An Economic Theory of Clubs," *Economica* (February 1965), pp. 1–14. Also see Todd Sandler and John T. Tschirhart, "The Economic Theory of Clubs: An Evaluative Survey," *Journal of Economic Literature* (December 1980), pp. 1481–1521.

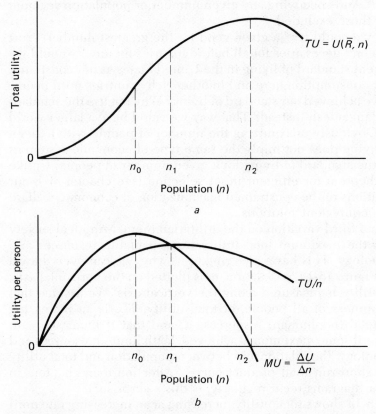

Figure 15-1
Utility and Population. *a*, Total utility schedule; *b*, average and marginal utility schedules.

lation might be restricted to n_1, where average utility is greatest. Figure 15-1*b* shows that average utility will be maximized when the marginal utility of the last person born equals the average utility for all persons. If people were equally efficient "utility generators," equal consumption would generate equal utility for each person at n_1. If individual (and social) utility is increasing at a decreasing rate, maximizing average utility would imply equal income or wealth distribution.[4] This, of course,

---

[4] In chapter three, diminishing marginal utility of wealth implied risk aversion. Abba Lerner, in his *Economics of Control: Principles of Welfare Economics* (New York: Macmillan, 1944), assumed ignorance of any individual's marginal utility of wealth but generally diminishing marginal utility of wealth to argue that a just society would distribute wealth equally. Milton Friedman and L. J. Savage, in "The Utility Analysis of Choices Involving Risk" (*Journal of Political Economy* [August 1948], pp. 279–304), argued that since diminishing marginal utility of wealth implied that individuals would not even play fair gambles, the fact that people engaged in unfair gambles denied the basis of Lerner's argument.

ignores the problem of how to motivate the creation of wealth when everyone is guaranteed an equal share.

But wait a minute! How do we know that people are equally efficient utility generators? Should a glutton and an esthetic be given equal shares? If not, who should get more? Should families with many children be given proportionately more than small families? Should the handicapped be given compensatory wealth; should people with natural advantages or special talents be otherwise handicapped?[5] It should be obvious that maximization of average utility is not a practical standard for judging the success of institutions or policies. We have no means of comparing different people's marginal utility. Most people prefer being rich to being poor and would rather be healthy than ill. But this is no basis for judging how taking wealth from some and giving it to others would affect total economic well-being.

Ultimately, whether or not a person prefers maximization of total utility or of average utility as a criterion for judging economic institutions depends, probably a great deal, on how he or she expects to fare under the operation of either rule. For obvious reasons, "more for me but less for you" is not an operational criterion of economic welfare likely to win universal approval.

Economic Individualism and Pareto Optimality

A criterion which agrees in spirit with "the greatest good for the greatest number" philosophy, but avoids the impractical aspects of the utilitarian ideal, is the **Pareto criterion**, named for the turn-of-the-century economist-sociologist, Vilfredo Pareto. An avid critic of the concept of measurable utility, Pareto nevertheless agreed that the basis for measuring social welfare should be the sum of individual well-being. Even if social welfare cannot be measured because there is no interpersonal standard of utility, it should still be possible to determine, at least in some circumstances, whether a policy change increases or decreases individual welfare, the utility of others remaining constant. If a change in policy would make at least *one person better off* (in his or her own estimation), while making *no one else worse off*, the change would *increase* social welfare. A policy which would constitute a Pareto improvement in social welfare is said to be **Pareto superior** to the status quo. Conversely, a policy change which *harmed one or more persons*, while making *no one else better off*, would *decrease* social welfare.

The Pareto criterion for measuring social welfare is uncontroversial

---

[5] The chilling image of a society operated on such extreme egalitarian principles is provided by Kurt Vonnegut, Jr.'s "Harrison Bergeron" in *Welcome to the Monkey House* (New York: Delacorte, 1968).

and practical, albeit limited. If one person objects that a policy change makes someone else better off, that person must be made worse off by the change. The Pareto criterion does not say what happens to social welfare when some are made better off while others are made worse off by a change in policy. If I rejoice in someone's misfortune, I must be made better off by the change which harmed him or her. Again, Pareto's criterion does not apply. To disagree with the criterion itself implies that the assumptions on which it is based are violated.

The Pareto criterion is practical in its use of individual actions to reveal changes in individual welfare. When individuals are free to choose which goods to consume, we may infer that the commodities purchased are preferred to other options encompassed by their budget constraint (see the appendix to chapter two). Changes which make people better off (in their own terms) will be reinforced by their assent, while changes which make people worse off will be resisted. Situations in which the Pareto criterion is relevant will be identified by their lack of controversy. When some are made better off at the expense of others, the irrelevance of the Pareto criterion will be evident in the discord.

Remember that we are seeking a unanimous standard for judging economic policies. That the Pareto criterion is not applicable to all policies reflects the clash of interests in a complex society. Were economists to go beyond the Pareto criterion and attempt to develop an absolute standard that would encompass changes which help some individuals while hurting others, the profession would align itself with one set of interests against another. Free entry into the economics profession would destroy the consensus of what *ought* to be done in controversial situations. If economists attempted to protect this arbitrary standard of social justice from "heretics" by forming an ideological cartel, they would find themselves in competition with members of the other social sciences over topics economists consider their scientific property.

There are a number of issues about which economists largely agree (at least in the abstract), even though these issues may be controversial among noneconomists. Most economists favor unrestricted international trade, deregulation of (would-be) competitive markets, and repeal of laws which prevent individuals from exchanging goods or services when others are not materially affected by that exchange (e.g., usury laws, blue laws, minimum wage laws). Granted that economists may differ about the scope of competitive markets, this is a disagreement in degree rather than in kind. The way economists think causes them to resist inefficient solutions to economic problems. The Pareto criterion is most dramatic when it inspires wisdom in the face of controversy. This wisdom is born of the insistence that when controversial decisions must be made, all possibilities for Pareto improvements should be exhausted before inevitable trade-offs between vested interests are confronted.

Operational significance of the Pareto criterion lies in the definition of a **Pareto optimum**: a situation in which it is *impossible to make anyone better off without making some other person worse off*. A Pareto optimum exists after all possible Pareto improvements in social welfare have been made. The somewhat ironic consequence of our definition of Pareto optimality is that no society should find itself in a situation where Pareto superior policy changes are possible, since that would imply that social welfare is unnecessarily lower than it has to be. Scarcity may indeed make sacrifice inevitable, but as a minimum performance standard, economic institutions should automatically bring society to a Pareto optimum.

It is a prediction of welfare economics that a perfectly competitive market economy will achieve all possible Pareto improvements in social welfare, thereby bringing society to a Pareto optimum. We shall see that since alternative Pareto optimal improvements in social welfare are often possible, the Pareto criterion does not imply unique solutions to economic problems.

Property Rights and Exchange

To reprise our discussion in chapter eight, a *commons* is said to exist when individuals can use scarce resources without experiencing the costs they impose on society. The "tragedy of the commons" is that while the absence of **property rights** may seem egalitarian, the commons arrangement favors the selfish.[6] It might be argued that the commons is a workable arrangement when people are motivated by altruism: religious communes and monastic orders are cited as proof. The easy answer is that if people were true altruists, having property rights would not be antisocial, since people would voluntarily share. (The more difficult question is whether the institution of private property *causes* egoistic behavior which makes the commons wasteful.[7]) But suppose that users of limited pastureland were able to graze their flocks without taking responsibility for overgrazing. Each selfish shepherd would understand that if grass were left by his or her livestock, someone else's flock would eat it. All selfish individuals would consider themselves better off if they owned a share of the pasture, from which other shepherds could be excluded. Then any grass preserved would belong to the person who preserved it. It is possible that no one would be made worse off by this arrangement since altruists would share their property, while a few sel-

---

[6] Garrett Hardin, "The Tragedy of the Commons," *Science* (December 1968), pp. 1243–1248.

[7] See Virginia Held, *Property, Profits and Economic Justice* (Belmont, California: Wadsworth, 1980), introduction, pp. 1–19.

fish individuals would have eventually ruined the commons for everyone anyway.

Since it would be possible to divide up limited pastureland in a way that would make all economic agents better off, or at the least make no one worse off, the commons is not Pareto optimal. However, since there are many possible ways that property rights could be assigned, it does not follow that achieving a Pareto optimum would necessarily result from a Pareto improvement in social welfare. One shepherd might usurp the position of overlord, policing use of the pasture in exchange for a share of others' flocks. Those peasants who died resisting enclosure of the commons—even if guided by erroneous economic principles—were clearly not made better off by the institution of property rights.

Economic theory ascribes egoistic motives to individuals. Each person is assumed to pursue his or her own interest while being indifferent to the welfare of others. It is the invisible hand, not human virtue, which achieves desirable social outcomes from selfish behavior. The ultimate issue of welfare economics is setting down necessary and sufficient conditions for a Pareto optimal allocation of scarce resources, which, generally speaking, is equivalent to an economically efficient allocation of scarce resources. If limited resources are being squandered, it will be possible to improve the lot of some members of society without harming others. After the conditions for optimality have been set forth, economic theorists then determine how an ideal market would achieve such an outcome.

As we have specified the tragedy of the commons, private property rights—or any equivalent arrangement (such as stewardship) that requires individuals to experience the consequences of their use of scarce resources—are necessary if egoistic individuals are to achieve a Pareto optimal allocation. That other character types may be able to live in communal harmony—say, in a monastic order or a kibbutz—is neither denied nor assumed. Once individuals have been assigned property rights over scarce resources, the stage is set for trade. But unless each person can exclude others from the use of his or her property, resource owners cannot expect *quid pro quo* (or "something for something"), which is the essence of exchange.

Imagine two individuals, Adam and Eve, who are the only inhabitants of a suburb of Eden. They have just ended a trial separation, having overcome their mutual blame for the apple incident. They find that each has a certain quantity of fish (q_1) and figs (q_2), which were collected between their eviction from the Garden and their reconciliation. By assuming away any missing links or snakes which might be lurking about, we can define a **closed economy**. Let q_{1_A} represent the fish Adam has and q_{2_A} represent his figs. In this two-person example, Eve's fish and figs are, respectively, $q_{1_E} = \overline{q}_1 - q_{1_A}$ and $q_{2_E} = \overline{q}_2 - q_{2_A}$, where $\overline{q}_1$ and $\overline{q}_2$ represent the total quantities of fish and figs, respectively.

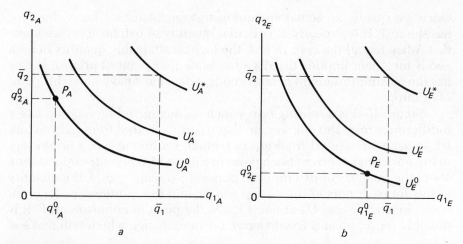

Figure 15-2
Indifference Curves for Two Traders—Adam (a) and Eve (b)—in a Closed Economy.

Figure 15-2a depicts Adam's indifference curve map: $q_{1_A}^0$ fish and $q_{2_A}^0$ figs place his initial endowment of commodities, point P_A, on his indifference curve U_A^0. To simplify the analysis, we are assuming that Adam and Eve are egoists, that each obtains satisfaction only from his or her own consumption. We assume that neither person's utility function contains the other's (estimated) welfare and that no commodity is consumed jointly. Hence, Adam would have been happier with all the fish and all the figs, since point $(\bar{q}_1, \bar{q}_2)$ is on his highest possible indifference curve, U_A^*. However, exclusivity of consumption means that Eve has rights to those fish which do not belong to Adam, $q_{1_E} = \bar{q}_1 - q_{1_A}$, and to those figs which are not Adam's, $q_{2_E} = \bar{q}_2 - q_{2_A}$.

Figure 15-2b shows Eve's endowment of fish (q_{1_E}) and figs (q_{2_E}) as point P_E on her indifference curve U_E^0. Like Adam, Eve is assumed to be an egoist who prefers more of either commodity to less of it, *ceteris paribus*: point $(\bar{q}_1, \bar{q}_2)$ is on a higher indifference curve, U_E^*, than her initial endowment.

If we look carefully at Figures 15-2a and 15-2b, we discover that one of them is redundant. Both graphs are constructed by plotting quantities of fish on the horizontal axis and figs on the vertical axis. Both have their origin in the lower left corner. More fish are shown by a rightward movement along the horizontal axis; more figs are shown by an upward movement along the vertical axis. Because the system is closed, each point shown in Figure 15-2a implies a particular point in Figure 15-2b.[8]

---

[8] Stated formally, the four equations describing fish and figs, $q_{1_A} = \bar{q}_1 - q_{1_E}$, $q_{2_A} = \bar{q}_2 - q_{2_E}$, $q_{1_E} = \bar{q}_1 - q_{1_A}$, and $q_{2_E} = \bar{q}_2 - q_{2_A}$, have only two degrees of freedom. Once we give a value to q_{1_A}, we have no freedom to choose the value of q_{1_E}, and vice versa. Once we give a value to q_{2_E}, we are forced to accept the implied value of q_{2_A}, and vice versa. Therefore, a point chosen in one diagram determines the only compatible point in the other diagram.

Once we specify an actual amount of figs for Adam, we know that Eve has the rest. If we specify a particular quantity of fish for Eve, we know that Adam has all the rest. In fact, the highest attainable quantity of both goods for Adam implies that Eve has none (her point of origin). If Eve has the maximum amount of both goods, Adam must have none (his point of origin).

Figure 15-3 is a *trading box*, which is constructed by rotating Eve's indifference map 180 degrees, so that q_{1E} is measured from right to left, while q_{2E} is measured from top to bottom, starting at Eve's origin (o_E) in the upper right corner. Each point in Figure 15-3 provides information about the quantity of fish for each person ($q_{1E} = \bar{q}_1 - q_{1A}$), the quantity of figs for each person ($q_{2E} = \bar{q}_2 - q_{2A}$), and the indifference level for each person (U_E^0 and U_A^0 at point P). At the point of endowment, P, it is possible for Adam and Eve to agree on an exchange which will make at

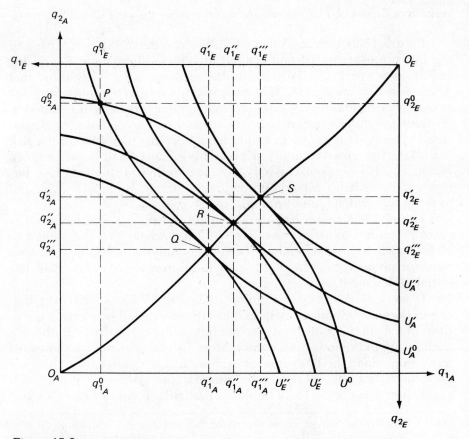

Figure 15-3
Trading Box for Two-Person, Two-Commodity Exchange. Points Q, R, and S are all Pareto superior to point P.

least one of them better off without making either worse off. Point P is not Pareto optimal.

In chapter eight we saw that the *ability to exchange* presupposes the *ability to exclude*. A trade is actually an exchange of property rights to commodities. Adam agrees to transfer the right to exclude others (including himself) from consuming his figs to Eve in exchange for the right to exclude others (including Eve) from consuming her fish. Unless each can exclude the other from consumption prior to trade, there will be no incentive to exchange. Ultimately, property rights create a frame of mind in which individuals confront the reality of scarcity in their use of resources. If Adam eats a fish, the cost is the fish which cannot be eaten later or the figs that he might have received in trade for that fish.

Figure 15-3, which illustrates the incentive to trade, is insufficient to determine the terms of trade that will emerge from a two-person bargaining process. If Eve is a very skilled trader, she may convince Adam to give her $q_{2_A}^0 - q_{2_A}'''$ figs in exchange for $q_{1_E}^0 - q_{1_E}'$ fish, so that the allocation of commodities moves from point P, at the intersection of two indifference curves, to point Q, where Adam's original indifference curve, U_A^0, is tangent to Eve's indifference curve U_E''. Because the new distribution of commodities would leave him on the same indifference curve, Adam would be made no worse off by the trade. However, Eve would move to a higher indifference curve. The move from point P to point Q would be a Pareto move, since Eve would be better off and Adam would be no worse off.

Point S is also Pareto superior to point P. If Adam were an adept bargainer, convincing Eve to part with $q_{1_E}^0 - q_{1_E}'''$ fish in exchange for $q_{2_A}^0 - q_{2_A}'$ figs, the distribution of commodities would move from point P to point S. In this case, Adam would have increased his satisfaction from U_A^0 to U_A''', while Eve's satisfaction remained at U_E^0. Finally, an exchange of $q_{1_E}^0 - q_{1_E}''$ of Eve's fish for $q_{2_A}^0 - q_{2_A}''$ of Adam's figs would increase the level of satisfaction for Eve and Adam to U_E' and U_A', respectively, when the allocation of commodities moved from point P to point R.

What distinguishes all three possible posttrade points—Q, R, and S—from point P is that the pretrade point occurs at an intersection of indifference curves for Adam and Eve, whereas each posttrade distribution point occurs at a tangency of indifference curves. At point P, indifference curves U_E^0 and U_A^0 have different slopes: Adam is willing to give up more figs to obtain an additional fish than Eve requires to remain indifferent. When two individuals have different marginal rates of substitution for commodities, a Pareto improvement in their welfare is possible. Voluntary exchange can make at least one of them better off without making the other worse off.

When an exchange has brought the distribution of commodities to a point where the resulting indifference curves are tangent, gains from voluntary exchange have been exhausted. At point R, a movement to a higher indifference curve for Eve (or Adam) implies moving to a lower indifference curve for Adam (Eve). Since people do not voluntarily submit to an exchange they consider unfair, allowing trade to proceed only as far as both parties consent should bring the distribution of commodities to a Pareto optimum.

Figure 15-3 shows that the Pareto criterion does not imply a unique trading solution. Points Q, R, and S are each a Pareto optimum: it is impossible to make one person better off without making the other person worse off. To take the analysis further, we must expand our two-person economy into one large enough to accommodate a competitive market system.

Before we bid farewell to this closed economy, we can state the first necessary condition for a Pareto optimal allocation of resources:

Efficient exchange: The distribution of commodities between two persons can be Pareto optimal only if the marginal rate of substitution between those commodities is the same for the two individuals:

$$(MRS_{12})_A = (MRS_{12})_B \quad \text{or} \quad -\frac{MU_{1_A}}{MU_{2_A}} = -\frac{MU_{1_E}}{MU_{2_E}}$$

As long as trade between two individuals is allowed to continue until one of them vetoes further exchange, we can be assured that they have exhausted their mutual gains from trade, or that the costs of reaching an agreement (called transaction costs) exceed the benefits that an exchange is expected to generate.

In Figure 15-3, the locus of Pareto optimal commodity distribution points is the line running from Adam's origin in the lower left corner to Eve's origin in the upper right. That this line passes through points Q, R, and S indicates that these points are potential termination points to voluntary trade. However, the subset of points between Q and S on this *contract curve* are the only Pareto optimal points which are Pareto superior to point P. All other points on the contract curve, although Pareto optimal, would cause either Adam or Eve to be worse off (in his or her own estimation) relative to point P.

Economic Welfare and Market Competition

We shall now proceed to explode our tranquil closed economy by showing how competitive markets for fish and figs lead to a unique trade equilibrium for our two individuals in an **open economy** (an economy which exchanges goods with the outside world). To apply the Pareto criterion to the voluntary actions of Adam and Eve, we will assume that all other economic agents are indifferent about the couple's division of property rights and that consumption of either fish or figs by either person has no impact on the welfare of people not involved in the trade. This is a simplifying assumption which will be acknowledged as a crucial assumption later. The reader's forbearance is appreciated.

In Figure 15-4, the dashed line passing through points P and R where Adam's indifference curve U'_A is tangent to Eve's indifference curve U'_E, represents the budget line given to our two traders by the relative prices of fish and figs in a competitive market. No longer is the outcome of a trade between Adam and Eve indeterminant. Although Adam would prefer a trade which culminated at point S, his incentive to hold out for better terms than those associated with moving from point P to point R has been preempted by the market. Since Eve can receive $q'_{2E} - q^0_{2E}$ figs for $q^0_{1E} - q'_{1E}$ fish by trading in the market instead of trading with Adam, Adam's veto of a trade would not interfere with Eve's ability to trade. Similarly, although Eve prefers terms that would move the distribution of commodities to point Q, her hopes of getting better

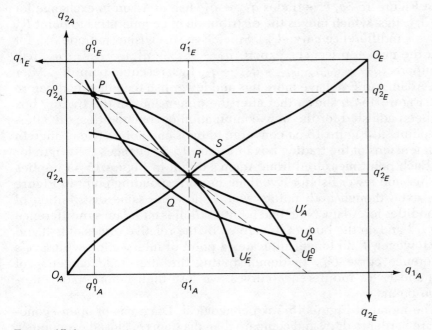

Figure 15-4
Unique Trade Equilibrium with Competitive Market. The dashed line passing through points P and R is the budget line for Adam and Eve created by competitive markets for fish and figs. Any terms offered by Eve which would move Adam to a point below U^*_A will cause him to use the market instead of trading with Eve; any terms from Adam which would cause Eve to move to a point below U^*_E will be vetoed by her, and she would trade in the market.

terms are dashed by Adam's access to a competitive market for fish and figs.

What is unrealistic about Figure 15-4 is the coincidental tangency of U'_A and U'_E at point R on the market-determined budget line. Figure 15-5a shows a much more likely outcome; Adam and Eve move to different points (R_A and R_E, respectively) on their common budget line, so that U'_A and U'_E are not (apparently) mutually tangent. The slope of the dashed budget line through points R_A and R_E is equal to the ratio of market prices: $\Delta q_2 / \Delta q_1 = -(p_1/p_2)$. That Adam and Eve move to different points on the budget line does not affect the attainment of a Pareto optimum. Since each person reorients his or her consumption of fish and figs so that his or her marginal rate of substitution equals the common price ratio of those commodities, it follows that $(MRS_{12})_A = (MRS_{12})_E$. In fact, one of the efficiency enhancing aspects of a competitive market is that, by preventing price discrimination, it results in the same set of prices for all consumers. Each consumer maximizing utility with respect to the consumption of two commodities will have the same marginal rate of substitution for those commodities.

In Figure 15-5a, Eve trades $q^0_{1_E} - q'_{1_E}$ fish to Adam in exchange for $q'_{2_E} - q^0_{2_E}$ figs, which moves the distribution of commodities to point R_A (on Eve's indifference curve U'_E). Since Eve still wishes to trade fish for figs at the market price, she exports $\overline{q}_1 - (q''_{1_E} + q'_{1_A}) = q'_{1_E} - q''_{1_E}$ fish and imports $(q''_{2_E} + q'_{2_A}) - \overline{q}_2 = q''_{2_E} - q'_{2_E}$ figs, reaching point R_E. After trade, Adam and Eve have more figs and fewer fish than they had before trade. Figure 15-5b shows that after the dimensions of the trading box have been adjusted for the new combination of commodities, the after-trade points in Figure 15-5a converge to the same point. The change in the dimensions of the trading box in Figure 15-5b changes the origin for Eve. Each point measured from Adam's origin in Figure 15-5b implies more figs and fewer fish for Eve than the corresponding point in Figure 15-5a, even though both points would show the same distribution of commodities for Adam. Note that point P still lies on Adam's indifference curve U^0_A and on the budget line given by the relative prices of fish and figs. However, P no longer indicates a point of intersection with Eve's indifference curve U^0_E. In demonstrating the after-trade tangency of Adam and Eve's indifference curves, we lose their before-trade intersection point.

The moral of Figure 15-5 is pedagogical. Diagrams of open economies are harder to draw and compare than diagrams of closed economies. Further analysis of the relationship between trade and economic welfare requires a choice. We must either abandon our fiction of a two-person, two-good economy or find a means of accommodating changes in the amounts of the two goods. We will follow the latter course for the present, dropping our assumption that the quantities of fish and figs are fixed in favor of bringing the production of commodities into the model. We will

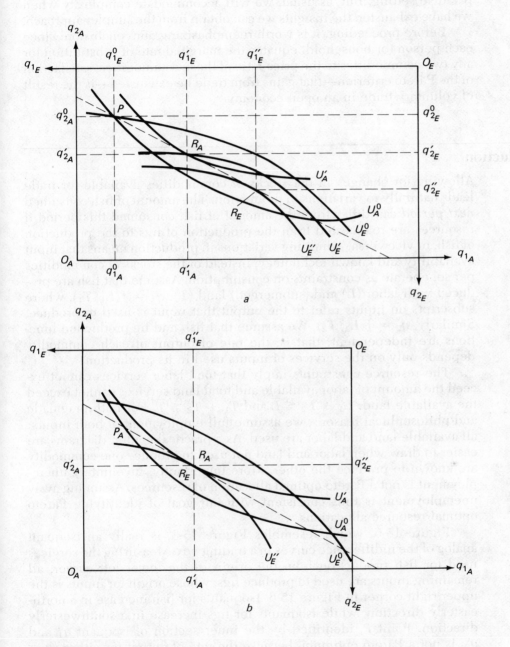

Figure 15-5
Competitive Trade. *a*, Opening of a closed economy; *b*, post-trade tangency
after dimension change.

eventually have to expand our horizon beyond this two-person, post-paradise setting. But, as usual, we will accommodate complexity when we have exhausted the insights we can obtain from the simpler approach.

Before proceeding, it is worth reemphasizing our conclusion: since each person (or household) equates the marginal rate of substitution for any two commodities to the price ratio of those commodities, satisfaction of the Pareto criterion—that gains from trade be exhausted—is the result of voluntary trade in an open economy.

Efficient Production

Allowing for changes in the stocks of commodities available for trade leads naturally to variations in production. The amount of fish consumed *next period* can differ from the amount of fish consumed this period if resources are reallocated from the production of figs to the production of fish, or vice versa. Admitting variations in production means that input availability and known technology, instead of the stocks of commodities per se, operate as constraints on consumption. Assume that fish are produced with labor (L) and (submerged) land (T): $q_1 = f(L_1, T_1)$, where subscripts on inputs refer to the output that input is used to produce. Similarly, $q_2 = f(L_2, T_2)$. We assume that fish and fig production functions are independent; that is, the rate of output of each commodity depends only on the services of inputs used in its production.

The resource constraints imply that total labor services cannot exceed the amount of labor available and total land services cannot exceed the available land: $L_1 + L_2 \leqq \overline{L}$ and $T_1 + T_2 \leqq \overline{T}$. For both pragmatic and philosophical reasons, we assume full employment of both inputs: all available land and labor are used. As a practical matter, diagrams are easier to draw when labor and land not used to produce one commodity are known to produce the other. More importantly, involuntary unemployment is not a Pareto optimal allocation of resources. Assuming away unemployment is thus consistent with our goal of identifying Pareto optimal resource allocations.

Figure 15-6, which resembles Figure 15-3, is really an isoquant analog of the indifference curves in a trading box. Measuring the services used for fish production from the origin in the lower left corner, all remaining inputs are used to produce figs, whose origin for inputs is the upper right corner in Figure 15-6. Isoquants for fish increase in a northeasterly direction, while isoquants for figs increase in a southwesterly direction. Point P, identified by the inner section of isoquant q_1^0 and q_2^0, is not a Pareto optimum, because the rate of output for either commodity could be increased by input substitution. Transferring a lot of labor from figs to fish and a little land from fish to figs—that is, moving output from point P to point Q—increases fish from q_1^0 to q_1', while the

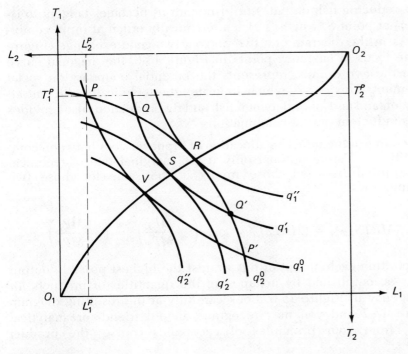

Figure 15-6
Technically Efficient Input Allocations. Points P and Q are technically inefficient: resource reallocation can increase the output of one commodity without reducing production of the other commodity. In contrast, points R, S, and V are each technically efficient; output of one commodity can be increased only if output of the other commodity is decreased.

production of figs remains at q_2^0. Although the marginal rate of technical substitution of labor for land would have declined (in absolute value) in fish production and risen in fig production (relative to point P), the intersection of isoquants q_1' and q_2^0 at point Q indicates that production of either good can be increased without reducing the output of the other. Point Q is superior to point P, but neither point is technically efficient.

Moving away from point Q, resources can continue to be reallocated along isoquant q_2^0. Transferring comparatively large amounts of labor from fig production to fish production while draining just enough land to hold fig production constant expands the output of fish until, at point R, isoquant q_2^0 is tangent to isoquant q_1''. Any further reallocation of resources would mean reducing the output of one commodity to increase the output of the other. Point R is technically efficient.

Alternatively, starting at point Q, fish output could be held constant at q_1' and relatively large amounts of land could be taken out of fish production, drained, and used to plant fig trees with a compensatory transfer of labor from fig to fish production to maintain fish output at q_1'. Reallocating resources along isoquant q_1' increases fig production (without reducing fish output) until isoquant q_1' becomes tangent to isoquant q_2' at point S, which is also a technically efficient input combination. As in the diagram of a two-person, two-good exchange (Figure 15-3), the locus of tangency points in Figure 15-6, the diagonal curve between the two origins, represents the potential boundary on social improvement. This curve, which indicates the technically efficient allocations of land and labor between fish and fig production, also provides a menu of efficient output combinations.

Efficient production: The allocation of input services between commodities is Pareto optimal only if the marginal rate of technical substitution between those inputs is the same for those two commodities:

$$(MRTS_{LT})_1 = (MRTS_{LT})_2 \quad \text{or} \quad \left(-\frac{MP_L}{MP_T}\right)_1 = \left(-\frac{MP_L}{MP_T}\right)_2$$

By plotting each output of figs against the highest possible output of fish is accomplished by juxtaposing the quantities of products for each tangency in Figure 15-6. Look carefully at the resulting diagram in Figure 15-7 and you may recognize an old friend (or analytical nemesis) from your principles of economics course: the **product**

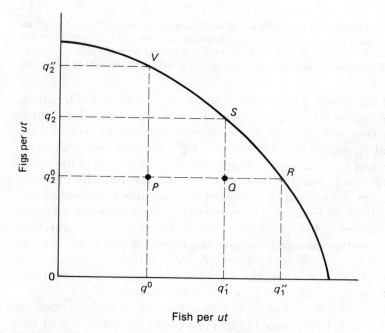

Figure 15-7
Product Transformation Curve: The Combinations of Commodities Resulting from Technically Efficient Combinations of Inputs.

transformation curve, also known as the **production possibility frontier**. By whatever name you know it, the curve in Figure 15-7 shows the maximum output of figs for each chosen output of fish (or vice versa). Each point on the production transformation curve implies that increasing the output of fish requires a decrease in the output of figs (or vice versa), given available inputs and knowledge of technical possibilities. Note that points P and Q in Figure 15-6 correspond to points inside the production possibility frontier; in fact, both points P and P' in Figure 15-6 plot to point P in Figure 15-7. Points Q and Q' in Figure 15-6 plot to point Q in Figure 15-7. From input combinations which produce q_1^0 fish and q_2^0 figs, it is possible to increase fish output to q_1'' (point R), or to increase fig output to q_2'' (point V), or to increase output of both goods to q_1' and q_2' (point S).

General Equilibrium

Accounting for changes in the mix of outputs provides a link between efficiency of resource allocation and attainment of a Pareto optimum. This bridge is the long-run competitive equilibrium. A **general equilibrium** exists when all markets—for both inputs and outputs—are in long-run competitive equilibrium. Each firm hires inputs so that the marginal rate of technical substitution between any two inputs equals the ratio of the prices of their services. When all firms confront uniform prices for inputs, the marginal rate of technical substitution between any two inputs will be the same for any two commodities which use those inputs. Each household allocates its income so that the marginal rate of substitution for any two commodities equals their (negative) price ratio. As long as households buy their commodities in competitive markets, all will face the same prices for any two commodities purchased, so that the marginal rate of substitution for any two commodities will be the same for all households which buy them. To link the equilibria between input markets and output markets, we will show that the ratio of the marginal costs of two commodities must equal the ratio of their market prices.

For the sake of simple analysis, imagine that Adam and Eve are paid in kind, receiving fish and figs in return for their labor services and for leasing their land to the production of those commodities. In Figure 15-8, point $\alpha(O_E)$ represents the point of production on the product transformation curve, resulting in q_1^0 fish and q_2^0 figs. We can represent the initial distribution of commodities as a point within the trading box bounded by the two commodity axes and the perpendicular lines to point $\alpha(O_E)$. If point P (measured from the origin in the lower left corner) represents Adam's initial income of $q_{1_A}^0$ fish and $q_{2_A}^0$ figs, point $\alpha(O_E)$ becomes Eve's origin—the reference point for measuring her income of

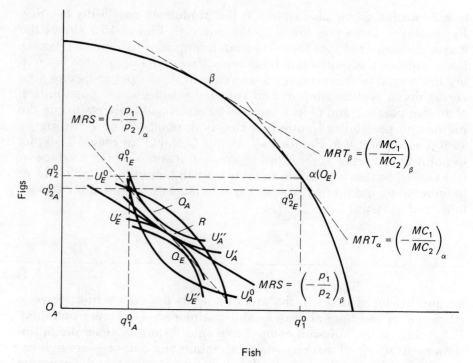

Figure 15-8
Product Transformation Curve and Trade Opportunities. Inequality between the marginal rate of substitution and the marginal rate of transformation is not Pareto optimal.

$q^0_{1_E}$ fish and $q^0_{2_E}$ figs. The intersection of indifference curves U^0_A and U^0_E at point P is a portent of mutual gains from trade. Obviously, point P is not a Pareto optimal distribution of the commodities.

The existence of competitive markets for fish and figs generates the dashed budget line through point P. The price ratio of the two commodities, which determines the slope of the budget line, equals the ratio of the marginal costs of those goods, given by the slope of the transformation curve at point α: $\Delta q_2 / \Delta q_1 = -p_1/p_2 = -(MC_1/MC_2)$. The **marginal rate of transformation**, the name given to the slope of the product transformation curve, equals the negative ratio of the marginal costs of the commodities in question:

$$MRT_{21} = \frac{\Delta q_2}{\Delta q_1} = -\frac{MC_1}{MC_2}$$

In a competitive industry, output is determined by the equality of marginal cost and price. Merely by assuming a brief time lag between when goods are produced (in response to prices prevailing then) and when they are sold, we can see the consequences of market disequilibrium. In Figure 15-8, Adam attempts to exchange figs for fish and move from point P to point Q_A, while Eve wishes to transfer her combination of goods from point P to point Q_E. Eve wants to exchange more fish for figs than Adam is willing to exchange at the prevailing price ratio. The tangencies of indifference curves U_E'' and U_A'' with the trading line do not coincide with the contract curve, the locus of tangencies of indifference curves indicating the limits of voluntary transactions. There is a shortage of figs and a surplus of fish at the price ratio determined by the ratio of the marginal costs of the two goods at point α. Arbitrage could eliminate the exchange disequilibrium by establishing a price ratio consistent with the mutual tangency of U_E' and U_A' on the contract curve, at point R.

Clearly, point R is Pareto superior to point P. However, although the gains from trade have been exhausted at point R, it is not a Pareto optimum. At point R, the marginal rate of substitution of fish for figs differs from the marginal rate of transformation at point α. By reallocating land and labor from fish to fig production (moving production from point α to β), the mix of outputs can be made to approximate more closely the preferences revealed through exchange.

Figure 15-9 depicts a Pareto optimum. The marginal rate of transformation, $MRT_{21} = \Delta q_2/\Delta q_1 = -(MC_1/MC_2)$, at point β is equal to the marginal rate of substitution for both Adam and Eve after trade;

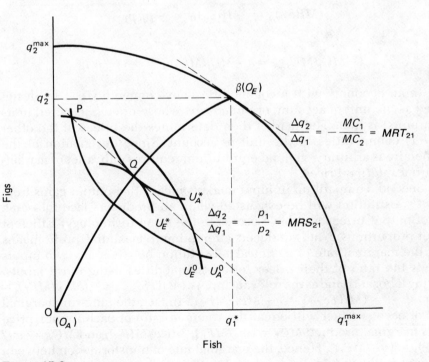

Figure 15-9
General Equilibrium in Two-Person, Two-Good Economy.

$(MRS_{21})_A = (MRS_{21})_E = -(MU_1/MU_2)$ at point Q. Since output has been adjusted so that producers and consumers face the same price ratio:

$$-\frac{MC_1}{MC_2} = -\frac{p_1}{p_2} = -\frac{MU_1}{MU_2}$$

Given the output and distribution of commodities depicted in Figure 15-9, it would be impossible to make Adam better off unless Eve were made worse off (or vice versa).

The situation depicted in Figure 15-9 is identical to a long-run equilibrium under perfect competition in all input and output markets. By letting our imaginations take over where two-dimensional diagrams leave off, we can extrapolate the characteristics of a general competitive equilibrium in all markets in an economy with many products, inputs, and consumers. First, competition in product markets means that gains from trade between any two consumers would be exhausted for all commodities. All consumers of any two goods would equate the marginal rate of substitution of those two commodities to the equilibrium price ratio. Taking any two goods (q_i and q_j) for any two persons (say, A and B) who consume both:

$$(MRS_{ji})_A = (MRS_{ji})_B = -p_i/p_j$$

or

$$(-MU_i/MU_j)_A = (-MU_i/MU_j)_B = -(p_i/p_j)$$

In an economy with n commodities, any commodity can be designated as the unit of account, or *numeraire*, whose price (measured in its own units) is one. The market then determines the prices of the other $(n-1)$ commodities in the unit of account. Since designation of the numeraire is arbitrary, general equilibrium requires only a set of market-clearing *relative prices*.

Second, competition in input markets means that output gains from input substitution will be exhausted when all producers face the same set of output prices and have access to the same technology. Efficient input proportions by all producers attempting to maximize profit means that the marginal rate of technical substitution between any two inputs equals the ratio of their prices for all commodities using those inputs. Taking labor and land as the relevant inputs, $(MRTS_{LT})_i = -(MP_L/MP_T)_i = -(w_L/w_T) = (MRTS_{LT})_j = -(MP_L/MP_T)_j$. In fact, the long-run marginal cost of each product will equal the common ratio of each input's price to its marginal product: $MC_i = (w_L/MP_L)_i = (w_T/MP_T)_i$ and $MC_j = (w_L/MP_L)_j = (w_T/MP_t)_j$. Hence, the marginal rate of transformation between two commodities is given by the ratio of their long-run marginal costs.

Finally, when all firms are in long-run competitive equilibrium,

Business Illustration
Allocational Efficiency for a Multiproduct Firm

The principles of efficient resource allocation have very important applications in plants where two or more outputs share one or more inputs. Whenever it is possible to produce more of one commodity without reducing the output of some other commodity, a multiproduct plant is operating inefficiently. In such circumstances, production costs could be cut without reducing revenue, or revenue could be increased without increasing costs. That may sound like a pleasant prospect, but it is advantageous only if someone else is manager and you are planning a bloodless coup.

Suppose that Econo-products makes two commodities: widgets, which require 10 hours of shaping on the lathe, 7.5 hours on the grinder, and 5 hours of polishing; and gadgets, which require 2 hours of shaping, 7.5 hours of grinding, and 20 hours of polishing. We shall assume that operating time of both lathes and grinders is limited to 3,000 hours per week, while polishers have a capacity of 6,000 hours per week. Since a product will be manufactured only if its market price at least covers its average variable cost, we also assume that the net price (price minus unit variable cost) of widgets is $50 each and the net price of a gadget is $40.

Formally, we may specify the selection of the optimal product mix as a linear programming problem (discussed in chapter seven) of the following form:

$$\text{Maximize } \Pi_g = 50q_1 + 40q_2$$

subject to:

$$10q_1 + 2q_2 + S_1 = 3{,}000$$
$$7.5q_1 + 7.5q_2 + S_2 = 3{,}000$$
$$5q_1 + 20q_2 + S_3 = 6{,}000$$

and

$$q_1, q_2, S_1, S_2, S_3 \geqq 0$$

where Π_g = gross profit, q_1 = widgets per week, q_2 = gadgets per week, S_1 = surplus shaping time, S_2 = surplus grinding time, and S_3 = surplus polishing time.

Since this is only an illustration, we will merely outline the linear programming solution to the optimal product mix problem. The accompanying figure shows feasible combinations of widgets (q_1) and gadgets (q_2) which satisfy all three input constraints. The line labeled $S_1 = 0$ represents combinations of q_1 and q_2 which use all available lathe time; combinations above or to the right of that line are not feasible because there is not enough shaping machinery. Where line $S_1 = 0$ intersects the horizontal axis, point D, determines the maximum output of widgets, $q_1 = 300$. Further, since one widget requires 5 times as much lathe time as a gadget does, the marginal rate of transformation along line S_1 is -5.

The grinder constraint line, $S_2 = 0$, intersects the shaping constraint line at point C, where $q_1 = 275$ and $q_2 = 125$. To the left of point C, there is too little grinding machinery to produce combinations of widgets and gadgets which would use shaping machinery to capacity. If fewer than 275 widgets or more than 125 gadgets are produced, some shaping machinery will be redundant, at least part of the week. Line $S_2 = 0$ intersects the

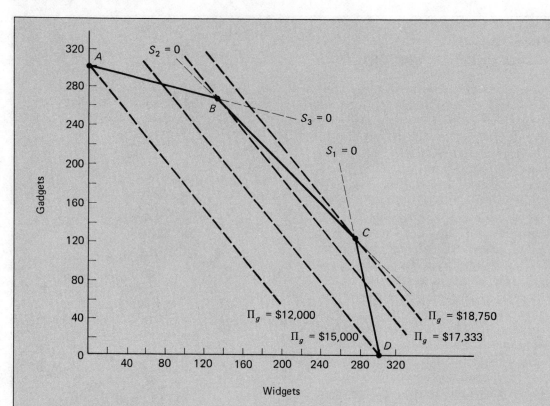

Production Possibility Frontier for Plant Producing Two Outputs with Three Fixed Input Services

polishing capacity line, $S_3 = 0$, at point B, where $q_1 = 133\frac{1}{3}$ and $q_2 = 266\frac{2}{3}$. If fewer than $133\frac{1}{3}$ widgets or more than $266\frac{2}{3}$ gadgets are produced, neither grinding nor shaping machinery will be used to capacity. Between points B and C, the cost of producing one more widget is producing one less gadget: $MRT_{21} = -1$.

The maximum production of gadgets is determined by the intersection of the polishing capacity line, $S_3 = 0$, with the vertical axis at point A, where $q_2 = 300$. Between points A and B, the marginal rate of transformation of gadgets into widgets is -0.25: for every four widgets produced, one gadget must be sacrificed.

The relative values of widgets and gadgets are given by the slope of the isoprofit lines, which represent combinations of q_1 and q_2 that result in the same gross profit: $\Pi_g = 50q_1 + 40q_2$.

Given the information in the figure, solution of the optimal product mix problem is straightforward. Since each widget is worth 25 percent more than each gadget, the firm's revenue increases when one gadget is sacrificed to get four more widgets: point B is more profitable than point A. To the right of point B, it costs one gadget to produce one more widget. Again, the slope of the isoprofit line is greater than the marginal rate of transformation.

By moving along the constraint line for grinding machinery (from point B to point C), the plant increases gross profit. However, once at point C, five gadgets must be sacrificed for each additional widget. The opportunity cost of widgets is too great at that point; no more should be produced at the expense of gadgets. Point C maximizes gross profit.

The three constraint lines in the figure describe a product transformation curve, whose slope, the marginal rate of transformation, is determined by the ratio of the marginal costs of the two commodities. When $-(p_1/p_2) < MRT_{21}$, where p_1 and p_2 are the net prices of widgets and gadgets, respectively, gross profit is increased by shifting inputs from widget to gadget production (transforming gadgets into widgets) until a corner is reached such that $p_1/p_2 < MC_1/MC_2$ to the right and $p_1/p_2 > MC_1/MC_2$ to the left. However, since variable costs have already been deducted, the relative marginal costs of widgets and gadgets reflect the opportunity cost of using fixed inputs to produce one commodity instead of the other.

such that $p_i = LRMC_i = LRAC_i$, it follows that the ratio of the marginal cost of any two products will equal the ratio of the prices of those two products: $MRT_{ji} = (-MC_i/MC_j) = (-p_i/p_j)$. This completes our list of requirements for a Pareto optimal allocation of resources:

Efficient allocation of resources: The mix of commodities produced is Pareto optimal only if the marginal rate of transformation between any two commodities equals the marginal rate of substitution between those commodities for all households consuming both, that is,

$$(MRT_{21}) = (MRS_{21})_A = (MRS_{21})_B$$

With all firms earning zero economic profit in long-run equilibrium, the total revenue generated by each commodity is exhausted on factor payments, whose prices are proportional to the value of that input's marginal product: $p_i q_i = w_1 v_1 + w_2 v_2 + \ldots + w_m v_m$.

"So what?" you ask. Let us take stock. We have shown that a competitive equilibrium in every market would correspond to a Pareto optimal allocation of resources. Given the distribution of property rights, consumer tastes, and available technology, any change in the pattern of resource allocation that would make anyone better off would make someone else worse off. That is because all possibilities for mutual gain have been eliminated by trade. Now the fun begins. The purpose of achieving a Pareto optimal allocation of resources was to exhaust all noncontroversial improvements in economic well-being. Ironically, economists' praise of universal competition brings them to a stage where advocating change means favoring one economic agent at the expense of another.

Property Failure: External Costs and Benefits

It is one thing to outline the conditions that would characterize a Pareto optimum; it is an entirely different matter whether those conditions are realized in our experience. Efficient resource allocation means that more of one commodity can be produced only by reducing the output of another commodity. To violate the efficiency criterion would mean making scarcity artificially severe. To fail to exhaust Pareto improvements in social welfare would mean allowing someone's utility level to be unnecessarily austere.

Achieving a Pareto optimum can be shown in another analysis of technical efficiency. In Figure 15-10a, an economic system is operating inside its production possibility frontier, at point Z. More of commodity i could be produced without reducing the output of commodity j, or vice versa. Nevertheless, producing inside the production possibility curve does not revoke scarcity, which is still evident in the opportunity cost of either commodity. Allocating unemployed or inefficiently used inputs to producing one commodity means society sacrifices the *potential* output increase of some other commodity.

Now consider the case of a Pareto inferior social state which results from incomplete property rights, such as point Ω in Figure 15-10b. Suppose that Cain, whose *ordinal utility* (utility measurable only to the extent of showing which prospects are preferred), U_C, is plotted on the vertical axis, threatens to steal some of Abel's corn. Abel, whose ordinal utility is plotted on the horizontal axis, must divert some of his time from

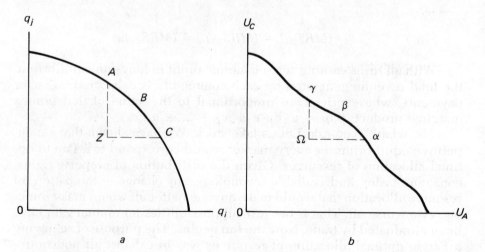

Figure 15-10
Consequences of Inefficient Resource Allocation. *a*, Artificial output scarcity; *b*, unnecessarily lost welfare.

production or leisure to guard his property. Both siblings are worse off than they might be under an alternative specification of property rights. Were Cain deterred from threatening Abel by his conscience or fear of punishment, Abel's utility would increase to the level indicated by point α on the utility possibility frontier. There are many points which are Pareto superior to Ω in Figure 15-10b. Abel might work the hours currently wasted guarding his property and use the output to pay Cain not to steal his corn. Extorted payments from Abel would make Cain better off, improving his welfare to that indicated by γ, while Abel would be no worse off than at Ω. Both α and γ are Pareto superior to Ω. But since Abel is better off at α and Cain is worse off, relative to γ, where Cain is better off and Abel worse off, α and γ cannot be compared using the Pareto criterion.

The reader may be perplexed that improving the welfare of a solid citizen at the expense of a would-be extortionist is not justified by the Pareto criterion. But we would have to embellish Pareto's criterion with a moral content not implied by him to make such a judgment. According to our specification, the Pareto criterion may not be used to select among Pareto optima, even if we are trying to determine how to move from a suboptimal social arrangement.

Consider another example, similar in its implications but different in its moral content. Cain raises cattle on his ranch, which is adjacent to Abel's cornfields. Steers being steers, some of Cain's herd wander into Abel's fields and trample his crops. Omitting from consideration any utility cattle may gain from vandalism, this state of incomplete property assignments is not Pareto optimal. If Cain could, without cost to himself, prevent his animals from straying, making him liable for crop damage would increase his watchfulness over his herd. Crop damage would be prevented, or at least reduced (and compensated), and Abel would be better off; assuming damage prevention, Cain would be no worse off. Abel's utility would increase as social welfare moved from Ω to α in Figure 15-10b.

But liability might be assigned to Abel, instead, exempting Cain from responsibility for crop damage. By installing a fence or bribing Cain to keep closer watch on his herd, crop damage could be lessened. If erecting a fence cost less than the crop damage it prevented, Abel would be better off with a fence while Cain would be no worse off. If Cain would prevent his cows from straying for a payment less than the cost of a fence, both Cain and Abel could be made better off (a movement from Ω to β). Even if Cain extorted the total value of the crops his cattle would have destroyed (a movement to γ), Abel would be no worse off than at Ω.

An important theorem, attributed to Ronald Coase, maintains that in a world of perfect competition and zero transaction costs, the situation existing under an incomplete specification of property rights could be improved upon by assigning liability for *external costs* to either party.[9] Further, in terms of our last example, the **Coase theorem** asserts that the same allocation of resources to corn and beef production would occur regardless of whether Cain compensated Abel for crop damage or Abel paid Cain to prevent crop damage. Imagine that Cain and Abel formed a partnership to raise beef and corn as joint products. Corn would either be sold on the market or used as feed, whichever maximized joint profit. The cost of crop damage would be *internalized*.

When one person's use of property imposes uncompensated costs on another, an **externality** is said to exist. Externalities are sometimes called *third-party effects* because they are outside the context of the usual buyer-seller (two-party) relationship involved in a voluntary trade. An externality is suboptimal; a more complete specification of property rights would improve the pattern of resource allocation, making at least one person better off without harming anyone else.

The Coase theorem is derived from the idea that a change in property rights which benefited one person but threatened to harm another would constitute a Pareto improvement in social welfare *if* winners compensated losers so that the latter were made at least no worse off by the change. Assigning liability would give one party veto power over some forms of resource allocation, while voluntary agreements would be used to assure that neither party was worse off because of a change in resource use. As long as the scope of the externality is limited, assigning liability to either of the parties would internalize the costs of resource allocation. If transaction costs are zero, the pattern of resource allocation would be unaffected by who bore liability. This is because producer behavior is assumed to be based on profit maximization, which implies that resource allocation patterns are independent of the producer's wealth. In long-run competitive equilibrium, revenue covers all opportunity costs of inputs, regardless of whether (to use our example) the marginal cost of raising a steer is measured in terms of its expected crop damage or the bribe its owner would have received for penning up the animal.

As with many models in microeconomics, differences exist over the scope of real-world problems the Coase theorem could alleviate. Although producer behavior may be independent of the entrepreneur's wealth, a household's wealth is likely to have an impact on the consumption decision. Suppose that my neighbor likes loud parties and I like peace and quiet. If I have the right to complain and have my neighbor fined for disturbing the peace, he bears liability. Perhaps I can be persuaded to ignore loud parties for a payment of $500, the cost of in-

[9] Ronald Coase, "The Problem of Social Cost," in William Breit and Harold Hochman, eds., *Readings in Microeconomics* (New York: Holt, Rinehart and Winston, 1971), pp. 484–517.

sulating my bedroom from sound. If having loud parties is worth more than $500 to my neighbor, a payment of $500 to me entitling him to my forbearance from complaining would be a Pareto move. Yet, if I bore liability (I could not legally stop noisy parties), I might not be willing to pay $500 for peace (to insulate my bedroom or bribe my neighbor to keep the noise level down) if quiet is a normal good.

As the scope of an externality increases, the likelihood of achieving Pareto moves by voluntary agreements diminishes. Some resources, such as clean air and unpolluted water, are squandered because individuals cannot be excluded from using them. For instance, producers of steel or chemicals find that their (private) production costs are minimized when wastes are dumped into the commons. Property rights, which are reasonably effective at enabling individuals to keep their goods, are not always as effective at forcing people to pay their social costs. On the other hand, were individual producers to incur the higher production costs of using nonpolluting techniques, they would not be able to recover those costs in the prices of their products, or from consumers of the cleaner environment.

As in the case of a localized externality, where the Coase theorem may be valid, large-scale externalities imply a suboptimal allocation of resources. However, prohibitive transaction costs prevent private agreements from achieving an improvement in social welfare. When a large number of arrangements are potentially Pareto superior to the commons, competition for property rights may prevent their being assigned.

The fact that whales are "free" threatens several species with extinction; excessive harvesting may prevent adequate reproduction. If, say, the Soviet Union were recognized as the owner of all unharvested whales, the state (a monopoly) could force Russian whalers to limit their catch to an optimal amount which left enough whales to replenish the supply. At the same time, as the recognized whale owner, the Soviet Union could police the catches of other countries. Given its powers of detection and enforcement, the U.S.S.R. might be reasonably successful at imposing an optimal harvest worldwide. A free-market country, say, Japan or Iceland, might be less willing or able to prevent poaching. Yet, in all likelihood, Japan and Iceland would rather own the unharvested whales than recognize Soviet property rights to them. In fact, it appears that each country prefers the commons and the potential extinction of whales to recognizing some other country's ownership rights.

When a **property failure** (a failure of exclusivity) occurs, private agreements and voluntary actions do not necessarily bring about an improvement in social welfare because individuals are not forced to consider the social costs of their actions. Generally, one of two solutions is proposed: monopoly power or government regulation. Actually, both solutions can be subsumed under the heading of market failure. Governments, to be effective, must have unchallenged authority in the markets they regulate. And another name for unchallenged market authority is monopoly.

Market Failure: Monopoly Power

There appear to be a considerable number of situations in complex economies which involve a trade-off between Pareto suboptimal social arrangements. For instance, should society allow a commons to exist in the realm of scientific discoveries? Knowledge is not usually scarce in the same way that other goods are scarce. If one person consumes an apple, there are fewer apples remaining for everyone else. But if one person learns of an idea developed by another, there is no less knowledge to go around. Knowledge, unlike most commodities, is not diminished by distribution.

The *value* of knowledge does depend, like the value of most commodities, on its relative scarcity. If one person invests resources and effort into the "production" of new information (for instance, development of a cost-saving production technique), usually those costs of research and development can be recovered only if *use* of information can be made exclusive. As shown in chapter eight, patents, which purport to be property rights to ideas and inventions, do not (cannot) grant exclusivity of knowledge. Patents constitute the right to exclude others from the market in which the protected idea is used. Property failure (a commons in ideas) is "solved" by mandating **market failure** (granting monopoly power in markets). What is paradoxical about solving property failure by generating market failure is that, like the commons, monopoly leads to a suboptimal allocation of resources.

Figure 15-11 illustrates the allocation of resources under pure competition and under monopoly, assuming a nondiscriminating monopolist operating multiple plants. In Figure 15-11a, a competitive equilibrium results in output Q_e at price p_e, determined at point B, where the market demand curve intersects both the short-run market supply curve, S_{SR}, and the long-run market supply curve, S_{LR}. The competitive equilibrium represents a Pareto optimum because consumer surplus is maximized. The marginal value of the commodity to consumers equals the opportunity cost of inputs needed to produce the commodity efficiently. If more of this good were produced, resources would be taken from production of some commodity consumers value more than the additional unit of this one. Producing less of this commodity would free resources which, if not unemployed, would be allocated to production of a less valued good. This is the importance of a *general* competitive equilibrium: marginal cost must equal price for all goods produced. As we shall see, when some markets are monopolized, or when external costs occur,

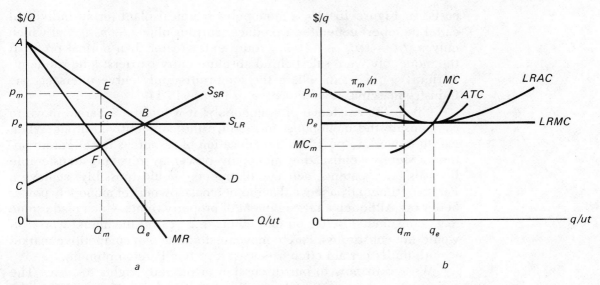

Figure 15-11
Welfare Effects of Monopoly Pricing. *a*, Monopolization of a competitive market; *b*, monopoly at the plant level.

a Pareto move may be possible by *not* imposing competitive rules on other markets.

Under a competitive market equilibrium, consumer surplus would be approximated by triangle ABp_e, while short-run producer surplus would equal triangle BCp_e (see the appendix to chapter four). In long-run equilibrium, producer surplus would equal zero, with the long-run supply curve, S_{LR}. All revenue over variable cost would equal the opportunity cost of (otherwise) fixed inputs.

A nondiscriminating monopolist would limit output to Q_m, charging price p_m. Consumer surplus would be reduced to triangle AEp_m. The net gain in producer surplus would be $(p_m - p_e)Q_m - BGF$. The cost of monopolizing a competitive market for consumers would be $(p_m - p_e)Q_m + EGB$, where EGB equals the portion of consumer surplus which does not become producer surplus. Triangle EGB is called the **excess burden of monopoly**. Because a nondiscriminating monopolist must reduce output to increase price, the lost consumer surplus on output not produced represents the inefficiency of monopoly. If consumers paid the firm its monopoly profit in exchange for the right to purchase the commodity at a constant price of p_e, the monopolist would be no worse off, while consumers would be better off by at least the additional consumer surplus represented by EGB.

Monopolization or cartelization of a structurally competitive industry would cause excess production capacity in the short run. Short-run producer surplus would be partly absorbed by higher than optimal fixed costs. In Figure 15-11b, a monopolist's typical plant (or an individual cartel member) generates a producer surplus of $(p_m - p_e)q_m$, of which only $\pi_m/n = (p_m - ATC)q_m$ represents greater than normal profit. If the monopoly were safe behind absolute entry barriers, long-run equilibrium would occur where the long-run supply curve intersects the industry marginal revenue curve in Figure 15-11a.

Given the existence of a monopoly, it would be a Pareto move to compensate the monopolist to produce the competitive output. When Pareto moves are possible, the allocation of resources is not Pareto optimal. Merely confiscating monopoly power by revoking transferable licenses (e.g., patents, acreage allotments) would (possibly) achieve a Pareto optimum by a move that did not make owners of monopoly power better off. Although a reassignment of property rights which made some (e.g., consumers) better off and others (e.g., cartel members) worse off would not constitute a Pareto move, restoration of a competitive market would, under certain circumstances, lead to a Pareto optimum.

We return now to our discussion of property rights to ideas. The argument in favor of patents maintains that inability to appropriate the potential benefits of an idea may deter inventive and innovative activities. In the absence of patents, if one firm in a competitive industry introduced cost-saving technology, that innovation would be duplicated by new firms or adapted by old firms which would otherwise be displaced, and the benefits the innovator anticipated would be short-lived. The experience which generated lower consumer prices in one industry might never occur again if each competitive producer feared that costs incurred in research would never be recovered through the difference between the product price and the reduced cost of production.

Granting an inventor a patent supposedly mitigates the disincentive toward inventive activity and innovation. Let us look at an example. Suppose that a producer of farm machinery develops and patents a cost-saving combine. An advertising blitz ("Don't be caught without a Conglomerate Products Combine!") could panic farmers into innovating quickly, thereby reducing the prices of various agricultural commodities as output increased (assuming no price supports or output restrictions). However, the monopoly producer of the improved combine would restrict its outputs to maximize profits. The demand for new equipment by producers in a competitive industry (here, farming) is related to the cost savings the equipment is expected to generate. If farmers expect no cost savings, no Conglomerate Products combines will be sold, and the patent is worthless. If the combine is sold for a price equal to its marginal production cost, no surplus will be generated to pay for research and development. Profit is maximized where marginal revenue equals the combine's marginal cost; only by coincidence would $(p_m - ATC)Q_m$ equal the sunk cost of research and development. Nevertheless, food prices will not fall as far as would have been the case had imitators been allowed to copy the design of the improved combine and market duplicates at marginal cost.

If the patent system is not Pareto optimal, we should seek some alternative means of rewarding inventive activity, one that avoids the monopolistic distortions of the patent system. Gary Becker has suggested an incentive for inventive activity which uses a lottery-type system to identify and reward social benefactors.[10] Since research is always risky, there is a lottery aspect in the patent system itself. However, because a patent is a monopoly license, lucky inventors who "win" patents extract their rewards from consumer surplus, causing an excess burden in the process.

Becker has suggested a reversal of his economic approach to crime as an alternative means of bestowing rewards on inventors. The criminal justice system, designed to deter undesirable activity, works like a lottery in a less than perfect world. Not every criminal is punished, nor is every person who is punished necessarily guilty, in either a legal or moral sense. Even people acquitted of crimes suffer considerable financial and psychological costs. According to Becker, the optimal criminal justice system would minimize the (expected) net social cost of crime, including harm to victims and the cost of apprehension, trial, and punishment. If fear of imprisonment deters most would-be offenders, society must allocate resources to punishing those who are not deterred; otherwise that deterrent will lose credibility. By analogy, if the prospect of economic reward stimulates inventive activity, at least some of those who produce social benefits must be rewarded if that inducement is to remain effective.

The social cost of rewarding inventive activity is, ironically, similar to the social cost of penalizing criminals. Since criminals hide and attempt to evade prosecution, resources must be allocated for sorting the guilty from the innocent, so that the probability of punishment is higher for the former. In addition to being just, a system of due process is also necessary for an optimal allocation of resources to the legal system. If the probability of punishment were independent of whether a person committed a crime, crimes themselves would be "free." Similarly, the prohibition against cruel and unusual punishment can be explained by society's need for a marginal deterrent. If a petty crime like shoplifting carried the death penalty, there would be few shoplifters, but arresting a shoplifter who had nothing to lose by murder would be dangerous.

The social cost of the patent system is the distortion in resource allocation which results from the exercise of monopoly power. Society rewards an inventor by giving that person (or the person or firm that purchases the patent) the right to create an artificial shortage of the

---

[10] "Crime and Punishment: An Economic Approach," *The Economic Approach to Human Behavior* (Chicago: University of Chicago Press, 1976), pp. 71–74.

patented commodity. Were some agency, such as the National Academy of Science or the Nobel Prize Committee, to "apprehend" social benefactors and bestow money and honors on them, inventive activity could be encouraged without impairing economic efficiency. Of course, the committee charged with identifying the originator of an idea would have to sift through fraudulent claims, but the patent office already must wrestle with this problem.

The reason Becker's system is not used to reward innovation is fairly clear. Patents already exist; the market value of a patent equals the present value of the monopoly profit it is expected to generate. Were patents to be displaced by a system of cash transfers, many patent owners would experience a loss of wealth. If taxes were collected to buy up monopoly licenses (thus making patent holders no worse off), many taxpayers would be understandably upset. Once again, achieving a Pareto optimum does not necessarily involve a Pareto move, and competition over who should benefit most from the elimination of a system that is not Pareto optimal may prevent any Pareto optimum from being achieved.

General Theory of the Second Best

There is no sharp division between the exclusivity of property rights and the openness of markets. This leads to the practice of solving property failure by means of market failure: externalities which result from too narrow a scope for property rights give way to monopoly, whereby property rights are widened to encompass markets themselves. An economic system in which property rights are optimally specified and markets are perfectly competitive may be a technical impossibility. If that is true, we may never be absolutely sure that social arrangements are Pareto optimal. If the specter of incomplete property rights makes monopoly unavoidable in one or more markets (e.g., patents and occupational licensing are legally sanctioned), how might Pareto moves be made? According to the **general theory of the second best**, if competitive behavior cannot be achieved in all markets, it *may* be optimal to allow otherwise competitive markets to deviate from competitive results.[11]

Figure 15-12 illustrates the general theory of the second best through a reprise of the bilateral monopoly model encountered in chapter fourteen. Unlike Figure 15-11, the long-run supply curve in Figure 15-12 is

---

[11] Richard G. Lipsey and Kelvin Lancaster, "The General Theory of the Second Best," *Review of Economic Studies* 24 (1956–57), 11–32. The theory of the second best is similar to John Kenneth Galbraith's concept of countervailing power, developed three years earlier in his *American Capitalism: The Concept of Countervailing Power* (Boston: Houghton Mifflin, 1953).

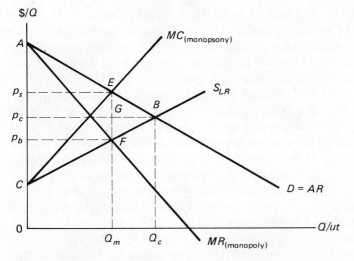

Figure 15-12
Bilateral Monopoly and the Theory of the Second Best

positively sloped, implying that some input owners will be receiving more than the opportunity costs of inputs they own. In long-run competitive equilibrium, resource suppliers would be receiving economic rent—also called the *producer surplus*—equal to the area of triangle $p_c BC$. A monopolist confronting a competitive input market and many buyers in the output market would offer Q_m units for sale at price p_s (the seller's best price). The monopolist's gross gain would consist of $(p_s - p_c)Q_m$ in confiscated consumer surplus and $(p_c - p_b)Q_m$ of lost economic rent by other input suppliers. (Of course, economic rent on inputs the monopolist owned would be "lost" only in the trivial sense that the monopolist's profit in part displaces what would have been its economic rent.) Total excess burden with a positively sloped long-run supply curve consists of the area of triangle EBF, of which the area of triangle EGB represents squandered consumer surplus and the area of triangle GBF represents economic rent which is lost, without generating compensatory monopoly profit.

Figure 15-12 is drawn so that a monopsony buyer, confronting competitive sellers, would purchase Q_m units at a price of p_b (the buyer's best price), receiving a monopsony profit of $(p_s - p_b)Q_m$—exactly equal to what a monopolist would receive. Since sellers would not be offered sufficient inducement to produce Q_c units, lost producer and consumer surpluses equal to the area of triangle EFB would be the excess burden of monopsony.

Suppose the monopsony buyer confronted a monopoly seller. The seller would offer Q_m units at price p_s; the buyer would counter with an offer of p_b. A standoff would make both parties worse off than any trade at a price between p_b and p_s. Even if the buyer gave in to the seller, the buyer would obtain a surplus of p_sAE. If the buyer prevailed and paid price p_b, the seller would gain a surplus of P_bCF. But neither would obtain a surplus if no trade took place.

A standoff would occur if both parties demanded the maximum surplus of $(p_s - p_b)Q_m$. If a compromise price of p_c were struck, the total surplus shared by buyer and seller would exceed the surplus either party could obtain dealing with a powerless trading partner. This is the insight of the general theory of the second best. In compensation for dropping its claim on $(p_s - p_c)Q_m$ of the disputed surplus, the seller would receive additional producer surplus equal to the area of triangle GFB. In lieu of the disputed share $(p_c - p_b)Q_m$, the buyer would receive additional consumer surplus equal to triangle GEB.

As under pure competition, the outcome p_c, Q_c is a Pareto optimum. Since this is a *possible* outcome of bilateral monopoly, it is possible that a bilateral monopoly market could reach a Pareto optimum. On the other hand, the most common example of bilateral monopoly—labor-management collective bargaining—sometimes results in a strike or lockout. There is no guarantee that a bilateral monopoly market will reach a Pareto optimum. Bluffs and threats may lead to an outcome which would be Pareto inferior to what would be achieved under unchallenged monopoly or monopsony. That is what is frustrating about bilateral monopoly: there is no guarantee that it will allocate resources efficiently. There is only the possibility that bilateral monopoly might be better than one-sided monopoly or monopsony. Monopolists, of course, prefer to sell to competitive buyers, while monopsonists prefer to buy from competitive sellers.

The final question we consider is whether or not price discrimination by monopoly sellers (or monopsony buyers) leads to a more efficient allocation of resources than nondiscriminating monopoly. Although the issue may seem trivial at first, recall from chapter ten that price discrimination leads to *greater* output. Put crudely, price (wage) discriminators are more efficient at confiscating consumer surplus (or economic rent by resource suppliers), thereby creating less excess burden. Given the reluctance of economists to make interpersonal comparisons of well-being, might it not be possible that a perfectly discriminating monopoly would be just as efficient as a perfectly competitive market, since a perfect discriminator would be able to turn every dollar of consumer surplus into a dollar of producer surplus?

Figure 15-13a repeats the model of an ideal competitive market in long-run equilibrium. To simplify, we assume a constant-cost industry, which implies no producer surplus or economic rent. The equilibrium price-quantity of p_e, Q_e leads to a consumer surplus of ABp_e. There is no producer surplus in the sense that all inputs used to produce this

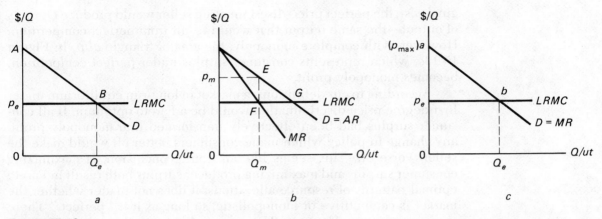

Figure 15-13
Consumer and Producer Surplus under Competition and Monopoly. *a,* Perfect competition: maximum consumer surplus; *b,* nondiscriminating monopoly: excess burden; *c,* perfect price discrimination: maximum producer surplus.

output are receiving a payment which is equal to both the market value of the factor's marginal product and the opportunity cost of the factor's services (i.e., the market value of its marginal product in another industry).

Figure 15-13*b* shows the conventional multiplant monopoly or cartel in which price discrimination is not feasible. The increased monopoly revenue on the first Q_m units (above long-run average cost) results in an excess burden equal to the area of triangle *EFG*. Hence, nondiscriminating monopoly is an inefficient method of redistribution. A conventional monopoly in long-run equilibrium is Pareto inferior to a competitive market in long-run equilibrium.

Figure 15-13*c* depicts complete monopoly power in the abstract and highly unlikely case of perfect, or first-degree, price discrimination. The type of discrimination encountered in chapter ten is known as third-degree price discrimination: different groups of consumers pay different prices, but each consumer within a group pays the same price for each unit purchased. Second-degree price discrimination occurs when each consumer pays a different price, but any consumer's price is the same for each unit he or she purchases. First-degree price discrimination would occur if the monopolist were able to charge the highest price the market would bear for each unit of output. If the market average revenue curve were given by $p = a - bQ$, where $-b = \Delta p/\Delta Q$, the first unit would be sold for $a - b$ dollars, the second unit for $a - 2b$ dollars, and so forth. The perfect price-discriminating monopolist would not have to reduce price on inframarginal units in order to sell one more unit. The inverse demand schedule confronting a perfectly discriminating monopolist is also the seller's marginal revenue curve. By producing where marginal revenue (price charged for the last unit) equals long-run marginal cost, the perfect price-discriminating seller would produce Q_e units of output—the same output that would result from perfect competition. However, with complete monopoly, the area of triangle abp_e in Figure 15-13c, which represents consumer surplus under perfect competition, becomes monopoly profit.

According to our definitions, a market in long-run equilibrium under first-degree price discrimination would be a Pareto optimum. If all consumer surplus had been effectively transformed into monopoly profit, any change in policy which made consumers better off would make the seller worse off. This seems like an ironic conclusion. If maximizing consumer surplus and maximizing producer surplus both result in Pareto optimal patterns of resource allocations, it does not matter whether the market is competitive or monopolistic, so long as it is "perfect." There must be a catch. There is: However unlikely, a general competitive equilibrium is logically possible, whereas it is logically impossible to define a "general equilibrium" of perfect monopolists, making such an outcome unattainable. If a monopolist (monopsonist) gains at the expense of others, the advantages to being a monopolist are limited by the extent that other markets are not perfect monopolies. Monopolization of all markets by perfect price discriminators would mean that no consumer surplus existed—not even for monopoly sellers. Instead of a welfare maximum, this state would constitute a welfare minimum. This state of affairs is also known as the commons.

Beyond Microeconomics: Property Rights versus Efficiency

We have seen that economics revolves around the influence of scarcity on human behavior. Microeconomics approaches problems from the perspective of individual economic units: how do individual firms and households respond to incentives in a way that generates socially desirable outcomes? The commons is "bad" because it encourages individuals to ignore scarcity in pursuing their own ends. Exclusivity in the use of inputs and outputs forces individuals to think in terms of opportunity cost. Figure 15-14 relates the extent of property rights to market efficiency. The origin depicts the commons: without property rights there can be no markets. As property rights are created to give owners the ability to exclude, limited markets emerge, but only simple barter in which exchange is simultaneous. Without additional legal guarantees, the party who gave up property rights first would have to depend on the good will of the other party to reciprocate. Workers would be at the mercy of employers if labor occurred before wages; employers would be unsure of workers' services if wages were advanced. Only with the enforcement of contracts can the ability to exchange truly be said to exist.

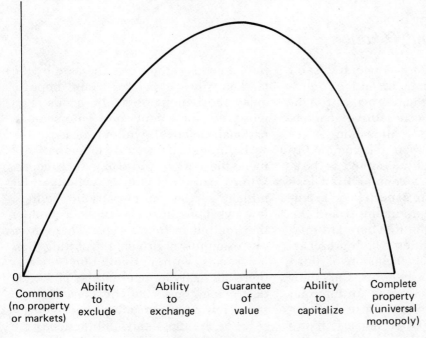

Figure 15-14
Trade-off between Property Rights and Markets
Adapted from Carroll et al., "The Market as a Commons," p. 616.

As long as exchange is voluntary, the ability to exchange enables individuals to reach mutually advantageous exchanges. If all markets are competitive, market equilibria will be Pareto optimal. However, when the assumptions of perfect competition are violated, the relation between extending property rights and market efficiency becomes murky. The tensions between property rights and market efficiency help explain the controversial status of market models between the extremes of perfect competition and pure monopoly. Product differentiation destroys market anonymity as consumers associate commodity characteristics or product quality with the name of the producer. Since unrestricted market entry would allow inferior products to undermine the reputations of distinguished sellers, property rights are extended to encompass brand-name and trademark exclusivity. Temporary monopoly advantages usually cannot be capitalized because of the constant influx of close substitutes—what Joseph Schumpeter referred to as "gales of creative destruction."

Although it is generally agreed that a monopolistically competitive market tends toward a zero profit long-run equilibrium, there is controversy about whether long-run equilibrium under monopolistic compe-

Policy Illustration
Public Goods and Taxation

Microeconomic theory concentrates on the impact of economic incentives on individual households and firms, whose interactions through competitive markets result in an efficient allocation of resources. For that reason, the commodity in question is usually assumed to be a pure private good—a commodity whose costs and benefits are experienced exclusively by the firm producing it and the household consuming it. There are relatively few commodities which are characterized by perfect exclusion of third parties from costs or benefits. Cars emit pollutants and occasionally run into one another. The value of my house depends on the upkeep of other houses in my neighborhood. The clothes we wear, the movies we see, the music we hear are determined to an extent by the tastes of others.

At the opposite extreme from pure private goods are pure public goods—commodities for which consumption by one implies consumption by all. The most obvious example of a pure public good is national defense. If a hostile nation is deterred from dropping a nuclear bomb on my house, you will benefit if you live next door. Perhaps an even better example of a pure public good is the institution of property rights: the property of all must be protected. If each person is responsible for protecting his or her own property, the commons will result. The strong will stop producing and try to steal from the weak; the weak will stop producing because there is no point to it.

Paradoxically, there cannot be a completely private market system because public goods cannot be generated by the market. Since everyone would hope to enjoy the benefit of public goods (e.g., mosquito abatement, law enforcement, national defense) without bearing the cost, individuals would not voluntarily incur the cost of providing such goods. While many individuals volunteer for military service out of patriotic feelings, few weapons manufacturers volunteer their output in time of war. There are a few examples of drivers retrofitting their older cars with antipollution devices; there are many more examples of drivers destroying their catalytic converters to save a few cents per gallon on leaded gas.

For the most part, public goods are financed by governments through taxes, rather than by voluntary exchange. Because of its position as guarantor of property and enforcer of laws, the government can use its taxing powers to coerce payment. The federal income tax is an (imperfect) example of an ability-to-pay tax. Ideally, as a household's income increases, the percentage of income paid in taxes increases. On the other hand, the federal and state taxes on gasoline used to finance highways represent a benefit tax. Roughly speaking, the more a person uses the highways, the more gasoline that person buys and therefore the more taxes he or she pays.

The obvious problem of government financing of public goods and services is that it is difficult to determine exactly what the breakdown between public and private goods ought to be, as the simple production possibility frontier in the accompanying figure illustrates. First, no-

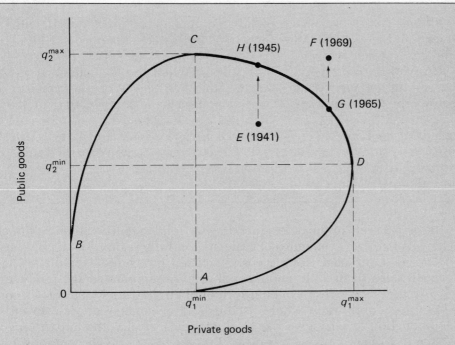

Alternative Combinations of Public and Private Goods in a Mixed Economy

tice that, unlike Figure 15-7, the accompanying figure has two positively sloped portions. Point A indicates that a society with only private goods would suffer the tragedy of the commons. Without universal property rights, enforcement of contracts, national defense, and other public goods, society would degenerate into fortress households living off nuts and berries. Point B suggests a similar problem with public financing of all commodities. In a society with millions of households, my contribution to total output is insignificant. If I stopped working, my share of output would remain virtually the same. However, if most households stopped producing, all would share a pittance. Obviously, Pareto optimality implies that society operate between points C (maximum public goods) and D (max-

imum private goods) in such a way that producing more public goods requires the sacrifice of some private goods.

There are many other difficulties in defining the optimal combination of public and private goods. As we saw in chapter fourteen, the Pentagon's monopsony position in the market for military personnel tends to keep wages for recruits too low and encourages direct confiscation of labor resources (the draft). Ironically, the end to monopsony distortion may not mean a return to efficient factor prices, given the incentives faced by elected decision makers. While a mayor and city council may have initially run for office on a pledge to keep taxes low (e.g., by paying monopsony wage rates for police, firefighters, and elementary-school teachers), institution of effective collective bargaining will make a new strategy necessary for reelection. Instead of fighting pay hikes for government workers, politicians may see workers on government payrolls as an important voting block and "give away the store" in wage negotiations.

Finally, if a mixed economy is operating at a point such as *E* in the figure, there are unemployed resources which could be used for either public or private goods. By financing World War II with new and borrowed money, the United States government increased both guns and butter. When the Vietnam War escalated in 1965, the American economy was operating at a point similar to *G*; fighting a war without raising taxes increased private incomes relative to private goods; the result, as we learned painfully, was inflation.

tition is Pareto optimal. Production costs tend to remain above minimum levels because economies of scale are not fully realized by passive sellers. Also, although selling costs incurred by aggressive sellers might push sales to the rate corresponding to minimum average production cost, these costs result in equilibrium prices that are higher than a competitive equilibrium would establish. If economies of scale in either production or sales give rise to oligopolistic rivalry, the impact on economic welfare is even less clear. Firms give way to corporations, over which owners may have little control and whose control over the market is marred by extensive uncertainty. Indeed, a nearly ideal market for ownership rights to corporations (the stock market) means that owners will tend to receive a normal return on investment. The absence of clearly identifiable monopoly profits leads some economists to consider the modern corporation as the legitimate heir to the legacy of the invisible hand. The clear violation of the assumption of atomistic size leads others to consider oligopoly as indistinguishable from monopoly.

If society extends the *guarantee of value* with monopolistic entry restrictions, the next step is to permit trade in monopoly licenses. If Jones has a patent, but Smith would be more productive in exploiting it, both Smith and Jones would be made better off by a transfer of monopoly power. The ability to transfer monopoly power grants the owners the *ability to capitalize* what would otherwise be a continuous stream of monopoly profits. Because monopoly prices must be sustained to produce a normal return on the investment in monopoly power, capitalization tends to distort monopoly market distortions in the name of preserving the value of property rights. We have only to imagine what would happen to the value of farmland in the wake of an end to agricultural price supports to see how concern for guaranteeing property values can overturn market efficiency.

Complete market security would mean never having to worry about competition, either from other sellers or from other buyers. Complete property rights imply complete confiscation of consumer surplus. If one monopoly encroaches on otherwise competitive markets, the monopolist's gain is actually part of the consumer surplus in other markets. By creating an artificial shortage, the monopolistic firm is able to raise the relative price of its product; the monopolist obtains a larger share of society's output by contributing a smaller share. But what if all markets were monopolized? Each profit-maximizing monopolist-monopsonist would be an indifferent consumer, receiving no surplus on goods consumed and thus making each seller's surplus valueless. Ironically, while we can imagine a Pareto optimal market in which consumer surplus is maximized, we cannot imagine a maximum producer surplus. As we have seen, another name for a system in which everyone is trying to steal from everyone else is the commons.

The world is too complex for there to be a single explanation for all events, economic or otherwise. But one idea seems compelling. It is entirely possible that expansion of property rights has carried private enterprise societies past the apex of Figure 15-14. Having built a set of institutions to overcome the tragedy of the commons, we may be sliding toward an equivalent demise of the market. Microeconomic theory is continually struggling with a similar puzzle: whether further refinements in theories of ideal markets encourage or impede solutions to real-world problems. It is a question which no doubt will continue to intrigue the next generation of economists.

HIGHLIGHTS

1. The search for a workable measure of economic welfare forces us to abandon definitions which either violate scarcity (the greatest good for the greatest number) or require interpersonal comparisons of utility (maximization of average utility). The advantage of the Pareto criterion is that it allows us to infer changes in economic well-being from voluntary actions.

2. The voluntary exchange of goods requires the existence of property rights, or the ability to exclude. Mutual gains from trade can occur as long as two individuals or households have different marginal rates of substitution for commodities. When there is a competitive market for final goods, individuals adjust their purchases so that the marginal rate of substitution for any two commodities purchased equals their price ratio. Hence, if all individuals pay the same prices, the competitive mar-

ket will reach a Pareto optimal allocation of consumer goods.

3. In allocating inputs to produce outputs, efficiency requires that the marginal rate of technical substitution for any two inputs be the same in all production processes employing those inputs. Competitive input markets lead producers to select inputs so that the ratio of the marginal products of any two inputs equals the ratio of the market prices for their services. This, along with full employment, will move production ot the economy's production possibility frontier.

4. A general competitive equilibrium (i.e., all markets in long-run competitive equilibrium) would generate a Pareto optimal allocation of resources, since marginal cost would equal price for each commodity, implying equality between the marginal rate of transformation

for any two products and the common marginal rate of substitution for consumers. When a general competitive equilibrium exists, it is impossible to make anyone better off without making someone else worse off, even if beneficiaries tried to compensate victims of a policy change.

5. Monopoly is not a Pareto optimum because, without perfect price discrimination, the monopolist's surplus is smaller than the total surplus lost by consumers and input suppliers. Incomplete property rights, which create external benefits and/or costs, also generate a nonoptimal allocation of resources. Since the distinction between property and markets is blurred, however, property failure (externality) is frequently "solved" by creating market failure (monopoly).

6. According to the general theory of the second best, if one or more markets cannot be made to conform to competitive behavior, it may not be optimal to impose competitive structure or behavior on other parts of the economy. This proposition helps explain the lack of consensus about how to deal with less than ideal market structures.

GLOSSARY

Closed economy   An economy which contains all relevant production and exchange.

Coase theorem   The proposition, attributed to Ronald Coase, that as long as markets remain competitive and transaction costs are zero, assigning liability to one of the parties to a localized externality will have the same effect as if the two producers merged into a multiproduct firm; namely, the external effect will be internalized, and liability will influence only wealth distribution, not resource allocation (relative to the alternative assignment of liability).

Efficient allocation of resources   The mix of commodities produced is Pareto optimal only if the marginal rate of transformation between any two commodities equals the marginal rate of substitution between those commodities for all households consuming both.

Efficient exchange   The distribution of commodities between any two persons can be Pareto optimal only if the marginal rate of substitution between those commodities is the same for those two individuals.

Efficient production   The allocation of input services between any two commodities is Pareto optimal only if the marginal rate of substitution between those inputs is the same for those two commodities.

Excess burden of monopoly   The loss of consumer surplus (and possibly economic rent by resource suppliers) over and above the gain in monopoly profit due to monopolization of a market.

Externality   A situation in which some of the benefits or costs of the use or exchange of scarce resources are experienced by parties who are neither buyers nor sellers in the relevant market. Equivalent to **property failure**.

General equilibrium   A state of affairs in which all markets are in long-run competitive equilibrium, such that (1) all consumers' marginal rate of substitution for any two goods equals their price ratio; (2) the marginal rate of technical substitution is the same for any two inputs in the production of all outputs; and (3) the marginal rate of transformation for any two goods equals their price ratio.

General theory of the second best   The proposition, attributed to Kelvin Lancaster and Richard Lipsey, that when the conditions for allocational efficiency cannot be met in some market(s) (e.g., due to the use of monopoly to eliminate property failure), the second-best policy may not imply requiring that the optimality conditions be observed by other actors in the affected market(s) or in other markets.

Marginal rate of transformation   The slope of the product transformation curve: $MRT_{21} = \Delta q_2/\Delta q_1 = -(MC_1/MC_2)$.

Market failure   Failure of the market to operate as a commons, so that one or more sellers (or buyers, in the case of monopsony) are able to exclude others, that is, to exercise de facto ownership rights to the market.

Open economy An economy in which some portion of production and exchange results from interaction with other economies (e.g., international trade).

Pareto criterion A standard for judging policy changes in terms of relative social welfare, advanced by Vilfredo Pareto. If a policy change makes at least one person better off without making anyone worse off (each in his or her own estimation), the policy change is deemed an improvement in social welfare. If a policy change makes anyone worse off without making at least one person better off, the policy change is deemed detrimental to social welfare. The Pareto criterion cannot be applied directly to policy changes which make some people worse off while making others better off (unless some other policy change can be shown to be Pareto superior).

Pareto optimum A state of affairs in which all possibilities for Pareto improvements in social welfare have been exhausted: it is impossible to make anyone better off by a policy change unless someone else is made worse off, and it is impossible for the beneficiaries of the policy change to compensate victims completely (since such compensation would constitute a Pareto improvement). A general equi-

librium in a competitive system is a Pareto optimum characterized by (1) **efficient exchange,** (2) **efficient production,** and (3) **efficient allocation of resources.**

Pareto superior A state of affairs (policy) is said to be Pareto superior to another state of affairs (policy) if the former can be attained by a Pareto move from the latter (if the former policy results in at least one person being made better off and no one being made worse off than under the latter policy).

Product transformation curve The diagram of technically efficient combinations of two commodities, such that output of one commodity can be increased only if output of the other product is decreased. Also called the **production possibility frontier**.

Production possibility frontier See **product transformation curve**.

Property failure The failure of legal or social institutions to enforce exclusivity in the use or exchange of scarce inputs or outputs. Equivalent to **externality**.

Property rights The legally enforceable or socially sanctioned ability to exclude others from using a scarce resource or commodity.

Welfare economics That branch of economic theory dealing with the design of ideal economic systems and the analysis of policies meant to improve economic well-being.

SUGGESTED READINGS

Arrow, Kenneth J. *Social Choice and Individual Values.* 2nd ed. New Haven: Yale University Press, 1970.

Bator, Francis. "The Simple Analytics of Welfare Maximization." *American Economic Review* (March 1957), pp. 22–59. Reprinted in William Breit and Harold Hochman, eds. *Readings in Microeconomics.* 2nd ed. New York: Holt, Rinehart and Winston, 1971, pp. 455–483.

———. "The Anatomy of Market Failure." *Quarterly Journal of Economics* (August 1958), pp. 351–379. Reprinted in William Breit and Harold Hochman, eds. *Readings in Microecon-*

omics, 2nd ed. New York: Holt, Rinehart and Winston, 1971, pp. 518–537.

Baumol, William J. *Economic Theory and Operations Analysis.* 4th ed. Englewood Cliffs, New Jersey: Prentice-Hall, 1977, chapter 21.

Buchanan, James, and William Stubblebine. "Externality." *Economica* (November 1962), pp. 371–384.

Calabresi, Guido, and A. Douglas Melamed. "Property Rules, Liability Rules, and Inalienability: One View of the Cathedral." *Harvard Law Review* (1972), pp. 1089–1128. Reprinted in Bruce Ackerman, ed. *The Economic Foun-*

dations of *Property Law*. Boston: Little, Brown, 1975.

Carroll, Thomas M., David H. Ciscel, and Roger K. Chisholm. "The Market as a Commons: An Unconventional View of Property Rights." *Journal of Economic Issues* (June 1979), pp. 605–627.

Coase, Ronald. "The Problem of Social Cost." *Journal of Law and Economics* (October 1960), pp. 1–44. Reprinted in William Breit and Howard Hochman, eds. *Readings in Microeconomics*. New York: Holt, Rinehart and Winston, 1971, pp. 484–517.

Hardin, Garrett. "The Tragedy of the Commons." *Science* (December 1968), pp. 1243–1248. Reprinted in Bruce Ackerman, ed. *The Eco-*

nomic Foundations of Property Law. Boston: Little, Brown, 1975.

Lerner, Abba P. *The Economics of Control: Principles of Welfare Economics*. New York: Macmillan, 1944.

Little, I. M. D. *A Critique of Welfare Economics*. Oxford: The Clarendon Press, 1950.

Manne, Henry G., ed. *The Economics of Legal Relationships: Readings in the Theory of Property Rights*. St. Paul, Minnesota: West, 1975.

Mills, Edwin S. *The Economics of Environmental Quality*. New York: Norton, 1978.

Rawles, John. *A Theory of Justice*. Cambridge: Harvard University Press, 1971.

Scitovsky, Tibor. *Welfare and Competition*. 2nd ed. Homewood, Illinois: Irwin, 1971.

EXERCISES

Evaluate

Indicate whether each of the following questions is true (agrees with economic theory), false (is contradicted by theory), or uncertain (could be true or false, given additional information). Explain your answer.

1. There is no excess burden if a monopolist is able to practice price discrimination.
2. The only real solution for monopoly is monopsony, and vice versa.
3. The only way to achieve a Pareto optimum is by a Pareto improvement in economic welfare.
4. The fact that research takes place in academic institutions without monopolization of knowledge proves that patent laws are not Pareto optimal.
5. A Pareto optimum means "the greatest good for the greatest number."
6. According to the Pareto criterion, society should never instigate a policy unless those made better off are able to compensate those made worse off.
7. Allowing individuals to contribute to charities voluntarily is Pareto superior to forcing a redistribution of income through government taxes and transfers.

8. Allowing individuals to exchange monopoly licenses for money removes the allocational inefficiencies of monopolistic markets.
9. The general theory of the second best implies that general equilibrium theory is irrelevant to real-world problems.
10. Allowing thieves to steal, as long as they pay fines equal to the harm done to victims, is Pareto superior to putting criminals in jail.

Contemplate

Answer each of the following in a brief but complete essay.

11. Indicate whether each of the following policy changes would be a Pareto improvement of social welfare. Briefly explain your reasoning and your assumptions.
    a. The government reduces an import tariff below a previously prohibitive rate (i.e., no goods were imported, so that the tariff raised no revenue) to that rate which maximizes government revenue. The tax revenue is used to compensate domestic producers for profits lost to foreign competition.
    b. The government gradually reduces the tariff in part *a* to zero, after using revenue

from it to retrain workers in the affected industries.

c. The state legislature passes a right-to-work law, whereby workers cannot be forced to join a union which represents them in collective bargaining.

d. Draftees into the armed forces are permitted to hire replacements.

e. Employers are given complete freedom to hire any workers they wish, regardless of race, religion, sex, physical handicaps, or educational background.

f. A minimum wage law is repealed in favor of a negative income tax (see chapter three) which distributes the same income to the working poor by giving them a fraction of the difference between the repealed minimum wage and their market wage.

g. The government runs a budget surplus after cutting wasteful spending to reduce the rate of inflation without reducing business investment.

12. Evaluate this statement: Welfare economics has as much relevance to real-world problems as asking how many angels can dance on the head of a pin.

13. Suppose that medical science discovered a "utility gland" in the middle of the human brain, and its electrical impulses could be measured on a pain-pleasure scale, much like a temperature scale for body heat. Would economists be justified in using these (hypothetically accurate) measures of human happiness to determine the greatest good for the greatest number? Briefly explain your answer.

14. If, as the text suggests, there exists a trade-off between the scope of property rights and the degree of market efficiency, how would economists go about defining the optimal degree of monopoly? What sort of tests might they use to determine whether property failure or market failure created greater potential loss of economic welfare?

Appendix A

Calculus: The Algebra of Change

Imagine that you and a good friend are out for a drive in your new car. A short while ago, at your suggestion, he took the wheel, and now the two of you are rolling merrily along. Out of the corner of your eye you spot a police car parked on a side road; a check shows that the speedometer is registering 65 miles per hour. "Slow down," you suggest, calmly. "This looks like a speed trap."

Your friend nods passively, lifts his foot from the accelerator and slams on the brake, leaving 400 feet of tire tread and a pile-up of 15 cars on the freeway behind. "Speed up, you fool!" you shout, as you struggle to pull your seat belt from around your neck.

Another nod from your friend. He hunches his shoulders, tightens his grip on the steering wheel, and tromps down on the accelerator. Within 20 seconds you are moving at 100 miles per hour. The police car has pulled out onto the highway and is obviously following your car.

Do you dare tell your friend to slow down and risk another panic stop? You realize that he lacks the ability to make small changes in the car's velocity. You resolve that, should you survive, you will recommend that he enroll in a course in calculus.

Some Basic Concepts

Most decisions involve moving from a known situation to a different set of circumstances, based on anticipation of how an action will affect attainment of one or more goals (revenue, cost, profits, or happiness). Rarely does life have to come to a grinding halt, so the impact of the new action can be measured from absolute zero. If your firm is producing 500 pairs of shoes per day and you want to determine the profit from producing 501 pairs per day, you do not shut down operations, send your employees home, and hire a team of accountants to recalibrate your overhead. It is sufficient to hire enough additional inputs to

A-1

raise the rate of output by one more pair of shoes per hour and then to compare the resulting change in cost with the change in revenue.

Differential calculus, which we study in this appendix, is the algebra of change. If you have taken a course in economic theory before, or if you have skimmed through this book, you have encountered such terms as marginal cost, marginal revenue, marginal productivity, and marginal utility. Each of these concepts is *derived* from a relationship between the value of one variable (output, input, or consumption) and the resulting value of another variable. Algebra shows us how to determine the value of one variable given the value of another variable. Calculus enables us to derive the change in one variable due to the change in the causal variable.

This text is sprinkled with footnotes which show how various concepts can be derived with the use of calculus. Calculus is the natural habitat of microeconomic theory. Students who are able to employ calculus as one tool in learning microeconomics are urged to do so by following the quantitative footnotes. On the other hand, students without knowledge of calculus will find this no handicap. An understanding of basic algebra and simple geometry will suffice to master all the concepts covered.

Let us begin with a few simple definitions. A *set* is a collection of anything: a set of golf clubs, tennis games, real numbers, efficient methods of producing a commodity. A set is designated by a pair of braces { }, which enclose the *elements*, or members, of the set. The set {Tom, Regina, Michael} includes as elements the members of the Carroll family. This set is *finite*, meaning that the elements in it can be counted. The set $\{6, 7, 8, 9, \ldots, 978, \ldots\}$, denoting all integers greater than five, can also be written $\{x \mid x \in \text{integers} \,\&\, x > 5\}$, where ϵ, the Greek letter *epsilon*, means "is an element of" the set of integers. This set is *infinite*; the elements in it cannot be counted because their number is unlimited. As children are told, there is no end to counting.

A *relation* is a set which is established between elements of two or more sets. A marriage is a relation between elements of the set "husbands" and the set "wives." An affair is a relation between members of different marriages. An *ordered pair* is a relation in which the order of appearance of elements is important. If we define the set of ordered pairs $M = \{(f,m) \mid f \in \text{females} \,\&\, m \in \text{males}\}$, then (Bob,Carol) and (Ted,Alice) do *not* belong to set M, whereas (Alice,Ted) and (Carol,Bob) do belong to set M. The set $R = \{(x,y) \mid x \text{ is married to } y\}$ is a set of pairs but not a set of ordered pairs, since the order in which individuals appear is arbitrary. Commonplace ordering rules include "ladies first," "age before beauty," and "first come, first served."

The set from which the first element of an ordered pair is drawn is called the *domain*. In economics, the domain of an ordered pair may be determined by common sense (a producer's average revenue is defined only for positive rates of output), or it may be specified by economic reality (a monopolist limits output to that range for which demand is price elastic). In some cases, the domain is itself an ordered pair or ordered "*n*-tuple": production is a consequence of combining various input services; utility is a consequence of consuming various quantities of goods. A production function, $q = f(L,K)$, relates the dependent variable, output (q), to combinations of inputs, labor (L), and capital (K). In set notation: $Q = \{(L,K,q) \mid q = f(L,K)\}$. The domain of such relations is often specified by some constraint: total spending on commodities must remain within the household's budget; a firm's output combinations may be limited by fixed productive capacity.

The set from which the second element of an ordered pair, or relation is drawn is called the *range*. The convention is to consider the second element of a relation as the consequence of the first, so that the range of a relation is generally determined by the specified domain. For instance, the household's budget constraint determines the range of possible utility levels. The domain of technically efficient input combinations determines the range of possible output levels.

When each element of the domain of a relation is associated with no more than one element of the range, that relation is called a *function*. Much of the groundwork to developing the theory of the firm (chapters eight through twelve) involves the definition of functional relationships by positing particular behavior for individual economic agents. First, all possible input combinations are screened so that only technically efficient combinations remain. Then the *production function* is determined by selecting the maximum possible output for each technically efficient combination of input services. Hence, a production function has only one rate of output for each member of the domain (technically efficient input combinations). The cost function is established by selecting the lowest cost input combination from among the technically efficient ones for each level of output.

In summary, economic theory is concerned with functional relations between causal variables (drawn from the domain of a function) and response variables (drawn from the range). Once a one-to-one correspondence between those variables has been established, economic theory turns to the maximization or minimization of those functions: once we have found least-cost combination of inputs for each rate of output, we relate the cost function to the firm's revenue function to determine which rate of output maximizes profit. Here is where calculus comes in. The optimal rate of output might be identified by trying all possible output levels and determining which rate generates the highest net gain. Or, output can be increased until profit does not change.

Marginal Analysis and Derivatives

Much of microeconomic theory is concerned with marginal analysis—determining how a change in one variable causes a change in another variable. In a conventional total cost (TC) figure, marginal cost (MC) is defined as the *slope* of the total cost curve. When we observe discrete changes in output (which cause noticeable changes in total cost), we actually calculate the slope of a line connecting two points on the total cost curve. If the relationship between output (q) and cost (C) is linear, as shown in Figure A-1a, any change in output—no matter how large or small—will always cause a proportional change in cost: $\Delta C / \Delta q$ = a constant. For a linear cost function, $C = a + bq$, a equals fixed cost (cost independent of output), and b equals marginal cost, the change in cost due to a one unit change in output.

Most total cost functions have different slopes at different points, due to diminishing marginal productivity of variable inputs in the short run and variable

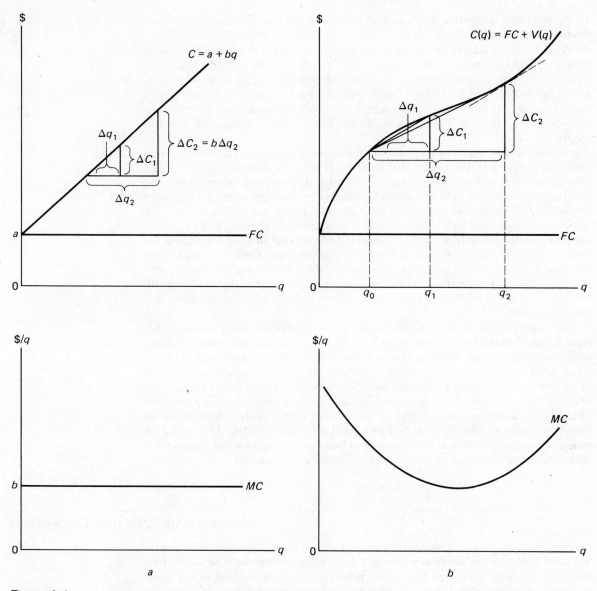

Figure A-1
Marginal Cost Curves for (a) Linear and (b) Nonlinear Cost Functions

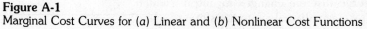

returns to scale in the long run. The total cost curve in Figure A-1*b* has a different slope at each level of output; making discrete observations of output leads us to infer discrete changes in cost. The ratio of the observed change in cost (ΔC) to the observed change in output (Δq) does not yield the slope of the total cost curve, $C(q)$, but measures the slope of the line (arc) connecting nonadjacent points on $C(q)$. The slope of $C(q)$ at q_2 in Figure A-1b is equal to the slope of the (dashed) tangent line at that point. The slope of the tangent differs considerably from the slope of the arc connecting points on $C(q)$ corresponding to q_0 and q_2.

It would be convenient for the producer to know the additional (i.e., marginal) cost of each level of output, so that the firm could produce the optimal rate of output (where marginal revenue equals marginal cost) without having to experience nonoptimal profits. If total cost changes smoothly and predictably with output,[1] we should be able to *derive* a smooth, predictable marginal cost function, which relates the rate at which cost is changing to output produced.

An expert and meticulous draftsman could carefully plot a two-variable relation; then, with the help of a straight edge, fit a tangent line to as many points on the graph as possible; and finally, with equal care, plot the slope of each tangent against the associated value of the independent variable. This process would reveal that a smooth function (e.g., total cost curve) is associated with a smooth plot of slopes of related tangency lines (e.g., marginal cost curve). However, the investment required to become an expert at drafting hardly seems justified if the sole purpose is to draw marginal cost curves. The more efficient approach would be to learn a trick from calculus. If the plot of a total cost function is based on a known formula, the formula for marginal cost can be derived directly, without the painstaking geometry just described.

Given a smooth function of the form $C = C(q)$, the change in cost due to a quantity change of Δq units is given by $\Delta C = C(q + \Delta q) - C(q)$, so that the slope of the arc connecting those two points on the total cost curve is:

$$\frac{\Delta C}{\Delta q} = \frac{C(q + \Delta q) - C(q)}{\Delta q} = \frac{\text{change in cost}}{\text{change in output}}$$

When $C(q)$ is not a linear function, the precise slope of the total cost curve equals the slope of the tangent line at each point. Since a tangent touches $C(q)$ at one point only, the change in the independent variable is, quite literally, zero along the tangent line. And, as every student of algebra knows, division by zero is impossible.

Here is where the development of calculus takes a clever turn. Suppose we imagine that the change in output becomes smaller and smaller—that it *approaches* zero. As long as the change in the independent variable is not actually zero (say, about 1 one-billionth), we can still divide by that quantity. Then, if, by dividing, we have been able to eliminate the Δq from the denominator of the ratio, we can pretend that the change in quantity goes all the way to zero, thereby eliminating from the slope formula any remaining terms still containing Δq. We use the notation "$\lim_{\Delta q \to 0}$" (read "the limit of . . . as Δq approaches zero") to allow the change in q to get arbitrarily close to zero without actually violating the conventions of algebra.

---

[1] In nontechnical terms, a function is said to be *continuous* when the change in the dependent variable from point to point is gradual, without the function being broken. More technically, a function, $C(q)$, is continuous at q_2 if q_2 is in the domain of C and $C(q)$ approaches $C(q_2)$ as q approaches q_2.

Definition of the Derivative

We define the *derivative* of a function as the function which relates the change in the dependent variable (due to infinitely small changes in the independent variable) to the value of the independent variable. The term "derivative" stems from the fact that it is a function derived from another function:

$$MC = \frac{dC}{dq} = \lim_{\Delta q \to 0} \frac{C(q + \Delta q) - C(q)}{\Delta q}$$

An example may demonstrate how the definition of a derivative can clarify concepts that appear baffling when explained verbally. Students are often perplexed that marginal revenue falls exactly twice as fast as average revenue (price) for a monopolist facing a linear demand curve. Why exactly twice as fast? Why not 1.5 or 3 times as fast? Can real-life economic relationships always be so regular?

As shown in chapter ten, a linear average revenue function has a formula of the form $p = a - bQ$ (which is really the inverse of a demand function of the form $Q_d = \alpha - \beta p$, where $a = \alpha/\beta$ and $b = 1/\beta$, with $a,b > 0$). Total revenue equals price times quantity sold: $TR = pQ$. Substituting the formula for average revenue for p, we get $TR = (a - bQ)Q = aQ - bQ^2$; total revenue can be expressed as a quadratic equation of output. Since marginal revenue is the change in total revenue due to a change in output, we find the equation for marginal revenue by finding the derivative of total revenue with respect to output:

$$
\begin{aligned}
MR = \frac{dTR}{dQ} &= \lim_{\Delta Q \to 0} \frac{a(Q + \Delta Q) - b(Q + \Delta Q)^2 - aQ + bQ^2}{\Delta Q} \\
&= \lim_{\Delta Q \to 0} \frac{aQ + a(\Delta Q) - bQ^2 - 2bQ(\Delta Q) - b(\Delta Q)^2 - aQ + bQ^2}{\Delta Q} \\
&= \lim_{\Delta Q \to 0} \frac{a(\Delta Q) - 2bQ(\Delta Q) - b(\Delta Q)^2}{\Delta Q} \\
&= \lim_{\Delta Q \to 0} a - 2bQ - b(\Delta Q) \\
&= a - 2bQ
\end{aligned}
$$

Note that when a function, like the average revenue function in Figure A-2, is a polynomial (the independent variable is multiplied by various constants and raised to integral powers), the subtraction of the original function from the functional value of $Q + \Delta Q$ removes all terms which do not contain ΔQ. Since all remaining terms in the numerator contain ΔQ, raised to the power of one or greater, ΔQ can be eliminated from the denominator, while, in each term in the numerator, the exponent on ΔQ is lowered by one power. Finally, since the denominator has been eliminated, we can imagine ΔQ going all the way to zero, its "limit." From this pattern we are able to infer some simplifying rules for taking derivatives.

For our purposes, probably the most useful rule applies to the derivative of a polynomial function: if y is a function of x such that $y = cx^n$, where c is a constant and n is a positive integer, then $dy/dx = ncx^{n-1}$. To take the derivative

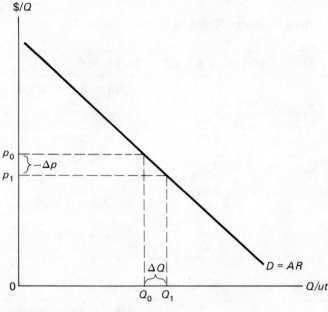

Figure A-2
Change in Revenue for a Monopolist

of y (the dependent variable) with respect to x (the independent variable) when y is given by x raised to a power and multiplied by a constant, we bring the exponent to the front of the constant, then reduce the exponent term by one. This is a very useful generalization.

Marginal Revenue and Total Revenue: A Numerical Simulation

In several chapters of the text, a new concept is explored using a numerical example (see chapters five, six, seven, nine, ten, and fourteen). In this appendix, we will pause a moment to simulate the derivation of the marginal revenue function from a firm's total revenue function. Imagine that Mom's Pizza Parlor can sell pizzas according to the average revenue (inverse demand) schedule: $p = \$12 - 0.05q$, where p is the price per pizza and q is the quantity of pizzas sold per day. Since total revenue equals price times quantity, $TR = 12q - 0.05q^2$. Marginal revenue—defined in principles courses as the change in total revenue divided by the change in output (that is, $MR = \Delta TR / \Delta q$)—is really the *rate* of change of revenue with respect to output: $MR = \lim_{\Delta q \to 0} [TR(q + \Delta q) - TR(q)]/\Delta q$. The smaller the change in output, the closer will be the ratio of the change in revenue to the change in cost be to the rate of change in which we are interested.

Table A-1 simulates the approximation of marginal revenue by taking smaller and smaller changes in output. First, we imagine that Mom is producing

TABLE A-1
Marginal Revenue at Three Different Rates of Output, $TR = 12q - 0.05q^2$

$q = 100$; $p = \$12 - 0.05(100) = \$7$; $TR = \$7(100) = \$700$

Δq	$TR(q + \Delta q)$	$TR(q + \Delta q) - TR(q)$	$\dfrac{TR(q + \Delta q) - TR(q)}{\Delta q}$
5	\$708.75	\$ 8.75	\$1.75
2	703.80	3.80	1.90
1	701.95	1.95	1.95
0.5	700.9875	0.9875	1.975
0.1	700.1995	0.1995	1.995
−0.1	699.7995	−0.2005	2.0005
−0.5	698.9875	−1.0125	2.005
−1	675.95	−2.05	2.05
−2	695.80	−4.20	2.10
−5	688.75	−11.25	2.25

$q = 120$; $p = \$12 - 0.05(120) = \$6$; $TR = \$6(120) = \$720$

Δq	$TR(q + \Delta q)$	$TR(q + \Delta q) - TR(q)$	$\dfrac{TR(q + \Delta q) - TR(q)}{\Delta q}$
5	\$718.75	−\$1.25	−\$0.25
2	719.80	− 0.20	− 0.10
1	719.95	− 0.05	− 0.05
0.5	719.9875	− 0.0125	− 0.025
0.1	719.9995	− 0.0005	− 0.005
−0.1	719.9995	− 0.0005	+ 0.005
−0.5	719.9875	− 0.0125	+ 0.025
−1	719.95	− 0.05	0.05
−2	719.80	− 0.20	0.10
−5	718.75	− 1.25	0.25

$q = 140$; $p = \$12 - 0.05(140) = \$5$; $TR = \$5(140) = \$700$

Δq	$TR(q + \Delta q)$	$TR(q + \Delta q) - TR(q)$	$\dfrac{TR(q + \Delta q) - TR(q)}{\Delta q}$
5	\$688.75	−\$11.25	−\$2.25
2	695.80	− 4.20	− 2.10
1	697.95	− 2.05	− 2.05
0.5	698.9875	− 1.0125	− 2.025
0.1	699.7995	− 0.2005	− 2.005
−0.1	700.1995	+ 0.1995	− 1.995
−0.5	700.9875	0.9875	− 1.975
−1	701.95	1.95	− 1.95
−2	703.80	3.80	− 1.90
−5	708.75	8.75	− 1.75

100 pizzas per day, selling each pizza for $7 and realizing $700 in revenue. If output were increased by 5 pizzas per day ($\Delta q = 5$), price would drop by $0.25 ($0.05 \times 5$) on all 105 pizzas. Hence, while $6.75(5) = \$33.75$ would be received on the last 5 pizzas produced, Mom would lose $25 ($0.25 \times 100$) on the first 100 pizzas which previously sold for $7 each. The net gain in revenue is only $8.75, making the average revenue gained for each of the last 5 pizzas $8.75/5, or $1.75 each.

If 102 pizzas were produced ($\Delta q = 2$), price would fall from $7 to $6.90, and total revenue would increase by $3.80. In this case, the net gain in revenue would average $1.90 per pizza; a smaller deviation from our reference point ($q = 100$) means a greater average increase in revenue per pizza. Indeed, if $\Delta q = 1$, the price of pizza falls by $0.05, meaning that $6.95 is received for the 101st pizza, while $5 is lost on the first 100 pizzas; the net gain in revenue is $1.95.

Since some pizza parlors sell pizza by the slice, we can imagine what would happen if $\Delta q = 0.5$: the price of pizza would fall by $0.05 \times 0.5 = \$0.025$, resulting in an increase in revenue of $0.9875, which amounts to $1.975 per pizza. Even slices equal to one-tenth of a pizza can be imagined, although lowering the price by half-a-penny per pizza begins to run afoul of the smallest unit of United States currency. The point of the example is to show that by taking smaller and smaller changes in output, the change in revenue converges on the slope of the tangent line to the total revenue curve at the point where $q = 100$ and $TR = \$700$. Indeed, by imagining that output is decreased by one-tenth of a unit per day we can calculate that, as changes get smaller in absolute value (Δq approaches zero from either direction), the ratio of the change in revenue to the change in output gets very close to $2.

Table A-1 also simulates the derivation of marginal revenue when $q = 120$ ($TR = \$720$) and $q = 140$ ($TR = \$700$). In each case, as the change in quantity gets smaller in absolute value, the ratio of the change in revenue to the change in output gets closer to the actual rate of change of revenue due to the change in output. As you ponder the pattern in Table A-1, let us return to the derivation of shortcuts for calculating derivatives.

Basic Rules of Derivatives

Since the purpose of this appendix is to give the uninitiated student a "feel" for calculus, we will not go to the trouble of rigorously proving the calculus concepts. The interested student might consult an instructor in the mathematics department, or perhaps an economics professor who teaches a course in mathematical methods for economists.

The change in a function of the form $y = cx^n$ due to a change in x is $c(x + \Delta x)^n - cx^n$. When we expand the expression $c(x + \Delta x)^n$, the first term will be cx^n. This term will disappear since cx^n is subtracted from $c(x + \Delta x)^n$. The second term will be $c(nx^{n-1}\Delta x)$; in the expansion, x^{n-1} will be multiplied by Δx n times. This second term contains Δx, which will disappear from this term when the numerator of the definition of the derivative is divided by the denominator. The third term and any subsequent terms (if $n \geq 3$) will contain

Δx raised to a power greater than one. After the denominator disappears and Δx is imagined to become zero, all these terms will disappear. The only term which will remain, regardless of the value of n, is cnx^{n-1}.

Exploring the rule further, we can rediscover the reason for some mathematical conventions. For instance, the derivative of x^3 is $3x^2$; if $y = x^2$, $dy/dx = 2x$, and so forth. Suppose we were working with the identity function $y = x$. Clearly, every time x changes by one unit, y changes by one unit, since the two are really the same variable. Therefore, if $y = x$, $dy/dx = 1$. Since x can be written as x^1, our rule implies $dx^1/dx = 1x^0$, since zero is one less than one. This implies the mathematical convention $x^0 = 1$. Since a constant can be expressed as $c = c \times 1 = cx^0$, it follows that $dc/dx = d(cx^0)/dx = 0 \times cx^{-1} = 0$.

If n is negative, x^n is the reciprocal of x^{-n} (e.g., if $n = -2$, $x^{-2} = 1/x^2$); as x becomes larger, x^n becomes smaller. The slope of x^n is negative when $n < 0$. If $y = x^{-2}$, $dy/dx = -2x^{-2-1} = -2x^{-3}$. (Remember, with negative numbers, "smaller" means getting farther away from zero.) If n is a fraction, the rule still holds; for $y = x^{1/2}$, $dy/dx = 1/2x^{-1/2}$. Even if n is an irrational number, the rule still holds; if $y = x^\pi$, $dy/dx = dx^\pi/dx = \pi x^{\pi-1}$.

A slight detour here. One of the driving forces of science is the compulsion to remove theoretical "holes," that is, to account for unexplained or undefined phenomena. We can account for virtually every polynomial term as the derivative of some other (higher powered) polynomial. For instance, $3x^2$ is the derivative of $x^3 \pm c$ (the "plus or minus a constant" is added since the derivative of a constant is zero). Reversing the process of taking derivatives (called differentiation) is integration (i.e., we are integrating a function we took apart). Now the problem: what function, when we take its derivative, gives us x^{-1}, or $1/x$? It might seem that the answer could be obtained easily. By adding one to the exponent, we should be able to find the function from which it was derived. Alas, $x^{-1+1} = x^0$, and x^0 is a constant, namely, one. The derivative of one, or any constant for that matter, is zero, not the reciprocal of x.

The reciprocal of a number enters into mathematics quite often; it will not do to remain ignorant of the function which gives $1/x$ as its derivative. Mathematicians, by means too complex to explore here, eventually discovered that the natural logarithm function had a derivative function equal to the reciprocal of the independent variable.[2] If $x = e^y$, so that $y = \log_e x$ (also expressed as $y = \ln x$), $dy/dx = d(\ln x)/dx = 1/x$.

In microeconomics, many phenomena involve the combination of two or more functions. We will now consider how the derivative of a "super function" is related to the derivatives of its constituents. The first rule we investigate is the *chain rule*: If $y = f(x)$ (read "y is given by the function f of x") and $x = g(w)$ (x is given by function g of w), $dy/dw = df(x)/dx \times dg(w)/dw$ or $dy/dw = dy/dx \times dx/dw$. If y changes when x changes, and x changes when w changes, the change in y with respect to w is the product of the change in y with respect

---

[2] The natural number, e, is the base of the natural logarithms and is an irrational number whose approximate value is 2.718281. This number is determined as the limit of $(1 + 1/n)^n$ as n approaches infinity. In economics, the natural number enters into the determination of the value of an asset when compounding is continuous: $V_t = P_0 e^{rt}$, where $e = \lim_{n\to\infty}(1 + 1/n)^n$, r is the rate of interest, and P_0 is the value of the asset at time $t = 0$.

to x and the change in x with respect to w. To take a trivial example, suppose that $y = 2x$ and $x = 3w$. Clearly, $y = 6w$, and $dy/dw = 6$, which can also be derived as $dy/dw = dy/dx \times dx/dw = 2 \times 3 = 6$.

A less trivial example from economics involves the *derived demand* for labor (see chapter thirteen). Firms hire workers, not because the entrepreneur is gregarious, but because firms sell the output workers produce. We have two relations: (1) the firm's revenue is a function of output, $TR = pq$, and (2) output is a function of the amount of labor employed, $q = f(L)$, assuming labor is the only variable input. If the firm is a price taker in the product market, price is treated as a constant: $d(pq)/dq = p$. We can therefore define the marginal revenue product of labor as $d(pq)/dL = d(pq)/dq \times dq/dL = MRP_L = pMP_L$.[3]

Another combination of functions frequently encountered in economics is the sum or difference of two functions of the same independent variable. Profit equals total revenue (a function of output) minus total cost (also a function of output). Luckily, the derivative of a function which is equal to the sum (difference) of two other functions is equal to the sum (difference) of the derivatives of those functions, an intuitively appealing result. Given $\pi(q) = pq - C(q)$ for a price-taking firm, the change in profit, π, with respect to output, q, is $d\pi/dq = d(pq)/dq - dC(q)/dq = p - MC$, where $MC = dC(q)/dq$.

Suppose a function is generated as the product of two other functions. Intuition suggests that the derivative of a function obtained by taking the product of two other functions should be the product of the derivatives of those functions. Unfortunately, intuition does not always lead to the correct answer. We have already learned that the chain rule gives the derivative of a function whose causal variable is really the function of another variable as the product of the derivatives of the constituent functions.

A diagramatic exposition from economics may be useful here. Total revenue is the product of price and quantity, but price is a function of output for the imperfectly competitive seller. On a demand (or average revenue) diagram, the rectangle formed by the price and quantity axes and the perpendicular lines from the relevant point on the demand curve to those axes gives an estimate of total revenue. In Figure A-2, output is assumed to increase from Q_0 to Q_1, resulting in a price decrease from p_0 to p_1 for a nondiscriminating monopolist. The change in total revenue is the net effect of two opposing consequences of the output increase. The firm is selling more units at price p_1 but is receiving less revenue on the first Q_0 units of output, which once sold for p_0 each.

The change in total revenue is:

$$\Delta TR = p_1 Q_1 - p_0 Q_0 = p_1(\Delta Q) + Q_0(\Delta p)$$

Dividing through by the change in quantity:

$$\frac{\Delta TR}{\Delta Q} = p_1 \frac{\Delta Q}{\Delta Q} + Q_0 \frac{\Delta p}{\Delta Q}$$

Letting ΔQ approach zero allows us to drop the subscripts on p_1 and Q_0, thereby

---

[3] Those familiar with calculus and microeconomic theory know that the marginal product of labor is a partial derivative. However, since that concept has yet to be covered, this example has been developed under *ceteris paribus* assumptions.

determining the general formula for marginal revenue:

$$MR = \frac{dTR}{dQ} = \lim_{\Delta Q \to 0} \left(p\,\frac{\Delta Q}{\Delta Q} + Q\,\frac{\Delta p}{\Delta Q} \right) = p\left(\lim_{\Delta Q \to 0} \frac{\Delta Q}{\Delta Q} \right) + Q\left(\lim_{\Delta Q \to 0} \frac{\Delta p}{\Delta Q} \right)$$

$$= \frac{d(pQ)}{dQ} = p\,\frac{dQ}{dQ} + Q\,\frac{dp}{dQ} = p + Q\,\frac{dp}{dQ}$$

The derivative of the product of two functions equals the sum of each function times the derivative of the other. If $y = f(x) \times g(x)$:

$$\frac{dy}{dx} = f(x)\,\frac{dg(x)}{dx} + g(x)\,\frac{df(x)}{dx}$$

Each function behaves as a *scaler* (i.e., a multiplicative constant) when the effect of a change in the other function on the dependent variable is being determined. We first find the effect of a change in x on $g(x)$, using $f(x)$ as a scaler, then add the effect of a change in x on $f(x)$, using $g(x)$ as a scaler.

Intuition really takes a holiday when we confront the next rule, which involves functions created by taking the ratio of two other functions. If we are given a function $y = f(x)/g(x)$:

$$\frac{dy}{dx} = \frac{g(x)\,\dfrac{df(x)}{dx} - f(x)\,\dfrac{dg(x)}{dx}}{[g(x)]^2}$$

If there weren't some practical reason for knowing how to take the derivative of the ratio of two functions, it would seem prudent to leave such nonintuitive relationships to mathematicians. But consider average cost; it is equal to total (or variable) cost, which is a function of output, divided by output, which is a function of itself. Understanding how average cost changes as output changes is just important enough to force us to learn how to take the derivative of a function composed of the ratio of two other functions.

Using concepts already developed—the chain rule and the derivative of a product of two functions—we can derive the formula for the derivative of a ratio of two functions for ourselves. Once we are able to figure something out, memorization is unnecessary; whenever we forget the formula, we can go back and derive it again. The function $y = f(x)/g(x)$ can also be written as $y = f(x) \times [g(x)]^{-1}$, where $[g(x)]^{-1}$ is clearly a "function of a function." Applying the rule for calculating the derivative of a product of two functions:

$$\frac{dy}{dx} = \frac{d\{f(x) \times [g(x)]^{-1}\}}{dx} = [g(x)]^{-1}\,\frac{df(x)}{dx} + f(x)\,\frac{d[g(x)]^{-1}}{dx}$$

$$= [g(x)]^{-1}\,\frac{df(x)}{dx} - f(x) \times [g(x)]^{-2}\,\frac{dg(x)}{dx} \quad \text{(by the chain rule)}$$

$$= \frac{g(x)\,\dfrac{df(x)}{dx} - f(x)\,\dfrac{dg(x)}{dx}}{[g(x)]^2} \quad \text{(factoring out } [g(x)]^{-2})$$

One final concept will establish the rules of derivatives which will guide the reader through the footnotes in this text. As long as a derivative of a smooth (continuous) function is itself a smooth (continuous) function, we can define the *second derivative* of a function as the result of taking a derivative of a derivative. Suppose that $Q = 100L - L^2$ is a short-run production function for a firm whose only variable input is labor. With each additional worker (up to $L = 50$), output will increase as employment increases. In deciding whether to hire an additional worker, the employer determines the marginal product of labor: $MP_L = dQ/dL = 100 - 2L$. The contribution to output of the last worker hired equals 100 units of output minus two times the number of workers employed. The marginal product of labor is declining by two units with each worker hired: $dMP_L/dL = -2$. Since the marginal product of labor is the first derivative of Q with respect to L, the derivative of marginal product with respect to labor is the second derivative of output with respect to labor: $d^2Q/dL^2 = dMP_L/dL$. Given $Q = 100L - L^2$, $dQ/dL = -2L$, and $d^2Q/dL^2 = d(100 - 2L)/dL = -2$.[4] The second derivative, also a function, can have a derivative, called the third derivative, and so forth. However, no footnote in this book involves derivatives of an order higher than two.

At this point, let us take stock and list the rules for derivatives we have developed:

1. If $y = cx^n$, $\dfrac{dy}{dx} = ncx^{n-1}$.

2. If $y = \log_e x$ (or $y = \ln x$), $\dfrac{dy}{dx} = \dfrac{d(\ln x)}{dx} = \dfrac{1}{x}$.

3. If $y = f(x)$ and $x = g(w)$, $\dfrac{dy}{dw} = \dfrac{dy}{dx} \times \dfrac{dx}{dw}$.

4. If $y = f(x) \pm g(x)$, $\dfrac{dy}{dx} = \dfrac{df(x)}{dx} \pm \dfrac{dg(x)}{dx}$.

5. If $y = f(x) \times g(x)$, $\dfrac{dy}{dx} = f(x)\dfrac{dg(x)}{dx} + g(x)\dfrac{df(x)}{dx}$.

6. If $y = \dfrac{f(x}{g(x)}$, $\dfrac{dy}{dx} = \dfrac{g(x)\dfrac{df(x)}{dx} - f(x)\dfrac{dg(x)}{dx}}{[g(x)]^2}$.

7. If $y = f(x)$ and $\dfrac{dy}{dx} = \dfrac{df(x)}{dx}$, $\dfrac{d^2y}{dx^2} = \dfrac{d\left(\dfrac{dy}{dx}\right)}{dx}$.

Maximizing and Minimizing

Anyone encountering calculus for the first time who has made it this far in the appendix has earned an honest answer to that ancient question: "So what good is all this junk?" If you recall your principles course, or if you have read the rest

[4] A careful distinction between the first and second derivatives of a (single variable input) production function will help avoid a common error. The law of *diminishing marginal productivity* indicates that the *second derivative* of output with respect to the variable input is *negative*; however, $d^2Q/dL^2 < 0$ does not imply that $dQ/dL < 0$.

of this book, you know that much of microeconomics is concerned with *optimizing* behavior: maximizing utility, minimizing cost, maximizing profit. As you are no doubt aware, implementing theoretical concepts is sometimes difficult: the data are poor or unavailable; forces held constant in theory vary continually and unpredictably; employers stubbornly resist advice from recent college graduates. Finding the "best" rate of output is an iterative process: produce something, change the rate of output, and see what happens to profit.

In Figure A-3, total profit, Π, equals the distance between total revenue (a linear function of output for a price taker) and total cost (a nonlinear function

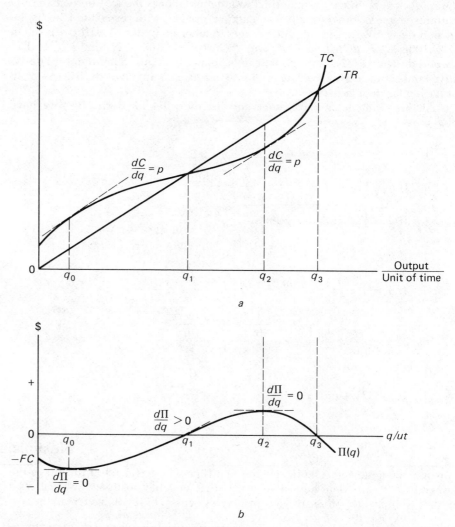

Figure A-3
Profit Maximum and Minimum: *a*, where $dTR/dq = dTC/dq$; *b*, $d\Pi/dq = 0$. When $d^2\Pi/dq > 0$, profit is at a minimum (q_0). When $d^2\Pi/dq < 0$, profit is at a maximum (q_2).

of output). Where $\Pi(q)$ is at its lowest (q_0) and at its highest (q_2), the slope of the total profit function, $d\Pi/dq$, is zero: at the top of a hill and at the bottom of a gully, the topography must be flat. When $\Pi(q)$ is increasing, its slope is positive; when $\Pi(q)$ is decreasing, its slope is negative. At its minimum point (q_0) and at its maximum point (q_2), profit is neither increasing nor decreasing: $d\Pi/dq = 0$.

In Figure A-3a, the slope of the total revenue function, $dTR/dq = p$, equals the slope of the total cost function, $dC(q)/dq$, at q_0 and q_2. By taking the derivative of profit with respect to output, the producer can sift the profit-maximizing output level from the infinite number of possible output rates. However, the profit function also has a zero slope at q_0, the output associated with minimum profit (maximum loss).

When the derivative of a function is zero, the function is neither increasing nor decreasing at that value of the independent variable. If a function has a maximum, it is likely to occur where the function is flat. (The only other possible maximum is a "corner solution," to be discussed below.) When a flat part of the curve is identified, further investigation is required to assure that it is a (local) maximum and not a minimum (or vice versa, if we wish to minimize a function).

Imagine that you are hired by a centrally planned economy to run a number of steel plants. You discover that your plant managers are all quite timid and literal minded—an understandable attitude for bureaucrats liable for punishment for sabotage if they question orders. You also realize (having read chapter fifteen of this book) that your plants would operate most efficiently if each plant manager behaved like a price-taking entrepreneur. You tell each manager, "Expand output until the cost of producing the last unit equals its (state determined) price." Six months later, you are on your way to Siberia. You wonder what went wrong.

Figure A-3 shows that if total revenue and total cost functions are moving apart when output is very small $(dC/dq > dTR/dq)$, the profit function is decreasing $(d\Pi/dq < 0)$. At q_0, the profit function has "bottomed out." If output were increased beyond q_0, losses would decrease and profit would increase. But your plant managers stopped at q_0 because you said to produce where marginal cost equals price. They should also have been told to check that profit would decrease if output were increased or decreased slightly. At q_0, a small increase in output would cause profit to increase $(d^2\Pi/dq^2 > 0)$—when you are at the bottom of a gully, a movement in any direction is up! At a maximum, the slope of the profit function must be decreasing. When profit is maximized, it is increasing below that level of output and profit is decreasing above that level of output $(d^2\Pi/dq^2 < 0)$.

The slope must be decreasing in the neighborhood of a local maximum (first you go up, then level off, then go down). The slope is increasing in the neighborhood of a local minimum (first you go down, then level off, then go up). Therefore, identifying the maximum or minimum value of a function is a two-step process. First, take the first derivative and solve for the values of the independent variable that make the slope of the objective function zero. Second, calculate the *value* of the second derivative at each of the *critical values* you just identified. If $df(x)/dx = 0$ and $d^2f(x)/dx^2 < 0$, the function is at a (local) maximum at that value of x. If $df(x)/dx = 0$ and $d^2f(x)/dx^2 > 0$, you have identified a (local) minimum of $f(x)$. If both the first and second derivatives equal zero (e.g., $y = x^3$ at $x = 0$), it is possible that the function is at neither a maximum nor a minimum but a "turning point"—a point where the second derivative changes sign, causing a "step" in the function itself.

There is one additional caution to consider when maximizing a function. As shown in Figure A-3, short-run profit begins at negative fixed costs and may actually fall lower before bottoming out. If things are going very badly for a firm, it is possible that the local profit maximum (where $d\Pi/dq = 0$ and $d^2\Pi/dq^2 < 0$) may result in greater losses than if the firm produced nothing; this is the case of the *corner solution*. Instead of occurring at a "flat place" on the profit function, the true (or "global") maximum occurs at the corner where the function emanates from the vertical axis (i.e., $q = 0$). As shown in chapter nine a competitive firm shuts down when price is less than average variable cost at the rate of output for which marginal cost equals price.

Partial Derivatives: Never Having to Say *Ceteris Paribus*

Few concepts in microeconomic theory are more derided by noneconomists than the idea of *ceteris paribus*—"all other things remaining the same." The prospect of all changes in taste, income, and other prices being postponed until the economist has had enough time to show how the market price and quantity sold respond to a change in supply conditions is enough to strain the credulity of even the A+ student. But the human mind is not designed to move in multiple directions at the same time. Human beings generally prefer to trace through each aspect of a process separately before tackling some grand synthesis.

We cannot long ignore the fact that most functions in economics (e.g., total cost) contain more than one potential causal variable (e.g., factor prices, factor quantities, output levels). But as long as the multiple causal variables are *independent* of one another, it is at least conceptually possible that one of them can change without *causing* a change in any other variable except the dependent variable. When variables are independent, their simultaneous change is coincidental rather than predictable. (When *ceteris paribus* logic cannot be used, *mutatis mutandis* logic is appropriate, as explained in chapter four.) While learning economic theory, it is much easier to concentrate on each independent variable separately, then add together their influences to obtain a complete picture.

Even though *ceteris paribus* analysis is more or less forced on us by the nature of the learning experience, we can use calculus to escape from verbal fables of time standing still. Furthermore, by enabling us to separate the influences of several independent variables on one or more dependent variables, calculus also frees us from the shackles of two-dimensional diagrams.

Suppose that $y = f(x_1, x_2, \ldots, x_n)$ is a function with one dependent variable (y) and n independent variables (x_1 through x_n). The *partial derivative* of y with respect to x_i, represented as $\partial y/\partial x_i$, is defined as the change in y due to a change in variable x_i, all other variables remaining constant. The partial derivative of a function is obtained by following the derivative rules for a change in one of the independent variables and treating all other independent variables as if they were constants. The partial derivative of y with respect to x_1 is:

$$\frac{\partial y}{\partial x_1} = \lim_{\Delta x_1 \to 0} \frac{f(x_1 + \Delta x_1, x_2, x_3, \ldots) - f(x_1, x_2, x_3, \ldots)}{\Delta x_1}$$

A simple illustration may help. Suppose that $y = xz$, where x and z are both independent variables. Note that $\partial y / \partial x = z$ and $\partial y / \partial z = x$: the impact of a change in x on y depends on the value of z, while the effect of a change in z on y depends on the value of x. Nevertheless, if x and z are truly independent, there is no reason to expect a change in one variable to cause a change in the other variable. For analytical convenience, other independent variables can be treated as constants. If $y = 3x + 2z$, $\partial y / \partial x = 3$ and $\partial y / \partial z = 2$. In this case, the influence of either independent variable on the dependent variable is invariant with respect to the value of the other variable. In fact, if $y = a + bz$, $\partial y / \partial x = 0$. If the variable y does not depend on the value of x, a change in x elicits no response from y.

Not surprisingly, partial derivatives are themselves functions of multiple independent variables, so that second and even higher order partial derivatives can be defined. The law of diminishing returns says that the second partial derivative of output with respect to any of the inputs in a production function must eventually become negative. If $q = f(L, K)$ relates the rate of output (q) to the services of two inputs, labor (L) and capital (K), the marginal product of labor is $\partial q / \partial L$, and the law of diminishing returns states that $\partial MP_L / \partial q = \partial^2 q / \partial L^2 < 0$ beyond some value of L. Once you have learned to think in terms of partial derivatives, you will be less likely to confuse negative marginal productivity ($\partial q / \partial L < 0$) and diminishing marginal productivity ($\partial^2 q / \partial L^2 < 0$).

With partial derivatives we can also express how a change in one independent variable influences the partial derivative formula of another independent variable. For instance, if an increase in capital services increases the marginal product of labor, we say that the cross partial derivative is positive: $\partial^2 q / \partial K \partial L = \partial(\partial q / \partial L) / \partial K > 0$. If, however, an increase in capital services reduced the marginal product of labor (e.g., automation made some labor skills obsolete), the partial derivative of the marginal product of labor with respect to capital would be negative: $\partial^2 q / \partial K \partial L = \partial(\partial q / \partial L) / \partial K < 0$.

Instead of holding all but one of the independent variables constant, we might wish to analyze what would happen if they all changed at the same time. In verbal or geometric analysis, this would create chaos. However, by using a fortunate characteristic of calculus, we can isolate the effect of each independent variable on the dependent variable, even when all variables are changing at once. We conclude this appendix with a study of the *total differential*, which is defined as the change in y (the dependent variable) when all of the x's (independent variables) change by small amounts:

$$dy = \frac{\partial y}{\partial x_1} dx_1 + \frac{\partial y}{\partial x_2} dx_2 + \cdots + \frac{\partial y}{\partial x_n} dx_n$$

The total change in $y (dy)$ is given by the sum of the partial derivative of y with respect to each independent variable times the change in that variable. The total differential vindicates our use of *ceteris paribus* analysis as a learning device; after the impact of each independent variable on the dependent variable has been determined, the total effect of all variables can be found by adding together the partial effects.

Suppose that an economist estimates a demand function of the form $Q_d = D(p_1, p_2, \ldots, p_n, y, \tau)$, which contains the prices of n goods (the commodity itself plus complements and substitutes), real income, y, and some proxy for tastes, τ. With sufficient data, the total change in quantity demanded could be forecast as:

$$dQ_d = \frac{\partial q}{\partial p_1}\, dp_1 + \frac{\partial q}{\partial p_2}\, dp_2 + \cdots + \frac{\partial Q}{\partial p_n}\, dp_n + \frac{\partial Q}{\partial y}\, dy + \frac{\partial Q}{\partial \tau}\, d\tau$$

Q.E.D.

It is traditional to end mathematical proofs with the initials Q.E.D., which stand for *quod erat demonstrandum*, literally, "which was to be proved." Think of this phrase as the mathematician's sign of relief—a stuffy equivalent of "I'm glad that's over."

This appendix is concluded and, by the order of topics presented, so is the book. If you have read this appendix as a preliminary to the text and are confused, take heart. Remember that learning often requires more than one pass over the course material. If you read through this appendix as if it were a novel (admittedly short on plot and lacking in character development), try again, only this time, plod. Then, if you are still confused, try once more after you have read the rest of the book. You may find you have greater aptitude for economics than for mathematics; many professional economists made a similar discovery when they were at the same point in their studies as you are now.

As stated in the introductory chapter, economics does not lend itself to memorization. If you have mastered calculus, it can help you understand, and hence remember, many of the concepts introduced in this book. If you are a novice at calculus, do not worry. None of the material presented in the main body of the text requires an understanding of calculus. In fact, an understanding of microeconomics may ultimately motivate you to learn calculus. Good luck.

Appendix B

Answers to Calculation Questions

Chapter 2

11. A bird in the hand is worth two in the bush. $MRS_{bh/bb} = -1/2$ (I will give up one bird in the hand for every two birds in the bush).
12. I like ice cream better than cake. $MRS_{c/ic} < -1$ (I will give up at least one portion of cake for another portion of ice cream).
13. Anita went shopping and found a sale on hats and gloves. Hats were $15 each and gloves were $10 per pair. She bought four hats and two pairs of gloves. $MRS_{h/g} = -2/3$ ($MRS = -p_g/p_h$ in equilibrium).
14. "A horse! A horse! My kingdom for a horse!" $MRS_{k/h} \leq -1$ (Richard III might have been willing to give up more than his kingdom for a horse).
15. I would give anything for a cigarette. $MRS_{x/c} = -\infty$, where x is "anything" (this statement shows the danger of having an offer taken literally).
16. Five dollars for this piece of junk! You must be joking! $MRS_{x/j} > -\$5/p_x$, where x is commodity actually purchased with the $5 not spent on the piece of junk.
17. "'Tis better to have loved and lost, than never to have loved at all." $MRS_{x/love} < 0$ (love is a good, worth sacrificing something for).
18. Q. Your money or your life? A. Don't shoot! $MRS_{m/l} \leq -$money in pocket (you are willing to give up at least the amount of money in your pocket in exchange for your life).

11. An individual owns a $60,000 house and calculates that there is a 1 percent chance that the house will be destroyed by fire within one year.
    a. The expected payoff of the insurance policy is $0.01 \times \$60,000 = \$600$, which is the maximum a risk neutral household would pay as an annual insurance premium.
    b. Since a risk averse person would prefer equalizing wealth in prospective futures to taking the gamble posed by nature, such a person would pay

a premium in excess of actuarially fair rates (i.e., greater than $600 per year), although the maximum he or she would pay cannot be determined a priori.

c. If a homeowner paid $750 per year for a policy with an expected payoff of $600, we could infer that the person was risk averse or else was misinformed about the probability of fire.

d. If the government allowed premium payments for fire insurance to be deducted from taxable income, the premium a risk neutral person would be willing to pay is the expected payoff divided by $(1 - t)$, where t is the marginal tax rate. A risk neutral homeowner in a 25 percent tax bracket would pay up to $600/0.75 = 800; a risk neutral homeowner in a 40 percent bracket would pay up to $600/0.60 = $1,000$.

12. a. $C_{1\,\text{max}} = \$42,000; C_{0\,\text{max}} = \$38,000$
    b. $C_{1\,\text{max}} = \$41,500; C_{0\,\text{max}} = \$37,727.27$
    c. $C_{1\,\text{max}} = \$44,000; C_{0\,\text{max}} = \$40,000$
    d. $C_{1\,\text{max}} = \$40,000; C_{0\,\text{max}} = \$36,363.64$
    e. $C_{1\,\text{max}} = \$40,800; C_{0\,\text{max}} = \$35,862.07$ (budget line kinked at $C_1 = \$30,000; C_0 = \$10,000$)

Chapter 4

11. For the linear demand equation $Q_d = 800 - 50p$:
    a. $\Delta Q_d / \Delta p = -50$
    b. When $p = 0$, $Q_d = 800 - 50(0) = 800$.
    c. If $Q_d = 0$, $p \geq 800/50 = 16$.
    d. $\eta = -1$ implies $-50(p/Q_d) = -1$, or $-50[p/(800 - 50p)] = -1, 50p = 800 - 50p$, so that $p = 800/100 = 8$.

12. Arc elasticity for:

a. $p_1 = 100$ $p_2 = 75$
    $Q_1 = 50$ $Q_2 = 60$

$$E = \frac{(60 - 50)/(60 + 50)}{(75 - 100)/(75 + 100)}$$

$$= \frac{1/11}{-1/7} = -\frac{7}{11} = -0.636$$

b. $p_1 = 10$ $p_2 = 0$
    $Q_1 = 0$ $Q_2 = 100$

$$E = \frac{(100 - 0)/(100 + 0)}{(0 - 10)/(0 + 10)}$$

$$= \frac{1}{-1} = -1$$

c. $p_1 = 125$ $p_2 = 200$
    $Q_1 = 75$ $Q_2 = 50$

$$E = \frac{(50 - 75)/(50 + 75)}{(200 - 125)/(200 + 125)}$$

$$= \frac{-1/5}{3/13} = -\frac{13}{15} = -0.867$$

Chapter 5

11. a. Plan E is technically inefficient, since it requires more of both inputs than plan D. All other plans require more of one input and less of the other, relative to remaining efficient plans.

   b. Adjacent processes can be combined efficiently. The marginal rates of technical substitution between efficient pairs of processes are:

A to B	$MRTS_{KL} = -5$		D to C	$MRTS_{LK} = -0.2$
B to C	$MRTS_{KL} = -4$	or	C to B	$MRTS_{LK} = -0.25$
C to D	$MRTS_{KL} = -3$		B to A	$MRTS_{LK} = -0.33\frac{1}{3}$

12. a. The marginal and average products of labor are:

L	MP_L	AP_L	L	MP_L	AP_L
1	5.0	5.0	30	6.0	8.0
5	8.75	8.0	40	4.0	7.0
10	12.0	10.0	50	2.0	6.0
20	8.0	9.0	60	-2.0	4.67

   b. If $L = 1$, $Q_{max} = 10$ when $K = 10$. If $L = 5$, $Q_{max} = 50$ when $K = 50$.

   c. The marginal product of capital for each rate of employment of labor can be calculated by increasing K (used) so that $K/L = 10$, then calculating $MP_K = \Delta q/\Delta K$:

L	$q(K = 100)$	$q(K = 10L)$	MP_K
1	5	10	-0.056
5	40	50	-0.20
10	100	100	0.00
20	180	200	0.20
30	240	300	0.30
40	280	400	0.40
50	300	500	0.50
60	280	600	0.64

Chapter 6

11. a. If $w_l/w_k = 2$, plan D would be the minimum cost plan, since this is the corner solution where $MRTS_{KL}$ is closest to $-w/r$.

   b. Earnings of taxi drivers are irrelevant, since their wage rate is treated as an "overhead expense" by the firm.

12. a. $MC = AVC$ somewhere between $q = 100$ and $q = 200$, since $MP_L > AP_L$ when $q = 100$ and $MP_L < AP_L$ when $q = 200$.

   b. $MC = AVC = \$4$ as long as $K \leqq 100$.

   c. If 300 units of output were produced, 50 workers would be required if $K = 100$. Since $MP_L = 2$, $MC = \$40/2 = \$20$. The marginal product of capital is 0.5; hence, two units of capital are required to produce one more unit of output. Therefore, up to $10 would be paid for an extra unit of capital services.

Chapter 7

11. a. X: $L = 5$, $K = 10$; Y: $L = 10$, $K = 5$; Z: $L = 20$, $K = 2$.
     b. | $MRTS_{LK}$ | $MRTS_{KL}$ |
         |---|---|
         | -1.0 | -1.0 |
         | $-10/3$ | -0.3 |

     c. $w_l/w_k = 2$; process X is the least-cost process, since $MRTS_{LK} = -1.0 > -2$. $w_l/w_k = 0.5$; process Y is the least-cost process: $-1.0 < -w_l/w_k < -0.3$. $w_l/w_k = 0.25$; process Z is the least-cost process: $-0.3 < -w_l/w_k$.

12. a. Fixed cost $= 250.
     b. Since 20 units of output can be produced in capital-intensive process X with all capital available, 5 units of labor will be required. Variable cost $= $10 \times 5 = 50; total cost $= $250 + $50 = 300.
     c. To produce the 21st unit of output, capital must be transferred from process X to process Y. By reducing capital by 1/2 unit in process X, one unit of output is lost; by transferring 1/4 unit of labor and hiring an additional 3/4 unit of labor, two units of output can be produced in process Y. For a net increase of one unit of output, 0.75 units of labor must be hired, so that $MC = $10(0.75) = 7.50.
     d. To produce 40 units of output, all capital must be used in process Y. To produce the 41st unit, capital must be transferred from process Y to process Z. The linear production function resulting from combining processes Y and Z can be derived by solving the equation $Q = aL + bK$ for a and b, after substituting known values of L and K. Using efficient input combinations for $Q = 40$ in process Y ($L = 20$, $K = 10$) and process Z ($L = 40$, $K = 4$), we have:

$$20a + 10b = 40 \qquad 40a + 20b = 80 \qquad \therefore b = 40/16 = 2.5$$
$$\underline{40a + 4b = 40} \qquad \underline{40a + 4b = 40} \qquad a = \frac{40 - 10(2.5)}{20} = \frac{15}{20}$$
$$16b = 40 \qquad\qquad = 0.75$$

Solving $Q = 0.75L + 2.5K$ for L, with $Q = 41$ and $K = 10$, we have $L = [41 - 2.5(10)]/0.75 = (41 - 25)/0.75 = 16(4/3) = 64/3 = 21.33$. Since we know it takes 20 units of labor to produce 40 units of output, the marginal cost of the 41st unit is $10(1.33) = 13.33.

13. a. To produce 5 units of output, the firm minimizes variable cost by hiring 5 workers at $5 each and 1/2 hour of machine services, so that $VC = $5(5) + $25(1/2) = 37.50.
     b. As long as $w_l/w_k \leq 0.30$, as is the case up to 10 labor hours, process Z is the least-cost process. Using 10 labor hours and 1 capital hour, the firm produces 10 units of output. Labor costs equal $5(5) + $7.5(5) = $62.50, and capital costs are $25(1) = $25, so that $VC(10) = 87.50. For $0.30 < w_l/w_k < 1$, as is the case for the 11th through the 45th worker hired, process Y is the least-cost process. To produce 40 units of output,

20 labor hours are required, which cost $10(5) + $12.50(5) + $15(5) + $17.50(5) = $275. With 10 machine-hours hired for $250, it costs $525 to produce units 11 through 50. Total variable cost is $612.50.

c. If all workers must be paid the same wage rate, the marginal cost of labor equals the wage rate the last worker is paid plus the raise given to other workers who could otherwise have been paid a lower wage rate. The marginal cost of labor equals $25 when 25 labor hours have been hired. The firm produces 50 units of output in process Y, hiring 12.5 machine hours for $312.50 and 25 labor hours at $15 each, or $375. Total variable cost is $687.50.

Chapter 9

11. a. Since $AVC = 5 + q$, $p \geqq 5$ for output to occur.
    b. When $p = \$45$, q is given by $5 + 2q = 45$, or $2q = 40$, and $q = 20$.
    c. When $p = \$40$, $q = (40 - 5)/2 = 17.5$.

$$TR = 40(17.5) = \$700.00$$
$$TC = 500 + 5(17.5) + (17.5)^2 = \$893.75$$
$$\therefore \pi = -\$193.75$$

12. a. $MC = p$ implies $5 + 2q = p$, or $q_s = -2.5 + 0.5p$.
    b. With 1,000 identical firms, $Q_s = 1,000(q_s) = -2,500 + 500p$.
    c. Equilibrium means $Q_s = Q_d$ at the prevailing price, so that:

$$27,500 - 100p = -2,500 + 500p$$
$$600p = 30,000$$
$$p = \$50$$
$$Q = 27,500 - 100(50) = -2,500 + 500(50) = 22,500$$

d. With each firm producing 22.5 units, $TR = 50(22.5) = \$1,125$; $TC = 500 + 5(22.5) + (22.5)^2 = \$1,118.75$; and $\pi = \$6.25$. Slight entry is predicted.

Chapter 10

11. a. $MR_1 = p_1 - \dfrac{\Delta p_1}{\Delta Q_1} Q_1 = 100 - 2Q_1 - 2Q_1 = 100 - 4Q_1$

$MR_2 = p_2 - \dfrac{\Delta p_2}{\Delta Q_2} Q_2 = 80 - Q_2 - Q_2 = 80 - 2Q_2$

b. $MR_1 = MR_2 = 10$ implies:
$100 - 4Q_1 = 10$, or $Q_1 = 22.5$; $p_1 = 100 - 2(22.5) = \$55$; $\eta_1 = -1.22$

$80 - 2Q_2 = 10$, or $Q_2 = 35$; $p_2 = 80 - 35 = \$45$; $\eta_2 = -(1)\dfrac{45}{35} =$

-1.286

c. $TR = p_1Q_1 + p_2Q_2 = 55(22.5) + 45(35) = 1{,}237.5 + 1{,}575 = \$2{,}812.50$
    $TC = 100 + 10Q_1 + 10Q_2 = 100 + 10(22.5) + 10(35) = \$675.00$
    $\therefore \pi = \$2{,}137.50$

12. a. With $p_1 = \$55$ and $p_2 = \$45$, an initial profit of \$5 per unit could be made by shipping the product from market 2 to market 1. This would cause sales in market 2 to rise and sales in market 1 to fall, since customers in market 1 are now buying from a middleman.

   b. Given $p_h = p_L + 5$, Q_1 is not determined by optimal Q_2. Substituting:

$$100 - 2Q_1 = 80 + 5 - Q_2$$

$$2Q_1 = Q_2 + 15, \text{ or } Q_1 = 7.5 + 0.5Q_2$$

   $MR_2 = MC$ implies $80 - 2Q_2 = 10$, or $Q_2 = 35$, and $p_2 = \$45$; $p_1 = \$45 + 5 = \$50$, so $Q_1 = 50 - 0.5p_1 = 25$.
   $TR = 50(25) + 45(35) = 1{,}250 + 1{,}575 = \$4{,}075$
   $TC = 100 + 10(25) + 10(35) = \$700$
   $\therefore \pi = \$2{,}125$

Chapter 11

11. a. Given $q = 40\bar{p} - 20p_i$, $AR = p_i = 2\bar{p} - 0.05q$.

   b. $MR = p_i + q \dfrac{\Delta p}{\Delta q} = 2\bar{p} - 0.05q - 0.05q = 2\bar{p} - 0.1q$

   c. If $\bar{p} = 10$, $MR = 20 - 0.1q$. $MR = MC$ implies $20 - 0.1q = 3$ or $q = 10(20 - 3) = 170$; $p_i = 20 - 0.05(170) = 20 - 8.50 = \$11.50$.

   d. $TR = 11.50(170) = \$1{,}955$
       $TC = 500 + 3(170) = \underline{1{,}010}$
       $\pi = \$\overline{945}$

12. a. With a daily profit of \$945, Mom's experience will likely attract firms into the pizza business.

   b. If the average price of pizza fell to \$6.00, Mom's marginal revenue formula would become $MR = 12 - 0.1q$. $MR = MC$ implies $12 - 0.1q = 3$, or $q = 9/0.1 = 90$; $p_i = 12 - 0.05(90) = 12 - 4.5 = \$7.50$.
   $TR = 7.50(90) = \$675$
   $TC = 500 + 3(90) = \underline{770}$
   $\pi = -\$95$

Chapter 12

11. a. $MR_1 = p + \dfrac{\Delta p}{\Delta Q_1} Q_1 = 100 - 2Q_2 - 4Q_1$

   $MR_2 = p + \dfrac{\Delta p}{\Delta Q_2} Q_2 = 100 - 2Q_1 - 4Q_2$

b. $MR_i = MC_i$ implies $100 - 2Q_j - 4Q_i = 10$; $Q_i = (90 - 2Q_j)/4$, $Q_1 = (90 - 2Q_2)/4$, and $Q_2 = (90 - 2Q_1)/4$.

c. Cournot solution is obtained by simultaneous equations:

$$
\begin{array}{lll}
Q_1 = 22.5 - 0.5Q_2 & Q_1 = 22.5 - 0.5Q_2 & Q_2 = 22.5/1.5 \\
0.5Q_1 = 22.5 - Q_2 & Q_1 = 45.0 - 2Q_2 & Q_2 = Q_1 = 15
\end{array}
$$

$p = 100 - 2(15 + 15) = 100 - 60 = \$40$

d. Under collusion, $Q = Q_1 + Q_2$, $p = 100 - 2Q$, and $MR = 100 - 4Q$. $MR = MC$ implies $100 - 4Q = 10$, or $Q = 90/4 = 22.5$; $p = 100 - 2(22.5) = \$55$, and $TR = 55(22.5) = \$1,237.50$:

$$
\begin{array}{ll}
TR_1 = \$618.75 & TR_2 = \$618.75 \\
TC_1 = 212.50 & TC_2 = 212.50 \\
\pi_1 = \$\overline{406.25} & \pi_2 = \$\overline{406.25}
\end{array}
$$

With Cournot solution, each firm's profit is:

$$
\begin{array}{ll}
TR_1 = 40(15) = \$600 & TR_2 = \$600 \\
TC_1 = 100 + 150 = 250 & TC_2 = 250 \\
\pi_1 = \$\overline{350} & \pi_2 = \$\overline{350}
\end{array}
$$

Collusion would increase each firm's profit by \$56.25.

12. a. $\eta_{12} = \dfrac{\Delta Q_1/Q_1}{\Delta p_2/p_2} = \dfrac{\Delta Q_1}{\Delta p_2}\left(\dfrac{p_2}{Q_1}\right) = 2\left(\dfrac{p_2}{Q_1}\right) = \dfrac{2p_2}{Q_1}$

$\eta_{21} = \dfrac{\Delta Q_2/Q_2}{\Delta p_1/p_1} = \dfrac{\Delta Q_2}{\Delta p_1}\left(\dfrac{p_1}{Q_2}\right) = 2\left(\dfrac{p_1}{Q_2}\right) = \dfrac{2p_1}{Q_2}$

b. $\dfrac{\Delta p_1 Q_1}{\Delta p_1} = 88 - 4p_1 + 2p_2 + p_1\left(-4 + 2\dfrac{\Delta p_2}{\Delta p_1}\right)$

$\phantom{\dfrac{\Delta p_1 Q_1}{\Delta p_1}} = 88 - 8p_1 + 2p_2 + 2p_1\dfrac{\Delta p_2}{\Delta p_1}$

$\dfrac{\Delta p_2 Q_2}{\Delta p_1} = 56 - 4p_2 + 2p_1 + p_2\left(-4 + 2\dfrac{\Delta p_1}{\Delta p_2}\right)$

$\phantom{\dfrac{\Delta p_2 Q_2}{\Delta p_1}} = 56 - 8p_2 + 2p_1 + 2p_2\dfrac{\Delta p_1}{\Delta p_2}$

c. $\dfrac{\%\Delta R_1}{\%\Delta p_1} = 1 + \eta_{11} + \eta_{12} \times \theta_{21}$, where $\theta_{21} = \dfrac{\Delta p_2/p_2}{\Delta p_1/p_1}$

$\dfrac{\%\Delta R_2}{\%\Delta p_2} = 1 + \eta_{22} + \eta_{21} \times \theta_{12}$, where $\theta_{12} = \dfrac{\Delta p_1/p_1}{\Delta p_2/p_2}$

d. When $\theta_{ji} = 0$, $\%\Delta R_i/\%\Delta p_i = 1 + \eta_{ii}$; when $\theta_{ji} = 1$, $\%\Delta R_i/\%\Delta p_i = 1 + \eta_{ii} + \eta_{ij}$.

13. a. Given $MC_i = 10q_i$, $MC(Q) = Q$.

b. $MC = MR$ implies $100 - Q = Q$, $2Q = 100$, so that $Q = 50$, and $p = 100 - 0.5(50) = \$75$.

c. $TR_i = 5(75) = \$375$

$TC_i = 100 + 5(5)^2 = \$225$

$\pi_i = \$150$

d. If $\Delta q_i = -5$ (i.e., $q_i = 0$), $p_0 = \$77.50$, so that $p_i = 77.50 - 0.5q_i$, and $MR_i = 77.50 - q_i$. $MR_i = MC_i$ implies $77.50 - q_i = 10q_i$, or $11q_i = 77.50$, $q_i \approx 11$, $p = 77.50 - 0.5(7) = \$74 = 100 - 0.5(52)$.

e. If $Q - q_i = 45$ (undetected cheating), $TR_i = 7(74) = \$518$
$$TC_i = 100 + 5(7)^2 = \$345$$
$$\pi_i = \$173$$

If $Q - q_i = 63$ (other firms match output increase),
$$p = 100 - 0.5(70) = \$65, \text{ and } TR_i = \$455$$
$$TC_i = 345$$
$$\pi_i = \overline{\$110}$$

A risk neutral firm would consider cheating a reasonable gamble if $(1 - \rho)173 + \rho 110 \geq 150$, where ρ = probability of detection;

$$173 - 173\rho + 110\rho \geq 150$$
$$-63\rho \geq -23$$
$$\rho \leq \frac{-23}{-63} = 0.365$$

Chapter 14

11. a. The labor demand curve under competitive conditions would be given by the condition $w = MRP_L = 19 - 0.1L$. Solving for $L_d = (19 - w)/0.1 = 190 - 10w$. The labor supply function is given by $L_s = a + bw$ in general terms. Substituting two values of L and w when both men and women are employed, we can solve for a and b:

$$60 = a + 6b \; (L = 60 \text{ when } w = 6)$$
$$\underline{100 = a + 7b} \; (L = 100 \text{ when } w = 7)$$
$$40 = b \; a = 60 - 6(40) = -180$$

Since equilibrium in a competitive labor market ($L_d = L_s$) would maximize employment, we can solve for w:

$$-180 + 40w = 190 - 10w$$
$$50w = 370$$
$$w = \$7.40 \text{ per hour}$$
$$L = -180 + 40(7.4) = 190 - 10(7.4) = 116$$

b. The impact on male and female workers is given by the table below:

	w_f	L_f	Economic Rent	w_m	L_m	Economic Rent
Before union	$6.50	60	$300.00	$7.50	40	$30.00
After union	7.40	78	362.40	7.40	38	26.20

Men lose 2 workers, and 38 male workers each lose $0.10 in economic rent per hour, for a gross loss of $3.80 in economic rent. Women gain 18 workers, 60 females employed at $6.50 per hour gain economic rent of $0.90 each ($54), plus 16 of 18 additional workers receive economic rent ranging from $0.20 to $1.20 ($8.40), for a total gain of $62.40 in economic rent. Net gain by all workers is $58.60 if employment-maximizing wage is obtained through collective bargaining.

12. a. The competitive wage is given by:

$$-10{,}000 + 50w = 50{,}000 - 100w$$
$$150w = 60{,}000$$
$$w = \$400$$
$$L = 10{,}000$$

b. Economic rent would be maximized by setting $MR_l = w_r$:

$$500 - 0.02L = 200 + 0.02L$$
$$0.04L = 300$$
$$L = 300/0.04 = 7{,}500$$

c. The wage rate which maximizes economic rent is determined by substituting 7,500 for L in the inverse demand function: $w_l = 500 - 0.01(7{,}500) = \$425$

d. If plumbers' jobs were auctioned, 7,500 workers would be willing to work for a reservation wage determined by substituting 7,500 into $w = 200 + 0.02L = 200 + 0.02(7{,}500) = \$350$/week. (Note that maximum kickbacks would equal $(7{,}500)(75) = \$562{,}500$ per week.)

Index

Numbers in boldface indicate the page on which the term is defined.